Skilled interpersonal communication

Research, theory and practice

Sixth edition

Owen Hargie

 Routledge
Taylor & Francis Group

LONDON AND NEW YORK

Sixth edition published 2017
by Routledge
2 Park Square, Milton Park, Abingdon, Oxon OX14 4RN

and by Routledge
711 Third Avenue, New York, NY 10017

Routledge is an imprint of the Taylor & Francis Group, an informa business

First edition published 1981 by Croom Helm
Fifth edition published 2011 by Routledge

British Library Cataloguing in Publication Data
A catalogue record for this book is available from the British Library

Library of Congress Cataloging in Publication Data
Names: Hargie, Owen, author.
Title: Skilled interpersonal communication : research, theory and practice / Owen Hargie.
Description: 6th edition. | Abingdon, Oxon ; New York, NY : Routledge, 2017. | Includes bibliographical references and index.
Identifiers: LCCN 2016010249| ISBN 9781138823778 (pbk.) | ISBN 9781138823761 (hardback) | ISBN 9781315741901 (e-book)
Subjects: LCSH: Interpersonal communication.
Classification: LCC BF637.C45 H33 2017 | DDC 153.6—dc23
LC record available at https://lccn.loc.gov/2016010249

ISBN: 978-1-138-82376-1 (hbk)
ISBN: 978-1-138-82377-8 (pbk)
ISBN: 978-1-315-74190-1 (ebk)

153.6

Typeset in Century old Style
by Swales & Willis Ltd, Exeter, Devon, UK
Printed and bound by CPI Group (UK) Ltd, Croydon, CR0 4YY

For my wife, Patricia

Contents

CONTENTS

Figures

Boxes

Tables

Preface

The contribution of effective interpersonal communication to success in both personal and professional contexts is now widely recognised. Interpersonal training programmes are a component part of the training for all professional groups, and the contribution of communication to social and personal well-being has been extensively researched. It is clear that the ability to communicate effectively at an interpersonal level is a vital part of the human condition. As such, knowledge of various types of skills, and of their effects in social interaction, plays a pivotal role in interpersonal functioning. It is for this reason that interest in the study of skilled communication has grown so rapidly.

While the term 'social skill' tends to predominate within clinical contexts and in developmental/elementary educational fields, in academic and professional spheres the more common usage is 'interpersonal skill' or 'communication skill'. The title of this book reflects the fact that its heartland lies in the academic domain of interpersonal communication, as applied to higher-order contexts. It also reflects the fact that the treatment of skill in the book encompasses a comprehensive review of research findings and analyses of theoretical perspectives, as well as direct applications to practice in a range of settings.

The function of the book is to provide a key reference for the study of interpersonal communication *per se*. It is concerned with the identification, analysis and evaluation of a range of skills that are employed widely in interaction. As such, this text will be of interest both to students of interpersonal communication in general and to qualified personnel and trainees in many fields in particular. The book examines the central features of a range of core interpersonal skills. Chapters 1 and 2 provide a foundation for the text by examining the nature of interpersonal communication and interpersonal skill. Fourteen main skill areas are covered in the remaining chapters, beginning with nonverbal communication in Chapter 3. This aspect of interaction is the first to be examined, since all of the areas that follow contain nonverbal elements and so an understanding of the main facets of this channel facilitates the examination of the other skills. Chapter 4 incorporates an analysis of the skilled use of rewards and reinforcement, while the skill of questioning is reviewed in Chapter 5. In Chapter 6, an alternative strategy to questioning, namely reflecting, is investigated. Reflection consists of concentrating on what others are saying and reformulating back to them the central elements of their message.

The skill of listening is explored in Chapter 7, where its active nature is emphasised, while explaining is focused upon in Chapter 8. In Chapter 9, self-disclosure is examined from two perspectives: first, the appropriateness of personal self-disclosure, and second, methods for promoting maximum self-disclosure from others. Two important episodes in any action – the opening and closing sequences – are reviewed in Chapter 10. Techniques for protecting personal rights are discussed in Chapter 11 in terms of the skill of assertiveness. The skill area of influencing and persuading has attracted growing interest in recent years and this is covered in Chapter 12, while the related skill of negotiation is addressed in Chapter 13. Finally, in Chapter 14 the skills involved in interacting in, and leading, small group discussions are examined.

One striking difference between this sixth edition and the first edition of the book nearly four decades ago is that in the latter edition my problem was finding research studies into skilled interpersonal communication to include, whereas for the current edition my main difficulty was in deciding what to leave out. There is a mountain of research in this field and it is expanding exponentially. Academics across a wide range of disciplines are contributing to the growing body of work on interpersonal skills. It is simply impossible to reference all of this material. The filter method I have used therefore is to select what I consider to be key publications in each area and cite these for readers to pursue. While I would have liked to describe many of the interesting research studies in more detail, space simply does not permit this. There is also a large corpus of work on the application of many of these skills in mediated communication, especially via social media. However, while I mention some of this, it is not the focus of this text. Likewise, there is a developing literature in the field of human social neuroscience, but again this is outside the scope of the present text. *Skilled Interpersonal Communication* remains firmly centred on what occurs during face-to-face communication.

Furthermore, the skills included do not represent a completely comprehensive list, but they are generally regarded as being the central aspects of interpersonal communication. In addition, it is recognised that, while these skills are studied separately, in practice they overlap and complement one another. What is definitely the case is that knowledge of the repertoire of skilled behaviours covered in this text will enable readers to extend and refine their own pattern or style of interaction.

From a personal perspective, a poignant factor in writing this new edition has been the absence of my two former and founding co-authors, both of whom passed away prematurely, David Dickson on 24 May 2008 and Christine Saunders on 9 August 2002. David and Christine were irreplaceable co-workers and friends. Working with them never actually felt like work – it was fun. They were constant sources of inspiration, insight, intelligence, wisdom, support, creativity and, above all, endless good humour. In those days I actually looked forward to going to work! Together, we produced many books, book chapters, journal articles, videos, inventories and training scenarios, all of which informed our pedagogical innovations in the field of interpersonal communication. We were pioneers in the field of interpersonal skills and our work has had wide influence and impact. Working on this publication was a lonely task following the years of sharing and camaraderie with Christine and David when producing those earlier editions. I miss them and thought of them frequently as each chapter evoked cherished memories. I have felt the warm glow of their presence very strongly as I wrote this new edition and I see them often in my mind's eye. Their influence pervades the book. However, while I recognise with great gratitude and deep affection their role in forming and shaping this edition, I also fully accept sole responsibility for any of its flaws.

I would also like to acknowledge the assistance provided by the School of Communication, Ulster University. A special word of thanks is due to those members of staff in the School who have been closely involved in, and contributed to, the evolution of interpersonal communication programmes. In particular, I am indebted to Pauline Irving, Valerie Purchase and Karyn Stapleton, who have been constant sources of encouragement, support and advice, and to my good friend and former colleague Dennis Tourish for his ongoing insights and ideas. I would also like to thank the external reviewers of the fifth edition of the book, Anne Marie Bülow, Copenhagen Business School; Kate D'Arcy, University of Bedfordshire; Mark Davies, University of South Wales; Nelica La Gro, University of East London; Fred Morrison, Ulster University; Lilianne Potters, Utrecht University; and Su Steed, University Centre Doncaster, who provided very useful comments and suggestions for changes to this new edition. In addition, the invaluable feedback from students and trainees on my interpersonal communication modules and training programmes is recognised. Where possible, I have adopted the suggestions from all of these sources, but again I accept full responsibility for the final decisions on what has been included.

A special note of thanks is given to the editorial staff at Routledge, for all their help, support and expertise. Words of appreciation are due to Philip Burch and David Barr, graphic design technicians in the School of Communication at Ulster University, for their skill in producing some of the more intricate diagrams.

Finally, I am indebted to my wife, Patricia, who provided the necessary motivation, care and unending love to sustain me throughout the production of this text.

Owen Hargie
Jordanstown

Chapter 1

The features of interpersonal communication

THE IMPORTANCE OF BEING A SKILLED COMMUNICATOR

HUMANS HAVE A FUNDAMENTAL, powerful and universal drive to interact with one another. As expressed by Afifi and Guerrero (2000, p. 170):

> There is a long history of research establishing the importance that individuals place on connectedness … individuals' needs for initiating, developing and maintaining social ties, especially close ones, is reflected in a litany of studies and a host of theories.

The mere presence of another has been shown to be arousing and motivating and this in turn influences our behaviour – a process termed *compresence* (Burgoon *et al.*, 1996). We behave differently in company than when alone. When we meet others we are 'on stage' and so give a performance that differs from how we behave 'off stage'. We also enjoy interacting, and indeed the act of engaging in facilitative interpersonal communication has been shown to contribute to positive changes in emotional state (Gable and Shean, 2000). While our dealings with other people can sometimes be problematic or even contentious, we also seek, relish and obtain great reward from social interaction. Conversely, if we are unable to engage meaningfully with others, or are ostracised by them, the result is often loneliness, unhappiness and depression (Wood, 2014).

The seemingly innate need for relationships with others has been termed *sociation* (Wolff, 1950). As Ryff and Singer (2000, p. 31) put it: 'Across time and settings, people everywhere have subscribed to the view that close, meaningful ties to others is an essential

feature of what it means to be fully human'. In other words, individuals need to commune with others. Three core types of psychological need have been identified – competence, relatedness and autonomy – and the satisfaction of all three results in optimal well-being (Ryan *et al.*, 2013). The competence need comprises a wish to feel confident and effective in carrying out actions, in order to achieve one's goals. The relatedness need reflects a desire to have close connections and positive relationships with significant others. The autonomy need involves wanting to feel in control of one's own destiny, rather than being directed by others.

In order to satisfy all three psychological needs it is necessary to have an effective repertoire of interpersonal skills. In their review of the area, Spitzberg and Cupach (2011, p. 481) point out that, 'Social and interpersonal skills are the means through which all human relationships are initiated, negotiated, maintained, transformed, and dissolved'. These skills have always been important. Our early ancestors who lived in groups were more likely to survive than those who lived alone, and so the skills involved in developing and maintaining social bonds assumed a central role in human evolution (Leary, 1996). Forgas and Williams (2001, p. 7) noted that: '*Homo sapiens* is a highly sociable species... our impressive record of achievements owes a great deal to the highly elaborate strategies we have developed for getting along with each other and co-ordinating our interpersonal behaviors'. Indeed, Levinson (2006) argued that the human mind is specifically adapted to enable us to engage in social interaction, and that we could therefore be more accurately referred to as *Homo interagens*.

Another part of the reason for sociation is that: 'The essence of communication is the formation and expression of an identity. The formation of the self is not an independent event generated by an autonomous actor. Rather, the self emerges through social interaction' (Coover and Murphy, 2000, p. 125). In this way, 'a sense of personal identity is achieved through negotiation with others' (Postmes *et al.*, 2006, p. 226). In other words, we become the people we are as a result of our interchanges with others (this issue is explored in detail in Chapter 9). Interaction is the essential nutrient that nourishes and sustains the social milieu. Furthermore, since communication is a pre-requisite for learning, without the capacity for sophisticated methods and channels for sharing knowledge, both within and between generations, our advanced human civilisation would simply not exist. Communication therefore represents the very essence of the human condition. Indeed, one of the harshest punishments available within most penal systems is that of solitary confinement – the removal of any possibility of interpersonal contact.

Thus, people have a deep-seated need to communicate and the greater their ability in this regard, the more satisfying and rewarding will be their existence. Research has shown that those with higher levels of interpersonal skill have many advantages in life (Segrin *et al.*, 2007; Hybels and Weaver, 2011; Spitzberg and Cupach, 2011; Lievens and Sackett, 2012). They cope more readily with stress, adapt and adjust better to major life transitions and have higher self-efficacy in social situations, greater satisfaction in their close personal relationships, more friends, and are less likely to suffer from depression, loneliness or anxiety. Those with a higher repertoire of interpersonal skills are sensitive to the needs of those with whom they interact, and this in turn leads to them being liked by others, who will seek out their company. By contrast, the *social skills deficit hypothesis* purports that those who lack adequate social skills are at risk of depression because of their inability to foster positive interpersonal experiences and avoid negative social experiences (Segrin and Flora, 2011).

In a review of research, Segrin (2000) concluded that interactive skills have a 'prophylactic effect' in that socially competent people are resilient to the ill effects of life crises, whereas individuals with poor skills experience a worsening of psychosocial problems when faced with stressors in life. As summarised by Segrin and Taylor (2007, p. 645), 'human beings seek and desire quality interpersonal relationships and experiences. Social skills appear to be an important mechanism for acquiring such relationships, and where they are experienced, obvious signs of positive psychological states are abundantly evident'. Many of the benefits here are, of course, inter-related, and so it is probable that the network of friendships developed by skilled individuals helps to buffer and support them in times of personal trauma. Those with high levels of skill also act as positive communication role models for others, and so they are more likely to be effective parents, colleagues or managers.

There are other tangible rewards to be gained from developing an effective interpersonal skill repertoire. These begin from an early age, since children who develop good interactive skills perform better academically (Rhoades *et al.*, 2011; Whitted, 2011). Skilled children know how to communicate effectively with the teacher and so are more likely to receive help and attention in the classroom. Their interactive flair also enables them to develop peer friendships and thereby make school a more enjoyable experience. The benefits then continue in many walks of life after school. For example, Epstein *et al.* (2013) found that in romantic relationships the perceived effectiveness of the communication skills of one's partner is the best predictor of self-reported satisfaction with the relationship.

In the business sphere there are considerable advantages to be gained from good communication (Robbins and Judge, 2014), and effective managers have been shown to have a strong repertoire of interpersonal skills (Clampitt, 2013; Bedwell *et al.*, 2014). Surveys of employers also consistently show that they rate the ability to communicate effectively as a key criterion in recruiting new staff (CBI, 2012; UKCES, 2012). In their research into entry into the elite professions, Ashley *et al.* (2015, p. 6) found that 'elite firms define "talent" according to a number of factors such as drive, resilience, strong communication skills and above all confidence and "polish"'. Individuals also need to pay attention to their *social capital*, which refers to the benefits that accrue from being socially skilled, fostering a large network of conducive and committed relationships characterised by good will, trust and reciprocity, forging commitments and developing a good social reputation (Song, 2011; Boyas *et al.*, 2012).

The relationship between social capital and interpersonal skill has been compared to that between resource stock and resource flow in organisations, in that social capital can be regarded as an accumulated asset, while interpersonal skill is one of the key factors that determine the value of this asset (Baron and Markman, 2000). Entrepreneurs who possess high levels of interpersonal skill have advantages in a range of areas, such as obtaining funding, attracting quality employees, maintaining good relationships with co-founders of the business and producing better results from customers and suppliers (Hitt *et al.*, 2011). Not surprisingly, therefore, skilled communicators have been shown to be upwardly mobile and more likely to receive pay rises and gain promotions (Burleson, 2007).

Likewise, in health care, the importance for professionals of having a 'good bedside manner' has long been realised. In 400 BC, Hippocrates noted how the patient 'may recover his health simply through his contentment with the goodness of the physician'. In recent years, this belief in the power of communication to contribute to the healing process has been borne out by research. Di Blasi *et al.* (2001) carried out a systematic review of studies in Europe, the USA and Canada that investigated the effects of doctor–patient relationships. They found that practitioner interpersonal skills made a significant difference to patient well-being. Practitioners with good interpersonal skills, who formed a warm, friendly relationship with their patients and provided reassurance, were more effective in terms of patient well-being than those who kept consultations impersonal or formal. Bensing *et al.* (2013) also found that patients prefer doctors who are empathic, take time to listen and foster a good relationship with them. Similarly, Rider and Keefer (2006) and Tallman *et al.* (2007) have shown that high levels of practitioner interpersonal skill are positively correlated with increases in the quality of care and effective health outcomes, while ineffective skills are associated with decreased patient satisfaction and increased medication errors and malpractice claims. These findings are corroborated in the field of nursing, where effective interpersonal communication has been shown to be related to improved health outcomes, such as greater patient satisfaction and quality of life (Klakovich and dela Cruz, 2006). Similar findings recur across professions. Thus, in teaching, interpersonal skills have been shown to be critical for optimum classroom performance (Worley *et al.*, 2007).

As aptly summarised by Orbe and Bruess (2005, p. 6), 'the quality of our communication and the quality of our lives are directly related...Our lives are a direct reflection of the quality of the communication in them'. This means that interpersonal skills are at the very epicentre of our social existence. We ignore them at our peril. But the good news is that we can improve our ability to communicate. A great deal is now known about the key constituents of the DNA of interactive life. Indeed, the academic study of interpersonal communication has a very long and rich tradition, spanning some 5,000 years. The oldest essay ever discovered, written about 3,000 BC, consisted of advice to Kagemni, the eldest son of Pharaoh Huni, on speaking effectively in public. Similarly, the oldest book, the *Precepts*, written in Egypt by Ptah-Hotep, *circa* 2,675 BC, is a treatise on effective communication.

In the intervening years, the fairly obvious observation that some individuals are better social interactors than others led to carefully formulated and systematic investigations into the nature and function of interpersonal interaction. Indeed, Segrin (1992) pointed out that the concept of social skill had been investigated by researchers in virtually all fields of social science. This has occurred at three levels:

1   Theoretical analyses of how and why people behave as they do have resulted in various conceptualisations of skilled behaviour (see Hargie, 2006a).

2   Research has been conducted into the identification and effects of different types of social behaviour. It is this level that the present book addresses.

3   Several approaches to training in communication skills have been introduced in order to ascertain whether it is possible to improve the social performance of the individual (for a review of these, see Hargie, 2006b).

Given the early historical focus on communication, it is perhaps surprising that this area was subsequently largely neglected in terms of academic study in higher education, until its resurgence in the late twentieth century. As noted by Bull (2002, p. vii), 'Communication is of central importance to many aspects of human life, yet it is only in recent years that it has become the focus of scientific investigation'. For example, it was not until 1960 that the notion of communication as a form of skilled activity was first suggested (Hargie, 2006a).

However, recent years have witnessed a vast outpouring of research and scholarship in this field. An important part of this work has involved an analysis of the skills approach to communication. This will be explored in depth in Chapter 2. In the present chapter we now focus upon the process of interpersonal communication *per se*, as this provides the necessary foundation upon which the skills-based approach is built.

WHAT IS INTERPERSONAL COMMUNICATION?

As a concept, communication is notoriously difficult to pin down. It represents a phenomenon that is at one and the same time ubiquitous yet elusive, prosaic yet mysterious, straightforward yet frustratingly prone to failure. The complexity of the process has created difficulties when it comes to reaching agreement over matters of formal definition. Holli and Beto (2014) attributed the problem to the vast range of activities that can be legitimately subsumed under the label. Traced back to its Latin roots, the verb 'to communicate' means 'to share', 'to make common', meanings reflected in much of the current literature. In this way, Hamilton (2014) defined communication as the process whereby people share ideas, thoughts and feelings in commonly comprehensible ways. Hewes (1995) identified two central themes at the core of communication: *intersubjectivity*, which has to do with striving to understand others and being understood in turn; and, *impact*, which represents the extent to which a message brings about change in thoughts, feelings or behaviour.

In this book the focus is upon interpersonal communication. In his review of the field, and while recognising that there are wide variations in how the concept has been interpreted, the definition proffered by Burleson (2010a, p. 151) was that, 'Interpersonal communication is a complex situated social process in which people who have established a communicative relationship exchange messages in an effort to generate shared meanings and accomplish social goals'. A number of key features of the process have been identified (Hartley, 1999; Adler *et al.*, 2013a).When compared with other forms of communication, this sub-category is typified by the:

- face-to-face (nonmediated) nature and physical closeness of the interaction;
- dyadic (one-to-one) or small-group setting in which it occurs;
- fact that it is shaped by, and conveys information about, the personal qualities of the interlocutors as well as their social roles and relationships;
- multiplicity of communication channels that are available;
- interdependence of the interactors;
- instantaneity of feedback available;
- extent of self-disclosure engendered;
- intrinsic nature of rewards stemming from intensive person-to-person contact.

In simple terms, Brooks and Heath (1993, p. 7) defined interpersonal communication as, 'the process by which information, meanings and feelings are shared by persons through the exchange of verbal and nonverbal messages'. This leads on to the first defining feature of communication.

Communication is a process

A distinct tradition within communication theory is that of conceptualising what takes place as a process of sending and receiving messages (Stewart *et al.*, 2005; DeVito, 2011). Communication requires that at least two contributors are involved in an ongoing and dynamic sequence of events, in which each affects and is affected by the other in a system of reciprocal determination. Each at the same time perceives the other in context, makes some sort of sense of what is happening, comes to a decision as to how to react and responds accordingly. Being more specific, the components of the communicative process have been identified as including communicators, message, medium, channel, code, noise, feedback and context (Adler and Proctor, 2014). Each of these will now be examined in turn.

Communicators

The centrality of communicators to the process is fairly obvious. A range of factors pertaining to the people involved in interaction directly affect the process. As will be demonstrated throughout this text, interpersonal skills are influenced by *inter alia* the gender, age, ethnicity, physical appearance and personality of those involved.

Message

The message can be thought of as the content of communication, containing whatever it is that the interlocutors wish to share. Gouran (1990, p. 6) described it as, 'a pattern of thought, configuration of ideas, or other response to internal conditions about which individuals express themselves'. Such expression, however, presupposes some form of behavioural manifestation: thoughts and feelings, to be made known, must be encoded or organised into a physical form capable of being transmitted to others. Decoding, the counterpart of encoding, is the process whereby recipients attach meaning to what they have just experienced (O'Hair *et al.*, 2011).

Medium

The medium is the particular means of conveying the message. In a seminal contribution, Fiske (1990) described three types of media:

1   *presentational*, e.g. voice, face, body;
2   *representational*, e.g. books, paintings, architecture, photographs;
3   *technological/mechanical*, e.g. internet, phone, television, radio.

The first of these is pivotal to interpersonal communication. Media differ in the levels of *social presence* afforded. As explained by Stevens-Long and McClintock (2008, p. 22), this is 'the degree to which the medium is experienced as sociable, warm, sensitive, or personal, creating the impression that the person communicating is *real*'. *Media richness* is a similar concept, suggesting that media differ in the wealth of information that they carry. Actually talking to someone face to face provides a greater richness of social cues and a fuller experience of the individual than, for example, messaging or e-mailing. Choices as to the most suitable medium to use depend upon a range of factors (Korda and Itani, 2013). In organisations, face-to-face rather than mediated (telephone, letters, e-mail, etc.) communication is the medium consistently preferred by employees (Meehan, 2013).

Channel

Differences between channel and medium are sometimes blurred in the literature, and, indeed, the two terms are often used interchangeably. 'Channel' refers to that which 'connects' interlocutors and accommodates the medium. DeVito (2013) described it as operating like a bridge between the sender and receiver. Fiske (1990) gave as examples light waves, sound waves, radio waves, as well as cables of different types, capable of carrying pulses of light or electrical energy. Likewise, DeVito (2013) distinguished between the:

- *vocal-auditory* channel, which carries speech;
- *gestural-visual* channel, which facilitates much nonverbal communication;
- *chemical-olfactory* channel, accommodating smell;
- *cutaneous-tactile* channel, which enables us to make interpersonal use of touch.

These different channels are typically utilised simultaneously in the course of face-to-face communication.

Code

A code is a system of meaning shared by a group. It designates signs and symbols peculiar to that code and specifies rules and conventions for their use (Klüver and Klüver, 2007). The English language, for example, is a code in accordance with which the accepted meaning of 'dog' is an animal with four legs that barks. Other codes are Morse, French, Braille.

Noise

Here the word 'noise' has a rather special meaning, which is more than mere sound. It refers to any interference with the success of the communicative act that distorts or degrades the message so that the meaning taken is not that intended. As such, noise may originate in the source, the channel, the receiver or the context. It may be external and take the form of intrusive sound, which masks what is being said, or it may be internal, stemming from intrapersonal distractions. Ethnic or cultural differences can cause communication 'noise', in that meanings attached to particular choices of word or forms of expression can vary considerably, causing unintended confusion, misunderstanding, insult or hurt (Holliday *et al.*, 2010).

Feedback

By means of feedback, the sender is able to ascertain the extent to which the message has been successfully received and the impact that it has had. Monitoring receiver reactions enables subsequent communications to be adapted and regulated to achieve a desired effect. Feedback, therefore, is vitally important to successful social outcomes. It plays a central role in the model of skilful interaction presented in Chapter 2 and more will be said about it then.

Context

Communication always occurs within a particular context, and this can have a powerful influence upon the interaction and the outcomes (Adler *et al.*, 2012). To be more accurate, communication takes place within intermeshing frameworks. Contexts include the physical, social, chronological and cultural, although a relational context could be added as well. An inescapable instance, geographical location, provides a physical setting for what takes place. For example, people in lifts often behave in rather restrained ways that match the physical constraints of their surroundings. The temporal context is also important. Thus, a college seminar may be held late on a Friday afternoon or early on Monday morning and the arousal level and enthusiasm of students can be influenced as a result. The relationship provides a further framework for interaction. For example, unmarried males tend to react more positively to touch from a significant other than unmarried females, but this pattern is reversed for married individuals (Hanzal *et al.,* 2008). It is also possible to envisage a range of psychosocial factors such as status relationship, which constitute a different, but equally significant, framework for communication.

So far, context has been depicted as exerting an influence upon communication. But it should not be overlooked that, in many respects, interlocutors can also serve to shape aspects of their situation through communication. The concept of context features prominently in the skills approach to communication and this will be fully discussed in Chapter 2.

Communication is inevitable

This is a contentious point. Communication has long been held, by those theorists who adopt a broad view of what constitutes the phenomenon (e.g. Scheflen, 1974; DeVito, 2012), to be inevitable in social situations where each is aware of the other's presence and is influenced in what is done as a result. Watzlawick *et al.* (1967, p. 49) were responsible for the much-quoted maxim that, under such circumstances, 'one cannot *not* communicate'. But are all actions communication? What if I display behaviour that I have little control over and do not mean to display – am I communicating? For some theorists, unless conditions are imposed, then all behaviour becomes communication, so rendering the term largely redundant (Trenholm and Jensen, 2007). The debate concerns issues such as communicative behaviour being intentional, performed with conscious awareness and being code-based (Knapp *et al.,* 2014). Applying such conditions in their most extreme form would confine communication to those acts:

- performed with the intention of sharing meaning;
- perceived as such by the recipient;
- executed with conscious understanding;
- accomplished by means of a shared arbitrary code; arbitrary in this sense means that the relationship between the behaviour and what it represents is a matter of agreed convention.

But does the encoder have to be consciously aware of the intention? What if the decoder fails to recognise that the witnessed behaviour was enacted intentionally and reacts (or fails to act) accordingly?

For many, these impositions are too extreme and create particular problems for the concept of *nonverbal* communication. Some nonverbal behaviour may best be described as informative rather than communicative. Thus, different sets of more relaxed restrictions have been suggested. Burgoon *et al.* (1996, pp. 13–14), for instance, advocated that those actions be accepted as communicative that, '(a) are typically sent with intent, (b) are used with regularity among members of a given social community, society or culture, (c) are typically interpreted as intentional, and (d) have consensually recognised meaning'. As such, an unconscious, unintentional facial expression could still be accepted as communicative.

Remland (2009) additionally argued that communication does not have to rely upon an arbitrary code. Such codes are made up of symbols whose relationship to the thing in the world that they represent is merely a matter of agreed convention. Taking a previous example, there is no obvious reason why 'dog' should be the word symbol that represents the animal to which it refers. Indeed, the Spanish use *perro*. Intrinsic codes that are biologically rather than socially based are also acceptable. This would include blushes being recognised as symptoms of embarrassment, despite the fact that they do not share this same type of arbitrary relationship.

Communication is purposeful

Another commonly cited characteristic of communication is its purposefulness. It is now widely accepted that, 'action is directed by goals that reliably control and motivate the behavioral system' (Aarts and Elliott, 2012a, p. vii). People interact with some end in mind; they want to effect some desired outcome. In other words, communication is far from idle or aimless, but is conducted to make something happen – to achieve a goal. As expressed by Westmyer and Rubin (1998, p. 28):

> To understand why people engage in interpersonal communication, we must remember that communication is goal directed. Interpersonal needs establish expectations for communication behaviour. Communicators are mindful in that they are capable of acknowledging their needs and motives, and realize that they can choose particular communication behaviors to fulfil these needs.

It is this that both adds impetus to and provides direction for the transaction. A pivotal implication of casting communication as purposeful activity is that it must also be thought of as 'adjusted' (Kellermann, 1992). That is, communicators fashion what they say and do, on an ongoing basis, in response to the goals that they are pursuing and the likelihood of their attainment (Wilson, 2006; Palomares, 2008). Adjusted performance presupposes the possibility of selection and choice amongst alternative courses of action. In other words, communication is a strategic enterprise. Dillard (1998) claimed that even the affective dimension of communication is in some respects managed strategically. While not denying an expressive element that may be more difficult to control, Planalp (1998, p. 44) agreed. She maintained that:

> people communicate their emotions to others for some purpose, whether intentionally or unintentionally…They may communicate emotion in order to get support (e.g. sadness, loneliness), negotiate social roles (anger, jealousy), deflect criticism (shame, embarrassment), reinforce social bonds (love), or for any number of other reasons.

The goal-directed nature of communication is central to the notion of skilled communication and so will be discussed in more detail in Chapter 2.

Communication is transactional

In early linear models of how communication took place (e.g. Shannon and Weaver, 1949), one person was designated the *source*, the other the *receiver*, and the process was held to commence when the former transmitted a message to the latter. This is a good example of what Clampitt (2013) called 'arrow' communication, i.e. communication that goes in one direction only. The limitations of such linear conceptualisations of face-to-face interaction are now widely recognised. Communicators are, at one and the same time, senders and receivers of messages. While person A is speaking, he or she is usually also monitoring the effects of the utterance, requiring information from B to be simultaneously received. Correspondingly, person B, in listening to A, is also reacting to A's contribution. The notion of 'source–receiver' is therefore a more accurate representation of the role of each participant (DeVito, 2016). Recent models of communication are based upon a *transactional* conceptualisation that stresses dynamic interplay and the changing and evolving nature of the process (Adler *et al.*, 2013a). In this way, interlocutors continually affect and are affected by one another, in a system of reciprocal influence.

Communication is multi-dimensional

Another significant feature of communication is its multi-dimensionality: messages exchanged are seldom unitary or discrete. Communication scholars have long concurred about two separate but inter-related levels to the process (Watzlawick *et al.*, 1967; Adler *et al.*, 2012). One concerns *content* and has to do with substantive matters (e.g. discussing a recent film; explaining Attribution Theory). These issues form the topic of conversation and usually spring to mind when thinking about what we do when communicating. But this is seldom, if ever, all that we do when communicating. Another less obvious level addresses the *relationship* between the interlocutors. Matters such as identity projection and confirmation are part and parcel of the interchange.

Identity projection and confirmation

In their choice of topic for discussion (and topics avoided), particular words and forms of expression adopted, manicured accents, speed of speech and a whole complex of nonverbal behaviours and characteristics, interactors work at designing the messages they send about themselves. These messages are to do with who and what they are, and how they wish to be received and reacted to by others. According to Wetherell (1996, p. 305) 'As people live their lives they are continually making themselves as characters or personalities through the ways in which they reconcile and work with the raw material of their social situation'. Communication is at the forefront of this endeavour. Our identity is formulated and evolves as a result of our interactions with others (McConnell and Strain, 2007).

In this sense, identity is not only something that we convey but a reality that is created in our dealings with others (this is further discussed in Chapter 9).

Impression management and *self-presentation* are the terms used to refer to the process of behaving in such a way as to get others to ratify the particular image of self being presented (Guerrero *et al.*, 2014). A direct approach is talking about oneself, and strategies for introducing self as a topic into conversation have been analysed by Bangerter (2000). For the quest to be successful, however, it has to be carried out with subtlety. Being seen as boastful and self-opinionated could well spoil the effect. Less conspicuous ways are therefore frequently utilised, often relying on the nonverbal channel (see Chapter 3). If the attempt is seen (or seen through) as a flagrant attempt at self-aggrandisement or ingratiation, it will backfire and a less than attractive impression be created.

Succeeding in conveying the right impression can confer several sorts of possible advantage (Leary, 1996). It can lead to material rewards as well as social benefits such as approval, friendship and power. Goffman (1959) emphasised the importance of social actors maintaining *face*, which can be thought of as a statement of the positive value claimed for self – a public expression of self-worth. He observed that actors characteristically engage not only in self-focused facework but are careful not to invalidate the face being presented by the interlocutor. In a highly influential book chapter, Brown and Levinson (1978) analysed how politeness operates as a strategy intended to reduce the likelihood of this being thought to have happened. Giving criticism is an example of a face-threatening situation. Metts and Cupach (2008) outlined how both verbal and nonverbal cues of politeness help to mitigate the possible negative effects of verbal criticism.

Relationship negotiation

Communication also serves relational ends in other ways by helping to determine how participants define their association (Foley and Duck, 2006). It is widely agreed that relationships are shaped around two main dimensions that have to do with *affiliation* (or liking) and *dominance*, although a third, concerning level of involvement or the *intensity* of the association, also seems to be important (Tusing and Dillard, 2000). Status differences are often negotiated and maintained by subtle (and not so subtle) means. The two directives, 'Shut that damned window!' and 'I wonder would you mind closing the window, please' are functionally equivalent on the content dimension (i.e. the speaker obviously wishes the person addressed to close the window), but a different type of relationship is presupposed in each case.

Power is also an important factor in human relationships (Robertson, 2013; Sturm and Antonakis, 2015). When people with relatively little social power, occupying inferior status positions, interact with those enjoying power over them, the former have been shown (Berger, 1994; Fiske and Berdahl, 2007) to manifest their increased 'accessibility' by, among other things:

- initiating fewer topics for discussion
- being more hesitant in what they say
- being asked more questions

- providing more self-disclosures
- engaging in less eye contact while speaking
- using politer forms of address
- using more restrained touch.

Sets of expectations are constructed around these parameters. It is not only the case that people with little power behave in these ways; there are norms or implicit expectations that they *should* do so.

These two communicative dimensions, content and relationship, are complexly inter-woven and inter-related (Knapp and Vangelisti, 2009). Statements have relational significance and the orchestration of relationships is typically achieved in this 'indirect' way. Indeed, Hanna and Wilson (1998) argued that every communication episode represents some defining element of the relationship. While the relationship itself may become the topic of conversation (i.e. form the content of talk), this usually only happens if it has become problematic.

Communication is irreversible

Simply put, once something is said, it cannot be 'taken back'. In this sense, communication is like the glue in a tube – once it is out, it cannot easily be retracted and there is usually mess involved in trying to do so. Take the example of a confidence that is broken by a secret being revealed – once that revelation has taken place, it cannot be undone. Of course, efforts can be made to mitigate the personal and relational consequences of the act. We can work at redefining what has taken place in order to make it more palatable and ourselves less blameworthy. The *account* is one mechanism used to this end. Accounts in this sense can be regarded as explanations for troublesome acts (Cody and McLaughlin, 1988; Buttny and Morris, 2001). Possibilities include apologies, justifications and excuses (Bousfield, 2008; Hargie *et al.*, 2010). In the case of the latter, the untoward action is attributed to the intervention of some external influence (e.g. that the information was extracted under threat or torture). Nevertheless, once information is in the public domain, it cannot be re-privatised.

OVERVIEW

This chapter has underscored the importance of interpersonal communication as a core part of our *raison d'être*. Most of us need, seek, enjoy and learn from interactions with others; we are stimulated by their presence and suffer psychologically if we are denied this contact. While the ability to communicate is not unique to humans, we have a sophistication that far surpasses all other species. We can share knowledge, beliefs and opinions about happenings in the distant past and possibilities for the future, about events here or in some other place, about the particular or the general, and the concrete or the abstract. It also enables us to develop deep, meaningful and lasting relationships. The more skilled we are in communicating with others, the more successful we are likely to be, both personally and professionally. Skilled interpersonal communication is therefore of the utmost importance in life.

However, despite its significance, communication is a notoriously difficult concept to define precisely. Nevertheless, as discussed in this chapter, a number of key defining attributes have been identified. Interpersonal communication is a transactional process in which messages are both sent and received simultaneously. It takes place within a set context and involves communicators who send messages that are delivered through various media and channels. It is inevitable, purposeful, multi-dimensional and irreversible. These key components of communication will be further analysed in the next chapter, where the focus will be on the nature of skilled interpersonal communication.

Chapter 2

A conceptual model of skilled interpersonal communication

INTRODUCTION

NUMEROUS CONTRASTING THEORIES and models have been formulated to represent and make sense of what happens when people engage in social interchange (see, for example, Berger *et al.*, 2010; Smith and Wilson, 2010; Heath and Bryant, 2012; Griffin *et al.*, 2014). Building upon the analysis in Chapter 1, in the present chapter a model of interpersonal communication is presented, in which the activity is conceptualised as a form of skilled performance. This represents what takes place when two people interact as a learned process that is undergirded by perceptual, cognitive, affective and behavioural operations, all of which function within and are influenced by the contextual framework. The activity is driven and directed by the desire to achieve particular goals and is accomplished by the ongoing monitoring of personal, social and environmental circumstances. The chapter begins by examining exactly what is meant by the term 'interpersonal skill' and delineates the key features of the activity; it then explicates the skill model of interpersonal communication.

COMMUNICATION AS INTERPERSONAL SKILL

In terms of nomenclature, different terms are used synonymously to describe the skilled nature of communication. The terms 'social skills', 'interpersonal skills' and 'communication skills' are often used interchangeably. The last term, however, can encompass written as well as interpersonal skills, while the first term is generally used to refer to developmental or clinical applications. In this the focus will therefore be upon the 'interpersonal' descriptor. Thus, interpersonal skills, in a global sense, can be defined as the skills we employ when interacting with other people. This definition is not very informative, however, since it really indicates what skills are *used for* rather than what they *are*. It is rather like defining an aeroplane as something that gets you from one city to another.

Attempts to define the term 'interpersonal skill' proliferate within the literature. In order to illustrate this point it is useful to examine some of the definitions that have been put forward by different theorists. In his early work in this area, Phillips (1978, p. 13) concluded that a person is skilled according to:

> the extent to which he or she can communicate with others, in a manner that fulfils one's rights, requirements, satisfactions, or obligations to a reasonable degree without damaging the interlocutor's similar rights, requirements, satisfactions, or obligations, and hopefully shares these rights etc. with others in free and open exchange.

This definition emphasises the macro-elements of social encounters, in terms of reciprocation between participants. This theme is also found in the definition given by Schlundt and McFall (1985, p. 23), who defined social skills as: 'the specific component processes that enable an individual to behave in a manner that will be judged as "competent". Skills are the abilities necessary for producing behavior that will accomplish the objectives of a task'.

These definitions tend to view skill as an *ability* that the individual may possess to a greater or lesser extent. A somewhat different focus has been proffered by other theorists, who define skill in terms of the *behaviour* of the individual. For example, Robbins and Hunsaker (2014, p. 6) iterated that 'A skill is a system of behavior that can be applied in a wide range of situations', while Cameron (2000, p. 86) stated that 'The term *skill* connotes *practical expertise*, the ability to *do* something'. Proctor and Dutta (1995, p. 18) extended this behavioural emphasis, to encompass the *goals* of the individual: 'Skill is goal-directed, well-organized behavior', while Kelly (1982, p. 3) emphasised the dimension of *learning* by defining skills as 'those identifiable, learned behaviors that individuals use in interpersonal situations to obtain or maintain reinforcement from their environment'. These elements were summarised by Robbins and Hunsaker (2014, p. 6), who argued that, to gain competence in a skill, 'people need to understand the skill conceptually and behaviorally, have opportunities to practice the skill, get feedback on how well they are performing the skill, and use the skill often enough to integrate it into their behavioral repertoires'.

In his review of definitions of skilled behaviour, Hargie (2006a, p. 13) defined interpersonal skill as: 'a process in which the individual implements a set of goal-directed, inter-related, situationally appropriate social behaviours, which are learned and controlled'. This is the definition adopted in this book. It emphasises seven separate components of skill.

1   Skilled performance is part of a transactional *process*.
2   Skilled behaviours are *goal-directed*.
3   Skilled behaviours are *inter-related*.
4   Skills should be *appropriate* to the *situation*.
5   Skills are defined in terms of identifiable units of *behaviour*.
6   Skilled behaviours are *learned*.
7   Skills are under the cognitive *control* of the individual.

Skilled performance is part of a transactional process

As discussed above, interpersonal communication is a process that is characterised by an ongoing verbal and nonverbal exchange of collaborative meaning making. In this sense, interaction requires skilled co-ordination, as each person regulates his or her actions in line with others (Arundale, 2013). This involves what Pickering (2006) referred to as 'the dance of dialogue', wherein individuals align their talk with one another, and construct shared meaning from the conversation. Balachandra *et al.* (2005) likened certain forms of interaction, such as negotiation, to the process of improvised performance (similar to improvised jazz or theatre), where those involved must pay attention to the moves of others and be flexible in how they respond. As will be discussed more fully later in the chapter, skilled performance is a transactional process that involves:

• formulating appropriate goals
• devising related action plans
• implementing these plans
• monitoring the effects of behaviour
• being aware of, and interpreting, the responses of others
• taking cognisance of the context in which the interaction occurs
• adjusting, adapting or abandoning goals and responses in the light of outcomes.

Skilled behaviours are goal-directed

Goals are at the very epicentre of the skills process and we will therefore discuss them more fully later when examining the conceptual model of skilled interpersonal communication. In terms of definition, goals are those behaviours the individual employs in order to achieve a desired outcome, and are therefore purposeful, as opposed to chance, or unintentional. As expressed by Carnevale and De Dreu (2006, p. 55), 'the human being is an *intentional system*', designed to pursue goals. In their analysis of the field, Brataas *et al.* (2010, p. 185) emphasised the pivotal nature of goals, pointing out that 'All other aspects of the interactive process relate to and can only be fully understood in the light of the goals being pursued'.

Goals both motivate and navigate the interpersonal process (Berger, 2002; Oettingen *et al.*, 2004). For example, if A wishes to encourage B to talk freely, A will look at B, use head nods when B speaks, refrain from interrupting B and utter 'guggles' ('hmm hmm'; 'uh, hu'; etc.) periodically. In this instance these *behaviours* are *directed* towards the *goal* of encouraging participation.

The goals we pursue are not always conscious, and indeed one feature of skilled performance is that behaviour is often executed automatically (Moors and De Houwer, 2007; Osman, 2015). Once responses are learned they tend to become hard-wired or habitual, and goal-directed behaviour is then under what Dijksterhuis *et al.* (2007) refer to as 'unconscious control'. In this way, people automatically and subconsciously regulate their behaviour in order to achieve their goals (Chen *et al.*, 2007). When we know how to drive, we no longer have to think about actions such as how to start the car, brake, reverse, and so on. Yet, when learning to drive, these actions are consciously monitored as they are performed. A distinction is made here between individuals' conscious awareness of the goal they wish to achieve and their comparative lack of consciousness of precisely how they are trying to achieve it. In their analysis of this distinction, Wyer *et al.* (2012, p. 240) give an example of this: 'People often consciously decide the point they want to make in an argument without being conscious of how they construct the statements they use to convey this point'.

In the successful learning of new skills we move through the stages of *unconscious incompetence* (we are totally unaware of the fact that we are behaving in an incompetent manner), *conscious incompetence* (we know what we should be doing and we know we are not doing it very well), *conscious competence* (we know we are performing at a satisfactory level) and finally, *unconscious competence* (we just do it without thinking about it and we succeed). This is also true of interpersonal skills. During free-flowing social encounters conversational pauses rarely reach 3 seconds and less than 200 milliseconds typically elapses between the responses of speakers (Heldner and Edlund, 2010). As a result, some elements, such as exact choice of words used and use of gestures, almost always occur without conscious reflection (Wilson *et al.*, 2000). In relation to the negotiation context, McRae (1998, p. 123) explained how: 'Expert negotiators become so proficient at certain skills in the negotiating process that they do not have to consciously think about using these skills. It's as if the responses become second nature.'

However, an awareness of relevant goals does not ensure success. As expressed by Greene (2000, p. 147):

> action may not be so readily instantiated in overt behavior...the inept athlete, dancer, actor or public speaker may well have a perfectly adequate abstract representation of what he or she needs to do, but what actually gets enacted is rather divergent from his or her image of that action.

Thus, skill involves not just the ability to formulate appropriate goals; it necessitates being able to implement them successfully in practice (Stafford and Dewar, 2014). In other words, '*skill* refers to the degree to which a performed behavior proves successful' (Miczo *et al.*, 2001, p. 40). An important part of this, as will be discussed in more detail later in the chapter, is the ability to detect accurately the goals being pursued by those with whom we interact (Palomares, 2009a).

Skilled behaviours are inter-related

Skilled behaviours are co-ordinated in order to achieve a particular goal. For example, as mentioned previously, when encouraging B to talk, A may smile, use head nods and look directly at B, and all of these signals will be interpreted by B as signs of encouragement to continue speaking. Each behaviour relates to this common goal, and so the behaviours are inter-related and synchronised.

Skills should be appropriate to the situation

Our behaviour is influenced to a very large degree by situational demands (Snyder and Stukas, 2007), and skilled individuals employ context-appropriate behaviours (Gearhart *et al.*, 2014). Dickson and McCartan (2005) referred to this aspect of skilled performance as *contextual propriety*. In their review of this area, White and Burgoon (2001) concluded that the key feature of social interaction is that it necessitates adaptation. Indeed, linguistic conceptualisations purport that skill is mutually constructed through dialogue and so can only be understood by an interpretation of how narratives develop in any particular context (Holman, 2000).

From an interpersonal communication perspective, Wilson *et al.* (2000, pp. 136–137) illustrated how effective interaction involves adaptation at all levels:

> Speakers coordinate their own behavior with that of their interactive partner. Interparty coordination is evident at microlevels, such as in the timing of mutual smiles…[and]…at more macrolevels, such as in the adjustment of one's own plans to the apparent plans of one's conversational partner.

In many routine situations, such as filling stations or fast-food counters, participants have a good idea of one another's goals and so adaptation is easy. However, in more complex contexts, such as psychotherapy or negotiation, the interlocutors have to spend considerable time establishing one another's agendas and agreeing mutual goals for the encounter, so that they can adjust and adapt their responses accordingly (Berger, 2000). The role of context in skilled performance will be returned to later in the chapter.

Skills are defined in terms of identifiable units of behaviour

We judge whether or not people are skilled based upon how they actually *behave*. Accordingly, 'Skill is reflected in the performance of communicative behaviors. It is the *enactment* of knowledge and motivation' (Cupach and Canary, 1997, p. 28). Verbal and nonverbal behaviour therefore represent the oxygen of the communicating organism. Skilled responses are hierarchically organised in such a way that large elements, like being interviewed, are comprised of smaller behavioural units, such as looking at the interviewer and answering questions. The development of interpersonal skills can be facilitated by training the individual to acquire these smaller responses before combining them into larger repertoires. Indeed, this technique is also used in the learning of many motor skills.

Skilled behaviours are learned

The sixth aspect of the definition is that behaviours are *learned*. Although some academics still purport that 'communication is intuitive' (Salmon and Young, 2011, p. 220), it is now widely accepted that most forms of behaviour displayed in social contexts are learned. As Verderber *et al.* (2014, p. 17) put it: 'Just as we learn to walk so do we learn to communicate. Because communication is learned, we can always improve our ability to communicate'. From birth, infants are communicated with as if they can understand. Parents and other carers talk to them and ascribe intentionality to their behaviour (e.g. 'You are hungry and are looking for some milk, aren't you?' 'There, you wanted your rattle, didn't you?'). The function here is to bring the infant into 'personhood' by treating it as a communicating being (Penman, 2000). This is a very important step in the social development of the individual. For example, as the child grows it is taught to read. This begins with the social process of slowly reading and speaking the words aloud, which eventually results in the child learning to read silently. The skill of talking to oneself in silence takes time to master, and is predicated upon the earlier social dynamic of reading with others. In this way, communication is central to the development of cognitive abilities.

Children reared in isolation miss out on these essential learning experiences. As a result they display distorted, socially unacceptable forms of behaviour (Newton, 2002). At a less extreme level, there is evidence to indicate that children from culturally richer home environments tend to develop more appropriate social behaviours than those from socially deprived backgrounds (Messer, 1995). This is exemplified by findings in relation to vocabulary development. By the age of 4 years a child from a high socioeconomic background will have been exposed to an accumulated total of around 42 million words as compared to 13 million words for a child from a low socioeconomic family (Hart and Risley, 2003). At school entry this leads to an average difference of about 15,000 words, with disadvantaged children having a vocabulary of some 5,000 words compared to 20,000 words for children from more advantaged backgrounds (Marulis and Newman, 2010). This is part of the process of intergenerational transmission of interpersonal skills, wherein the parent's communicative ability is predictive of the child's ability (Burke *et al.*, 2013).

Bandura's (1986) social cognitive theory purports that all repertoires of behaviour, with the exception of elementary reflexes (such as eye blinks), are learned. This process of social learning involves the *modelling* and *imitation* of the behaviour of significant others, such as parents, teachers, siblings or peers. From an early age, children tend to walk, talk and act like their same-sex parent. At a later stage, however, the child may develop the accent of his or her peers and begin to talk in a similar fashion – despite the accent of parents. In addition to modelling and imitation, a second major element in the learning of social behaviour is the *reinforcement*, by significant others, of these behaviours (see Chapter 4 for a full discussion of reinforcement). In childhood, for example, parents encourage, discourage or ignore various behaviours that the child displays. As a general rule, the child learns, and employs more frequently, those behaviours that are encouraged, while tending to display less often those that are discouraged or ignored. In this sense, feedback is crucial to effective performance.

Skills are under the cognitive control of the individual

The final element in the definition of skills, and another feature of social cognitive theory, is that they are under the cognitive *control* of the individual. As expressed by Cameron (2000, p. 86):

> A 'skilled' person does not only know how to do certain things, but also understands *why* those things are done the way they are. S/he is acquainted with the general principles of the activity s/he is skilled in, and so is able to modify what s/he does in response to the exigencies of any specific situation.

Thus a socially inadequate individual may have learned the basic elements of skills but may not have developed the appropriate thought processes necessary to control the utilisation of these elements in interpersonal encounters. An important dimension of control relates to the timing of behaviours. Skilled behaviour involves implementing behaviours at the most apposite juncture. Learning *when* to employ behaviours is just as crucial as learning *what* these behaviours are and *how* to use them. As expressed by Wolvin and Coakley (1996, p. 52), 'Communication skills combine with communicator *knowledge* – information and understanding – to influence the entire process'.

Zimmerman (2000) identified four key stages in the learning of skills.

1   *Observation.* Here the person watches others perform the skill, and also pays attention to other dimensions such as the motivational orientation, values and performance standards of the actors, as well as how the repertoires used vary across target persons.
2   *Emulation.* At this stage the individual is able to execute a behavioural display to approximate that observed. The display is emulated but not replicated. For example, the *style* of praise used may be similar but the *actual words used* will differ.
3   *Self-control.* This involves the actor beginning to *master* the skill. Thus, the tennis player will practise serving until this is fully developed, while a barrister will likewise practise questioning technique.

4 *Self-regulation.* Finally, the person learns to use the skill appropriately across different personal and contextual conditions. To continue the analogies, here the tennis player is concerned with placing the serve where it is likely to find the opponent's weak point, while the barrister will consider appropriate questions to achieve the best outcomes from different witnesses.

The acronym CLIPS is useful for remembering the key features of interpersonal skill. Skilled performance is:

- Controlled by the individual
- Learned behaviour that improves with practise and feedback
- Integrated and inter-related verbal and nonverbal responses
- Purposive and goal-directed
- Smooth in the manner in which the performance is executed.

Building upon these key features of skill, a model of skilled interpersonal communication will now be discussed.

A SKILL MODEL OF INTERPERSONAL COMMUNICATION

This model builds upon related skill-based models developed, *inter alia*, by Hargie (2006c), Bull (2006), Bull and Feldman (2012) and Dickson *et al.* (1997), based upon earlier theorising by Argyle (1983). As shown in Figure 2.1, it is based upon six elements of skilled interpersonal interaction. These are:

1 person–situation context
2 goals
3 mediating processes

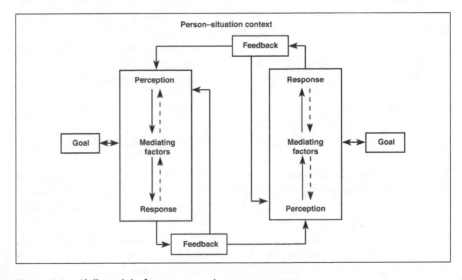

Figure 2.1 Skill model of interpersonal communication.

4   responses
5   feedback
6   perception.

By way of an overview, the skill model of interpersonal communication rests upon three basic assumptions. The first is that people act purposefully; second, that they are sensitive to the effects of their actions; and, third, that they take steps to modify subsequent action in the light of this information. Dyadic interaction is depicted within a person–situation framework wherein what takes place when people engage in communication is shaped both by the particular attributes and characteristics of the individual and by the impinging demands of the shared situation.

As discussed above, a widely agreed feature of social activity is that it is goal-directed. People establish and pursue goals in the situations within which they interact, even if this amounts to little more than the pleasure to be had from conversing. In a quest to realise the adopted goal, mediating processes are operationalised. Accordingly, possible strategies for actualising these outcomes are formulated, their projected effects evaluated, a decision is made about a plan of action and the plan is executed in terms of responses implemented. The interactive nature of the process is such that each person provides feedback to the other that is of relevance to decisions about whether or not goals are being achieved. In addition, the individual has a direct channel of feedback on performance, enabling monitoring of self to take place.

While feedback is available, it can only be acted upon if it is actually perceived. Perception is therefore central to skilful interaction, yet its intrinsically selective and subjective nature often results in perceptual inaccuracy and miscommunication (Hinton, 2015). The model also recognises the inter-relationship between goals and mediation, perception and responses. In this way, our mediating processes may cause us to evaluate our current goals as unattainable and so we will formulate new ones. Furthermore, the way in which we perceive others is influenced by our prevailing emotional state and cognitive structure; and, our responses play a part in shaping our thoughts and feelings (as shown by the dashed arrows in Figure 2.1).

To sum up, and in keeping with cognitive theories of interpersonal communication in general, 'people are assumed to be actors and to have goals...these actors are endowed with complex mental machinery. The machinery is deployed in pursuit of those goals' (Hewes, 1995, p. 164). It should be remembered that, due to the dynamic and changing character of communication, both participants are, at one and the same time, senders and receivers of information. Each is, even when silent, acting and reacting to the other. Furthermore, potential barriers to successful communication exist at each of the different stages outlined. A more detailed consideration of each of these components of the model will now be presented.

Person–situation context

Participants bring considerable personal 'baggage' to social encounters. This includes their attitudes, values, expectations and dispositions. The way in which they have come to regard themselves (*self-concept*) and the beliefs that they have formed about their abilities to succeed in various types of enterprise (*self-efficacy*) will determine the sorts of encounters contemplated, goals selected, how these are pursued and anticipated rewards derivable from them.

Interaction is also co-determined by parameters of the situation within which individuals find themselves, including role demands and the rules that pertain (Clarke, 2013). Take, for example, a priest and a parishioner in the confessional. Each is personally unique, yet the respective roles inherent in this highly restricted situation dictate that, regardless of the individuals involved, much the same sort of activity will be entered into by priests and parishioners. The implicit rules governing how both parties should conduct themselves under these circumstances will, by condoning certain actions and reproving others, regulate the interaction that unfolds.

There has long been debate about whether our behaviour is determined by the types of people we are or by the situation in which we find ourselves (Krueger, 2009; Sailer and McCulloh, 2012). It is now generally recognised that personal and situational sources of influence are bi-directional (Wortley, 2012; Vlăduţescu, 2014; Rauthmann *et al.*, 2015). As summarised by Hirsh (2009, p. 755), 'Although researchers examining the situational and dispositional determinants of behaviour have traditionally been at odds with one another, contemporary models acknowledge the importance of adopting an interactionist framework'. Furthermore, it is not only the case that personal characteristics and situational factors combine to determine behaviour, since what transpires during social contact can also effect changes in interactors. Involvement with others can lead to modifications in individual knowledge, beliefs and attitudes (indeed, the success of educational and counselling interventions depends upon it) and can also, within limits, serve to redefine the social situation (Smith and Boster, 2009). Thus, interlocutors may decide to dispense with the customary formality surrounding situations such as the selection interview, summit meetings, etc., and turn them into much more relaxed occasions. While acknowledging the interactive nature of the person–situation context, it is useful to examine each separately.

Personal characteristics

A complex of personal factors, including attitudes, personality, appearance, age and gender, shape the interactive process in respect of goals pursued, perceptions and interaction patterns.

Attitudes

How our attitudes are structured and the extent to which they determine what we do are topics of ongoing debate (Albarracin *et al.*, 2005; Bohner and Dickel, 2011). A long-standing way of thinking about attitudes (Katz and Stotland, 1959) is in terms of three constituent elements, sometimes referred to as ABC:

- *Affective*: how one feels about the target, either positive or negative, liking or disliking. Indeed, for some this is the most important attribute.
- *Behavioural*: one's predisposition to respond in a certain way towards the target.
- *Cognitive*: one's knowledge or beliefs about the target.

For example, I may have a particular attitude towards my next-door neighbour such that I believe that he is jealous of me and out to do me down (cognitive), which makes me dislike him (affective) so I avoid his company (behavioural). Note, however, that attitudes only define a tendency to behave in a particular way in respect of an attitude object. According to the *theory of planned behaviour* (Ajzen, 1991), additional considerations such as *perceived behavioural control* (the ease with which we feel we can accomplish the behaviour) and *subjective norms* (our appreciation of the prevailing expectations regarding that behaviour and our motivation to comply) are likely to shape our intentions to behave accordingly. It is these intentions that directly lead to behaviour in line with attitudes (the relationship between attitudes and behaviour is explored further in Chapter 12).

In any situation therefore there may not be a direct correspondence between attitude and actual behaviour. Attitudes interact with other personal characteristics, including values and other attitudes, together with situational forces, to influence responses. Furthermore, not all attitudes are equally accessible or held with the same strength of feeling (Maio and Haddock, 2015).

Personality

Personality is the complex of unique traits and characteristics of an individual that shape interaction with the environment and the ability to relate to oneself; it allows us to predict behaviour across time and situations (Carducci, 2015). A large number of personality traits has been identified. There is now wide consensus regarding the validity of what has been termed the 'big five' personality traits, often known by the OCEAN acronym, of openness, conscientiousness, extraversion, agreeableness and neuroticism (Rauthmann *et al.*, 2015). To take just one of these, extraversion–introversion is a dimension along which individuals can be placed that has implications for communicative behaviour. There is evidence that introverts tend to speak less, make more frequent use of pauses, engage in lower frequencies of gaze at their partners, are less accurate at encoding emotion and prefer to interact at greater interpersonal distances (John *et al.*, 2008; Knapp *et al.*, 2014).

Appearance

Physical appearance plays an important role in the interpersonal process. We make judgements about others based upon their height, weight, dress, attractiveness, skin colour, and so on. As we will discuss in more detail in

Chapters 3 and 10, the first impressions that we make based upon appearance have an important influence on how we evaluate others and respond to them. Furthermore, there is increasing evidence that the judgements we form of others based upon appearance are often accurate. While we are told that we should not judge a book by its cover, research has shown that naïve observers can accurately judge the personality traits of a person from a single photograph. As Di Domenico *et al.* (2015, p. 340) explain, 'The accuracy of such appearance-based judgments is mediated by observers' use of distinct physical cues that validly portray the traits of target individuals'. For example, judgements about levels of the trait of conscientiousness are higher if the person is wearing a more formal type of dress.

Age

The relative ages of participants will influence their behaviour and the expectations that each has of the other (Spisak *et al.*, 2014). Particular ways in which communication is used by and towards older people and issues surrounding intergeneration talk has attracted considerable research interest (Nussbaum and Coupland, 2004). The elderly are frequently subjected to forms of speech that can be seen as patronising (Dickson and McCartan, 2005; Lin *et al.*, 2008). Examples of some of these are presented in Box 2.1.

Negative stereotypes of older people seem to be the reason for this way of relating. Picking up on cues denoting advanced years can activate a stereotype suggesting incompetence, decline or senility, such that younger

---

Box 2.1 Examples of patronising communication with the elderly

- *Simplification strategies* – using a simplified register as one might with a child (e.g. basic vocabulary, short sentences, simple sentence structure, more restricted range of sentence patterns)
- *Clarification strategies* – ways of making yourself heard and understood (e.g. speaking more loudly, slowly and with exaggerated intonation; using repetition)
- *Diminutives* – being dismissively familiar or patronising; includes calling the person 'honey', 'love' or 'dear', or describing a thing or event, such as a nap, as 'little' (e.g. 'It's time for a little nap, dear')
- *Demeaning emotional tone* – acting superciliously
- *Secondary baby talk* – talking as one would to a baby (e.g. 'Just a teensy-weensy bit more?')
- *Avoidance* – discussing the older person, in his or her presence, with a relative rather than addressing the older person directly
- *Overly controlling* – being impatient or assuming the person's needs are already known

---

speakers may tailor what they say in keeping with this set of beliefs. One example of this is a tendency to use simplified or patronising talk with mature adults (Hehman *et al.*, 2012; Samuelsson *et al.*, 2013). Older people tend to have frequent contact with healthcare workers. Does communication in this context, therefore, reveal these same trends? The answer is yes. In working with institutionalised older people, 'secondary baby talk' or 'elderspeak' has been found to be a feature of carers' communication, and often regardless of the level of personal competence of the receiver (Carpiac-Claver and Levy-Storms, 2007; Christian *et al.*, 2014). However, the elderly tend to rate carers more favourably when nonpatronising speech is used (Draper, 2005). There is a caveat here, however, in that the lower the older person's level of cognitive functioning, the more favourably this type of elderspeak is rated (Roter and Hall, 2006).

Gender

Numerous studies have documented differences in how males and females communicate verbally and nonverbally (Pichler and Coates, 2011; Knapp *et al.*, 2014). These, however, should not be overstated, nor should it be assumed that they apply to each and every individual (Tenenbaum *et al.*, 2011; Chu, 2014). With that in mind (and other things being equal), females, compared with males, typically tend to:

- interact at closer interpersonal distances;
- be more tolerant of spatial intrusion;
- make greater use of eye contact and touch;
- smile more and are more facially, gesticularly and vocally expressive;
- be more adept at both encoding and decoding nonverbal messages;
- have deeper insights into their relational goals.

Males and females express themselves differently in language. Researchers commonly report that 'women are more likely than men to use language to form and maintain connections with others (i.e. affiliation), whereas men are more likely to use language to assert dominance and to achieve utilitarian goals (i.e. self-assertion)' (Leaper and Ayres, 2007, pp. 328–329). This was shown by Tannen (1995), who analysed how males and females typically respond to 'trouble talk' – being told about some personal problem or difficulty. When women disclose personal predicaments, they primarily expect (and tend to get from other women) a listening ear, confirmation of their concerns and an understanding reaction. Indeed, this type of talk serves, in part, to strengthen interpersonal bonds between friends. Men, however, respond by tackling the problem head-on in an attempt to solve it through giving information or offering advice. Miscommunication is such that men tend to see women wallowing in their problems rather than discussing practical steps to solve them. Women, on the other hand, can feel that men don't understand them and are not prepared to make the effort to do so. Frustration is shared equally. This issue of gender differences is further discussed in several chapters, particularly Chapter 9.

Situational factors

Various attempts have been made to delineate the essential constituents of situations (Miller *et al.*, 1994; Gosling *et al.*, 2008; Rauthmann, 2012). Perhaps the simplest categorisation is that by Pervin (1978), who proposed that the key elements are:

- who is involved
- what is happening
- where the action is taking place.

A more highly differentiated analysis of social situations, derived from extensive research, is that offered by Argyle *et al.* (1981) and elaborated by Hargie (2006c). They identified eight key features of the situations within which people interact.

1   *Goal structure.* Situations have goal implications. Not only do we seek out situations with goal satisfaction in mind, but particular situations will place constraints on the goals that can be legitimately pursued.
2   *Roles.* In most situations individuals act in accordance with more or less clearly recognised sets of expectations centring upon their social position and status. Behaviour is governed by the roles people play (e.g. doctor, teacher, priest, spouse) and this is in turn central to an understanding of the situation.
3   *Rules.* Situations are rule-governed. There are (often implicit) stipulations that govern what is acceptable conduct for participants. It may be perfectly acceptable for two friends at a student party to sing, shout, dance and drink alcohol from a bottle. But were such behaviour transferred to a lecture theatre or place of worship it would be in strict contravention of the contrasting rules that prevail in those contexts.
4   *Repertoire of elements.* This refers to the range of behaviours that may be called upon for the situation to be competently handled.
5   *Sequences of behaviour.* In many situations interaction unfolds in a quite predictable sequence of acts on the part of participants (e.g. checking in at a hotel, visiting the GP surgery). As already mentioned, people often function in highly routine instances according to scripts.
6   *Situational concepts.* As discussed earlier in relation to schemas, individuals possess knowledge which enables them to make sense of situations and perform appropriately in them.
7   *Language and speech.* There are linguistic variations associated with social situations. Some, for example, public speaking, require a more formal speech style than others, such as having a casual conversation.
8   *Physical environment.* The physical setting, including furniture, decor, lighting and layout, often influences who talks to whom, how they feel, how much they say and how the talk is regulated.

Culture

At a broader level, cultural background is a highly significant contextualising factor. Culture can be regarded as the way of life, customs and script of a group of people. Cultural and sub-cultural variables have a bearing on the different features of the communicative process. In turn, communication shapes culture (Arasaratnam, 2014). Intercultural differences therefore run much deeper than possible differences in language, encompassing not only much of the nonverbal channel of communication but beyond to the underlying social order itself and the meanings and values that give it form (Asante *et al.*, 2014). When two people from radically different cultures come together, not only may they be attempting to use different language codes to represent a shared world, but the respective social worlds themselves may have little overlap.

Cultural influences permeate values, beliefs and cherished practices. Indeed, so pervasive are cultural effects that they shape individuals' entire understanding of their social worlds. A classic study conducted by Hofstede (1980) revealed four underlying dimensions along which a large sample of different national groups could be plotted in respect of fundamental values espoused. These dimensions were:

1   *power distance* – the amount of respect and deference displayed by those in different positions on a status hierarchy;
2   *individualism–collectivism* – the extent to which one's identity is shaped by individual choices and achievements or a feature of the collective group to which one belongs;
3   *uncertainty avoidance* – the degree to which life's uncertainties can be controlled through planning and foresight;
4   *masculinity–femininity* – this has to do with the relative focus upon competitive, task-centred achievement versus co-operation and harmonious relationships.

European and North American cultures scored high on individualism and low on power distance, while those from Latin American and Asian countries were low on individualism but high on power distance. These cultural dimensions have been shown to influence communication in a myriad of ways (Samovar *et al.*, 2012; Taras *et al.*, 2012).

At another level, culturally prescribed norms govern how people conduct themselves during social encounters. These norms determine punctuality, interpersonal distance, touch, use of gestures, facial expressions, gaze patterns – indeed, all the nonverbal codes (Manusov and Patterson, 2006; Remland, 2009). Machismo in Hispanic cultures, for example, imposes display rules that forbid male expressions of pain. In Muslim cultures there are gender difficulties surrounding touch by a male health worker in the course of a physical examination of a female patient. Aspects of culture are explored in future chapters, and particularly in Chapter 11.

Having considered the person–situation context of communication, the other components of the model will now be explored.

Goals

As discussed earlier, goals are central to skilled performance. Moskowitz (2012, p. 1) defined a goal as, 'an end state that the organism has not yet attained (and is focused toward attaining in the future) and that the organism is committed to'. Put another way, the goals that we have in mind are mental representations of future end-states that we would like to make happen (Fishbach and Ferguson, 2007). Goals are related to motivation, needs and wants. The goals that we pursue are shaped by what we want or need, while our motivation to continue to pursue a particular goal is influenced by its importance for us. Effective salespeople are well aware of these distinctions. A customer may not *need* a 60-inch TV but if he or she really *wants* it then the motivation to buy will be high.

Different ways of analysing and categorising human goals have been documented (e.g. Moskowitz and Grant, 2009; Caughlin and Scott, 2010; Aarts and Elliott, 2012b). Some of the most significant elements will now be examined.

Content and process elements

Maes and Gebhardt (2000) specified that goals have *content* and *process* properties. The former defines *what* is to be attained, the latter addresses *how* this is to be effected and commitment to the objective. Content goals can often be achieved using a variety of different processes, some of which may be more or less effective.

Task and relational goals

For most professionals, when fulfilling one's task role it is also very important to maintain a facilitative relationship with one's clients. Indeed, both functions are usually closely related. One of the assumptions underlying many goal-based accounts of human endeavour is that individuals are, often concurrently, striving to actualise a multiplicity of outcomes (Dillard, 2008). For example, Samp and Solomon (1998) identified seven categories of goal behind communicative responses to problematic events in close relationships. These are to:

1   maintain the relationship
2   accept fault for the event
3   ensure positive face
4   avoid addressing the event
5   manage the conversation
6   cope with emotion
7   restore negative face.

Referring back to what was said earlier about the multi-dimensionality of communication, Tracy and Coupland (1990) identified one of the most basic distinctions as that between task goals and face or relational goals. In certain situations it may be difficult to satisfy both and yet be vitally important to do so. For example, health care presents a myriad of occasions when face can be compromised (Brataas *et al.*, 2009). As a result, instances of humour being used as a face-giving strategy, to stave off awkward embarrassment in situations such as nakedness, have been reported in medical contexts (Foot and McCreaddie, 2006). Such tactics enable both task and relational goals to be achieved. As aptly summarised by Lawler (2006, p. 197), 'Skill is required by the nurse to construct a context in which it is permissible to see other people's nakedness and genitalia, to undress others and handle other people's bodies'.

Instrumental and consummatory goals

Along similar lines, Ruffner and Burgoon (1981) distinguished between goals that are *instrumental* and those that are *consummatory*. Instrumental goals are carried out in order to achieve some further outcome (e.g. a supervisor may reward effort to increase productivity). Consummatory communication, on the other hand, satisfies the communicator's goal without the *active* intervention of another: e.g. the supervisor may reward in order to experience the feeling of satisfaction or power when distributing largesse.

Implicit and explicit goals

Some of the goals that we try to achieve in interaction are readily available to us. We are consciously aware of them and, if asked, could articulate them with little effort. Not all goals are like this, but rather, many operate in a reflexive, automatic manner (Bargh, 2005). While they are influential in what we do, we would find these more difficult to account for. As explained by Berger (1995, p. 144):

> Given that conscious awareness is a relatively scarce cognitive resource, it is almost a certainty that, in any social-interaction situation, several goals will be implicit for the actors involved, and that goals at the focal point of conscious awareness will change during the course of most social-interaction episodes.

Does attributing purposefulness to the communicative act presuppose consciousness? For some the answer is in the affirmative: purposive behaviour implies conscious awareness. Klinger *et al.* (1981, p. 171) believed that convictions of the existence of unconscious goals do not match the evidence, concluding that 'life would be far more chaotic than it is if substantial portions of people's goal strivings were for goals about which the striver was unconscious'. Emmons (1989) summarised this thinking by suggesting that it is commonly accepted that people have considerable access to their goals and can readily report them but are less aware of the underlying motivational basis upon which they are founded.

On the other hand, Langer *et al.* (1978), in their early work in the field, argued that much of communication is 'mindless'. They distinguished between *mindful* activity where 'people attend to their world and derive behavioral strategies based upon current incoming information' and *mindlessness*, where 'new information is not actually being processed. Instead prior scripts, written when similar information was once new, are stereotypically reenacted' (p. 363). More recently this concept of mindfulness has been used as the basis for therapeutic interventions (Hasson, 2013; Penman and Burch, 2013). Burgoon and Langer (1995) explored the various ways in which language itself can predispose to mindlessness in its capacity to mould thought. Similarly, Monahan (1998) demonstrated how interlocutors' evaluations of others can be influenced by nonconscious feelings derived from information sources of which they have little awareness. Consistent with this thesis, Kellermann (1992) argued that communication is at one and the same time purposeful/strategic *and* also primarily automatic. Likewise, Lakin (2006, p. 63) concluded that 'consciousness is not required for behavior to be either strategic or adaptive'. As stressed by Burgoon (2005, p. 238), 'strategic activity should not be construed as requiring a high degree of cognitive awareness or mindfulness'.

Circumstances under which we tend to become aware of customarily nonconscious encoding decisions (Motley, 1992; Burgoon and Langer, 1995) include:

- novel situations;
- situations where carrying out a routinely scripted performance becomes effortful;
- conflict between two or more message goals;
- anticipations of undesirable consequences for a formulated version of a message, thus requiring reformulation;
- some unexpected intervention (such as a failed attempt to 'take the floor' or experiencing the 'tip-of-the-tongue' phenomenon) between the initial decision to transmit a message and the opportunity to do so;
- the goals of the communication being difficult to actualise or the situation being troublesome in some other way.

Hierarchical organisation

Goals are hierarchically structured, with some being more widely encompassing than others (Oettingen and Gollwitzer, 2001). This theme is common in the literature, although some authors have countenanced more complex arrangements than others. Dillard (1990) believed that a three-level structure was adequate, with broad motives leading to goals that, in turn, governed sub-goals. Berger (1995) also identified *metagoals* that over-arch more specific instances. These include quests for *efficiency* – a requirement to achieve the objective by the most economical means, and *social appropriateness* – a stipulation not to violate prevailing norms and expectations.

Furthermore, primary and secondary goals may be at work in specific interactive episodes (Wilson, 2010). *Primary goals* are the ostensible reason for the interaction taking place; they give it meaning and establish expectations and responsibilities. *Secondary goals* span different episodes, shaping and placing constraints around the pursuit of primary goals (e.g. maintaining face or reducing anxiety). These are also referred to as long-term and short-term goals.

Hargie (2006a) gave the example of an employment interviewer interviewing a job applicant. The long-term goal here is to reach a decision as to the suitability of the interviewee. Appropriate related short-term goals are to welcome the candidate, make introductions and ask relevant questions.

Goal importance

We attach more weight to some goals than others, and so these have most impact upon our actions at any particular juncture. Decisions about goal selection are in turn determined by the desirability and attractiveness of a particular goal, estimates about the feasibility of achieving it, the projected immediacy of gratification, possible costs which may ensue, and so on (Shah and Kruglanski, 2000; Oettingen *et al.*, 2004). One implication of recognising that goals differ in importance is the need for a prioritising mechanism to regulate goal selection. This allows for ongoing assessment and re-prioritising as some outcomes are attained, others abandoned or alternative means formulated for achievement, as circumstances alter (Bandura, 1997; Brataas *et al.*, 2010).

Level of precision

Carver and Scheier (2000) noted that goals differ in their level of concreteness/abstraction. Some may be quite specific and precise, others more vague and indeterminate. Thus a junior nurse may have as a goal to be more assertive in transactions with other staff, or politely but firmly to refuse to swap shifts with Jo the next time the request is made. In the context of the identification of objectives for educational or therapeutic interventions, one of the commonly accepted recommendations is that they be precisely articulated in assessable terms (Millar *et al.*, 1992).

Goal compatibility

How well the goals of interlocutors align has obvious and extremely important implications for the encounter and what transpires. Goals may be:

- *similar* – here both are striving to achieve the same or similar goal but in so doing each may coincidentally thwart the other (e.g. both friends want to off-load about their relationship troubles);
- *complementary* – here goals are compatible (e.g. one friend wants to off-load, the other wants to listen);
- *opposed* – one's goal may be in direct opposition to that of the other (e.g. one friend wants to find out about the other's relationship, while the other does not want to reveal this information).

In terms of the individual, conflict can also take place between goals at a similar level and between goals at one hierarchical level and the next (Maes and

Gebhardt, 2000). In discussing metagoals in the strategic management of embarrassment, for example, Sharkey (1997) explained how social appropriateness may be forfeited in favour of efficiency when it is the intention of someone to deliberately cause embarrassment to another. Efficiency refers to how quickly and easily one can accomplish one's goal, while social appropriateness refers to being able to do so without causing loss of face for others. Sharkey gave the example of someone hogging the conversation among a group of friends, and one of the group saying, 'Have you always been a talkaholic?' Here, the response may be efficient in getting the person to stop talking, but it is low in social appropriateness, as it may anger the speaker as well as causing embarrassment for everyone present.

Once a goal has been decided upon, the next step is to devise a plan of action to achieve it. This involves a set of mediating processes.

Mediating processes

These processes mediate between the goal being pursued, our perceptions of events and what we decide to do about them. They also, as we have seen, play a part in the formulation of goals, influence how people and events are perceived and reflect the capacity of the individual to assimilate, deal with and respond to the circumstances of social encounters. The stage of mediation involves both cognitive and affective processes.

Cognitive processes

Discussions of the cognitive processes that make interpersonal communication possible can be readily found in the literature (e.g. Strack and Förster, 2009; Augoustinos et al., 2014). Knowledge is a key factor here. A distinction can be made between what is known, on the one hand, and the cognitive processes by means of which information is decoded, stored and retrieved from memory, on the other (Meyer, 1997; Roskos-Ewoldsen and Monahan, 2007). Knowledge of our social world and how it operates, of people and the circumstances in which they find themselves, together with shared communication codes, is fundamental to any contemplation of skilled interpersonal activity. Having relevant information upon which to draw is invaluable when deciding courses of action and pursuing them. Indeed, it is drawn upon at every stage of the communication process – from identifying goals that are likely to be within reach, through making sense of the situation and the actions of the other, to selecting and implementing a considered strategy. Psychologists and communication scholars have made use of the notion of *schema* in explaining how information is organised into a framework representing the world as experienced by the individual, and used to interpret current events (Wolvin, 2010a). A schema is a mental structure which provides us with expectations about how others are likely to behave in certain contexts (Augoustinos et al., 2014). Different types of schema (or schemata) have been identified (Fiske and Taylor, 2014):

- *self-schemas* concern our knowledge of ourselves;
- *event schemas* or *scripts* represent the sequences of events that characterise particular, frequently encountered, social occasions such as ordering a meal or buying a newspaper;
- *role schemas* involve concepts according to which we expect people, based upon occupation, gender, race and so forth, to abide by certain norms and behave within set parameters of appropriate conduct;
- *causal schemas* enable us to form judgements about cause-and-effect relationships in our physical and social environment, and to adopt courses of action based upon the anticipations which such schemata make possible;
- *person schemas* facilitate, as organised sets of knowledge about features and characteristics, the social categorisation of others.

The related concept *category* has also been used to explain how we structure information about others and impose meaning on the social world. Fiedler and Bless (2001, p. 123) defined a category as a 'grouping of two or more distinguishable objects that are treated in a similar way'. 'Party', for instance, is a category that you use to group particular social events with features that distinguish them in important ways from other social events such as lecture, concert or public meeting. The complexity of the social milieu makes categorising people, occasions and happenings inescapable. It would simply be chaotically impossible to treat every event we encountered in life as separate, uniquely different and distinct. We would find it impossible to function in this way. Categorising others, and our social world, is therefore inevitable.

But placing people in categories can have a negative side. It can lead to the application of *stereotypes*, whereby individual characteristics tend to be neglected and all members of the group are regarded in an undifferentiated manner, as sharing a set of generalised attributes (Nelson, 2009; Schneider and Bos, 2014). Under these circumstances individuality suffers and people or events are regarded as being largely interchangeable. The cost of this type of generalising 'is that we fail to appreciate the complete uniqueness of the whole person, ensuring that our stereotypes sometimes lead us into judgements that are both erroneous and biased' (Tourish, 1999, p. 193). Stereotypes may be widely held (social stereotypes) or peculiar to an individual (personal stereotypes). They can also become self-fulfilling. If we regard all red-haired people as aggressive we may act towards them in a belligerent way, and so precipitate an aggressive reaction that confirms our stereotype (this is further discussed in Chapter 10).

Wyer and Gruenfeld (1995) identified five key cognitive elements that guide information processing in interpersonal encounters:

1　*semantic encoding* – the interpretation of messages in keeping with available semantic concepts and structures;
2　*organisation* – the arranging of information into mental representations of the person, thing or event;
3　*storage and retrieval* – the storage of these representations in memory and their subsequent selective access as and when required;

4   *inference processes* – decisions to respond are shaped by inferences about the implications and consequences of that action. Assumptions and implications about the nature of the encounter, the communicators and their relationship are also important;

5   *response generation* – of over-riding importance here are the strategies selected to bring about targeted goals and objectives. Possibilities of responses sometimes being 'mindless' must also be acknowledged, as must the influence of emotion on performance.

Some of the processes that lead to the pursuit of a certain course of action are more cognitively demanding than others. Those involving 'mindful' problem solving or decision making are particularly challenging, and deserve further attention. A distinction can be made between descriptive and prescriptive models of problem solving and decision making, or between how decisions are arrived at and how they should be arrived at. Nelson-Jones (1996) recommended a seven-stage framework for rational decision making:

1   *Confront* – this includes recognising the need for a decision to be taken, clarifying what exactly it is that is hoped to be achieved, and being open to the circumstances, both internal and external, of the decision.

2   *Generate options and gather information* – try to think of as many options as possible, without any attempt at this point to evaluate their chances of success.

3   *Assess the predicted consequences of options* – projected advantages and disadvantages of each need to be thought through. One important consequence, of course, is the probability of that course of action successfully achieving the goal being pursued. Others have to do with judgements of self-efficacy – the belief in one's ability to implement that strategy successfully; implications for face – how one might be seen by the other or others; and personal costs – including the amount of difficulty and effort required. By reflecting upon the positive and negative features of each option according to these criteria, the best option under the circumstances can be logically and systematically revealed.

4   *Commit to the decision* – here, resolve to the course of action selected should be strengthened.

5   *Plan how to implement the decision* – a plan should be formulated in which goals and sub-goals are clearly stated, constituent tasks broken down, difficulties anticipated and sources of support identified.

6   *Implement the decision* – timing of implementation is one of the important factors to bear in mind. Other features of implementation will be taken up when the *response* element of the model is explicated.

7   *Assess consequences of implementation* – reflecting upon outcomes leads to improved future performance.

The complexities involved at this stage of cognitive processing are still the subject of much speculation (Fiske and Taylor, 2014). However, the process of 'thinking about thinking' is important. This involves *metacognition* and *mentalising*. Metacognition refers to the way in which we monitor and control our own cognitive processes, while mentalising denotes the process whereby we monitor and attempt to interpret the cognitive activities of others (Firth, 2012). The processes of metacognition and mentalising are also referred to as *theory of mind processes* (Bagozzi and Verbeke, 2014). In order to interact successfully we must be aware of our own goals, plans and perceptions, while also paying careful attention to how others are thinking. The way in which messages are encoded by skilled communicators will reflect judgements along these lines.

Affective processes

Affect has attracted considerable attention from scholars of communication (Philippot and Feldman, 2005; Burkitt, 2014). Just how emotion operates though, and the contributions of, for instance, physiological and neurofunctional constituents, on the one hand, and social, moral and cultural determinants, on the other, are matters of ongoing debate (Frijda, 2006; Schirmer, 2014). However, it is widely acknowledged that we cannot completely separate the affective and the cognitive – how we feel from how and what we think (Demetriou and Wilson, 2008). As expressed by Bless (2001, p. 392), 'Affective states have been shown to influence encoding, storage, retrieval, judgmental processes, and style of information processing. These processes are, of course, highly intertwined.'

Dillard (1998) identified three ways in which emotions can be involved in the communication process:

1   *Emotion-motivated* communication is behaviour caused by underlying emotion (e.g. one person shouts loudly and swears at another in a fit of anger).
2   *Emotion-manifesting* communication provides insights into a person's underlying emotional state (e.g. a patient's downcast look enables the health professional to make judgements about that person's 'spirits').
3   *Emotion-inducing* communication involves words and actions that trigger emotion in others (e.g. someone cries after being told a sad story).

Emotions play a key role in the mediation process. Hargie (2006c) charted both cognitive and affective elements that serve a mediating capacity in interaction, and demonstrated the close inter-relationship between the two systems. It is clear that the meanings we attach to events are often coloured by how we feel at the time (Demetriou and Wilson, 2008). Forgas (1994) discovered that people who were happy tended to locate causes of relational conflict in external and unstable sources while those who were sad looked to internal and stable alternatives. The former responded with active strategies for coping while the latter were more passive. Wyer and Gruenfeld (1995, p. 38) highlighted reciprocity as a further mediating role of emotion on behaviour, in that, 'individuals appear to reciprocate the affect or emotion that they perceive a communicator has conveyed to them' (this is further discussed in Chapter 3 in relation to the phenomenon of emotional contagion).

While the important end product of mediating processes is a strategy or plan of action designed with goal achievement in mind, this plan must always be tentative and open to revision. Given the inherent fluidity of interaction, Berger (1995, p. 149) argued that, 'reducing the actions necessary to reach social goals to a rigid, script-like formula may produce relatively ineffective social action'. Unfortunately, this is what sometimes characterises encounters with professionals, where interactions become ossified in repetitive, stereotyped rituals, carried out in a mechanical, habituated way with little affective warmth or care shown for the client. In contrast, skilled communication is adaptively and reflexively responsive to the emotional needs of the other.

Responses

Plans and strategies decided upon are implemented at this stage. There can be no guarantee, of course, that their translation into action will be flawless or indeed successful. Jordan (1998) identified two of the main errors that can occur: *slips* are actions that are not part of the plan, or are planned but performed out of sequence; *lapses* are planned actions that are omitted rather than enacted. According to the *hierarchy principle* (Knowlton and Berger, 1997), when people fail to achieve an interactional goal, but persist, they tend first to adjust low-level elements of the plan (e.g. volume or speed of speech) rather than more abstract higher-order elements (e.g. general strategy).

A common categorisation of social action is that of *verbal* and *nonverbal* communication. While closely connected, verbal communication has to do with the purely linguistic message, with the actual words used. Nonverbal communication is discussed in depth in the next chapter, while skilled components of both verbal and nonverbal behaviour are discussed in the following chapters.

Feedback

The concept of feedback has long been the subject of investigation in the social sciences (Hattie and Timperley, 2007; van de Ridder *et al.*, 2008; Wood, 2013). Feedback enables us to assess the effects of our communications. It is a fundamental feature of communication and without it skilled engagement would not be possible (Heath and Bryant, 2012). Having acted, individuals rely on knowledge of their performance together with outcomes that may have accrued in order to reach decisions as to what to do next and alter subsequent responses accordingly.

In the model in Figure 2.1, two sources of feedback are depicted. First, we obtain feedback from our own responses in that we have access, through internal receptors in muscles and joints, as well as visually (to a certain extent) and aurally (albeit with distortion), to what we do and say when communicating with others. Second, as interaction takes place, each person is, in what s/he says and does, providing the other with information which can act as feedback. Convergence towards mutual understanding and shared meaning is proportional to the degree to which feedback is put to effective use. Limited provision and/or reception increase the chances of divergence and misunderstanding.

Corresponding to the different aspects of responding, feedback can be provided verbally or nonverbally. Although both are typically implicated, nonverbal modes may be particularly salient when it comes to affective or evaluative matters, while cognitive or substantive feedback relies more heavily upon the verbal.

Perception

Not all information potentially available via feedback is perceived, and not all information received is perceived accurately. But it is only through the perceptual apparatus that information about the internal and external environment, including other people and the messages that they transmit, can be decoded and acted upon through making judgements and decisions in relation to the goals being sought.

In their review of this area, Skowronski *et al.* (2008, p. 313) pointed out that 'Perceptions of others are relevant to virtually every human endeavor'. How we perceive others is fundamental to skilful interaction, yet perception is a profoundly precarious activity (Teiford, 2007). Generally speaking, it is an active and highly selective process (Rutherford and Kuhlmeier, 2013). These qualities tend to be emphasised in particular with reference to social interaction (Jussim, 2012). We are actively involved in the perceptions that we make, rather than being merely passive recipients (Hess *et al.*, 2008). We seldom attend to all the stimuli available in any situation, but rather filter out the less conspicuous, less interesting or less personally involving elements. As such, perception is subjective. Despite naive assumptions, the belief that we perceive and observe other people in a correct, factual, unbiased, objective way is a myth. Rather, what we observe typically owes as much, if not more, to ourselves in perceiving, as it does to the other person in being perceived. As expressed by Wilmot (1995, p. 150): 'There is no "immutable reality" of the other person awaiting our discovery. We attribute qualities to the other based on the cues we have available, and the unique way we interpret them.'

The essentially selective and inferential nature of social perception and its heavy dependence upon the knowledge structures, expectations and attributional processes of the perceiver often results in perceptual inaccuracy and hence miscommunication (Hinton, 2015). This has direct ramifications for interpersonal relations, since research studies have shown that interpersonally accurate individuals have higher-quality relationships, greater psychological adjustment and a range of more favourable workplace outcomes (Hall *et al.*, 2015).

In addition to perceptions of others, skilled interpersonal behaviour also requires *metaperception*, which refers to 'a person's construal of the perception(s) that one or more others hold regarding that person' (Turner and Schabram, 2012, p. 10). Skilled communicators have the ability to make accurate perceptions of self and how one is being perceived by others. People differ in the extent to which they monitor their performance and under what conditions (Snyder, 1987). While high self-monitors endeavour to create and maintain an impression in keeping with the situation and to earn approval, low self-monitors are much less preoccupied by these concerns. Nevertheless, lax self-monitoring is likely to diminish one's communicative effectiveness (Metts and Mikucki, 2008).

OVERVIEW

Our identity and sense of purpose depend on us finding a 'place' in our social world. The ability to achieve this 'place', in turn, is dependent to a very large extent upon one's interactive skills. The fluent application of skill is a crucial feature of effective social interaction. The skill definition and model presented in this chapter emphasise that communication is context-bound. There are spatial, temporal, relational and sometimes organisational frameworks within which it is embedded. The personal characteristics of the participants combine with features of the situation to shape interaction. Likewise, goals pursued are determined by personal and situational factors. Plans and strategies to accomplish these derive from mediating processes and resulting tactics are enacted in manifested responses. A central premise of the model outlined is that participants are at one and the same time, in what they say and do, providing each other with information of relevance to decisions about the extent of goal attainment. Without such feedback, skilled interaction would be impossible, but it can only be acted upon if it is perceived. In this way, personal perception plays a pivotal role in interpersonal transactions.

Throughout the remaining chapters of this book, the central features of a range of core interpersonal skills will be examined, in terms of relevant aspects of goals, mediating factors, response repertoires, feedback, perception and central aspects of the person–situation context, as detailed in this chapter.

Chapter 3

Communicating without words: skilled nonverbal behaviour

INTRODUCTION

THE ACT OF COMMUNICATING usually conjures up images of what people variously say, text or e-mail to one another: that is, of the content exchanged in the delivery of messages. But communication is a more inclusive process. Studies of how much the average person talks per day show that the large majority of interaction time is not taken up by speech but by nonverbal communication (NVC). As such, relating interpersonally demands the ability to display skilled nonverbal behaviour and to be sensitive to the body language of others. This chapter is, accordingly, concerned with those forms and functions of face-to-face interaction that do not rely primarily upon what we say. Rather, the focus is upon how we communicate through, for example, the look on our faces, the direction and duration of our eye gaze, the nature of our gestures, the posture we adopt, and so forth. These messages can be more telling than the accompanying words. Interestingly, from an early age most of us are taught to 'watch what we say', and so develop a high level of awareness and control over our message content. By contrast, we are not taught to 'watch' our body language, and so are often unaware of how we are behaving nonverbally during interactions. Yet, there is evidence that our patterns of nonverbal behaviour remain more consistent over time than our verbal behaviour (Weisbuch *et al.*, 2010).

At the same time, distinguishing between verbal and NVC is not as conceptually straightforward as it might at first seem. Neither is it useful to think of the two as being operationally discrete (Grebelsky-Lichtman, 2014), and particularly when it comes to hand/arm gestures (Beattie, 2004). While some theorists support the conceptualisation of nonverbal behaviour as skill (e.g. Friedman, 1979), others have argued that it is not a discrete skilled area. Thus, Riggio (1992, p. 6) pointed out, while 'the communication skill framework separates skills in verbal and NVC, in reality, verbal and nonverbal skills are complexly intertwined'. For the most part, in our everyday social contact, verbal and nonverbal codes are indeed intermeshed, each to varying degrees defining and qualifying the other in the over-all process of conveying meaning (Matsumoto *et al.*, 2013; DeVito, 2016). However, nonverbal behaviour is undoubtedly a distinct form of communication which can be utilised alone or as part of other skills, and which involves both encoding (sending nonverbal messages) and decoding (interpreting nonverbal messages) skills (Burgoon *et al.*, 2011).

Fascination with nonverbal aspects of social intercourse can be traced back to scholars such as Aristotle, Cicero and Quintilian in the West and Confucius in the East. In classical and medieval times, forms of specific gesture were identified in the teaching of rhetoric along with their planned effects on audiences (Gordon et al., 2006). The concerted attention by social scientists to nonverbal matters has been shown to be much more recent, having a starting point in the 1960s (Knapp, 2013). This followed a long period during which the topic was deprecated as inconsequential, and those interested in it as academically suspect. For example, Aldous Huxley (1954, p. 77) described nonverbal education as a subject which was 'for academic and ecclesiastical purposes, non-existent and may be safely ignored altogether or left, with a patronising smile, to those whom the Pharisees of verbal orthodoxy call cranks, quacks, charlatans and unqualified amateurs'. Such milestones in the evolution of the subject as Charles Darwin's *The Expression of Emotion in Man and Animals* (Darwin, 1872/1955) only began to receive serious social scientific recognition in the past few decades (Ekman and Keltner, 1997).

But developments since then have been immense, and interest in the field has burgeoned, leading to significant conceptual and empirical advances as witnessed by countless publications of books, book chapters and journal articles (Patterson, 2014). What was once described by Burgoon (1980, p. 179) as the 'foundling child of the social sciences – disdained, neglected, even nameless', is now a well-established member of the family, and indeed has outgrown it. The multifaceted study of NVC currently draws inspiration from disciplines such as neurophysiology which lie well beyond the established boundaries of the social sciences. Thus, Segerstrale and Molnar (1997) identified NVC as one of the foremost sites of a *rapprochement* between biology and social science, with respective researchers investigating such fundamental issues as the extent to which nonverbal behaviour is culturally prescribed or naturally determined. Indeed, a bio-evolutionary paradigm, which attempts to explain aspects of nonverbal behaviour in terms of Darwinian concepts of heritability and survival value, has generated much interest amongst those theorising in the area (Floyd, 2006).

VERBAL AND NONVERBAL COMMUNICATION

At first sight, crafting a sharp definition of 'nonverbal' might seem like an easy task, but things are less than simple. As Matsumoto *et al.* (2013, p. 4) put it,

Table 3.1 Verbal and vocal communication

	Verbal communication	Nonverbal communication
Vocal	Content of talk	Intonation, pitch, volume, accent, rate of speech, etc.
Nonvocal	Sign language, writing, etc.	Body language (gestures, posture, facial expressions, gaze, etc.)

'The exact boundary of nonverbal communication, as part of communication, is a point of contention'. Although the division between verbal communication and NVC defies any sharp delineation, NVC is often thought of broadly as communication without words (DeVito, 2013). In a piece of early but still relevant work, Laver and Hutcheson (1972) distinguished between verbal and nonverbal, and vocal and nonvocal communication. As shown in Table 3.1, vocal behaviour refers to all aspects of speech, including content and accompanying expressions such as tone of voice, rate of speech and accent. Nonvocal behaviour, by contrast, refers to all other bodily activities that serve a communicative purpose, such as facial expressions, gestures and movements. These are often referred to as body language. Verbal communication, on the other hand, refers to the content of what is said – the actual words and language used, while nonverbal behaviour refers to all vocal and nonvocal behaviour that is not verbal in the sense defined above.

This system seems therefore to insert a sharp and clearly recognisable division between the verbal and the nonverbal, until it is realised that verbal communication has a nonvocal element. It encompasses types of gestural communication such as formal sign language that one may have expected to find listed as nonverbal. Correspondingly, and just as counter-intuitively, 'subtle aspects of speech frequently have been included in discussions of nonverbal phenomena' (Mehrabian, 2007, p. 1). Framing precise definitions based upon hard and fast distinctions between verbal communication and NVC, therefore, presents difficulties. Instead, some have teased the two forms apart by pointing up broad differences (Richmond and McCroskey, 2000; Andersen, 2008). As such, and by comparison with the nonverbal, verbal messages:

- rely much more heavily upon symbols (i.e. words) as part of an arbitrary code;
- tend to be discretely packaged in separate words (i.e. in digital form) rather than represented in continuous behaviour (i.e. in analogue form) as when gazing or holding a certain posture;
- make use of the vocal/aural channel of communication (at least in face-to-face interaction);
- for the most part carry meaning explicitly rather than implicitly;
- typically address cognitive/propositional rather than emotional/relational matters;
- are processed primarily by different hemispheric regions of the brain.

Remland (2006) further noted that verbal interchanges must take place sequentially (i.e. participants must take turns) but interactors can communicate simultaneously using a nonverbal code.

In this chapter, therefore, the focus is upon communication by, for instance, tone of voice, volume of speech and intonation. In addition to these nonverbal aspects of speech, information is transmitted and received through a whole range of body movements such as posture adopted. When seated, is the posture stiff, upright and symmetrical, suggesting tension or anxiety, or is the person sprawled out in the chair, suggesting a feeling of relaxation or familiarity? Faces, too, play an important role in social encounters by at times giving expression to our inner thoughts, such as showing delight when presented with an unexpected gift or displaying sadness when told about the death of a friend. A smile can also suggest approachability and availability for interaction.

Before we open our mouths to speak, our physical appearance conveys a great deal of information about our age, sex, occupation, status (if a certain uniform is worn) and personality. For someone with the unnerving perceptual acuity of a Sherlock Holmes in matters of social observation, such cues may become the veritable words of biography; Arthur Conan Doyle (2001, p. 20) placed the following words in the mouth of his great sleuth: 'By a man's finger-nails, by his coat-sleeve, by his boot, by his trouser-knees, by the callosities of his forefinger and thumb, by his expression, by his shirt-cuffs – by each of these things a man's calling is plainly revealed'. Not only are we concerned with the appearance and behaviour of the people involved in communication, but in addition, environmental factors such as architecture, furniture, decoration, colour and texture can provide insight into the nature of those inhabiting that space, and in turn shape interpersonal contact. These examples give some idea of the categories to which nonverbal behaviour attends. A more comprehensive range will be presented later in the chapter.

THE IMPORTANCE OF NONVERBAL COMMUNICATION

There is a reduced prospect of successful face-to-face interaction in situations where interactors have little appreciation of their own NVC, or a lack of sensitivity to the other person's body language. This is as applicable to work as it is to everyday social situations. The role of NVC has been acknowledged, *inter alia*, in management (Hamilton, 2014), education (McCroskey *et al.*, 2006), nursing (Dickson and McCartan, 2005), law (Brodsky *et al.*, 1999), pharmacy (Berger, 2005) and medicine (Robinson, 2006). In relation to the latter, a meta-analysis of research studies by Henry *et al.* (2012) found that positive nonverbal behaviour of clinicians is directly related to ratings of patient satisfaction, particularly in terms of showing warmth and listening.

Relative contribution of nonverbal and verbal communication

Difficulties in sharply separating the verbal from the nonverbal have already been noted. Attempting to treat each as distinct and independent with a view to making differential judgements about relative value is not particularly fruitful. Nevertheless, the verbal medium has often been set as a benchmark for assessing the significance of the nonverbal. Consider a situation where a person is saying something but conveying an altogether different message through NVC. Which holds sway? What are the relative contributions of the two to the overall message received? Mehrabian (2007) estimated that overall communication was made up of body language (55 per cent), paralanguage (the nonverbal aspects of speech) (38 per cent) and verbal content (7 per cent). It may come as something of a surprise to learn that *what* we say may contribute a mere 7 per cent to the overall message received. These proportions, however, should not be regarded as absolute and seriously underrepresent the contribution of verbal communication in circumstances where information from all three channels is largely congruent. Matsumoto *et al.* (2013) point out that estimates from different studies of the amount of information contributed by the nonverbal channel range between 65 and 95 per cent, while Guerrero and Floyd (2006) offered a more modest estimate of 60–65 per cent of meaning carried nonverbally during social exchanges. But qualifying conditions apply. The finding holds more for adults, in situations of message incongruity and where the message has to do with emotional, relational or impression-forming outcomes. It should also be emphasised, of course, that in any case NVC does not have to be shown to be *more* important than the verbal in order to be significant.

Trustworthiness and nonverbal communication

As mentioned earlier, we tend to be less aware of the nonverbal accompaniment to much of what we say than we are of the actual words spoken. While we often carefully monitor what is said to achieve the desired effect, how we are saying it may escape censor such that the reality of the situation is 'leaked' despite our best efforts. In this way, NVC can be thought of as a more 'truthful' form of communication through the insights that it affords into what may lie behind the verbal message. This is the 'window on the soul' assumption. It is only true to a point. Even in the case of facial expressions, it would be wrong to assume a simple, direct and unerring cause-and-effect relationship with underlying emotional states. Certain facial displays are regulated in keeping with the social context, making them more or less likely to be exhibited (Parkinson, 2013). Social intentions and motives can be at the root of such behaviour rather than these expressions being the simple, reflexive manifestation of emotional states (Scherer and Grandjean, 2007).

Skilled interactors can learn to control what their bodies say, as well as the messages sent in words. The work of 'spin doctors' with politicians and other influential people in the public eye does not stop merely at verbal manicure. Appropriate facial expressions, looks, gestures and tone of voice are all included in the 'branded' end product.

Phylogeny and nonverbal communication

Phylogeny concerns the evolution of a species. Taking an evolutionary view of our origins, NVC is undoubtedly an earlier, more primitive form of communication than language (Burgoon *et al.*, 2011). According to Leakey (1994), particularly telling evolutionary changes took place in the emergence of modern mankind during a period stretching between from half a million to some 35,000 years ago. The outcome was people with similar appearances and abilities to those we see around us today. The precise point at which language emerged and whether it developed rapidly or more slowly over a period extending beyond half a million years ago is a matter for debate. However, its emergence seems to have been associated with an increase in brain size, advances in tool-making skills and living in extended social collectives. A complex and sophisticated system of communication enabled individuals to become part of larger groups and to plan and execute successfully collaborative projects such as hunting. Indeed, this ability has been mooted as one reason behind the eventual displacement of Neanderthals in Europe by *Homo sapiens*, around about 30,000 years ago (Pitts and Roberts, 1997).

Earlier hominid species would, of course, have had basic ways of making themselves known. Some suggest that this was most likely in the form of body movements together with a range of vocalisations similar perhaps to those of the present-day, nonhuman primates (Papousek *et al.*, 2008). Lieberman (1998, pp. 84–85) proposed that, 'the earliest form of protolanguage used manual gestures, facial expressions (grin, lip protrusion, etc.) and posture – a sort of body language'. As such, it would be essentially restricted to expressing emotional states such as anger or fear, and perhaps fixing relational bonds as in grooming. Here, therefore, we have NVC enabling our early ancestors to regulate social life in small groups, albeit in less sophisticated ways than that made possible by the advent of modern language.

Ontogeny and nonverbal communication

Ontogeny refers to the development of the individual, and here again we find NVC, especially through visual, tactile and vocal cues, pre-dating language as a rudimentary means of making contact with others. Within the first few days of life, infants demonstrate a capacity to encode and decode nonverbal messages (Halberstadt *et al.*, 2013). As noted by Turner (2014, p. 23):

> newborn babies can read all of the primary emotions in their caretakers within weeks ... and they can imitate these emotions in their facial expressions whereas it takes two years of babbling before an infant can even begin to form sentences.

Important early interaction between mother and child takes place through both touch and synchronised exchanges of patterns of gaze and vocalisation. Increased levels of gaze between mother and child are associated with heightened vocal activity (Giles and Le Poire, 2006). In addition to synchronising early vocal exchanges with carers in ways that mimic conversational turn taking, infants a few months old display facial expressions that closely resemble those of adults in conveying emotions such as joy, surprise and interest, but especially pain (Kohut *et al.*, 2012). Once again we rely upon NVC when language is unavailable, this time in the evolution of the individual rather than the species.

Substance of nonverbal messages

Language is particularly suited to conveying ideas and information about our environment, together with our understandings and intentions in respect of it. Through the use of language we have succeeded in such spectacular feats of joint endeavour as building the pyramids and putting a man on the moon. Only through language can we access and meaningfully discuss the philosophy of Wittgenstein, plays of Shakespeare, songs of the Beatles, poetry of Keats or novels of Tolstoy. Nonverbal behaviour, in contrast, tends to convey information of a different type (although not exclusively so), to do with such matters as feelings and our attitudes towards those whom we meet (Adler *et al.*, 2012). Included are impression management and the projection of personal and social identity. It is largely through drawing upon such raw material that interpersonal relationships are built, sustained and sometimes terminated. These relationships, in turn, are the bedrock of institutions such as marriage, family and work, which go to make up society.

Universality of nonverbal communication

We can often make ourselves known in a rudimentary way through signs and gestures when communicating with people from differing cultural backgrounds who do not share a common language. NVC has therefore a greater universality than language. This is particularly so when it comes to the expression of primary emotions such as fear or anger (Andersen, 2008). But it would be misguided to assume that all NVC is similar. Failure to appreciate the nonverbal nuances of cultural diversity can lead to miscommunication and interaction breakdown (Matsumoto and Hwang, 2013a), which is just as real as failure to use the proper words. Body language and gestures are used in widely different forms as we move from culture to culture (Gesteland, 2012). For instance, while in most of Europe and North America shaking the head signals refusal and disagreement, in parts of India it indicates the opposite, and nodding the head means 'no'. However, in Japan nodding the head may mean neither agreement nor disagreement but merely ongoing attention to the speaker. A mistake made by business people travelling abroad, often to their cost, is to assume that those whom they meet will more or less observe the same social conventions with which they are accustomed (Hamilton, 2014).

PURPOSES OF NONVERBAL COMMUNICATION

Just why we should make use of NVC is an intriguing question. We are the only species with the sophisticated means of communicating that we call language. Other species display various forms of nonverbal behaviour. Through changes in,

---

Box 3.1 Purposes of nonverbal communication

Nonverbal communication is used to achieve a number of interpersonal goals, including to:

1 *replace verbal communication* in situations where it may be impossible or inappropriate to talk
2 *complement verbal communication*, thereby enhancing the overall message
3 *modify the spoken word*
4 *contradict*, either intentionally or unintentionally, what is said
5 *regulate conversation* by helping to mark speech turns
6 *express emotions and interpersonal attitudes*
7 *negotiate relationships* in respect of, for instance, dominance, control and liking
8 *convey personal and social identity* through features such as dress and adornments
9 *contextualise interaction* by creating a particular social setting

---

for example, real or apparent size, posture and movement, odour and skin colour, and in a myriad of barks, grunts, screams and roars, they convey information about bodily and emotional states, signal mating readiness, claim social status and announce territorial ownership. But language is different. It frees us from the here and now, from the physical and actual. Without it we would find it difficult or impossible to refer to, never mind take into account, abstract concepts such as love, loyalty or honour; happenings at this point in time in another place; happenings in the past; happenings in the future; and things that have never happened (including the whole literary genre of fiction).

The bulk of this chapter will be devoted to mapping different forms of nonverbal behaviour. Before doing so, however, it is necessary to address the question as to why we make use of NVC. In answering this question, we will examine the commonly identified purposes of NVC (Burgoon *et al.*, 2010; Knapp *et al.*, 2014). These are summarised in Box 3.1.

Replacing verbal communication

Some NVC, especially in the form of gestures, is used as a direct substitute for words under circumstances where speech is either not feasible or desirable. It may be that participants have neither hearing nor speech, relying entirely on the use of hand, arm or mouth movements as part of recognised signing systems allowing communication to take place. Sometimes, on the other hand, individuals are temporarily denied a suitable channel to facilitate speech, and so resort to some form of gesture-based contact (e.g. divers under water). In other situations, excessive ambient noise may make talking impossible. Alternatively, interactors may find themselves too far apart to have a normal conversation necessitating some alternative such as semaphore, or the tic-tac system of signalling used by racecourse bookmakers. Secrecy may be a further reason for not wishing to talk publicly. In different sports, team members can be seen using nonverbal cues to signal the proposed play at different stages of the game. On other occasions it may be that NVC is a more apposite channel; an example given by Cameron and Xu (2011) in their review of gestural communication is that a pointing finger can be more efficient than words if you want to explain where an object is located.

Complementing the spoken word

Nonverbal behaviour is often used alongside what is said in a way that is consistent with it. In so doing, the verbal message may be clarified, extended or enhanced. Some material, such as giving elaborate directions or describing an irregular shape, can be difficult to get across in words alone. In order to facilitate the overall message an imaginary map or outline is sometimes drawn in the air while describing the route or object. These gestures are known as illustrators and they will be examined later in the chapter. Nonverbal cues can also complement language in other ways involving propositional and emotional messages. Expressions of sympathy are much more convincing when the sympathiser's overall demeanour mirrors what is said.

Modifying talk

The verbally delivered message can be either nonverbally accentuated or attenuated. This is a further example of accompanying nonverbal cues serving to qualify what is said. Such behaviour can sometimes help to emphasise parts of the verbal messages. When a speaker puts more stress on certain words than others, uses pauses between words to convey gravity or interest, varies the tone and speed of utterances, the importance of certain words or phrases is underlined in the mind of the listener. In a sense it is analogous to the writer who puts words in italics or underlines them. In addition, body movements are frequently used to add more weight to the verbal message. Take, for example, the mother who in wanting to ensure that her son is listening closely and taking her seriously, swings him round to face her closely, puts both arms on his shoulders and looks at him straight in the eyes before beginning to speak. Alternatively, a benign smile may temper the overall message received in the context of a stern parental rebuke. All are examples of NVC working to deliver a more or less extreme message.

Contradicting the spoken word

There are occasions where a person says one thing but conveys an incongruous message nonverbally: where the two modes are at odds. This may or may not be done intentionally. Forms of discourse ranging from sarcasm to humour often rely upon something being said 'in a particular way'. The words suggest one interpretation but tone of voice and body language something different. The NVC provides a frame for interpreting what was said. Such subtlety may, however, be missed by children who have been found, when compared with adults, to place a more negative interpretation on a critical comment by an adult said with a smile. When exposed to contradictory verbal and nonverbal signals, we follow a three-step sequence. We typically become confused and uncertain, then we look for extra information to resolve the discrepancy and finally, if unsuccessful, we react negatively with displeasure or withdrawal (Knapp *et al.*, 2014).

Another aspect here is that when it is deemed that the discrepancy is unintentional, it may be construed as an attempt to deceive. As Granhag *et al.* (2015, p. xv) point out, 'Deception, a deliberate attempt to convince someone of something the liar believes is untrue, is a fact of everyday life'. It is often sparked by such self-serving motives as achieving goals, gaining influence and creating favourable impressions, but we can also resort to lying in the interests of others, in order to protect or support them (Guerrero *et al.*, 2014). The famous psychotherapist, Sigmund Freud (1905/1953, pp. 77–78), believed that deception can be detected nonverbally: 'no mortal can keep a secret. If his lips are silent, he chatters with his finger-tips; betrayal oozes out of him at every pore.' When asked to identify cues associated with deception, facial signals tend to be most frequently cited by people across a wide range of countries (Hurley and Frank, 2011). However, and despite popular belief, there is no telling cue or pattern of cues that directly, uniquely and unambiguously signal deception (Sorochinski *et al.*, 2014). For example, while there is some research to indicate that in high-stake contexts where people have a lot to lose (such as during interrogation) they tend to avoid eye contact and speak with a higher-pitched voice when lying (Gray, 2008), other studies have shown no difference between liars and truth tellers in patterns of eye gaze (Burgoon and Levine, 2010). Indeed, Monahan (2014) argues that because liars are strategic in how they communicate, they may actually engage in more eye contact when being deceptive because we trust others more when they look us in the eye. Despite advances in computer-based methods for the analysis of deceptive behaviours (Burgoon *et al.*, 2014), the reality is that 'the equivalent of Pinocchio's growing nose does not exist' to enable us to identify deception readily (Vrij, 2008, p. 4). Indeed, when consistencies have been found between nonverbal cues and lying, those cues have been interpreted as due to the underlying processes that accompany deception and attempts at control (such as physiological arousal, negative affect, cognitive demand), rather than to the deceit itself (Burgoon, 2005).

As such, lying can manifest itself in different ways, including increased autonomic arousal suggesting heightened stress (e.g. raised heart rate and sweating); conspicuous attempts to control performance (e.g. appearing 'wooden' or having a slow deliberate delivery); displaying emotion which may be either caused by the deception (e.g. signs of anxiety and guilt) or the basis of it (e.g. pretending to be happy when sad); and, increased cognitive processing of information (e.g. more concentrated thinking revealed in gaze avoidance) (Levine, 2013). There is some research, albeit based upon replies to forced-choice questions on computer, to suggest that when people lie their responses are longer than when they are being truthful (Gregg, 2007). The hypothesis here is that, while truth telling involves only the processing of true beliefs, deception necessitates two further processes – the decision to lie and the composition of the fabrication – and these two additional processes result in longer response times.

However, the extent to which dissembling triggers these processes depends upon such factors as the complexity of the deceit and the risks involved in being caught out. Furthermore, the processes just mentioned are not unique to deception and can emerge during interaction for other reasons (Frank and Svetieva, 2013). Again, some people may be less fazed or challenged than others at having to mislead (Rogers, 2008). Small wonder that our success is limited when it comes to relying upon nonverbal behaviour to detect deceit (Vrij, 2006; Bond et al., 2015). While Strömwall and Granhag (2007) found that adults could detect lying in children with a 62.5 per cent success rate, inconsistencies and contradictions in their statements (i.e. verbal cues) were the most telling giveaways. Verbal aspects of deception will be further discussed in Chapter 9.

It is important to reiterate, though, that when receiving mixed messages, where there is inconsistency between the verbal and the nonverbal channels, the latter normally hold sway (Verderber et al., 2014). This is in keeping with the assumption that NVC is a more 'truthful' channel. In some early studies reviewed by Remland (2009), vocal and facial cues, in particular, were relied upon heavily in forming judgements in such mixed-message situations.

Regulating conversations

How do we manage to conduct conversations so that we don't keep interrupting each other but at the same time there are no awkward silences between speech turns? The highly co-ordinated nature of interaction is an inescapable feature of the process (Cappella and Schreiber, 2006). Detailed analyses have revealed some of the strategies used to prevent over-talk, handle it when it occurs and generally manage turn taking (Schegloff, 2000). NVC is an important part of this process. Conversationalists are able to anticipate when they will have an opportunity to take the floor. Duncan and Fiske (1977) identified a number of nonverbal indices that offer a speaking turn to the interlocutor. These include a rise or fall in pitch at the end of a clause, a drop in voice volume, termination of hand gestures and change in gaze pattern. In addition, they found that if a speaker persisted with a gesticulation even when not actually talking at that point, it essentially eliminated attempts by the listener to take over the turn. Hence someone (but depending on the person's culture) coming to the end of a speech turn will typically introduce a downward vocal inflection (unless the individual has just asked a question), stop gesticulating and look at the partner. This information can, of course, be made use of in situations where one is keen not to hand over the floor. Since high status and interpersonal influence are usually positively correlated with extent of verbal contribution, those with higher power are less likely to employ turn-yielding cues.

Expressing emotions and interpersonal attitudes

A key purpose of the nonverbal channel is to convey emotional states (App *et al.*, 2011). One reason for this is that expressing emotion is tightly bound up with managing relationships and NVC is a crucial source of information both about how we feel, and how we feel about others (Graham *et al.*, 2008). Furthermore, relating successfully depends upon competence in both encoding and decoding NVC. In relation to the latter point, Bryon *et al.* (2007) found that salespersons who were better at recognising emotion from nonverbal cues sold more and recorded higher average annual salary increases. However, the extent to which affective information is managed intentionally and with awareness can vary (Bull, 2002). Some emotional indices, such as pupil dilation in response to heightened arousal or sweating when anxious, are largely outside our control. Others suggesting anger or sadness are more manageable. Facial expressions represent an important emotional signalling system, although body movements and gestures are also implicated. Six basic emotional states that can reliably be read from facial patterns are sadness, anger, disgust, fear, surprise and happiness (Scherer *et al.*, 2011). Contempt may be a possible seventh. A substantial body of evidence, following the earlier work of Charles Darwin, claimed that these are reasonably universal across cultures (Ekman and O'Sullivan, 1991). Nevertheless, questions have been raised over the extent to which facial expressions can be thought of as the direct products of underlying biologically determined affective states, unaffected by social and cultural influences in their expression, perception and interpretation (Scherer and Grandjean, 2007; Parkinson, 2013). An alternative way of viewing them is as a means of signalling behavioural intent. This issue will be returned to later, in the section on facial expressions.

We also reveal attitudes about others in our nonverbal behaviour towards them. For example, direct displays of positive affect have been shown to be communicated through smiles, eye contact, facial expressiveness, touch, posture and voice (Guerrero and Floyd, 2006).

Negotiating relationships

As shown in Chapter 2, communication is a multi-faceted activity. Two people discussing an issue are doing other interpersonal things at the same time, both in what they say and how they say it. One of these 'other things' that can become the topic of conversation, but seldom does outside of intimate partnerships or problematic encounters (e.g. a conflict about role responsibilities at work), is the nature of the relationship itself. Aspects of social power, dominance and affiliation are conveyed through nonverbal channels. Amount of talk (talk time), loudness of speech, seating location, posture, touch, gestures and proximity are instrumental in conveying who is controlling the situation as the dominant party in an interaction (Burgoon and Dunbar, 2006). In all these ways actions can speak louder than words.

Through largely nonverbal means, people establish, sustain, strengthen or indeed terminate a relational position. This can be done on an ongoing basis, as adjustments are made to ensure that levels of involvement are acceptable. *Immediacy* or psychological closeness is a feature of interaction that is regulated in part nonverbally and indeed has been singled out as arguably the most important function of NVC (Bodie and Jones, 2012). Immediacy has to do with warmth, depth of involvement or degree of intensity characterising an encounter. It is expressed through a range of indices including eye contact, interpersonal distance, smiling and touch and must be appropriate to the encounter. Violating expectations in respect of these by, for example, coming too close, gazing too much, leaning too far forward or orienting too directly can lead to discomfort on the part of the recipient, compensatory shifts by that person and negative evaluations of the violator (Houser, 2005). This has been explained in terms of equilibrium theory (Argyle and Dean, 1965), which contends that certain behaviours, particularly eye contact and proximity, combine to create a level of intimacy, and to avoid discomfort these behaviours must achieve equilibrium. In this way, it is argued, individuals will compensate for an increase in one level of intimacy by effecting a decrease in another level (Sullivan and Goodfriend, 2013). For example, in an elevator, strangers often have to stand at an intimate level of proximity, and so to achieve equilibrium they completely avoid eye contact.

These compensatory behavioural adjustments re-establish the status quo, thereby maintaining a level of involvement that is both predictable and comfortable. More generally, and according to *communication accommodation theory*, interlocutors convey their attitudes about one another and indicate their relational aspirations by the extent to which they tailor aspects of their communicative performance to make these more compatible with those of the other (Hargie, 2014). For example, they may adjust their initial discrepant speech rate to find a balanced compromise, or alternatively accentuate difference if they find they have little desire to promote commonality. When individuals are actively managing personal relationships it would often be too disturbing to state openly that the other was not liked or thought to be inferior. Nonverbal cues can be exchanged about these states but without the message ever being made explicit. In addition, initial relationships can change over time so that an original dominant–submissive relationship can become more egalitarian. Change would not come about as readily if it had been explicitly stated at the beginning how each felt towards the other.

Conveying personal and social identity

In a complex of ways involving habitat, dress, deportment and accent, we send messages about ourselves including the groups and social categories to which we belong. In so doing we also implicitly suggest how we would like to be perceived, received and related to. This is a further role for NVC (Afifi, 2006). While not all nonverbal behaviour is strategically deployed in this quest, among cues that are, those promoting judgements of physical attractiveness, warmth and pleasantness, likability, credibility and power are particularly salient. In business organisations with steep hierarchical structures of authority, projecting suitable images of status forms an inevitable part of dealing with others both within and outwith the company. Features such as size of office and opulence of furnishings take on a special significance in this process. Organisations often have standards stipulating the minimum size and type of office for employees at a particular level in the management pecking order.

Contextualising interaction

Finally, in the ways that people communicate they create social situations. Through chosen dress code, arrangement of office space, and so on, opportunities are created for a meeting to become a very formal interview or a more casual chit-chat. Appropriate forms of conduct will be correspondingly suggested. All social settings, from the familiar, such as Sunday lunch, staff meeting or a visit to the dentist, to the more elaborate, such as a graduation ceremony or a funeral, carry with them acceptable codes of conduct. Someone who deviates from these common patterns of behaviour and so upsets the social order may be called upon either to apologise or offer an excuse or explanation for his or her wayward behaviour.

These various purposes of NVC do not always occur independently, nor are they separately served by specific behavioural cues. It is quite possible for several to be exercised simultaneously. The remainder of this chapter will examine more closely the various forms that nonverbal behaviour can take. These are presented in Box 3.2.

HAPTICS

Haptics refers to the analysis of the use of touch in communication. It is a field of study that has attracted a rapid growth in research investigation in recent years (Hertenstein and Weiss, 2011). Touch is a primitive form of communication

---

Box 3.2 Types of nonverbal communication

Nonverbal communication can take the following forms:

- *Haptics* – communication through physical touch
- *Kinesics* – communication through body movement (e.g. gestures, head nods, posture, eye contact, facial expression)
- *Proxemics* – messages conveyed through the perception and use of personal and social space (e.g. interpersonal distance, territoriality)
- *Physical characteristics* – information revealed through body shape, size and adornments
- *Environmental factors* – messages carried by features of the social surroundings such as furniture, décor and lighting
- *Vocalics* – communication by means of the nonverbal elements of speech (e.g. voice pitch, resonance, and so on)

---

in respect of both evolutionary (phylogenic) and personal (ontogenic) development. It is one of the earliest and most basic forms of stimulation that we experience, the first of our senses to develop, and it functions even when our other senses begin to atrophy in later life (Field, 2014). It is widely recognised that positive physical contact is crucial to the psychological and biological well-being of infants and to their subsequent social and intellectual development (Richmond and McCroskey, 2000). Benefits of massage in accelerating growth and weight gain among premature babies have been documented (Adler, 1993). The profound effects of tactile stimulation extend throughout life (Jones, 2005). Apart from its specialised therapeutic use ('the healing touch') in a health context, touch has been found to affect heart rate, blood pressure and nutritional intake of patients. It can also have a comforting or calming effect. In more specific circumstances a number of beneficial outcomes have been documented in research studies. In situations where it is used appropriately, the person touching is more likely to:

- be more positively evaluated (Erceau and Guéguen, 2007; Guéguen, 2010)
- receive preferential treatment (Guéguen and Fisher-Lokou, 2003)
- have money returned (Kleinke, 1977)
- receive tips from customers when waiting at tables (Hertenstein, 2011)
- have others comply with requests (Andersen, 2011; Guéguen, 2014).

In relation to the last of these points, there is a growing body of research to support the potency of what has been termed 'incidental touch' or the 'Midas touch', where a brief, light touch on the shoulder or upper arm from someone making a request increases the recipient's willingness to comply (Guéguen, 2010; Haans et al., 2014). The recipient is not usually consciously aware of having being touched, yet is influenced by the contact. Hence the derivation of the expression that someone is 'an easy touch'. However, tactile contact is not always well received. *Touch avoidance* is a general predisposition distinguishing those who like this form of contact and engage in it from others who devalue and largely shun tactile communication (Andersen, 2005). That apart, physical contact can be an extremely ambiguous, multi-layered and highly gendered act that is used to convey a range of emotions (Hertenstein and Keltner, 2011). Probably for this reason it is strictly rule-bound and taboo-ridden. One cannot go touching anyone, anywhere, at any time, in any place – at least not without getting into trouble. In an early and frequently cited study, students reported that they were touched most often on the hands and arms, although who was doing the touching also made a difference (Jourard, 1966).

Touching is used to achieve a number of goals relating to both the context in which it occurs and the relationship of the interactors. Heslin and Alper (1983) identified five such purposes:

1   *Functional/professional.* A number of professionals touch people in the normal course of their work: nurses, dentists, doctors, opticians, chiropodists, airport security staff and hairdressers, to name but a few. A common distinction here is between *instrumental* and *expressive* touch (Dickson

et al., 1997; Weiss and Niemann, 2011). The former happens in the normal course of carrying out a task and does not carry any further connotations (e.g. nurse taking a patient's pulse). Expressive touching, on the other hand, conveys interpersonal messages to do with emotion, attitude or association (e.g. a nurse holding a child's hand during an uncomfortable procedure conducted by a doctor). Montague *et al.* (2013) found that clinicians were perceived by patients to be more empathic when they used some social touch (e.g. handshake, pat on the back).

2   *Social/polite.* We have different culturally prescribed forms of contact used as part of the greeting ritual (see Chapter 10). They serve to acknowledge the other and ascribe to that person a social involvement. In Western culture a handshake is typically used in formal situations. In other cultures kissing, embracing or nose rubbing may be more common. Being in direct, ongoing contact may also signal to others that these two are together: that they form a pair (or couple). Examples of these *tie signs* include linking arms and holding hands, which express a certain shared relational intimacy (Afifi and Johnson, 2005).

3   *Friendship/warmth.* This includes contacts such as a friendly pat on the back, or a comforting touch on the hand, aimed at establishing amicable relationships. It is a way of showing interest in others and positive feelings towards them. This can be very rewarding in terms of giving encouragement, expressing care and concern, and showing emotional support and understanding. It has been pointed out that, in standard Western culture, friends are unlikely to engage in much touching when alone, because it tends to be associated more with sexual motives (Richmond and McCroskey, 2000).

4   *Love/intimacy.* In close relationships touching is a very profound way of conveying depth of feeling (Hertenstein, 2011). The love, of course, may be that for a child, spouse or parent. Even with a partner, love can take on different guises, from the passion of early romance to the enduring commitment of old age. Each set of circumstances will be marked quite differently through type and extent of physical contact. Again there may be close friendships that we could describe as intimate but not necessarily involving love, as such. Once more, touching will likely be one of the features that sets these apart from mere acquaintances.

5   *Sexual arousal.* The famous sex therapists Masters and Johnson (1970) claimed that sex is the ultimate form of human communication. Here we have touch being used in its most intense form involving parts of the body only accessible to certain others and typically when in private.

Several other types of contact, as identified by Jones (1999), can be added to the above list. They include touch:

- in the context of play (e.g. tickling);
- as an expression of negative feelings (e.g. slapping or throttling);
- as a way of managing interaction (e.g. placing a hand on someone's shoulder to get attention);

- to gain influence and control (e.g. touching someone lightly as we ask a favour);
- as a symbolic or ritualistic act (e.g. two heads of state shaking hands to symbolise accord between their nations);
- that is accidental (e.g. bumping into someone).

Various factors, including culture, status, gender and age, help to determine who touches whom, under what circumstances, how much and where (Knapp *et al.*, 2014). Touch features much more extensively in social encounters in some parts of the world than in others. So-called *contact* cultures, where touching is more prevalent, include southern Europe, the Middle East and Central America, while among noncontact counterparts can be listed northern Europe, North America and Japan.

Issues of status also influence touching (Hall, 2011). Powerful individuals, when interacting with subordinates, tend to indulge in more nonreciprocated touch (Burgoon and Bacue, 2003). Those displaying such behaviour also attract higher ratings of power and dominance than the recipients of that contact. In a study by Hall (1996) of actual touching at academic meetings, while there was no evidence that high-status participants touched low-status participants with greater frequency than vice versa, differences did emerge in the type of contact initiated. High-status academics tended to touch arms and shoulders in what was judged to be a sign of affection. Low-status counterparts were more likely to shake hands, which was regarded as essentially a formal expression. Implications of power and control could also be the basis of some findings suggesting that female patients react more favourably than males to expressive touch by nurses (Dickson, 1999). That said, Andersen (2008) concluded from his review of the evidence that touch had actually more to do with conveying immediacy and intimacy than with status and dominance.

Males and females differ in how they communicate by tactile means, at least in Western societies. Generally men are less touch-oriented and when they do make physical contact are more likely to engage in hand touching than non-hand touching (DiBiase and Gunnoe, 2004). This trend extends to professional interaction, with male nurses touching less and male patients being touched less (Routasalo, 1999). However, the social setting within which touch occurs is an important factor. Sporting contexts, for example, seem to be largely exempt from the normal trend downplaying male touch. Again, it should be noted that most of this research has focused on 'friendly or at least innocuous touches' (Hall, 2006, p. 206). We know a lot less about the use of other forms of touch to do with, for instance, aggression.

Finally, haptic communication seems to change across the lifespan. Younger men (under 30 years) and those in dating relationships (rather than being married) have been found to touch more than females (Willis and Dodds, 1998). As noted in Chapter 2, marital status is also important, in that unmarried men have more favourable reactions to touch than unmarried women, while for married males and females this pattern is reversed. In old age, there may be a blurring of functional and expressive forms of touch due to declining health with increased care needs. However, there is evidence that, when hospitalised, the elderly receive the least amount of tactile contact; Hollinger and

Buschmann (1993) showed that their perception of being touched, when it did occur, was found to be most positive when it:

- was appropriate to the situation
- did not impose a greater level of intimacy than desired
- was not condescending
- did not detract from their sense of independence and autonomy.

KINESICS

Kinesics, as the name suggests, is the analysis of communication through bodily motion. When observing individuals or groups interacting, one is often struck by the sheer dynamism of what goes on. Even if seated, arms and hands are typically busy; heads and bodies are moving with the conversation; eyes are switching from one person to another in the group, including some in the discourse while excluding others, monitoring reactions; and, all the while facial expressions are conveying interest, boredom or liking. Kinesics can be divided into five main areas: gestures, head nods, posture, eye gaze and facial expression.

Gestures

As defined by Kong et al. (2015, p. 111), 'Gesture refers to the arm and hand movements that synchronize with speech'. Matsumoto and Hwang (2013b, p. 1), in noting that children who are born blind also use this form of communication, refer to gestures as 'a form of embodied cognition – movements that express thought or the process of thinking'. Gestures are used in almost every conversation across all cultures (albeit with cultural and situational variations), leading Cutica and Bucciarelli (2015, p. 289) to conclude that, 'gestures and speech form an integrated system of communication'. However, gestures are very useful for communicating certain types of information (e.g. direction, shape, size) but not others (e.g. colour, name, flavour) (Bavelas et al., 2014). Different attempts have been made to categorise gestures (e.g. Beattie, 2004; McNeill, 2005), but the most-cited classification is that by Ekman and Friesen (1969), which identified five main types: *emblems*, *illustrators*, *regulators*, *affect displays* and *adaptors*.

Emblems

Emblems have a direct verbal translation and so are one of the few nonverbal cues to function, to all intents and purposes, like words. Examples include the signs used by police officers to direct the flow of traffic (e.g. hand upwards, palm facing, meaning 'stop'), by those communicating with the deaf and by diners who signal to the waiter that they want the bill by holding out the palm of one hand and pretending to write on it with the other. While emblems have a direct verbal translation, like words, the meaning can differ from culture to culture.

For example, crossing one's fingers, an emblem peculiar to Christian cultures, originated as a secret 'sign of the cross' to indicate to others that one was a Christian, then became a sign of the cross to ward off Satan, and later just a signal of hoping for good luck (Matsumoto and Hwang, 2013b). Other emblems are universal, such as the 'telephone gesture' with the thumb and little finger extended, other fingers curled, thumb close to the ear and little finger close to the mouth. However, since some emblems have obscene meanings in a specific context, one must also be careful (Knapp *et al.*, 2014). For example, the sign with the thumb touching the tip of the index finger to form a ring, palm facing out, in the UK and USA means 'A-okay', in Japan means money, in France means that the thing referred to is worthless and in Turkey and Greece, the gesture represents an insulting sexual invitation with the ring representing an orifice – invariably the anus. Further examples of emblems from around the world have been documented (e.g. Hogg and Vaughn, 2008; Gesteland, 2012).

Illustrators

These are directly linked to speech and so are also termed *co-verbal gestures*. Not only are they linked to speech but they co-occur in a tightly synchronised manner (Bavelas and Chovil, 2006). On their own they make little sense but take their meaning from the conversational context (Suppes *et al.*, 2015). For example, a fisherman when describing a fish that got away may say, 'It was this big,' while holding his two hands apart. Illustrators are used in a variety of ways to facilitate and emphasise what is said. For this reason, teachers make extensive use of such gestures (White and Gardner, 2012). One reason for this is that, as shown by Alibali *et al.* (2014, p. 68) in their review of the area, 'teachers' gestures can have a substantial impact on students' learning from instruction'. Indeed, research into the use of gestures in classrooms reveals that students as well as teachers make frequent use of gestures to engage with and enhance learning (Alibali and Nathan, 2012).

Gestures can also provide illustrations of the verbal content of a message. Lausberg *et al.* (2007) noted that *ideographic gestures*, as well as enunciating abstract concepts or ideas (e.g. cupped hands when explaining love), can be used to trace the pattern of thought as it unfolds. *Pantomimes* act out some occurrence, or imagined subject or circumstance. On the other hand, pointing to an object or place while referring to it involves *deictic gestures*; these can also be self-focused (*self-deictics*).

Regulators

These orchestrate conversation and ensure that turn taking is switched smoothly. As speakers finish a speech turn they will usually drop their hand as they bring a gesture to an end. Not to do so, despite the fact that they may have stopped speaking, is usually enough to signal that they still have something left to say and have not conceded the floor. *Baton gestures* or *beat gestures* are a slightly different type used by the speaker, among other things, to mark out the beat of the delivery (Hostetter and Skirving, 2011). They can be thought of as regulating an individual's contribution rather than the to and fro of exchange. It is as if the speaker is conducting the orchestra of his/her own voice with an invisible baton.

Affect displays

Hand movements also convey affective states, although the face is a richer source of such information. Gestures can reveal emotional dispositions such as embarrassment (e.g. hand over the mouth); anger (e.g. white knuckles); aggression (e.g. fist clenching); shame (e.g. hands covering the eyes); nervousness (e.g. nail and finger biting); boredom (e.g. hair preening); despair (e.g. hand wringing). Professionals should be sensitive to these hand signals which, because of their often spontaneous nature, may reveal more about a client's feelings than words would permit.

Adaptors

Feldman *et al.* (1991) distinguished between gestures that are linked with speech (*illustrators*) and directed towards objects or events, and those which are more socially related. The latter involve four main types:

1   *object-adaptors* – fiddling with something (e.g. playing with a pen or paper cup);
2   *self-adaptors* – these are more self-focused, involving one part of the body such as a hand or arm coming into moving contact with another part (e.g. scratching or hand wringing);
3   *alter-adaptors* – gestures used in a defensive, self-protective manner (e.g. clasping hands or folding arms in front of chest);
4   *other-adaptors* – these are targeted towards another (e.g. picking lint off someone's clothing or a mother stroking a child).

The first two, in particular, act as a form of tension release and are characteristically performed unintentionally and with little awareness. These are thought to be the echoes of early childhood attempts to satisfy needs. One school of thought suggests that they are signs of anxiety or unease (Bernieri, 2005). They may also be associated with negative feelings toward self or others (Knapp *et al.*, 2014). Alternatively, it has been found that self-adaptors can create impressions of honesty, genuineness and warmth (Harrigan, 2005).

Gestures aiding communication

Those who supplement their dialogue with good use of hand and arm movements usually arouse and maintain the attention of their listeners, indicate their interest and enthusiasm and make the interaction sequence a stimulating experience for participants (Cutica and Bucciarelli, 2015). Kendon (1984) focused on the various conditions under which individuals use the gestural expressive mode and concluded that the speaker divides the task of conveying meaning between words and gestures in such a way as to achieve either economy of expression or a particular effect on the listener. For instance, a gesture can be used as a device for completing a sentence that, if spoken, might prove embarrassing to the speaker. It can also be used as a means of telescoping what one wants to say, when the available time is shorter than one would like. Gestures can also be employed to clarify some potentially ambiguous word or as an additional component when the verbal account is inadequate to represent truly the information being shared. Feyereisen and Havard (1999) discovered that adults made greater use of representational gestures when responding to questions requiring them to draw upon mental images that were motor (e.g. 'Could you explain how to wrap a box in paper for a present?') rather than visual (e.g. 'Could you describe the room in which you live most often?').

It is now well established that the use of appropriate gestures increases the clarity and comprehension of explanations (Hostetter and Skirving, 2011). But we often see speakers gesticulate even when they cannot be seen by listeners, such as when on the telephone, and therefore under circumstances where gesticulations can have no evident communicative advantage for the audience. It has been found that doing so can benefit *speakers* in enhancing speech and cognition (Stevanoni and Salmon, 2005). In this way, gestures fulfil speaker-related cognitive functions, including the facilitation of conceptual planning and lexical access (Holler and Wilkin, 2011). Gesturing therefore not only aids the receiver's comprehension of the message, but also enhances the speaker's level of fluency and retrieval of cognitive information (Goldin-Meadow and Albali, 2013).

Head nods

Head movements can replace or be associated with talk. They are a ubiquitous feature of the interactive process and are related to the roles of speaker and listener in quite involved ways (Aoki, 2011). In relation to the listener's role, interest in the speaker can be communicated by head movements. Head nodding is an important 'back-channel' signal from the listener indicating that the speaker should continue talking. Positive associations have been found between ratings of physicians' head nodding when interacting with patients and impressions of their levels of rapport (Robinson, 2006). Ishi *et al.* (2014) found that the use of head nods was influenced by the closeness of the relationship between interactors, in that fewer nods were employed when interacting with someone with whom the listener had a close relationship (such as a family member), whereas the frequency of nods, and especially multiple nods, increased when the relationship between the interactors was more distant.

There are also status and gender differences in the use of head nods, in that in interactions between lower- and higher-status individuals the former use more of them, while in general females use them more than males (Helweg-Larsen *et al.*, 2004). In terms of cross-cultural communication, people from some countries, such as Sweden, use nods as signs of listening but not necessarily concurring (Von Glinow *et al.*, 2004). They are also used extensively by Japanese speakers, who synchronise their use of nods to help establish rapport and togetherness, with one study showing that in a 6-second period each interlocutor used six head nods (Oshima, 2014). Also, a comparative study of dyadic interaction revealed that the Japanese used on average one head nod every 5.75 seconds, as opposed to one nod every 22.5 seconds for Americans (McClave, 2000).

As mentioned earlier, NVC serves to regulate turn taking during conversation. Based upon fine-grained analysis of doctor–patient interaction, Robinson (2006) reported that physicians tended to head nod at junctures where it seemed that patients were completing or could potentially complete their speech turn. Examining the role of the speaker, Duncan and Fiske (1977) found that two cues, head turning away from the other person and beginning to gesture, were significantly associated with taking the role of speaker. This was confirmed by Thomas and Bull (1981), examining conversations between mixed-sex pairs of British students, who found that, prior to asking a question, the students typically either raised the head or turned the head towards the listener. Just before answering a question the speaker turned the head away from the listener. This latter finding may be due to the effects of cognitive planning on the part of the listener prior to taking up the speaker's role.

Posture

As we will see in this section, posture can be revealing of status, attitudes, emotions, interpersonal attitudes and gender. Heller (1997) charted four main categories of human posture: standing, sitting, squatting and lying. Everyday interpersonal communication, of course, predominantly concerns the first two.

Status

Posture is one of the cues used to make decisions about the relative status of those we observe and deal with, at least when status is accompanied by power and the potential for dominance (Brey and Shutts, 2015). The degree of relaxation exuded seems to be the telling feature (Andersen, 2008). High-status individuals characteristically adopt a more relaxed position when they are seated (e.g. body tilting sideways; lying slumped in a chair) than low-status subjects, who are more upright and rigid. When standing, people in a position of power and influence again appear more relaxed, often with arms crossed or hands in pockets, than those in subordinate positions, who are generally 'straighter' and 'stiffer'. Those with high status are also likely to take up more expansive postures, standing at their full height, chest expanded and with hands on hips.

Interpersonal attitudes

A seated person who leans forward towards the other is deemed to have a more positive attitude towards both the person and the topic under discussion than when leaning backwards (Knapp *et al.*, 2014). Thus, Dowell and Berman (2013) found that the joint use of a forward lean and eye contact by therapists led to increased client perceptions of therapist empathy, the therapeutic alliance and treatment efficacy. The reason is probably that forward leaning is a component of the complex of interpersonal behaviour, already mentioned, called immediacy that signals close psychological contact (Guerrero, 2005). It is also interesting to note that most prolonged interactions are conducted with both participants either sitting or standing, rather than one standing and the other sitting. Where the latter situation does occur, communication usually is cursory (e.g. information desks), pedagogical (e.g. the teacher in a classroom) or strained (e.g. interrogation sessions). Posture can signal a positive attitude, so that one study of tipping behaviour by restaurant clientele in the US Midwest found that the waitress achieved greater rewards when she either sat down at or leaned over the table (Leodoro and Lynn, 2007).

Relative posture adopted is a significant marker of how interactors feel about one another and of the relationship between them. *Postural congruence* or *mirroring* occurs when similar or mirror-image postures are taken up, with ongoing adjustments to maintain synchrony. Common matched behaviours include leg positions, leaning forward, head propping, facial expressions and hand and arm movements. This form of 'mimicry', which is usually carried out subconsciously, is a positive sign that the exchange is harmonious (Farley, 2014). Research findings show that behavioural mimicry plays a very important role in relational development and maintenance (Chartrand and Lakin, 2013). One reason for this is that we are more likely to mimic the verbal and nonverbal behaviour of people that we like or are attracted to (Gonzales *et al.*, 2010). This means that we are in turn more likely to be attracted to those who mirror our behaviours. Thus, therapists who use matching postures are perceived by clients to be affiliative and empathic, and this in turn encourages greater interviewee disclosure (Hess *et al.*, 1999). Likewise, in positive doctor–patient exchanges, nonverbal mirroring has been shown to be prevalent, particularly in relation to reciprocation of head nods and smiles (Duggan and Bradshaw, 2008).

Emotions

In a series of experiments, Bull and Frederikson (1995) illustrated how particular listener emotions are encoded by posture, so that boredom, for example, was associated with a backward lean, legs outstretched and head dropped and supported on one hand. Early studies suggested that bodily posture communicated the intensity of emotion, rather than the specific emotional state, which was regarded as more the domain of facial expressions (Ekman, 1985). However, more recent research shows that posture can in fact also convey emotion-specific information (Dael *et al.*, 2012). Thus, in one study adults could successfully identify emotions depicted by actors playing emotional scenes on videotape, even when facial and vocal cues were denied them (Montepare *et al.*, 1999). Nevertheless, the presence of congruent facial expressions has been shown to enhance the accuracy of emotional judgements of posture (Mondloch *et al.*, 2013).

Personality

We make a range of judgements about the personality of others based upon their nonverbal behaviour, although these are not always accurate (Gifford, 2013). Dysphoria (sadness or depression) has been shown to be characterised by distinctive gait and postural patterns (Michalak *et al.*, 2009). The typical gait of depressed individuals involves reduced walking speed, vertical head movements and arm swing. Moreover, depressed and sad walkers display greater sideways-swaying movements of the upper body and a more slumped posture. The diagnostic value of NVC in the clinical/therapeutic setting has been commented upon by Knapp *et al.* (2014), who affirmed the validity of much of the popular stereotype of the depressed person as being downcast and generally sluggish in movement. In their study into posture and personality, Guimond and Massrieh (2012) were able to distinguish between introverts and extraverts based upon posture, and their findings also indicated that those with personalities that are less flexible and adaptable are more likely to exhibit a posture that is less flexible and relaxed.

Eye gaze

Obsession with gaze, looking and being looked at, together with its potent effects on social behaviour is deep-rooted in the human condition (Seppänen, 2006). This occurs at a very early stage of development, with newborn infants from about the age of 2 days showing a preference for looking at eyes with direct gaze (Puce, 2013). They also learn very quickly to 'keep an eye' on things – watching both other people and their surroundings. Gaze refers primarily to looking at another in the facial area. *Mutual gaze* happens when the other reciprocates. This is sometimes also referred to as *eye contact* when the eyes are the specific target, although just how accurate we can judge whether someone is looking us directly in the eye or merely in that region of the face is open to debate. Associated terms are *gaze omission,* where gaze is absent, and *gaze avoidance,* where it is intentionally being withheld. When gaze becomes fixed and focused in an intrusive way that may infringe norms of politeness, it becomes a *stare* and is associated with a different set of social meanings and potential reactions.

Gazing during social interaction can serve a variety of purposes (Tang and Schmeichel, 2015). In an early analysis, Kendon (1967) suggested these were primarily to do with expressing emotional information, regulating interaction, revealing cognitive activity and monitoring feedback from the other. More recent classifications (e.g. Richmond and McCroskey, 2000; Knapp *et al.*, 2014) are elaborate differentiations of these core functions, but add the further purpose of marking the relationship.

Expressing emotional information

The region of the eyes is a particularly significant part of the face when it comes to expressing fear and surprise (Ekman and Friesen, 2003). The direction of gaze also shapes judgements about emotion revealed facially (Adams and

Kleck, 2003). In an experiment into nonverbal manifestations of pain, involving four different procedures – electric shock, cold, pressure and muscle ischaemia – Prkachin (1997) found that closing the eyes was a consistent pain expression, while other signals were narrowing of the eyes and blinking.

Initiating and regulating interaction

Catching someone's eye is the necessary first step to opening up channels of communication and seeking contact with them. Direct eye gaze increases the psychological arousal level of and often evokes blushing in the recipient, who is aware of being the focus of attention and so feels under scrutiny (Drummond and Bailey, 2013; Helminen *et al.*, 2016). In a group discussion, patterns of gazing are used to orchestrate the flow of conversation, with members being brought into play at particular points. In dyads, a typical interactive sequence would be person A coming towards the end of an utterance looking at person B to signal that it is B's turn to speak. B, in turn, looks away after a short period of mutual gaze to begin responding, especially if intending to speak for a long time, or if the message is difficult to formulate in words. Person A will continue to look reasonably consistently while B, as speaker, will have a more broken pattern of glances.

Revealing cognitive activity

Eye behaviour can be used to infer underlying thought processes (Gray and Ambady, 2006). What we do with our eyes can reveal how cognitively taxed we are at that point in time. We tend to avoid gaze when processing difficult material in order to minimise distractions. Thus, there is a greater likelihood of gaze being avoided when attempting to answer more difficult questions (Glenberg *et al.*, 1998). By examining patterns of eye movements, Mogg *et al.* (2000) showed how the hypervigilance of anxious subjects predisposed them to shift their gaze quickly toward angry faces.

Monitoring feedback

Research has shown that, in Western society, people look more as they listen than as they speak, and the duration of looking is longer during listening than talking (Griffin, 2016). But speakers gaze periodically to obtain feedback and make judgements about how their message is being received and adjustments that may need to be made to their delivery.

Culture and gender are two highly significant determinants of levels and patterns of social looking. Culture helps to shape expectations of eye behaviour, especially the frequency and target of gazing (Schofield *et al.*, 2008), although duration may also be pertinent (Matsumoto, 2006). While Swedes gaze less frequently than the English, they do so for longer. At a general level, Arab culture tends to be more gaze-oriented than either English or North American. Even within the latter it seems that Afro-Americans, compared to Whites, look more while speaking and away when listening. In India, gaze avoidance is a mark of deference when talking to someone of much higher status.

Women tend to look and be looked at more than men. Based on a review of studies involving children and adults, Hall (2006) found that females gazed more in conversations than did males, with the difference more pronounced amongst adults. Different explanations for this phenomenon include the view that women display a greater need for inclusion and affiliation than men, and that desire for affiliation promotes more looking (Argyle and Cook, 1976). Alternatively, it is contended that eye contact is seen as less threatening to females than males, with the result that they are less likely to break eye contact in similar situations. A further explanation is along the lines that these gender variations are really a reflection of traditional differences in dominance/submissiveness.

Marking the relationship

The extent of our involvement with another is reflected in our eye behaviour. We make more and longer eye contact with people we regard positively and from whom we expect a positive reaction, leading Andersen and Andersen (2005, p. 115) to assert that 'Eye contact is at the heart of the immediacy construct, as it can signal interest, approach, involvement, warmth, and connection simultaneously'. Professionals such as counsellors (Ivey *et al.*, 2014) and physicians (D'Agostino and Bylund, 2014) are encouraged to make use of eye contact to signal not only positive affect but also attention to and interest in the client. Thus, Montague *et al.* (2013) found that duration of eye contact between clinicians and patients was positively related to patient ratings of clinician empathy. Reduced levels of eye contact amongst couples can be variously interpreted as disapproval, less power and dominance, or lowered levels of intimacy, depending upon the context (Feeney *et al.*, 1999). Paradoxically, we also sometimes look extensively at those with whom we are in conflict (e.g. staring or glaring). Noller (1980) documented how marital couples in conflict gazed more at each other during episodes of disagreement.

In addition to conveying relational information in respect of liking, affiliation and interest, gaze signals differences in status, power and dominance. High-status and dominant individuals (both males and female) have been shown to engage in greater levels of gaze (Dunbar and Burgoon, 2005; Tang and Schmeichel, 2015). However, the ratio of looking while speaking to looking when listening is a more telling indicator of dominance than absolute levels of this type of behaviour. According to this visual dominance ratio, those in higher-status positions look about the same while speaking and listening, while their subordinates gaze much more while listening (Burgoon and Bacue, 2003).

Facial expressions

Studies of facial expressions have a long history, spanning at least two centuries (e.g. Bell, 1806). As shown by Puce (2013, p. 150), 'Over the years, a very large body of literature has stressed the importance of the face in human interactions'. At present it probably attracts more research and scholarly debate than any other aspect of NVC. This is because the face is an incredibly powerful source of information about us, our attitudes towards others and how we relate to them (Calder *et al.*, 2011; Bruce and Young, 2012; Vernon *et al.*, 2014). For instance, counsellor facial expressions have been found to be predictive of clients' perceptions of rapport during helping interviews (Sharpley *et al.*, 2006). Likewise, studies have shown that leaders as opposed to nonleaders in a range of fields (military, business, sports) can be identified solely from facial characteristics (Olivola *et al.*, 2014). We also infer judgements about how trustworthy others are from their faces, and these judgements have been shown both to have a high degree of consensus and to influence significantly how we respond to the interlocutor (Wilson and Rule, 2015).

However, many of these studies have used ratings of still photographs to gauge judgements of individuals along a range of characteristics and outcomes, and there have been criticisms of this approach. In their review of this area, Todorov *et al.* (2105, p. 538) conclude that, 'The relationships between facial appearance and social outcomes depend critically on a host of interpersonal and contextual factors'. Another problem with still photograph research is that, as Krumhuber *et al.* (2013, p. 44) have shown, 'A key feature of facial behavior is its dynamic nature'. Over 20 different muscles responsible for producing in excess of 1,000 distinct expressions make the face a rich and dynamic source of detail, particularly in relation to emotion. There are three key parts: the brows and forehead; the eyes and bridge of the nose; and the cheeks and mouth. Variations here are highly salient, as in Figure 3.1, where emotional

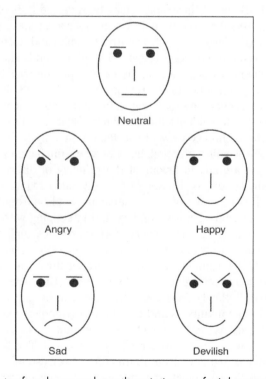

Figure 3.1 Effects of eyebrow and mouth variations on facial expressions.

states (such as sadness and happiness) can readily be interpreted from basic schematic facial representations (as evidenced by the ubiquitous happy/sad emoticons included in e-mails and texts).

Research into facial width-to-height ratio (fWHR) has shown that males have a higher fWHR than females, and that males with a higher fWHR tend to be more aggressive across a range of contexts than those with a lower fWHR (Haselhuhn *et al.*, 2014). The complexity of the face is also witnessed in *affect blends* or configurations that convey more than one basic emotion at the same time: the mouth may be smiling while the eyes are sad. The traditional view, which can be traced back to Charles Darwin, emphasises facial *affect displays* as biologically based, direct expressions of underlying emotional states that have some sort of adaptive value. Darwin wrote, 'that in the case of the chief expressive actions they are not learned but are present from the earliest days and throughout life are quite beyond our control' (Darwin, 1872/1955, p. 352).

Consistent with this thinking is an emphasis on the universality of emotional expression: people reveal and recognise the same states in the same way regardless of where they live. As previously mentioned, the six basic emotions consistently decodable are sadness, anger, disgust, fear, surprise and happiness, with contempt as a possible seventh. There is evidence that we may be specially attuned to process certain types of emotional information, leading to the rapid recognition of anger and threat (Kret *et al.*, 2011). Of course, our emotional experiences are not confined to the above seven, since how a range of other emotions are depicted and perceived has also attracted considerable interest (Hummert, 2014). Some of these states may be revealed in fleeting, *micromomentary expressions* that pass with little conscious awareness in a fraction of a second and are particularly difficult to control (Ekman and Rosenberg, 2005). A microexpression lasts for between 170 and 500 milliseconds and is defined as 'a brief facial movement revealing an emotion that a person tries to conceal' (Yan *et al.*, 2013, p. 218). They are of interest in relation to the study of deception, as it is argued that the person's mask slips during this split second to reveal true information about the individual's inner feelings (Egan, 2014).

However, the orthodox view of the face as mainly a direct, biologically based system for revealing emotion has not gone unchallenged (Jack *et al.*, 2012). Rather than arguing in favour of the primacy of discrete categories of emotion (e.g. sadness, anger), Russell (1997) advanced a view that we first process emotional NVC in terms of the dimensions of pleasure and arousal. Any specific emotions attributed are secondary and in keeping with situational and additional detail about the person observed. Here, social signalling functions are accentuated over the purely biological. A view of facial expressions has been proposed as culturally determined, circumstantially sensitive ways of communicating that are shaped by social motives and intentions (Kupperbusch *et al.*, 1999; Fridlund and Russell, 2006). Perhaps both views can be accommodated. Buck (1994) argued that spontaneous and deliberate (symbolic) expressions represent two parallel systems, both of which are important.

But of course we do not always reveal how we feel. The fact that showing emotion on the face is regulated by *display rules* is well established (Ekman and Friesen, 1969; Afifi, 2006). Social pressures mean that it is not always acceptable to make affective states public, particularly in certain cultures. The inscrutable face is often associated with the Japanese stereotype. In an often-cited experiment, Friesen (1972) had American and Japanese students watch alone a gruesome piece of film while being videotaped. Similar expressions of disgust were revealed but, when later interviewed about the film, only the American students persisted with these negative facial displays. Japanese are also less approving of showing disgust and sadness in the company of close friends. Later cross-cultural work revealed that Russian and South Korean participants reported higher levels of control over their emotional expressions compared with the Japanese, while American subjects were the least censorious (Matsumoto, 2006).

Facial expressions play a crucial role in *emotional contagion*, the process whereby emotion spreads from one person to another (Hatfield *et al.*, 2014). TV producers of comedy shows are well aware of this contagion effect when they use 'canned laughter' to encourage audiences to laugh along. In close relationships, as we interact with others we emotionally converge with them by automatically and continuously mimicking their facial expressions, posture, gestures and paralanguage (Coco *et al.*, 2014). Facial mimicry is a common phenomenon, as we mirror the expressions of our interactive partner to facilitate a positive relationship (Krumhuber *et al.*, 2014). As shown by Lundqvist and Dimberg (1995, p. 203), 'facial expressions are contagious'. While emotional contagion is a common phenomenon, it is also the case that there are individual differences in the extent to which individuals have the capacity to identify and reflect the emotions of others (Vijayalakshmi and Bhattacharyya, 2012). One theory of emotional contagion suggests a two-step process. First, we mimic the expression of the interlocutor. Second, feedback from our facial (and other) muscles leads to experiences of those corresponding emotions – we then feel as the other person feels.

Smiles

Smiles are one of the most common and easily recognised forms of facial expression, and the most widely studied facial expression of emotion (Johnston *et al.*, 2010). They also have many and diverse meanings (LaFrance, 2011; Jensen, 2014). While enjoyment is one obvious interpretation, smiling can also signal appeasement or even contempt. For this reason, smiles are interpreted differently according to the context in which they are displayed (Barrett *et al.*, 2011). Gender and status are further factors here, with females smiling more than males across situations and cultures (Adams *et al.*, 2015), and low-status people seemingly more pressured into using more smiles (Smith *et al.*, 2015). Among men, those with higher testosterone levels and those who wish to appear dominant have fewer and less pronounced smiles (Kraus and Chen, 2013).

Spontaneous as opposed to contrived (or social) smiles can be readily differentiated, with the former, Duchenne smile, involving not only the mouth but also the eyes. It is achieved through contraction of both the zygomaticus major muscle, which pulls the lip corners up into a typical smile, and the orbicularis oculi, pars lateralis muscle, which narrows the eye aperture by raising the cheeks and lowering the eye cover fold, giving the appearance of wrinkles at the sides of the eyes. With a polite or posed smile we only use one muscle – the zygomaticus major. Interestingly, Matsumoto and Willingham (2009) found no differences in the winning and losing facial expressions of noncongenitally blind, congenitally blind and sighted athletes, in that all of them used a social smile when they lost, but a Duchenne smile when they won. This indicates that such facial expressions are not dependent on observational learning, and that other learning modalities, including reinforcement not involving the visual channel, may be sufficient for learning the facial display rules in this context. The other alternative is that that there may be an evolved, possibly genetic, basis for these responses. The fact that the blind newborn child uses smiles lends support to this latter perspective (Jones, 2008). Duchenne smiles are preferred to social smiles, result in a more positive appraisal of the sender and people using them have been shown to be more persuasive (Shore and Heerey, 2011; Reed et al., 2012; Quadflieg et al., 2013; Gunnery and Hall, 2014). Although Duchenne smiles can be employed deliberately rather than spontaneously, the evidence indicates that perceivers can distinguish between the genuine and posed versions (Krumhuber et al., 2014).

While this sub-section has been about the fluidity of the face as a means of communicating, fixed features can also be informative and influential. A key factor in recognising gender from photographs is the distance from eyelid to brow, which is smaller in men (Campbell et al., 1999). Additionally, personality attributes are influenced by facial structure and expression, with a wide consensus about the traits inferred; for example, baby-faced as compared to mature-faced females are perceived to be warmer and less dominant (Sparko and Zebrowitz, 2011). Finally, factors that increase ratings of attractiveness in both males and females are symmetry (the extent to which both sides of the face are similar), averageness (the extent to which the face reflects the majority of faces within a given population), sexually dimorphic shape cues (very masculine or very feminine face shapes) and skin health and colour (Little et al., 2011; Morrison et al., 2013).

PROXEMICS

Proxemics refers to the process whereby we perceive and make use of personal and social space. It has been studied in relation to the dimensions of territoriality, personal space and interpersonal distance, orientation and seating arrangements. All of these have a direct bearing on the interactive process.

Territoriality

Territory refers to a geographical area over which individuals claim some particular set of rights for a period of time by way of access, occupancy or utilisation. It invokes associated concepts such as encroachment, invasion and defence. There are four main sub-divisions:

1   *Primary territory* is associated with the occupier who has exclusive use of it. This could be a house, or even a bedroom which others may not enter without seeking permission and through invitation. It is an area of privacy that one can retreat to and where one has control. Ashkanasy *et al.* (2014) demonstrated how, in open-plan shared offices, workers use *marking* and *defending* tactics to set up and protect their primary territory. Marking involves drawing boundaries around objects by erecting a barrier to designate personal space and using personalisation strategies such as leaving personal possessions around one's area or displaying photographs or awards. Defending involves taking steps to protect against possible intrusions by, for example, locking one's desk drawers or filing cabinets, and password-protecting one's computer.

2   *Secondary territory* is less strongly linked with an individual or group. People may, out of habit, sit in the same seat in a lecture room or in the pub, but this cannot be backed up by claims of 'ownership' and exclusivity. Nevertheless, it can result in feelings of irritation if the space is occupied by someone else. One interesting example of this type of space is in coffee bars or restaurants. Imagine that you are sitting alone at a table for two having a coffee, the café is very busy, and someone arrives and asks permission to sit at the free space. What would you do? Well, *territorial customers* would regard this as an intrusion into their space and respond with deliberate deceptions, such as saying that they are keeping the chair for someone who will be joining them shortly (Wu *et al.*, 2014). They also try to pre-empt intrusions by spreading out personal possessions (e.g. hanging a coat over the free chair).

3   *Public territory* is space that is available to all to make use of for limited periods of time and is therefore particularly difficult to control. Park benches, library seats and parking spaces are examples. Nevertheless, we have a tendency to claim more rights here than we are entitled to: we often relinquish our occupancy begrudgingly. Most people park in the same space in the work carpark every morning and often feel annoyed if they arrive to find someone else is occupying that space. Again, using marking tactics to delineate boundaries is one way of defending one's 'patch' and preventing occupancy. By way of an example, Afifi (2006) observed how students often place books or personal belongings on the seat next to them to stop others from sitting there.

4   *Interaction territory* is a special type of space that is created by others when interacting (e.g. a group having a conversation on the footpath). It lasts only as long as the interaction, but during that period others tend to walk around rather than through the gathering. This is more likely in the overall context of public space (e.g. students in conversation in a corridor in the library) rather than secondary territory to which the interactors have limited claims (e.g. nonresident students in conversation in the corridor of the halls of residence).

Personal space and interpersonal distance

Personal space is an area of space immediately surrounding the body, and slightly larger at the front, that 'travels' with us as we move around. It can grow or shrink depending upon our personality, the situation in which we find our-selves or our relationship with the person with whom we are dealing – but we feel very uncomfortable when it is encroached upon. Even in conditions where we anticipate crowding, such as the subway at rush hour, we display annoyance in our body language and facial expressions when our space is invaded by bodily contact (Aranguren and Tonnelat, 2014). Introverts, violent offenders, type A personalities (i.e. very driven, time-conscious, competitive individuals) and the highly anxious tend to claim larger personal spaces (Argyle, 1988), although no significant sex differences have been consistently found (Akande, 1997).

Linked to personal space is interpersonal distance. This is the distance that interactors maintain when having a conversation. It is shaped by a nexus of factors such as social setting, culture, gender, age, status, topic of conversation, relation-ship shared and physical features of interlocutors (Knapp *et al.*, 2014). In turn it has implications for how comfortable we feel about the encounter as well as our interpersonal attitudes towards, and relationship with, the other (McCall *et al.*, 2009). Contact cultures, as well as engaging in more haptic communication, tend to permit closer interpersonal distances. In general, females are approached more closely than males (Andersen *et al.*, 2013), and also interact at a closer distance, although under conditions of threat or discomfort they tend to take up larger distances than males (Hall, 1984). This could account for the finding that females waiting to use an ATM approached males less closely than vice versa (Kaya and Erkip, 1999). Interpersonal distance has also been found to be closer in same-sex interactions (Jacobson, 1999; Kaya and Erkip, 1999). Interestingly, Uzell and Horne (2006) discovered that gender, as a personality factor, was a more impor-tant determinant of this measure than biological sex, *per se*, with those men and women sharing more feminine traits communicating at closer distances.

Interactors of equal status tend to take up a closer distance than those of unequal status (Zahn, 1991). In fact, where a status differential exists, lower-status individuals will typically permit those of higher status to approach more closely than they would feel privileged to do. As the topic of conversation shifts to become more intimate than is comfortable for the other, that person may increase distance. Interpersonal distance is, therefore, part of this dynamic of nonverbal cues, including gaze and orientation, serving to regulate levels of inti-macy and involvement (Buck and Miller, 2015). As expressed by Andersen and Andersen (2005, p. 114), 'Immediacy can be signaled through several proxemic or spatial channels. Most primary is interpersonal distance (i.e. Proxemics). Closer distances can be both an indication and a cause of closer interpersonal relationships.' Presenting a fuller picture, evidence is cited by Andersen *et al.* (2006) that closer distances only lead to greater immediacy when the other is positively experienced as being rewarding.

The anthropologist Edward Hall (1966) identified four distinct categories of distance common in Western society. These are:

1   *Intimate*, ranging from touching to about 18 inches (45 centimetres) – reserved for very close friends and family.
2   *Casual-personal*, from 18 inches to 4 foot (45 centimetres to 1.2 metres) – typifies informal conversations with friends and acquaintants.

3   *Social-consultative*, from 4 to 12 foot (1.2 to 3.7 metres) – used for more impersonal professional transactions.
4   *Public*, from 12 foot (3.7 metres) to the range of sound and vision – used for making speeches and addressing large groups at formal gatherings.

Finally, physical characteristics of participants also determine, to some extent, the distance between interactors. For example, research studies have shown that people select greater distances for interactions with those with physical deformities or facial disfigurement (Ryan *et al.*, 2012).

Orientation and seating arrangements

Orientation refers to body angles adopted when people talk face to face, such as directly facing or shoulder to shoulder. As such, it concerns the position of the trunk, rather than head, and marks the degree of intimacy in the conversation and levels of friendship. It is useful to look at proximity and orientation together since it has been found that there can be an inverse relationship between them: that is, direct face-to-face alignment is linked to greater interpersonal distance and sideways angling to closer distance, especially in situations where orientation is being used to compensate for excessive closeness. Orientation can also be altered to include or exclude others from the group during discussion.

Early studies of seating behaviour by Sommer (1969) in North America, replicated by Cook (1970) in the UK, pointed to some interesting differences when individuals are given a choice of where to sit when engaged in different sorts of activities. People were asked how they would position themselves at a rectangular table, if asked to carry out a series of tasks with a friend of the same sex. The tasks were:

- *conversation* (sitting chatting for a few minutes before work)
- *co-operation* (sitting completing a crossword together or such like)
- *co-action* (sitting at the same table individually reading)
- *competition* (competing to see who would be first to solve a number of puzzles).

As Figure 3.2 shows, a side-by-side position was considered to be co-operative, while a face-to-face orientation was regarded as competitive. A 90° angle in relation to one another was selected for conversations, while for co-action (studying or working independently) a location across the table but at the opposite ends was chosen.

Finally, seating can be arranged in such a way as to encourage or discourage interaction. A layout that promotes interchange is called *sociopetal*; one that has the opposite effect, *sociofugal*. It is important, therefore, that seating for a group discussion is arranged using a sociopetal pattern to make it easier for open interchange and sharing. On the other hand, a sociofugal variant would be more suited if the intention is for a presenter to play a centrally dominant role by

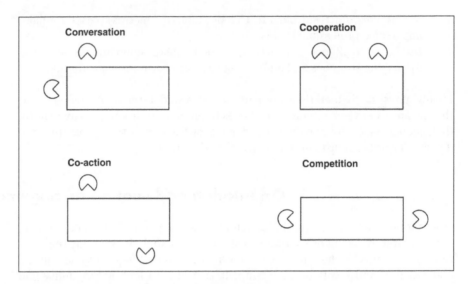

Figure 3.2 Types of task and seating arrangements.

making more use of one-way communication. Examples of types of seating varying along the sociopetal–sociofugal dimension are shown in Figure 3.3. Further elements of spatial arrangement in respect of office design will be presented later, in the section on environmental factors.

PHYSICAL CHARACTERISTICS

Included under this rubric are a vast array of bodily features, some of which are more easily altered than others, but all of which are used to make judgements about the person in respect of, for instance, ethnicity, gender, age, occupation, status and attraction. This includes body size and shape, and height. Aspects of dress and attractiveness will be discussed in Chapter 10.

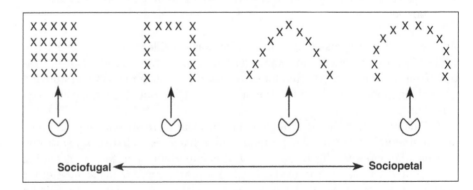

Figure 3.3 Seating arrangements and interaction.

Body size and shape

Evaluations of female physical attraction based upon body size and shape favour the slender. In a study by Swami *et al.* (2007a), in which males in three European countries (Britain, Spain and Portugal) rated images of women, body mass index (BMI), a measure of weight in relation to height, was the most important factor in judgements of the females' physical attractiveness. Those with low BMIs were rated as more appealing. According to Margo (1997), 'Barbie doll' features are universally appealing and represent stereotyped features of the human form that have become more prevalent during recent evolutionary history. In keeping with the Barbie doll image, men have been shown to tend to express a preference for females with medium to larger breasts (Zelazniewicz and Pawlowski, 2011).

But there are cultural factors that can affect ideals of attractiveness. It has often been reported that men favour women with a low waist-to-hip ratio (WHR), ideally around 0.7 (i.e. curvaceous body shape), and particularly as romantic partners in one-off encounters (Braun and Bryan, 2006; Dixson *et al.*, 2011). This preference, though, could be more typical of male choice in affluent, developed Western society (Swami, 2015). What about those in subsistence economies? Marlowe and Wetsman (2001) found that Hazda men in Tanzania, who were hunter-gatherers, preferred heavier women with higher WHRs (i.e. with fuller waists). These researchers argued that, in subsistence situations such as these, where women's work is physically demanding and energy sapping, thinness could indicate poor health or inability to cope with the harsh conditions. From an evolutionary perspective such women would be less likely to conceive and successfully raise children. The topic of attractiveness will be returned to in Chapter 10.

Height

It is well established that tall people are regarded more positively than short people (Hensley and Cooper, 1987). For example, Stulp *et al.* (2013) analysed data from all the US presidential elections and found that height was a key factor. As much as 15 per cent of the variance in votes between candidates could be attributed to height differentials. Taller Presidents received significantly more popular votes than their opponents. In addition, those Presidents who were re-elected were significantly taller than those who failed to be re-elected. Presidents were also found to be some 7 centimetres (2.7 inches) taller than the average Caucasian US male of their generation. This height effect has become more marked in recent years, probably because of increased visibility on broadcast media. Stulp *et al.* explain these 'heightism' findings by hypothesising that 'taller' is equated with 'greater'.

These expectations can influence job success (Case *et al.*, 2009). For example, Melamed and Bozionelos (1992) discovered that height was a key determinant of promotion among British civil service managers. In terms of earnings, Judge and Cable (2004) found that, in the US workplace, those who were 6 foot (1.83 metres) tall could expect to earn $166,000 more, over a 30-year career span, than those who were 7 inches (17.8 centimetres) shorter. Similarly, Case and Paxson (2008) showed that, in both the USA and UK, for every additional 10-centimetre (4-inches) height advantage, males earned 4–10 per cent more, and females 5–8 per cent more. These results were confirmed in a large Australian study, where Kortt and Leigh (2010) illustrated how a 10-centimetre (3.9-inch) increase in height was linked to a 3 per cent increase in pay for men, and a 2 per cent increase for women.

ENVIRONMENTAL FACTORS

Environmental communication is an important area of study, examining as it does the meanings associated with the various places and spaces which form the backdrop to, and in turn shape, interaction (Strongman, 2012). The physical setting can influence our mood, how we perceive the social situation and judgements about the person who occupies, or has responsibility for, that space. It also helps to determine our likelihood of interacting with others, the form that interaction will take and how long it is likely to last. Hall (1966) distinguished between *fixed-feature* and *semifixed-feature* elements of the environment. The former include everything that is relatively permanent or not easily changed, like the architectural layout of a house, size and shape of rooms and materials used in their construction. Semifixed features are much easier to move around or modify, and include furniture, lighting, temperature and colour of décor. Based upon such characteristics, we form impressions of our surroundings, organised around six dimensions (Knapp *et al.*, 2014):

1   *Formality* – concerns cues leading to decisions about how casual one can be in what is said and done or if a more ritualised or stylised performance is demanded.
2   *Warmth* – this is the extent to which we feel comfortable, secure and at ease in this location.
3   *Privacy* – has to do with the degree to which interactors feel that they have the space to themselves or whether others may intrude or eavesdrop.
4   *Familiarity* – involves impressions of having encountered this type of setting before and knowing how to deal with it (or not, as the case may be).
5   *Constraint* – concerns perceptions of how easy it is to enter and leave the situation.
6   *Distance* – addresses how close, either physically or psychologically, we feel to those with whom we share the space.

These perceptions will, in turn, shape the types of interaction we engage in and how we experience them. The ways in which work space is arranged and utilised can send strong signals about the status and authority of occupants, the sorts of tasks and activities being implicitly proposed, and indeed, the desirability and appropriateness of communication in that situation.

Those in authority and control in organisations commonly have their status acknowledged by the way that they position themselves *vis-à-vis* others with whom they associate (DuBrin, 2011). As a rule, they tend to adopt positions that are more central and elevated than their lesser-ranking colleagues. They are also privileged with greater space and more privacy (Guerrero and Floyd, 2006). It is common for the seats of power in organisations to be located in palatial surroundings in the top floors of buildings. CEOs of large corporations rarely occupy a small, dark room in the basement. In his book on power, Korda (1975) identified how one of the factors that determines the power afforded by an office arrangement is the extent to which the manager can control space and readily restrict access to visitors. Furthermore, he believed that the organisation and use of office space are more impactful in this sense than the size of the office *per se* or how it is furnished. Other factors, such as having access monitored on one's behalf by someone of lesser status (e.g. a gate-keeping secretary), not being exposed, being able to look directly at visitors and seeing them before being seen, are also held to be important. In relation to the latter points, from the office plans in Figure 3.4, it can be seen that person A communicates most power and control, B next, with C the least.

In larger offices, separate areas are often set side for distinct purposes, enabling temporary adjustments to be made to suggest power and control. What Korda (1975) called the *pressure area* is centred on the desk and is the site of formal business transactions. It is here that hard bargaining and difficult decision making take place. The *semisocial area* is furnished differently with, for example, a sofa or easy chairs, coffee table and drinks cabinet, and can be used to stall, ingratiate or mollify a visitor, as necessary.

Furthermore, it seems that, apart from impressions of power and authority, personality judgements are frequently based upon how office space is utilised. Comfort in dealing with others, friendliness and extraversion tend to be attributed to occupants of more *open* office arrangements in which, for example, the desk, as with B and C in Figure 3.4, is moved against a wall rather than used as a barrier. Additionally, variations in the arrangements of environmental factors, such as architectural style, interior décor, lighting conditions, colours, sounds, and so on, can be influential on the outcome of interpersonal communication.

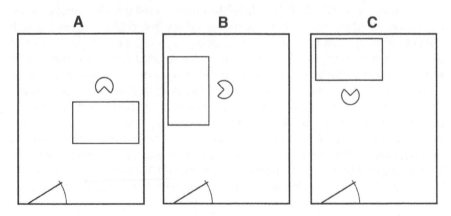

Figure 3.4 Office designs communicating power.

VOCALICS

NVC, it will be recalled, includes aspects of speech as well as body language. These are the parts that accompany the spoken word, but are not verbal. From accompanying vocalic indices, impressions can be formed, with varying degrees of veracity, about age, gender, size, personality, emotional state, and, to some extent, occupation (Scherer *et al.*, 2003; Ko *et al.*, 2006; Imhof, 2010; Bänziger *et al.*, 2014). As Kreiman and Sidtis (2011) point out in their text on vocalics, when we hear someone talk, without seeing the person, we can accurately judge a range of characteristics, such as whether the speaker is male or female, young or old, drunk or sober, happy or sad, excited or bored, ill or healthy, from England or the USA, and so on. The general term *paralinguistics* includes such features as speech rate and intensity; volume; emphasis; pitch, modulation and quality of voice; and articulation and rhythm control. Other features, such as speech dysfluencies and vocalisations such as 'uh', 'er' and 'um', are also included within the study of paralanguage (these are discussed in Chapter 8). The vocalics sometimes contain a meta-message that lets the listener know how the verbal content is to be taken (e.g. 'tongue in cheek', soberly, respectfully, seductively).

Knapp *et al.* (2014) reviewed evidence to show that judgements are made from paralanguage about different elements of the communication process. Speech rate, for instance, has been linked to messages about emotions, relationships and social influence, although how it is used between interlocutors rather than by either individually is a more important feature (Buller, 2005). Research studies have also shown that subjects are able to judge accurately the height, weight, physical strength and age of speakers by listening to their voice (Hughes *et al.*, 2014). However, our preference for aspects of paralanguage can change across the life cycle. For example, Saxton *et al.* (2009) found that pre-teen girls (11 years) favoured higher-pitched rather than deep male voices, but from the age of 13 years, and especially with the onset of puberty, this preference had been reversed, and the older girls found a deeper, mature male voice more attractive.

Drahota *et al.* (2008) found that subjects could tell from listening to audio recordings whether the speaker was smiling or not, and could judge with a high level of accuracy what type of smile the speaker was using (the types employed were Duchenne smile, non-Duchenne smile, suppressed smile, nonsmile). This was confirmed by Xu *et al.* (2013, p. 39), in their review of emotional expressions associated with vocalics, who concluded that, 'smiles during speech are clearly audible'. Some other examples of emotions associated with speech are that rate of speech can be directly related to anger: 'hot' anger has a notably fast tempo, while 'cool' anger is more moderate in pace. Fear is characterised by a high pitch. There are two main types of sadness – a depressed form that is characterised by very low energy and a grieving form associated with a sobbing voice. Mean amplitude (associated closely with loudness) and the extent to which amplitude varies around a mean value have been shown to be positively related to perceived dominance of the speaker; speech rate, on the other hand, is negatively associated (i.e. the faster the rate, the lower the estimation of dominance) (Tusing and Dillard, 2000). Finally, anxiety is an emotional state that is characterised by speech errors.

Prosody is the term used to refer to those vocal variations associated with the words that help convey the meaning of what is said (Hancil and Hirst, 2013). This can be exemplified in the statement: 'John's lending me his guitar'. If we decide to place more vocal emphasis on certain words we can alter its meaning:

1   *John's* lending me his guitar.
     (*John* is the one giving the guitar: no one else.)
2   John's *lending* me his guitar.
     (John's *lending,* not giving, or selling his guitar.)
3   John's lending *me* his guitar.
     (*I* am the recipient and no one else.)
4   John's lending me *his* guitar.
     (The guitar being lent does not belong to anyone but *John.*)
5   John's lending me his *guitar.*
     (Nothing else is being loaned, only his *guitar.*)

Finally, accent is an important marker of social identity and a rich source of opinions and value judgements about people. By the age of 6 years children have developed the ability to distinguish between accents (Wagner *et al.*, 2014). It is a readily accessible cue that can be used to place an individual in a particular social category. Once a person is located by accent, corresponding stereotypes are triggered that in turn can evoke favourable or unfavourable attributions (Kinzler and DeJesus, 2013). This includes judgements such as how friendly, trustworthy, warm or intelligent the speaker is. As summarised by Wagner *et al.* (2014, p. 1063) in their review of the area, 'a speaker's regional dialect is a rich source of information about that person'. Adults show preferences for the accent of in-group members and an accent that they consider as being of higher status. It is also a speech characteristic that we sometimes modify in line with that of our conversational partner. According to *communication accommodation theory*, as mentioned earlier in the chapter, we tend to bring our speech more into line with that of our partner when we are seeking approval, creating a positive association or signalling in-group membership (Dainton and Zelley, 2015). For example, I now live in the city of Belfast but I grew up in the small seaside town of Ballycastle, also in Northern Ireland, that has a different dialect. When I return on my regular visits there I accommodate to the local accent – usually subconsciously, but on occasions I am aware of so doing.

OVERVIEW

When we think about the communicative process and how it operates, the nonverbal tends to be overshadowed by the verbal. Little wonder that the contribution of nonverbal elements is often downplayed in our estimation of their role in the overall activity. However, it would be mistaken to assume that the verbal and nonverbal are two distinct systems of communication. Nothing could be further from the truth. As shown by Grebelsky-Lichtman (2014, p. 416), 'The two communication modes (verbal–nonverbal) have expressive and receptive aspects, which interact with and modify one another'. Even reaching neatly defined conceptual distinctions is difficult. In broad terms, though, NVC compared to language tends to rely less on a symbolic code, is often represented in continuous behaviour, carries meaning less explicitly and typically conveys emotional/relational rather than cognitive/propositional information.

Riggio (2005) noted that being nonverbally skilful involved an expressive element, an element of sensitivity and one of regulation or control over performance. By means of NVC, we can replace, complement, modify or contradict the spoken word. When it is suspected that the latter was done unintentionally and deceit is possible, nonverbal cues are often regarded as more truthful. We also regulate conversations through gestures, gaze and vocal inflection. Revealing emotions and interpersonal attitudes, negotiating relationships, signalling personal and social identity and contextualising interaction are further uses served by means of haptics, proxemics, kinesics and vocalics, together with physical characteristics of the person and the environment. We need information about other people's qualities, attributes, attitudes and values in order to know how to deal with them. We often infer personality, attitudes, emotions and social status from the behavioural cues presented to us. Of course, the situation also works in reverse; not only do we gather information about others from the way they present themselves to us, but if we are skilled, we go to great lengths to present others with a certain type of picture of ourselves.

Knowledge of the various facets of NVC, and of their effects in social interaction, can enable us to improve our ability to deal with others successfully. The skilled use of nonverbal behaviour is a key facet of success in interpersonal encounters. It must also be stressed, however, that much of nonverbal meaning is inferred and can be easily misconstrued. It only suggests possibilities and must be interpreted in the overall context of not only verbal but also personal and circumstantial information. Many of the elements of NVC that have been discussed in this chapter will be returned to in the remaining chapters of this book.

Chapter 4

Rewarding others:
the skill of reinforcing

INTRODUCTION

FROM EARLY CHILDHOOD THE role of social rewards, in the
form of verbal and nonverbal reinforcement, is crucial. The
smiles, hugs and soothing vocalisations of a mother are important
reinforcers for her child, and likewise the eye contact, smiles and
paralinguistic messages of the infant are key rewards for the mother,
during the mother–child bonding process. In addition, the mother's
social reinforcement is usually directly related to the satisfaction of
the child's biological needs (food, heat, etc.), and so an associative
link is formed. When the child is being changed, kept warm or fed
it is simultaneously receiving social reinforcers (smiles, etc.). Thus,
the connection between social and material reinforcers is established from the earliest stage of development. Indeed, research
in neuroscience has confirmed the connection between social and
material rewards, in that both processes involve overlapping neural
substrates (Lin *et al.*, 2012). The power of social reinforcement is
quickly learned by the child and used to shape the behaviour of the
mother or caregiver. Goldstein *et al.* (2009, p. 636) showed that, by
the age of 5 months, infants, 'have learned the social efficacy of their
vocalizations on caregivers' behavior'.

Throughout life, a fundamental principle governing behaviour is that people tend to do things associated with positively
valued outcomes for them. By contrast, they usually do not persist with actions that from past experience have produced little
of positive consequence, or even unwanted negative effects. As
noted by Skinner (1971, p. 199), reinforcement is based 'on the
simple principle that whenever something reinforces a particular
activity of an organism, it increases the chances that the organism
will repeat that behavior'. This is summarised by the maxim in the
business world: 'What gets rewarded gets done'. Positively valued
outcomes can of course take many forms. Some (e.g. obtaining

food, water and shelter) are necessary for physical survival, while others (e.g. attractive company) are less vital but still important. Events that are even less tangible, yet highly valued just the same, include positive features of interpersonal contact, as shown in Box 4.1. Friendly smiles, words of approval or praise, warm congratulations, generous applause or an enthusiastic response from an attentive listener are all reactions that are generally desired. As expressed by Granhag *et al.* (2015, p. xv): 'Social relationships benefit from people making each other compliments now and again because people like to be liked and like to receive compliments'. Not only do we find social rewards appealing, we tend to act in ways that bring them about. The fact that these positive reactions can influence what we do, by making it more likely that we will engage in such behaviours in preference to others, is central to the concept of reinforcement as an interpersonal skill.

It will be recalled from Chapter 2 that the ability to obtain and provide rewards features prominently in attempts to define interpersonal skill. Deficits in this respect can have negative personal and interpersonal consequences. Reviews of the area have shown correlations between interpersonal skill deficits, inability to gain positive reinforcement and poor psychological well-being (Segrin and Taylor, 2007; Segrin *et al.*, 2007). Having the ability to reward (i.e. reward-ingness) is a key dimension of interaction that plays a central role in friendship formation and personal attraction (Foley and Duck, 2006; Smith and Mackie, 2007). In professional circles the ability to reinforce effectively, during dealings

---

Box 4.1 Everyday examples of reinforcement

- An infant makes its first attempt at 'Mummy' and the adoring mother responds with enraptured smiles, hugs and kisses
- A pupil who has been struggling with quadratic equations gets them all right for the first time and the attentive teacher lavishes generous praise
- The striker for the home team scores a goal and is mobbed by his team mates while the frenetic fans chant his name in exultation
- Someone in the group tells a funny story and the other members erupt in laughter
- A sales executive beats the monthly target and earns the heart-felt congratulations of the sales team
- A learner driver manages to complete a U-turn for the first time and the instructor smiles in recognition and gives a 'thumbs-up' sign

In all of these cases it is likely that the person reacted to in each of these positive ways will be influenced subsequently to strive to do similar things in future situations. When the individual does so, his or her actions (scoring goals, telling funny stories, saying 'Mummy', etc.) are said to have been reinforced.

---

with those availing of the service on offer, has been heavily stressed (Dickson *et al.*, 1997; Arnold and Boggs, 2016). This is because rewards in social situations serve 'to keep others in the relationship, to increase the other's attraction to ego, and to make greater influence possible, when reinforcement is contingent upon the desired behaviour' (Argyle, 1995, p. 82). The term 'contingent' in the reinforcement literature refers to a direct linkage between the behaviour and the reinforcement – the reinforcer occurs as a causal consequence of the behaviour. By contrast, noncontingent reinforcement occurs when reinforcers are randomly given, regardless of the behaviour of the interlocutor.

REINFORCEMENT AND PROFESSIONAL PRACTICE

In their analysis of generic communication styles, de Vries *et al.* (2009) identified one of the core dimensions as 'supportiveness', which involves complimenting, praising, encouraging and comforting others. This style is important, since, in his research into 'comforting communication', Burleson (2010b, p. 161) found that 'people who are skilled at providing emotional support are more popular, better liked, and have more lasting friendships and intimate relationships'. Thus, a core skill common to professional practice in a range of settings involves responding positively to others so as to reward and reinforce appropriately. In education, for instance, reinforcement has been found to be a powerful tool for teachers to use to improve pupils' social behaviour in class and promote academic achievement (Sutherland and Wehby, 2001; Woolfolk, 2005). In their review of research into effective teaching, Harbour *et al.* (2015, p. 9) found that, 'When teachers use positive feedback at increased rates, a number of benefits arise, including improvements in student achievement, engagement, and behavior'. Numerous classroom studies have also shown that increases in the use of teacher positive reinforcement result in concomitant decreases in disruptive pupil behaviours (Pisacreta *et al.*, 2011). In their pioneering research into teaching skills, Turney *et al.* (1983) charted how through reinforcement teachers could increase pupils' attention and motivation, improve classroom behaviour and promote achievement, by various verbal and nonverbal means, including:

* praise and encouragement
* gestures
* adjusting physical proximity
* opportunities to take part in other activities such as playing class games with peers.

Shifting the focus from teaching to psychotherapy, a view has been advanced of the psychotherapist as a powerful source of social reinforcement that is used during the consultation to shape change (Castonquay and Beutler, 2005). For Beier and Young (1998), while clients' maladaptive patterns of relating may elicit painful responses from others, those same patterns may also meet a more compelling need for predictability and consistency in dealings with them. In this way dysfunctional behaviour is sustained through interpersonal reinforcement. The therapist's task is to reshape more productive and satisfying styles of interaction. Accordingly, the role of reinforcement in Parent–Child Interaction Therapy has been highlighted, as has the crucial role of the therapist as a purveyor of reinforcement therein (Pemberton *et al.*, 2013).

In the related field of counselling, Ivey *et al.* (2014) attributed special status to 'attending' in their taxonomy of constituent microskills, going so far as to label it 'the foundation skill' (p. 64) of the interviewing and counselling process. Attending to the client in this sense involves:

- following the conversational lead offered
- adopting appropriate body language
- engaging visually
- being vocally responsive.

Based on the premise that people will only talk about what others are prepared to listen to, clients can be encouraged to disclose issues of concern through the judicious use of attending behaviour and the reinforcing effects of selective listening on the part of the counsellor or interviewer.

Reinforcement has also been identified as playing a prominent role in physiotherapists' interactions with patients (Adams *et al.*, 1994). In this study, physiotherapy sessions involving both adults and children in outpatient, obstetrics and gynaecology, neurology and paediatric departments were videotaped for fine-grained analysis. Reinforcement was identified as an important element of the task-oriented dimension of practice. It featured in work with both adults and children and comprised, for example, praise, acknowledging increased effort, positive feedback, smiling and eye contact. This piece of research was closely based upon earlier work by Saunders and Caves (1986), who used a similar methodology to unearth the key communication skills of a different professional group, speech and language therapists. 'Using positive reinforcement' was one of the categories to emerge from interactions with children and adults. Verbal and nonverbal sub-types were specified. Using the same approach, Hargie *et al.* (2000) charted the key communication skills of community pharmacists and found that reinforcement, in the context of explaining to patients, was rank-ordered as the second most important pharmacist skill, after rapport building.

In other areas of health care, health-worker social rewards in the form of attention, praise, approval, compliments, and so on, can increase patient satisfaction and improve adherence to prescribed drug regimens and recommended courses of action. This may include sticking to a set diet and maintaining healthy eating patterns (Holli and Beto, 2014). By taking steps to monitor patient behaviour and reinforce adherence when it does take place, health professionals can go some way to ensuring that patients co-operate fully in their treatment. This can have particular impact in cases of difficult or unpleasant courses of action. In controlling difficult long-term medical conditions, according to Warren and Hixenbaugh (1998, p. 441):

It is the role of the doctor to convince the patient that the discomfort or inconvenience in the short term will bring rewards (by avoiding complications) in the long term...In order to achieve this, reinforcements, such as praise for appropriate behaviour, must be immediate.

Fisher (2001) emphasised that influencing change along these lines presupposes the prior establishment of a relationship of trust, acceptance and respect. It is only in this context that praise and approval are likely to be valued. In a similar vein, Buckmann (1997) argued that using rewards like selective positive feedback, benevolent behaviour and acceptance statements that convey to patients that they are held in high regard, can act indirectly to enhance adherence. These ways of relating strengthen health professionals' referent power (i.e. the social power bestowed upon them as people to be identified with or 'looked up to'). This, together with their expert power (i.e. the influence they command due to their expertise), serves to strengthen patients' self-esteem and sense of self-efficacy (these aspects of influence are further addressed in Chapter 12). Following the argument through, patients who have a better sense of their own worth and a greater belief in their ability to succeed in the task are more likely to co-operate in their treatment.

Rewards, including praise, make a potentially beneficial contribution to other and diverse areas of professional activity, such as management and organisational operations. Those intent on building effectively functioning teams in the workplace have been advised to be particularly attentive to the power of social rewards (Hargie *et al.*, 2004). When systematically applied, improvements in staff absenteeism, motivation, job satisfaction, productivity and safety can result (for reviews see, for example, Austin and Carr, 2000; Pershing, 2006). The findings were summarised by Reid and Parsons (2000, p. 281), with reference to human service settings:

> A variety of consequences have been demonstrated through OBM [Organizational Behavior Management] research to have reinforcing effects on desired staff performance including, for example, money, free meals, commercial trading stamps, discount coupons, and work duties, trips away from the work site, and special recognition ceremonies.

However, as always, reinforcement is a two-way street and in the workplace rewards work both ways, as employees attempt to influence and shape the behaviour of managers. Hargie *et al.* (2004, pp. 85–86) showed how:

> Subordinates influence managers through rewards such as social approval (praise, nonverbal acknowledgment, etc.), and by their work rate and volume of output. Conversely they can punish managers by withdrawing verbal and nonverbal rewards and by reducing their work efforts.

Finally, sports coaches who employ rewarding techniques have been found to be popular, and have also been shown to enhance levels of skill and improve results (Smith and Smoll, 2007; Freeman *et al.*, 2009). Furthermore, Justine and Howe (1998) reported that, among adolescent female field hockey players, frequent praise from the coach was associated with greater perceptions of self-competence and satisfaction with both the coach and general team involvement.

BEHAVIOUR AND ITS CONSEQUENCES

Since Ivan Pavlov, the eminent Russian physiologist, introduced the term (Pavlov, 1927), the concept of reinforcement has been the subject of much heated debate in psychology. One psychologist who was at the forefront of much of this was B.F. Skinner (1953). Skinner preferred the term 'reinforcement' to 'reward' due to the greater semantic precision which it afforded, together with its lack of mentalistic trappings. As such, a reinforcer, by definition, has the effect of increasing the probability of the preceding behaviour. The application of reinforcement procedures in keeping with Skinnerian principles is known as *instrumental* or *operant conditioning*. The central tenet of this process focuses on the ability of the consequences of behaviour to increase the probability of subsequent manifestations of that behaviour, relative to some preconditioned level (Lieberman, 2012).

For any particular piece of behaviour there are environmental stimuli that precede or accompany it and other stimuli that follow it. Consider the classroom example of a teacher asking the class a question, to which Mary raises her hand. As far as the pupil's act is concerned, the most conspicuous antecedent stimulus is obviously the posed question. The response also takes place within the context of a plethora of accompanying stimuli which constitute the classroom environment. Other stimuli follow on from it and are made available as a consequence of the behaviour having been performed (e.g. the teacher may react enthusiastically, the child may be offered the opportunity to display knowledge by answering, other classmates may marvel at her brilliance, etc.). Further significant factors have to do with, for instance, how hungry Mary is for this sort of attention. The role of antecedent stimuli will be returned to, but for the moment let us stay with the outcomes of performance.

In broadest terms, the relationship between a response and its consequences may lead to that response subsequently being:

1   increased in frequency
2   decreased in frequency
3   left largely unchanged.

As to the first of these eventualities, reinforcement is the process taking place. Reinforcers serve to make preceding actions more likely to recur. Reinforcement can take a positive or a negative form, as will be explained shortly. Before doing so though, it is useful to consider two outcomes that serve to reduce the likelihood of similar future actions – punishment and extinction.

Punishment

This has the effect of suppressing behaviour so that it is less likely that those acts leading to the punishment will be repeated. Indeed, it too can operate in either a positive or a negative way. *Positive punishment* involves the introduction of something unpleasant (a noxious stimulus), such as a physical blow or hurtful criticism, contingent upon the appearance of the targeted behaviour. *Negative punishment* involves withdrawing some benefit that, had the individual not acted in that way, would have continued to be enjoyed. Removing privileges, such as access to the computer, is an example. Attempts at control and influence through punishment are common in everyday interaction and may be subtly exercised. They can involve sarcasm, ridicule, derision, reprimands and threats, to specify but a few. However, a number of undesirable side-effects have been associated with punishment (Durrant and Ensom, 2012; Martin *et al.*, 2013). It can produce negative emotional reactions such as fear and avoidance, which may generalise beyond the response being punished to the punishing agent, for example a teacher, and then have a further dysfunctional impact upon attitude to the subject being taught and even to school itself. In most contexts it is clear that the carrot is better than the stick.

Extinction

When actions previously reinforced cease, for whatever reason, to produce customary outcomes that are positively valued, the likely long-term effect will also be a reduction in those activities. This occurs through the phenomenon of extinction. Thus, while there are important differences between punishment and extinction, both serve to reduce the likelihood of a response (Newman and Newman, 2007).

Positive reinforcement

So, reinforcement can be engineered through positive or negative means. The positive reinforcement principle states that, 'if someone in a given situation does something that is followed immediately by a positive reinforcer, then that person is more likely to do the same thing the next time he or she encounters a similar situation' (Martin and Pear, 2015, p. 32). As noted by Nicholas (2008), positive reinforcers take many forms, including a verbal or nonverbal reward, a material object, money, a privilege or valued activity. For example, Mary, the pupil in the earlier example, may have received a positive reinforcer in the form of having her contribution to the lesson praised by the teacher, making her more prepared to offer further contributions.

It is positive reinforcement and rewards that are commonly referred to when reinforcement is conceptualised as an interpersonal skill, and this will therefore be the focus of much of the analysis in this chapter. Before moving on, the relationship between positive reinforcement and reward needs to be clarified. For some, such as Martin and Pear (2015), the terms are roughly synonymous. Indeed, Nelson-Jones (2014), operating within a counselling framework, declared a preference for 'reward', believing it to be more in keeping with the language of helping. Technically speaking, however, a reinforcer must, by definition, act to increase the frequency of the behaviour upon which it is contingent. For Kazdin (2013), a reward, in contrast, is something given and received in return for something done. While it may act as a reinforcer, whether or not it actually does reinforce is an empirical question. On this point, and in the classroom context, Zirpoli and Melloy (2015) stressed that teachers should not assume that a particular stimulus or activity will be reinforcing for a pupil. Indeed, Capstick (2005) showed that there are often marked differences between what teachers and pupils perceive to be the most potent forms of reward.

Negative reinforcement

Here, a response is associated with the avoidance, termination or reduction of an aversive stimulus that would have either occurred or continued at some level had the response not taken place. Negative reinforcement and punishment should not be confused. Although both involve aversive states, in the case of punishment this state is made contingent on the occurrence of the behaviour under focus and has the effect of making that behaviour less likely to recur. With negative reinforcement, the behaviour that results in the noxious stimulus being reduced, eliminated or avoided will be more probable in future.

Examples of negative reinforcement in everyday life are common. We have a headache, take FeelFine analgesic and the pain disappears, making it more likely that we will take FeelFine the next time a headache strikes. The TV becomes uncomfortably loud when the adverts come on, spurring us to grab the remote control to turn down the volume. One theory is that habit-forming behaviours like drinking alcohol or smoking are maintained through their effect in reducing tension (Stroebe, 2000). Experimental evidence was produced by Craighead et al. (1996) that college women with bulimia nervosa and past depression had higher rates of learning on a computerised mental maze task when provided with negative social feedback for errors made, rather than positive feedback for correct responses. It was thought that avoidance or minimisation of negative reactions was the key factor.

Much of our interpersonal interaction is shaped in a similar way through negative reinforcement (Cipani and Schock, 2011). Bringing to an end as quickly as possible an interchange with someone found unpleasant, uninteresting or just difficult to relate to could be accounted for in this way. A similar explanation may explain why we speak back in defence of our position in conversations where it has been challenged. An argument can be thought of as a logical, reasoned debate or, alternatively, as a quarrel between two people, each of whom is out to vanquish the other (Billing, 2001). Contemporary society is increasingly typified by arguments, with associated confrontation and threats to face (Tannen et al., 2007). As such, disagreement with our point of view and the prospect of being shown to be wrong can make us feel vulnerable, threatened and humiliated. Having the chance to defend our beliefs and opinions successfully often brings relief and therefore makes responding more likely.

Conversational repair is a further feature of talk, in that corrections, apologies and disclaimers are brought into play when participants unwittingly break a conversational or societal rule, thereby running the risk of causing confusion or even losing face (Hayashi *et al.*, 2013). Viewed as the application of negative reinforcement, breaking the rule may cause embarrassment or discomfort, which in turn can be assuaged by an apology or disclaimer. This then makes it likely that these forms of repair will be relied upon again in similar situations.

Allen and Stokes (1987) reported a more formal application of negative reinforcement in managing the disruptive and unco-operative behaviour of children receiving restorative dental treatment. In this case, children were asked to be 'big helpers' by staying still and being quiet while the dentist worked. This led to the temporary suspension of treatment. Gradually children had to be 'big helpers' for longer periods of time in order to have the dentist suspend treatment for a period. Not only were children markedly more compliant by the last visit but, from readings of heart rate and blood pressure, were significantly less stressed by the experience.

The different types of behavioural consequence outlined in this section are depicted in Figure 4.1 and summarised in Box 4.2.

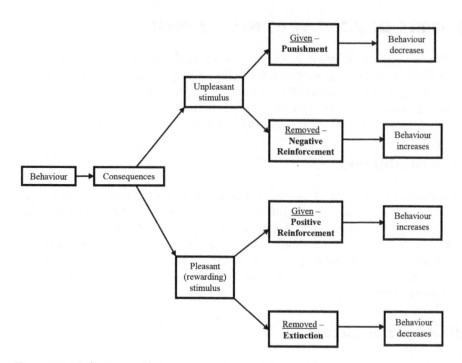

Figure 4.1 Behaviour and its consequences.

Box 4.2 Consequences of behaviour

Punishment – suppresses targeted behaviour

Positive punishment – involves the introduction of something unpleasant (e.g. being scolded, slapped, made to feel uncomfortable)

Negative punishment – involves the removal of something desired (e.g. TV confiscated, credit card withdrawn, car keys taken away)

Extinction

Extinction eliminates targeted behaviour (e.g. you will stop putting a coin in a particular dispensing machine that consistently fails to deliver a can of soft drink)

Reinforcement – promotes targeted behaviour

Positive reinforcement – involves the introduction of something pleasant (e.g. receiving praise, chocolate, attention, money, playing a favourite computer game)

Negative reinforcement – involves the removal of something undesirable (e.g. stopping pain, boredom, embarrassment, stress)

CATEGORIES OF POSITIVE REINFORCEMENT

The vast range of things that we do as we go about our daily lives gives rise to a multiplicity of differing outcomes, both physical and social. Many of these exert a controlling influence through the operation of positive reinforcement. Psychologists have proposed different systems of classification. Sherman (1990) suggested five core reinforcement categories – primary, conditioned, social, sensory and activity.

Primary reinforcers

These can be thought of as stimuli that are inherently valued, and the positive value and reinforcing potential of which do not rely upon a process of prior learning. Examples include food, drink, shelter, air, sex, and so on. These are things that we depend on for survival, due to our biological make-up. Despite their fundamental indispensability, they have limitations as a direct means of influencing the complexities of everyday person-to-person interaction, where the rewards tend to be more subtle.

Conditioned reinforcers

This grouping, also called *secondary reinforcers*, is in sharp contrast to the previous. It includes events that have no intrinsic worth but whose power to control behaviour is ultimately derived from an earlier association with primary reinforcers. We learn to value conditioned reinforcers. Tokens, stickers, vouchers, medals, stamps, badges, stars, and such like, can be incorporated into organised programmes called *token economies* where they are earned for engaging in particular tasks and subsequently exchanged for more basic back-up reinforcers (Kazdin, 2013). Under particular circumstances, an originally neutral stimulus can become associated with a number of primary reinforcers. Money, to cite one example, can be used to obtain food, drink, shelter, heat and sex. Skinner (1953) called this special class *generalised reinforcers*. Since these are particularly applicable in relation to social reinforcement they are discussed further under the next sub-heading.

Social reinforcers

Lieberman (2012, p. 149) defined social reinforcers as, 'stimuli whose reinforcing properties derive uniquely from the behaviour of other members of the same species'. Social behaviour, by definition, presupposes the involvement of others. In the main, the types of rewards that govern and shape it are also contributed by those with whom we mix and intermingle and are a powerful, though often subtle, influence on our actions. Buss (1983) further categorised these rewards as either process or content.

Social process rewards

These are an inherent part of interpersonal contact and include, in order of increasing potency, the mere presence of others, attention from them and their conversational responsivity. An interesting observation is that too much or too little of these activities can be aversive; it is only at a notional intermediate level that they become reinforcing. The attention given by a teacher to a pupil in the same environment may well change from being reinforcing to punishing if it is either withdrawn totally or, at the other extreme, becomes intrusively persistent.

Social content rewards

What takes place within interaction also has rewarding ramifications. Here Buss paid particular heed to the acts of showing deference, praising, extending sympathy and expressing approval, confirmation or affection. Unlike their process equivalents, these presuppose a certain type of interpersonal relationship to be relevant and effective. Thus, we seldom express affection to complete strangers.

As well as process and content rewards, individuals can find variously reinforcing opportunities to compare themselves to others, compete, dominate or self-disclose, and may seek out situations and occasions to indulge themselves accordingly.

Generalised reinforcers

Individuals are moulded as social beings through the influence of the social milieu of which they are a part. As we have seen, the subtleties of the process involve the judicious distribution, by significant others, of such mechanisms as attention, interest, approval and affection. It is these sorts of activities that lie at the heart of positive responding conceived of as an interpersonal skill. Through them one person can influence what another does without using actual or threatened physical force. According to Skinner, positive social reactions can be used to shape interpersonal behaviour because they serve as generalised reinforcers. The approval and attention of others are examples. Of approval, he wrote, 'A common generalised reinforcer is approval...It may be little more than a nod of the head or a smile on the part of someone who characteristically supplies a variety of reinforcers. Sometimes...it has a verbal form "Right!" or "Good!"' (Skinner, 1957, p. 53). In the case of attention, he noted that, 'The attention of people is reinforcing because it is a necessary condition for other reinforcements from them. In general, only those who are attending to us reinforce our behaviour' (Skinner, 1953, p. 78).

For Lieberman (2012), among others, these aspects of social performance, in that they can be thought of at all as reinforcers in the Skinnerian sense, embrace both learned and unlearned dimensions. To be more specific, the suggestion is that some of the nonverbal features, such as smiles and hugs, may not depend upon prior experience to be positively valued. In other words, they are a blend of primary and conditioned reinforcers.

Sensory reinforcers

Listening to beautiful music, looking at a striking painting, attending the theatre or watching an exciting sporting event are all attractive possibilities, albeit to varying extents for different individuals. We need only think of the costs and inconveniences that devotees will endure to indulge themselves in these activities to appreciate that certain quantities and qualities of sensory stimulation can be highly rewarding. This fact was exploited by Mizes (1985) in treating an adolescent girl who was hospitalised following complaints of chronic lower-back pain. The extent of this pain was such that she was virtually bed-ridden. Tests and examinations failed to locate any physical cause, and the case was treated as an abnormal behaviour disorder which was being inadvertently held in place through operant conditioning. When opportunities to watch TV, have access to the telephone and receive parental visits were made conditional upon demonstrably increased mobility, symptoms gradually subsided.

Activity reinforcers

For Premack (1965), activities rather than things are reinforcing. It is eating and drinking that is of significance, rather than food or drink, as such. Stated formally, the *Premack principle* proposes that activities of low probability can be increased in likelihood if activities of high probability are made contingent upon them. Activity reinforcement can be a powerful means of organising work routines and maximising commitment in a diversity of professional settings, including management, health care, sport and education. Holli and Beto (2014) highlighted the benefits in the management of patients with eating disorders of walking, gardening or reading (or whatever the client finds attractive) as rewards to be earned by sticking to agreed dietary habits. In sport, the example is given by Martin and Pear (2015) of a swimming coach who produced a 150 per cent improvement in the practice of racing turns at both ends of the pool together with the number of swimming sets completed without stopping. The reinforcing activity was being allowed to take part in a final 10-minute fun activity in the pool, which was made contingent upon these elements of training.

In school, pupils may prefer, for example, more practical classes to didactic instruction. Lessons can be arranged in such a way that to get to do practical activities, the theory must be understood. The 'Good Behaviour Game', for use with younger pupils, has been employed as a way of improving behaviour in class (Dijkman *et al.*, 2014). If the group record fewer than, say, 5 tally marks for breaking classroom rules during the day, they win privileges such as a period of 'free time', before going home. More generally, Burden and Byrd (2012) pointed out that being permitted to carry out classroom tasks, such as operating equipment, taking a note to the office or checking attendance can be prized activities in the classroom.

The potential for these principles to enhance managerial effectiveness and raise output has been recognised for some time (e.g. Komaki, 1982). Increasing productivity was demonstrated in an early study by Gupton and Le Bow (1971), through an internal rearrangement of the various types of task that workers carried out. In this case the workers were part-time telephone sales personnel in industry who sold both new and renewal service contracts. On average, the success rate for attempts at renewals was more than twice that for new sales, so sales personnel tended to devote most of their energies to the former. As far as the firm was concerned this resulted in a general failure to attract new customers. A new regime was imposed whereby five new calls were required before the representatives had an opportunity to make attempts at renewal sales. This contingency resulted in a substantial increase, not only in the number of new contracts sold, but in renewals as well.

STIMULUS CONTROL

It was mentioned earlier in the chapter that behaviour can be set in a context of, on the one hand, preceding and accompanying stimuli and, on the other, consequent events. The probability of responding can be affected by the presence or absence of a stimulus as well as by the response to one's behaviour. When a certain action only succeeds in eliciting reinforcement in the presence of particular accompanying stimuli, then that piece of behaviour is said to be under *stimulus control* and those stimuli have become *discriminative stimuli* in respect of it (Donahoe, 2014). They signal the availability of a reinforcer for behaving in that way. When the overall context acts in this way, then *contextual control* is in operation (Sarafino, 2004).

Many examples of stimulus control spring to mind. The doctor–patient consultation is traditionally a one-sided affair, especially with male doctors (Dickson and McCartan, 2005; Imber, 2008). The high-control style of doctors involves interrupting frequently, asking almost all of the questions (see Chapter 5) and setting the agenda. Attempts by patients to negotiate their own agendas usually meet with little success. In this setting, doctor questions may serve as discriminative stimuli indicating to patients when their contributions will be welcomed and when not. Hooper (1995) analysed differences between expert and novice nurses when taking the pulse and blood pressure of senior citizens. She discovered that discriminative stimuli such as casual conversation, client comfort and health-related information differentiated between the two groups in respect of such elements of practice as eye contact, verbal interaction, use of touch, attending to the client and obtaining the measurement. In the business sphere, the perspicacious employee who learns to read the subtle cues that suggest the likelihood of the manager being receptive to new ideas, and accordingly picks an opportunity to propose some innovation, is also being influenced by stimulus control.

Discriminative stimuli, therefore, signal the occasion for particular behaviours to be reinforced and must not be confused with reinforcing stimuli. The latter always function as a *consequence* of the targeted behaviour.

VICARIOUS REINFORCERS

So far the focus has been upon the direct impact of a positive outcome on the acquisition and regulation of the behaviour that brought it about. But the influence of rewards is wide-ranging and can be indirect. Vicarious reinforcement is the process whereby individuals are more likely to adopt particular behaviours if they see others being rewarded for engaging in them (Kazdin, 2013). Through observing the actions of others we learn not only what to do, but how to do it; we benefit from their successes (Bandura, 2006). Rewards, vicariously experienced, can influence learning, motivation and emotions. Seeing others rewarded for some behaviour (e.g. observing other pupils being rewarded by the teacher for answering questions in the classroom) can act as a strong inducement for the observer to do likewise, when it is inferred that similar outcomes will accrue by behaving similarly (Gureghian, 2013). Furthermore, when the consequences of actions are socially mediated, a basis is established for reassessing the attractiveness of experienced outcomes through witnessing what happens to others under comparable conditions. For example, receiving recognition from a supervisor will mean much more once it is realised, from observations of interactions with others, that this person rarely acknowledges effort. Receiving rewards and punishments is associated with the creation of pleasant and unpleasant emotional states. Awareness of these states and circumstances in other people can be emotionally arousing and this facility is believed to account for empathic responsivity to them (Bandura, 1986). The ability to engage empathically with others is, of course, fundamental to effective counselling (Egan, 2014).

The consequences here are far-reaching. For example, Rebellon (2006, p. 403), in a study of adolescent delinquency, illustrated the potency of vicarious reinforcement, finding that: 'a delinquent attracts the attention of peers, that audience members take note of this phenomenon, and that they therefore increase their delinquency in proportion to their own desire for peer attention'. Vicarious reinforcement has important implications for professional practice. A teacher, in a large and busy classroom, may find difficulty in providing reinforcement on an individual basis for appropriate behaviour and accomplishments. Under these circumstances much of the teacher-based reinforcement that pupils receive is likely to be vicarious, as they observe other pupils being rewarded for particular responses. In relation to management, the maxim of 'praise publicly – punish privately' articulates the potentially vicarious benefits of bestowing rewards in the presence of others (Prue and Fairbank, 1981).

On a more cautionary note, however, two possible downsides of vicarious reinforcement are that:

- praising in public can cause embarrassment for some and so may produce negative rather than positive effects;
- watching others persistently rewarded for something that the observer has done equally competently, but without comparable recompense, may cause resentment and de-motivation. This has been referred to as the implicit effects of observed consequences and, as such, distinguished from vicarious facets (Bandura, 1986).

INTERPERSONAL EFFECTS OF SOCIAL REWARDS AND REINFORCERS

A range of goals tends to be served by social rewards and reinforcers (Dickson *et al.*, 1993; Cairns, 2006). These are summarised in Box 4.3, and will now be examined in more detail.

Box 4.3 Purposes of reinforcement

The main goals served by the skill of reinforcement are to:

- promote interaction and maintain relationships
- increase the participation of the interactive partner
- influence the nature and content of the contribution of the interlocutor
- demonstrate a genuine interest in the ideas, thoughts and feelings of the other
- make interaction interesting and enjoyable
- create an impression of warmth and understanding
- increase one's own social attractiveness as the source of rewards
- display one's own power, as the controller of rewards
- improve the confidence and self-esteem of the other person

Promoting interaction and maintaining relationships

During social encounters we not only welcome but demand a certain basic level of reward. If it is not forthcoming we may treat this as sufficient grounds for abandoning the relationship in favour of more attractive alternatives. Research into friendship and peer relations in children shows that an important characteristic that distinguishes popular from unpopular children is being rewarding and supportive (Bagwell and Schmidt, 2011). Conversely, Jones *et al.* (1982) discovered that college students who were lonely, in comparison to their more gregarious peers, were found to be strikingly less attentive to conversational partners. More extremely, Argyle (1995) noted the marked lack of reinforcement typifying the interpersonal performance of certain categories of patients with mental disorder, such as schizophrenia and depression. He described them as unrewarding to the point of being 'socially bankrupt'. These individuals do not show interest and attention, with the result that interacting with them is unrewarding (Hammen, 1997). Impoverished social contact may produce a further deterioration in mental state, with fewer opportunities for interpersonal involvement, thus creating a debilitating downward spiral: 'As the individual becomes more depressed, social avoidance leads to further reductions in exposure to positive reinforcement and the problem is compounded' (Walker, 2001, p. 162).

Increasing the active involvement of the interactive partner

For professionals who work mainly with other people, it is important that recipients of the service are encouraged to be fully involved in what takes place, if the goals of the encounter are to be achieved. Promoting active participation in the classroom is a good example. Costs incurred by pupils, in the form of energy expended, lack of opportunity to devote time to competing activities and fear of getting it wrong, amongst others, must be offset by the availability of rewards. In some learning situations (e.g. acquiring a novel skill), intrinsic rewards from efficient task performance may be initially limited. Teacher reinforcement is therefore one method of increasing pupil commitment to what is taking place.

Influencing the nature and content of contribution

Apart from extending the general level of participation, rewards can be administered in a planned and systematic fashion to reinforce and shape contributions selectively along particular lines. Interviewees can be influenced by selective interviewer reinforcement to continue with the detailed exploration of certain topics or issues to the exclusion of others regarded by the interviewer as being of lesser relevance or even counter-productive. In a medical setting, for instance, White and Saunders (1986) demonstrated how patients suffering from chronic pain conversationally focused more on their pain when the interviewer responded with attention and praise. Selectively reinforcing 'well talk', on the other hand, had the opposite effect.

Martin and Pear (2015) gave an interesting example of a 13-year-old girl who began to complain of severe headaches. Over a number of years this attracted considerable attention in the form of concern from family, friends and eventually, as the migraine-like condition worsened, from health workers. Various medical treatments were attempted but no organic cause could be found for her complaint. At the age of 26 years she was still experiencing incapacitating headaches and it was felt that these could in fact be due to them being reinforced. So,with her agreement, a behaviour treatment programme was introduced in which all those with whom she came in contact ignored 'pain behaviour' (e.g. complaining, taking tablets, going to bed) and praised 'well behaviour' (e.g. engaging in exercise, completing domestic tasks) whenever it was manifested. The mean number of pain behaviours dropped from a baseline of eight to fewer than one per day after 3 weeks of treatment, and were totally eliminated by the end of the programme. Using the same principles, teachers can increase the incidence of appropriate pupil behaviour in class (Zirpoli and Melloy, 2015).

Before progressing, it should be acknowledged that, when worded in this way, there is little which is either original or profound in the proposition that people are inclined to do things that lead to positive outcomes and avoid other courses of action that produce unwanted consequences. This much is widely known. Indeed, the statement may seem so obvious as to be trivial. But, despite this general awareness, individuals are often remarkably unsuccessful in bringing about behavioural change both in them and in other people. Indeed, it has been found that partners of drug abusers often unwittingly encourage the very behaviour that they are trying to eliminate through their inconsistent use of reinforcement and punishment (LePoire et al., 2000). The conclusion drawn by Lieberman (2012, p. 141) is that, 'Clearly the principle of reward cannot be quite as simple as it sounds'.

Many professionals make surprisingly poor use of this interpersonal skill. Cannell et al. (1977), investigating the performance of survey interviewers, found that adequate or appropriate responses received proportionately less positive interviewer reinforcement than did less desirable reactions. Refusal to respond, the least desirable response, received proportionately the highest levels of reinforcement. Furthermore, during investigative interviews, interviewer reinforcement can distort the information-gathering process, leading to false accounts of what took place, especially with child witnesses (Talwar and Crossman, 2012). For example, Garven et al. (1998) analysed several hundred interview transcripts conducted with children as part of an inquiry into alleged child abuse by seven Californian teachers. They found evidence of several suggestive techniques employed, including praising or rewarding children when they said or did something that fitted in with interviewers' assumptions (see Chapter 5 for a further discussion of interviews with children).

Classroom studies have shown that the use of reinforcement by teachers tends to be at very low rates (Harbour et al., 2015). Reviewing a number of studies, Brophy (1981, p. 8) concluded that its use is 'typically infrequent, noncontingent, global rather than specific, and determined more by students' personal qualities or teachers' perceptions of students' need for praise than by the quality of student conduct or achievement'. Likewise, educators may administer praise on the basis of answers they expect to receive rather than those actually given (Eggen and Kauchak, 2012).

Demonstrating interest in the other person, making interaction enjoyable and creating an impression of warmth and understanding

In addition to influencing what recipients say or do, bestowing rewards also conveys information about the giver. Providers of substantial amounts of social reinforcement are usually perceived to be keenly interested in those with whom they interact and what they have to say. They also typically create an impression of being warm, accepting and understanding. Teacher praise and encouragement have been associated with positive pupil ratings of the teacher (Kelly and Daniels, 1997; Bakx *et al.*, 2015) and of satisfaction with the course (Worland, 1998). By contrast, teachers who dispense few social rewards are regarded as cold, aloof, depressed or bored – as well as boring.

Increasing one's own social attractiveness as the source of rewards

Some investigators, such as Clore and Byrne (1974), have made use of the concept of reinforcement in attempting to account for interpersonal attraction. Responses and pleasurable feelings that stem from receiving rewards become associated with the provider, or even with a third party who happens to be consistently present when they are dispensed. Such attraction, however, is neither universal nor unconditional, depending as it does upon how what is taking place is construed by the recipient. The source is more likely to be found to be attractive if the action being praised is regarded by the recipient as praiseworthy; praise from that individual is valued, and if it reflects a positive change from a more negative disposition by the source towards the recipient (Raven and Rubin, 1983). If, on the other hand, it is suspected that there are ulterior motives for lavish praise or compliments, and ingratiation or manipulation is suspected, liking for the source will deteriorate (Aronson, 2008).

Displaying one's power

The distribution of rewards can be conceptualised as an exercise in power and authority. Being in a position to determine whether or not another receives something of value confers on the bestower the ability to exert influence, and the power to set the conditions to be met for the rewards to be given. When the allocation of rewards is viewed by the recipient as an attempt at control, however, resistance to such manipulation may result. This can be a manifestation of *psychological reactance*, and an attempt to assert personal freedom and autonomy when these are threatened (see Chapter 12 for a fuller discussion of power and reactance).

Improving the confidence and self-esteem of the other person

Finally, positive reactions may not only produce more favourable impressions towards those who offer them, but can also result in heightened feelings of self-esteem and self-efficacy in the recipient. Self-esteem refers to the sense of personal worth that an individual holds, ranging from love and acceptance to hate and rejection. Self-efficacy is a belief in one's ability to accomplish a task or reach a goal successfully (Bandura, 1997). Being given positive information about levels of skill possessed can make us think differently about tackling a particular task. More generally, Sullivan (1953) believed that one's concept of self develops out of the reflected appraisals of significant others. Thus, positive rewarding experiences with parents and other key adults lead to positive views of self, while being subjected to negative experiences, including blame, constant reprimands and ridicule, results in feelings of worthlessness. Does this mean then that those receiving praise invariably assume that they are better or more able than those who don't? This is an important question, to be returned to shortly.

Self-enhancement versus self-verification

People are not merely passive recipients of the reactions of others. Rather, they often make a deliberate effort to present themselves in such a way as to attract a particular type of evaluative response. One motive for this is *self-enhancement*. Through a process of *impression management* or *self-presentation* individuals go out of their way to make themselves as appealing as possible to others (Stapleton and Hargie, 2011). The importance of promoting a positive assessment of self, and being looked upon favourably by others has been stressed (Pilkington and Smith, 2000; Tesser, 2001). Attention, praise, approval and various other rewards will be valued on these grounds. But what if such reactions clash with our existing perceptions of self and the suggested positive self-evaluations are inconsistent with how we already see ourselves? For some, under certain circumstances, *self-verification* rather than self-enhancement is what counts (Gómez *et al.*, 2007; Swann, 2009). Here, it is not necessarily a positive evaluation that is being sought, but rather one that is consistent with the individual's existing self-referenced views and beliefs (Seih *et al.*, 2013). According to Taylor *et al.* (1995), a range of factors, including personality and culture, as well as situational aspects, will make self-enhancement or self-verification salient. For those with negative views of themselves, receiving information from others that back up these perceptions (i.e. self-verification) seems to be stressed (Ayduk *et al.*, 2013). These findings have interesting and significant ramifications for rewarding and reinforcing. For those with a poor self-concept and low self-esteem, praise and other positive reactions incongruent with how they regard themselves may not be appreciated and fail to have a reinforcing influence. Indeed, the opposite may be the case. Before leaving the topic, though, it should be mentioned that people vary, more generally, in the extent to which their sense of self-esteem is contingent upon external factors such as praise or criticism (Wolfe, 2007).

Locus of control

A further dimension of personality that is of functional relevance to social rewards is locus of control. This term refers to the extent to which individuals regard themselves, rather than powerful others, or mere chance, as having control over what happens to them (Francis, 2014). The originator of the term, Rotter (1966) developed the following formula to determine the behaviour potential of a response – that is, the likelihood of a particular response being chosen in a specific situation:

$$behaviour\ potential = reinforcement\ value \times expectancy$$

Here, reinforcement value refers to one's personal evaluation of the reward, while expectancy refers to one's subjective estimation of the likelihood of actually receiving the reinforcement in this context. Those who believe that they can personally influence the extent to which they will receive reinforcement have a high internal locus of control. These individuals believe that rewards gained are contingent upon their own performance and a reflection of their relatively enduring characteristics and qualities. At the other extreme, those who think that reinforcement is determined by external forces have a high external locus of control; this is typified by the idea that any successes that may occasionally happen are due largely to chance, luck or some external influence rather than to their own efforts. Those with an internal locus of control tend to attain higher levels of reward (Kormanik and Rocco, 2009). This leads to success in life. In their review of research in a range of areas, such as physical and mental well-being, educational attainment and organisational achievement, Maltby *et al.* (2013, p. 86) concluded that, 'With very few exceptions, it appears that internals are more successful than externals in most situations'.

BEHAVIOURAL COMPONENTS OF SOCIAL REINFORCEMENT

Given that, in theory, anything that increases the frequency of the preceding piece of behaviour can be considered a reinforcer, even if this list is restricted to elements of interpersonal behaviour, the resulting number of potential reinforcers could be extensive. Coverage will, therefore, be restricted to the more widely recognised elements featured in the literature. In doing so, a conceptual distinction will be made between components that are essentially verbal and those that are nonverbal. While this is a convenient way of structuring the section, as discussed in Chapter 3, in practice these two channels are closely interwoven.

Verbal components

The verbal channel of communication is a powerful source of social reinforcement. Things said can provide feedback, validate self-views and strengthen feelings of self-esteem and self-worth, or have the opposite effect. Verbal components of reinforcement range in sophistication from simple expressions such as 'OK', to more elaborate responses that relate to some aspect of the functioning of the interlocutor.

Acknowledgement/confirmation

This category includes words and phrases that acknowledge, confirm or agree with what has been said or done. Examples include verbalisations such as 'OK', 'Yes', 'Right', 'Fine', 'I see', 'That's it', as well as nonlexical vocalisations like 'mm-hmm' and 'uh-huh' (strictly speaking, the latter would be more appropriately listed under the nonverbal heading but, since they have often been grouped along with the other verbal utterances exemplified, it is more convenient to include them here). These responses are a common feature of conversations, since they signal that the listener is paying attention to the speaker (Brownell, 2012). They have also been shown to be crucial to the regulation of interaction when people talk over the telephone (Hargie *et al.*, 2004). Within the sphere of nursing, Balzer Riley (2012) illustrated the importance of phrases such as 'Mm-hmm', 'Yeah', 'I see', as signals of attention to patients and colleagues. From a counselling perspective, Ivey *et al.* (2014) referred to these types of responses as 'minimal verbal utterances' (p. 157) and described them as one way of encouraging clients to continue with their explication of personal concern during interviews. Together with nonverbal responses such as head nods and smiles, they have also been termed 'minimal encouragers', which 'work by using the "minimal" amount of feedback necessary to encourage clients to keep talking' (Blonna and Water, 2005, p. 62).

The reinforcing consequences of these attending utterances have been revealed in a number of classic experimental investigations, one of the most widely reported of which was that conducted by Greenspoon (1955), in which he simply asked subjects to produce as many individual words as they could think of. By responding with 'mm-hmm' each time a subject gave a plural noun and ignoring all other types of words, the number of plural nouns mentioned by subjects increased considerably over the course of the experiment. Not all subsequent investigations, though, have produced such positive outcomes. Rosenfeld (1987) suggests that at least some of these failures could be accounted for by the fact that social reinforcers were administered on a noncontingent basis (subjects were exposed to them regardless of whether they were engaging in lengthy speech turns). For a stimulus to serve as a reinforcer for any specific piece of behaviour and conditioning to take place, it must occur in conjunction with that behaviour (Lieberman, 2012).

Praise/encouragement

Unlike the previous category, here listener reactions go beyond the simple acknowledgement and confirmation of what has been said or done, to express praise or support overtly. Praise is most commonly defined as an expression of approval or admiration (Dozier *et al.*, 2012). Instances of this category of reward range from one-word utterances, e.g. 'Good', 'Excellent', 'Fantastic' (and various other superlatives), through phrases like 'Well done', 'How interesting', 'Keep it up', to more elaborate avowals of appreciation. Professional areas where such effects have been examined are as diverse as organisational management, interviewing and coaching. Martin and Pear (2015) presented, as an example, the case of a basketball coach who used praise to increase the number of supportive comments made by players to other team members, thereby strengthening team spirit. Practice drills were also enhanced in this way. Alternatively, Thompson and Born (1999) demonstrated how praise and verbal prompting could be effective with elderly people suffering from dementia or brain injury in getting them to take part correctly in exercise sessions while attending an adult day-care programme.

Teaching is an activity where opportunities abound for putting praise and approval to good use in rewarding effort and accomplishment in the classroom (Zirpoli and Melloy, 2015). It represents probably the most extensively researched area of application of this type of social reinforcer and numerous reviews of research have been carried out (e.g. Cameron and Pierce, 1996; Hancock, 2000; Cairns, 2006; Robins, 2012; Cavanaugh, 2013). Through the judicious use of reinforcement, significant and beneficial changes can be brought about in:

- student attentiveness
- on-task behaviour in class
- student time spent on homework assignments
- motivation to learn
- levels of academic achievement
- pupils' and students' evaluations of praise and of the teachers who use it.

As a general conclusion, therefore, it would appear that praise in the classroom can pay dividends. In practice, though, there is evidence that:

- teachers put praise to a number of uses apart from rewarding and reinforcing
- pupils are aware of this
- praise is not always administered effectively
- some pupils are more appreciative than others of praise and respond to it differentially.

Good and Brophy (2008) questioned the extent to which techniques such as praise are a prominent feature of the day-to-day classroom discourse of teachers or are skilfully used with reinforcing effect. Alternative purposes of praise include encouraging, directing and gaining rapport (Brown *et al.*, 2103). Whether teacher praise acts as an effective reinforcer depends upon a number of qualifying variables, including:

- features of the pupil, such as reinforcement history
- the type of task undertaken
- the pupil's actual performance

- the nature of the praise
- the manner in which the praise is administered
- characteristics of the source.

Pupils are also sensitive to the plurality of uses to which teachers put praise and interpret it accordingly. Taylor (1997) found that they applied labels such as deserved (when the performance was good) versus instructional. The latter included (1) encouraging; (2) signalling to others to do the same; and (3) increasing co-operation and participation.

The effects of praise can be maximised (Hancock, 2000; Burden and Byrd, 2012) by ensuring that it:

- is applied contingently
- specifies clearly the particular behaviour being reinforced
- is contiguous, in that it is offered soon after the targeted behaviour
- is credible to the recipient
- is restricted to those students who respond best to it. Not all do, with some finding this type of reward patronising or embarrassing when delivered in the presence of peers.

Praise, culture and socioeconomic status

The influence of culture and socioeconomic status on children's reactions to praise has been the subject of concerted enquiry. There are clear cultural differences in reinforcement (Cairns, 2006). For example, in Eastern cultures such as Japan and Taiwan, teacher reinforcement in schools is much less prevalent than in American classrooms (Weirzbicka, 2004). Furthermore, Weirzbicka showed how the expressions 'good girl' and 'good boy', which are widely used in Anglo adult speech to praise children, do not have equivalents in other European languages. She argues that these terms have their roots in the English and American puritanical past. Weirzbicka also noted that, in some cultures, such as the Gusii culture in Kenya, parents tend not to praise their children because it is felt that it would make the child disobedient, rude and conceited. In China there is an attitude that children are resilient and so benefit from being criticised for failure and only rewarded for very special efforts (Chua, 2011), while 'parents in Hong Kong commonly believe in the notion of "spare the rod and spoil the child", making them unable to recognise the harmful effects of harsh parenting' (Li et al., 2013, p. 3).

In relation to socioeconomic status, Hart and Risley (2003) carried out a major observational study of the behaviour of families from different backgrounds in Kansas City, where all communications in the home were tape-recorded for a period of over 2 years. They found large differences in levels of praise. The average child in a professional family received 32 instances of encouragement and 5 discouragements per hour (a positive ratio of over 6 to 1), in a working-class family it was 12 rewards and 7 discouragements per hour (a positive ratio of around 2 to 1) and for families on welfare the figures were 5 encouragements and 11 discouragements per hour (a negative ratio of about 2 to 1).

Factoring up from their observations, they estimated that, during the first 4 years of life, an average child in a professional family would receive 560,000 more instances of encouragement than discouragement; in a working-class family the figures were 100,000 more encouragements than discouragements; but in a family on welfare the figures were 125,000 more discouragements than encouragements. This helps to explain the conclusion by Russell (1971, p. 39) that, 'One of the most consistent findings is that there is a social class difference in response to reinforcement'. Middle-class children respond better to praise and approval as compared with their lower-class compatriots (Wilson and Conyers, 2013). Since the latter are less likely to be exposed to this type of reinforcement they are less likely to attach value to it, favouring instead tangible rewards like money, food or toys.

Praise and age

Marisi and Helmy (1984) found age differences to be implicated in determining how praise is reacted to. Comparing the effects of this incentive on performances of 6-year-old boys with those of 11 and 17 years on a motor task, they discovered that it was only with the youngest group that praise proved beneficial. Likewise, Burnett and Mandel (2010) showed how younger children between the ages of 4 and 9 years old tend to accept teacher praise at face value, whereas children above the age of 11 years are more likely to examine critically the rationale for the praise. Miller and Hom (1997) found that older pupils (eighth grade) compared to younger (fourth and sixth grades) generally see praised children as being less able. On the other hand, Wheldall and Glynn (1989) have shown that the behaviour of adolescents in class can be effectively managed by the teacher praising acceptable conduct in keeping with rules previously agreed by members, and largely ignoring minor infringements. We will return to the issue of age later, in relation to person and process praise.

Praise and personality

Several personality factors have been found to mediate the reinforcing impact of praise. The first of these is pupils' locus of control. As previously mentioned, people who are essentially internally set hold a belief in their own ability to extract reinforcers from the environment, whereas externals are inclined to put any rewards that come their way down to chance or luck. Kennelly and Mount (1985) found that internality of control, and an appreciation of the contingency of teacher rewards, was predictive of good academic achievement and teacher ratings of pupil competence. By contrast, Baron et al. (1974) and Henry et al. (1979) associated an external orientation with receptivity to verbal reinforcement.

Self-efficacy, it will be remembered, refers to a belief in one's ability to succeed at some task or undertaking. Kang (1998) reported a complex relationship between praise, age, gender, academic status and self-efficacy. Praise was positively related to self-efficacy among regular students but negatively so for those at the bottom end in classes with a large spread of ability. This pattern was reversed in groups with a narrow spread of ability. Generally, girls and students at the bottom of the class had lower levels of self-efficacy.

There is good reason to believe, at least with older individuals, that the personality dimension extraversion/introversion may play a further salient role. In particular, it seems that extraverts may be more receptive to the effects of praise, while for introverts, the punishment of inappropriate responses can produce better results (Boddy *et al.*, 1986; Gupta and Shukla, 1989). Susceptibility to such interpersonal rewards from others seems to be strengthened among those who display a heightened need for approval, and therefore have a predilection to act in ways that will increase the chances of others reacting favourably towards them.

Is praise always good?

While praise is undoubtedly a potent force in social interaction, as already alluded to in this chapter, there can be downsides to this phenomenon. The claims that praise boosts motivation for the rewarded activity, results in more of it, promotes learning and improves self-image have been challenged (Deci *et al.*, 1999; Bayat, 2011). One criticism is that intrinsic motivation to engage in a task may suffer when external rewards are offered (McLean, 2009; Murtagh, 2014). This perspective purports that, by having the motivational basis for completing an activity switched from an intrinsic interest in it to some external reward such as money, we may gradually come to carry out that activity only for the remuneration. Once the reward ceases, it is argued, so too will the behaviour. Internal motivators, such as a sense of satisfaction or pride, are powerful impellents to action, and anything that minimises their influence can seriously undermine long-term commitment. Consider the scenario in Box 4.4.

So far it has been assumed that praise, among other things, strengthens belief in ability and promotes self-esteem. Meyer *et al.* (1986) argued that just

---

Box 4.4 An example of intrinsic rewards driving performance

A group of cross-country runners meet up each lunch time to cover a 4-mile (6-kilometre) course before getting quickly showered and returning to work. This means that they have only time to grab a quick snack and the lunch hour is one endless rush – but they enjoy it. One winter's day they meet up as usual. By the end of the second mile, the weather turns very cold and they find themselves facing driving rain while under foot the mud is ankle deep. The usual banter gradually dies as the group struggles up a steep rise with 2 miles (3 kilometres) still to go. They begin to get colder, wetter and more exhausted. One of the runners is finally heard to grumble through chattering teeth, 'If I was being paid to do this, I would be asking for a wage increase!'

the opposite may sometimes occur and showed that those subjects praised for success at an easy task and not blamed for failure at a difficult task inferred that their ability for that type of work was low. When praise for success at the easy task was withheld and failure at the difficult task blamed, subjects assessed their ability as being much higher. Other studies have shown that children may attribute teacher praise for success at an easy task to low ability on their part (Miller and Hom, 1997; Coe *et al.*, 2014). Students who were praised for a good academic performance by an evaluator who lacked knowledge of their level assumed that the evaluator had lower expectations of them, and rated the evaluator less favourably than students not praised (Lawrence, 2001). Furthermore, Derevensky and Leckerman (1997) discovered that pupils in special education classes tended to receive more praise and positive reinforcement than those in regular classes. Similarly, weaker pupils in classrooms have been shown to receive more praise from teachers (Hattie and Timperley, 2007). As succinctly summarised by Kaspar and Stelz (2013, p. 1), 'Blame and praise sometimes have a seemingly paradoxical effect: blame after failure sometimes leads to the impression that the recipient has a high ability. In contrast, praise after success can lead to an inference of low ability'. Thus, praise does not always carry positive messages as far as inferences about ability levels are concerned. In particular, this type of support 'may be ineffective, or even associated with negative outcomes if it reduces the recipient's sense of autonomy, control, or self-efficacy' (Freeman *et al.*, 2009, p. 197). Pupils' understanding of the reason for praise being given will determine what they make of it.

Another possible downside of praise was highlighted by Twenge (2014), who argued that many parents over-praise their children. In their review of the area, Brummelman *et al.* (2014a, p. 728) illustrated how, 'In current Western society, children are often lavished with inflated praise (e.g. "You made an *incredibly* beautiful drawing!")'. It has been shown that such over-valuations from parents lead to the development of narcissism in children, who internalise their parents' overstated views by forming self-beliefs such as, 'I am superior to others' (Brummelman *et al.*, 2015). The children then develop a misguided sense of their actual abilities as well as becoming 'praise junkies' expecting rewards for completing even minor tasks (Suissa, 2013). This can be witnessed in the educational system, where there is a reluctance to fail students. Many elementary schools in the UK employ a token economy system, whereby teachers distribute stickers as rewards to children for good behaviour. However, research has shown that these are often allocated freely and for minimal efforts (such as sitting in your seat) in an attempt to allocate approval to all children, with the result that they lose their rewarding potential (MacLure and Jones, 2009). As one 4-year-old pupil put it, 'What's the point of doing anything if you're praised for just sitting?' (Henry, 2009). It is argued that these classroom reward systems seem to be guided by the maxim of the dodo in *Alice's Adventures in Wonderland*, whose decision at the end of a race was that 'EVERYBODY has won, and all must have prizes' (Phillips, 1998). As a result of parental and educational over-allocation of reward, young people can face later disappointment and disillusionment as they crash on the hard rock of reality when confronted with some of the harsher difficulties in life. A reward for doing very little provides no useful feedback and does not increase the individual's sense of competence. In addition, receiving such a reward can convey to the child that the activity has been carried out just to please the teacher – the child feels less in control and so less committed to the activity.

Person process and product praise

There are differences across ages and gender in relation to differential forms of praise with children. Corpus and Lepper (2007) compared four forms of reinforcement:

1   product praise – for what someone has produced (e.g. 'This is a very good essay');
2   process praise – for effort expended (e.g. 'You have worked really well on this essay');
3   person praise – for a particular trait (e.g. 'You are very clever');
4   neutral feedback (e.g. a positive-sounding 'OK').

Results showed that 4–5-year-old children demonstrated increased motivation after receiving any of the first three types of praise, but not the fourth (neutral). However, girls aged 9–11 years actually showed decreased motivation after person praise, whereas boys in this age group reacted well to all four types of praise.

Person praise has been found to result in children, particularly those with low self-esteem, feeling ashamed when they fail (Brummelman et al., 2014b). Research also shows that children praised for their ability (person praise), rather than effort (process praise), are less likely to want to tackle tasks that would have greater learning potential but would not guarantee success, in favour of those that they know they can do successfully (Dweck, 2007; Pomerantz and Kempner, 2013). Receiving praise for ability also creates vulnerability; when faced with failure, such children express least enjoyment with the activity, show less perseverance and find the experience most aversive. Children praised by parents for their inherent ability have also been shown to be more likely to regard intelligence as a fixed trait rather than something that can be enhanced, whereas praise for effort increases their motivation to succeed – and this effect is long-lasting (Gunderson et al., 2013). Thus, there are two patterns of reaction here, which are heavily shaped by the reinforcement people have received: they may display a *helpless* response wherein they attribute failure to a lack of personal ability and so give up, or they may develop a *mastery-oriented* pattern by increasing their level of effort when faced with potential setbacks (Skipper and Douglas, 2012).

The extent to which praise can undermine intrinsic motivation and be detrimental to performance has, however, been the subject of considerable debate (Sansone and Harackiewicz, 2000; Bronson and Merryman, 2009). In an extensive review of some 100 experiments, Cameron and Pierce (1994, p. 394) concluded that, 'our overall findings suggest that there is no detrimental effect [of extrinsic rewards] on intrinsic motivation'. Nevertheless, Good and Brophy (2008) cautioned that, in the classroom, reinforcement must always be applied in such a way as to complement natural outcomes of performance and not under-mine intrinsic interest. According to Lieberman (2012), praise and other social rewards are less likely to have this negative effect than are material alternatives.

A useful summary of the research findings into praise was given by Henderlong and Lepper (2002, p. 774): 'Provided that praise is perceived as sin-cere, it is particularly beneficial to motivation when it encourages performance attributions to controllable causes, promotes autonomy, enhances competence without an overreliance on social comparisons, and conveys attainable stand-ards and expectations'. In order to overcome some of the potential downsides of reinforcement, the research findings suggest a number of guidelines to fol-low when using reinforcement in the classroom. It is better to use praise rather than material rewards, and to attribute the praise to the child's own motivation. Rather than praising the child just for carrying out a task, make the reward contingent upon the attainment of a certain level or standard. Link the praise directly to improvements in performance, and include specific feedback infor-mation on improvement as part of the reward. Finally, encourage the child to reflect on why s/he is being praised. For example, an English teacher could reward a child by saying:

> Well done! Your essay mark has improved from a C grade to a B grade [attainment of higher level]. The overall structure is much better, as is your use of grammar and spelling, and the story itself shows good creativity [feedback information]. Your enjoyment in writing this really comes across [reward linked to internal motivation]. How do you feel about the essay this time? [encouraging child to reflect on reasons for the reward].

Response development

There is a progressive sequence of rewards, which commences with the mere acknowledgement of a response, continues with the positive evaluation of it through praise and proceeds to the further exploration and development of the content. In this way, having an idea or action accepted as part of the agenda for the ongoing discourse may be looked upon as the highest form of praise. It is quite easy for a teacher, manager, interviewer or coach to express a few perfunctory words of acknowledgement or commendation before continuing on a completely different tack. However, the development of one's response indicates (1) that the listener must have been carefully attending, and (2) that the content must have been considered worthy of the listener's time and effort to make it part of 'the talk'.

A response can be developed in a number of ways. In the classroom, Burden and Byrd (2012) recommended that teachers should follow up pupils' contributions by encouraging them to elucidate their initial response, develop it, move their ideas to higher levels and provide support for their opinions. This is a powerful means of providing reinforcement during a lesson, even if it is less frequently used than alternatives already considered. On the other hand, teach-ers may develop a pupil's contribution by elaborating upon it themselves. The potential reward for pupils of having their ideas form part of the lesson will be readily appreciated. In a group, members may be asked to contribute their suggestions and be reinforced by having their responses further explored by other members. In a coaching context, certain individuals can be selected to demonstrate a skill or technique to the other participants for them to develop. If tactfully handled, this form of response development can be highly motivating and positively valued.

Clearly there is a whole range of possibilities for developing responses. Dickson *et al.* (1993), in reviewing some conditioning-type studies, suggested that reflective statements (see Chapter 6) and self-disclosures (see Chapter 9) may function in this way. In general, though, research concerning the reinforcing effects of response development is less prevalent than that involving reinforcers included in the previous two categories.

Nonverbal components

The administration of reinforcement is not solely dependent upon the verbal channel of communication. It has been established that a number of nonverbal behaviours, such as a warm smile or an enthusiastic nod of the head, can also have reinforcing impact on the behaviour of the other person during interaction (see Chapter 3). For instance, Rosenfarb (1992, p. 343) believed that positive change in client behaviour during psychotherapy can be accounted for in this way. He explained how this might operate:

> Often, subtle therapeutic cues serve to reinforce selected aspects of client behavior. A therapist's turn of the head, a change in eye contact, or a change in voice tone may reinforce selected client behavior…One therapist, for example, may lean forward in her chair whenever a client begins to discuss interpersonal difficulties with his mother. Another therapist may begin to nod his head as clients begin to discuss such material. A third may maintain more eye contact. In all three cases, each therapist's behavior may be serving as both a reinforcing stimulus for previous client behavior and as a discriminative stimulus for the further discussion of such relevant material.

The fact that nonverbal cues can operate to influence behaviour is no surprise, given that the nonverbal channel of communication is frequently more important than the verbal channel with regard to the conveying of information of an emotional or attitudinal nature. The nonverbal channel is particularly adept at communicating states and attitudes such as interest, liking, warmth and involvement.

Gestural reinforcement

This category includes relatively small movements of specific parts of the body. 'Gestural' in this sense is broadly defined to encompass not only movements of the hands, arms and head, but also the facial region. Concerning the latter, two of the most frequently identified reinforcers are smiles and eye contact.

Smiles

A genuine, or Duchenne, smile, as opposed to a polite, or social, smile, has been shown in a number of studies to be one of the most potent of all reinforcers (Krumhuber *et al.*, 2014). While both types of smile are widely used in social encounters, there is clear evidence that, 'genuine smiles have a higher social-reward value than do polite ones' (Heerey and Crossley, 2013, pp. 1146–1147). Indeed, in their experimental study, Shore and Heerey (2011) found that subjects were willing to forgo the opportunity of a monetary reward in order to receive the reward of a genuine smile. One reason for the power of a genuine smile as a reinforcer is that subjects have been shown to be significantly more likely to co-operate with people displaying a Duchenne smile than those displaying a non-Duchenne smile (Johnston *et al.*, 2010; Reed *et al.*, 2012; Gunnery and Hall, 2014). See Chapter 3 for further discussion of the Duchenne smile.

Eye contact

This is an important reinforcer, given that the establishment of eye contact is the foundation for interpersonal interaction (Senju and Johnson, 2009) and a key indicator of social attention (Freeth *et al.*, 2013). During conversation, continued use of this behaviour is an indicator of our responsiveness to the other, and level of involvement in the exchange. It has been found that, when individuals engage in eye contact, they experience increased levels of cortical activity associated with the intensity of attention and interest (Honma, 2013). Its selective use can, therefore, have strong reinforcing potential. For example, D'Agostino and Bylund (2014) found eye contact to be a core nonverbal indicator of communication accommodation during physician–patient interactions. The over-use of eye contact or gaze, though, can also be threatening and cause discomfort or distress (see Chapter 3).

Gestures

Certain movements of the hands and arms can signal appreciation and approval. Probably the most frequently used gestures of this type are applause and the 'thumbs-up' sign. Head nods are a type of gesture that have a wider relevance (Aoki, 2011). As discussed in Chapter 3, they belong to a group of attention-giving behaviours known as 'back-channel' communication that are used to regulate and control the interactive flow. Their frequent use can be seen during practically any interactive episode, being commonly used to show acknowledgement, agreement, affection and understanding (Sherman *et al.*, 2013; Oshima, 2014).

Proximity reinforcement

Unlike the previous category, this includes gross movements of the whole body or substantial parts of it. Proximity reinforcement refers to the reinforcing effects that can accrue from altering the distance between oneself and another during interaction. A reduction in interpersonal distance usually signifies a desire for greater intimacy and involvement. However, while someone who adopts a position at some distance from the interlocutor may be seen as being unreceptive and detached, a person who approaches too closely may be regarded as over-familiar, dominant or even threatening. In a study by Goldman (1980), attitudes of subjects were more successfully modified by means of verbal reinforcers when the interviewer stood at a moderate (4 to 5 foot: 1.2 to 1.5 metres) rather than a close (2 to 3 foot: 0.6 to 0.9 metres) interpersonal distance.

With participants who are seated, as professionals often are during encounters, it is obviously much more difficult to effect sizeable variations in interpersonal distance. However, changes can be accomplished by adopting forward- or backward-leaning postures. A forward-leaning posture has been found to be reinforcing, and has been shown to be apposite for conveying acceptance, attention and receptivity in a range of fields such as therapy (Dowell and Berman, 2013) and health care (Stepanikova, 2014). Communicating at closer proximity was identified by Mehrabian (2007) as part of a complex of behaviours which he labelled 'immediacy', which denotes a positive attitude towards the interlocutor.

Touch

Used appropriately, touch can be a powerful form of reinforcement (Hertenstein and Weiss, 2011). It can be construed in a number of ways as conveying, among other things, affection, appreciation and support (Field, 2014). As such, the relevance of touch to health care delivery is evident and its rewarding effects in the nursing setting have been well documented (Routasalo, 1999; Connor and Howett, 2009). In the classroom, Wheldall *et al.* (1986) found that, when teachers of mixed-gender infant classes used positive contingent touch when praising good 'on-task' classroom behaviour, rates of this type of behaviour rose by some 20 per cent. Nevertheless, as with many forms of nonverbal behaviour, 'Touch and the lack of touch are intriguing and complex entities because the meaning of touch can vary from one situation to the next' (Davidhizar and Giger, 1997, p. 204). In many contexts, of course, touch is inappropriate, even socially forbidden, and must be used with discretion (see Chapter 3).

HOW DO REINFORCERS REINFORCE?

The key feature of reinforcement is that it increases the future probability of the behaviour that led to it. There is much less agreement, however, about just how this is brought about. Three main possibilities will be briefly considered here: reinforcement as a direct modifier of behaviour; reinforcement as motivation; and reinforcement as information.

Reinforcement as a direct modifier of behaviour

Favoured by theorists such as Skinner (1953), this view is that essentially reinforcers function directly and automatically to bring about behavioural change.

Two important implications stem from this view. The first is that the individual's awareness of what is taking place is not a pre-requisite for reinforcement – the person does not need to be able to talk about or show an understanding of why he or she was reinforced (Martin and Pear, 2015). While reporting findings to substantiate this proposition, Lieberman (2012) nevertheless concluded that the circumstances under which reinforcement without awareness takes place tend to be rather contrived or extraordinary. The second implication concerns the nature of the relationship between the targeted response and the reinforcing event. Does reinforcement depend on the behaviour in question bringing about a positive outcome (contingency) or simply being followed in time by it (contiguity)? A belief in contiguity as a necessary and sufficient condition for reinforcement to take place is commonly associated with its unconscious operation. Skinner (1977, p. 4), for instance, wrote that, 'Coincidence is the heart of operant conditioning. A response is strengthened by certain kinds of consequences, but not necessarily because they are actually produced by it.' The precise nature of the relationship between behaviour and subsequent events in respect of contingency and contiguity is not entirely clear, such that a causal relationship can sometimes be inferred where none exists.

Reinforcement as motivation

A second possibility is that reinforcers serve largely to motivate. In this way, the expectation of receiving a reward for succeeding in a task spurs on further efforts in that direction and makes it more likely that this type of task will be undertaken again. Such incentives may be external and represent the projected attainment of a tangible outcome (e.g. money, food, praise), or, as Bandura (1989) stressed, be internal and derivable from anticipated positive self-evaluations at the prospect of succeeding in the task at hand.

Reinforcement as information

The third interpretation adopts the cognitive stance that reinforcers function by providing information on task performance. Sarafino (2004) pointed out that feedback is implicit in many of the forms of reward that we obtain. Thus, if we receive a material reward or praise for some action, this in itself also tells us that we performed well. However, Hattie and Timperley (2007) and Wentzel and Brophy (2014) have argued that the two are inherently different processes. Fagan (2014) pointed out that, while positive feedback tends to be associated with praise, this is not always its main purpose. For example, it is used as a teacher management tool to provide pupils with information to guide them towards an understanding of what is being explained. Likewise, conditioning studies are often arranged so that response-contingent points are allocated, which can then be exchanged by subjects for back-up reinforcers, like food or money. The material value of these reinforcers is usually small, and in some instances subjects work diligently for paltry financial remuneration. When food is the reward it is often left unconsumed, indeed, sometimes discarded without being tasted, and yet at the same time subjects continue to work for more. These findings are difficult to reconcile in motivational terms, if money or food is thought of as the key inducement. Perceiving the conditioning procedure as a problem-solving exercise in the eyes of the subjects is a more plausible explanation. Points received for an appropriate response are prized, not hedonistically through association with money or food, but on account of the information they contribute to finding a solution to the 'puzzle'. In this way, conditioning results are explained in terms of subjects trying to figure out the connection between what they do and the outcomes they experience in a sort of puzzle-solving exercise.

While conclusive proof to resolve these differences in position is lacking, the present consensus of opinion appears to be that, as far as social performance in everyday situations is concerned, probably little instrumental conditioning takes place without at least some minimal level of conscious involvement (Lieberman, 2012). The effects of reinforcement seem to rely more upon a contingent than a mere contiguous association between behaviour and reward (Schwartz and Robbins, 1995). Furthermore, recipients' understanding of why they received the reward also seems to matter (Miller and Hom, 1997).

GUIDELINES FOR THE USE OF THE SKILL OF REINFORCEMENT

Sets of recommendation for enhancing the effectiveness of reinforcing procedures can be found in different sources (e.g. Maag, 2003; Cairns, 2006; Burden and Byrd, 2012; Zirpoli and Melloy, 2015). The main aspects will now be highlighted.

Appropriateness of rewards

Throughout this chapter an attempt has been made to stress the fact that stimuli that may have reinforcing properties in some situations may not have the same effects in others. Bearing in mind the model discussed in Chapter 2, it is important that one remains sensitive to the characteristics of the situation, including the other people involved, when choosing the type of reinforcement to use. Thus, some forms of praise that would be quite appropriate when used with a child would seem extremely patronising if used with an adult. Attention should, in addition, be paid to the reinforcement history of the individual. Not all rewards will be prized equally. Different people may prefer certain reinforcers to others, and the same individual on different occasions may find the same reinforcer differentially attractive.

Reinforcement given should also be appropriate to the task undertaken and the degree of success achieved. As shown in this chapter, consideration should be given to the recipient's perceptions of equity and self-verification. At least with material rewards, less satisfaction is expressed when there are discrepancies between what is received and what is felt to be deserved, even when the inequity results in higher recompense than was thought to be merited. Furthermore, people who receive praise for completing a relatively easy task may conclude they have low ability at this type of work. This is also the case with the well-known expression 'damned with faint praise', where the reinforcement proffered actually indicates a lack of ability on the part of the recipient (e.g. where a sports coach says to a pupil 'That's not too bad for you, John').

Genuineness of application

It is important that social rewards are perceived as genuinely reflecting the source's reaction to the targeted person or performance. If not, they may come across as sarcasm, veiled criticism or bored habit. Complementarity of verbal and nonverbal behaviour is important in this regard. When seen as an attempt at cynical manipulation, rewards are also likely to be counter-productive (Aronson, 2008). This is exemplified by the phrase 'too sweet to be wholesome', which refers to someone who over-reinforces, well beyond the sub-cultural norm, and so is viewed as having ulterior motives – the rewards are then not regarded as genuine and the person is viewed with suspicion.

Contingency of reinforcement

In order for the various social behaviours reviewed in this chapter to function as effective reinforcers, their application must be made contingent upon the desired action (Martin and Pear, 2015). This does not mean that the random use of such behaviour will fail to produce an effect. It may well serve to create a particular impression of the provider or the situation, or put the recipient at ease. It is highly improbable, however, that it will selectively reinforce as desired. In many situations, it is prudent to specify, quite precisely, the behavioural focus of attention.

Frequency of reinforcement

It is not necessary to reinforce each and every instance of a specific response for that class of response to be increased. It has been found that, following an initial period of continual reinforcement to establish the behaviour, the frequency of reinforcement can be reduced without resulting in a corresponding reduction in target behaviour. This is called intermittent reinforcement, and many real-life activities (such as gambling) are maintained in this way. Frequencies of performance do not decline in the face of intermittent reinforcement, but rather they actually increase and become more resistant to extinction (Leslie and O'Reilly, 1999). Accordingly, Maag (2003) recommended that rewards should be used sparingly to maximise their reinforcing efficacy. A related recommendation is that recipients have access to these only after performing the desired behaviour. Along similar lines, *gain/loss theory* predicts that, when the receipt of a reward is set against a backdrop of a general paucity of positive reaction from that source, its effect will be enhanced (Aronson, 2008).

Variety of reinforcement

The continual and inflexible use of a specific reinforcer will quickly lead to that reinforcer losing its reinforcing properties. The recipient will become satiated. If an interviewer responds to each interviewee statement with, for example, 'good', this utterance will gradually become denuded of any evaluative connotations, and consequently will rapidly cease to have reinforcing effects. An attempt should therefore be made to employ a variety of reinforcing expressions and behaviours while ensuring that they do not violate the requirement of appropriateness.

Timing of reinforcement

A broadly agreed recommendation is that a reinforcing stimulus should be applied directly following the target response. As shown by Zirpoli and Melloy (2015), a delay between behaviour and reinforcement usually leads to a decrease in the relative effectiveness of the reinforcement. If reinforcement is delayed there is a danger that other responses may intervene between the one to be promoted and the presentation of the reinforcer. Making the individual aware of the basis upon which the delayed reinforcement is being given can help to reduce any negative effects of delay (Trolinder *et al.*, 2004). This is not to overlook the fact that, from a motivational viewpoint, the availability of immediate payoff is likely to have greater incentive value than the prospect of having to wait for some time for personal benefits to materialise.

Selective reinforcement

In this context selective reinforcement refers to the fact that it is possible to reinforce selectively certain elements of a response without necessarily rein-forcing it in total. This can be effected during the actual response. Nonverbal reinforcers, such as head nods and verbal reinforcers like 'mm-hmm', are of particular relevance in this respect since they can be used without interrupting the speaker. Selective reinforcement can also be applied following the termi-nation of a response. Thus a teacher may partially reinforce a pupil who has almost produced the correct answer to a question (e.g. 'Yes, Narinder, you are right, Kilimanjaro is a mountain, but is it in the Andes?'). By so doing the teacher reinforces that portion of the answer which is accurate, while causing the pupil to rethink the element which is not. Allied to this process, *shaping* permits nascent attempts at an ultimately acceptable end performance to be rewarded. By systematically demanding higher standards for rewards to be granted, performances can be shaped to attain requisite levels of excellence. The acquisition of most everyday skills like swimming, driving a car or playing a musical instrument involve an element of shaping. If reinforcers were withheld until the full-blown skilful activity was performed, learning could take a long time and be an extremely thankless task for the learner.

OVERVIEW

Reinforcement as an interpersonal skill plays a fundamental role in our lives. What people do, what they learn, the decisions that they take, their feelings and attitudes towards themselves and others, indeed, the sorts of individuals they become, can be shaped and moulded by the reactions of others. While the basic notion that people tend to behave in ways that bring about positive outcomes for them is scarcely iconoclastic, it does seem that, in many professional circles, reinforcement is not used skilfully. Good and Brophy (2008), for example, question whether teachers routinely use praise in the classroom in such a way as to be maximally reinforcing of desired behaviour and achievement.

The types of social reinforcers concentrated upon in this chapter were divided into verbal and nonverbal for the purpose of analysis. In practice, however, these two channels intermesh. Verbal reinforcers include such reactions as acknowledging, confirming, praising, supporting and developing the interlocutor's responses in a variety of ways. Nonverbally, gestures such as smiles, head nods and eye contact, together with larger body movements, including reducing interpersonal distance, forward posture leans and touch, have been found to have reinforcing potential.

When utilised in accordance with the guidelines outlined above, reinforcement can serve to promote interaction and maintain relationships; increase the involvement of the interactive partner; make interaction interesting and enjoyable; demonstrate a genuine interest in the ideas, thoughts and feelings of the other; create an impression of warmth and understanding; enhance the interpersonal attractiveness of the source; and improve the confidence and self-esteem of the recipient. At the same time, the effectiveness of reinforcement is determined by a complex array of interwoven factors, including those to do with the source, the recipient, the context, the nature of the reward itself and the way in which it is delivered.

Chapter 5

Finding out about others: the skill of questioning

INTRODUCTION

THE QUESTION IS A key constituent of the DNA of interactional life. In one of my communication classes I use an exercise in which I ask four volunteers to come to the front of the class. I then instruct them to carry on a conversation about 'the events of the week'. The only rule is that no one is allowed to ask a question. Two things happen. First, the interaction is very stilted and difficult. Second, someone very quickly asks a question. To continue with the above analogy, in the absence of questioning DNA, the communication organism becomes unstable and eventually dies.

Questions are at the heart of interpersonal encounters. Information seeking is a core human activity that is central to learning, decision making and problem solving (Mokros and Aakhus, 2002). In most social encounters questions are asked and responses reinforced – this is the method whereby information is gathered and conversation encouraged. Thus, questioning is one of the most widely used interactive skills, and one of the easiest to identify in general terms. However, as cautioned by Dickson and Hargie (2006, p. 121), 'While at a surface level questioning seems to be a straightforward feature of communication, deeper analysis, at functional, structural, and textual levels, reveals questioning to be a complex and multifaceted phenomenon'.

Society is fascinated by questions and answers. Those involved in public question-and-answer sessions have become the gladiators of the electronic era. Let us take a few examples. Contestants in TV quiz shows can win fame and fortune just by knowing the answers to questions they are asked. Their 'hosts', or interrogators, on these shows are already household names. TV and radio interviewers also become celebrities because they are good at asking the right questions, albeit in an entertaining fashion. Courtroom dramas, in which lawyers thrust rapier-like questions at innocent and guilty defendants or witnesses, are ubiquitous. So, too, with police films where the skilled detective eventually breaks down the recalcitrant suspect through insightful and incisive questioning. Question Time in the UK House of Commons and Senate Investigations in the USA, both of which involve hard and often harsh questioning (Bull, 2013), have a special type of fascination for viewers.

The above examples underline the ultimate power and potential of questions as contributors to success or failure across different contexts. They also reflect the fact that this is a core interpersonal skill. Those who can use questions in a fluent, unobtrusive and helpful manner will be more successful in their interactions. This chapter examines the nature, function and effects of various forms and types of questions across a range of social contexts.

DEFINITION OF 'QUESTION'

The first question we need to ask is, perhaps paradoxically, what exactly is a question? As de Ruiter (2012) has shown, there is no simple answer here. A question can be defined in interactional, functional, grammatical, sociolinguistic or semantic terms. Wang (2006) noted that grammatically a question is interrogative in form, syntactically it is a sentence in which the subject and the first verb in the verb phrase are inverted and semantically it communicates a desire for further information. The latter meaning is in line with the skills perspective, wherein a question is defined as a request for information, whether factual or otherwise. In this way, a question can be regarded as a statement or nonverbal act that invites a response (Stewart and Cash, 2013). For example, a high-pitched 'guggle' such as 'hmmm?' after someone has made a statement is a form of request to the speaker to continue speaking. Similarly, a directional nod of the head, after asking one member of a group a question, can indicate to another group member that the question is being redirected and a response expected. Questions, then, may be nonverbal signals urging another to respond. They may also be statements uttered in an inquisitive fashion, e.g.:

- 'Tell me more'.
- 'You do realise what will happen'.

Statements that request information have been termed declarative questions (Stivers, 2012) and implied questions (Miles, 2013); they are also referred to as prosodic questions, defined as 'declarative sentences containing question cues that may be intonational, or these utterances are marked as questions by means of a variety of contextual cues' (Woodbury, 1984, p. 203). In the legal context, prosodic questions are widely used by attorneys (e.g. 'You were still in your home at that time?'), especially during the cross-examination of witnesses (Dillon, 1990). Conversely, as these examples given by Wang (2006, p. 533) illustrate, what seem like questions may in fact be statements:

- Who cares? (I don't care)
- What difference does it make? (It makes no difference)

Although, as discussed by Clark (2012), a question can be posed nonverbally in a variety of ways, most questions in social interaction are verbal in nature. At the same time, there are certain nonverbal signals that should accompany the verbal message, if a question is to be recognised as such. One paralinguistic signal is the raising or lowering of the vocal inflection on the last syllable of the question. Other nonverbal behaviours include head movements, rapidly raising or lowering the eyebrows and direct eye contact at the end of the question accompanied by a pause. The function of these nonverbal behaviours is to emphasise to the interlocutor that a question is being asked and a response expected.

QUESTIONS IN CONTEXT

The skill of questioning is to be found at every level in social interaction. Young children, exploring a new environment, seem to be naturally inquisitive, always seeking answers to an ever-increasing number of questions. At this stage, questions play a crucial role in their learning and maturation process, as they attempt to assimilate information in order to make sense of their surroundings. It is very important for the child's development that parents take time to answer these questions (Cook, 2009). This rewards the child for asking questions, inculcates a sense of curiosity and provides answers to what are perceived to be important issues.

The role of questions in human interchange has long been studied in a range of academic disciplines, including psychology, communication, philosophy and linguistics (Miles, 2013). Investigations into the use of questions in various professional contexts have also been carried out for decades (Freed and Ehrlich, 2010). As Waterman *et al.* (2001, p. 477) noted, 'Asking questions is a fundamental part of communication, and as such will be an important factor in the work of many professionals'. In the education context, Margutti (2006, p. 314) pointed out that:

> Questions and answers are the most prevalent instructional tools in a long standing pedagogic tradition in which the centrality of questions in teaching is widely recognized...and which is claimed, by some, to have come down all the way from Socrates.

A large volume of research into the effects of teacher questions in the classroom has now been accumulated (e.g. Gayle *et al.*, 2006; Hardman, 2011; Reinsvold and Cochran, 2012; Coe *et al.*, 2014). In her text in this field, Pagliaro (2011, p. ix) concluded: 'Researchers have consistently reported that questioning is one of the teaching skills that has the greatest effect on student achievement'. An early study was conducted by Corey (1940), in which she had an expert stenographer make verbatim records of all classroom talk in six classes. It was found that, on average, the teacher asked a question once every 72 seconds. Some 30 years later, Resnick (1972), working with teachers and pupils in an infant school (serving 5–7-year-old children) in south-east London, found that 36 per cent of all teacher remarks were questions. Furthermore, this figure increased to 59 per cent when only extended interactions were analysed. More recently, this rapid rate of teacher questioning was confirmed by Siraj-Blatchford and Manni (2008), who discovered that, over an observation period of 400 hours, the 28 teachers being recorded asked a huge total of 5,808 questions. Likewise, Reinsvold and Cochran (2012) found that teachers asked 93 per cent of all classroom questions compared to 7 per cent by pupils.

Hardman (2011) reports that pupil questions account for less than 5 per cent of total classroom questions, and that most of these relate to procedural issues where the pupil seeks information from the teacher. In a review of such studies, Dillon (1982) presents results to show that teachers ask about two questions per minute, while their pupils taken as a whole only ask around two questions per hour, giving an average of one question per pupil per month. When the teachers were surveyed about their use of questions, it was found that they actually asked three times as many questions as they estimated they had, and received only one-sixth the number of pupil questions estimated. However, as previously mentioned, reticence at asking questions is not the general norm for children. For example, Tizard et al. (1983) radio-recorded 4-year-old girls at home and at school and found that on average per hour the children asked 24 questions at home and only 1.4 at school. Interestingly, one major reason given by students for their reluctance to ask questions in class is fear of a negative reaction from classmates (Dillon, 1988). Daly et al. (1994), in a study in the USA, found a significant and negative correlation between question asking and age in pupils between 13 and 16 years. As pupils got older they felt less comfortable about asking questions in class. Daly et al. also found that in terms of question asking the following felt more at ease:

- males
- Whites
- higher-income groups
- those with higher self-esteem
- those who felt accepted by the teacher.

A three-part IRF or IRE (initiation–response–feedback/evaluation) sequence has long been the norm in classrooms (Waring, 2012; Molinari et al., 2013). This consists of a teacher initiation, usually a question, followed by a brief pupil response, and a teacher follow-up where some type of feedback or evaluation is given to the student's answer. As summarised by Smith et al. (2006), the IRF structure 'often consists of closed teacher questions, brief pupil answers which teachers do not build upon, superficial praise rather than diagnostic feedback, and an emphasis on recalling information rather than genuine exploration of a topic' (p. 444). However, Zemel and Koschmann (2011) illustrated how part of the follow-up or evaluation stage of this sequence can involve teachers becoming aware that incorrect student answers may be caused by a lack of clarity in their initial question, with the result that they then use replacement questions. Such findings indicate that teachers need to be more mindful of the many nuances pertaining to classroom questioning.

An analysis of the use of questions by doctors reveals parallel findings. As Brashers *et al.* (2002, p. 259), in their review of information exchange in the consultation, put it: 'Physicians ask most of the questions and patients provide most of the information'. Indeed, West (1983) found that, out of a total of 773 questions identified in 21 doctor–patient consultations, only 68 (9 per cent) were initiated by patients. Furthermore, when patients did ask questions, nearly half of these were marked by speech disturbances, indicating discomfort at requesting information from the doctor. Likewise, Sanchez (2001) cited a study in which, during an average consultation time per patient of 2.1 minutes, doctors asked 27.3 questions. Such a pattern and volume of doctor questions mean that patients have little scope to reply, let alone formulate a question. Yet, one of the key elements rated most highly by patients when receiving bad news is the opportunity to ask questions (Hind, 1997). This is important, as shown in a survey involving 45,700 participants across 24 European countries, in which it was found that patient reluctance to ask questions of the doctor was significantly related to their nonadherence to medication (Stavropoulou, 2011). If patients have concerns about their medication but feel unable to raise these with the doctor, then they are more likely to resolve their uncertainties by just not taking the medication.

The difficulties faced by patients in asking questions have been well documented (Katz *et al.*, 2007; Deen *et al.*, 2011). When asked, the main reason given by patients for not requesting information from doctors is a fear of appearing to be ignorant (Roter and Hall, 2006). In particular, less-well-educated and lower-income patients have been shown to ask fewer questions of doctors (Siminoff *et al.*, 2006). Skelton and Hobbs (1999) found that patients often prefaced their questions with the phrase 'I was wondering...'. Doctors never used this expression with patients. Interestingly, the only time they did use it was when they telephoned colleagues. Similarly, Wynn (1996) found that medical students quickly learned how to handle patient-initiated questions – by adopting the strategy of asking unrelated doctor-initiated ones. In this way, they maintained control of the consultation. However, Parrott *et al.* (1992), in a study of paediatrician–patient communication, found that while paediatricians generally asked more questions than patients, during consultations in which they specifically addressed concerns raised by patients more questions were subsequently asked by the latter. It would therefore seem that patient questions can be encouraged (and, of course, discouraged) by the approach of the doctor.

In relation to community pharmacy, Morrow *et al.* (1993) carried out a UK study in which they recorded a series of community pharmacist–patient consultations. They found that patients asked on average 2.5 questions per consultation compared to an average of 4.1 for pharmacists. This ratio of patient questions is much higher than that found in doctor–patient consultations. Interestingly, a number of the questions asked by these patients related to requests for clarification about what the doctor had previously told them. This suggests that either they felt more at ease asking questions of the pharmacist than indicating lack of understanding to the doctor, or that they had subsequently thought of questions they would have liked to have been able to ask the doctor. Morrow *et al.* argued that the public may have a view that, since pharmacies are readily and easily accessible, pharmacists are probably 'approachable' professionals. Furthermore, the fact that in most instances clients are paying directly for the services they receive may mean that they feel more empowered to ask questions in community pharmacies.

QUESTIONS AND CONTROL

The above findings reflect the control differential in relation to questioner and respondent. In a review of questions as a form of power, Wang (2006, p. 531) illustrated how: 'The inborn features of questions make them naturally bound up with power in that questions possess the ability to dominate and control'. As shown by Gee *et al.* (1999), there is usually a considerable difference between interviewer and interviewee in terms of expertise, status and power. Indeed, this power imbalance was noted in a humorous fashion by Lewis Carroll in *Alice's Adventures in Wonderland*, where a father responds to his child's questions as follows:

> 'I have answered three questions and that is enough,'
> Said his father 'don't give yourself airs!
> Do you think I can listen all day to such stuff?
> Be off, or I'll kick you down stairs.'

Bolden (2009, p. 122) noted that questions allow the questioner to control the conversation, 'by requesting the addressee to engage with a specific topic and/ or perform a particular responsive action'. In most contexts it is the person of higher status, or the person in control, who asks the questions. Thus, the majority of questions are asked by teachers in classrooms, doctors in surgeries, nurses on the ward, lawyers in court, detectives in interrogation rooms, and so on. For this reason, some counselling theorists have long argued that counsellors should try not to ask any questions at all of clients, to avoid being seen as the controller of the interaction (Rogers, 1951). A related power factor here is the attitude of the questioner. For example, Baxter *et al.* (2006) found that, when people were interviewed in a firm, formal manner, they were more likely to alter their initial answers than when interviewed in a friendly, relaxed fashion. The manner in which interviewees are questioned also affects how they are judged by observers. As noted by Fiedler (1993, p. 362), 'The way in which a person is questioned may have a substantial effect on his or her credibility, regardless of what he/she actually says'. For example, witnesses in court or candidates at selection interviews may be treated with the utmost respect when being questioned, or alternatively dealt with in an offhand manner. As well as directly impacting upon the interlocutor's self-esteem and confidence, such treatment is in turn likely to have an impact upon how the jury or selection panel respectively evaluate the responses.

To compound the problem, the respondent in many instances feels under stress when being questioned. This is certainly true in the above examples, where apprehension and anxiety are often experienced by patients on the ward or in the surgery, suspects in police stations, pupils in classrooms and defendants in court. Furthermore, in the latter two cases, the person asking the questions already knows the answers, and this makes these situations even more stressful and removed from normal interaction. In everyday conversation, we do not ask questions to which we already know the answers, or if we do we employ elaborate verbalisations to explain our behaviour ('I was surprised to discover something...; Let me see if you can guess...').

In the courtroom, it is a long-known maxim that lawyers should only ask questions to which they already know the answers. In this context, the creation of stress in witnesses is regarded as a legitimate tactic, and this is developed by a rapid-fire questioning approach, where one question is asked every few seconds, the respondent does not know what to expect next and the answers are already known by the questioner. This would undoubtedly put most people under pressure. In the classroom, however, the heightened anxiety of pupils may be dysfunctional, and detrimental both to learning and to pupil–teacher attitudes. Teachers should bear this in mind when employing this skill. Professionals also need to be careful in relation to the overall volume of questions used since, as shown by Benn *et al.* (2008, p. 57), 'too many questions may inhibit the development of a collaborative relationship'.

PURPOSES OF QUESTIONS

Bolden (2009, p. 122) pointed out that, 'Questions and answers are among the most readily recognizable and pervasive ways through which participants achieve and negotiate their communicative goals'. In fact, questions serve a range of purposes, depending upon the context of the interaction (Miles, 2013). For example, questions are asked by:

- salespeople to assess customer needs and relate their sales pitch to the satisfaction of these needs;
- teachers to check for pupil understanding;
- negotiators to slow the pace of the interaction and put pressure on their opponents;
- doctors to facilitate diagnoses.

The main general goals of questions are outlined in Box 5.1.

However, it should be realised that the type of question asked influences the extent to which each of these various goals can be fulfilled. Indeed, it is the responses made to questions that determine whether or not the objective has been achieved. In this sense, a question is only as good as the answer it evokes.

Box 5.1 Goals of questioning

The main goals served by the skill of questioning are to:

1 obtain information
2 initiate interaction
3 maintain control of an interaction
4 arouse interest and curiosity concerning a topic
5 diagnose specific difficulties the respondent may have
6 express an interest in the interlocutor
7 ascertain the attitudes, feelings and opinions of the respondent
8 encourage maximum participation from respondents
9 assess the extent of the interlocutor's knowledge
10 encourage critical thought and evaluation
11 communicate, in group discussions, that involvement and overt participation by all group members are expected and valued
12 encourage group members to comment on the responses of other members of the group
13 maintain the attention of group members (e.g. by asking questions periodically without advance warning)

TYPES OF QUESTION

Several different classifications of question types have been proposed. Rudyard Kipling (1902) put forward the following early categorisation:

> I keep six honest serving men,
> (They taught me all I knew);
> Their names are What and Why and When,
> And How and Where and Who.

As will be seen, these lines reflect, to a fair degree, the different classifications of questions that have been identified.

Closed/open questions

The most common division of questions relates to the degree of freedom, or scope, given to the respondent in answering. Those that leave the respondent open to choose any one of a number of ways in which to reply are referred to as open questions, while those that require a short response of a specific nature are termed closed questions.

Closed questions

These usually have a correct answer, or can be answered with a short response selected from a limited number of possible options. There are three main types:

1   *Selection question.* Here the respondent is presented with two or more alternative responses, from which to choose. As a result, this is also known as an *alternative question* (Gazdik, 2011) or *forced-choice question*. Examples include:

- 'Would you rather have Fyfe, Cameron or Rodgers as the next President?'
- 'Do you want to travel by sea or by air?'

2   *Yes–no question.* As the name suggests, this question may be adequately answered by a 'yes' or 'no', or some equivalent affirmative or negative. This type of question is also known as a *polar question* (Heritage and Raymond, 2012). Examples include:

- 'Did you go to university?'
- 'Has there been any bleeding?'

3   *Identification question.* This requires the respondent to identify the answer to a factual question and present this as the response. This may involve:

- recall of information, e.g. 'Where were you born?'
- identification of present circumstances, e.g. 'Where exactly is the pain occurring now?'
- queries about future events, e.g. 'Where are you going on holiday?'

Closed questions are usually easy to answer, and so are useful in encouraging early participation in an interaction. They can usually be answered adequately in one or a very few words, since they are restricted in nature, imposing limitations on the possible responses that the respondent can make. They give the questioner a high degree of control over the interaction, so that a series of such questions can be prepared in advance in order to structure the encounter, and the answers that the respondent may give can usually be anticipated. Where time is limited and a diagnosis has to be made, or information gathered, closed questions are often the preferred mode. They have a number of applications across contexts.

In fact-finding encounters, they are of particular value and so are often used in a variety of research and assessment-type interviews. In the research interview, answers to closed questions are more concise and therefore easier to record and code than replies to open questions (Breakwell *et al.*, 2006). This in turn facilitates comparisons between the responses of different subjects. In many assessment interviews, the interviewer has to ascertain whether or not the client is suitable for some form of grant or assistance and so find out whether the person meets a number of specified requirements (e.g. a social welfare official has to ask a client about financial affairs, family background, etc., before deciding upon eligibility for state allowances). Here again, closed questions are of value.

In the medical sphere it has been shown that doctors are two to three times more likely to ask yes–no questions than any other type of question (Raymond,

2003). Similarly, research findings show that only between 1 and 3 per cent of pharmacist questions are open in nature (Greenhill *et al.*, 2011). Furthermore, Morrow *et al.* (1993) found that, while almost all pharmacist questions were closed in nature, some 69 per cent of these were of the yes–no variety. They argued that pharmacists were following the clinical algorithm approach of eliminative questioning for diagnosis. While this approach, if carried out expertly, should result in the correct clinical conclusion, it is not without drawbacks in that important information may be missed. For example, one of the clients in their study was suffering from severe toothache for which the pharmacist had recommended a product and was completing the sale when the client asked: 'What about if you've taken any other tablets? I've taken Paracodol.' This unsolicited enquiry provoked further questions and subsequently altered the pharmacist's dosage recommendations.

Their potential for structured control is one of the reasons that teachers use significantly more closed than open questions in classrooms (Reinsvold and Cochran, 2012), and why this pattern is more marked in numeracy than in literacy classes (Smith *et al.*, 2006). This pattern of closed questioning in the classroom emerges at the initial stage of education; in the pre-school setting Siraj-Blatchford and Manni (2008, p. 7) found that: '94.5% of all the questions asked by the early childhood staff were closed questions that required a recall of fact, experience or expected behaviour'.

Open questions

These can be answered in a number of ways, with the response being left open to the respondent. Here, the respondent is given a higher degree of freedom in deciding which answer to give. Open questions are broad in nature, and require more than one or two words for an adequate answer. In general they have the effect of encouraging the interlocutor to respond in more detail about his or her concerns (Hill, 2014). They are useful in allowing a respondent to express opinions, attitudes, thoughts and feelings. They do not require any prior knowledge on the part of questioners, who can ask open questions about topics or events with which they are not familiar. They also encourage the respondent to talk, thereby leaving the questioner free to listen and observe. This means that the respondent has a greater degree of control over the interaction and can determine to a greater extent what is to be discussed. It also means that the questioner has to listen carefully to what is being said in order to follow up on responses.

An important advantage of open questions is that the respondent may reveal information that the questioner had not anticipated. Where a respondent has a body of specialised knowledge to relate, the use of open questions can facilitate the transmission of this knowledge. As noted by Kidwell (2009), closed questions merely require respondents to 'fill in' the specific detail requested, whereas open questions encourage them to 'fill out' whatever information they wish to provide. For this reason, however, where time is limited, or with over-talkative clients, they may be less appropriate. Answers to open questions may be time consuming, and may also contain irrelevant, or less vital, information.

Open/closed sequences

Some open questions place more restriction upon respondents than others. Consider the following examples of open questions asked by a detective of a suspect:

1   'Tell me about your spare-time activities.'
2   'What do you do in the evenings?'
3   'What do you do on Saturday evenings?'
4   'What did you do on the evening of Saturday 19 January?'

In these examples, the focus of the questions has narrowed gradually from the initial, very open question to the more restricted type of open question. This could then lead into more specific closed questions, such as:

5   'Who were you with on the evening of Saturday 19 January?'
6   'Where were you at 7.00 p.m. that evening?'

This approach, of beginning an interaction with a very open question, and gradually reducing the level of openness, is termed a funnel sequence (Kahn and Cannell, 1957; Miles, 2013) (Figure 5.1). It has been recommended in investigative interviewing, where there is evidence that a structure that begins by encouraging a free-narrative response from interviewees ('Tell me all you know about *X*') and then progressively narrowing the focus, is most effective (Powell *et al.*, 2007). A funnel structure is also common in counselling interviews, where the helper does not want to impose any restrictions on the helpee about what is to be discussed, and may begin a session by asking a very open question, such as, 'What would you like to talk about?' or 'How have things been since we last met?' Once the helpee begins to talk, the helper may then want to focus in on certain aspects of the responses given. Likewise, in the medical interview, Cohen-Cole and Bird (1991, p. 13) pointed out that:

> A considerable body of literature supports the use of open-ended questioning as an efficient and effective vehicle to gain understanding of patients' problems. To be sure, after an initial nondirective phase...the doctor must ask progressively more focused questions to explore specific diagnostic hypotheses. This...has been called an 'open-to-closed cone'.

An alternative approach is to use an *inverted funnel* (or *pyramid*) *sequence*, whereby an interaction begins with very closed questions and gradually opens out to embrace wider issues. Such an approach is often adopted in careers guidance interviews in which the interviewer may want to build up a picture of the client (e.g. academic achievements, family background, interests) before progressing to possible choice of career and the reasons for this choice. By using closed questions initially to obtain information, the careers interviewer may then be in a better position to help the client evaluate possible, and feasible, career options.

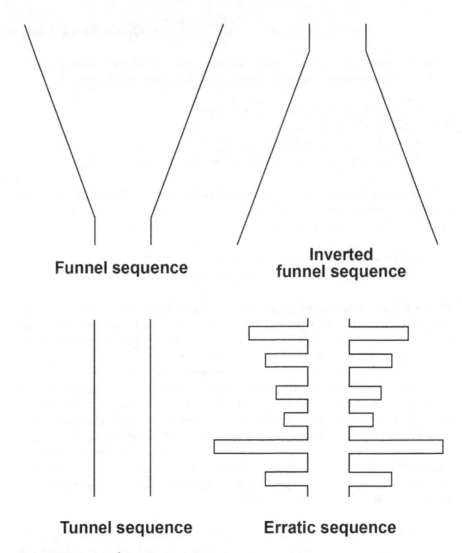

Figure 5.1 Types of questioning sequence.

A third type is the *tunnel sequence*, also referred to as the *string of beads* (Stewart and Cash, 2013). Here, all of the questions employed are at the same level and are usually closed. Such a sequence may be used in certain types of assessment interview, wherein the objective is to establish a set of factual responses. This type of closed tunnelling for information is often characteristic of screening interviews, where the respondent has to be matched against some pre-set criteria (e.g. eligibility for state welfare benefit or grant). A closed tunnel sequence of questions is also used by lawyers in court when they wish to direct a witness along a pre-determined set of answers.

There is research evidence to suggest that a consistent sequence of questions facilitates participation and understanding in respondents, whether the sequence be of a tunnel, funnel or inverted funnel nature. On the other hand, an *erratic sequence* of open and closed questions is likely to confuse the respondent and reduce the level of participation. Erratic sequences of questions (also known as rapid variations in the level of cognitive demand) are common in interrogative interviews where the purpose is to confuse suspects and 'throw them off guard' since they do not know what type of question to expect next. Indeed, in courtrooms, Kestler (1982, p. 156) recommended that when lawyers wish to trap witnesses they should use an erratic sequence, involving 'a quick change of focus designed to catch the witness off-balance, with thoughts out of context'.

Comparing open and closed questions

Several research studies have examined the relative effects of open and closed questions in different situations. In an early investigation, Dohrenwend (1965) found that, in research interviews, responses to open questions were some three times longer than those to closed ones, as measured by amounts of verbalisation. She concluded that closed questions offer more definite advantages than open questions in research interviews because they exert a tighter control over respondents' answers. Open questions, while answered in more detail, tended to result in responses that deviated from the topic of the question, whereas with closed questions the respondent was more likely to answer the question in a direct fashion. However, although closed questions may facilitate control, they also have disadvantages in research interviews. Dillon (1997) illustrated how both types of question may result in missing or inaccurate information being gathered. He showed that, when asked the open question of what they preferred in a job, only half as many respondents mentioned a 'feeling of accomplishment' as those who selected it when it was presented as one of the alternatives in closed format. On the other hand, good pay was the most frequently volunteered answer to the open question, but the least frequently selected alternative in the closed. If the factor a subject considers most important is missing from the list attached to a closed question, it is not likely to be mentioned and instead some of the presented factors will be offered as the answer. This is because the respondent perceives one of the 'rules' of the task to be that of having to make a choice from the presented list. Unless told otherwise, the subject assumes that the items on the list are the sole focus of the experimenter. On the other hand, if only the open question is used, the respondent may simply overlook one or more important factors. Dillon therefore recommended the use of open questions with a range of respondents in order to produce an exhaustive list of alternatives for later inclusion in closed-question format in survey interviews.

Generalisations about the relative efficacy of open or closed questions are difficult, since the intellectual capacity of the respondent must be taken into consideration. It has long been known that open questions may not be as appropriate with respondents of lower intellect. Schatzman and Strauss (1956) compared respondents who had not gone beyond secondary school level with those who had spent at least 1 year at college. They found that open questions tended to be more effective with the latter group than with the former, as judged by the questioning behaviour of experienced interviewers who were given a certain degree of freedom about what type of questions to employ. The interviewers used more open questions with the respondents of higher education than with those of lower education.

Research comparing the use of open and closed questions in counselling (Dickson *et al.*, 1997) has found that open questions are more effective in:

- promoting interviewee self-disclosures
- producing more accurate responses
- increasing perceived counsellor empathy.

Thus, most texts in the area recommend that counsellors should concentrate on asking open questions that require a more extended response. As noted by Strong (2006, p. 1005), 'There is a common proverb in counseling that a good question is one that requires a lengthy pause to answer'. Egan (2014, p. 139) concurred with this advice, and proffered the following guidance to helpers: 'As a general rule, ask open-ended questions ... Counselors who ask closed questions find themselves asking more and more questions. One closed question begets another.' Given this backdrop, Forrester *et al.* (2008) were surprised to discover that social workers, who are often perceived to have a counselling role, asked on average twice as many closed questions as open ones during interviews. The relevance of the advice given by Egan was substantiated by the fact that one of the social workers in the Forrester *et al.* study ended up asking ten times as many closed as open questions.

Likewise, in the medical sphere, research in the USA (where the consultation with the doctor is normally preceded by a consultation with a nurse or medical assistant) has shown that patients show significantly greater satisfaction with the relational aspect of doctors' communication when the physician begins the consultation with an open (e.g. 'How can I help?' 'What brings you in today?') as opposed to a closed (e.g. 'I see you have sinus problems?' 'I understand you're having some leg problems?') question (Robinson and Heritage, 2006). In addition, such initial open questions by doctors have been shown to result in significantly longer patient answers, which in turn reveal significantly more symptoms (Heritage and Robinson, 2006).

In a different context, Loftus (1982) found that, in the questioning of eye witnesses, open questions produced more accurate information, but less overall detail, than specific closed questions. As a result, she recommended that, in this context, questions should be open initially ('Tell me what happened') to obtain accuracy of information, followed by specific closed questions ('What age was he?') to obtain a fuller picture. This recommendation has been consistently supported in studies of investigative interviewing (Memon and Bull, 1999; Wright and Powell, 2006).

In terms of response times, it has been found that, as open questions require greater effort in the formulation of an answer, respondents take more time to answer them in comparison to closed questions (Strömbergsson *et al.*, 2013). However, a related feature that needs to be taken into consideration here is the length of the question itself. There is evidence to indicate that duration of responses is related to length of questions, in that longer answers tend to be given to longer questions (Wilson, 1990). One explanation for this may be that, as the length of a question increases, it is likely to contain an increased number of propositions, each of which then needs to be addressed by the interlocutor. It could also be that the respondent judges the length of reply expected by the questioner in proportion to the duration of the question, and responds in line with this perceived implicit expectancy.

The linguistic context of questions is also important. For example, Allwinn (1991) demonstrated how closed questions could be elaborated on by skilled people through the use of pre-remarks (e.g. 'I'm not very knowledgeable about this, so could I ask you...?') to indicate that a detailed response is required, despite the fact that the question could logically be answered in one or a few words. Also, the context and rules of the interaction may mean that, although a question has been phrased in a closed fashion, it is clear that an open reply is expected. Thus, the perceived purpose of a question is influenced by a range of factors, each of which may influence how it is interpreted.

Recall/process questions

This categorisation refers to the cognitive level at which questions are pitched. Recall questions are also known as lower-order cognitive, and process as higher-order cognitive, questions. The distinction between recall and process questions is most commonly made within education, and can be found primarily in classroom interaction research studies.

Recall questions

As the name suggests, these involve the simple recall of information. They are pitched at a lower level of cognitive demand since they only test the ability of the respondent to recall facts, for example:

- 'Where were you born?'
- 'When was the Battle of Waterloo?'

Recall questions serve a number of useful purposes in different settings. A teacher may employ them at the beginning of a lesson to ascertain the extent of pupil knowledge about the topic. Such questions provide feedback for the teacher and also encourage pupil participation at the outset. They can also be used intermittently to check that the class has understood what has been covered so far and is ready to move on to the next stage. In this way their function is 'to share facts in order to establish a firm foundation for further work' (Morgan and Saxton, 2006, p. 48). Similarly, at the end of a lesson the teacher may use this type of question to determine the extent of pupil learning that has taken place as a result of the lesson, and also to highlight to pupils that such learning has occurred.

In interviewing contexts, recall questions may be employed at the beginning of an interview as a form of 'ice breaker' to get the interviewee talking. As mentioned earlier, they are also important when questioning eye witnesses to crimes. In medicine, recall questions are also of relevance in the diagnosis of an illness. Thus a doctor will use questions such as:

- 'When did the pain first begin?'
- 'Have you had any dizzy spells?'

Process questions

These are so called because they require the respondent to use some *higher mental process* in order to respond. This may involve giving opinions, justifications, judgements or evaluations, making predictions, analysing information, interpreting situations or forming generalisations. As stated by Tofade *et al.* (2013, p. 1), 'Higher-order questions elicit deeper and critical thinking'. In other words, the respondent is required to think, at a higher-order level, about the answer. For example: 'How do you think you could improve your relationship with your wife?' Such questions require the respondent to go beyond the simple recall of information and usually there is no correct answer. Furthermore, they require longer responses and can seldom be answered in one or two words. They are employed in situations where someone is being encouraged to think more deeply about a topic. For this reason they are often utilised to assess the ability of an individual to think at a higher-order level. In executive-type selection interviews, they are frequently used in this assessment function, e.g.:

- 'What can you offer this company that other applicants cannot?'
- 'What have been your main strengths and weaknesses as a manager?'

In teaching, they encourage pupils to reflect upon the material being presented. Research reviews of questioning in the classroom context have consistently found that teachers ask considerably more recall than process questions (Hargie, 1983; Dickson and Hargie, 2006; Morgan and Saxton, 2006; Khan and Inamullah, 2011). These are somewhat disconcerting findings, since the type of question asked by teachers affects the degree of creativity or expressiveness available to pupils, and process questions provide more scope than recall questions. In a world where technological advances move at a rapid pace, facts can quickly become outdated and the ability to evaluate new information is of great importance. Morgan and Saxton (2006, p. 46) advised that, if teachers want 'students to think about what they are learning so that learning becomes part of their view of themselves and their world, you have to ask questions that will help them understand...and help them think about the meanings being made'. For this reason, Hargie (1983, p. 190) argued that, during training, 'attention should be given to means whereby teachers can increase their use of thought-provoking questions as opposed to factual or recall questions'. There is firm research evidence to support such a proposal, since Rousseau and Redfield (1980, p. 52), in reviewing a total of 20 studies, showed that 'gains in achievement over a control group may be expected for groups of children who participate in programmes where teachers are trained in questioning skills…gains are greatest when higher cognitive questions are used during instruction'.

However, caution should be exercised in attempting to generalise about the use of process as opposed to recall questions. Research tends to suggest that process questions are more effective in increasing both participation and achievement of individuals of high intellectual ability, whereas recall questions appear to be more appropriate for individuals at lower ability levels. For example, Rubie-Davies (2007) found that teachers who held above-average expectations for their pupils used more higher-order questions than those with below-average expectations. For teachers with mixed-ability classes, there are some particular difficulties here, in that the consistent use of process questions is likely to stimulate pupils with a high IQ but may be inappropriate for, or confuse, pupils with a low IQ.

At first sight, there would appear to be little difference between the recall/process and the closed/open categorisations of questions, and indeed, many closed questions are of a recall nature, while many process questions are open. However, it is possible to have closed process questions and open recall questions. Consider a science teacher who has explained to pupils the properties of water and limestone, and then asks, 'Will the water pass through the limestone?' While the question is process, it is also closed. Similarly, a question such as 'What did you do during the holidays?' is both open and recall.

Affective questions

These are questions that relate specifically to the emotions, attitudes, feelings or preferences of the respondent – that is, to the *affective* domain. An affective question can be recall, process, open or closed, depending upon which aspect of feelings is being explored. Where an attempt is being made to ascertain reactions to a past event, a recall question may be employed (e.g. 'Who was your favourite teacher at school?'). On the other hand, when present feelings are being explored, a closed question may be used (e.g. 'Do you feel a little embarrassed talking about this?').

The utilisation of recall or closed questions, however, places restrictions upon respondents in terms of what they are expected to relate about their feelings. Where it is important that the client be given time and freedom to discuss emotions, open questions are more advantageous. Open affective questions facilitate the expression of feelings. These can relate to past emotions (e.g. 'How did you feel when your mother died?') or to the present emotional state ('How are you coping with this now?'). To encourage a respondent to think more deeply about feelings, and about the underlying reasons for these, process questions may be applicable. Rather than merely asking for feelings to be reported, they further tap into an evaluation of possible underlying causes (e.g. 'What caused you to hate your father so much?'). This type of question encourages the respondent to interpret reasons for feelings and perhaps become more rational in exploring them.

Affective questions are particularly relevant in counselling contexts where the discussion of feelings is very important. They are also important in health care, where it has been shown that skilled doctors use more questions that address the psychosocial aspects of the patient's condition than their less skilled colleagues (Ford and Hall, 2004; Tallman *et al.*, 2007).

Leading questions

All questions contain assumptions or presuppositions. Fiedler (2007, p. 15) defined presuppositions as 'silent implications or taken-for-granted inferences' within questions. As a very simple example, if I ask you 'What time is it?' the pre-suppositions are that: (1) you have access to this information; (2) you can read the time; and (3) you are willing to give me this information. Likewise you would usually assume that: (1) I genuinely do not know the time; (2) I do not have ready access to this information; and (3) I really wish to find out this information. However, if the interaction is between a pair of young adult strangers, the target might then make the assumption that the questioner is really attempting to open dialogue as the first step in relational development, and respond accordingly. Alternatively, if the target is the spouse of the questioner, both are at a party and the hour is late, the question might be read as a signal that it is time to go home, as the baby-sitter will be ready to leave. Adler *et al.* (2013b) termed these latter examples *counterfeit questions* in that they are not what they appear at first sight, since they carry hidden agendas. Question assumptions can also, of course, be true or false. For example, a detective in attempting to trap a suspect who claims to have been at a particular cinema on the evening of a crime may ask 'What did you do when the power failed in the cinema at 8.45 p.m.?' There was no power failure, and so this false assumption places the suspect in a difficult position if being deceitful.

Leading questions are assumption-laden. By the way they are worded they lead the respondent towards an expected response. The anticipated answer is implied or assumed within the question, and may or may not be immediately obvious to the respondent, depending upon the phrasing. For this reason, they have also been termed *misleading questions* or *suggestive questions* (Gee *et al.*, 1999). There are four different types: (1) conversational leads; (2) simple leads; (3) implication leads; and (4) subtle leads.

Conversational leads

As the name suggests, these are used in common parlance. Everyday conversa-tions typically contain comments that anticipate a certain type of response, e.g.:

- 'Isn't this a lovely day?'
- 'Wasn't that a terrible accident yesterday?'

These lubricate the flow of conversation since they anticipate the response that the interlocutor would have been likely to give and so demonstrate shared understanding. In interviews, conversational leads convey the impression of friendliness and interest on the part of the interviewer, providing, of course, they accurately anticipate the respondent's answer. Correct conversational leading questions create the feeling that the interlocutor is 'in tune' with us.

Simple leads

These are unambiguously intended to lead the respondent to give an answer that the questioner expects to receive. Unlike the conversational lead, the simple lead assumes the answer the questioner expects, as opposed to the answer that the respondent would have given in any case. The simple lead, then, takes little cognisance of the respondent's thoughts and feelings, e.g.:

- 'Surely you don't support the communists?'
- 'You do want to go to university, don't you?'

The latter example includes a *tag question* ('...don't you?'). This type of question, tagged on at the end, turns a statement into a leading question. As noted by Lester (2008), 'The question created by adding the question tag is not usually a genuine request for information. It is typically a request for confirmation that the information in the main body of the sentence is correct' (p. 306). Tag questions have been shown to reduce evaluations of speaker credibility and power and so should be used with caution (Hosman and Siltanen, 2011).

Simple leads can have advantages. It has been known for some time that the use of simple leads that are obviously incorrect can induce respondents to participate fully in an interview, in order to correct any misconceptions inherent in the question. Beezer (1956), for example, conducted interviews with refugees from the then East Germany in which he found that simple leading questions that were clearly incorrect yielded more information from respondents than did questions that were not leading. Thus, when respondents were asked, 'I understand you don't have to pay very much for food in the East Zone because it is rationed?' most replied by trying to correct the interviewer's mistaken impressions about general living conditions.

The blatantly incorrect simple leading question serves to place the respondent in the position of expert *vis-à-vis* the misinformed interviewer. As a result, the respondent feels obliged to provide information that will enlighten the interviewer. Some of this information may involve the introduction of new and insightful material. While they can be effective in encouraging participation, it is not possible to state how, and in what contexts, simple leading questions can be most gainfully employed. In certain situations, and with particular types of respondent, their use is counter-productive. Most authors of texts on interviewing have eschewed this form of questioning as bad practice. Furthermore, in the courtroom, leading questions are not permitted in the direct examination of a witness by the counsel for the side calling the witness, although they are allowed during cross-examination of the other side's witnesses.

Kestler (1982, p. 59) positively recommended the use of leading questions by lawyers during cross-examination since they 'permit control of the subject matter and scope of the response. The witness is constrained to answer "yes" or "no".' They are also used by detectives to encourage suspects to confess to crimes. Here, what are known as *minimisation strategies* are employed to reduce the suspect's perceived responsibility for what happened. These involve 'offering legal or moral face-saving excuses for actions, conceptualizing actions as accidental, blaming the victim and underplaying the seriousness of the charges' (Klaver *et al.*, 2008, p. 73). Examples of leading questions using minimisation strategies with a suspect in a rape case are:

- 'She led you on and on and look at the way she was dressed, what else would you have thought?'
- 'She's a bit of a slag, she was asking for it really, wasn't she?'

Research findings show that minimisation strategies result in suspects believing that they will be treated more leniently if they confess, even when no such leniency is explicitly offered.

Implication leads

These lead the respondent to answer in a specific fashion, or accept a negative implication if the response given is contrary to that suggested. Implication leads exert a much greater degree of pressure on the respondent to reply in the expected manner than simple leads, and for this reason they are also known as *complex leading questions* and *given-that questions*. An example of this type of question (where the 'given-that' part is implied rather than stated) is: 'Anyone who cared for their country would not want to see it destroyed in a nuclear attack or invaded by a foreign power, so don't you think any expenditure on an effective defensive deterrent is money well spent?' In this case, a negative answer places the respondent in the position of apparently being unpatriotic.

If a respondent disagrees with the assumed response, a justification is usually expected by the questioner. For this reason, implication leads are often used by radio and television interviewers when interviewing political, or controversial, individuals. Similarly, in arguments and debates, they are employed in order to put opponents under pressure, and emphasise a certain point of view. Loftus (1982) provided another example of an implication lead, namely 'Did you know that what you were doing was dishonest?' This type of 'trick question' puts the respondent under pressure either to accept the negative implication of dishonesty or respond at length. It is a variant of the well-known and oft-cited implication question, 'When did you stop beating your wife?'

Subtle leads

A humorous example of the effects of subtle leads is the story about the Dominican and Jesuit priests who debated whether it was permissible to say their daily prayers and smoke their pipes at the same time. Unable to reach a definitive conclusion, each agreed to consult his superior for guidance. The Jesuit returned very satisfied, saying he had obtained permission. The Dominican bemoaned this outcome, saying his superior had refused his request. 'What did you ask him?' enquired the Jesuit. 'Well, obviously, if it was OK for me to smoke while praying.' 'Ah,' said the Jesuit, 'that was your mistake. I asked mine if it was permissible to pray while smoking.' As this story indicates, subtle leads may not be instantly recognisable as leading questions, but nevertheless they are worded in such a way as to elicit a certain type of response. They are also known as *directional questions* in that the respondent is being subtly directed towards a particular type of answer. This is because, as summarised by Loftus (2006, p. 3), 'just changing a single word or two in a question can sometimes have a sizeable effect on the answer'.

In the sphere of interrogation, Buckwalter (1983) illustrated that suspects of crimes are more forthcoming when asked to 'tell the truth' rather than 'confess your crime'. Similarly, in cases of murder, motives are given more readily to the question 'Why did you do it?' than to 'Why did you murder him?' Buckwalter advised interviewers to avoid terms such as kill, steal, rape, and replace them with words such as shoot, take, sex. In fact, it is a myth that the key to effective interrogation is to accuse, confuse, hurt or embarrass the suspect. Such Gestapo-like techniques just do not work. Rather, they make the person afraid, resentful, reluctant, hostile and defensive – all of which reduces the likelihood of truthful disclosure. Texts on interrogation recommend that the best guide is not to think of oneself as asking questions, but as being questioned. Their advice is to put yourself in the position of the respondent and consider what would make you tell the truth in this context. Research in interrogation consistently reveals that, to be successful, the interviewer must build up a rapport with the interviewee and appear to be nonjudgemental (Williamson, 2005). Good interrogators possess qualities such as: genuineness, trustworthiness, concern, courtesy, tact, empathy, compassion, respect, friendliness, gentleness, receptivity, warmth and understanding. We disclose to such people – they seem to care and do not judge (see Chapter 9 for further discussion of disclosure).

An early example of how a subtle change in the wording of a question can influence the respondent to answer in a particular way was reported by Harris (1973). In an abstract study into the accuracy of guessing measurements (i.e. no films or photographs were shown), when subjects were asked either 'How tall was the basket-ball player?' or 'How short was the basket-ball player?' they guessed about 79 inches (2 metres) and 69 inches (1.7 metres), respectively. Other questions asked by Harris along the same lines produced similar results – thus, the question 'How long was the movie?' resulted in average estimates of 130 minutes, whereas 'How short was the movie?' produced an average of 100 minutes. Loftus (1975) reported similar findings. When subjects were asked either 'Do you get headaches frequently, and if so, how often?' or 'Do you get headaches occasionally, and if so, how often?' the respective reported averages were 2.2 and 0.7 headaches per week.

This is part of the *acquiescence effect*, wherein respondents comply with or acquiesce to the explicit or implicit direction of the question (Bhattacharya and Isen, 2008). Most people, when asked, 'How many animals of each kind did

Moses take on the ark?' will reply 'two', even though they are aware that in the biblical story it was Noah who took animals on the ark. This phenomenon, termed *The Moses Illusion* (Erickson and Mattson, 1981), illustrates how respondents attempt to gauge and anticipate the answer that the questioner is seeking and so demonstrate helpfulness by supplying it. Gibbs and Bryant (2008, p. 368) noted that part of the question-and-answer process involves 'understanding the questioner's plans and goals when formulating appropriate replies'. We are not just passive recipients of questions. Rather, we actively search for and interpret the meanings and assumptions behind the inquisitive words being used. Indeed, as Wänke (2007, p. 234) noted: 'respondents will use any cue in the provided information to infer the intended meaning of a question...Previous questions, introductions, the question wording, answer formats, and any other information may serve this purpose'.

The desire to give the 'right' answer is a powerful force in human nature. This is one of the reasons why 'researchers have long known that people tend to agree with one-sided statements, and that the same subject may agree to two opposite statements on different occasions' (Kunda and Fong, 1993, p. 65). A practical application of the acquiescence effect can be found in retail contexts, where staff are trained to ask directional questions. For example, in a fast-food outlet when a customer orders a meal, the person taking the order will often be told to use a directional assumptive question, such as 'Coke with your meal?' The customer often accepts the suggestion, and so profits are maximised. In restaurants, waiting staff are trained to use subtle leads such as: 'Are you enjoying your meal?' or 'Is everything OK?' and so encourage a positive response from, and 'feel-good' factor in, diners.

How questions are contextualised can also influence acquiescence. For example, in interviews into earliest memory, Hirt *et al.* (1999) showed that low-expectancy conditions (e.g. saying to the person 'If you don't remember, it's all right') as compared to high-expectancy conditions (e.g. 'Tell me when you get an earlier memory') produced earliest-reported life memories from respondents of 3.45 years and 2.28 years, respectively. Furthermore, when college students were initially asked to report their earliest memory, the mean recall age was 3.7 years. However, students were then told that most people could recall their second birthday, if they were really willing to let themselves go, focus and concentrate. When then asked for memories of second birthday and earlier memories, 59 per cent of subjects reported a memory of their second birthday, and the mean recall age fell to 1.6 years. In addition, when fed a piece of false information (i.e. getting lost in a shopping mall) together with three actual events (as supplied by parents or siblings), some 25 per cent then claimed to have memories of this false event.

An important related phenomenon here is what is known as *anchor bias* (Brewer *et al.*, 2007). This occurs when the initial question contains a suggested figure. For example, a subject is asked: 'Do you think the chance that you will get the flu is more or less than 90 per cent?' Subjects are then asked the subsequent question 'What do you think the percentage chance is that you will get the flu?' The suggested anchor number of 90 per cent influences the subject in formulating an answer to the second question, which as a result will be closer to this figure. The fact that this figure has been stated leads the respondent to make the assumption that it must somehow be close to the actuality. Otherwise, why would the questioner cite it? Variations of this anchoring effect have been studied for decades. Thus, Loftus (1975) asked subjects either 'In terms of the total number of products, how many other products have you tried? one? two? three?' or 'In terms of the total number of products, how many other products have you tried? one? five? ten?' Responses to these questions averaged 3.3 and 5.2 other products, respectively. Likewise, Gaskell *et al.* (1993) showed how, when asked about annoyance with TV adverts, subjects given high alternatives (every day, most days, once a week, once a month, less often, never) reported significantly higher frequencies of feeling annoyed than those given low alternatives (once a week or more often, once a month, about every few months, once a year, less often, never). The values in a given scale are assumed to reflect average, typical or normative behaviour, and so respondents wishing to be seen as 'normal' choose a figure near the mid-point.

Furthermore, Bless *et al.* (1992) cited evidence to demonstrate that the more demanding the computation of a requested frequency response, the more likely it is that respondents are led by the alternatives suggested in the question. Interestingly, Hetsroni (2007) found that subjects given an open-question format produced significantly higher estimates than those provided with fixed-response alternatives. One reason for this may have been that the absence of possible answers meant there was no standard against which subjects could estimate normative responses. It has also been shown that the nature of the given response scale can affect perceived definitions of terms. Thus, in one study two groups of subjects were asked to report how often they felt 'really annoyed' (Wright *et al.*, 1997). Subjects either received a set of low response frequencies (from 'less than once a year' to 'more than every 3 months') or high response frequencies (from 'less than twice a week' to 'several times a day'). Respondents were then asked to define 'annoyed' and it was found that those in the low response frequency group described it as a more severe disturbance than those in the high-frequency condition.

Another example of subtle leads lies in the use of implicit verb causality. Action verbs, such as 'attack' or 'assist', imply that the subject is the initiator, or cause, of the behaviour. In contrast, state verbs, such as 'admire' or 'abhor', suggest that the object of the statement is the cause of the event. Thus, 'Why did Stephen attack Helen?' suggests that Stephen is the aggressor, whereas 'Why did Stephen abhor Helen?' suggests that Helen was in some way responsible for Stephen's reaction. Research has shown (Fiedler, 2007) that the degree of guilt attributed to a defendant is lower when state rather than action verbs are used in questions. In addition, answering questions containing state verbs about whether someone depicted on video attacked or ridiculed others has been shown to induce greater negative judgements of the depicted person, even when the respondent denies that the event occurred. This is because the implicit verb causality in the phrasing of the question influences later judgements.

Another feature associated with subtle leads is the *misinformation effect*, which occurs when respondents are led by questions in such a way as to confirm aspects of an event that never happened. In their review of this field, Zaragoza *et al.* (2006, p. 35) concluded that the misinformation effect 'is one of the best-known and most influential findings in psychology'. In an early study, Loftus and

Palmer (1974) had subjects view films of car accidents, and then questioned them about what they had seen. The question 'About how fast were the cars going when they smashed into each other?' produced higher estimates of speed than when the verb 'smashed' was replaced by 'hit', 'bumped', 'collided' or 'contacted'. One week later those subjects who had been asked the former question were also more likely to say 'yes' to the question 'Did you see broken glass?', even though no glass was broken in the accident. In a related piece of research, Loftus and Zanni (1975) compared the effects of questions containing an indefinite article with the same questions containing a definite article. In this study 100 graduate students were shown a short film of a car accident and then asked questions about this. It was found that questions which contained a definite article (e.g. 'Did you see *the* broken headlight?') produced fewer uncertain or 'I don't know' responses, and more false recognition of events which never in fact occurred, than did questions which contained an indefinite article (e.g. 'Did you see *a* broken headlight?').

This *false recognition* was also reported in the Loftus (1975) study. Loftus conducted four different experiments, each of which highlighted the way in which the wording of questions, asked immediately after an event, influenced the responses to questions asked considerably later. In one of these experiments students were shown a videotape of a car accident and asked a number of questions about the accident. Half of the subjects were asked, 'How fast was the white sports car going when it passed the barn while travelling along the country road?' while half were asked 'How fast was the white sports car going while travelling along the country road?' Although no barn appeared in the film, 17.3 per cent of those asked the former question responded 'yes' when later asked 'Did you see a barn?', as opposed to only 2.7 per cent of those asked the latter question.

The concept of *recovered memory* has caused much debate in this area. Here, people are interviewed in depth until they eventually recall past experiences, often of abuse, which had previously been repressed. However, it has been argued that such recovered memory is often in fact *false memory* planted as a result of biased questioning (Pezdek and Banks, 1996). In particular, questions that encourage respondents to think about an event can lead to a process termed *imagination inflation*. As defined by Loftus (2001, p. 584), this is 'the phenomenon that imagining an event increases subjective confidence that the event actually happened'. Interestingly, getting people to write down their constructed experiences greatly increases their belief in the veracity of these fictitious events. Loftus further showed that certain people are more susceptible to such inflation, including those who:

- have a tendency to confuse fact with fiction
- more often experience lapses in attention and memory
- possess more acute powers of imagery.

The implications of the above findings have ramifications for anyone concerned with obtaining accurate information from others, but they are of particular import for those who have to interview children.

Effects of leading questions upon children

There is a growing volume of research to show that leading questions have a particularly distorting effect upon the responses of children (Zajac *et al.*, 2003; Krähenbühl and Blades, 2006; Spencer and Lamb, 2012; Bowles and Sharman, 2014; Pipe *et al.*, 2014). One reason for this is that the acquiescence effect is very strong with young children. Furthermore, Milne (1999, p. 175) showed how children with intellectual disabilities 'were significantly more likely to go along with misleading questions (i.e. questions which lead the child to the wrong answer)'. This finding was confirmed in a later study by Ternes and Yuille (2008). Furthermore, Hardy and van Leeuwen (2004) demonstrated that younger children (3 to 5.5 years) were less able to resist suggestion than older ones (5.5 to 8 years). Loukusa *et al.* (2008) also showed that the ability of children to interpret the contextual dimensions of questions developed over time between the ages of 3 and 9 years. Given the research findings in this area, they concluded: 'It is imperative that interviewers avoid contaminating children's statements through use of inappropriate interviewing techniques such as leading questions' (p. 155).

Leading questions need to be used with caution, or avoided altogether, by those who interview children. For those on the receiving end of such questions, Gee *et al.* (1999) showed how young people could be inoculated against the effects of misleading questions by receiving training in how to deal with them. Endres *et al.* (1999) similarly illustrated that giving children advance warning about 'tricky' questions, and explicitly allowing them to reject a question by saying 'I don't know' when unsure about the answer, led to a reduction in errors in responses to suggestive questions. These results have been confirmed in other research which shows that encouraging children to say 'Don't know' and giving them clear prior instructions about how to deal with questions resulted in more accurate recall by them of events (Ghetti and Goodman, 2001; Waterman and Blades, 2011; Scoboria, 2012).

Research has also supported the use of open questions with children (Holliday and Albon, 2004). In their detailed work in this area, Waterman *et al.* (2001) showed how children were less accurate in reporting events they had experienced when answering closed questions than when answering open ones. They further found that yes–no questions could produce distorted responses. For example, when asked nonsensical yes–no questions (e.g. 'Is a fork happier than a knife?' 'Is red heavier than yellow?'), 75 per cent of 5–8-year-olds answered either 'yes' or 'no'. Yet, when later questioned about their responses, it was clear that many children who answered 'no' were simply indicating that they did not agree with the assumption inherent in the question. But they did not say so at the time. The problem is that a yes–no question presupposes a pre-determined response (either 'yes' or 'no') and the child acquiesces with this (Waterman *et al.*, 2004).

Furthermore, the social demands of the situation are such that children assume that adults will ask reasonable questions, and so they feel under pressure to respond to the expectations inherent in these questions (Okanda and

Itakura, 2008). When asked open-format nonsensical questions (e.g. 'What do feet have for breakfast?'), 95 per cent of children said they did not understand the question. This was particularly the case when children were told that it was OK to say if they did not understand. In their review of this area, Powell and Snow (2007, p. 57) showed that the most effective approach for professionals interviewing children involved 'the use of non-leading open-ended questions and other prompts that encourage elaborate responses, but allow the interviewee flexibility to report what information they remember'. Likewise, in their analysis, Krähenbühl and Blades (2006, p. 326) concluded: 'researchers have found that the use of open-ended questions has indeed improved the accuracy levels in recall'.

Young children have a particular problem with the use of *embedded questions* such as 'Can you tell me who was there?' (Hardy and van Leeuwen, 2004). These are confusing for children because they contain two questions – in this case, 'Are you able to tell me?' and 'Who was there?' Embedded questions are also known as *indirect probes*, and so those interviewing children should avoid these and use direct probes. In the latter example it is best just to use the direct probe, 'Who was there?' Likewise, hypothetical questions (e.g. 'What if I told you he wasn't tall enough to reach the window from the garden?') have been shown to confuse children, who until the age of about 11 years do not have the abstract reasoning abilities to deal with them (Sas, 2002). These findings have obvious implications for those involved in questioning children in forensic situations, such as child abuse investigations. Yet, in practice, children are often subjected to very difficult questioning routines. For example, in 2009 a court case at the London Old Bailey attracted immense media interest. A 4-year-old girl (the youngest child ever to give evidence in this court) was required to testify against a man who she claimed had raped her. She gave evidence from an adjoining room via a video link. It transpired that the accused, who was later found guilty, had previously been convicted of torturing and killing an 18-month-old child. However, what provoked particular outcry in this case was the way in which the barrister questioned the child. Among a series of leading questions, multiple questions and difficult tag questions that he asked her were the following:

- 'He didn't touch you, did he? Did he? I have to ask you one more time. We have to have an answer from you, he didn't touch you, did he?…[and after a considerable delay]…I have to wait until I get your answer. He didn't touch you, did he?'
- 'Do you remember that you said to me that you didn't tell fibs? Is that true or a fib? What is truth?'
- 'Was it something someone told you to say? Was it something you made up?'

Not surprisingly, one journalist reporting on this case concluded, 'there has to be a better system for gaining justice for infants than cross-examination in court' (Anthony, 2008).

As summarised by Lamb *et al.* (1999, p. 261), 'researchers agree that the manner in which children are questioned can have profound implications for what is "remembered"'. The title of a book chapter by Walker and Hunt (1998) neatly sums it up, 'Interviewing child victim-witnesses: How you ask is what you get'. Yet it has been shown that closed questions predominate in many such interview contexts (Wright and Powell, 2006; Powell and Snow, 2007), and that children often respond to the assumptions in the questions they are asked without making their real answers clearly known. In their study into the experiences of young witnesses in court cases in England, Wales and Northern Ireland, Plotnikoff and Woolfson (2009) interviewed 182 children and 172 parents. They found that some 65 per cent of the young people interviewed reported problems relating to how they were questioned in court by lawyers, including the complexity of questions, a related lack of comprehension, a rapid or repetitive questioning style, having 'words put in their mouth' and having their answers interrupted. Among the key recommendations from this study was that, when dealing with child witnesses, steps need to be taken by the judicial system to improve standards of questioning overall, and in particular to control inappropriate questioning of children by lawyers. This was also emphasised by Smith *et al.* (2011).

Probing questions

These are follow-up questions designed to encourage respondents to expand upon initial responses. Stewart and Cash (2013) referred to them as *secondary questions* in that they follow on from the main, or primary, question. They are ubiquitous, so that in group discussions, some 90 per cent of all questions asked are probes (Hawkins and Power, 1999). They are also very important in dyadic contexts, leading Bernard (2006, p. 217) to conclude, 'The key to successful interviewing is learning how to probe'. Once a respondent has given an initial answer it can be explored further by using one of the following types of probe: clarification; justification; relevance; exemplification; extension; accuracy; restatement; echo; nonverbal; consensus; and clearinghouse probes.

Clarification probes

These are used to elicit a clearer, more concisely phrased response, in situations where the questioner is either confused or uncertain about the content or meaning of the initial responses. Since an important purpose here is to obtain more detail, they are also known as *informational probes* (Miles, 2013). Examples include:

- 'What exactly do you mean?'
- 'Could you explain that to me again?'

As noted by Stewart *et al.* (2005), this type of clarifying question is 'motivated by a need to understand more clearly' (pp. 167–168). In the medical context, Tallman *et al.* (2007) found that doctors who used this type of probing question in order to understand the patient's situation fully received higher ratings of patient satisfaction.

Justification probes

These require respondents to explain and expand upon initial responses by giving an explanation or reason for what they have said, e.g.:

- 'Why do you say that?'
- 'How did you reach that conclusion?'

However, care must to be taken when using this type of question, which requests that the respondent further accounts for his or her initial response, so that it is not interpreted as an accusation, criticism or challenge by the interlocutor (Bolden and Robinson, 2011).

Relevance probes

These give respondents an opportunity to reassess the appropriateness of a response and/or make its relevance to the main topic under consideration more obvious. This enables the inquirer to ascertain which relationships are being made between objects, people or events, and in addition encourages the respondent to reflect on the validity of these. Relevance probes include:

- 'How does this relate to your home background?'
- 'Is this relevant to what we discussed earlier?'

Exemplification probes

These require respondents to provide concrete or specific instances of what they mean by what may, at first, appear to be a rather vague statement. Asking for an example to illustrate a general comment often helps to clarify the precise nature of the point being made. Included here are questions such as:

- 'Could you give me an instance of that?'
- 'Where have you shown leadership qualities in the past?'

Extension probes

These are used to encourage a respondent to expand upon an initial answer by providing further information pertinent to the topic under discussion. In classroom research these have been termed *uptake questions*, in that the teacher uses the pupil's answer in the follow-up question (Hardman, 2011). An extension question is best employed in situations where it is felt that the interlocutor should be able to make further responses that will facilitate the development of the discussion. Examples include:

- 'That's interesting, tell me more'.
- 'Is there anything else that you can remember about it?'

The simple, brief form of this type of question ('And...?' 'So...?' 'Go on') is referred to as a *nudging probe* (Stewart and Cash, 2013).

Accuracy probes

These questions draw the respondent's attention to a possible error in fact that has been made. This offers the interlocutor the option to adjust or restructure the response where necessary. As they afford an opportunity for the person to think about what has just been said, they are also known as *reflective probes*. They are most useful in situations where either it is absolutely vital that the respondent is certain about the accuracy of responses (e.g. an eye witness being cross-examined in court), or where the questioner knows the correct answer and wishes to give the respondent a chance to reflect upon an initial response (e.g. a teacher questioning pupils). Accuracy probes include:

- 'Are you quite sure about that?'
- 'It definitely happened before 3.00 p.m.?'

Restatement probes

These are used to encourage a respondent to give an adequate answer, following either an unrelated response or no answer at all to an initial question. This form of probe is also known as *prompting*. Depending upon the hypothesised cause of the respondent's failure, the questioner may prompt in different ways. If it is thought that the person did not hear the initial question correctly, it can simply be restated. If it is thought that the person did not understand the initial phrasing of the question, it may be rephrased either in parallel fashion, or at a simpler level. It may, however, be deemed necessary to prompt the respondent either by reviewing information previously covered (e.g. 'You remember what we talked about last week') or by giving a clue which will help to focus attention in the right direction. An example of this latter type of prompt is included in the following excerpt from a radio 'phone-in' quiz:

> *Q:* With what country would you associate pasta?
> *A:* Spain.
> *Q:* No, you might drink some Chianti with the pasta [prompt].
> *A:* Yes, of course, Italy.

Echo probes

These are so called because they are questions that 'echo' the words used by the respondent in the initial response, by repeating these in the follow-up probe (Gazdik, 2011). They are often employed in everyday interaction, but if over-used they are counter-productive, since, if every answer is parroted back, the interlocutor will soon become very aware of this and, in all probability, stop responding. As cautioned by (Bernard, 2006, p. 219), 'If you use the echo probe too often, though, you'll hear an exasperated informant asking, "Why do you keep repeating what I just said?"'. Examples of echo probes are included in the following:

> *A:* After the meal he became very romantic, and told me that he loved me.
> *Q:* He told you that he loved you?
> *A:* Yes, and then he took my hand and asked me to marry him.
> *Q:* He asked you to *marry* him?

Nonverbal probes

Also known as *silence probes* (Miles, 2013), these are nonverbal behaviours employed in such a manner as to indicate to the respondent a desire for further information (Clark, 2012). Included here is the use of appropriate paralanguage to accompany expressions such as 'Oh?!', or 'Never?!' together with inquisitive nonverbal behaviours (e.g. raising or lowering of eyebrows, sideways tilt of the head and eye contact). An attentive pause following an initial response can be used as a silent probe, indicating a desire for further responses. Indeed, interviewer pauses can put pressure on interviewees to respond in order to fill the silence.

Consensus probes

These give an opportunity for a group to pause in a discussion and for individuals to express their agreement or disagreement with an initial response. Asking consensus questions is a useful technique for a group leader to employ in order to gauge the extent of support within the group for any proposed idea or line of action. By asking, 'Does everyone agree with that?' or 'Is there anyone not happy with that?' the level of group consensus can be evaluated.

Clearinghouse probes

The purpose of this type of probe was described by Stewart (2009, p. 191): 'a *clearinghouse* probe is designed to make sure all important information has been covered'. These are very open questions that allow respondents to answer as they wish and provide any remaining information not yet covered (Miles, 2013). Stewart and Cash (2013) recommended the use of clearinghouse probes at the end of interviews. For example, during the closing stage of a selection interview the interviewer may ask the candidate, 'Is there anything we haven't asked you that you would like to have been asked, or anything you would like to add before we finish?'

Probes must be used skilfully, and as a result of ineptitude or faulty listening by the questioner this is not always the case. The ability to probe effectively is at the core of effective questioning. Fowler and Mangione (1990) illustrated how probing is one of the most difficult techniques for interviewers to acquire, while Millar *et al.* (1992, p. 131) noted that: 'Novice interviewers often find that they have obtained a wealth of superficial information because they have failed to explore interviewee responses in any depth'. In one study of groups, Hawkins and Power (1999) found that females used more probing questions than males. They speculated that this is because women value connection and co-operation more than men. Males may be more sensitive to what they see as 'intrusions' into their personal and private life. Indeed, Millar and Gallagher (2000) illustrated how some interviewees may resent interviewers who probe too deeply, especially about sensitive topics, since they then feel an increase in vulnerability and a need to defend themselves. Likewise, Egan (2014) underscored the importance of sensitivity when using probing questions in a helping context, and recommended they be employed as 'gentle nudges' to help keep the interviewee focused, rather than as a way of extorting information from reluctant clients. Probes therefore must be used with care. When skilfully employed they invite elaboration of arguments, sharing of information and opinions, and result in increased participation.

One interesting aspect here is what is known as the *probing effect*. This refers to the fact that a respondent who is probed is rated as being more honest, both by the questioner and by observers, as compared to someone who is not probed. This unusual finding has been well corroborated across a range of conditions and contexts (Levine and McCornack, 2001). There is no consensus about why this probing effect should occur. One explanation is that probing produces in respondents a heightened state of awareness, as they realise they are under scrutiny. As a result, they carefully monitor and adapt their verbal and nonverbal behaviours to make these appear more truthful, and thereby convey a greater impression of honesty. The probing effect has implications across many situations, not least for lawyers who have to make decisions about the questioning of individuals in the courtroom (Heller, 2006).

Rhetorical questions

These do not expect a response, either because the speaker intends to answer the question, or because the question is equivalent to a statement (as in, 'Who would not wish their children well?' to mean, 'Everyone wishes their children well'), or is used as a rebuke which does not anticipate a response (as in, 'How could you?'). In the former case, rhetorical questions are often used by public speakers to stimulate interest in their presentation by encouraging the audience to 'think things through' with them. With large audiences, interactive questions are usually not appropriate since only a few people would be given a chance to answer, and the rest may have difficulty in hearing their responses. For this reason, lecturers, politicians and other individuals, when addressing large groups, often employ rhetorical questions. As Turk (1985, p. 75) put it: 'Asking questions is the best way to promote thought . . . We are so conditioned to provide answers to sentences in question form, that our minds are subconsciously aroused towards an answer, even if we remain silent'. In this way, rhetorical questions have been shown to impact upon the type of thinking engaged in by listeners (Whaley and Wagner, 2000). Charismatic leaders in the business setting use rhetorical questions during meetings with staff as a way of encouraging their engagement and motivation (Antonakis *et al.*, 2012).

Multiple questions

These are two or more questions phrased as one (e.g. 'When and where will we meet up and how will we get there?'). In terms of their linguistic structure being either mono-clausal or bi-clausal and the question word being co-ordinated or not, eight types of multiple question structures have been identified (see Gazdik, 2011). While a multiple question may contain a number of questions of the same type, quite often it comprises an open question followed by a closed one to narrow the focus (e.g. 'How is your project progressing? Did you get all of the data collected?'). Multiple questions may be useful where time is limited and it is important to get some answer from a respondent. For this reason they are often used by radio and television interviewers who have a given (often brief) period of time in which to conduct the interview, and so just getting the interviewee to respond is often the priority. In most situations, however, they are wasteful – especially where the questions subsumed within the multiple question are unrelated. In the clinical interview setting, Morrison (2008, p. 57) referred to these as double questions and noted that they 'may seem efficient but they are often confusing. The patient may respond to one part of the question and ignore the other without you realising it.' In essence, multiple questions are liable to confuse the respondent, and/or the responses given may confuse the questioner, who may be unclear exactly which question has been answered. They can also cause frustration.

In an early classroom study, Wright and Nuthall (1970) found that the tendency on the part of a teacher to ask one question at a time was positively related to pupil achievement, whereas the tendency to ask more than one question at a time was negatively related to achievement. In the field of health, Dickson *et al.* (1997) showed how patients have difficulties in formulating a reply when asked multiple questions. They serve to pressurise and confuse the patient and they also decrease the probability of receiving accurate information.

RELATED ASPECTS OF QUESTIONING

Effective communicators are concerned with how they ask questions. In particular, they pay attention to the following issues.

Structuring

In certain social situations where a large number of questions will be used, it is useful to structure the interaction in such a way as to indicate what questions are likely to be asked, and why it is necessary to ask them (e.g. 'In order to help me advise you about possible future jobs I would like to find out about your qualifications, experience and interests. If I could begin with your qualifications…'). By structuring the interaction in this way, the respondent knows why the questions are required, and what type of questions to expect. Once the interlocutor is aware of the immediate goals of the questioner, and recognises these as acceptable, the interaction will flow more smoothly (see the skill of set induction in Chapter 10 for a fuller discussion of this type of structuring).

Pausing

The function of pausing as a form of silent probe has already been mentioned. However, as well as pausing after receiving a response, pauses both before and after asking a question can be advantageous. By pausing before asking a question, the attention of the listener can be stimulated and the question given greater impact. For example, Margutti (2006) found that, in the classroom setting, a long pause by the teacher was often the signal to pupils that a new question-and-answer sequence was about to begin, whereas during questioning-and-answer sequences teachers tended to use very brief 'micropauses'. By pausing after asking a question, the interlocutor is given the distinct impression of being expected to provide some form of response. The use of pauses after asking a question also overcomes the possibility of multiple questions. Finally, pausing after a respondent gives an initial answer encourages the person to continue talking.

The importance of pausing was investigated in early studies by Rowe (1969, 1974a, b). She found that, when teachers increased the average 'wait time' after pupil responses, the length of these responses increased from 7 words when the pause was 1 second to 28 words when the pause was 3 seconds. Other positive benefits were that:

- the teacher tended to ask more process questions
- pupils asked more questions
- those pupils who did not tend to say much started talking and produced novel ideas.

The benefits of teacher pauses of some 3 seconds were confirmed by Tobin (1987). Yet there is evidence to indicate that the average teacher pauses following a teacher question and a pupil response are 1.26 seconds and 0.55 seconds, respectively (Swift et al., 1988). The disadvantages of such short wait times were highlighted by Dillon (1990, p. 221) who, in a review of research into the benefits of pausing across a range of professional contexts, concluded that pauses need to be a minimum of 3 seconds' duration in order 'to enhance the partner's participation and cognition'.

Distribution

In group contexts, leaders should try to involve as many members as possible in the discussion (see Chapter 14 for more information on group leadership).

One method whereby this can be achieved is by distributing questions to all members, so that everyone's point of view is heard. This is a useful technique, especially with individuals who may be reluctant to express their views unless given a specific invitation. The redirection of a question from one group member to another may be of particular value in achieving a discrete distribution of questions, without exerting undue pressure, or embarrassing any individual.

Distribution has also been found to be important in the medical context. For example, in paediatric consultations, research has shown that the recipient of the initial physician question determines the extent to which the child is likely to participate in the encounter (Stivers, 2001). When this is addressed directly to the child (e.g. 'Well, Patricia, and how can I help you today?') rather than to the parent ('Well, Mrs Jones, and how is Patricia today?'), the child is likely to become a more active participant. Stivers and Majid (2007) extended this research to examine factors associated with the direction of questions to children rather than parents. They found that, in the US context, paediatricians were less likely to direct questions to Black or Latino children of low-education parents as compared to their White peers. Professionals therefore need to be aware of possible implicit biases in their distribution of questions. In another related study, Stivers (2012) found that children were more likely to respond to questions when the doctor directed social (nontask-related) questions to them early in the consultation, employed yes–no questions and used direct eye contact with the child when asking a question.

Responses

Jacobs and Coghlan (2005) illustrated how the study of questioning has taken primacy over the process of answering. Few theories of communication incorporate an explicit model of answering. Yet, just as there is a wide variation in types of questions that can be asked, so too is there a broad range of possible responses (Bolden, 2009). As shown by Hayashi (2009, p. 2122), 'Answering a question is not a simple matter of providing the information requested by the questioner...respondents to questions have at their disposal a variety of ways to display their stance toward the question'. Respondents can display overt or covert resistance to answering questions for a variety of reasons (Miles, 2013). Responses to questions have been divided into *preferred*, where the reply fits with the expectations of the question, and *dispreferred*, where the answer runs contrary to these expectations (Raymond, 2003). The latter form is often communicated in subtle ways. For example, prefacing the answer to a question by 'Oh' can indicate that the question is perceived to be inapposite, unexpected or unwarranted. It may also signify that this is not a topic the respondent wishes to discuss at any length (Heritage, 1998). However, there is one context where the opposite is the case. This is in relation to the HAY ('How are you?') question, used as part of the greeting ritual, where no depth of reply is expected (see Chapter 10 for further discussion of the HAY question). Here, an Oh-prefaced response (e.g. 'Oh, fine') tends to indicate that in fact the interlocutor does not really feel fine and wishes to discuss this further.

Dillon (1990) identified a large number of possible answers to questions, the main types of which can be summarised as follows:

1 *Silence.* The respondent may choose to say nothing.
2 *Overt refusal to answer,* e.g. 'I'd rather not say'.
3 *Unconnected response.* The interlocutor may change the topic completely.
4 *Humour.* For example, to the question 'How old are you?' the respondent may reply 'Not as old as I feel'.
5 *Lying.* The respondent may simply give a false answer.
6 *Stalling.* Again, to the question 'How old are you?' the person may reply 'How old do you think I am?' Answering a question with a question is a classic stalling technique.
7 *Evading.* Bull (2003, 2011) has identified techniques used by politicians to evade having to answer questions directly. These include questioning the question, attacking the interviewer or stating that the question has already been answered.
8 *Selective ambiguity.* Thus, to the question about age, the interlocutor may reply, 'Don't worry, I'll finish the marathon OK'. In other words, the respondent pretends to recognise the 'real' question, and answers it.
9 *Withholding and concealing.* In this instance, people attempt to avoid disclosing information that may be damaging to them or those close to them. This is a problem commonly faced by investigators (criminal, insurance, etc.), but is also applicable to those professionals who have to deal with sensitive or taboo issues such as child abuse, incest, drug abuse, and so on.
10 *Distortion.* Respondents in many instances give the answers that they feel are socially desirable, often without consciously realising they are doing so. Thus in survey interviews, subjects tend to over-estimate behaviours such as voting, reading books and giving to charity, and under-estimate illnesses, financial status, illegal behaviour and money spent on gambling (Wood and Williams, 2007).
11 *Direct honest response.* Here, the person gives a direct, truthful answer to the question.

OVERVIEW

Although, at first sight, questioning would seem to be a straightforward interpersonal skill, upon further examination it can be seen that, in fact, it is more complex. Most of us employ a barrage of questions in everyday parlance without giving them a great deal of thought, but becoming a skilled questioner requires much more effort. As aptly summarised by Morgan and Saxton (2006, p. 12): 'We all know how to ask questions – after all, we have been doing it since we could talk – but as you likely realize, becoming an *effective* questioner is hard. It takes time and vigilance.'

As shown in this chapter, there is a large variety of different types of question that can be asked in any given situation, and the answers received are markedly affected by both the wording and the type of question asked. However, no hard-and-fast rules about which type of question to use in particular social encounters exist, since much more situation-specific research is needed in order to investigate the effects of aspects such as the nature of the respondent and the effects of the social context. Nevertheless, the categorisations of questions contained in this chapter provide a useful template for the analysis of the effects of questions in social interaction. Furthermore, the examples given, and the research reviewed, provide the reader with insight into the different modes of usage, and the accompanying effects, of different types of question.

It is clear that questions are powerful tools for finding out about others. However, they can also constitute a useful and subtle method for regulating the participation levels of respondents, maintaining control of the conversation, getting the answers we want and encouraging conformity. In other words, questions need to be used skilfully. There is a great deal of truth in the advice given by Voltaire that we should 'Judge a man not by his answers but by his questions'.

Chapter 6

Showing understanding for others: the skill of reflecting

INTRODUCTION

AS WITH THE SKILL of questioning, reviewed in the previous chapter, the skill of reflecting is a way of encouraging partici-pation and gaining information. However, the two skills differ in a number of important respects. To use a motoring analogy, when using questions the interviewer is driving the interaction and the inter-viewee is the passenger, whereas the use of reflections encourages the interviewee to become the driver with the interviewer as a fellow traveller. Reflecting involves responding to the other person in a non-directive manner, while at the same time conveying interest, under-standing and engagement. Although some inconsistencies have been identified among the definitions presented in the literature (Dickson, 2006), reflections can be defined as statements, in the interviewer's own words, that encapsulate and re-present the essence of the inter-viewee's previous message. As shown in Figure 6.1, when the empha-sis is exclusively upon reflecting back the factual component, this is termed 'paraphrasing' (or 'reflection of content'); where it is solely upon the affective or emotional component it is 'reflection of feeling'; and where both facts and feelings are involved it is referred to as 'reflection'. Some theorists make a further distinction between *sim-ple reflections*, which focus upon what the interlocutor has just said, and *complex reflections*, which go beyond this to include some per-tinent aspects of earlier interviewee responses beyond the previous speech turn (Moyers *et al.*, 2003; Forrester *et al.*, 2008).

Carl Rogers, the founder of person-centred counselling (Rogers, 1980, 1991), is commonly credited with coining the term, although the technique is, of course, used in other approaches to counselling (see Strong, 2006; Ivey *et al.*, 2014) and in a variety of settings that have nothing to do with counselling. For example, Rautalinko and Lisper (2004) reported positive results from a training programme

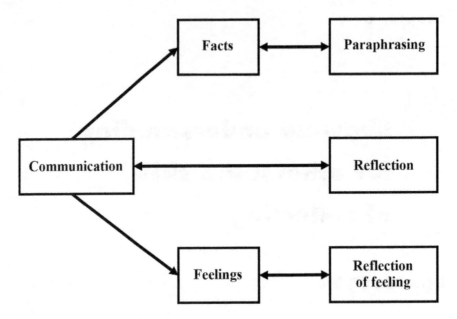

Figure 6.1 Types of reflection.

designed to improve the reflective listening of insurance company personnel during conversations with clients. The importance of the skill of reflecting has also been highlighted in the contexts of business (Ding, 2006), engineering (Whitcomb and Whitcomb, 2013), social work (Koprowska, 2014), therapy (Corey, 2005), medicine (Roter and Hall, 2006), nursing (Kagee, 2013) and interviewing (Stewart and Cash, 2013).

STYLES OF INTERACTING

Before examining reflecting in detail, it is useful to consider the contrasting styles that people can adopt when dealing with others. While different models accounting for style can be found, they all share the premise that there are recurring patterns in a person's behaviour that are evident to others during interaction (Snavely and McNeil, 2008). Style, in this sense, refers to the characteristic manner in which the content of communication is delivered (Norton, 1983; Dinsbach *et al.*, 2007; de Vries *et al.*, 2013) or, more generally, how someone handles an interpersonal episode. It refers to *how* what is done is done. Cameron (2000) emphasised its expressive function in creating a particular 'aesthetic' presence for the other. As such, the importance of paying attention to communication style in business interactions has been stressed (Kenman, 2007). Conversational style includes aspects such as degree of formality (Mayer *et al.*, 2004), assumed dominance (Martin and Gayle, 2004), as well as elaboration and directness (Adler *et al.*, 2013b).

The latter characteristic, directness, is most relevant here. Directness involves the degree of explicit influence and control exercised or attempted and, correspondingly, the extent to which the conversational partner is constrained in responding (DeVito, 2016). The interviewer following a direct style will determine the form, content and pace of the encounter. By contrast, when employing an indirect style the interviewer encourages the interviewee to decide upon these features of the discussion. According to Benjamin (2001), a direct style is typified by the use of interviewer leads, while an indirect style is characterised by responses. Although both terms are difficult to define unambiguously, responding has to do with reacting to the thoughts and feelings of interviewees, exploring their worlds and keeping them at the centre of things. On the other hand, the interviewer who leads tends to replace the interviewee on centre stage and become the dominant feature in the interaction. Benjamin (2001, p. 206) explained it as follows: 'When leading, I make use of my own life space; when responding, I tend more to utilize the life space of the client. Responses keep the client at the center of things; leads make the interviewer central.'

Reflections are accordingly a type of response. As defined by Forrester *et al.* (2008, p. 43), 'A reflection is a hypothesis about what the client means or feels expressed as a statement'. When reflecting, the interviewer strives to capture the significant message in the respondent's previous contribution and re-presents this understanding. This has been described as the interviewer 'mirroring back' to interviewees what they have just said. As noted earlier, reflections can be contrasted with questions, which are often used to lead the conversation. It is useful, at this point, to consider some examples. Read the two short fictional scenarios in Boxes 6.1 and 6.2.

Box 6.1 Strangers on a train: scene I

Karen is a first-year student travelling home by train for the weekend. During the journey she falls into conversation at different times with two fellow passengers, both of whom are strangers to her. The first conversation is with Anna and this is how it progresses:

Anna:	'Good book, is it?'
Karen:	'Sorry?'
Anna:	'That book you're reading…Good, is it?'
Karen:	'No, not really.'
Anna:	'Why are you reading it then?'
Karen:	'I have to, in a way. It's part of my course.'
Anna:	'Oh…are you a student?'
Karen:	'Yes…at the university.'
Anna:	'What are you studying?'
Karen:	'Law…and I must have this book finished before my tutorial next week.'
Anna:	'Enjoy it, do you…university?'
Karen:	'I suppose so, in a way.'
Anna:	'What do you intend to do then…when you finish?'
Karen:	'I don't really know…'

Box 6.2 Strangers on a train: scene II

After Anna leaves the train, Fay enters the carriage and joins Karen. Let us now eavesdrop on their conversation:

Fay:	'You're not really reading it, are you?'
Karen:	'Pardon?'
Fay:	'The book…you haven't turned a page in the last 10 minutes.'
Karen (smiling):	'No, I suppose I haven't. I need to get through it though, but I keep drifting away.'
Fay:	'It doesn't really hold your interest.'
Karen:	'No, not really. I wouldn't bother with it, to be honest, but I have to have it read for a tutorial. I'm at the university.'
Fay (smiling):	'It's a labour of labour then, rather than a labour of love.'
Karen:	'I should say! I don't enjoy it at all…Indeed, I'm getting to like the whole course less and less…'
Fay:	'So it's not just the book, it's the whole programme as well.'
Karen:	'Yes, in a way…although the course itself isn't really bad…some of it is pretty good, in fact, and the lecturers are fine. It's me, I suppose. You see, I wanted to do English rather than Law…but my parents talked me out of it.'
Fay:	'So the course is OK, as such, it's just that, had it been left to you, you would have chosen a different one.'
Karen:	'Oh, they had my best interests at heart, of course, my parents. They always do, don't they? They believed that my job prospects would have been limited with a degree in English. And they give me a really generous allowance…but I'm beginning to feel that I'm wasting my time…and their money. They would be so disappointed, though, if I told them I was quitting my legal studies…'

These two conversations with Karen differ markedly in the approaches adopted by Anna and Fay, respectively. In the first situation (Box 6.1), Anna probes for mainly factual information to do with Karen's book, her course and what she intends to do after university. Anna and her agenda are very much the dominating features of the conversation with Karen doing little more than passively acting as the information source. Questioning is the tactic used exclusively to direct the interchange from one topic to the next, and each question does little to develop the previous response. There is minimal encouragement for Karen to furnish information other than what is directly relevant to Anna's line of enquiry. By contrast, the second exchange (Box 6.2) centres very much upon Karen and the difficulties she is experiencing, with Fay staying, conversationally, much more in the background. Rather than directly leading Karen into areas that are not of her choosing, Fay guides the conversation in ways that facilitate Karen's discussion of personal issues that seem important for her to ventilate. Unlike the first exchange, here there are no questions asked by Fay, apart from her opening query. Rather, her interjections take the form of statements – these statements are reflections.

Apart from contributing examples of the technique of reflecting, the two contrasting conversational excerpts serve to make two additional points. The first is that it is not always necessary to ask questions to get in-depth information from others. The second, more general, point is that verbal styles adopted during interaction can differ markedly. The particular style adopted by an interviewer is, in part, dependent upon the type of interview being conducted (Keats, 2000). A more direct, questioning style is more appropriate where:

- the interviewee has accepted the interviewer's role as interrogator;
- the information required is, basically, factual in nature;
- the amount of time to be devoted to the interview is limited;
- a long-term relationship need not be established;
- the information is directly for the benefit of the interviewer.

In contrast, a more indirect, responsive style is typically used to best advantage when:

- the interviewee is the participant who stands to gain from the encounter;
- exchanges have a significant affective dimension;
- the information is confused, fragmented and hazy – due, perhaps, to the fact that it involves a problem never fully thought through before;
- it is important to build a harmonious, egalitarian relationship with the interviewee.

Despite this distinction it would be inappropriate to assume that a more direct style of operating is never used under the latter set of conditions or that questions should not form part of the range of skills employed. Equally it would be mistaken to conclude that in the former circumstances a reflective statement should never be contemplated. Indeed, counsellors vary in the directness of their style depending upon the particular school of counselling to which they subscribe so that some are likely to be more direct than others across a range of contexts. Nevertheless, as a generality, the above distinction holds.

Some of the disadvantages of relying on questions have been pointed out in counselling (Inskipp, 2006; Egan, 2014), teaching (Dickson and Hargie, 2006; Smith *et al.*, 2006) and interviewing (Hartley, 1999; Stewart and Cash, 2013). Questions can:

- socialise the interviewee to speak only in response, and just to reveal information directly requested;
- encourage the interviewee to let the interviewer take complete responsibility for the interaction, and for finding a satisfactory solution to the problems or difficulties presented by the interviewee;

- inhibit the development of a warm, understanding relationship, conducive to the exploration of important, but perhaps intimate and, for the interviewee, potentially embarrassing details;
- direct the conversation in ways that are shaped by the interviewer's underlying assumptions.

Despite these disadvantages many professionals rely upon a predominantly questioning style (see Chapter 5). For example, in one study of interviewing skills employed by social workers, the number of questions used outnumbered reflections by a ratio of more than 15 to 1 (Forrester *et al.*, 2008).

FACTUAL AND AFFECTIVE COMMUNICATION

Reflecting has been regarded by some theorists as a unitary phenomenon and labelled accordingly, while others have conceived of it as encompassing a varying number of related processes, including *reflection of content* (Manthei, 1997), *reflecting experience* (Brammer and MacDonald, 2003), *reflection of meaning* (Freshwater, 2003; Ivey *et al.*, 2014) and *restatement* (Hill, 2014). Some have conceptualised reflection as a form of *dialogic practice* through which interviewer and interviewee co-construct meaning (Strong, 2006). However, the most commonly cited distinction is between *reflection of feeling* and *paraphrasing* (Dickson, 2006). Most of the messages that we send and receive provide different types of information. One type of information is basically *factual* or *cognitive*, concerning things, places, people, happenings, and so on. A second is predominantly *feeling-based* or *affective*, concerning our emotional states or attitudinal reactions to ourselves, to others or to our environment. Almost all statements have two types of message: a content message that concentrates on the subject matter under discussion, and a relational message that focuses upon how the parties feel about one another (Adler *et al.*, 2013b).

Some messages are predominantly factual, others essentially affective. An example of the former would be, 'It's 4.30 p.m.', in response to a request for the correct time. An example of the latter would be 'Oh no!' uttered by someone who has just been informed of a tragic event. This is obviously an expression of shocked grief, rather than a challenging of the fact that the event occurred, and is therefore fundamentally affective. The majority of messages, however, contain elements of both types of information. Consider the following statement:

> Mornings could not come soon enough for me, that summer. I was always up well before the others. I could scarcely wait for them to rise and the fun to begin. Breakfast was eaten swiftly and we ran to the beach. Each day seemed to hold endlessly exciting possibilities. The time just flew past.

The factual parts of the message are that the person had a daily routine of getting up early, waiting for the others, grabbing some breakfast and heading for the beach. The affective part conveys the sense of pleasure, happiness, excited anticipation and general *joie de vivre* of that period.

The emotive component of a message can take three basic forms:

1   *Explicitly stated.* Here the feeling aspect is directly mentioned in the verbal content. For example, 'I was ecstatic'.
2   *Implicitly mentioned.* In this case feelings are not directly stated but rather the affective information is implicitly contained in what is said. Egan (2014) distinguished between *discussed* and *expressed* feelings and emphasised that emotional experience that is expressed 'is part of the message and needs to be identified and understood' (p. 104). Thus, take someone who has recently suffered loss, and says listlessly, 'Most days I just don't even get up...I don't have the energy to do anything. I can't concentrate...not even think straight. I've lost all interest – everything just seems so pointless. I keep having these really black thoughts...' Here, depression, while not explicitly mentioned, is a palpable emotional message carried by the words. In other instances, though, the implicit emotional message 'written between the lines' may be less clear.
3   *Inferred.* The affective component of a message can be inferred from the manner in which the verbal content is delivered – from the nonverbal and paralinguistic accompaniments. However, it can be difficult to decode affect accurately when it has not been explicitly stated and, in these cases, care is recommended (Jones, 2005).

PURPOSES OF REFLECTING

Reflecting serves a number of purposes (Brammer and MacDonald, 2003; Dickson, 2006; Hill, 2014). Some of these were summarised by Forrester *et al.* (2008, p. 43): 'They are central to the expression of accurate empathy; they encourage deeper exploration of emotional content; and they allow the worker or counsellor sensitively to manage the interview, e.g. by summarizing one stage and opening up another'. The overall goals served by reflecting are presented in Box 6.3. While a number of these are common to both paraphrasing and reflection of feeling, some are obviously more relevant to one than the other.

Box 6.3 Purposes of reflecting

The main goals served by the skill of reflecting are to:

1   demonstrate interest in and involvement with the other person
2   display close attention to what is being communicated
3   show that you are trying to understand fully what the other is saying
4   check your perceptions and ensure accuracy of understanding
5   facilitate the other person's comprehension of issues involved and clarity of thinking on these matters

(continued)

(continued)

6   focus attention upon particular aspects and encourage further exploration
7   communicate a deep concern for what the other person considers to be important
8   place the major emphasis upon the interviewee, rather than the interviewer
9   indicate that it is acceptable for the other person to have and express feelings in this situation and so facilitate the person's ventilation
10 allow the other person to 'own' feelings expressed
11 enable the other person to realise that feelings can be an important cause of behaviour
12 help the other person to scrutinise underlying reasons and motives
13 operate from within the other's frame of reference and demonstrate empathy

PARAPHRASING

Paraphrasing can be defined as the process of feeding back to another, in your own words, the essential factual part of the other's message. The emphasis here is upon content (events, thoughts, ideas, descriptions, etc.) rather than affect. Paraphrasing is most appropriate when the message received carries little emotion to be dealt with, or when it may be inappropriately premature to begin to explore the affective undertow in depth and so initially dealing with the facts is a safer option (Cormier *et al.*, 2008; Egan, 2014). Paraphrases therefore have three important pre-requisites.

1   The focus is primarily upon the factual information received; the word 'primarily' is used purposefully, however, since it is often difficult to eliminate affective aspects entirely.
2   Paraphrases do not simply involve repeating what has just been said. One type of probing technique, echoing, involves the straight repetition of the interviewee's previous statement, or a part of it (see Chapter 5). Such restatement, however, does not constitute a paraphrase. If, when paraphrasing, the interviewer continually repeats the interviewee's words it can quickly lead to the latter becoming frustrated (Blando, 2011). As aptly expressed by Inskipp (2006, p. 80) 'Paraphrasing is not parroting'. Instead, interviewers should respond using their own terms, while not violating or misrepresenting the original meaning (Wood, 2014).
3   They should be reformulations of the essence of the interlocutor's previous message (Koprowska, 2014). This requires the speaker to identify the core of the statement embedded in the communication. The key question to consider is, 'What is this person really trying to communicate?' It should, therefore, not be assumed that the paraphrase must encompass everything that has just been said, some of which may well be tangential.

In the conversation between Rio and Sahla in Box 6.4, all of Sahla's responses are paraphrases. These examples of paraphrasing manifest, 'in action', the defining characteristics of the skill, and help to illustrate some of its advantages. By demonstrating that she can accurately reproduce the fundamentally important parts of what Rio has just said, Sahla demonstrates that she:

- is attending single-mindedly
- recognises that it is important to understand fully what Rio is striving to relate, hence conveying respect
- has accurately 'tuned in' to Rio's narrative.

By so doing, Rio is also made aware of the fact that Sahla is interested in his present difficulty and is prepared to become involved in helping him to explore it further. According to Hill (2014), responding with this type of reflective statement, in

---

Box 6.4 Rio, Rebecca and the party that went wrong

Rio: 'I'm not sure whether or not to phone Rebecca, after what happened at the party on Saturday night...and the row, and that.'

Sahla: 'You had an argument with Rebecca at the weekend?'

Rio: 'Yes. I didn't know Vicky would be there. There's nothing between Vicky and me now, but you know the way she always comes on strong...trying to make other girls jealous?'

Sahla: 'Ah, so Rebecca thought that you and Vicky had something going on.'

Rio: 'Yes, and Rebecca started to talk to Dirk and one thing led to another. Dirk didn't know that we were together...and the next thing they were getting cozy on the sofa. Dirk couldn't believe his luck! She only did it to get back at me, though.'

Sahla: 'Right, Rebecca didn't really fancy Dirk, she was simply retaliating, as she saw it ...'

Rio: 'Yeah. At the time though, I didn't realise what was going on. Dirk and I are mates and I thought he was trying to make a move on my girl. So I grabbed him by the shirt and dragged him out of the chair...He thought I had gone mad. So he hit me and I hit him...Mind you, we were both fairly drunk as well.'

Sahla: 'You thought that Dirk was taking liberties, so you initiated a drunken row.'

Rio: 'Yeah...when I think of it now, I feel so stupid...so embarrassed... neither Rebecca nor Dirk has been in touch since. If I phone they might ring off, but the longer I leave it, the worse it could get. On the other hand, I suppose, waiting until the weekend could give everyone a chance to simmer down and forget it.'

Sahla: 'So, you are keen to mend fences with Rebecca and Dirk but are unsure when is best to make a start.'

---

a formal helping setting, affords clients the opportunity to evaluate what they are thinking and saying and contemplate their thoughts and feelings at a deeper level.

One of the foremost uses of paraphrasing is to let clients know they are being listened to (Cormier *et al.*, 2008). As summarised by Weger *et al.* (2014, p. 39), 'Reflecting a speaker's message through paraphrasing demonstrates that the listener has understood what the speaker is trying to communicate, thereby confirming the speaker's experience as valid and significant'. Indeed, Orbe and Bruess (2005, p. 166) described a 'great listener' as someone who is capable of paraphrasing without changing the meaning of what has just been said. From the interviewer's point of view, the subsequent reaction of the interviewee to the paraphrase offered also confirms (assuming it is accurate) that the interviewer is on the proper 'wavelength'. Indeed, paraphrases are often used for this very purpose – as a check on accurate understanding. Broadcast journalists employ this skill frequently when interviewing – they paraphrase the interviewee's responses to clarify and check the precise meaning of these for both parties immediately involved, and also for the listeners. Likewise, in the classroom, teachers frequently paraphrase pupil contributions. By so doing they not only establish that they have fully understood what was said, but also clarify the information provided for the rest of the class. Again, it is not uncommon to hear someone who has just received directions to get to a particular place paraphrase back what was told, e.g. 'So I go to the end of the road, turn right, second on the left, and then right again'. In this case, paraphrasing serves the dual purpose of checking accuracy and promoting the memorisation of the information.

By encapsulating, and unobtrusively presenting to the interviewee, in a clear and unambiguous manner, a key facet of their previous communication, the speaker also gently guides and encourages the continuation of this theme and the exploration of it in greater depth. Interviewees' thoughts, especially when dealing with an apparently intractable problem, are often inchoate and ambiguous. An accurate paraphrase, by condensing and crystallising what has been said, can often help the interviewee to see more clearly the exigencies of the predicament (Lindon and Lindon, 2007). Paraphrasing also enables interviewers to keep interviewees and their concerns front stage, by responding and guiding rather than leading and directing. It indicates that interviewers, rather than imposing their own agenda, are actively trying to make sense of what is being heard from within the interviewee's frame of reference (Hough, 2006). In the sports context, it has often been said that a good referee is one who controls the game and lets it flow, while remaining in the background. In many situations the same holds true for a good interviewer. Using Benjamin's (2001) terminology, the interviewer uses the interviewee's life space rather than that of the interviewer. By keeping the focus upon those issues which the interviewee wants to ventilate, the interviewer also says, metaphorically, that their importance is acknowledged.

REFLECTION OF FEELING

Reflection of feeling can be defined as the process of feeding back, in your own words, the essence of the feelings expressed in the other person's previous communication. The similarity between this definition and that of paraphrasing will be noted and many of the features of the latter, outlined above, are applicable. The major difference between the two definitions is, of course, the concern with affective matters peculiar to reflection of feeling, including those messages conveyed nonverbally (Inskipp, 2006). As expressed by Nelson-Jones (2014, p. 102), 'Reflecting feelings means responding to clients' music and not just to their words'. The most important steps in the use of the skill are regarded by Brammer and MacDonald (2003) to be:

- recognising the feeling being expressed
- labelling and describing this feeling clearly and accurately
- observing the reaction of the other
- evaluating the extent to which the reflection was helpful.

Thus, a necessary pre-requisite for the successful use of this skill is the ability to identify accurately, and label, the feelings being expressed by the interlocutor. Unless this initial procedure can be accomplished, the likelihood that the subsequent reflection of those feelings will achieve its desired purpose is greatly reduced.

A number of relevant distinctions to do with expressing feelings have been identified by Nelson-Jones (2014). He pointed out that feelings can be simple or complex, and that sometimes what comes across is a range of mixed emotions. For example, two common combinations of affect identified by Teyber (2006) are:

1   anger–sadness–shame
2   sadness–anger–guilt.

In the first, predominating anger may be a reaction to hurt, invoking sadness, with both combining to trigger shame. In the second, sadness is the primary emotion, connected to repressed anger, leading to guilt. In each case, the presenting feeling of anger or sadness is buttressed by a much more involved constellation of emotions and experiences, some of which are easier for the individual to recognise and discuss than others. This multi-dimensionality makes the task of identifying and reflecting feeling that much more demanding. Again, and with respect to the objects of feelings, they may be self-focused, directed towards the interviewer, or be vented on a third party, thing or event. Furthermore, feelings discussed may have been experienced in the past or be current in the here and now of the encounter. Concentrating upon the latter is referred to as immediacy (Egan, 2014). Present-tense reflections of here-and-now states create more powerful experiencing and can often be most useful.

Turning to inferred emotional states, some are more readily identifiable than others from nonverbal cues such as facial expressions (Ekman and O'Sullivan, 1991; Remland, 2009) and vocal features (Banse and Scherer, 1996). In an early series of experiments, Davitz (1964) had actors read verbally neutral sentences in such a way as to convey different emotions. Tapes of these were presented to judges for decoding. Fear and anger were most readily recognisable. In general, however, positive emotions are more easily discerned than unpleasant ones, and females tend to be more successful than males at recognising emotional cues (Kret and de Gelder, 2012). It is also possible to train individuals to improve their performance. As far as reflecting back feelings based solely upon nonverbal cues is concerned, though, Lindon and Lindon (2007) recommended a cautious approach. Until a certain level of familiarity and trust has been established, recipients may be made to feel embarrassingly transparent and quite vulnerable, if feelings are reflected prematurely. Thus, in his research into actual counsellor–client exchanges, Strong (2006) found that counsellors used such reflections later in the process, once rapport had been established.

While the terms 'feelings' and 'emotions' are sometimes used synonymously, feelings often refer to more subtle emotional or attitudinal states. For this reason they are typically more difficult to label accurately. It has been suggested that one cause of this difficulty is that some interviewers do not possess a sufficient repertoire of feeling terms, thereby making fine discrimination and identification problematic. Cormier *et al.* (2008) advocated that interviewers should have at their disposal a number of broad categories of feeling words. Each of these can be expressed at a low, moderate or intense level. For example, 'petrified' could accurately describe someone in intense fear; 'scared' if that feeling is more moderate; and 'frightened' if it is experienced at a lower level. Other examples of feeling continuums are given in Box 6.5. By initially determining the broad category and then the intensity level, subtle feelings can more easily be deciphered, thereby facilitating the process of reflecting them back. Feelings should be reflected at the appropriate level of intensity to demonstrate that the interviewer is on the same wavelength as, and fully in touch with, the interviewee (Van der Molen and Gramsbergen-Hoogland, 2005).

An excerpt from a helping interview is provided in Box 6.6. Compare the helper responses in this excerpt with the examples of paraphrases provided previously. Here, the interviewer's primary focus is upon exploration and

---

Box 6.5 Examples of continuum of feelings

Low	*Moderate*	*Intense*
Surprised	Shocked	Stunned
Happy	Delighted	Ecstatic
Annoyed	Angry	Furious
Like	Love	Adore
Unhappy	Sad	Depressed
Joy	Delight	Jubilation
Dislike	Hate	Despise
Interested	Absorbed	Enthralled
Ignored	Rejected	Abandoned

Box 6.6 Examples of reflecting feeling

Client: Well, my wife finally left. As you know, she had threatened this on and off for a while but I never dreamed she would actually walk out. But, to my amazement, she did. I can't believe it.

Helper: You are shocked.

Client: Yes. She was everything I ever wanted and, although she had that affair last year, I had begun to put that behind me.

Helper: You had started to move on.

Client: More or less. It was very hurtful at the time but I know I had been taking her for granted. I was working all hours, trying to earn as much money as I could – for us. I tried to change and pay her more attention and this is the thanks I get.

Helper: You are clearly very upset.

Client: Yeah. I don't know where I go from here. I still care for her but part of me is also very angry at what she has done. That's the thanks I get. I'm not sure that I even want her back.

Helper: You have mixed feelings. You have affection for her but there is also a sense of betrayal.

Client: Indeed. She was my first love but she has treated me terribly… (Client continues to discuss his situation)

---

understanding of the feelings being conveyed by the client. While these examples were drawn from a helping session, it should be realised that this skill has a much broader application. For instance, in the negotiating process the role of emotion in shaping proceedings is very important (Shapiro, 2000). Here, reflecting the feelings of the other side assists in the process of exploring their needs, building rapport and mutual respect and preventing a buildup of emotional negativity (Gray, 2003; Hargie *et al.*, 2004) (see Chapter 13 for further discussion of negotiation). Reflection of feeling is therefore appropriate across a range of social settings in promoting the examination of feelings, emotions and attitudes.

Reflection of feeling shares a number of features in common with the skill of paraphrasing. By responding in this way, attention to and interest in the other is demonstrated. It helps clients to feel understood, and to sense that both they and their concerns are important and respected. Burleson (2003) reviewed the beneficial effects on psychological, relational, physical and health outcomes of providing emotional support to those in distressed states; in a class of supportive response that encourages the further elaboration of difficult circumstances and associated feelings, he included 'reflections or restatements of the target's emotive expressions' (p. 566). Such messages are high in person-centredness, and, as Burleson (2008, p. 208) pointed out, messages that are high in person-centredness 'explicitly recognize and legitimize the other's feelings, help the other to articulate those feelings, elaborate reasons why those feelings might be felt, and assist the other to see how those feelings fit in a broader context'. In this way, reflecting back the central feeling element of what they have just communicated can enable recipients to think more clearly and objectively about issues that previously were vague and confused.

Another key benefit of this skill is that it acts as a means whereby the speaker can check for accuracy of understanding (Wilkins, 2003). Going beyond aspects held in common with paraphrasing, reflection of feeling indicates to others that it is acceptable for them to have and express feelings in that situation – it validates their affective experiences (Hill, 2014). This is important, since in many everyday conversations the factual element of communication is stressed, to the neglect, and even active avoidance, of the affective dimension. People often need to be 'given permission' before they will reveal emotionally laden detail. But when they do unburden themselves the release can heighten energy and promote a sense of well-being (Cormier et al., 2008). By reflecting the other's feelings, a speaker acknowledges that person's right both to have and disclose such emotions.

Another goal of reflection of feeling is to help people to 'own' their feelings – to appreciate that ultimately they are the source of, and can take responsibility for, their affective states. Various ploys commonly used by people to disown their feelings include speaking in the second person (e.g. 'You get depressed being on your own all the time'), or third (e.g. 'One gets depressed...'), rather than in the first person (e.g. 'I get depressed...'). Sometimes a feeling state is depersonalised by referring to 'it' (e.g. 'It's not easy being all alone', rather than, 'I find it difficult being all alone'). Lindon and Lindon (2007) recommended helping the other to personalise feelings through reflecting. Since reflective statements make explicit the others' affective experiences, and label those statements as clearly belonging to them, they help them to acknowledge and come to terms with their emotions. Indeed, it has been contended that helping clients to progress towards maximum self-awareness and understanding is the primary aim of this skill (Manthei, 1997). Recipients are also encouraged to examine and identify underlying reasons and motives for behaviour, of which they previously may not have been completely aware. Furthermore, they begin to realise that feelings can have important causal influences upon their actions.

The use of this skill can also serve to foster a facilitative relationship. Interviewers who reflect feeling accurately are more likely to be regarded as empathic (Lang and van der Molen, 1990; Hough, 2006). As noted by Teyber (2006, p. 53), clients experience a deep sense of being empathised with when, 'the therapist can reflect the most basic feeling or capture the key issue in what the client has just said'. However, it should not be assumed that reflection of feeling and empathy are one and the same; empathy is a broad concept involving several sub-processes (Chakrabarti and Baron-Cohen, 2008), so that being empathic involves much more than reflecting feeling (Gallagher and Hargie, 1992). Nevertheless, an appropriate, well-chosen reflection can be one way of manifesting empathic understanding and adopting the other's internal frame of reference (Irving and Dickson, 2006). Interviewees consequently feel deeply understood, sensing that the interviewer is with them and is able to perceive the world from their perspective. The interviewee in such a relationship is motivated to relate more freely to the interviewer and divulge information that has deep personal meaning.

Practices to avoid when reflecting feeling

For reflection of feeling to be used to best effect, the following pitfalls need to be avoided:

1   *Inaccuracy.* Accuracy is important when labelling feelings expressed by the respondent. If feelings are reflected that were neither experienced nor expressed, the other's sense of confusion and failure to be understood can be heightened. This does not mean that failing, occasionally, to 'hit the nail on the head' is necessarily disastrous.

2   *Moving too quickly.* This happens when the reflection begins to surface sensed emotion that the listener is not yet ready either to acknowledge or discuss in any depth in that situation or at that stage of the relationship.

3   *Emotional abandonment.* Interviewers should avoid bringing deep feelings to the surface without assisting the interviewee to deal with them. This can sometimes happen at the end of an interview when the interviewer leaves the interviewee 'in mid-air' (see Chapter 10 for a discussion of effective closure techniques).

4   *Ossified expression.* There is a tendency among many inexperienced practitioners consistently to begin their reflection with a phrase such as 'You feel...' While such a sentence structure may be a useful way of learning the skill, its monotonous use can appear mechanical and, indeed, 'unfeeling' over time and can have an adverse effect on the recipient. For this reason a greater variety of types of opening phrases should be developed.

5   *Parroting.* The interviewer should not simply repeat back feeling words employed by the interviewee. Such 'parroting' of emotional labels should be distinguished from reflecting feeling. As was highlighted in relation to paraphrasing, 'Parroting only irritates speakers and implies that you have not really processed or understood their situation and subsequent reaction' (Balzer Riley, 2012, p. 111).

6   *Over-inclusion.* This occurs when the reflection goes beyond what was actually communicated by including unwarranted suppositions, or speculations.

7   *Emotional mismatch.* Perhaps one of the most difficult features of the skill is trying to match the depth of feeling included in the reflection to that initially expressed. If the level of feeling of the reflection is too shallow the recipient is less likely to feel fully understood or inclined to examine these issues more profoundly. If it is too deep the person may feel threatened and anxious, resulting in denial and alienation. More generally, the reflective statement should mirror the same type of language and forms of expression of the other, without being patronising. The latter, together with the other potential pitfalls mentioned above, can only be overcome by careful practice, coupled with a critical awareness of one's performance.

RESEARCH OUTCOMES OF A REFLECTIVE STYLE

Comparisons of the outcomes of an indirect, reflective style with a range of alternatives have been carried out in empirical studies for several decades. The trends from these investigations have been generally positive. Interviewers who use a reflective style make interviewees feel more comfortable (Silver, 1970), encourage greater revelation of intimate details (Ellison and Firestone, 1974) and are regarded as having a greater understanding of their clients (Zimmer and Anderson, 1968; Turkat and Alpher, 1984). A significant relationship between reflection of feeling and ratings of empathic understanding has also been shown (Uhlemann et al., 1976). Likewise, Ehrlich et al. (1979) found that interviewers who reflected feelings that had not yet been named by interviewees were regarded by the latter as being more expert and trustworthy. A similar procedure, labelled 'sensing unstated feelings', emerged as a significant predictor of counsellor effectiveness in a study by Nagata et al. (1983).

From the analyses of therapy sessions undertaken by Hill and her colleagues (Hill et al., 1988; Hill, 1989), not only was reflecting discovered to be one of the most common of the identified techniques utilised by therapists, but clients reported that they found it one of the most helpful. They regarded it as providing support and seldom reacted negatively to its use. Such reflections assisted clients in becoming more deeply attuned to their emotional and personal experiences, leading to more profound levels of exploration and greater insights into their circumstances and difficulties. One of the most marked outcomes was an association with significantly reduced levels of anxiety.

A number of studies have found that reflections increase the amount of interviewee self-statements (e.g., Powell, 1968; Kennedy et al., 1971; Haase and Di Mattia, 1976; Mills, 1983; Forrester et al., 2008) and depth of intimacy of these disclosures (Vondracek, 1969; Beharry, 1976). When reflections of feeling are employed, this has been shown to promote substantial increases in interviewee affective disclosures (Merbaum, 1963; Highlen and Baccus, 1977; Highlen and Nicholas, 1978). As summarised by Forrester et al. (2012, p. 126), reflections 'elicit more disclosure from clients. They are at least as good as a question for exploring an issue, and they are a better way of exploring in depth something of importance'.

There seems to be an individual difference factor influencing reactions and outcomes to reflective versus directive styles of engagement. Some evidence reviewed by Hill (1992) suggests that locus of control, cognitive complexity and reactance of clients may be important. Locus of control, it will be recalled from Chapter 4, refers to a belief in personally significant events being shaped by either internal or external sources, while reactance is a predisposition to perceive and respond to events as restrictions on personal autonomy and freedom (see Chapter 12). Cognitive complexity relates to the conceptual differentiation and sophistication with which individuals make sense of their circumstances. Hill (1992) came to the conclusion that those high on internality of control and cognitive complexity, and low on reactance, were more suited to less directive interventions such as reflecting.

Studies investigating the effects of a reflecting technique on attitudes towards the interviewer have also reported favourable outcomes. A positive relationship was shown by Dickson (1981) between the proportion of paraphrases to questions asked by employment advisory personnel and ratings of interviewer competency provided by independent, experienced judges. A comparable outcome emerged when client perceptions of interviewer effectiveness were examined by Nagata *et al.* (1983). Likewise, in studies of the effects of paraphrases upon interviewee responses, Weger *et al.* (2010, 2014) found that interviewers employing this technique received significantly higher ratings of likeability than when they simply used acknowledgements (e.g. 'OK', 'That's great'). Weger *et al.* suggest that it may be that listeners view paraphrases as a form of verbal mimicry similar to nonverbal mirroring (see Chapter 3) and so perceptions of likeability increase because we tend to like people who mirror what we say or do.

In sum, these findings indicate that the use of a reflective style tends to have a range of positive effects on interviewees. At a behavioural level, this technique can produce increases in the amount, intimacy and affective degree of information which interviewees reveal about themselves. In the therapeutic context there is evidence linking reflecting with positive outcome measures for clients. However, the intervening effects of individual differences in demographic and personality factors should not be overlooked.

OVERVIEW

Reflection is a powerful skill. It puts respondents at centre stage in the interaction, allows them to develop and evaluate their thoughts, ideas and feelings and helps to establish a close bond between the interlocutors. At first blush it seems deceptively simple, but it is a skill that many novices find difficult to master. In the numerous training programmes that I have conducted in well over three decades, I have found that it is the most difficult skill for trainees to acquire. This often only becomes evident to them when they attempt to put the skill into practice. Trainees tend to revert to asking questions rather than reflecting; this is because in everyday life they use questions profusely but reflections rarely.

To obtain optimum effect, the following points should be remembered when adopting a reflective style.

1   *Use your own words.* Reflecting is not merely a process of echoing back the words just heard. Some analysts include repetition as part of their definition, for example: 'reflection of feelings is defined as repeating or rephrasing of the client's statements, including an explicit identification of feelings' (Chui *et al.*, 2014, p. 762). However, it is generally recognised that speakers should strive to reformulate the message using their own terminology. In addition, Ivey *et al.* (2014) recommended using a sentence stem that includes, as far as possible, a word in keeping with the other's characteristic mode of receiving information. For example, assuming that the

other is a 'visualiser' (i.e. someone who relies mainly upon visual images as a means of gathering and processing information and who uses expressions such as; 'I *see* what you mean...'; 'The *picture* that I am getting...'), it would be more appropriate to begin a reflection with 'It *appears* that...' or 'It *looks* like...' By contrast, with someone who prioritises the aural channel (and uses expressions like 'I *hear* what you are saying...'; 'I can't *tune in* to what she is saying...'), then reflections beginning with, 'It *sounds* to me that...' or 'As I *listen* to you, what seems to be *coming through* is...' may be more apposite.

2   *Do not go beyond the information communicated by the interlocutor.* Remember, reflecting is a process of only feeding back information already given by the speaker. The reflection should not add to or take away from the meaning as presented. Reflections should not include speculations or suppositions which represent an attempt to impose meaning on what was communicated, and, while based upon it, may not be strictly warranted by it. The speaker, therefore, when reflecting, should not try to interpret or psychoanalyse. Interpretation may be useful on occasion, but it is not reflection. For example:

A: 'I suppose I have never had a successful relationship with men. I never seemed to get on with my father when I was a child...I always had problems with the male teachers when I was at school...'
B: 'You saw the male teachers as extensions of your father'.

Note that this statement by B is not a reflection. It is an interpretation that goes beyond what was said by A.

3   *Be concise.* The objective is not to include everything said but to select what appear to be the most salient elements of the preceding message. It is only the core or essence of what the other was trying to communicate that the speaker should strive to reflect. Reflections should be short statements rather than long, involved or rambling.

4   *Be specific.* One of the goals of reflecting is to promote understanding. Frequently interviewees, perhaps due to never having previously fully thought through that particular issue, will tend to express themselves in a rather vague, confused and abstract manner. It is more beneficial if, when reflecting, interviewers try to be as simple, concrete and specific as possible, thereby ensuring that both they and the interviewees successfully comprehend what is being said.

5   *Be accurate.* Accuracy depends upon careful listening (see Chapter 7). While person B is talking, person A should be listening single-mindedly, rather than considering what to say next, or entertaining other thoughts less directly relevant to the encounter. The inclusion of a 'check-out' phrase as part of the reflective utterance has been advised as a means of assessing accuracy of understanding, when the affective message received has not been explicitly stated (Ivey *et al.*, 2012). For instance, 'Deep down I sense a feeling of relief...would that be part of what you are saying?' In addition to inviting corrective feedback, by offering the opportunity to comment on

the accuracy of understanding, the speaker avoids giving the impression of assumed omniscience or of imposing meaning on the other. If a practitioner is frequently inaccurate in reflections proffered, the client will quickly realise that further prolongation of the interaction is pointless, since the practitioner does not seem able to appreciate what is being said. This does not mean that an occasional inaccuracy by a generally and genuinely concerned interviewer will damage the relationship. Rather, in such a case the recipient, realising the speaker's determination to grasp meaning, will generally be motivated to provide additional information and rectify the misconception. Indeed, Hill (2014) argued that helpers should not be too worried about evaluating the accuracy of a particular reflection, but rather should communicate to clients that they are endeavouring to understand their concerns.

6   *Do not over-use reflections.* Not all contributions should be reflected. To attempt to do so would restrict rather than help the other person. Reflections need to be used in conjunction with the other skills that an interviewer should have available (e.g. questioning, reinforcing, self-disclosure). In some instances it is only after rapport has been established that reflection of feeling can be used without the interviewee feeling awkward or threatened.

7   *Focus upon the immediately preceding message.* Reflections typically reflect what is contained in the other's immediately preceding statement. It is possible, and indeed desirable on occasion, for reflections to be wider-ranging and to cover a number of interjections. The interviewer may wish, for example, at the end of the interview, to reflect the facts and feelings expressed by the interviewee during its entire course. Reflections such as these, that have a broader perspective, are called *summaries of content* and *summaries of feeling*, and are a useful means of identifying themes expressed by the interviewee during the complete interview, or parts of it (see Chapter 10 for more detail on closure).

8   *Combining facts and feelings.* Reflection contains two essential component skills – reflection of feeling and paraphrasing. It is, of course, possible to combine both factual and feeling material in a single reflection if this is felt to be the most appropriate response. Indeed, this is often how the skill is used in practice. As an introductory tool for those unused to conveying empathic understanding, Egan (2014, p. 113) recommended what he called 'the basic formula: "You feel ... [here name the correct emotion expressed by the client] because ... [here indicate the correct thoughts, experiences, and behaviors that give rise to the feelings]"'. Feelings and facts are brought together in this format, with one type of information complementing the other and enabling the recipient to perceive the relationship between them. Moreover, Ivey *et al.* (2014) identified how, in this way, deeper meanings underlying expressed experiences can be located and sensitively surfaced – a process they termed 'reflection of meaning'.

Chapter 7

Paying attention to others: the skill of listening

INTRODUCTION

IN SOCIAL INTERACTION THE process of listening is of crucial importance. As Mark Twain famously observed: 'If we were supposed to talk more than we listen, we would have two tongues and one ear'. To respond appropriately to others, we must pay attention to the messages they are sending and link our responses to these. In Chapter 3 it was noted that the average person does not actually speak for long periods in each day, and indeed several studies into the percentage of time spent in different forms of communication have found listening to be the predominant interpersonal activity. Adults spend about 70 per cent of their waking time communicating (Adler *et al.*, 2013a). Of this, some 45 per cent of communication time is spent listening, 30 per cent speaking, 16 per cent reading and 9 per cent writing.

The importance of listening is now widely recognised across many contexts (Rautalinko and Lisper, 2004; Moore, 2005; Gable, 2007; Flynn *et al.*, 2008; Hargie, 2009; Bodie, 2012). Classroom research has shown that those students who score highest in listening ability achieve higher levels of academic attainment (Beall *et al.*, 2008). In her review of research in this area, Jalongo (2010, p. 4) concluded: 'Listening comprehension, defined as the young child's ability to understand what he or she hears, is highly predictive of overall academic achievement'. In the business sphere, Bambacas and Patrickson (2008) found that senior Human Resource executives rated the listening ability of candidates as a key criterion when recruiting prospective managers. Likewise, McCallum and O'Connell (2009) showed that listening ability is a key competency in organisational leadership. Peterson (2007, p. 286) highlighted how, through listening, managers can 'attain information and insights that are needed for well-grounded decision making'.

This was confirmed by Goby and Lewis (2000) in a study of the insurance industry, where staff at all levels, as well as customers (policyholders), regarded listening as the primary communication skill. Similarly, in a study of 1,000 sales-people, Rosenbaum (2001) found that the ability to listen in depth to client needs was a defining characteristic of success. However, surveys of hundreds of companies in the USA show that poor listening skills cause problems at all levels in organisations, from new employees through to CEOs (Stewart and Cash, 2013). Other research has confirmed that many managers are poor listeners, and that this is particularly the case in relation to receptiveness to difficult information being raised by employees. In their review of the area, Barwise and Meehan (2008, p. 22) argue that a main reason for this is that, 'managers often unwittingly signal that they don't want to hear bad news – for instance, by changing the subject or avoiding interaction – and subordinates tend to censor themselves'.

For professionals in most fields, listening is therefore a core skill, since knowledge of and expertise in listening techniques are central to success in interactions with clients and other professionals (Bodie, 2011; Koprowska, 2014). For example, in their empirical investigation of this area, Hargie *et al.* (2000) identified listening as a key skill in community pharmacy practice. In their study of medical skills, Rider and Keefer (2006, p. 626) illustrated how a core competency for doctors was the ability to: 'demonstrate effective listening by hearing and understanding in a way that the patient feels heard and understood'. This was borne out in a major empirical study of doctor–patient communication by Tallman *et al.* (2007), where the ability to display active listening was found to be a key determinant of physician effectiveness. Likewise, studies have shown that patients rate listening as the most important skill they look for in health professionals (Channa and Siddiqi, 2008; Davis *et al.*, 2008a; Boudreau *et al.*, 2009), and a meta-analysis of research studies by Henry *et al.* (2012) showed that greater clinician listening was significantly related to greater patient satisfaction. Jagosh *et al.* (2011) illustrated how effective listening serves three key objectives in the medical sphere: ensuring accurate clinical data gathering and diagnosis; serving as a core part of the therapeutic and healing process; and building a conducive doctor–patient relationship. As summarised by Davis *et al.* (2008b, p. 168), 'Research indicates that when healthcare providers listen to patients, there is more compliance with medical regimens, patient satisfaction is increased, and physicians are less vulnerable to malpractice lawsuits'. More generally, for those whose job involves a helping or facilitative dimension, it has been argued that the capacity to be a good listener is the most fundamental of all skills (Nelson-Jones, 2014).

In terms of personal well-being, 'Not only is listening a valuable skill, it is also conducive to good health. Studies have shown that when we talk our blood pressure goes up; when we listen it goes down' (Borisoff and Purdy, 1991a, p. 5). However, this may also depend upon the amount of effort we devote to the activity. Galanes and Adams (2012) reviewed research that showed how those who are actively trying to listen to, remember and understand what another person is saying show signs of concerted physical activity, including accelerated heart beat, whereas those not listening at all to the speaker have heart rates that often drop to the level of sleep.

Box 7.1 Benefits of effective listening	
At work	Personally
✓ Greater customer satisfaction	✓ Better family relationships
✓ Increased employee satisfaction	✓ Improved social network
✓ Higher levels of productivity	✓ Greater interpersonal enjoyment
✓ Fewer mistakes	✓ Improved self-esteem
✓ Improved sales figures	✓ Higher grades at school/college
✓ More information sharing	✓ More close friends
✓ Greater innovation and creativity	✓ An enriched life

Listening is a central skill at the earliest stage of personal development. The infant begins to respond to a new world by hearing and listening, with neonates showing a clear preference for listening to human speech (Vouloumanos and Werker, 2007). Newborns have also been shown to prefer speakers of their native language (Kinzler et al., 2007). Wilding et al. (2000) illustrated how neonates are able to discriminate between their father's voice and that of a male stranger, and infants prefer to look at their mother's face rather than a stranger's. They showed how babies rapidly develop the ability to combine visual and auditory stimuli, so at age 6–12 weeks they become distressed when shown a video of their mother in which the speech and visual content are discrepant.

In fact, listening is at the heart of communicative development, since the child has to learn to listen before learning to speak, learns to speak before learning to read, and learns to read before learning to write. In this sense, listening is a fundamental skill and the foundation for other communication skills. For this reason, listening can be regarded as a *pre-requisite skill* upon which other interactive skills are predicated. To ask the right questions, be assertive, give appropriate rewards, employ apposite self-disclosure, negotiate effectively, open and close interactions, and so on, you must engage in concerted listening. As aptly expressed by Robbins and Hunsaker (2014, p. 94), 'If you aren't an effective listener, you're going to have consistent trouble developing all the other interpersonal skills'. Indeed, many of the problems encountered during social interchange are caused by ineffective listening. Not surprisingly, research studies have shown a range of benefits that accrue from effective listening in both personal and commercial contexts (see Box 7.1 for a summary of these).

DEFINING THE TERM

Academic interest in listening can be traced back to the mid-twentieth-century work of Wiksell (1946) and Nichols (1947). Since that time, the volume of literature in this area has expanded rapidly (Wolvin, 2010a). But what is the exact meaning of the term 'listening'? In their analysis, Wolff et al. (1983) noted that the term 'listen' is based upon an amalgam of the Anglo-Saxon words: _hylstan_ (hearing) and _hlosnian_ (wait in suspense). However, there is a lack of consensus in the literature with regard to the precise meaning of the term and how it should be measured (Rost, 2011; Bodie, 2013). One reason for this is that listening is performed cognitively but evaluated behaviourally (Janusik, 2007). As a result, different definitions emphasise either the covert cognitive aspect or the overt behavioural dimension. Thus, some theorists regard listening as a purely cognitive auditory activity in which we attempt to comprehend and remember acoustic information (Gamble and Gamble, 2012). In this sense it is 'the process of receiving and interpreting aural stimuli' (Pearson and Nelson, 2000, p. 99). More specifically, listening is viewed as 'the complex, learned human process of sensing, interpreting, evaluating, storing and responding to oral messages' (Steil, 1991, p. 203).

In terms of interpersonal interaction, the focus of study for those who hold this perspective has been upon 'the process by which spoken language is converted to meaning in the mind' (Lundsteen, 1971, p. 1). As Bostrom (2006), in his systematic overview of the field, demonstrated, this approach emanated from the cognitive tradition and was significantly influenced by the supposition that reading and listening are different aspects of what are regarded as the same process – that of acquiring and retaining information. In this paradigm, listening is perceived as being parallel to, and the social equivalent of, reading: when we read we attempt to understand and assimilate the written word; when we listen we attempt to understand and assimilate the spoken word. Both are seen as cognitive, linguistic, abilities.

This cognitive, or information-processing, perspective made an important distinction between hearing and listening, in that hearing was regarded as a physical activity and listening as a mental process. In this sense, we may use our visual pathways to see but we read with our brains (and, indeed, blind people read using tactile pathways and Braille), and we activate our neurosensory pathways to hear but we listen with our brains. As shown by Boudreau _et al._ (2009), the cortex is not simply a passive receiver of sensory input – it actively modulates it. We do not need to learn to see but we need to learn to read. Similarly, we do not have to learn how to hear, but we have to learn how to listen. Roach and Wyatt (1999, p. 197) pointed out that, 'Far from being a natural process, listening is clearly a consciously purposive activity for which we need systematic training and supervision to learn to do well'. A key difference between hearing and listening is that: 'Whereas the former refers to a physiological receptivity at an individual level...the latter refers to an intersubjective orientation at a discursive, thus social level' (Jacobs and Coghlan, 2005, p. 120).

But aural definitions of listening ignore the important nonverbal cues emitted by the speaker. Yet such cues help to determine the actual meaning of the message being conveyed (see Chapter 3). For this reason, researchers in interpersonal communication have focused upon a communication competency model, underscoring the importance of all interactive behaviour in listening, encompassing both verbal and nonverbal responses (Bostrom, 2011; Hill, 2014). Thus, Bostrom (2006, p. 279) asserted that 'the best definition of listening is the _acquisition, processing, and retention of information in the interpersonal context_'.

It is 'the process of becoming aware of all the cues that another person emits' (Van Slyke, 1999, p. 98). The definition adopted by the International Listening Association (2015) is: 'the process of receiving, constructing meaning from, and responding to spoken and/or nonverbal messages'. Likewise, Jones (2011), in arguing that interpersonal listening is a multidimensional construct, includes not just cognitive and behavioural dimensions in her analysis, but also affective processes, such as feeling motivated to attend to and care about the speaker's messages. A similar perspective is followed in this chapter, where listening is regarded as *the process whereby one person pays careful overt and covert attention to, and attempts to assimilate, understand and retain, the verbal and nonverbal signals being emitted by another.*

Scholars in this field also distinguish between two other usages of the term. The first sense emphasises the visible nature of the process, and is referred to as *active listening* (Weger *et al.*, 2010). This occurs when an individual displays behaviours that signal overt attention to another. The second usage emphasises the cognitive process of assimilating information. This does not imply anything about the overt behaviour of the individual, but rather is concerned with the covert aspects. An individual may be listening covertly without displaying outward signs of so doing, and so is engaged in *passive listening* (Verderber *et al.*, 2014). In terms of interpersonal skill, it is the former meaning of the term that is utilised, and it is therefore important to identify those verbal and nonverbal aspects of behaviour that convey the impression of active listening. We will explore these in more depth later in the chapter.

Adler *et al.* (2013a) identified the key sub-processes involved in listening as attending to the message, attempting to understand it, responding appropriately and remembering the key components. While listening is often portrayed as a linear activity, these sub-processes are in fact all inter-related (Figure 7.1).

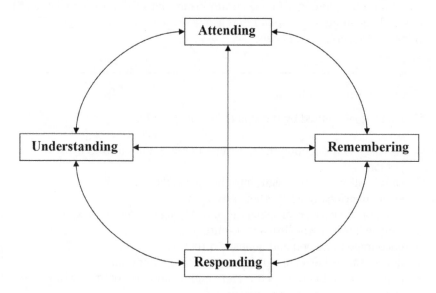

Figure 7.1 Main processes involved in listening.

Thus, for example, we are less likely to attend to, respond appropriately to or remember messages we cannot understand.

PURPOSES OF LISTENING

The skill of listening serves a number of purposes in social interaction, as summarised in Box 7.2. The specific goals vary depending upon the context. For example, in the sphere of management, Alvesson and Sveningsson (2003) found that managers perceived listening as serving a range of purposes, including, *inter alia*, as a way of:

- gathering, structuring and understanding information;
- demonstrating interest in, and respect for, employees;
- affirming the value of individuals and their right to 'be heard';
- making people feel included and respected, thereby increasing a sense of 'belonging';
- enabling the manager to ascertain and overcome negative employee experiences;
- providing reassurance and reducing anxiety;
- finding the appropriate emotional tone for an interaction;
- facilitating the decision-making process.

One recurring problem is that we often listen with the intention of responding, rather than with the objective of understanding what the speaker is saying (Van Slyke, 1999). In other words, our main concern is with our own point of view rather than with gaining a deeper insight into the other person's perspective. As shown in Box 7.2, our objectives when listening should include conveying attention and interest, gaining a full, accurate insight into the perspectives held by others and encouraging an open interchange of views, leading to agreed understanding and acceptance of goals.

Box 7.2 Purposes of listening

The main goals served by the skill of listening are to:

1 focus specifically upon the messages being communicated by the other person
2 gain a full, accurate insight into the speaker's communication
3 evaluate critically what others are saying
4 monitor the nonverbal signals accompanying the verbal messages
5 convey interest, concern and attention
6 encourage full, open and honest expression
7 develop an 'other-centred' approach during interaction
8 reach a shared and agreed understanding and acceptance with others about both sides' goals and priorities

---

ASSIMILATING INFORMATION

The processes of feedback, perception and cognition are all of importance in the assimilation of information during listening. In interpersonal interaction a constant stream of feedback impinges upon us, both from the stimuli received from other people and from the physical environment. Not all of this feedback is consciously perceived, since there is simply too much information to manage. As a result, a *selective perception filter* (Figure 7.2) is operative, and its main function is to filter only a limited amount of information into the conscious, while some of the remainder may be stored at a subconscious level. Evidence that such subconscious storage occurs can be found from studies into *subliminal perception*, which refers to the perception of stimuli below the threshold of awareness; this research demonstrates that these perceptions can have a priming effect on our judgements, attitudes and behaviour (Smith and McCulloch, 2012). For example, information flashed on to a screen for a split second, so fast that it cannot be read consciously, can influence how we respond.

Figure 7.2 illustrates how, from the large number of stimuli in the environment, a certain amount is presented as feedback. These are represented by the arrows on the extreme left of the diagram. Some stimuli are not perceived

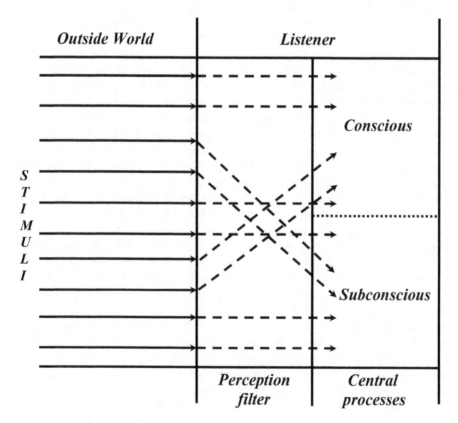

Figure 7.2 Selective perception process.

at all, or are filtered into the subconscious at a very early stage. Within the physical environment, the ticking of clocks, the hum of central-heating systems, the pressure of one's body on the chair, etc., are usually filtered into the sub-conscious during social encounters, if these are interesting. If, however, one is bored during an encounter, such as sitting through a dull lecture, then these items may be consciously perceived, and the social 'noises' from the lecturer given less attention.

Unfortunately, in interpersonal interaction, vital information can be filtered out, in that we may miss important social signals emitted by others. Where this occurs, effective listening skills are not displayed. In order to listen successfully we must be sensitive to verbal and nonverbal cues, and select the most relevant of these to focus upon. By observing closely the actions and reactions of others, it is possible to improve one's ability to demonstrate concerted and accurate listening. Dichotomous listening should also be avoided. This occurs when we attempt to assimilate information simultaneously from two different sources. Examples include trying to listen to two people in a group who are speaking at the same time, using a mobile device while engaged in face-to-face interaction or when distracted by some form of extraneous noise. In all of these instances the dichoto-mous nature of the listening interferes with the ability of the listener to interact effectively, since messages may be either received inaccurately or not received at all. Effective listening is facilitated by focusing solely on the interlocutor, and by manipulating the environment in order to ensure that extraneous distractions are minimised (e.g. by closing doors or switching off one's mobile device).

The listening process begins when our senses register incoming stimuli. The sensory register receives large amounts of information but holds it for a brief period of time. Visual sensory storage is highly transitory, lasting only a few hundred milliseconds. Auditory sensory data is held in the register for slightly longer – up to 4 seconds. To be retained, stimuli must be filtered from the sen-sory register into the individual's level of consciousness and held in memory. The short-term memory store retains stimuli for up to 1 minute. In an early and highly influential paper, Miller (1956) suggested that short-term memory could only cope with some 7 units, ± 2, of information. However, later work indicated that remembering is a complex process and that it is difficult to quantify pre-cisely how many 'units' can be remembered (Cowan et al., 2007).

In remembering, a process of 'chunking' occurs, in that groups of data are arranged together based on previous learning patterns. Thus, the set of letters UNOPECNATO may at first sight look like ten separate units. But it can read-ily be chunked into three separate acronyms by anyone who knows these – UN (United Nations), OPEC (Organization of the Petroleum Exporting Countries) and NATO (North Atlantic Treaty Organization), making the letter string easier to remember. Likewise, a new telephone number is retained for only a short period as each digit is assimilated as a separate unit; if this number is used fre-quently, it becomes one single unit (or chunk) of information and is transferred to the long-term memory store. Long-term memory is a permanent storage facil-ity that can retain information literally for a lifetime.

Social encounters involve declarative memory, which in turn can be coded and stored as semantic memory (e.g. remembering what someone said) and episodic memory (e.g. remembering what someone did) (Ratnayake and Broderick, 2014). Working memory is also important in listening. As explained by Gathercole *et al.* (2004, p. 2), 'The term "working memory" is used to refer to a mental workplace in which information can be stored and processed for brief periods of time in the course of demanding cognitive activities'. Working memory posits a duality system whereby both storage/memory and attentional/ computational functions combine in the creation of meaning. These two functional components respectively enable the individual to organise and manipulate incoming information during complex cognitive tasks (Conway *et al.*, 2007; Shipstead *et al.*, 2012). As expressed by Baddeley *et al.* (2009, p. 9), those with greater working-memory capacities have a higher ability to 'keep things in mind' during information processing. This means that they are better able to manage and deal with incoming verbal and visual information (Gathercole, 2008), which in turn facilitates listening (McInnes *et al.*, 2003; Janusik, 2007). In this way, people with high working-memory capacity have the ability to remember relevant details during interpersonal encounters and to bring these into play at apposite moments during interaction (Wolvin, 2010b).

Bostrom (2006) reviewed a range of research studies that found a link between capacity for short-term listening (STL) and success in various contexts. Good short-term listeners asked more questions in interviews, performed better in oral presentations, were rated as being better managers and had a higher rate of upward mobility within their organisation. However, while the importance of short-term memory for the listening process has been illustrated, the exact nature of any causal relationship between short-term memory, listening ability and overt listening behaviour is unclear (Ohata, 2005; Bostrom, 2006). Thomas and Levine (1996) found a positive and significant correlation between recall ability and use of head nods, gaze duration and short backchannel behaviours ('uh hu', 'mmm', etc.), but concluded, 'there is more to listening than simply recall. The reverse is also true. There is obviously more to recall than listening' (p. 121). Likewise, Bostrom (2006, p. 274) concluded that, although 'research indicates that STL is closely implicated in interpersonal activities…just how these abilities relate to one another is not known'. It should be noted that no link exists between long-term memory and listening ability. In other words, there is no relationship between having a good memory for distant events and being an effective listener. Fans of *The Simpsons* TV cartoon series will be aware of the Grandpa Simpson character, who frequently regales the family with detailed memories of days of yore, while blissfully ignoring what others are saying to him in the here and now.

TYPES OF LISTENING

Galanes and Adams (2012) distinguished between four types of listener (Box 7.3). These typologies are reflected in the main categories of listening that have been delineated. The core type, as emphasised in most texts in this area, is active listening, so this will be examined in some depth. However, six related types of listening that are important in different contexts will first be described: discriminative, comprehension, evaluative, appreciative, empathic and dialogic.

Box 7.3 Four types of listener

1 *People-oriented listeners.* Their primary concern is for others' feelings and needs. Can be distracted away from the task owing to this focus on psycho-emotional perspectives. We seek them out when we need a listening ear. Are good helpers
2 *Task-oriented listeners.* Are mainly concerned with getting the business done. Do not like discussing what they see as irrelevant information or having to listen to 'long-winded' people or 'whingers'. Can be insensitive to the emotional needs of others
3 *Content-oriented listeners.* These are analytical people who enjoy dissecting information and carefully scrutinising it. They often focus on the literal meaning of what has been said. They want to hear all sides and leave no stone unturned, however long the process. Can be slow to make decisions as they are never quite sure if they have garnered all the necessary information. Are good mediators
4 *Time-oriented listeners.* Their main focus is upon getting tasks completed within set time frames. They see time as a valuable commodity, not to be wasted. Are impatient with what they see as 'prevaricators' and can be prone to jump to conclusions before they have heard all of the information

---

Discriminative listening

This is the most basic form of listening, where the goal is simply to scan and monitor auditory and/or visual stimuli (Wolvin, 2009). Examples include scrutinising an interactive partner's facial expressions to ascertain his or her reactions to what we have just said, or listening to hear if the baby is crying upstairs. In each case the objective is to focus upon, or *discriminate*, incoming stimuli for feedback purposes. For some professionals, of course, discriminative listening is vital. This is especially the case with health professionals in a hospital context who have to monitor the well-being of patients on a regular basis, and make crucial discriminative decisions based upon the stimuli received.

Comprehension listening

The emphasis here is upon listening for central facts, main ideas and critical themes in order to *comprehend* fully the messages being received. This occurs when we listen to informative or instructive messages in order to increase our understanding, enhance our experience and acquire data that will be of future use to us. We may practise this type of listening at the 'getting-to-know-you' stage of relationships, while attending lectures, conducting fact-finding interviews or watching TV documentaries. This form of listening has also been termed *content listening* (Kramer, 2001) and *informational listening* (Orbe and Bruess, 2005).

Evaluative listening

This takes place when a speaker is trying to persuade us, by attempting to influence our attitudes, beliefs or actions. We listen evaluatively to enable us to make appropriate judgements concerning such persuasive messages. Interpretation of the messages we receive is an integral part of the listening process (Burleson, 2011; Edwards, 2011). As part of this, we listen for the spin or slant that the speaker puts on the message (Egan, 2014). We may practise this type of listening when dealing with salespeople, negotiating at meetings, listening to party political speeches, watching TV adverts or even when deciding with friends which pub to go to for the evening. In all of these instances we have to listen to the available evidence and the supporting arguments, weigh these up and *evaluate* them, before making a decision. The emphasis here is therefore upon listening for the central propositions being made, and being able to determine the strengths and weaknesses of each. This form of listening has also been referred to as *interpretive listening* (Bostrom, 2006) and *critical listening* in that it 'challenges the speaker's message by evaluating its accuracy, meaningfulness, and utility' (Pearson *et al.*, 2006, p. 111).

Appreciative listening

This occurs when we seek out certain signals or messages in order to gain pleasure from, or *appreciate*, their reception (Brownell, 2012). We may listen appreciatively to relax and unwind, to enjoy ourselves, to gain inner peace, to increase emotional or cultural understanding or to obtain spiritual satisfaction. This type of listening occurs when we play music which appeals to us, when we decide to attend a church service, when sitting in a park or walking in the country while assimilating the sounds of nature, or when we attend a public meeting in order to hear a charismatic speaker.

Empathic listening

Empathic listening takes place when we listen to someone who has a need to talk, and be understood by another (Floyd, 2014). Here the listener demonstrates a willingness to attend to and attempt to understand the thoughts, beliefs and feelings of the speaker (Bodie *et al.*, 2013). One in-depth study of listening dyads found that what speakers most wanted was for the listener to understand what they were saying, and to care about and empathise with them – their recommendation was to 'listen with your heart' (Halone and Pecchioni, 2001, p. 64). Empathic listening involves responding in a manner that is warm, reassuring and comforting and that shows respect and regard for the speaker (Stewart and Cash, 2013). While the first four types of listening are intrinsic in that they are for the benefit of the listener, empathic listening is extrinsic in that the listener is seeking to help the speaker (Walker, 1997). This type of listening is common between close friends and spouses. It is at the core of formal helping situations, and hence has also been referred to as *therapeutic listening* (Wolvin, 2009), *reflective listening* (Rautalinko and Lisper, 2004) and *supportive listening* (Jones, 2011; Bodie *et al.*, 2014). In their analysis of the area, Keaton *et al.* (2015, p. 482) showed how 'Supportive listeners are actively and non-judgmentally focused on concerns of others and are seen as generally likable'.

Dialogic listening

The term dialogue comes from the Greek words *dia* ('through') and *logos* ('meaning', or 'understanding'). In dialogic listening, meaning emerges and is shaped from conversational interchange (Shotter, 2009). For this reason it is also known as *relational listening* (Halone and Pecchioni, 2001). As summarised by Jacobs and Coghlan (2005, p. 115), this type of listening, 'involves the constitution of a relational basis that allows for intersubjective meaning generation'. Dialogic listening is two-way and of benefit to both sides, as views are shared in an attempt to reach a mutually agreed position. It is argued that the intense engagement involved allows interactors to reach a stage of *transcendence* in the listening process (Solomon and Theiss, 2013). All of us carry large amounts of cultural, national and racial baggage with us when we enter into discussions. We also bring our own ethnocentric slant, which means that we tend to perceive and judge other viewpoints from the perspective of our own. In dialogic listening we need to adopt a more cosmopolitan attitude that does not assume that the values and beliefs of any particular group are the only possible alternative. Rather, we must suspend judgement and be open and receptive to the views of others. As Stewart *et al.* (2005, p. 176) expressed it, 'The first step towards dialogic listening is to recognize that each communication event is a ride on a tandem bicycle, and you may or may not be in the front seat'. This type of listening is central to negotiations, where to reach effective outcomes the needs and goals of both sides must be jointly explored (see Chapter 13).

Rehling (2008) argued that what she termed *compassionate listening* is a sub-set of dialogic listening, for those who communicate in depth with the very seriously ill. As she describes it:

> Grounding our listening in compassion suggests listening to someone who is seriously ill with an openness and acceptance of human suffering, a hope to better understand that suffering and a desire to act to relieve the isolation and loneliness so often reported during serious illness.
>
> (p. 87)

Compassionate listening involves developing a sense of 'we-ness' during dialogue, in which shared humanity is emphasised, and there is recognition of the common struggles that characterise life, such as serious illness and death. The listener shares her or his own sense of vulnerability and mortality. Through discussion, a new sense of joint understanding is achieved. However, as emphasised by Rehling, compassionate listening can only take place when both parties are ready to participate. For example, some seriously ill people may not want to engage at this level of depth of sharing.

While appreciative listening is not so applicable in the social context, knowledge of discriminative, comprehension, evaluative, empathic and dialogic listening skills is of key import. But all of these listening types are predicated on an active approach to listening.

Active listening

Research has shown that speakers want listeners to respond appropriately to what they are saying, and who will 'really listen' (Virtanen and Isotalus, 2013) rather than 'just listen' (Halone and Pecchioni, 2001). In other words, they desire active listening in the form of both verbal and nonverbal engagement (Bodie *et al.*, 2012). Active listening requires concerted effort and attention (Orbe and Bruess, 2005), as it involves showing that we have both heard and understood what the interlocutor has communicated (Kagan, 2007). Duck and McMahan (2012) argue that what they term *engaged listening* is the key to relational success; this involves trusting and caring for others, wanting to know more about them and responding appropriately to what they say. The importance of engaged listening was demonstrated in a study by Beukeboom (2009), who showed university students a neutral film clip about a kiosk owner, and then had confederates interview them about what they had seen. Some interviewers used a positive listening style, with smiles, open posture and head nods, while others used a negative style involving frowns, unsmiling expression and closed posture. Results showed that listening style significantly affected how the subjects responded. Those interviewed with a positive listening style gave more of their own opinions and included more abstractions and interpretations (e.g. 'He doesn't trust people any more'), whereas those interviewed with the stern, negative style stuck to the descriptive and concrete facts of the film (e.g. 'He arranges newspapers in his stand'). The process of emotional contagion (see Chapter 3) probably plays a part here. When the listener shows warmth and enthusiasm for what we are saying this attitude influences us and so we are likely to become more expressive and expansive. By contrast, when the listener is cold and formal we are more likely to provide basic, factual responses. Thus, the ability to employ active listening has been associated with a range of positive relational outcomes (Gearhart and Bodie, 2011; Weger *et al.*, 2014).

Although verbal responses are the main indicators of successful listening, if accompanying nonverbal behaviours are not displayed it is usually assumed that an individual is not paying attention, and *ipso facto* not listening. While these nonverbal signs may not be crucial to the assimilation of verbal messages, they are expected by others. The first part of listening can be viewed as a silent response that precedes the spoken reply, and has been described as a type of initial answer (Jacobs and Coghlan, 2005). Furthermore, the nonverbal information conveyed by the speaker adds to, and provides emphasis for, the verbal message. An early example of this was shown in a study by Strong *et al.* (1971), who asked college students to listen only, or both view and listen, to tapes of counsellors and rate them on a 100-item checklist. Results indicated that when the counsellors were both seen and heard they were described as more cold, bored, awkward, unreasonable and uninterested than when they were heard only.

Verbal indicators of listening are discussed in many of the skills reviewed throughout this book. As noted earlier, listening is a pre-requisite skill that is part of all other skills. Within the skill of reinforcement, for example, *verbal reinforcers* are often regarded as being associated with attending (see Chapter 4). In terms of listening, however, it has long been known that caution is needed when employing verbal reinforcement. Thus, Rosenshine (1971) found that the curve of the relationship between amount of verbal reinforcement by teachers and degree of pupil participation in classroom lessons was bell-shaped. While verbal reinforcers (e.g. 'very good', 'yes') initially had the effect of increasing pupil participation, if this reinforcement was continued in its basic form, pupils began to regard it with indifference. Rosenshine pointed out that it is simple to administer positive reinforcers without much thought, but to demonstrate genuine listening some reasons have to be given for their use. Pupils need to be told why their responses are good for the reinforcement to be regarded as genuine.

Another aspect of reinforcement that is a potent indicator of effective listening is *reference to past statements*. This can range from simply remembering someone's name to remembering other details about facts, feelings or ideas they have expressed in the past. This shows a willingness to pay attention to what was previously discussed and in turn is likely to encourage the person to participate more fully in the present interaction. This is part of the process of *verbal following*, whereby the listener matches verbal responses closely to those of the speaker, so that they 'follow on' in a coherent fashion. If the listener makes linked statements that build upon the ideas expressed by the speaker, this is an indication of attentiveness and interest.

However, a distinction needs to be made between *coherent topic shifts*, which occur once the previous topic has been exhausted, and *noncoherent topic shifts*, which are abrupt changes of conversation that are not explained. We often use *disjunct markers* to signal a change of topic ('Incidentally...', 'Can I ask you a different question?' 'Before I forget...'). In the early stages of a relationship, individuals usually ensure that a disjunct marker is used before making a noncoherent topic shift, whereas once a relationship has been developed the need for such disjunct markers recedes. Thus, long-term partners often use unmarked noncoherent topic shifts during conversation without this unduly affecting their relationship. However, in professional interactions disjunct markers are advisable where verbal following does not take place.

It is also important to keep *interruptions* to a minimum. The words of the ancient Greek philosopher Xenocrates should be borne in mind: 'I have often regretted my speech, never my silence'. Research studies have shown that interruptions are not well received during interactive episodes (Halone and Pecchioni, 2001; Farley, 2008), and that the more frequent the number of interruptions, the greater the negative effect on the speaker (Gnisci *et al.*, 2012). In their study of doctor–patient consultations, Tallman *et al.* (2007) found that physician interruptions were related to patient dissatisfaction. Doctors who received low satisfaction ratings from patients interrupted after one or two sentences, whereas those who were given high ratings allowed the patient up to five uninterrupted sentences during storytelling. Interruptions often result in inattentive clients with unfinished business. As Tallman *et al.* (2007, p. 22) cautioned,

> An interrupted story doesn't simply drift away. It stays with the patient. Sometimes the patient's issue was not important medically, but it *so occupied the patient's attention* that the patient did not attend to what the doctor had to say.

Within the skill of questioning (see Chapter 5) the use of *probing questions* is a direct form of listening, wherein the questioner follows up the responses of the respondent by asking related questions. What Kramer (2001) termed 'verbal door openers' are also useful (e.g. 'Would you like to talk about that a little bit more?'). Similarly, the skill of *reflecting* (see Chapter 6) represents a powerful form of response development. In order to reflect accurately the feeling, or the content, of what someone has said, it is necessary to listen carefully before formulating a succinct reflecting statement. The use of *summarisation* during periods of closure is further evidence of prolonged listening throughout an interaction sequence (see Chapter 10).

Nonverbal responses are important during listening (Bodie and Jones, 2012). A key feature of effective listening is the ability to combine the meaning from body language and paralanguage with the linguistic message (Burley-Allen, 1995; Rost, 2011). Certain nonverbal behaviours are associated with attending while others are associated with lack of listening. Thus, Rosenfeld and Hancks (1980) showed how head nods, forward-leaning posture, visual attention and eyebrow raises were all correlated with positive ratings of listening responsiveness. They also found the most prevalent vocalisation to be the guggle 'mm hmm', with the most frequent nonverbal listening indicator being the head nod. This latter finding was confirmed by Duggan and Parrott (2001), who showed that head nods and smiles were very potent indicators of listening in doctor–patient interchanges. The main nonverbal listening responses are shown in Box 7.4.

Parallel and contrasting nonverbal cues have been identified as signs of inattentiveness or lack of listening (Duggan and Parrott, 2001). The most common of these are:

- inappropriate facial expressions
- lack of eye contact
- poor use of paralanguage (e.g. flat tone of voice, no emphasis)

- slouched or shifting posture
- absence of head nods
- the use of distracting behaviours (e.g. rubbing the eyes, yawning, writing or using a mobile device while the speaker is talking).

In fact, an effective technique to induce someone to stop talking is to use these indicators of nonlistening. These nonverbal signals can of course be deceiving, in that someone who is assimilating the verbal message may not appear to be listening. Most teachers have experienced the situation where a pupil appears to be inattentive and yet when asked a question is able to give an appropriate response. Conversely, people may engage in pretend listening, or *pseudo-listening*, where they show all of the overt signs of attending but are not actually listening at all (Sandow and Allen, 2005). This was referred to by Orbe and Bruess (2005, p. 181) as 'a masquerade for real listening'.

Although it is possible to listen without overtly so indicating, in most social settings it is important to demonstrate such attentiveness. Thus both the verbal and nonverbal determinants of active listening play a key role in social interaction. In fact, these signs are integrated in such a fashion that, in most cases, if either channel signals lack of attention this is taken as an overall indication of poor listening. Bearing the above types of listening in mind, a useful acronym for effective interpersonal listening is *PACIER*:

Box 7.4 Nonverbal signs of listening

1 *Smiles*: used as indicators of willingness to follow the conversation or pleasure at what is being said
2 *Direct eye contact*: In Western society, the listener usually looks more at the speaker than vice versa (in other cultures this may not be the case, and direct eye gaze may be viewed as disrespectful or challenging)
3 *Using appropriate paralanguage* to convey enthusiasm for the speaker's thoughts and ideas (e.g. tone of voice, emphasis on certain words, lack of interruption)
4 *Reflecting the facial expressions* of the speaker, in order to show sympathy and empathy with the emotional message being conveyed
5 *Adopting an attentive posture,* such as a forward or sideways lean on a chair. Similarly, a sideways tilt of the head (often with the head resting on one hand) is an indicator of listening. What is known as *sympathetic communication* involves the mirroring of overall posture, as well as facial expressions. Indeed, where problems arise in communication, such mirroring usually ceases to occur (see Chapter 6 for a fuller discussion of mirroring)
6 *Head nods* to indicate agreement or willingness to listen
7 *Refraining from distracting mannerisms*, such as doodling with a pen, fidgeting or looking at a watch

---

*P*erceive the other person's verbal and nonverbal communication.
*A*ttend carefully to gain maximum information.
*C*omprehend and assimilate the verbal message.
*I*nterpret the meaning of the accompanying nonverbals.
*E*valuate what is being said and, where appropriate, empathise.
*R*espond appropriately.

THE LISTENING PROCESS

At first sight listening may be regarded as a simple process (Figure 7.3) in which both sides take turns to respond and listen, but in fact this perspective needs to be extended to take full account of all of the processes involved (Figure 7.4). As we talk we also scan for feedback to see how our messages are being received. When we listen we evaluate what is being said, plan our response, rehearse this, and then execute it. While the processes of evaluation, planning and rehearsal usually occur subconsciously, they are important because they can interfere with the pure listening activity. Thus we may have decided what we are going to say before the other person has stopped speaking, and as a result may not be listening effectively. It is, therefore, important to ensure that those activities that mediate between listening and speaking do not interfere with the listening process itself.

In terms of the verbal message being received, listening is influenced by two main factors – reductionism and rationalisation.

Reductionism

The human memory is notoriously fallible. On average, we have forgotten about half of what we hear immediately after hearing it, and within 8 hours we remember only 35 per cent of the message (Adler *et al.*, 2013a). After 24 hours we have forgotten up to 80 per cent of the information received (Wilson, 2004). Since we can only

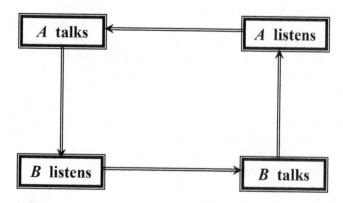

Figure 7.3 Basic model of listening.

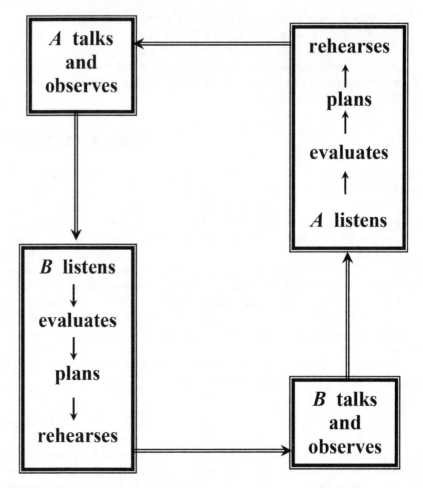

Figure 7.4 Extended model of listening.

assimilate a limited amount of data the messages we receive have to be reduced, sometimes at the expense of vital information. For this reason it is important to attempt to ensure that the central information being conveyed is remembered. Material should be organised into main themes, ideas and categories, and into a chronological sequence where possible. Such organisation must not, of course, interfere with the act of listening, but where time is available during interaction (as is usually the case), then this type of 'conceptual filing' can facilitate later recall.

Obviously, where it is possible to video- or audio-record the interaction this provides verbatim recall. However, this is not always feasible. Retention can also be facilitated by taking written notes of the main points emanating from the inter-action. As Bostrom (1990, p. 29) pointed out: 'Notetaking may enhance memory by enabling the receiver to transform the message so that it corresponds more closely with his or her own cognitive structure'. Such transformation involves several sub-processes, including the:

- increased mental activity involved in writing and listening;
- selection and reduction of material;
- repetition of the core features being presented;
- adaptation or translation of the message into more personally meaningful and accessible terminology.

These processes involved in note taking should enable the message to be more readily assimilated. Watson and Barker (1984) reported that note taking interchanged, rather than concurrent, with listening was more effective in terms of remembering what has been said. It is also socially more appropriate if note taking does not dominate the interaction, but is rather something that occurs sporadically, and is explained to the speaker ('Can I just note down some details before I forget them?'). Care needs to be taken, however, since it has been shown that note taking by doctors is regarded by patients as problematic. In particular, when the doctor consults medical records or makes notes therein, patients have been shown to become unsure about whether the doctor is actually listening or not (Ruusuvuori, 2001).

A range of memory device techniques can also serve as aids to memory. Dickson *et al.* (1997) highlighted three main mnemonics:

1 *acronyms,* such as PAIL for the four types of skin cuts: puncture, abrasion, incision, laceration;
2 *rhymes* to remember names, such as:
   'Big Bobby Blair,
   Very fat, red hair';
3 *visualisation,* whereby the listener creates a mental picture of what the speaker is saying – for example, trying to visualise a client's home environment and relationships as they are being described.

In a review of this area, Gellatly (1986) illustrated how mnemonics were a key part of early Greek and Roman education, and pointed out that mnemonics work by imposing organisation or order on the information to be remembered. While there is some research evidence to vindicate the use of these memory aids (Gregg, 1986), it would appear that their success is dependent both on the ability of the listener to use them, and upon the nature of the message being communicated.

The use of intrapersonal dialogue, wherein the listener engages in covert self-talk to heighten receptivity, can also facilitate retention. Egan (2014, p. 96) referred to this as 'listening to oneself', or having an 'internal conversation'. This may involve the use of:

- covert coaching (e.g. 'I'm not paying enough attention. I need to listen more carefully');
- self-reinforcement (e.g. 'I'm listening well and understanding what he is saying');
- asking covert questions (e.g. 'Why is she telling me this now?').

There is some evidence that, when listening to lectures, the latter technique of self-questioning may be most effective. King (1992) carried out a study in which she found that undergraduates trained to use self-questions (asking themselves questions during the lecture, such as 'What is the main idea of...?' 'How is this related to what we studied earlier?') remembered more about the lecture content 1 week later than either those taught to summarise the lecture in writing or those who simply took notes.

Rationalisation

As we listen, we assimilate information in such a way as to make it fit with our own situation and experience. If it does not fit immediately we may rationalise what we hear in order to make it more acceptable, but by so doing distort the facts. This occurs in four main ways.

1   We *attribute different causes* to those presented. Thus a patient may attribute a troublesome cough to the weather, or argue that it 'runs in the family', rather than accepting a practitioner's explanation that it is due to heavy smoking.

2   *Transformation of language* is a common form of rationalisation. This is often due to what Gregg (1986) termed *acoustic confusions,* caused by close similarity in the sounds of certain words. In the medical field products with similar-sounding names can be mixed up by doctors, nurses and pharmacists, with potentially tragic consequences (for example, in one case a Belgian patient died after being given the diuretic Lasix instead of the anti-ulcer drug Losec).

3   Paradoxically, given the aforementioned reductionism, there may be the *addition of material*. A classical instance of this occurs in everyday gossip, whereby a basic story is enlarged and embroidered upon during each re-telling, until it eventually becomes a sensational story. Care needs to be taken in professional situations to avoid 'reading too much into' what the client has said.

4   *Change in the order of events*. This is a common occurrence in the assimilation of information, whereby data becomes jumbled and remembered in the wrong order. Thus, 'Take two tablets three times daily after meals' is remembered as 'Take three tablets twice daily before meals'; or 'He lost his job and then started to drink heavily' becomes 'He started to drink heavily and then lost his job as a result'. Such transpositions can be obviated by the careful conceptual organisation of material being received.

FACTORS THAT INFLUENCE LISTENING

A number of factors influence the extent to which listening is effective. The main ones are personal factors, environmental factors, speech rate and delivery, emotionality, motivation and mental set.

Personal factors

Three main personal factors are relevant here: gender, age, and personality and disposition.

In relation to gender, there is now a substantial body of research to substantiate the view that females are more perceptive at recognising and interpreting nonverbal messages. Borisoff and Merrill (1991, p. 65), after reviewing the available evidence, concluded: 'Numerous studies have established women's superior abilities as both decoders and encoders of nonverbal messages when compared with men'. They suggested that part of the reason for these differences may be attributable to a status factor, in that lower-status people spend more time listening to higher-status people than vice versa and males may therefore conceptualise the listening role as being of lower status. However, this view is not in line with research findings by Johnson and Bechler (1998). They conducted a study at a Midwestern US university, where undergraduate students met in leaderless groups and were rated on leadership skills and on listening skills by separate teams of raters. Results showed that those rated high in listening behaviours by one set of coders were also rated high in leadership by a different set of coders. Interestingly, no differences were found in recall ability among subjects, and so it was the display of listening behaviour that was important. Johnson and Bechler concluded that their results confirm the general finding that leaders demonstrate more effective listening skills than other group members.

What may be the case is that each gender tends to tune into different aspects of a message, and indeed Adler *et al.* (2012) argued that often a female focuses more upon the relational dimension of the message while a male pays greater attention to the content. This was borne out in a study of 860 health professional students by Brown *et al.* (2010), where it was found that females had a stronger preference for people-oriented listening while males preferred a more content-oriented style (Box 7.3). Another difference is that males may be more likely to use head nods as a sign of agreement, whereas females often use them as indicators of attention but not necessarily agreement with the speaker (Stewart and Logan, 1998). This can lead to gender confusion if a male takes nods as agreement and then becomes annoyed when the female proceeds to express disagreement. However, much more research is required in order to chart the precise nature and extent of gender influence on listening ability.

Turning to age, findings show that some older people have greater difficulty with listening. One reason for this is due to a decline in working-memory capacity in some older individuals (Jost *et al.*, 2011). In his review of communication problems, Giordano (2000) noted that a reduced capacity for information processing can be problematic in this age group. However, he also emphasised that there are wide differences between older people, so that some will be more adversely affected than others. Indeed, age also brings positive changes, such as an increased vocabulary and a wealth of experience of dealing with people in various situations. Thus, listening faculties may be reduced or enhanced, depending upon the individual. The reaction to noise by age is, however, relatively consistent. Many young people enjoy noisy, rapidly changing environments with high levels of stimulation, and become bored if this is not available. With age our need for such levels of arousal decreases. Older adults in general prefer quiet, peaceful and tranquil surroundings and find noise off-putting. This is because they experience greater difficulty in coping with the cognitive interference caused by the intrusive stimuli. They are less able to manage divided attention, and so tend to be more susceptible to distraction from the effects of extraneous noise. So, when dealing with this age group the importance of securing a quiet location should be borne in mind. Likewise, reaction time and speech discrimination decrease with age, so that older people tend to need more time to process information and respond. This means that a slower rate of speech may be desirable. Giordano also recommended the use of periods of silence to allow the older person time for reflection. However, as discussed in Chapter 2, when communicating with the elderly, the dangers of *ageism* must be avoided, so that we should treat each person as an individual and not as an age.

In relation to personality and disposition, while more research is required to chart the nature of the relationship between personality and listening prowess, there are some trends. Highly anxious individuals have been shown to perform less well in listening (King and Behnke, 2004; Golchi, 2012), since they tend to be too worried about factors apart from the speaker to listen carefully to what is being said. As noted by Beck (1999, p. 63), 'Anxiety makes the mind wander from the current communication situation'. Golchi found that, in particular, higher levels of anxiety affected the ability to engage in appropriate metacognitive listening strategies (see Chapter 2). Likewise, those who are more susceptible to distractions are not good listeners, an extreme example being the hyperactive child. What Adler *et al.* (2013a) referred to as 'stage hogs' or 'conversational narcissists' are also poor listeners. These are dominating, self-centred, egotistical individuals who only want to talk and have no real interest in what others have to say. Introverts have been found to be better listeners than extraverts (Alavinia and Sameei, 2012), probably because they are content to sit back and let the speaker be the centre of attention. As would be anticipated, content-oriented listeners (Box 7.3) have been shown to have a higher *need for cognition* (Worthington, 2008), which is the desire to structure incoming information in a co-ordinated manner, sometimes referred to as the need to understand. Finally, those with a wider vocabulary are better listeners, since they can more readily understand and assimilate a greater range of concepts.

Environmental factors

Aspects of the environment affect listening. For example, listening is more difficult if the environment is either unpleasantly warm or cold (Kennedy *et al.*, 2006). Likewise, noise can be a major distraction (Beebe *et al.*, 2014). In a study of the impact of music on performance, Ransdell and Gilroy (2001) investigated the effects of music upon students' ability to write essays on computer. They found that music disrupted writing fluency. However, in this study the (perhaps unusual) choice of music (slow ballads taken from a Nelson Riddle Orchestra tape) was not self-selected by the students. By contrast, Bowman *et al.* (2007) found that listening to slow (but not fast) Mozart music, as compared to listening to rock music, improved students' listening comprehension on a videotaped lecture they viewed.

Again, however, the selection of rock music was not self-selected by subjects and was rather esoteric (Chuck Berry, Elton John and Billy Joel). In terms of inter-personal encounters, comprehension deteriorates when there is loud, intrusive noise that interferes with the assimilation process (such as building work going on outside). However, it remains unclear whether nonintrusive or self-selected back-ground noise has an adverse effect on listening or indeed facilitates it. For example, most pubs, restaurants and hotel lounges play background music to encourage con-versation. The level of noise is important, since background noise may be filtered out, whereas intrusive sounds cannot. However, the nature of the interaction is also relevant, so that a lecturer would not encourage even background noise if total concentration from students was desired. Dentists, on the other hand, often play background music to encourage patients to relax while in surgery.

Another factor is seating. Perhaps not surprisingly, one empirical study of 123 interactive dyads found that being seated was regarded as a facilitator to effec-tive listening (Halone and Pecchioni, 2001). If someone is expected to listen for a prolonged period, as in lecture theatres or classrooms, comfortable seating has been shown to be an important factor for listening effectiveness (Kennedy *et al.*, 2006). In group contexts, a compact seating arrangement is more effective than a scattered one. People pay more attention and recall more when they are brought close together physically, as opposed to when they are spread out around the room.

Speech rate and delivery

While the average rate of speech is 125–175 words per minute, the average 'thought rate' at which information is cognitively processed is 400–800 words per minute. The differential between speech and thought rate gives the listener an opportunity to assimilate, organise, retain and covertly respond to the speaker. However, this differential may also encourage the listener to fill up the spare time with other unrelated mental processes (such as daydreaming). Listening can be improved by using this spare thought time positively, by, for example, asking covert questions such as:

- 'What are the main points being made?'
- 'What reasons are being given?'
- 'In what frame of reference should this be viewed?'
- 'What further information is necessary?'

Where a speaker exceeds 300 words per minute, listening can be problematic. It is difficult to listen effectively for an extended period to a very rapid speaker, since we cannot handle the volume of information being received. Wolff *et al.* (1983, p. 155), in reviewing the literature on speech rate, however, concluded that listeners:

> prefer to listen, can comprehend better, and are more likely to believe a message that is presented at the rate of 190 words or more per minute... They demonstrate marked efficiency when listening to a speaker talking at 280 words per minute – twice the rate of normal speech.

Interestingly, as a result of such findings, television advertisers speeded up the rate of verbal presentation in their adverts, with positive results in terms of viewer comprehension and recall. However, here, listeners are only exposed to short blasts of material, accompanied by other visual and audio stimulation. In social contexts, a word of caution was noted by Janse (2004), who, following experimental studies in this field, concluded that speakers should only increase their speech rate if they are sure that listeners are able and willing to exert considerable effort to listening. The current findings also suggest that we have problems paying attention for lengthy periods to people who talk at, or below, the normal rate of speech. Professionals who have to deal with depressed clients will be aware of the problems involved in maintaining concentration with someone who says very little. Thus, when long pauses and a slow speech rate are used by a client, concentrated listening is required from the professional.

The topic of conversation and its degree of difficulty need to be factored into the equation. A slow speed may be appropriate with a complex issue, whereas with more basic material a faster pace is usually the norm. This was confirmed in a study by Robinson *et al.* (1997), where undergraduates were presented with taped lectures delivered at slow, moderate or fast rates. The results indicated that students receiving the slower speed comprehended the lectures better and rated the material as more important than those receiving the faster delivery. As a result of their findings Robinson *et al.* recommended that, for lectures, a speech rate of around 100 words per minute is most appropriate. One reason for this was identified by Dabbs (1985, p. 191), who observed: 'Long pauses are accepted by the participants in intellectual conversation as a normal result of trying to "figure things out", while long pauses in social conversation indicate things are not going well and will tend to be avoided'.

The clarity, fluency and audibility of the speaker all have an influence on listener comprehension. Thus, it requires effort to listen to, and comprehend, someone who speaks with a pronounced foreign accent, or who has a strong, unfamiliar, regional dialect. It is also difficult to listen to someone with a severe speech dysfluency, both because the message being delivered is disjointed, and because the listener is preoccupied thinking about how to respond to the dysfluency. Finally, it is not easy to pay attention to an individual who speaks in a dull monotone (as most students will testify), or who mumbles and does not have good voice projection.

Emotionality

If the speaker displays high levels of emotion, the listener may be distracted by this and cease to listen accurately to the content of the verbal message. In situations where individuals are in extreme emotional states, their communication is inevitably highly charged. It is often necessary to sustain an interaction in these circumstances. Sustaining can be defined as the process whereby someone experiencing an extreme emotional state is encouraged to ventilate, talk about and understand his or her emotions. When faced with a person experiencing extreme emotions (e.g. of depression or aggression) it is often not advisable either to reinforce positively or to rebuke the individual for this behaviour, since such reactions may well be counter-productive. For example, by rebuking an individual who is displaying aggressive behaviour, it is likely that this will only serve to heighten the aggression. A more reasoned response is to react in a calm fashion, demonstrating an interest in, without overtly reinforcing, the emotional person, but also showing a willingness to listen and attempt to understand what exactly has caused this to occur.

Only when strong emotional feelings begin to decrease can a more rational discussion take place. Someone who is 'too emotional' about something is likely to be 'too worked up about it' to listen to reasoned arguments. When dealing with an individual who is displaying high levels of emotion, it may be necessary to be prepared to wait for a period of time before this is ventilated. During this period the anxiety of the listener may interfere with the ability to listen carefully. Too much attention may be paid to the emotional message being conveyed, and as a result important information of a more factual nature may not be assimilated.

Motivation

A listener who is highly motivated will remember more of the information presented. The importance that we attach to an issue has been shown to affect our motivation to attend to it (Lecheler et al., 2009). If the message is of particular interest, or of special significance, comprehension and recall are heightened. In an experimental study in this area, Schneider and Laurion (1993) investigated how well undergraduates listened to and recalled items on radio news. They found greatest recall for 'high-interest' items of particular relevance (e.g. student-related issues, stories about their university). In addition, when the message conveys similar values, attitudes or viewpoints to our own, listening is facilitated, since most of us like to have our beliefs and expectations confirmed. Paradoxically, however, it has also been found that if a message contains a significant disconfirmation of our expectations, listening can also be heightened, as we are then motivated to evaluate this unexpected message. Thus, Frick (1992), in an investigation of the concept of 'interestingness', discovered that people find most interesting those statements that change, or challenge confidence in, their existing beliefs. Results also suggested that statements that advance our understanding are attended to with particular interest. An example given by Frick was that: 'a clinician would find most interesting those statements by a client that further the clinician's understanding of the client' (p. 126). In a similar vein, a social worker who suspects a parent of child abuse is likely to pay concerted attention to both the parent and the child when they are discussing parent–child relationships. At the same time, it is also important to pay attention to those areas that a client does not initiate. Indeed, listening theorists often emphasise the importance of listening to what is not being said by the speaker. Thus, a child who steadfastly avoids or blocks any discussion about a parent may well be sending out an important message.

If the speaker is regarded as an important person, or a recognised authority on a topic, listening motivation is increased, as more credence will be attached to what is being said. Also, more attention tends to be paid if the speaker is in a position of superiority. Motivation is therefore greater if the listener has admiration and respect for a speaker of high credibility. Holmes and Stubbe (2015) demonstrated how interruptions in workplace meetings are a manifestation of power, in that higher-status speakers are more likely to interrupt those of lower status. Similarly, Farley (2008) found that those who interrupt are perceived to be of higher status than those who have been interrupted, and those who had been interrupted rated themselves as less influential than those who had not been interrupted. On the other hand, the interrupters were rated as less likeable.

In terms of research into memory, two types of inhibition affect listening motivation (Quinlan and Dyson, 2008). Proactive inhibition occurs when something that has already been learned interferes with attempts to learn new material. A parallel problem is retroactive inhibition, which is where material that has already been learned is impaired as a result of the impact of, and interference from, recent material. In interpersonal encounters inhibition also occurs. *Retroactive listening inhibition* is where the individual is still pondering over the ramifications of something that happened in the recent past, at the expense of listening to the speaker in the present interaction. *Proactive listening inhibition* takes place when someone has an important engagement looming, and a preoccupation with this militates against listening.

Those who are not motivated to listen may use the process of blocking to divert the conversation or end it as soon as possible. The main blocking techniques are presented in Box 7.5. On occasions, some of these are legitimate. For

Box 7.5 Blocking tactics to listening	
Tactic	Example
Rejecting involvement	'I don't wish to discuss this with you' 'That has nothing to do with me'
Denial of feelings	'You've nothing to worry about' 'You'll be all right'
Selective responding	Focusing only on specific aspects of the speaker's message, while ignoring other parts of it
Admitting insufficient knowledge	'I'm not really qualified to say' 'I'm only vaguely familiar with that subject'
Topic shift	Changing the topic away from that expressed by the speaker
Referring	'You should consult your doctor about that' 'Your course tutor will help you on that'
Deferring	'Come back and see me if the pain persists' 'We'll discuss that next week'
Pre-empting any communication	'I'm in a terrible rush. See you later' 'I can't talk now. I'm late for a meeting'

example, a pharmacist would be expected to refer a patient to a doctor immediately if a serious illness were suspected. However, it is where blocking is used negatively that it becomes a serious obstacle to effective listening.

Mental set

We are all affected by previous experiences, attitudes, values and feelings, and these in turn influence our mental set for any given situation (see Chapter 10). We evaluate others based on their appearance, initial statements or what they said during previous encounters. These influence the way the speaker is heard, in that statements may be screened so that only those aspects that fit with specific expectations are perceived. The process of stereotyping acts as a form of cognitive short-cut that enables us to deal swiftly with others without having to make the effort to find out about them (see Chapter 2). Here all members of a particular group are regarded as homogeneous and having identical traits and behaviour patterns. By ascribing a stereotype to the speaker (e.g. racist, delinquent) we then become less objective. Judgements tend to be based on who is speaking, rather than on what is being said. While it is often important to attempt to evaluate the motives and goals of the speaker, this should be achieved by a reasoned, rational process, rather than by an irrational or emotional reaction to a particular stereotype. The listener should not enforce ascribed meaning to what the speaker has said by forcefully imposing his or her interpretation upon the other, in statements such as 'I heard what you said, but I know what you really mean' (Galanes and Adams, 2012). It is important to listen both carefully and objectively to everything that is being communicated.

Oscar Wilde clearly identified one of the pitfalls of listening when he said: 'Listening is a very dangerous thing. If one listens one may be convinced.' Part of mental set is the biases that we possess; these are like comfort blankets – we do not like them to be threatened and cannot contemplate losing them. One study of what individuals wanted from others, in terms of listening, showed that two key features were that the listener should put personal biases aside and be open-minded (Halone and Pecchioni, 2001). Yet in reality it is almost impossible to listen to others in a totally unbiased way (Egan, 2014). The biases we have developed as part of our upbringing and socialisation are filters that can distort the messages we receive. Thus, we often evaluate a message not on what is being said but on who is saying it. Likewise, someone who does not want to recognise difficult realities may refuse to accept these when expressed by another – either by distorting the message or by refusing to listen to the speaker altogether. At another level, people may not respond accurately to questions or statements, simply because they wish to make a separate point when given the floor. One example of this is politicians who want to ensure, at all costs, that they get their message across, and when asked questions in public meetings frequently do not answer these accurately, but rather take the opportunity to state their own point of view.

The above factors can constitute obstacles to effective listening, as shown in Figure 7.5.

Listening stage	Obstacles
Sensing	External noise (e.g. roadworks outside) Physical impairments (e.g. hard of hearing) Information overload
Attending	Poor speaker delivery (e.g. monotone) Overly long messages Lack of message coherence or structure Fatigue Uncomfortable environment Poor attending habits or disposition Negative attitudes to the speaker
Understanding	Low academic or linguistic ability Selective listening Mental set and biases of the listener Inability to empathise Different speaker/listener backgrounds
Remembering	Poor short-term listening ability Memory store limitations Proactive and retroactive inhibition

Figure 7.5 Obstacles to listening.

OVERVIEW

There is a well-known story about the main difference between the two nineteenth-century UK prime ministers Benjamin Disraeli and William Gladstone. This purported that when you dined with Gladstone you left feeling he was the most intelligent, charming and witty person in England, but when you dined with Disraeli, you left feeling that you were the most intelligent, charming and witty person in England. The difference was in the listening ability of the two individuals. Listening is a fundamental component of interpersonal communication. In a survey of attitudes to various communication behaviours, Glynn and Huge (2008, p. 564) concluded, 'there are obvious social costs for those who always talk more than they listen in conversation'. One of the dangers was aptly noted by the former US president Calvin Coolidge, when he remarked: 'No man ever listened himself out of a job'. It is important to realise that listening is not something that just happens, but rather is an active process in which the listener decides to pay careful attention to the speaker. It involves focusing upon the speaker's verbal and nonverbal messages, while at the same time actively portraying verbal and nonverbal signs of listening. The following guidelines should be borne in mind:

1   *Get physically prepared to listen.* If the interaction is taking place in your own environment, provide an appropriate physical layout of furniture, ensure adequate temperature and ventilation and keep intrusive noise and other distractions to a minimum.

2   *Be mentally prepared to listen objectively.* Try to remove all other thoughts from your mind, and concentrate fully. Be aware of your own biases, avoid preconceptions and do not stereotype the speaker.

3   *Use spare thought time positively.* Keep your thoughts entirely on the message being delivered, by asking covert questions, constructing mental images of what is being said or employing other concentration techniques.

4   *Do not interrupt.* There is a Native American Indian proverb that advises: 'Listen or your tongue will make you deaf'. It is therefore important to 'hold your tongue' and let the other person contribute fully. Develop a system of *mental banking*, where ideas you wish to pursue can be cognitively 'deposited' and 'withdrawn' later. This allows the speaker to have a continuous flow, and the fact that you can later refer back to what has been said is a potent indicator of active listening.

5   *Organise the speaker's messages* into appropriate categories and, where relevant, chronological order. Identify the main thrust and any supporting arguments. This process facilitates comprehension and recall of what was said.

6   *Do not overuse blocking tactics.* These are often employed subconsciously to prevent the speaker from controlling an interaction.

7   *Remember that listening is hard work.* Winston Churchill once remarked: 'Courage is what it takes to stand up and speak. Courage is also what it takes to sit down and listen.' It takes energy and commitment to listen actively. It has been said the only place you will find easy listening is as a specialist section in music retail. Professionals who spend their working day listening will testify that it is an exhausting activity, and one that requires discipline and determination. Indeed, as Figley (2002) has shown, those who work in the therapeutic sphere (counsellors, health professionals, etc.) can suffer from the phenomenon of *compassion fatigue* as a result of concerted listening to accounts of traumatic experiences.

In concluding this chapter, it is useful to bear in mind one of the precepts proffered by Polonius to his son Laertes in Shakespeare's *Hamlet, Prince of Denmark*: 'Give every man thine ear, but few thy voice'.

Chapter 8

Getting your message across: the skill of explaining

INTRODUCTION

THE AMOUNT OF INFORMATION in circulation seems to grow like Topsy. The electronic blizzard of information technology, epitomised by the internet, produces an unending flow of material in the form of facts, theories, speculations and opinions variously intended to inform, entertain, sell, shock or persuade. Billions of texts and e-mails are sent daily. At the same time, and despite predictions to the contrary, the volume of printed paper continues to increase exponentially. For example, about one million new books are published every year, and there are over 60,000 academic journals publishing numerous editions annually. Not surprisingly, information overload is a condition experienced by many. Being exposed in this way to a mish-mash of data, of course, does not automatically make us better informed. For this to happen, we need more than to have material simply 'dumped' upon us. Rather, it has to be delivered in such a way that we can sort it out and make sense of it. This chapter is devoted to the processes involved in delivering information in such a way as to maximise comprehension. The focus will be upon the task of sharing detail and educing understanding. Presentations that rely more upon emotion and are intended primarily to persuade (rather than enlighten) through creating changes in attitude or opinion (rather than knowledge) will be dealt with in Chapter 12.

Referring to communication within organisations, Clampitt (2013) highlighted three different dimensions: *data*, *information* and *knowledge*. While recognising difficulties in providing precise definitions of each, data is said to concern particular representations of reality, not all of which may be accurate or relevant to that person at that time. Information is created when certain elements are focused upon and isolated from background data, so enabling their potential contribution to decision making to be delineated.

Finally, knowledge relies upon recognising patterns and consistencies in information, thereby making possible the development of theories that can be tested. It is only such knowledge that produces effective action. There is, therefore, a need to give thought to the organisation of material, how it is delivered and to whom, if we are to benefit from what we read and hear, as well as successfully getting our own message across.

Explaining is a standard feature of everyday casual talk as well as forming the substance of more formal addresses to large gatherings attending lectures or public presentations. It is also a crucial part of skilled professional practice in areas such as education, health, medicine, technology, architecture, business and law (Brown, 2006). The importance of teachers being able to put across material in a way that pupils can readily grasp is obvious and has long been an abiding concern of educationalists (Thyne, 1963). Indeed, in their review of the area, Grant *et al.* (2010, p. 5) concluded that there is, 'compelling evidence regarding the influence of the classroom teacher on student learning...out of all the factors that are within the control of schools, teachers have the greatest impact on student achievement'. In the health context, patients have a need for information about diagnosis, prognosis, condition or treatment to be delivered in ways that they can understand (Pawlikowska *et al.*, 2012). Hajek *et al.* (2007) produced evidence linking patients' judgements of doctors' ability to explain matters in language familiar to them with patients' estimates of their likelihood of subsequently complying with received medical advice. Likewise, in the world of law, advice and instruction that may be couched in arcane (indeed, archaic) language has to be communicated clearly if recipients are not to be disadvantaged.

In the modern corporate environment professionals must be effective communicators. It is pointless having good ideas if others cannot grasp or appreciate them. In their analysis of communication styles, Bakker-Pieper and de Vries (2013) identified 'expressiveness' as a style that involves being articulate, energetic, eloquent, fluent and assured. This obviously links directly to the ability to deliver effective explanations. However, explaining is an activity often performed poorly by many professionals. This was summarised, in early work in the field of teaching, by Gage *et al.* (1968, p. 3):

> Some people explain aptly, getting to the heart of the matter with just the right terminology, examples and organization of ideas. Other explainers, on the contrary, get us and themselves all mixed up, use terms beyond our level of comprehension, draw inept analogies and even employ concepts and principles that cannot be understood without an understanding of the very thing being explained.

But teachers need not be singled out for special attention. Instances of health care professional–patient conversation have been pinpointed where deficiencies in information giving lie at the heart of poor levels of communication (Dickson and McCartan, 2005; Hagihara *et al.*, 2006; Office of the Health Services Commissioner, 2008). Patients often complain about not being told enough by doctors, and not understanding what is said when they are given explanations

(Brataas *et al.*, 2009). As noted by McSherry and Pearce (2011, p. 73): 'For healthcare professionals and organisations to deliver quality standards, effective communication and information-giving are essential'.

Moving from health to law, doubts have been expressed about how well the law system works in some US courts (Baum, 2013). At the centre of the process of criminal justice is a trial overseen by a judge, whose task it is to apply the appropriate law and make the jury familiar with it. The jury in turn is charged with applying that law to the evidence in reaching a verdict. The extent to which this is effectively achieved can be limited by the extent to which jury members comprehend the instructions received. Specific problems of comprehension have to do with vocabulary and the technical meaning of some terms that can be at odds with everyday interpretations. Additionally, instructional material can be poorly structured and awkwardly expressed (Solan and Tiersma, 2005). Referring specifically to jurors' difficulties in grasping the nuances of patent law, Caliendo (2004, p. 210) concluded that 'there exists a common failure to communicate to juries a statement of the law that is both clear and correct'.

In the world of management, the ability to get facts, ideas and judgements across in a clear and pithy way is no less valued (Hartley and Chatterton, 2015). As summarised by Rowan (2003, p. 404): 'just as good informative and explanatory communication is appreciated, the effects of poor informing and explaining are feared ... poor informative and explanatory communication skills lead to frustration between shift employees, lost revenue, and misunderstood employee benefit provisions'. Managers can be expected to give numerous formal presentations every year, and this aspect of the managerial role gains even greater prominence as careers progress (Adler *et al.*, 2012; Chesebro, 2014). Not surprisingly, surveys of employers consistently show that a key skill they seek in potential managers is the ability to explain and present material in a coherent, convincing and stimulating manner (Guffey and Loewy, 2013; Hamilton, 2014). Employees prefer communication from their line managers to be direct, easily understood and succinct (Hargie and Tourish, 2009). Oral briefings mostly fail because they are too long-winded, include too few examples, are unattractively delivered and have content that is poorly organised and contains too much technical jargon.

It is therefore essential that a broad range of professionals have the skills necessary to deliver effective explanations that are comprehensible to a variety of audiences. But, first, let us examine the nature of explanations *per se*.

WHAT IS AN EXPLANATION?

This is a deceptively simple question, but one that has occupied philosophers and social scientists for some time (Achinstein, 1983; Brown, 2006; Faye, 2014). One particular semantic knot to be unravelled is whether 'explaining' is essentially the same as other activities, such as 'describing', 'instructing' and 'relating', involving the giving of information, or in some way different from these. A further difficulty centres upon whether anything has to be understood for an explanation to have occurred. But let us leave this matter aside for the moment and tackle the first issue.

Some take a very broad and inclusive approach to defining what represents an explanation. For Hamilton (2014), an explanation involves activities such as defining a word or term, giving instructions on how to do something or describing the relationship between items. Even more broadly defined by Martin (1970, p. 59), 'the job of someone who explains something to someone…is to fill in the gap between his audience's knowledge or beliefs about some phenomena and what he takes to be the actual state of affairs'. Here we see that what counts is leaving the audience knowing or believing something of which they were previously uninformed. In a sense it does not really matter if information given is strictly accurate, provided that the explainer takes what is told to be the case. At the other extreme, explaining has been thought of in a much more restrictive sense as a special type of 'telling'. Here an explanation is different from a description, instruction or speculation. What is peculiar about it is that it goes beyond mere description to give reasons or reveal causes for the facts or events under discussion. In other words, answering the question 'why?' is an implicit or explicit feature of the process.

One way around this definitional dilemma is to think of categories of explanation rather than just explanations versus nonexplanations. Some, but not all, of these may have to do with presenting cause-and-effect relationships. One of the most pragmatic and robust typologies is that provided by Brown (2006), who outlined *descriptive*, *interpretive* and *reason-giving* varieties (Box 8.1).

- *Descriptive explanations* are provided when presenting information about specific procedures, structures, processes or directions. They typically address the question 'how?'
- *Interpretive explanations* define or clarify issues, meanings or statements. Here, the question that is mainly being responded to is 'what?'
- *Reason-giving explanations* specify the cause-and-effect relationships that account for some phenomenon or the reasons behind some action or event. They are commonly occasioned by the question 'why?' Within this category, Pavitt (2000) made a further distinction between *functional* and *causal* explanations. Functional explanations are required when the audience is confused about the purpose of some phenomenon. Causal explanations set out cause-and-effect relationships and often invoke laws or general principles.

But the term 'to explain' has two further meanings, one referring to the intention of the speaker, the other the success of the outcome (Turney *et al.*, 1983). Adopting the former, but not the latter, it makes sense to say, 'I explained it to him but he did not understand'. What counts for Achinstein (1983) in this respect is that:

- The speaker intends to answer the listener's question.
- The speaker believes that what is said is a correct answer to the question.
- The intention is to answer the question directly.
- The listener appreciates the speaker's intentions in these respects.

Box 8.1 Examples of types of explanation

Descriptive

- Going over the steps of how to bath a baby
- Outlining how to operate a new computer program

Interpretive

- Making clear the significance of a white line on an X-ray of a damaged leg
- Providing the meaning of the word 'oxymoron'

Reason giving

- Pointing out why wage rises that are not linked to productivity can trigger inflation
- Explaining why some trees lose their leaves in winter

Causal

- Outlining why sunbathing can lead to skin cancer
- Setting out the sequence of steps leading from turning the key in the ignition to a car engine firing up

Functional

- Explaining why flamingos have funny-shaped bills
- Presenting reasons why racing cars have broad wheels and spoilers

Note that there is no mention here of the listener's consequent level of comprehension. In professional contexts, however, this usage is clearly not sufficient. Rather, when it is said that something has been explained by a teacher or doctor, not only is it an expectation but a requirement that it be understood by the pupil or patient. As such, the claim, 'I explained it to him but he did not understand' would be inherently contradictory. This stipulation is partly reflected in the working definition proffered by Brown and Edmunds (2009, p. 76) that, 'Explaining is concerned with giving understanding to others'. This way of thinking also sits foursquare with the original meaning of the word as derived from the Latin verb *explanare*, 'to make plain'.

ABOUT EXPLAINING

Any particular explanation may involve elements that are descriptive, interpretive, causal or functional. It may also take place in the context of an impromptu encounter with another, as for instance when a manager clarifies some aspect of company policy to a member of staff. Alternatively, it can be a well-prepared, formal presentation to a group. Explanations can also take contrasting forms.

We tend to think of the *monologue* approach with the explainer delivering a 'lecture' while the recipient listens. But the *Socratic technique* can be very effective when it comes to creating understanding. Named after the Greek philosopher renowned for his technique of responding with a whole series of questions when asked to explain some abstract idea, such as 'justice', we can often lead others to understanding in a dialogue where we do most of the questioning (Box 8.2). This approach has the advantage of affording the listener an active role in the learning process.

Three principal modes of explaining can be employed:

1   *Verbal explanations* rely exclusively upon the spoken (or written) word to carry meaning and create understanding.
2   *Illustrations* supplement verbal presentations with pictures, models, graphs, videos, and so on.
3   *Demonstrations* involve 'explaining by doing'. They are a very practical and applied way of getting information across, usually about some process or technique.

It is difficult to legislate for skilful explaining. Regardless of the particular topic, there is no one proper way of presenting it that guarantees success. Adequacy is directly related to the recipient's age, background knowledge and ability (Jucks *et al.*, 2012). How finely should the concept be broken down? At what level should it be pitched? How can it be related to other material? What activities can the audience benefit from engaging in? These are the sorts of decisions faced by many professionals on a day-to-day basis.

Box 8.2 The Socratic technique

Why have camels got flat feet?

Mother: 'Well, Jane, where do camels live?'
Jane: 'In the desert'.
Mother: 'That's right. What is the ground like in the desert?'
Jane: 'It's all sandy'.
Mother: 'Where else can sand be found?'
Jane: 'At the beach'.
Mother: 'Yes, do you remember last summer on the beach when we played ball?'
Jane: 'Oh yes!'
Mother: 'What was it like trying to run on the soft sand?'
Jane: 'It was really hard. My feet dug in.'
Mother: 'Yes, so did mine. What though if we had large, flat feet like a camel?'
Jane: 'Oh, so that is why camels have flat feet'.

Box 8.3 Purposes of explaining

The main goals served by the skill of explaining are to:

1 provide others with information otherwise unavailable
2 simplify complexity
3 illustrate the essential features of particular phenomena
4 clarify uncertainties revealed during interaction
5 express opinions regarding particular attitudes, facts or values
6 reach some common understanding
7 demonstrate how to execute a specific skill or technique
8 empower others through giving understanding and increased autonomy
9 ensure learning

What may work as a clear and concise outline for one individual can get another person confused and frustrated, while a third may find it insultingly patronising. Perhaps the most fundamental rule is that explanations must be tailored to the needs, abilities and backgrounds of the audience. The onus is on the explainer to establish at what level an explanation should be pitched and how it can best be delivered.

PURPOSES OF EXPLAINING

The main goals of explaining are listed in Box 8.3. Some of these take precedence, depending upon the context of the interaction. Successfully meeting the needs and wants of recipients, particularly in professional contexts, is an important guiding principle. In health care, research reviews demonstrate that many patients positively value and benefit from the presentation of information by health professionals about their condition (Dickson and McCartan, 2005; Bensing *et al.*, 2013). This is particularly so for 'monitors' – patients who actively search out and request such information. 'Blunters', by contrast, deliberately avoid this detail, especially when news may be unpleasant (Miller *et al.*, 1988; Duncan *et al.*, 2013). Moreover, while cancer patients want information pertaining to diagnosis and treatment, some do not want extensive detail at all stages of their illness (Leydon *et al.*, 2000; Brataas *et al.*, 2010).

Being able to impart information to patients in terms that they can readily grasp is a crucial communication skill for doctors (Schirmer *et al.*, 2005) and nurses (Arnold and Boggs, 2016). Giving adequate and relevant information and explanation can:

- promote patient adherence to treatment regimens (Phillips *et al.*, 2012);
- result in tangible benefits to patients in terms of reduced pain and discomfort and earlier recovery (Thompson, 1998; Carlson *et al.*, 2005);

- help to reassure patients and decrease their stress levels before a procedure is performed (Zhou and Humphris, 2014);
- reduce levels of nonattendance for medical appointments (Hamilton et al., 1999).

One study found that the explanation given by doctors before and after the procedure was a key determinant of patient satisfaction with endoscopy (Yanai et al., 2008). Indeed, in a large-scale survey of patients with the eye condition glaucoma, 60 per cent of those who reported changing doctors did so due to poor communication (Herndon et al., 2006). Deficient explanations have contributed to findings, such as that patients in general forget some 50 per cent of the information given by practitioners (Morrow and Hargie, 2001), and that many patients fail to adhere to medication regimens (Ratanawongsa et al., 2013).

Usable information is an important source of social power (see Chapter 12). It follows that informing and training are ways of self-empowering others through enabling them to make more informed decisions over matters affecting their lives without having to seek help and guidance. Personal autonomy is promoted as a result. As already discussed, explaining is a way of creating understanding on behalf of the audience. But having to explain material after being exposed to it can also be an effective way for the explainer to learn it. Hence, the old maxim: 'The best way to learn something is to have to teach it'. This was demonstrated in an experiment by Coleman et al. (1997), who discovered that setting students the task of subsequently explaining Darwin's theory of evolution through natural selection produced more learning and understanding of that material than asking them to summarise it, or merely listening to it. Rittle-Johnson (2006) also discovered self-explanation, or generating explanations for oneself, was effective in promoting learning among school pupils and in facilitating its subsequent transfer to the solving of new problems.

THE EXPLAINING PROCESS

We can think of the key features of explaining in terms of the 5-Ps model – pre-assessment, planning, preparation, presentation and postmortem. Each of these will be developed with the aid of a diagram (Figure 8.1) that extends the work of French (1994) and Kagan and Evans (1995). Although the first three are often overlooked in a rush to 'get on with it', when explanations go wrong it is often on account of inadequate forethought. Admittedly, the unexpected can often knock off course even the most carefully crafted presentation. However, studies have shown that competent planning and preparation are linked to clarity of explanations (Brown, 2006). Someone who has a firm grasp of the material to be put across, and has given thought to how best to do so, is much more likely to explain effectively.

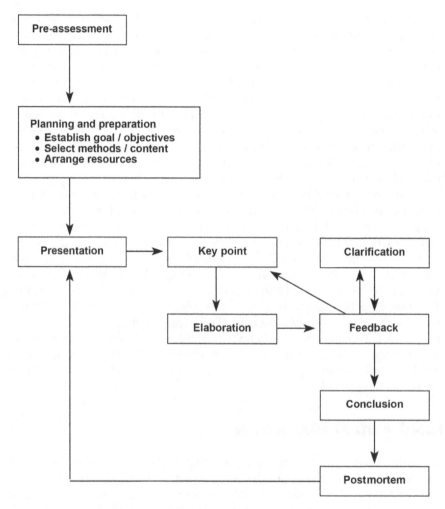

Figure 8.1 The '5-Ps' model of explaining.

PRE-ASSESSMENT

This has to do with finding out about the recipient and the circumstances that pertain before embarking on the mission to inform. Neglecting these considerations can result in much wasted effort – or worse. A quick checklist of what to assess includes:

- what the others want or need to know
- what they already know
- their ability to make sense of what they are about to hear
- the potential emotional impact of the material.

Referring to scientific explanations, Gilbert *et al.* (1998) claimed that an audience's judgement of the adequacy of an explanation is a feature of the extent to which it meets a need. This will depend on the degree to which prior relevant knowledge and understanding are taken into account, and the use that can be made of the explanation in the future. Professionals such as doctors (Thompson, 1998) and judges (Solan and Tiersma, 2005) often make the mistake of overestimating what patients and jurors already know. Health workers should establish, at the outset, whether what appears to be a request for information is indeed that, rather than, perhaps, a plea for reassurance (Brataas *et al.*, 2009). Nurses sometimes respond to the former with reassurance and to the latter with a factual explanation (Kagan and Evans, 1995).

Finding out what is already known makes sense not only from the point of view of avoiding needless repetition but also in establishing a suitable starting point from which to launch the explanation. Again, without some appreciation of the audience's linguistic code and cognitive abilities, it is highly probable that information will be pitched at entirely the wrong level. Thus, successful teachers build pupil understanding, other pupil characteristics and available resources into their planning. To explain effectively requires a certain empathic understanding of the other, in that the explainee's perspective must be taken into account. The explainer must develop a feel for how what is being proposed will be received and experienced. For example, in situations where the patient is not ready to receive further detail about condition or treatment, attempting an explanation along these lines is a futile exercise (Berger, 2005).

PLANNING AND PREPARATION

Monarth and Kase (2007) made the point that, in general, the more time available for preparation, the better the performance is likely to be. Likewise, Duck and McMahan (2012) illustrated how the success of presentations is largely dependent upon what takes place during the planning stage. But time available to plan and make adequate preparation will obviously differ depending upon settings and circumstances. Nevertheless, it is usually the case that the more thought that can be given to what needs to be covered and how best to do so, the better the end result. This is realised by the more experienced professional. Carter (1990) noted that novice teachers tend to jump in without giving adequate thought and planning to the task in hand. More expert teachers on the other hand develop:

- *cognitive schemata* which rely on the integration of specialised knowledge linked to specific situations (see Chapter 2);
- *organisational knowledge* in terms of how concepts are related and form a pattern;
- *tacit knowledge*, which is constructed from repeated experiences over time.

Planning and preparation comprise several sequenced and inter-dependent sub-tasks.

Establish goals/objectives

An explanation may be triggered by a direct request from someone who needs or wants to know something. Alternatively it may be the explainer who initiates the exchange. In the latter case, an important first step may be to create a 'felt need' on the part of recipients. They should have a sense that listening to what is about to be said will be worthwhile (see the section on motivational set in Chapter 10). Regardless of who initiates the episode, the explainer must have a firm grasp of the issue to be dealt with and what the explanation should achieve (Hamilton, 2014). A broad goal may be broken down into specific objectives and thought of in terms of changes brought about in recipients (Bradbury, 2010). These may relate to:

* what they should be able to *do* (*behavioural objective*);
* what they should *know and understand* (*cognitive objective*);
* *feelings* and *attitudes* that they should hold (*affective objective*).

Identify content and select methods

Here decisions are taken about the content of the explanation (the actual material to be put across) and how best to deliver this. Linked in turn to the material to be covered are the boundaries that circumscribe it, marking the relevant from the irrelevant. There is a logic that connects this set of judgements with those concerning goals and objectives. Each type of objective will suggest a somewhat different approach to giving information. For example, if the intention is that the audience should be able to complete some manual task involving an element of skill, a demonstration coupled with practise opportunities may be required. A need simply to know, on the other hand, could probably be satisfied with a verbal explanation or illustration.

Organise content

In discussing the importance of preparing your presentation and structuring the content, Beagrie (2007) cautioned that without a 'map' both you and your audience, in trying to reach your destination, will probably only succeed in getting lost. Once subject matter is firmly located, several other processes come into play. They include:

* selecting the key elements
* determining how these key elements are related
* structuring and linking the explanation to the particular audience.

Any body of information will have key elements that really must be grasped. In identifying these, Adler *et al.* (2012) advocated teasing out no more than five such elements. A greater number poses problems for the audience's powers of memory and will most likely be quickly forgotten. But it is not just presenting the main points that matters – how they inter-relate is also important. This in turn will suggest a sensible approach to structuring the explanation so that it moves, for instance, from the simple to the complex, and is easy to follow. Research in the teaching context shows that the teacher's ability to prepare, structure, organise and sequence facts and ideas with the maximum of logical coherence is positively related to pupil achievement (Wragg and Brown, 2001). Some alternative strategies to be adopted when it comes to structuring material can be found in Box 8.4.

Box 8.4 Strategies for organising content

1 *Topical arrangement.* Here the issue is analysed into related topics and sub-topics to be presented – the key elements. These have no particular relationship to one another, apart from shared relevance. The order in which they are covered is typically shaped by going from (1) the known to the unknown, and (2) the simple to the complex

2 *Chronological sequence.* In this case the key elements contained are ordered in relation to a timeline (e.g. describing how the company evolved to its present state, or outlining the steps involved in a manufacturing process)

3 *Logical sequence.* There are two alternatives here. The deductive sequence moves from general principles to what needs to be done in certain specific cases of relevance to the group. The converse, inductive sequence, begins with specific cases and from them moves to the derivation of broad principles that should be accepted and applied

4 *Causal pattern.* Here the material is ordered in terms of a sequence of cause-and-effect relationships that explains events and why they came about. It can be extended into the next possibility

5 *Problem–solution.* This option structures the presentation into two sections. The first sketches the nature of the problem. The second maps the solution

6 *Motivated sequence.* This is a more elaborate alternative than the previous. It is particularly suited when the intention is to change attitudes, beliefs or practices. It follows the sequence of gaining attention, establishing need, outlining how that need can be satisfied, helping the audience to visualise the satisfied need and finally stipulating what has to be done to accomplish that state

---

Arrange resources

This point is particularly apt in the context of a more formal presentation. Part of preparation is arranging for all the various resources to be available, and in working order, when and where you need them. If possible, it is also worthwhile checking out the location of the presentation in advance and the actual room which has been set aside. This includes familiarising oneself with the size and layout of the room, lighting and equipment. These can all influence levels of comfort and be more or less conducive to learning. They will also shape what it is possible to do with the group.

PRESENTATION

While the potential of an explanation will be enhanced as a result of the above preparatory processes, effectiveness ultimately depends upon the flow of the discourse and levels of clarity created. As shown in Figure 8.1, sequenced and ordered key points should be presented one at a time. After making a key point, this should be elaborated upon and understanding checked before moving on to the next. If necessary, clarification can be provided. Although relatively few studies have been concerned with the identification of effective planning and structuring aspects, a great deal of research has focused on presentation skills and tactics. An examination of these research findings has revealed a number of crucial features.

Clarity

A key goal of any explanation is to clarify the subject matter under focus. Such clarification of content also requires clarity of delivery. Clear explanations tend to be understood: those that are unclear simply cause confusion. Not surprisingly, having the ability to get one's message across clearly has been shown to a key feature of effective explaining (Engleberg and Daly, 2006; Bambacas and Patrickson, 2008). Of course, explainers need to know their subject, but while this may be necessary, it is not a sufficient condition for success. Their knowledge base is only one part of the equation. The topic still has to be communicated to an audience in a clear, unambiguous and structured way. Instructional clarity encompasses two inter-related elements: first, the structure of content and how different elements that make up the body of material are organised and, second, how that content is delivered. As far as the first element is concerned, Brown (2006) identified four structuring moves associated with clarity.

1   *Signposts.* These are statements that provide the listener with an advanced framework for structuring the information to come. As the name suggests, their function is to point the direction ahead and chart the path that will be taken. For example, a fitness instructor may begin explaining why a pulse

monitor is being used by saying, 'Let me first explain what a pulse monitor does in measuring your heart rate, then the importance of knowing how hard you are working when you train. Finally, I will go over how this information can be used to work out different training schedules for you.' In essence, these comments are the equivalent of the introduction in a report or essay.

2   *Frames*. These are words or phrases that mark the beginnings and endings of sections within the body of the talk. They are used to indicate the boundaries of specific topics or sub-topics contained in the explanation. Frames are particularly useful when the material is complex, with different embedded sub-elements. To continue with the example, a frame would be, 'OK. That covers what the pulse monitor does in picking up an electrical signal from the heart, each time it beats. Moving on from there to why that information is useful to you as you train...'

3   *Foci*. Foci statements highlight or emphasise key features of the explanation and help to make these 'stand out' from a backdrop of lesser material. Foci statements in relation to the ongoing example would be:

> 'Don't forget, you should always make sure someone is with you if you try to check your maximum pulse'.
> 'So remember, never turn training sessions into races'.
> 'It's very important that you include some recovery sessions in your regime as well'.

4   *Links*. Most talks or explanations cover a series of sub-topics, each designed to contribute to the listener's overall knowledge of a subject. Links are important in two respects. First, clarity of comprehension is improved if the speaker links the sub-topics into a meaningful whole. Second, speakers should try to link their explanation to the experience, previously acquired knowledge and observations of the audience. Using our ongoing example, links might include:

> Now you see, given that the heart adapts to higher levels of demand, why it is important to organise training so that you are continually asking a little more of it each time, to notice improvements in your fitness level. It's just like any other muscle, in that sense. The pulse monitor lets you check accurately how hard your heart is working.

There is classroom-based evidence that greater clarity of exposition is associated with increased liking by students of both teacher and course, lower levels of learner apprehension and heightened student motivation; moreover, students also tend to learn more under these circumstances (Comadena *et al.*, 2007; Stronge *et al.*, 2011; Orlich *et al.*, 2013). In the higher-education sector, among the main sources of dissatisfaction that students have with lectures are incoherence and failure of the lecturer to pitch the material at a level appropriate to the group (Brown, 2006).

Concision

The old maxim that 'A little remembered is better than a lot forgotten' has much to commend it when it comes to giving information. An explanation that carries more detail than is necessary is just as defective as one that does not carry enough – a key feature of effective explanations is that they are succinct (Harper, 2004). Thus, one study of first-year college students found that the introduction of additional quantitative material, in the form of illustrations and formulae not directly germane to the task, produced less effective learning (Mayer and Jackson, 2005). It has long been known that, in relation to the lecture context in colleges, 'learning begins to diminish seriously after fifteen minutes' (Verner and Dickinson, 1967, p. 90). In health-care situations where patients may be distracted by pain or have little energy, the crucial time period will be considerably shorter. Providing too much detail has been shown to be a communication problem in community care (Groogan, 1999). Indeed, Clampitt (2013, p. 144), in his analysis of organisations, likened information to food, and asserted that, 'There are far too many managers who have grown fat on information, but are starved for knowledge'. One way to 'diet' strongly advocated by Blundel (1998) is by embracing the KISS principle – 'keep it short and simple'.

Fluency

A fluent delivery is essential to effective explanation. For example, successful politicians have a fluent, flowing style of presentation that helps to convey an image of competence in the speaker and confidence in the message. Based upon over 30 years' observation of lectures and conferences, Bassnett (2007) concluded that the key to improving the quality of such events lay with enhancing delivery, by not speaking too fast, being fluent, having good voice projection and looking at the audience. For presentations to be successful, sloppy speech, poor enunciation and imprecise diction need to be rectified (Beaver, 2006). It is not only annoying to listen to garbled, rambling sentences punctuated all the way through with speech dysfluencies, but this annoyance can very quickly lead to inattention. Christenfeld (1995), in a study of undergraduates, reported that impressions of quality were negatively affected when speakers used a profusion of 'ums', and attributed their over-use to anxiety or lack of preparation on the part of the speaker. In the school context, Wragg and Brown (2001) also found that a fluent delivery was associated with explaining effectiveness in terms of subsequent pupil achievement.

Some of the main types of dysfluency shown in Box 8.5, such as a lisp or stammer, may require specialised treatment, whereas others can be occasioned by particular circumstances. As noted by Crystal (1997, p. 280), 'everyone is prone to hesitation, especially in situations where they have to speak under pressure'. The occasional dysfluency will not have a negative impact upon a presentation; it is their overuse that is problematic, as they then interfere with the listener's ability to pay attention to the central message. One of the main causes

---

Box 8.5 Ten ways to be dysfluent

1 *Filled pauses* – 'um', 'uh', 'er'
2 *Discourse markers* – e.g. 'sort of', 'you know', 'anyway'
3 *Sloppy diction* – lack of clear enunciation of word sounds
4 *Articulation handicaps* – lisp, etc.
5 *Stammering* – difficulty in controlling the rhythm and timing of speech
6 *False starts* – e.g. 'I must mention…well, maybe first I should say…of course, you may already know…'
7 *Poorly organised sentences* – e.g. 'well, we didn't intend when we left…see, John had this ticket…oh, and Jane phoned me…'
8 *Hesitation* – 'Can I…say that…'
9 *Cluttering* – abnormally fast rate of speech, with syllables running into each other
10 *Lack of voice projection* – e.g. mumbling

---

of dysfluency is trying to put too many ideas or facts across in one sentence. It is better to use reasonably short sentences, with pauses in between, than long, rambling ones full of subordinate clauses. Another cause of dysfluency is lack of adequate planning and forethought. Being thoroughly familiar with the material to be delivered enhances one's confidence and increases the likelihood of a fluent presentation.

Two main types of dysfluency have been the subject of research: filled pauses (such as 'um' or 'uh') and discourse markers (words or phrases such as 'kind of', 'I mean', 'like'). Lasernal *et al.* (2014) found that, during natural conversations, discourse markers (the most common being 'like') were used more often by women and younger people, but there was no difference in the usage of filled pauses across genders and ages. There was also a developmental factor operative, in that post-college (after the age of 22 years), the rate of discourse markers for both males and females dropped, as did the difference in levels between the genders, suggesting that we may 'grow out of' the use of these.

However, while the evidence underlines the need for a verbal presentation to be as fluent as possible, paradoxically the skilled use of 'uh' and 'um', referred to jointly as 'UHM' in the research literature, can serve an important attention-gaining explanatory purpose. There is evidence that 'uh' tends to be used by a speaker to signal a brief delay in speech, whereas 'um' is used when a longer delay is intended (Clark and Fox Tree, 2002). They occur in regular locations during explanations, particularly as a prelude to the introduction of new and unfamiliar terms (Kidd *et al.*, 2011). Thus, when doctors explain new technical terms they often combine UHMs with frame devices such as 'what we call' or 'it's something like', to gain the attention of patients and encourage them to pay greater attention to the explanation of the medical terms to follow (Heath, 1984). As Hargie *et al.* (2004, p. 242) pointed out, 'when they are used skilfully and systematically, filled pauses help recipients understand and remember what immediately follows their use'. Perhaps this is one reason why UHMs have been shown to be used more by older and better-educated as compared to younger and less well-educated individuals (Tottie, 2014).

Pausing

Pausing briefly to collect and organise thought processes before embarking on an explanation can also facilitate fluent speech patterns. However, there are cultural variations in relation to what are acceptable or 'fluent' pauses. For example, in Japan and China pauses of 5 seconds during interaction are not perceived to be pragmatic breakdowns in conversation, whereas in Western cultures pauses of 4 seconds are regarded as problematic (Fitzmaurice and Purdy, 2015). Planned pausing can help to increase understanding of the explanation. Rosenshine (1968), in an early research review of those behaviours related to teacher effectiveness, found that teachers who used pauses following an explanation increased pupils' knowledge, by ensuring that not too much material was covered too rapidly. Brown and Bakhtar (1988), in their study of lecturing styles, provided further support for the use of pausing when presenting lengthy explanations. Their research showed that one of the five most common weaknesses of lecturers was speaking too quickly. Similarly, in the health context, a survey of 617 breast cancer patients found that one of the areas where they felt improvement was most needed in their care and treatment was that doctors need to take more time when giving explanations to patients (Oskay-Özcelik *et al.*, 2007).

Appropriate language

An explanation must contain language appropriate to the intellectual capacity, background and language code of the listener. This was recognised by Chaucer in the fourteenth century, when he advised clerics not to use 'heigh [high] style' but to 'speketh [speak] so pleyn [plain] at this time, I yow preye [pray you], that we may understone [understand] what ye seye [say]' (Preston, 2014). Professionals are bilingual; in addition to their native tongue, they learn the specialised and often highly technical language associated with their work. All practitioners have a stock-in-trade of jargon. Indeed, in many respects it can serve them well, as a means of facilitating in-group communication, acting as a very conspicuous marker of group identity and denying information access to non-group members. But jargon can get in the way of understanding.

Professionals sometimes forget that clients are excluded from the specialist language used by them. In the medical sphere, Farrington (2011, p. 231) illustrated how: 'healthcare professionals, and doctors in particular, have a tendency to indulge in medical jargon when communicating with patients'. Blocks to communication occur when what linguists call *code switching* takes place and technical jargon forms part of the dialogue with patients or clients not privy to this lexicon. The problem is further compounded by the fact that the same words sometimes appear in the vocabularies of both, but with different meanings. Tiersma (2006) gave examples of everyday words such as 'burglary' and 'mayhem' that have different and much more precise legal interpretations as well as common meanings. He stressed the importance of explaining to jurors the precise legal meanings of such terms. Similarly, in medicine, terms such as 'risk factor' are not particularly well understood by patients (Cho *et al.*, 2015). In their analysis of how quantitative risk information (e.g. percentage chance of contracting a flu bug) can most effectively be explained to the public, Skubisz *et al.* (2009) emphasised that communicators should avoid jargon, and recommended that they should not only explain exactly what a term means but also explicitly state what it does not mean.

Of course, it is sometimes difficult for professionals to eliminate completely all technical terms, and to do so may indeed even jeopardise the client's full grasp of issues. It is how these terms are introduced that counts. Possibilities noted by Hopper *et al.* (1992), in an interesting study of naturally occurring telephone conversations to do with medical advice, included: giving a term and (as an aside) asking about the caller's familiarity with it; giving a paraphrase with the term; observing the caller's problems with terminology used and following up with a brief explanation; and, applying a term to a condition that the caller described.

Language also reflects the culture of the people who use it. Differences are not only a matter of foreign-word usage. Communication styles may additionally be at odds in levels of formality, precision and directness. An emphasis on maintaining harmony and not causing offence sometimes means that members of high-context cultures, such as Koreans, use elaborate forms of circumlocution in conflict situations to avoid responding with a direct refusal; to say 'No' could compromise the other's *kibun*, or sense of personal harmony, and threaten his or her face (Adler *et al.*, 2012).

Reducing vagueness

An explanation characterised by vague, indeterminate words and expressions will be less successful than one that employs precise terms to present specific information. With particular reference to good practices when nurses communicate with their patients and health colleagues, Balzer Riley (2012, p. 136) pointed out that, 'Being specific means being detailed and clear in the content of our speech. It means being concrete, so that our communication is focused and logical.' Language, though, is inherently ambiguous and prone to confusion. In a famous 1952 trial in England, 19-year-old Derek Bentley was sentenced to be hanged for the murder of a policeman, although the shooting was carried out by his accomplice, the 16-year-old Christopher Craig. Since the latter was a minor he could not be sentenced to death. The verdict, still controversial, depended upon the interpretation of Bentley's alleged directive that night to his partner when they were confronted by the policeman – 'Let him have it, Chris'. The prosecution's position was that Bentley had told his accomplice to shoot: the defence argued that Bentley was in fact telling him to hand over the gun.

This 'slipperiness' of language is captured in the expression that 'Meanings are in people, not in words'. Holli and Beto (2014) argue that many of the misunderstandings and breakdowns that plague communication can be laid at this particular door. In English even simple words can have multiple interpretations:

'fast' has some 15 dictionary definitions. For patients, being told that an event is 'likely' may be translated by some numerically as a one in ten probability, for others one in two (Edwards *et al.*, 2002). But confusions and imprecision creep into other languages as well, sometimes with disastrous consequences. Strong (2005) related how confusion over the Japanese word *mokusatsu* may have led to the atomic bomb attacks on Hiroshima and Nagasaki in 1945. The word was used by Prime Minister Suzuki to describe cabinet policy on the Potsdam Declaration that would have brought war to an end. *Mokusatsu* can mean either to ignore or to keep silent on something. Suzuki had the latter in mind. The cabinet was withholding comment, given their difficulties in breaking the news of surrender to the Japanese people. The Allied nations interpreted the broadcasted message as the Declaration being ignored by the Japanese, hence precipitating the attack on Hiroshima some 8 days later.

Not all imprecision can be totally eliminated from verbal explanations on every occasion. Most people will have experienced a situation when they have groped to find the exact term, and failing to find it, have substituted a less precise, more general alternative. However, attempts should be made to remove vagueness if the goal is to promote understanding. Problematic words and phrases have been documented (Gage *et al.*, 1968; Miltz, 1972; Bradbury, 2010), and are listed in Box 8.6. Well-established findings by Hiller *et al.* (1969, p. 674) into teachers' explanations revealed that, 'the greater the number of words and phrases expressing haziness, qualification and ambiguity ('some', 'things', 'a couple', 'not necessarily', 'kind of'), the less clear the communication'. From a sample of 84 undergraduate student lessons, Land (1984) found that students could accurately distinguish teacher clarity on the basis of presence or absence of vague terms. In particular he found that high-clarity lessons were significantly related to high student ratings on achievement tests, along with high student ratings of perception of clarity.

Box 8.6 Being precise about vagueness

The following are common forms of vagueness in an explanation:

- *Ambiguous designation* – e.g. 'type of thing', 'all of this', 'sort of stuff'
- *Undefined comparisons* – e.g. 'our figures show a marked increase...'
- *Negative intensifiers* – e.g. 'was not too', 'was not hardly', 'was not quite', 'not infrequently'
- *Approximation* – e.g. 'about as much as', 'almost every', 'nearly'
- *Bluffing and recovery* – e.g. 'they say that', 'and so on', 'to cut a long story short'
- *Indeterminate numbers* – e.g. 'a couple of', 'a fair number', 'some'
- *Groups of items* – e.g. 'kinds', 'aspects', 'factors', 'things'
- *Possibility and probability* – e.g. 'are not necessarily', 'it could be that', 'probably'
- *Unattributed sources* – 'There are findings to confirm that the product works'++

Providing emphasis

Another telling feature when attempting to explain effectively is the need to provide emphasis. This helps to make prominent the key points and crucial features of content. By providing points of emphasis the speaker can direct the listener's attention to the most important or essential information in the presentation. Emphasis can be nonverbal and verbal.

Nonverbal emphasis

Effective public speakers, politicians and television presenters, versed in the skills of oratory, use purposeful variation in their voice to alert their audience's attention to key issues. Skilful speakers also employ appropriate speech-related gestures and movements to underline key features of their explanations. Varied movements of the eyes, head, face, fingers, hands and whole body can be used purposefully and in a focused manner to augment the verbal message. While speakers also use gestures to help them to regulate and 'conduct' their own delivery, in a meta-analysis of 63 research studies into the effects of gestures on speech comprehension, Hostetter (2011, p. 311) concluded that, 'Gestures do benefit comprehension, and this benefit is independent of any benefits gestures may have for a speaker's production'.

Verbal emphasis

Speakers employ three main verbal techniques to achieve emphasis: verbal cueing, mnemonics and planned repetition.

Verbal cueing

This occurs when an individual employs specific verbal 'markers' to preface that part of the message to which attention is being drawn. These can be individual words such as 'first ...second...third', 'important', 'finally', 'major', 'fundamental', or phrases such as 'listen carefully', 'the important point to remember is', 'take time before you answer this question'. Verbal cueing helps to differentiate between the relevant and the irrelevant, the more important and the less important and the specific detail from the general background information.

Mnemonics

Perhaps not so common as verbal cueing but in a sense equally effective in acting as an *aide-mémoire* to the listener is the use of a mnemonic. As pointed out in the previous chapter, these are useful devices to facilitate understanding. A mnemonic might use the fact that key words essential to the explanation all begin with the same letter of the alphabet, making it easy to recall them when needed. One example is the '5-Ps' of the explaining process used in this chapter.

An *acronym*, where the first letter of each point combines to make a word, can also be highly memorable; for example FARM-B for the five classes of vertebrate animals – fish, amphibian, reptile, mammal, bird.

Planned repetition

A third technique is that of planned repetition of selected points during the presentation. Repetition enables the recipient to experience a 'feeling of familiarity' with the material, which in turn facilitates cognitive processing (this aspect of repetition is further discussed in Chapter 12). This is especially useful if a great deal of new or unfamiliar material is being explained. Ley (1988), from a research review of patient compliance with doctors' prescriptions, suggested that one major way a doctor can increase patient compliance is to repeat the important points of the instructions. Structured summaries judiciously placed at various points throughout a lengthy explanation appear to be beneficial to the recipient.

Aids to explanation

The speaker should plan to include some form of visual aid to improve the quality of an explanation. Multimedia presentations are powerful in helping to get the message across in an illuminating, attractive and memorable manner (Mayer, 2014). Visual aids also facilitate the retrieval of information from memory. According to *dual-coding theory* (Paivio, 1971; Liaw, 2004), audiovisual information is coded in memory in two different but related ways – verbally and visually. Textual messages are only coded verbally. As a result, 'it has been demonstrated repeatedly that people learn more deeply from text and pictures than from text alone' (Schüler *et al.*, 2015, p. 62). The old adage often holds true that 'A picture is worth a thousand words'. Aids can range from physical objects and models, to pictures, tables, charts, graphs, diagrams and video material. People assimilate information using different sensory channels. Some favour looking, rather than listening, and are particularly likely to appreciate the benefits of a multimedia approach. Visual representations support the spoken word and, by introducing greater variety, make for a more attractive experience for the group.

The advantages of presenters using visual aids include being perceived more favourably by their audiences, taking less time to present concepts and producing greater retention of what is learned (Moody *et al.*, 2002; O'Hair *et al.*, 2011). Likewise, Downing and Garmon (2002) reviewed evidence attesting to the beneficial effects of technology-based presentations on ease of note taking and grasping the organisation of content material. Visual images also tend to 'stick' in the mind. Bradbury (2010) estimated that audiences may remember as little as 10 per cent of a verbal presentation after 3 days, but as much as 66 per cent over the same time span when the material is delivered in a mixed verbal/visual format. Additional benefits of visual material, identified by Pathak (2001), include:

- gaining and directing attention to key points;
- providing a veridical representation of what is being explained;
- helping to organise material provided in text by contributing a visual framework displaying inter-relationships, etc.;
- offering an interpretation by illuminating the meaning of dense text;
- compensating for limited reading skills.

PowerPoint is a ubiquitous medium for delivering presentations that has been shown to have both advantages and disadvantages, depending upon how it is employed (Penciner, 2013). Perhaps the golden rule when designing such presentations is to avoid the 'all bells and whistles' trap. In the hands of the overzealous, the huge range of options available for colour, design, font type and size, pictures, cartoons, animation and sound effects can quickly lead to a visual spectacular in which the core message gets lost amid the special effects, so that the presenter (and the core message) ends up side-lined. One study of the university sector found that a common failing is that lecturers whizz through far too many PowerPoint slides too rapidly, with the result that students soon become disengaged and switch off (Mann and Robinson, 2009). Another important facet here is that for aids to be effective they must be shared. Increasingly, explanations are mediated, e.g. through telephone or computer help lines. Jucks *et al.* (2007) found that, when the explainer has access to computer representations (such as graphics images and diagrams) relating to the topic being explained, but these are not available to the person making the enquiry, the quality of the explanation is impaired.

In preparing visual aids, advice proffered (e.g. Hargie *et al.*, 2004; Beaver, 2007; Hamilton, 2014) includes avoiding:

- having too many;
- cluttering slides with too much information – a general rule is no more than six lines of text per slide;
- using long sentences rather than pithy phrases – a general rule is no more than six words per line;
- employing a font size that is too small, or that is difficult to read; e.g. Song and Schwarz (2010) found that the Arial font was easy to read and facilitated assimilation of material as compared to a more difficult-to-read font such as Mistral;
- including colour on an arbitrary basis, or hues that are difficult to distinguish at a distance;
- letting the technology take over – remember, these are just aids.

Verbal examples

The simplest aid to use in an explanation is the verbal example, analogy or case study. Like a bridge, a carefully selected example should span the space between what the listeners already know and what they are about to learn. To work, it must have a firm foundation in the experiences that the listener brings to the situation. It is usually best to give more than one example at a time to clarify a point, or provide proof (Hamilton, 2014). By so doing, the chances are reduced of coincidentally creating strong semantic links between nonessential elements of the example and the concept under focus (Rowan, 2003). Concrete everyday scenarios make the subject 'come alive' for the listener. Rosenshine (1971) illustrated how explanations were more effective when a piece of information, rule, principle or concept was followed by an example or examples, leading to a re-statement of the initial detail. Thus a concept should be introduced as follows:

Statement of concept → Example → Statement of concept

A nurse might say,

Your blood pressure is the pressure of the blood against your artery walls as it flows. Anything that prevents that flow will increase the pressure [statement]. Think of turning on the garden hose and holding your thumb over the end. You could check the buildup of pressure by trying to press the hose in the middle [example]. In the same way, the pressure of your blood is increased when a narrowing in the artery hinders the flow [statement].

In a major study of teacher competencies, Zuljan *et al.* (2012) found that the rule–example–rule format was rated by learners as crucial to the learning of new material. However, Brown and Armstrong (1989), in an analysis of 48 video-recorded and transcribed lessons, found that the rule–example–rule model was more appropriate to interpretive explanations of unfamiliar topics than for other types of explanation aiming at restructuring ideas. This suggests that the pattern of examples should be related both to the type of explanation given and to the listeners' previous knowledge.

Conclusion

Conclusions are opportunities to draw together the various strands of the explanation in a neat summary statement. This may be particularly important when the material has been gone through on a point-by-point basis, so ensuring that the links binding the various sub-elements are firmly in place and a successful synthesis is achieved. On occasion, however, it may be appropriate to leave a 'loose thread' – perhaps an unanswered question, or some seeming inconsistency. This can motivate the group to continue reflecting on the issue, and can serve as a useful lead-in if it is intended to continue with the explanation at a later date. Widener (2005) also drew attention to opportunities when closing to add impact to what was related during the presentation and leave the audience with a lasting impression of its content (see Chapter 10 for further information on closure).

Managing anxiety

So far the discussion about explaining has concentrated upon the more cognitive/ rational aspects of the task. But there is also a crucial visceral/emotional dimension that should not be ignored, especially when delivering formal presentations to large audiences. The fear of speaking in public, or *glossophobia*, is widespread (Souter, 2011). Public-speaking anxiety occurs when 'individuals experience physiological arousal (e.g., increased heart rate), negative self-focused cognitions (e.g., "I'm concerned I'll appear incompetent"), and/or behavioral concomitants (e.g., trembling) in response to an expected or actual presentation' (Bodie, 2010, p. 71). Surveys of the general population have consistently found that fear of public speaking ranks high in the list of most nerve-racking activities (Beagrie, 2007), being described by Beaver (2005) as one of the most prevalent of all fears. The phenomenon of *speech apprehension* (Gamble and Gamble, 2012) is a particular manifestation of a more general unease in relating to others, termed *communication apprehension* (Daly *et al.*, 1997). Such apprehension about speaking in public can be dysfunctional if not properly managed (Horwitz, 2001). In his review of research, Bodie (2010) identified the type of response patterns associated with public-speaking anxiety, the instruments available to measure these and the effectiveness of the various types of intervention that have been employed to help remediate this problem.

While inability to handle dysfunctional anxiety can present difficulties, the point also needs to be made that experiencing *some* level of stress when about to present is neither abnormal nor dysfunctional and is familiar to even the most experienced speakers. Indeed, it is often even desirable. Without it we probably would not be sufficiently on our toes to give of our best. Keeping stress positive and within constructive boundaries is what matters. Public-speaking anxiety has four interwoven components (Monarth and Kase, 2007). These involve:

1   *physiology* – increased blood pressure and heart rate, rapid breathing, trembling, feeling weak, sweating;
2   *mood* – feeling nervous, depressed, agitated, panicky;
3   *cognitions* – convincing yourself in advance that you can't do it, that it will go horribly wrong, that if you make the slightest slip it will be a disaster;
4   *behaviour* – avoiding presentations if possible, displaying nervous mannerisms, overcompensating by perhaps trying to memorise the speech, thus eliminating all spontaneity.

Steps to manage such dysfunctional affect include:

• *Finding out how to present effectively and becoming more skilled at it.* Often fear is a consequence of knowing or suspecting that you have not the resources to deliver a competent performance. The confidence that comes from planning and being well prepared also helps.
• *Learning to relax.* Anxiety is often learnt. This may be from being 'spooked' by listening to others or perhaps, as children, sensing their unease about speaking in public; watching others' faltering attempts; or

giving a presentation that went horribly wrong and being humiliated in this way, so that a lot of trepidation and little self-confidence have formed around this activity. But relaxing can likewise be learned. It is always good advice that, when preparing for a tense situation, you should avoid those who might heighten your level of tension – panic can be very contagious. Rather, seek out more relaxed company.

- *Desisting from talking yourself down.* Often those who are cruelly tormented at the thought of having to talk in public engage in negative self-statements such as:

> I'll never be able to do this. I'll make a complete fool of myself. They will see right through me, and think that I'm stupid. I'll dry up in the middle of it. My mind will go blank. I'll never be able to face them again

and so forth. In other words, these people convincingly 'talk' themselves into believing that they are going to do poorly, and then get extremely agitated at the prospect. This serves to make them even more certain that failure is inevitable: and in truth, under these circumstances, a self-fulfilling prophecy comes into play, and so failure probably results. Negative ruminations should be replaced with constructive alternatives (McCarthy and Hatcher, 2002). Positive self-statements should be employed, such as: 'I'm very well prepared for this talk. I have good visual aids that they will enjoy. I have answers to questions I may be asked. I'm looking forward to it.'

POSTMORTEM

So the explanation has been given, but the task is not yet over. Evaluating the outcome is indispensable. Taking pains to assess learning and doing so in a systematic way is a crucial part of the instructional process. The explainer must reflect upon what took place and evaluate to what extent the identified objectives were successfully achieved. If necessary, and as represented in Figure 8.1, the material may have to be gone over again, once some thought has been given to what went wrong and why. In their analysis of best practice in oncology, Reich *et al.* (2014) emphasise that patient understanding must be checked on an ongoing basis and can never be taken for granted. However, in their study of health professionals, Baker *et al.* (2007) found that few actually took pains to check patients' understanding of what had been explained.

In presentations, obtaining feedback from the audience is important both in checking levels of understanding and, by association, the adequacy of the explanation (Dickson *et al.*, 1997). Completeness of feedback was shown by Schroth (1992) to affect the speed significantly at which complex concepts were initially acquired. Subjects who were given verbal feedback after each response, irrespective of whether the response was correct or incorrect, did better than subjects receiving feedback only after correct responses or those receiving feedback only after incorrect responses. There are four main ways to check the efficacy of an explanation:

1   Note the nonverbal behaviour of the listener or listeners, since this is a rich source of evidence. Experienced and successful presenters constantly scan the faces and movements of explainees, both during and after the explanation, to detect signs of puzzlement, confusion or lack of interest. However, since individuals vary in the amount and kind of behaviour they overtly display, it is not always easy, or even possible, to deduce the efficacy of explanations by nonverbal means alone. Furthermore, some listeners may show nonverbal signs of attention and understanding out of politeness or not wanting to appear stupid, although they do not actually understand what is being said.

2   Another method of obtaining knowledge of comprehension is to ask a series of related questions. In the study by Baker *et al.* (2007), those health professionals who failed to check patient understanding through asking questions gave as a reason a lack of confidence in their ability to do so. They also reported failing to be convinced that using questions in this way was indeed an effective technique for improving patient understanding.

3   Alternatively, feedback can be gleaned by inviting listeners to ask questions on any aspect of an explanation they feel requires further clarification. This would appear to be more valid in terms of 'real' problems encountered by listeners, yet there is a danger that explainees may not respond for fear of seeming obtuse. In addition, where there is a status difference, people are reluctant to ask questions of those of a higher status (see Chapter 5).

4   It is also possible to ask the listener to summarise what has been heard. Although this is often an effective technique with pupils in school, it can sometimes be less so in situations with adults, where an impression of 'being tested' would be inappropriate. This possible interpretation can be overcome by phrasing the request so it seems that the speaker is accepting responsibility for any failure (e.g. 'I'm not sure how well I have explained that, would you tell me what you understand from it?').

At a broader level, and taking feedback into account, there is advantage in adopting a reflective approach to presentations (Burton and Dimbleby, 2006). This involves setting time aside to think back over what parts went well or not so well, together with trying to pinpoint reasons for successes and failures. Why was the audience still confused and unsure at the end? How could this be improved upon next time? Are there general lessons to be learned about explaining this type of material to this type of audience? It is only by adopting this approach that ongoing improvement will be brought about.

DEMONSTRATIONS

Illustrations make use of the sorts of audiovisual aids already mentioned to supplement speech. Demonstrations go further. Here an activity or process is explained by being carried out. It is explaining through doing. When the material is of a practical nature (e.g. a new skill or technique) and the learning objective is behavioural or performative (i.e. the audience being able to carry out the skill or technique), then this form of explanation is often called for. If a picture is worth a thousand words, then a demonstration is worth a thousand pictures. 'Hear one, see one, do one' has a long tradition in medical training. The medical student is told about a procedure, sees it carried out and is then expected to attempt it.

If an explanation does require a demonstration, there are several specific points that should be borne in mind in order to achieve effective results. They can be examined under three familiar headings: planning and preparation, presenting and obtaining feedback.

Planning and preparation

First, before proceeding with the demonstration, it is important to check that all items of equipment needed are prepared and available for use. In addition, the chief steps involved in the demonstration should be listed in the sequence in which they are to be presented.

Presenting

Having devised the procedures to be used in the demonstration, the next step is to present it in action. Initially, observers must be alerted to the purpose of the demonstration and what they will be expected to accomplish once it has been completed. When the viewers are prepared for the demonstration they should be guided step by step through the action with accompanying verbal descriptions of the essential features at each stage of the process (e.g. 'The first point to remember is, keep your feet shoulder-width apart…'). In addition, the linkage between one step and the next should be clearly illustrated, so that observers can see how each step fits into the overall action. Depending upon the complexity of the demonstration, it can be worked through completely, followed by a repeat performance emphasising the vital features at each stage. If, however, the skill or technique being explained is more complicated, the complete action can be broken down into coherent segments which the observer can practise in parts.

Obtaining feedback

Finally, it is important to assess whether or not the demonstration has been enacted effectively. Feedback can be obtained by a number of methods:

- having the observer or observers repeat the demonstration;
- repeating the demonstration slowly but requesting the onlookers to give the appropriate directions at each stage;
- requesting viewers to verbalise the salient features of the demonstration following the initial enactment.

OVERVIEW

This chapter has explored the nature, functions and techniques of explaining in a variety of professional and social contexts. Explaining is an attempt to create understanding, thus going beyond the mere giving of information. Different types of explanation were identified, including those that reveal causes, reasons, justifications and motives underlying the problem or event being analysed. Whilst the bulk of research into the skill of explaining has its roots in educational settings, it is by no means the sole prerogative of that profession. Other professions, both on a group or one-to-one basis, are also involved in providing relevant and interesting explanations for their consumers or colleagues. For example, the role and effectiveness of explanation have attracted considerable interest in health care and in legal settings. Likewise, the scientific community has begun to embark on the daunting quest of making knowledge of scientific advances accessible to a wider audience.

The explaining process can be analysed using the 5-Ps model of pre-assessment, planning, preparation, presentation and postmortem. Studies have uncovered that well-planned or structured explanations result in greater understanding, that clear, unambiguous explanations are highly valued by listeners and that summaries or feedback checks are effective in aiding retention. In conclusion, it should be remembered that the success of an explanation is measured not by the amount of detail conveyed but by the degree of understanding demonstrated by the listener. As such, the activity must be built around the particular needs, capacities and resources of the audience.

Chapter 9

Telling others about yourself: the skill of self-disclosure

INTRODUCTION

THE TERM SELF-DISCLOSURE is an amalgam of two elements. First, there is the intriguing entity of the 'self', and what exactly this comprises. Second, there is the process of 'disclosure', whereby the individual opens up some aspect of self to others. This chapter will examine both of these concepts, but with the main focus upon the latter. However, before exploring the fascinating world of how, what, when, where and why people disclose information about themselves, let us begin by examining the notion of self.

One major difference between *Homo sapiens* and other species is that humans possess a complex sense of self (Tracy and Robins, 2007). Not surprisingly, therefore, investigations of the self are as old as social science. In the nineteenth century the psychologist James (1890, 1892), in attempting to map the terrain, made a distinction between two types of self:

1   the 'I' self, which he saw as a knowing self in that it generates all of the knowledge we have of ourselves;
2   the 'me' self, which he viewed as being composed of three dimensions:

   *   a material self, relating to our evaluations of our physical bodies and possessions (home, car, etc.);
   *   a social self, concerned with how we see ourselves relating to and with others;
   *   a spiritual self, which is comprised of our ideas, thoughts, values and beliefs.

More recently, the concept of self has attracted an enormous amount of attention. Different conceptualisations have been put

---

Box 9.1 Dimensions of self: two examples

1 *Reflexive consciousness* – the ability to think introspectively about who we are
2 *Interpersonal being* – the self as it relates to and with other people
3 *Executive function* – how the self makes plans and behaves in such a way as to attempt to exert control over the outside world

(adapted from Beaumeister, 1999)

1 *Personal self*: you as a unique individual – your ideas, emotions, values, beliefs, etc.
2 *Social self*: your social roles and how you 'fit' with others
3 *Cultural self*: your identification with ethnic, religious, gender, social class or other grouping

(adapted from Stewart and Logan, 1998)

---

forward as to what exactly constitute its main components (Box 9.1). However, agreement on the definition of 'self' has proven difficult. It takes many forms and can be analysed from a myriad of perspectives (Sedikides and Spencer, 2007; Elliott, 2014). As an illustration of this, one conceptualisation of the different sides to self is presented in Figure 9.1.

Early notions about the existence of a self-contained, individual, unitary or 'sovereign self', that reveals or leaks information about 'inner reality' through disclosure, have been replaced by the concept of a social or dialogic self. While

Me as:	*Type of self*
I really am	True self
I would really like to be	Ideal self
I want others to think I am	Social self
I used to be	Past self
A new person	Reconstructed self
I should be	Ought self
I hope to become	Expected self
I am afraid of becoming	Feared self
I could have been	Missed self
Unwanted by one or more others	Rejected self

Figure 9.1 Types of self.

activity in certain regions of the brain has been associated with the functioning of the self (Heatherton *et al.*, 2007), it is generally recognised that the self is a relational entity (Carmichael *et al.*, 2007). How we present our self is adaptable and dynamic across situations (Amiot *et al.*, 2007). As noted by Tsekeris (2015, p. 1), 'it is widely acknowledged that the individual self is *social to the core*'. Indeed, some would argue that what we present is a reflected self that is shaped by others, so that eventually we come to see ourselves as we think others see us (Tice and Wallace, 2005). As explained by Jackson *et al.* (2012, p. 697), 'how we come to see ourselves is partially a reflection of how others see us, hence the idea of the "looking glass self"'. In this way, self is constructed and reconstructed through interaction; others play a pivotal role in creating and maintaining our concept of self.

Thus, self can be thought of as a social construction and self-disclosure is a process between individuals in which selves are shared, shaped, negotiated and altered. In this way, identity is formed by a combination of how we see ourselves and how others see us. For example, when two people get married they do not have given roles to guide their behaviour. Rather, these are formulated, developed, adjusted and agreed, both as a result of interactions within marriage, and following consultations with significant others. Recent perspectives conceptualise the self as being composed of a number of context-dependent self-aspects (e.g. partner, parent, student, manager, church treasurer, golf club member), any of which may be activated by the social situation. There is a considerable volume of research to show that people who play a large number of roles enjoy many benefits compared to those with only a few defining identities. The 'role-rich' cope more readily with change and stress, have better physical health and are more satisfied with their lot in life than the 'role-poor' (McKenna and Bargh, 2000).

Given that the self is social, others (family, friends, work colleagues, and so on) are almost always involved or in some way affected by our disclosures (Aron *et al.*, 2004). In this sense, information is often co-owned by a relevant circle of people, who need to be considered before it is revealed. One example of this occurs following marriage, when newly weds have to take cognisance of the expectations of their in-laws, including rules to do with information sharing, family secrets and appropriate disclosure. In this instance, research shows that disclosure of the family's private information to the new in-law serves to signify that this person is accepted as a family member (Serewicz and Canary, 2008). Disclosure from in-laws has also been shown to be related to marital harmony (Serewicz *et al.*, 2008).

There are also inner tensions between what Rosenfeld (2000) termed 'integration versus separation' and 'expression versus privacy', in that part of us wants to engage fully with others and another part wishes to hold something back. Thus, there is a need to strike a balance between 'revealing and concealing just enough to satisfy both the individual and society' (Buslig and Burgoon, 2000, p. 181). We like to have a group identity but at the same time have private aspects of ourselves that we keep from others. There is a unique essence to each person, such that, 'the inner self may well be shaped by social communication, but the self is far from a passive acceptance of feedback. Instead, the self actively

Box 9.2 Three 'sides' to place identity

1 *Physical insideness*: knowing one's way around and being familiar with the physical details of one's environment. Having a sense of personal 'territory'
2 *Social insideness*: feeling a sense of being connected to and part of a place. Knowing other people and being known and accepted by them
3 *Autobiographical insideness*: the idiosyncratic sense of 'having roots' to a place. Knowing 'where you come from' and 'who you are'

processes and selects (and sometimes distorts) information from the social world' (Beaumeister, 1999, p. 10). Furthermore, the notion of 'place identity' is also important. As Dixon and Durrheim (2004) point out, the term place identity 'denotes how individuals' sense of self arises in part through their transactions with material environments' (p. 457) in such a way that 'material environments not only underpin but also become *part of* the self' (p. 458). We use a variety of terms to express place identity, such as feeling 'out of place' or 'at home'. Place identity involves having a sense of 'insideness' (Box 9.2).

A great deal of social interaction consists of participants making statements, or disclosures, about a wide variety of issues. These disclosures may either be objective statements about other people, places or events, or subjective disclosures about the self. This latter type of statement, whereby the speaker reveals some personal information to others, is referred to as self-disclosure. As humans, we have an intrinsic need to talk about ourselves, with between 30 and 40 per cent of all our verbal communications involving the revelation of personal details about our actions, thoughts, feelings and beliefs (Tamir and Mitchell, 2012). Self-disclosure is also the cement that binds the parts together in the structure of interpersonal relationships (Guerrero *et al.*, 2014). Without disclosure, the whole relational edifice will collapse and so knowledge of this field is of key importance for effective interpersonal functioning (Brehm *et al.*, 2006). In this chapter we will examine definitional issues, the main features and elements of disclosure, its key purposes, core theoretical perspectives and factors that influence the extent to which disclosure will occur.

WHAT IS SELF-DISCLOSURE?

There is disagreement about the exact meaning of the term. Some definitions restrict the field of study to verbal disclosures only. Here, self-disclosure is defined as 'the process of communicating information about oneself verbally to another person' (Brohan *et al.*, 2012, p. 1). Other definitions further restrict the sphere of study to deeper levels of disclosure in terms of 'the revealing of intimate information about the self in conversation' (Cooks, 2000, p. 199). Hoffman's definition (1995, p. 238) highlighted the issues of veracity and accessibility:

'the revelation of information about the self that is verbally delivered, truthful, significantly revealing, and difficult or impossible to attain through other means'. Others underscore the importance of intentionality on the part of the discloser, so that Greene *et al.* (2006, p. 411) defined self-disclosure as occurring when 'one intends to deliberately divulge something personal to another'. Indeed, Fisher (1984) argued that information disclosed unintentionally, or by mistake, is a *self-revelation* rather than a self-disclosure. Mader and Mader (1990, p. 210) added the aspect of relational consequences: 'You self-disclose when you (1) intentionally give another person information about yourself (2) that the other person is not likely to get on his own and (3) that you realize could significantly affect your relationship to this person'. Pearson and Spitzberg (1987, p. 142) limited the scope even further by defining self-disclosure as 'communication in which a person voluntarily and intentionally tells another person accurate information about himself or herself', thereby excluding disclosures made under any form of threat.

But these definitions tend to exclude the study of nonverbal self-disclosures, which can be an important channel for communicating personal information – especially about feelings and emotions. In this chapter a wider perspective is held and self-disclosure is defined as the process whereby person A verbally and/or nonverbally communicates to person B some item of personal information that was previously unknown to B. In this sense, telling a close friend your name would not be a self-disclosure since this information would be already known, whereas telling a complete stranger your name would be a self-disclosure. Likewise, nonverbal disclosures, whether intentional or not, are included since this is a key form of communication and information (see Chapter 3). One important difference between verbal and nonverbal self-disclosure is that we have greater control over the former than the latter.

The recognition of self-disclosure as a central interpersonal skill began with the pioneering work of Sidney Jourard (1964, 1971), who stressed the need for a high degree of openness between individuals in many contexts, and illustrated the potency of self-disclosure as a technique for encouraging deep levels of interpersonal sharing. Since that time, an enormous amount of interest was generated in this area, to the point where it became one of the most researched topics in the fields of interpersonal communication and social psychology (Baxter and Sahlstein, 2000). Indeed, 'The pervasiveness and importance of self-disclosure accounts for the intense interest in this phenomenon shown by social scientists. Literally thousands of quantitative studies have been conducted over a period extending forty years' (Tardy and Dindia, 2006, p. 229).

Self-disclosure has been analysed and measured in various ways. Thus, McKay *et al.* (2009) identified four main disclosure categories:

1   *Observations.* Reporting what you have done or experienced: 'I graduated in 2011'.
2   *Thoughts.* These go beyond simple observations to reveal judgements about what has been experienced: 'If I had it to do again I would take the opportunity to study abroad as part of my degree'.

3   *Feelings.* The expression of affect: 'I really loved university – it was probably the happiest period of my life'.

4   *Needs.* Here the focus is upon needs and wants: 'I miss the challenges of academic life and feel that I want to take a postgraduate course now'.

Furthermore, there is a large number of pen-and-paper inventories designed to measure different aspects of self-disclosure, including:

* as a personality factor (Derlega and Chaikin, 1975)
* as varying across specific situations (Chelune, 1976)
* as a function of the target person (Miller *et al.*, 1983)
* specifically within feminist therapy (Simi and Mahalik, 1997)
* between spouses within marriage (Waring *et al.*, 1998).

An awareness of the nuances of self-disclosure is important in professional communication, for two main reasons. First, it is vital to be aware of contexts in which it is appropriate to self-disclose to clients. Second, professionals need to be aware of the benefits that accrue from, and the methods whereby they can encourage, full, open and honest self-disclosures from clients.

FEATURES OF SELF-DISCLOSURE

There are four key features of self-disclosures: they involve the use of a personal pronoun, can be about facts or feelings, can focus upon self or other, and can be about the past, present or future.

Personal pronoun

Verbal self-disclosures involve the use of the personal pronoun 'I', or some other personal self-reference pronoun such as 'my' or 'mine'. While these words may be implied from the context of the speaker's utterances, their presence serves to remove any ambiguity about whether or not the statement being made is intrapersonal (relating to personal experiences). Compare, for example, the statements:

A: Selection interviews can create a great amount of stress.
B: I find selection interviews very stressful.

In A it is not immediately clear whether the speaker is referring to selection interviews in general or to personal feelings about attending selection interviews. The use of the personal pronoun 'I' in B, however, serves to clarify the nature of the statement as a self-disclosure.

A personal self-reference pronoun is often the criterion used in research investigations as evidence of disclosure (Harper and Harper, 2006). This is one of the following three methods used to measure the phenomenon:

1   observer or recipient estimates of disclosure;
2   self-report measures such as inventories, self-ratings or sentence completion tasks;
3   objective counts of actual disclosures made during interaction.

One problem is that different research investigations use a range of measures, some tailored specifically for a particular investigation. Some investigations focus on one dimension of disclosure while others examine several aspects. This makes generalisations across studies very difficult (Omarzu, 2000). Even studies that use the 'objective' approach may not be directly comparable owing to differing definitions about what exactly constitutes a self-disclosure. While the counting of self-reference pronouns is one measurement criterion, another definition of self-disclosure used in research studies is: 'a verbal response (thought unit) which describes the subject in some way, tells something about the subject, or refers to some affect the subject experiences' (Tardy, 1988, p. 331). This definition obviously requires detailed training on the part of observers to ensure accuracy and agreement about instances of disclosure. Such differences need to be borne in mind when evaluating research findings in this field. Furthermore, much research on self-disclosure has been conducted in the artificial 'laboratory' situation, and often with undergraduate students, and so the results of these studies need to be treated with caution, since the extent to which they generalise to real-life contexts is unclear.

Facts or feelings

When two people meet for the first time, it is more likely that they will focus upon factual disclosures (name, occupation, place of residence) while keeping any feeling disclosures at a fairly superficial level ('I hate crowded parties'; 'I like rock music'). This is largely because the expression of personal feelings involves greater risk and places the discloser in a more vulnerable position. At the same time, deep levels of disclosure may be made to a stranger in a one-off encounter providing we feel sure that we will never meet the person again, and that we do not have friends or acquaintances in common. This was initially termed the 'stranger-on-the-train phenomenon' (Thibaut and Kelley, 1959) and, in later years as travel preferences changed, 'in-flight intimacy' (DeVito, 2016). This phenomenon can also apply to some professional situations. For example, a client may be reluctant to return for a second visit, following an initial session in which deep self-disclosures have been made to a counsellor who is in effect a complete stranger. Counsellors should therefore employ appropriate closure skills in order to help overcome this problem (see Chapter 10).

A gradual progression from low to high levels of self-disclosure leads to better relationship development. The expression of deep feeling or of high levels of factual disclosure (e.g. 'I was in prison for 5 years') increases as a relationship develops. Factual and feeling disclosures at a deeper level can be regarded as a sign of commitment to a relationship. Two people who are in love usually expect to give and receive disclosures about their feelings – especially towards one another (Kassin *et al.*, 2011). They also want to know everything about one another. In such a relationship there is a high level of trust, just as there is in the confession box, a doctor's surgery or a counsellor's office (areas where disclosures are also high). *Social Penetration Theory* (Altman and Taylor, 1973; Taylor and Altman, 1987) postulates that relationships progress through a number of stages:

- *Orientation.* When people meet for the first time shallow information about self is disclosed more readily than intimate details. For the relationship to develop, disclosures must be reciprocal. Some estimate will be made of the likely rewards and costs of pursuing the relationship, and for progression to occur the anticipated rewards must outweigh the costs.
- *Exploratory affective exchange.* More intimate details, especially at the feeling level, begin to be reciprocated. In relationships, disclosures gradually become more intimate (Aron *et al.*, 2006).
- *Affective exchange.* High levels of disclosure are exchanged as people get to know one another in depth (Denes, 2012).
- *Stable exchange.* Once a relationship has been firmly established, it should be characterised by continuing openness.
- *Depenetration.* If a relationship begins to fail as the costs start to outweigh the benefits, there begins a gradual process of withdrawal of disclosure, leading to relational termination.

Object of the statement

A self-disclosure can be about one's own personal experience, or it can be about one's personal reaction to the experiences being related by another. Consider the following interaction:

> *John*: 'I haven't been sleeping too well recently. I work from early morning until after midnight every day, and yet nothing seems to sink in. I'm really worried about these exams. What would I do if I failed them?'
>
> *Mary*: 'You know, John, I am very concerned about you. It seems to me that you are working too much, and not getting enough rest.'

This is an example of a self-disclosure as a personal reaction to the experiences of another person, since Mary is expressing concern and giving an opinion about the statements made by John. This is sometimes referred to as a *self-involving* statement, as opposed to a disclosure about oneself (Knox *et al.*, 1997). A professional can use this type of self-disclosure to express feelings about a client. Such disclosures can serve as a potent form of reinforcement (see Chapter 4). In this way, disclosure is a skill employed by effective negotiators as a way of building trust with the other side (see Chapter 13 for further information on this aspect of negotiation). Mary could have chosen to give a parallel self-disclosure about her own experience by saying something like,

I remember when I was sitting my final exams. I was worried about them too. What I did was to make sure I stopped working in time to get out of the house and meet other people. This took my mind off the exams...

Past, present or future

Self-disclosure can be about the past ('I was born in 1999'; 'I was really grief-stricken when my father died'), present ('I am a vegan'; 'I am very happy') or future ('I hope to get a promotion'; 'I want to get married and have a family'). One situation in which people are expected to self-disclose in terms of facts and feelings about the past, present and future is in the selection interview. Candidates will be asked to talk about their previous experience or education, to say why they have applied for the job and to outline their aspirations. Not only are interviewees expected to give details about themselves; they will more often than not be expected to relate their attitudes and feelings towards their experiences.

ELEMENTS OF SELF-DISCLOSURE

There are five main elements of self-disclosure that need to be taken into consideration. These relate to valence, informativeness, appropriateness, honesty and disclosure avoidance.

Valence

This is the degree to which the disclosure is positive or negative for both discloser and listener. In the early stages of relationship development, disclosures are mainly positive and negative self-disclosures usually only emerge once a relationship has been established. Negative self-disclosures have been shown to be marked by paralinguistic cues such as stuttering, stammering, repetition, mumbling and low, 'feeble' voice quality, whereas positive disclosures tend to be characterised by rapid, flowing, melodious speech (Bloch, 1996).

Lazowski and Andersen (1991) found that negative disclosures were regarded as having more informative power than positive ones. They postulated one reason for this finding as being that, since it is less acceptable for people to disclose negative information, such disclosures are likely to be more heartfelt and revealing. This is also true of positive and negative attributions, in that we only make a positive attribution about a person after repeated observations, whereas we readily ascribe negative evaluations after only a single instance (Fiedler, 2007). For example, we may say that someone is dishonest after witnessing one lie, but we only say they are honest when we have had considerable experience of their response patterns. In addition, what is known as the *Pollyanna principle* (Matlin and Stang, 1978) means that we tend to seek out positive rather than negative stimuli, and expect and report more positive than negative experiences. In like vein, we expect others to make positive self-disclosures and so we become more alert upon receiving a negative disclosure. This is because what is known as the *negativity effect* means that negative information is attributed as possessing greater relevance than positive information (Yoo, 2009). Thus, the comparative rarity of negative disclosures, and their greater inferential power, means that we need to use them with caution.

Research evidence shows that negative disclosures can be disadvantageous. Lazowski and Andersen (1991) carried out a study in which they had university undergraduates watch videotapes of an individual self-disclosing to someone off-camera. They found that the use of negative disclosures (e.g. 'I felt like telling him that I practically hated him, that I disliked him more than anyone I'd met in a long time'), when compared to positive disclosures (e.g. 'I felt like telling him that he was really a pretty nice guy'), led both male and female viewers to like the male speaker significantly less and to expect to be less comfortable when interacting with him. In a later study, Yoo (2009) confirmed that the use of negative disclosures tends to lead to more negative evaluations of the discloser. These differences were illustrated in a study by Miller *et al.* (1992), who contrasted the relative effects of negative, positive and bragging disclosures. The latter contained more superlatives (e.g. 'best' rather than 'good'); reference to doing better than others or having power over them; less emphasis on working hard and more on being a 'wonderful' person; and, less credit given to group efforts and more to personal achievements. Examples of each of the three categories used in this study were:

> *Positive:* 'I even got the most valuable player award. Boy, was I surprised...I was pleased to get the award and the recognition. I was glad to help my team finish the season so well.'

> *Negative:* 'I didn't play well this season. I was embarrassed...I tried to look like I was having fun but I kept thinking how lousy I played and that I shouldn't have come.'

> *Bragging:* 'I was the leading player all summer. Actually, I'm the best all-round player this league has ever seen. I could have my choice to play in any team I want next year.'

The results indicated that, to be rated as competent and successful, the use of bragging disclosures was a better strategy than negative disclosures, whereas the latter were seen as being more socially sensitive. However, the highest overall evaluations were given for positive disclosures, which were viewed as being both successful and socially sensitive. Thus the optimum approach would seem to be a mid-point between being self-deprecating at one extreme and boastful at the other. Bragging about accomplishments as a disclosure strategy was not popular in a study of dating behaviour among undergraduates, where other tactics such as emotional disclosure (e.g. 'I care about you') were regarded as more appropriate (Wildermuth *et al.*, 2007). But one context where self-promotion and a degree of bragging is the expected social norm is the employment interview. The rules of this form of interview are such that interviewers expect candidates to sell themselves in the best possible light. Here, two particular behaviours are commonly employed.

1   *Entitlements* refer to attempts to associate oneself with successful events or people (e.g. 'I was at EagleAir when we developed the breakthrough XJ521 jet fighter'; 'I took my degree at London when Eysenck was Head of Department'). This indirect self-presentation technique, known as 'association' or 'basking in reflected glory', can influence the perceptions of others if used skilfully (Carter and Sanna, 2006). However, it tends to be used more by males than females (Guadagno and Cialdini, 2007).

2   *Enhancements* are attempts to augment or exaggerate the importance of one's achievements (e.g. 'My degree programme was one of the hardest to gain entry to'; 'The senior manager was off ill quite a lot and so in reality I ran the department').

While the continuous and indiscriminant use of negative self-disclosure is dysfunctional, their judicious application can actually facilitate relational development. For example, disclosing negative emotions when one is in need of support (such as being nervous before giving a talk) can be perceived as the sharing of an important experience and a mark of friendship (Graham *et al.*, 2008). It can indicate that the discloser perceives the recipient as someone to be trusted not to take advantage of a revealed weakness. It also highlights the discloser's needs and enables the recipient to reciprocate by showing concern for these, thereby enhancing the relational bond. However, for this to be effective, Graham *et al.* noted that negative emotions should be expressed to those with whom one has a relationship, the depth of disclosed emotional state should be concomitant with the level of friendship and the intensity of the disclosure should reflect the degree of emotional need. Given these parameters, the disclosure of appropriate negative emotions increased ratings of likeability, offers of help and the level of relational intimacy.

Another interesting dimension of valence relates to the phenomenon of gossip, which has attracted increasing research attention (Yao *et al.*, 2014). An important function of self-disclosure is to influence and guide how others talk and gossip about us. Thus, we are aware of the wider implications beyond the immediate encounter (Smith, 2014). Gossip also serves a social comparison function in that it enables us to 'gain information about the validity of our opinions and abilities by talking with or about similar others' (Wert and Salovey, 2004, p. 132). This aspect of social comparison will be discussed later in the chapter.

Informativeness

Here, self-disclosure is assessed along three main dimensions:

1   *Breadth* – the total number of disclosures used. This is measured by counts of self-reference pronouns or topics covered, or by self-report instruments.

2   *Depth* – the level of intimacy of the disclosure. In general, emotionally intense, negative or embarrassing information tends to be rated as higher in intimacy (Omarzu, 2000). Depth is measured either using self-report instruments, or by rating actual disclosures made for intimacy level.

3   *Duration* – this is measured either by the total amount of time the person spends disclosing, or by a word count of disclosing statements.

The Derlega and Chaikin Inventory (1975) was designed to measure breadth and depth of disclosures. Examples of shallow levels of disclosure given in this inventory include: 'How often my aunts and uncles and family get together', 'Whether or not I have ever gone to a church other than my own', and deeper levels, such as 'How frequently I like to engage in sexual activity', 'The kinds of things I do that I don't want people to watch'.

In the Lazowski and Andersen (1991) study, mentioned earlier, it was found that disclosures about thoughts and feelings were viewed as deeper and more informative than those concerned with actions and they surmised that this is because: 'it is access to otherwise hidden cognitions and affects that gives listeners the feeling that they have heard something significant about the speaker' (p. 146). Two taboo topics that are difficult for most people to discuss are death and sex. The widespread avoidance of any discussion about death in most contexts (apart from the context of terminal illness) has resulted in Western society being portrayed as 'death-denying' (Wildfeuer *et al.*, 2015). In arguing for a more open approach to the discussion of death, Corr and Corr (2013) point out that for a long time there was a view that death has to be 'quarantined' lest it infects our life. For example, a survey carried out by the US National Hospice Foundation found that parents find it easier to talk to their children about sex than to talk to their own parents about dying with dignity (Levy, 1999). In fact, sex is the second taboo area, and in particular discussing details of sexual activities with one's partner. Rehman *et al.* (2013), in highlighting the finding that those who self-disclose more about sexual activity have greater sexual satisfaction, identified six main reasons why people are loath to so disclose. First, the worry that to do so may create feelings of guilt, embarrassment or shame. Second, a belief that discussing such matters is in some way immoral. Third, a fear that if one discloses one's sexual desires and pleasures these may be regarded as discrepant by one's partner and so the relationship could be damaged. Fourth, some people have feelings of inadequacy about being able to discuss sexual activities openly and skilfully. Fifth, a belief that it is not necessary or appropriate to discuss such intimate matters at all. Finally, the view that it is emotional rather than sexual intimacy that is at the core of a relationship.

Appropriateness

This is perhaps the most crucial aspect of self-disclosure. Each disclosure needs to be evaluated in the light of the context in which it occurs. While there are no hard and fast rules about the exact appropriateness of self-disclosure, there are some general indicators. Self-disclosures are more appropriate:

- from low-status to high-status individuals but not vice versa. Where there is a high degree of asymmetry in status, disclosure tends to be in one direction (Bochner, 2000). Thus, workers may disclose personal problems to their supervisors, but the reverse does not usually happen. This is because for a supervisor to disclose personal information to a subordinate would cause a loss of face which would affect the status relationship. Research findings indicate that self-disclosures are most often employed between people of equal status (Tardy and Dindia, 2006). However, Phillips *et al.* (2009) demonstrated that people make decisions about whether or not to disclose certain information either to underline existing status differences or serve to reduce them. For example, a senior manager in a corporation may attempt to reduce status differentials by disclosing to a shop-floor employee details of coming from a low-socioeconomic family background;

- when the listener is not flooded with them. There would seem to be a relationship between psychological adjustment and self-disclosure in that individuals who are extremely high or low disclosers are regarded as less socially skilled;

- when they are compatible with the roles of the interactors. We may disclose information to our spouses that we would not disclose to our children. Similarly, clients will often discuss a problem with a 'neutral' counsellor that they would not wish to discuss with their spouse or with close friends. Patients disclose answers to highly personal questions from doctors, such as 'Do you take drugs?' or 'How often do you have sexual intercourse?' that they would be unlikely to tolerate in other contexts. Nor would they expect the doctor to reciprocate with similar information. Even in close relationships there can be dangers with deep disclosures, especially of a highly sensitive nature. This is shown in studies of the difficulties faced by those diagnosed with HIV/AIDS in disclosing this to partners and family (Derlega *et al.*, 2000; Allen *et al.*, 2008; Hogwood *et al.*, 2013);

- when acceptable in the particular social context. We would be unlikely to disclose that we are suffering from severe diarrhoea during an intimate dinner on a first date, but we would do so in a doctor's surgery.

Honesty

As Bond *et al.* (2015) point out, there has been a fascination with deception since ancient times, as it is very important to be able to decipher whether someone is telling us the truth or lying. In terms of the veracity of disclosures, lies can be divided into three broad categories (Ennis *et al.*, 2008):

1   self-centred lies – used to protect oneself ('I was not there when it happened');
2   other-oriented lies – employed to protect a second person in the interaction ('I think that dress really suits you');
3   altruistic lies – used to protect a third party ('I was with James at that time, and so he could not have done that').

More specifically, the main reasons for making dishonest disclosures have been shown (DePaulo *et al.* 1996, 2003a, b) to be to:

- create a favourable impression
- influence and persuade others
- save face

- support and reassure others
- avoid conflict
- increase or reduce interaction with others.

Since these functions are central to the preservation of harmonious relationships, it is no wonder that deception is widespread (Granhag and Vrij, 2007). As Vrij (2007, p. 335) concluded, lies 'often serve as a social lubricant. Given this positive aspect of deception, it is not surprising that lying is a daily life event.' Indeed, some form of deception, often in the form of 'white lies', has been shown to occur in at least one-quarter of all conversations (Buller and Burgoon, 1996). One example of this is research into what is known as *avoidance-avoidance conflict* (Bull, 2002). Avoidance-avoidance conflict occurs in a situation where the person has to choose between disclosing a hurtful truth, telling a face-saving lie or giving an equivocal response (Edwards and Bello, 2001). For example, a close friend produces a painting that her 10-year-old son has just finished and asks for your opinion. You could respond:

- 'I think it's really beautiful. He has an obvious talent and flair for art.' (lie)
- 'I think it's very poor. The perspective is all wrong and there isn't enough contrast in the shading to give a three-dimensional feel to the painting.' (truth)
- 'Oh, so he's interested in art. You must be very proud of him.' (equivocation)

When faced with avoidance-avoidance conflict, research shows that the overwhelming majority of people opt for equivocation (Rosenfeld, 2000). The truth may be unpleasant for the recipient and damaging for the relationship, a lie can cause stress for the discloser and may cause problems if unveiled later, while an equivocal response often saves face all round.

In specialised circumstances, such as police interviewing, disclosures need to be examined carefully. Gudjonsson (1999) illustrated how confessions made by suspects are disputed in court for one of three reasons:

1   It is claimed that the confession was never actually made, but was fabricated either by the police or by a third party to whom the defendant is alleged to have confessed.
2   The confession is retracted – the defendant claims that, although a confession was made, this was done under some form of duress and is actually false.
3   The defence counsel disputes a confession that the defendant maintains is true, on the grounds that the person is not fit to plead because of intellectual impairment or psychological incapacity.

But, as discussed in Chapter 3, deception is difficult to detect. In fact, research has consistently shown that people are on average only 47 per cent accurate in detecting deception – that is, less than chance. Furthermore, there is a strong human propensity to judge messages as truthful – a process known as the *truth bias* or *veracity bias* (Burgoon and Levine, 2010). This means that most people can more accurately judge when messages are truthful than when they are deceptive, although for certain groups, such as police officers, parole board officers and social workers, there also seems to be a *lie bias* or *investigator bias*, which is the tendency to judge messages as deceptive (Bond *et al.*, 2005; Hauch *et al.*, 2016). The truth bias is most marked during face-to-face encounters and with those with whom we have a close relationship. There is also a lack of consistency in the results of research studies into deception (Ali and Levine, 2008). In reviewing this area, Vrij (2008, p. 4) concluded that 'not a single nonverbal, verbal, or physiological response is uniquely associated with deception'. Rather, deceptive behaviour depends on a range of personal and contextual factors. The deceiver's degree of motivation is important, in relation to the consequences of the lie being detected (Gray, 2008). If I tell you (falsely) that the bottle of wine you have brought to my house is one that I like and that I will enjoy drinking it at a later time, the costs associated with being found out are relatively small. On the other hand, a perpetrator trying to convince a detective of personal innocence following a brutal murder has a great deal at stake.

Knowledge of the baseline or 'normal' pattern of individual behaviour has been shown to be crucial before decisions about deviations therein can be made in judging the veracity of disclosures (Malone and de Paulo, 2001). We also tend to be more successful in detecting deceit when in situations with which we are highly familiar (Reinhard *et al.*, 2011). In general terms, however, the following behaviours seem to have some association with deception (Dickson *et al.*, 1997; Vrij, 2008; Warmelink *et al.*, 2012):

- more indirect answers that do not specifically refer to self (e.g. replying to the question 'Do you drink?' with 'Nobody in my family takes drink');
- increased use of negative statements ('I am not guilty' rather than 'I am innocent');
- greater degree of 'levelling' (use of terms such as 'all', 'every', 'none', 'nobody');
- fewer 'exclusive' words (e.g. without, but, except), which require cognitive effort;
- more general statements with fewer specific details given.

However, in a review of the field, Vrij and Granhag (2012, p. 110) warned that, since 'most verbal and nonverbal cues do not appear to be related to deception at all and that those that are only show a weak relationship with deception, we conclude that cues to deception are faint and unreliable'.

Smith *et al.* (2014) found that deception in mediated communication was very similar to what occurs in face-to-face interaction. In their study of deception in text messages they concluded that 'the degree to which these lies hue to patterns observed in face-to-face lying is remarkable' (p. 227). What are termed 'butler lies' are particularly common in mediated communication. So called because in former times this type of lie used to be told by the butler when someone called at the door (e.g. 'Sir is not at home'), these lies are concerned with availability management, which refers to behaviours that we use to enable us to decide how, when and where we interact with others (Birnholtz *et al.*, 2012). Thus, if we want to end a mediated communication we may tell a butler lie like 'someone has just knocked at the door', or if we do not want to meet someone at a suggested time we may say we cannot because we 'have an assignment to finish'.

Disclosure avoidance

The corollary of self-disclosure is self-suppression, and Hastings (2000a) illustrated how suppression, or avoidance, of certain talk and actions is culturally universal. She used the term *egocasting* to describe the intrapersonal process whereby the individual decides what side of self to display and portray to others (Hastings, 2000b). She argued that, when the person has to decide whether to disclose something that could cause potential personal harm, the self (or 'ego') makes a decision based upon the probable reaction of others and how this will in turn impact upon self and self-image. One example of this is the phenomenon of *self-silencing*, wherein the individual consistently suppresses personal opinions because of the fear that self-expression could have negative outcomes (Harper and Welsh, 2007). In identifying the main general aim of suppression as to protect the individual against harm, Afifi and Guerrero (2000) charted a number of more specific reasons for disclosure avoidance. These were later confirmed in a study by Derlega *et al.* (2008):

- Need for privacy. As expressed by a young female in the Afifi and Guerrero (2000) study:

  > My mom wants me to tell her everything. She thinks she has to know everything about me all the time. I get sick of it. Sometimes I want to tell her it's just not her business. I am almost an adult. I have my own life. I need my privacy.
  >
  > (p. 176)

- Social inappropriateness of the disclosure (e.g. we are unlikely to disclose details of our sexual proclivities to our parents over dinner).
- Futility (e.g. 'We've discussed this hundreds of times before and got nowhere'). In student dating relationships, a correlation has been found between degree of topic avoidance and dissatisfaction with the relationship (Merrill and Afifi, 2012).
- Wanting to avoid criticism, punishment or embarrassment. Fear of stigma has been shown to be a major determining feature here – particularly for those suffering from certain conditions, such as HIV/AIDS (Ostrom *et al.*, 2006).
- A desire to avoid conflict (so we may not tell aggressive others that we disagree with what they are saying).
- Protection of the relationship (e.g. we would be unlikely to tell our partner that we found someone else more attractive).
- Dissimilarity (nothing in common with the other person).

Many people have a fear of disclosing too much about their thoughts and feelings, since there is the risk of:

- being rejected, not understood or subjected to ridicule
- causing embarrassment or offence to the listener
- expressing and presenting oneself so badly that a negative image of self is portrayed.

The fear of disclosure is so great in some people, termed 'inhibitors' or 'suppressors', that they avoid revealing anything negative to others (Kowalski, 1999). Indeed, in many sub-cultures self-disclosure is actively discouraged, with the child being told 'Don't let others know your business' or 'Tell people only what they need to know'. This attitude then persists into later life where respect is often given to the person who 'plays cards close to the chest'. While in a game of poker it is wise not to disclose too much, either verbally or nonverbally, the attitude of avoiding self-disclosure can cause problems for people when they may have a need to talk about personal matters. Often, before we make a deep disclosure, there is a strategic process of *testing* (Kelly and McKillop, 1996) or *advance pre-testing* (Duck, 1999), whereby we 'trail' the topic with potential confidants and observe their reactions. If these are favourable, then we continue with the revelations; if not, we move on to a new topic.

Research into the issue of secrecy has also been explored in relation to disclosure avoidance. Afifi *et al.* (2007, p. 63) described a secret as, 'the type of private information that is viewed as risky enough that it is worth intentionally concealing'. Secrets involve a *secret keeper* and a *secret target* – the person from whom the information is kept. For example, a wife (secret keeper) tells her husband (secret target) that their 18-year-old daughter is going steady with a boy at college, but does not tell him that they are sleeping together. Those in the secret-keeper position often have a benign attitude to secrecy, yet this usually changes to resentment when they find themselves in the secret-target position. This is because being in the former position tends to give one a feeling of control and power, while being 'kept in the dark' leads to feelings of exclusion, rejection or betrayal. However, secret keepers experience stress as they undergo a process of *rumination*, whereby they are trying to suppress the information but at the same time find it difficult not to think (or ruminate) about it. Indeed, there is a paradox here, in that while they may try not to think about the information, they must at the same time think about it so that they do not unwittingly reveal it (Afifi and Caughlin, 2006).

Individuals are more likely to reveal a secret where three conditions prevail: the target has a right or need to know this information, the discloser has a high need for catharsis and others, including the target, are persuading the person to divulge the information (Afifi and Steuber, 2009). While, in general, secrecy can be damaging for relationships (Finkenauer *et al.*, 2005; Smetana *et al.*, 2006), under certain circumstances it is beneficial. For example, Vangelisti and Caughlin (1997) found that, within families, secrets kept to protect family members from hurt or pain were positively correlated with relational satisfaction, while secrets held as a result of poor intra-family communication or a desire to avoid evaluation had negative effects upon familial relationships. However, the distinction is not always easy to make and requires a deeper knowledge of those involved. In the earlier example, is the wife withholding the secret to protect her husband from pain, or because she is afraid of how he would then evaluate their daughter or is it just one more instance of poor communications generally within the family? In their study of marriage, Finkenauer and Hazam (2000) found that both disclosure and secrecy were important potential sources of marital satisfaction, and it was the appropriate use, and goal, of each that was most important.

In therapy, it has been shown that many clients conceal certain types of information (Farber, 2003). Among the information that is less likely to be revealed to therapists are matters to do with sex, personal failures and aggression. By comparison, aspects of oneself and one's parents that are most disliked tend to be the topics most commonly discussed by clients. In the medical sphere, while open disclosure to patients about their condition is the norm, there are occasions where therapeutic nondisclosure (also referred to as therapeutic privilege or therapeutic exception) may be considered (Berger, 2005). This is where disclosure would be likely to cause emotional distress such that the patient's capacity for decision making would be impaired, or where it would violate the patient's expressed cultural requirements.

PURPOSES OF SELF-DISCLOSURE

The goals of the discloser appear to be of paramount importance in determining the amount, content and intimacy of disclosure in different contexts (Oguchi, 1991; Derlega *et al.*, 2008). For example, research has shown (Rosenfeld, 2000) that with friends the top two reasons for self-disclosure are (1) relationship maintenance and enhancement, and (2) self-clarification – to learn more about one's thoughts and feelings. With strangers, however, the top two purposes are (1) reciprocity – to facilitate social interchange, and (2) impression formation – to present oneself in the best light. The main goals of self-disclosure are as follows.

To develop relationships

The appropriate use of self-disclosure is crucial to the development and maintenance of long-term relationships (Foley and Duck, 2006; Greene *et al.*, 2006). Those who either disclose too much or too little tend to have problems in establishing and sustaining relationships.

To encourage reciprocation

The *norm of reciprocity* is a powerful force in human interaction (Şener, 2011; Belmi and Pfeffer, 2015). When we receive something from another person we experience a feeling of obligation to reciprocate. In everyday interaction, reciprocation of self-disclosures is the norm. We will return to this aspect of disclosure later, in relation to theories of self-disclosure reciprocation.

To share experiences

In certain instances, a professional will have had similar experiences to the client, and can share these to underline the fact that there is a depth of understanding between the two. This also helps to portray the professional as 'human'. Thus a health professional visiting a young mother who has just had her first child may say, 'I know the problems associated with becoming a parent since I have three children myself', thereby establishing a common bond, and providing a foundation for a discussion of the particular problems faced by this mother. However, this type of 'me too' approach needs to be used appropriately and should not be taken to the extreme of what Yager and Beck (1985) termed the 'We could have been twins' level. As we will see later, by self-disclosing, the practitioner can also act as a role model for the client to disclose.

To facilitate self-expression

It can become a burden not being able to tell others about personal matters, and having to keep things 'bottled up'. Self-disclosure can have a therapeutic effect, by enabling us to 'get it off our chest' by 'letting go' (Kassin and Gudjonsson, 2004), which is why counselling, the confessional or discussing something with a close friend can all make us feel better. There is indeed some truth in the old maxim that 'A problem shared is a problem halved'. As summarised by Kim and Ko (2007, p. 325): 'Self-expression allows people to distinguish themselves from others, to reflect their own beliefs and needs, and validate their own self-concepts'. Stewart et al. (2005) referred to self-disclosure as part of a process of social *exhaling* (as opposed to listening, which they termed *inhaling*). Professionals should be aware both of the existence of the need for clients to exhale, and of ways to allow them to satisfy it. It is interesting to note that, when people are not able to utilise interpersonal channels for disclosure, they often use substitutes such as keeping a personal diary, talking to a pet or conversing with God. Indeed, this need can be observed at an early stage in young children, who often disclose to a teddy bear or doll.

Often, after a traumatic event the victim attempts to suppress or inhibit thoughts about it, and avoid discussing it with others. However, the more disturbing the event, the greater is the need to talk about it and ventilate one's feelings. If this process is not facilitated, then adverse health effects are likely to occur, as the person continually ruminates about what has happened (Kowalski, 1999). Trying to keep it inside tends to result in thoughts of the experience beginning to dominate – a phenomenon referred to as the 'hyperaccessibility of unwanted cognitions' (Garland and Howard, 2014). Interestingly, Kowalski illustrated how, while disclosure after a stressful event provides a necessary catharsis, disclosure before a stressful event may not be beneficial as it can serve to magnify feelings of anxiety.

In a comprehensive review of the research on a range of illnesses (such as cardiovascular diseases, HIV, cancer), Tardy (2000, p. 121) found considerable evidence to show that self-disclosure has positive effects upon health, concluding that: 'self-disclosure facilitates health by not only eliminating the deleterious consequences of inhibition but also by organizing thoughts and memories in more productive ways'. Derlega et al. (2014) found that patients regarded disclosure about their illness to their primary medical provider to be particularly helpful. One reason for this is that disclosure has been shown to boost immunological functioning (Petrie *et al.*, 1995). These findings are particularly important for health professionals, since it is clear that, for patients to disclose fully, the most important pre-requisite is the sensitivity shown by health caregivers, who must be aware that 'the messages they convey – even when they are saying nothing at all – will guide patients in their decision making about whether to tell the whole truth, or only that part which the caregiver seems most receptive to hearing' (Parrott *et al.*, 2000, p. 147).

There is increasing evidence that written emotional disclosures (WED) are also beneficial (Ashley *et al.*, 2013). It would appear that writing about personal stress or trauma experiences can contribute to the healing process because the written task necessitates the person having to work through the event and come to terms with thoughts and feelings about it. As noted by Creswell *et al.* (2007, p. 238): 'Writing about major life events and traumatic experiences can have significant benefits for mental and physical health. Throughout the past two decades, a large literature has shown that expressive writing improves physical health'. For example, Pennebaker and Francis (1996) found that first-year students who were asked to write about their thoughts and feelings about coming to college, in comparison to a control group, had a reduced level of illness visits to the health centre, coupled with improved grade point averages. In a later study, Yang *et al.* (2015) also found that undergraduates who were requested to engage in WEDs about stress or trauma events they had experienced showed significant improvements in psychological, social and physical health in comparison to a control group who were just requested to write about what they had done in the past week. Likewise, Warner *et al.* (2006) carried out a study of adolescents with asthma, and found that those who engaged in written disclosure, compared to control subjects, experienced a number of benefits, including decreases in asthmatic symptoms and functional disability, and improvements in positive affect.

However, it is also the case that, 'a relatively large number of studies have failed to find positive results of the WED intervention' (O'Connor *et al.*, 2014, p. 1068). Possible reasons for this include differences in research design and individual differences across samples. In their review of the research, Stroebe *et al.* (2006) conclude that WEDs may be of greater benefit for more vulnerable, insecurely attached individuals who have fewer opportunities for disclosure in their everyday lives. By comparison, securely attached adults are less likely to benefit from WED, as they have developed relationships in which they have regular opportunities for self-disclosure about stress or trauma to facilitate their personal adjustment.

On the other hand, Greenberg and Stone (1992) argued that the written expression of feelings on occasions can be superior to oral disclosures, since the recipient of interpersonal disclosures may respond inappropriately. They cite the example of how when incest victims tell their mothers about the event a high proportion of mothers respond by disbelieving or blaming them. This occurs in other areas. Victims of abuse in childhood often face threats about what will happen if they disclose and may not be believed when they do tell (Walker and Antony-Black, 1999). Studies of the gay population also reveal difficulties with disclosure or 'coming out', in terms of negative reactions from family and friends (Ryan *et al.*, 2015).

Overall, however, these findings are interesting for the process of therapy. People seem to benefit from discussing or writing about their deepest feelings, and this can be a key step in the process of coping with the trauma. As Tubbs (1998, p. 229) aptly summarised it: 'Part of returning to mental health involves sharing oneself with others'.

To heighten personal knowledge

An important function of disclosure is the process of *self-clarification* (Orbe and Bruess, 2005). This is exemplified by the saying, 'How do I know what I think until I hear what I say?' The value of the 'talking cure' in therapy is a good example of how the process of allowing someone to express their thoughts, ideas, fears and problems freely actually facilitates the individual's self-awareness (Forrest, 2010). The importance of self-disclosure in therapy was explained by Stricker (1990, p. 289):

> It is through the self-disclosure of the patient to the therapist that he can begin to recognize previously hidden and unacceptable aspects of himself, to recognize the acceptability of what had been experienced as forbidden secrets, and to grow in a healthier fashion.

Thus, self-disclosure can help people to clarify and understand their feelings and the reasons for them; in other words it encourages them to know themselves more fully. This view was confirmed in a study of adults (aged 33–48 years old) in Japan and the USA, where it was shown that in both countries levels of self-knowledge and self-disclosure were positively correlated (Asai and Barnlund, 1998). In therapy training there is also a need for supervisors of trainee therapists to encourage self-disclosure in the supervisory relationship, since research has shown that the quality of this relationship affects supervisee disclosure (Knight, 2014; Sweeney and Creaner, 2014).

The benefits of disclosure can be illustrated with reference to the Johari window (Luft, 1970) developed by two psychologists, Joseph Luft and Harry Ingram (and named after the initial letters of both first names). As depicted in Figure 9.2, this indicates four dimensions of the self. There are aspects that are:

- known both by self and by others (A), such as statements one has made;
- unknown by the self but known to others (B), including personal mannerisms, annoying habits, and so on;
- personally known but not revealed to others (C), including embarrassing thoughts or feelings;
- unknown both to self and others (D), such as how one would behave in a particular crisis context.

One of the effects of self-disclosing is that the size of segment A is increased and the size of segments B, C and D reduced. In other words, by encouraging clients

	Known to self	*Unknown to self*
Known to others	A	B
Unknown to others	C	D

Figure 9.2 The Johari window.

to self-disclose, not only do they find out more about themselves, but the professional also gains valuable knowledge about them, and thereby understands them more fully.

To promote social comparison

A key process in interpersonal interaction is that of *social comparison*, in that we evaluate ourselves in terms of how we compare to others. In particular, we engage in two types of comparison (Adler *et al.*, 2013b). First, we decide whether we are *superior or inferior* to others on certain dimensions (attractiveness, intelligence, popularity, etc.) Here, the important aspect is to compare with an appropriate reference group. For example, modest joggers should not compare their performance with Olympic-standard marathon runners. Second, we judge the extent to which we are the *same as or different from* others. At certain stages of life, especially adolescence, the pressure to fit in with and be seen as similar to peers is immense. Thus, wearing the right brand of clothes or shoes may be of the utmost importance. We also need to know whether our thoughts, beliefs and ideas are in line with and acceptable to those of other people. This is part of the process of *self-validation,* whereby we employ self-disclosures to seek support for our self-concept (Orbe and Bruess, 2005). Another aspect of social comparison in the counselling context relates to a technique known as *normalising.* This is the process whereby helpers provide reassurance to clients that what they are experiencing is not abnormal or atypical, but is a normal reaction shared by others when facing such circumstances (Dickson *et al.*, 1997). Patient disclosure, encouraged by the therapist, seems to facilitate the process of normalising (Munro and Randall, 2007).

People who do not have access to a good listener may not only be denied the opportunity to heighten their self-awareness; they are also denied valuable feedback as to the validity and acceptability of their inner thoughts and feelings. By discussing these with others, we receive feedback as to whether these are experiences which others have as well, or whether they are less common. Furthermore, by gauging the reactions to our self-disclosures, we learn what types are acceptable or unacceptable with particular people and in specific situations.

To ingratiate and manipulate

Some clients use self-disclosures in an attempt to ingratiate themselves with the professional. This type of client tends to disclose quite a lot, and say very positive things about the professional ('You are the only person who understands me'; 'I don't know what I would do without you'). In a sense, the client is 'coming on too strong', and this can be very difficult to deal with. The purpose may be to manipulate the professional for some form of personal gain. On the other hand, if this type of revelation is genuine, it can be a signal that the client is becoming over-dependent. Either way, it is advisable to be aware of this function of manipulative disclosure.

SELF-DISCLOSURE THEORIES

Three main theories have been proposed to explain the process of disclosure reciprocation during interaction. These are trust–attraction, social exchange and modelling. Each has been shown to have explanatory power (Archer, 1979). There is no firm evidence to support one of these theories over the other two and different studies have lent support to one or other. Indeed, it is likely that all three explanations can partially account for reciprocation and that the relative importance of each will vary across situations. We will now examine these theories and the related concepts upon which they are based.

Trust–attraction

This theory is built upon two of the supporting pillars of disclosure – trust and attraction. The trust–attraction hypothesis argues that, when A discloses, B perceives this as conveying trust; as a result, B is likely to be more attracted to A and this increased liking in turn leads B to disclose to A. Trust and attraction have indeed been shown to be very important determinants of disclosure.

Trust is central to the establishment of relationships. We trust our friends and so if we do not trust someone then that person will not become one of our friends. In terms of trust, when we self-disclose we make ourselves vulnerable to the other person (Korsgaard et al., 2014). This means that we need to trust others before we will disclose to them. Interestingly, however, a paradox here is that self-disclosure requires trust, but also creates it. If the discloser trusts the recipient to keep disclosures in confidence, and not misuse them, then more self-disclosures will occur. In certain contexts professionals can be faced with an ethical dilemma when receiving self-disclosures. For example, if a client discloses having committed a crime of some sort, there may be a legal requirement for the professional to inform the police, yet to do so could well destroy the relationship of trust that has been developed. How such ethical dilemmas are resolved will, of course, depend upon the particular circumstances involved.

Petronio and Bantz (1991) investigated the use of prior restraint phrases, such as 'Don't tell anyone' or 'This is only between ourselves', on disclosures. Their study revealed that a large percentage of both disclosers and receivers of such private disclosure anticipated that the recipient would pass on that information. This was confirmed in a survey of 1,500 office workers by the company Office Angels (2000), where some 93 per cent admitted to imparting to others information that they had been asked specifically not to disclose to anyone else.

Over three-quarters (77 per cent) of workers would have told at least two others by the end of the working day in which they received the disclosure. The main reason (36 per cent) given for so doing was the attention and recognition obtained from having 'inside' information, although 20 per cent of staff had a more Machiavellian motive, reporting that they would use the new knowledge as a means of demonstrating power. People tend to regard secrecy as a relative dimension in relation to revealing information they have been told, even when privacy rules are invoked by the discloser (Venetis *et al.*, 2012).

The use of prior restraint phrases is part of what Petronio (2002) termed 'communication privacy management' (CPM), whereby we attempt to place a border around who will have access to private information about ourself. Communication privacy management purports that individuals regulate access to personal information using a rule-based system guided by five key criteria: cultural norms; contextual aspects (the physical and social situation); gender; motivational expectations (e.g. relationship development); and risk–benefit analysis. This process is also known as 'communication boundary management' (CBM). As explained by Dillow *et al.* (2009), 'CBM theory proposes that all individuals construct metaphorical boundaries around information that they consider private or sensitive' (p. 206). These boundaries are important, given that when one self-discloses information of a highly private nature there is both the possibility and temptation of betrayal by the recipient, while for the discloser there is the external danger of being discovered and the internal danger of giving oneself away. This makes such disclosures particularly fascinating elements of interpersonal encounters.

Interestingly, a gender difference emerged in the Petronio and Bantz (1991) study, in that males were more likely to expect subsequent disclosure when a prior restraint phrase was not used, whereas females were more likely to expect subsequent disclosure when a prior restraint phrase was used. It was also found that the five types of people most likely to receive disclosures were (in order and for both genders)

1   best female friend
2   nonmarital significant other
3   best male friend
4   mutual friend
5   spouse.

Those most unlikely to be told were strangers and the recipient's father. This latter finding is compatible with other research findings, which show that fathers are often the least likely recipients of disclosure (Mathews *et al.*, 2006; Derlega *et al.*, 2008, 2014). In addition, one study of parents' disclosures about their own lives and concerns to their late-adolescent children (freshers at university) found that fathers disclosed less than mothers, and the self-stated purpose of their disclosures was more likely to relate to attempts at changing the behaviour of the children. Mothers, on the other hand, cited venting, seeking advice and looking for emotional support as their main reasons for disclosing (Dolgin, 1996). These findings were confirmed by the same author in a parallel survey of freshers themselves, who rated mothers as disclosing more than fathers, especially about their problems and emotions (Dolgin and Berndt, 1997).

The attractiveness of the listener is the second element in this theory of self-disclosure. We disclose more to attractive individuals. Part of the reason for this is simply that we like attractive people. We also like people more once they have disclosed to us (Sprecher *et al.*, 2013). Thus, Tardy and Dindia (2006) illustrated how self-disclosure impacts upon attraction in three related ways, 'we like people who self-disclose to us, we disclose more to people we like, and we like others as a result of having disclosed to them' (p. 237). Not surprisingly, therefore, more self-disclosures tend to be made to individuals who are perceived as being similar to us (in attitudes, values, beliefs, etc.), since such individuals are usually better liked. Evidence that this is a two-way link was found in a study by Vittengl and Holt (2000), where a positive correlation occurred between self-disclosure and ratings of attractiveness, even in brief 'get acquainted' 10-minute conversations between strangers. It is therefore clear that appropriate disclosure is a key element in the establishment of positive relationships. Dress is also part of attractiveness. Thus, one study showed that patients were significantly more likely to disclose their sexual and psychological problems to doctors wearing 'professional' dress (i.e. a white coat), as this was their preferred mode of dress for physicians (Rehman *et al.*, 2005).

Social exchange

It has been argued that the theoretical foundations of self-disclosure are embedded within social exchange theory (Krasnova *et al.*, 2010). Interpersonal encounters have been conceptualised as a form of joint economic activity or social exchange in which both sides seek rewards and try to minimise costs, which may be in the form of money, services, goods, status, love or affection (Kelley and Thibaut, 1978). As Mitchell *et al.* (2012, p. 99) point out, 'According to this theory individuals engage in a series of interdependent interactions that generate obligations among the exchange parties'. The social exchange theory of disclosure purports that, when A discloses to B, this is a form of investment in the relationship and so there is a reciprocal disclosure obligation placed on B, and for the relationship to continue this needs to be fulfilled (Worthy *et al.*, 1969). As noted by Harper and Harper (2006, p. 251), 'one feature of self-disclosure is its reciprocity; meaning that a person's disclosure increases the likelihood that the other party will also disclose'. Indeed, there is evidence that the *norm of reciprocity* holds even when the recipient of disclosure is a computer pre-programmed to respond in specific ways (Moon, 2000). People are also more likely to reciprocate fully if they believe they were individually sought out by the discloser to receive the initial disclosure, rather than being just another in a whole line of people being told the story (Omarzu, 2000). If these rules are broken then not only will the reciprocity effect not occur, but the relationship between disclosure and attraction is also broken. There also tends to be a *norm of equity* between people, which means that we do not like to feel in debt or beholden to others and so B feels under pressure to reciprocate the initial disclosure at a similar level of intimacy in order to return the investment made by A.

As Kowalski (1996) illustrated, such exchange can sometimes take the form of one-upmanship. For example, if I tell you about my experience of being burgled and what I had stolen, you may top this by telling me about how when you were burgled you lost considerably more than me. Also, in everyday interaction if A makes an intimate self-disclosure, this influences the depth of disclosure reciprocated by B. Where reciprocal exchange of self-disclosures does not occur, one of three types of situations prevails:

1   The person making the disclosures is not really interested in the listener. This type of person's need to tell all is so great that the effect on the listener is not considered. The speaker is simply using the listener as a receptacle into which to pour disclosures. This is quite common when someone is undergoing some form of inner turmoil, and needs a friendly ear to encourage the ventilation of fears and emotions. To use another analogy, the listener becomes a 'wailing wall' for the speaker. In certain professional contexts this is acceptable, as in counselling and therapy (Forrest, 2010).

2   The person who is receiving the disclosures does not care about the speaker. In this case the speaker is foolish to continue disclosing, since it is possible that the listener may use the disclosures against the speaker, either at the time of the disclosure or later.

3   Neither one cares about the disclosures of the other. In this case there is no real relationship. If one person discloses, it is a monologue; if both disclose it is a dialogue in which exchanges are superficial. A great deal of everyday, fleeting conversation falls into the latter category.

Modelling

As explained in Chapter 2, Bandura's (1986) social cognitive theory argues that two key features of social learning are the modelling and imitation of the behaviour of significant others. Especially in situations where we are unsure about how to behave, we observe the behaviour of important others and are inclined to copy what they do. In this way, modelling theory purports that, by disclosing, A is providing B with a model of appropriate and perhaps expected behaviour in that context. B then is more likely to follow the model as provided and so also self-disclose. In this way, by self-disclosing, the professional can act as a role model for the client to do likewise. The initial dangers of self-disclosure are such that in everyday encounters we expect an equal commitment to this process from people with whom we may wish to develop a relationship (Greene *et al.*, 2006). For this reason, professionals should expect clients to experience difficulties in self-disclosing at any depth at the early stage of an encounter. Even if the client has a deep-rooted need to 'tell someone', such an experience is inevitably embarrassing, or at least awkward, where the disclosures relate to very personal details. On occasions it is the fear that certain disclosures may be unacceptable to family or friends that motivates an individual to seek professional help. The anxiety about disclosing personal information can be overcome partially by a self-disclosure from the professional to the effect that this type of problem has been dealt with often, or that it is quite acceptable for the client to have the problem. They can also be overcome by the professional acting as a role model through using self-disclosure.

Within the field of therapy, the issue of therapist self-disclosure (TSD) to clients is a contentious topic that is viewed differently across diverse therapeutic traditions (Gibson, 2012; Ziv-Beiman, 2013; Lee, 2014), and for which there are no real guidelines for the therapist to follow (Brody, 2013). In general, research findings support the use of TSDs (Baldwin, 2000; Bochner, 2000; Bitar et al., 2014), with clients appreciating and benefitting from appropriate TSDs (Burkard et al., 2006; Audet and Everall, 2010; Henretty et al., 2014). However, Hill (2014) demonstrated that, whereas clients tended to rate TSDs as helpful, counsellors were more likely to rate them as unhelpful. In their study of clients currently in long-term therapy, at one extreme they identified a minority of clients who preferred no TSDs at all, while at the other some were voracious in their desire to know as much as possible about the helper – even to the extent of seeking out other clients of the same therapist to share information. A number of advantages of TSDs have been identified from the research literature (Henretty and Leavitt, 2010) (Box 9.3). Knox et al. (1997) found that the most effective therapist disclosures occurred when:

- clients were discussing important personal issues;
- they were personal as opposed to self-involving; they were often about past experiences, and none was concerned with feelings or opinions about the therapy relationship *per se*. Three main categories of disclosure emerged here: (1) family (e.g. one therapist revealed having a son); (2) leisure activities (one talked about fly fishing); and (3) shared difficult experiences (one revealed the problems she experienced with her family when she 'came out' as a lesbian);
- clients felt that the helper had disclosed to offer reassurance that their feelings were understandable.

While it is recognised that TSDs can have advantages and disadvantages depending upon how they are employed, and that the decision to disclose depends upon the context and the therapeutic orientation of the therapist (Farber, 2006; Gibson, 2012; Ruddle and Dilks, 2015), it has been recommended (Knox and Hill, 2003; Burkard et al., 2006; Egan, 2014) that helpers:

- let clients know at the outset if they intend to disclose their own experiences – this should form part of the initial 'contract';
- time the disclosures to fit with the flow and content of the interaction;
- do not disclose too much or too often – disclosures should be focused;

- ensure that disclosures are culturally appropriate, given the client's background;
- disclose solely for the client's benefit; role reversal is not the purpose here – helpers should not burden the client with their problems;
- do not disclose too much, but be selective and to the point rather than rambling;
- are flexible – disclosure will be appropriate for some clients, but not others.

However, research also shows that professionals in many fields rarely act as disclosure role models. For example, Hargie *et al.* (2000) found that self-disclosure was recognised by pharmacists as a core skill, but in their study, which involved video-recording community pharmacist–patient interactions, few pharmacist disclosures actually occurred. Likewise, Fisher and Groce (1990) analysed 43 medical interviews and found that doctors rarely disclosed information about themselves. The pattern of low disclosure by health professionals seems to evolve at an early stage. Thus, Ashmore and Banks (2001) found that student nurses were less willing to disclose to patients than to any other target person. Yet, the use of some disclosures can help practitioners to present a more 'human' face to patients. Tallman *et al.* (2007) videotaped 92 primary care consultations and related the behaviour of doctors to patient satisfaction ratings. They found that physicians who received higher satisfaction ratings were also more likely to self-disclose. Examples of disclosure included female doctors telling patients that they too had children, and a physician telling a patient that her husband was on statins. However, disclosures need to be skilled, since in a study of 113 doctor–patient consultations, McDaniel *et al.* (2007) found that most disclosures by physicians were not really helpful for the

---

Box 9.3 Advantages of counsellor disclosure

When used appropriately, counsellor disclosures:

- act as a role model for clients to disclose
- help to normalise client problems
- serve to foster a sense of 'mutuality', or equality, with clients
- decrease the therapist–client hierarchy and help to balance the power differential
- make the helper seem more human and more authentic
- are beneficial for the overall relationship
- offer new insights to clients
- can reassure clients
- give clients a feeling of *universality*, through reassurance that they are not alone in how they feel and that their feelings are neither abnormal nor unexpected
- show clients that things can and do work out

patient, as they often switched the focus away from and failed to return to the patient topic that preceded the doctor's disclosure. Thus, in the Tallman *et al.* (2007) study, successful physicians used self-disclosure selectively, and they were always relevant to the patient's situation.

Self-disclosure by the professional can be advantageous in other contexts. For example, appropriate teacher disclosures have benefits in the classroom (Cayanus and Martin, 2008). When teachers use positive disclosures that are directly linked to the lesson material, these are well received by students and increase motivation, engagement and learning. In terms of valence, it can be acceptable for instructors to reveal some negative experiences. For example, a sports teacher may detail an instance of having played badly and lost a game, or an art teacher may describe the production of a painting that did not turn out as well as expected. Teacher disclosures that are mildly negative can have a number of advantages: they underline the fact that no one is perfect or flawless, but that we learn from our mistakes; they show a 'human' side to the teacher and this, in turn, can facilitate student liking and engagement; and, if teachers only use positive disclosures they may be perceived as narcissistic, and students may feel inferior (Cayanus *et al.*, 2009). However, teachers should avoid using too many negative disclosures. They should also definitely refrain from revealing deeply negative details (such as having stolen, told lies or cheated in examinations), as these have an adverse impact on students (Cayanus and Martin, 2008). Thus, studies by McBride and Wahl (2005) and Hosek and Thompson (2009) showed that, while instructors made self-disclosures about their personal histories, families and everyday activities, they did not reveal information on personal matters, such as salary, or information that could damage their credibility or lead to negative evaluations (such as sexual activity or drug taking).

FACTORS INFLUENCING SELF-DISCLOSURE

A number of personal and contextual factors influence the extent to which self-disclosure is employed.

Personal factors

Age

First-born children tend to disclose less than later-born children. This difference may be due to later-borns being more socially skilled, because their parents have more experience of child rearing, and they have older siblings to interact with. It may also be the case that the eldest child has higher status and is therefore less likely to disclose to lower-status siblings. More generally, in a study of 212 undergraduates in the USA, Dolgin and Lindsay (1999) found that there was less disclosure to siblings who were 5 years younger. They also found that, while younger siblings reported disclosure to seek advice and emotional support from older siblings, the latter reported more disclosures aimed at teaching their younger brothers or sisters. Another difference was that females reported making more disclosures for emotional support than males. One important factor here is the nature of the relationship between siblings. Thus, Howe *et al.* (2000), in a study of Canadian fifth- and sixth-grade children (mean age 11.5 years), found that warmth of the relationship was a key determinant of sibling disclosure.

Disclosure tends to increase with age. As Archer (1979) pointed out, this finding has been reported in studies of children between the age of 6 and 12 years, and in college students between the ages of 17 and 55 years. However, Sinha (1972), in a study of adolescent females, found that 12–14-year-old girls disclosed most, followed by 17–18-year-olds, with 15–16-year-olds disclosing least. Sinha argued that, at this latter stage, the adolescent is at a stage of transition, from girl to woman, and may need more time to 'find herself'. In a study of 174 adolescents in the USA, Papini *et al.* (1990) found that self-disclosures about emotional matters to best friends increased from 12 to 15 years of age. They also found that, at the age of 12 years, adolescents preferred to disclose emotionally to parents, but by the age of 15 years they preferred to disclose to friends. It was further discovered that adolescents with high self-esteem and the esteem of peers were more likely to disclose their emotional concerns to friends, whereas those who felt 'psychosocially adrift' did not communicate such worries in this way. The adolescents in this study disclosed more about their concerns to parents who were perceived to be open to discussion, warm and caring. Adolescents have been shown to decide not to disclose to parents in order to avoid criticism or punishment, to develop autonomy from them or for emotional reasons (Smetana, 2008).

Coupland *et al.* (1991) conducted a series of studies on 'painful self-disclosure' (PSD) in interactions between women aged 70–87 years and women in their mid-30s. PSD refers to the revelation of intimate information on ill health, bereavement, immobility, loneliness, etc. They found that the older women revealed more PSDs, initiated more of them and were less likely to close such disclosing sequences. Since older women usually have experienced more painful events simply by virtue of longevity, it is perhaps not surprising that they disclose more of them than younger women. It could also be related to a reduced need for approval from others, in that the older individual may be less concerned with what other people think, and so more willing to voice an opinion. Coupland *et al.* suggested that PSDs can have positive effects for older women in terms of earning credit for having coped successfully with difficult life events. They speculated that such PSDs can help the older person to 'locate oneself in relation to past experiences, to one's own state of health, to chronological age and perhaps to projectable future decrement and death' (p. 191). The responses of young adults to the PSDs of older people range from pro-social engagement to active disengagement (Fowler and Soliz, 2013).

Many older people clearly enjoy and benefit from talking about their past and indeed such reminiscence is a positive method of therapy for this age group (Williams and Nussbaum, 2001). The experiences of loss are of particular import at this life stage (Suganuma, 1997). However, their greatest recall (the 'personal memory bump') is for life events that occur between the ages of 10 and 30

(Thorne, 2000). During this span, identity is shaped for adult life. It is also a time of highly charged emotional events, such as going to high school, dating, college, starting employment, finding a partner, setting up home, having children. Hence, many of the memories recalled are of 'firsts' (first love, first job, etc.).

Gender

Studies have been carried out to ascertain gender differences in talk. For example, in one study 396 students in the USA were fitted with digital devices which, every 12.5 minutes, automatically recorded what they said for a 30-second period (Mehl *et al.*, 2007). Factoring up from these recorded samples, the researchers found gender differences in that women used some 16,215 words and men 15,669 words over an assumed period of 17 waking hours per day. However, this study has been criticised both on the relatively small sample size and on the skewed nature of the sample, in that university students may well be more verbose than the remainder of the population. Furthermore, very large within-sample differences were also evident. For example, follow-up investigation revealed that the most talkative male was estimated to use 47,000 words per day and the least talkative male only 500 words (*Science Daily*, 2007).

In their meta-analysis of research studies into gender differences in adults' language use, Leaper and Ayres (2007) found that women used more self-disclosures than men. Likewise, Dindia (2000), in an earlier meta-analytical study, also found that females disclosed more than males, but this was moderated by the gender of the recipient, so that:

- females do not disclose to males any more than males do to males
- females disclose more to females than males do to males
- females disclose more to females than males do to females
- females disclose more to males than males do to females.

Kowalski (1999) highlighted another gender difference, in that while men tend to be more careful with regard to the content of their self-disclosures, women are more concerned about the recipient of their disclosures. There are several impinging variables that interact with gender to determine disclosure levels.

Situational factors

The topic, gender of recipient and relationship between discloser and recipient are all determinants of disclosure. For example, battered women specifically want to talk to another female about their experiences (Dieckmann, 2000).

Gender role identity

This relates to how strongly a person feels male or female. It would seem that individuals, either male or female, who regard themselves as possessing female attributes disclose more. Shaffer *et al.* (1992) ascertained that measures of sex role identity were better predictors of self-disclosure to same-sex strangers than was gender *per se* (which failed to predict willingness to disclose). Both males and females high in femininity self-disclosed more. Masculinity had no effect upon disclosure levels, while androgynous subjects (high in both male and female traits) demonstrated high levels of intimacy and flexibility in their disclosures across various contexts.

Gender role attitudes

This refers to how one believes a male or female should behave. We learn to display what we feel are the appropriate behaviours for our gender role (Richardson and Hammock, 2007). These will have been influenced by same-sex parent and significant others. Thus, if a male believes his role to be the solid, strong, silent type he is unlikely to be a high discloser.

Gender role norms of the culture or sub-culture

Grigsby and Weatherley (1983) found that women were significantly more intimate in their disclosures than men. It would seem that it is more acceptable in Western society for females to discuss personal problems and feelings. Males disclose more about their traits, work and personal opinions while females disclose more about their tastes, interests and relationships. Males have also been shown to be less willing to disclose distressing information than females (Ward *et al.*, 2007). It is therefore important to be aware that males may find difficulty in discussing personal matters, and may need more help, support and encouragement to do so.

Ethnic and religious group

Differences in disclosure have been found between different ethnic groups (Asai and Barnlund, 1998; Harris *et al.*, 1999). In the USA, European Americans tend to disclose more than African Americans, who in turn disclose more than Latin Americans. In general, Americans have been found to be more disclosing than similar groups in Japan, Germany, the UK and the Middle East. Yet Wheeless *et al.* (1986), in a study of 360 students, found no difference in disclosure levels between American students and students of non-Western cultural origin studying in the USA. Likewise, Rubin *et al.* (2000) compared 44 North Americans with 40 Chinese students studying in the USA for less than 3 years, and found that target person and nature of topic were much more powerful determinants of disclosure than either gender or nationality.

In another study, Hastings (2000a) investigated disclosure among Asian Indian postgraduate students at university in the USA. She found clear cultural differences in nature and pattern of disclosure. Role relationships played a very large part in determining disclosure amongst Asian Indians. Hindus believe that God has decreed the roles occupied by individuals and so the hierarchy is sacred and one's position deserved. Therefore, subordinates should not question those in authority. As a result, the Indians found difficulties with the propensity for US students to make demands of, or challenge, those in authority (their professors). They also disliked perceived American traits of extensive talk, overt expressions of self and the direct, forcible statement of personal viewpoints. As summarised by Hastings: 'Whereas American friendship is enacted through expressing oneself, Indian friendship is enacted through suppressing oneself' (p. 105).

The traditional Japanese trait of humility and a deep reluctance to disagree with others or say 'no' has caused difficulty in the operation of effective focus groups (Flintoff, 2001; Cullen and Parboteeah, 2010). This means it is very difficult to get participants to express strong views, and if someone does so the other group members tend to concur with this opinion. In an attempt to over-come prevailing disclosure norms, focus group leaders have asked participants to write down their views and then read them out. But this is far from ideal, removing as it does the dynamic interchange of ideas that characterises this method.

There is little evidence regarding the effects of religious affiliation upon disclosure levels. One early study was conducted by Jourard (1961) at the University of Florida, in which he investigated differences between affiliates of the Baptist, Methodist, Catholic and Jewish faiths in relation to level of disclosures to parents and closest friends of both genders. No significant differences were found between denominations for females, although Jewish males were significantly higher disclosers than members of the other denominations, none of whom differed from one another. Jourard speculated that this difference may have been due to closer family ties in the Jewish community and therefore could have been a factor of sub-culture rather than religion *per se*.

In another American study, Long and Long (1976) found that attire (presence or absence of a habit) but not religious status (nun versus non-nun) produced significant differences in interviewee responses. Males were more open in the presence of an interviewer not in habit, whereas the opposite was true for females. Thus, religious dedication appeared to be less important than the impact of clothing whereby such dedication is usually signalled. A similar 'identification' effect was reported by Chesner and Beaumeister (1985), in a study of disclosures by clients to counsellors who identified themselves as devout Christians or Jews compared to counsellors who did not disclose religious convictions. It was found that Jewish subjects disclosed significantly less to the counsellor who declared himself a devout Christian. Chesner and Beaumeister conclude that counsellor disclosure of religion does not facilitate client disclosure and may in fact reduce it.

In the Northern Ireland context, a study of Protestant and Catholic undergraduates revealed that both Catholic and Protestant students were significantly more likely to disclose to those of the same religion than to those of the other religion (Dickson *et al.*, 2000). Interestingly, gender differences emerged here, in that females were significantly more likely than males to disclose to those from the opposite religion. In another part of this study, actual interactions between same- and opposite-religion dyads revealed a greater breadth of disclosure (number of topics discussed) in same-religion pairs. Also in the Northern Ireland context, Hargie *et al.* (2008) found that the decision of Protestants and

Catholics to disclose to those from the outgroup was mediated by degree of trust held for that group.

Personality and disposition

Personality variables have been shown to relate to disclosure level (Reno and Kenny, 1992; Suganuma, 1997; Waldo and Kemp, 1997; Matsushima *et al.*, 2000; Omarzu, 2000). Shy, introverted, types, those with low self-esteem and individuals with high need for social approval disclose less, while social desirability is negatively related to depth of disclosure. Also those with an external locus of control (who believe their destiny is shaped by events 'outside' themselves over which they have no control) disclose less than those with an internal locus of control (who believe they can largely shape their own destiny). A significant and positive correlation between Machiavellianism and disclosure has been reported for females but not for males (O'Connor and Simms, 1990). Lonely individuals have been found to disclose less (Schwab *et al.*, 1998), while neurotics tend to have low self-disclosure flexibility, in that they disclose the same amount, regardless of the situation. Self-disclosure flexibility refers to the ability of an individual to vary the breadth and depth of disclosures across situations. Highly flexible disclosers are able to modify the nature and level of their self-disclosures whereas less flexible disclosers tend to disclose at the same level regardless of context. Miller and Kenny (1986) illustrated how 'blabber-mouths' who disclose in an undifferentiated fashion are not the recipients of high levels of disclosure from others. Such individuals, also referred to as *talkaholics*, have a tendency to communicate compulsively, and so are very high disclosers (Long *et al.*, 2000). In a similar vein, 'blurters' have problems in communication as they engage in disclosures that are spontaneous and unedited, and so are likely to have negative consequences (Hample *et al.*, 2013).

A number of research studies have shown that accepting/empathic people receive more disclosures (Westwood *et al.*, 2011). Miller *et al.* (1983) identified what they termed 'openers', who are able to elicit intimate disclosures from others. They developed an 'Opener Scale' to measure this ability, containing items such as 'I'm very accepting of others' and 'I encourage people to tell me how they are feeling'. The nonverbal behaviour of openers is very important. For example, Duggan and Parrott (2001) found that head nods and appropriate smiles and related facial expressions from physicians encouraged greater levels of disclosure from patients. Also in the medical sphere, in the Tallman *et al.* (2007) study mentioned earlier, it was found that doctors who encouraged patients to disclose their concerns fully received higher patient satisfaction ratings. Forrester *et al.* (2008) reported similar findings with social workers. Stefanko and Ferjencik (2000) identified five dimensions that were characteristic of openers:

1   *communicativeness and reciprocity*: the ability to engage with others readily and to reciprocate disclosure appropriately;

2   *emotional stability*: showing appropriate reactions and avoiding any rapid mood swings;

3   *perspective-taking ability*: being able to see things from the other person's point of view;
4   *spontaneity in communication*: showing acceptance of disclosure, especially about intimate or embarrassing topics;
5   *being sympathetic*: showing understanding and concern for the other.

In her study of people who had survived a near-death experience, Hoffman (1995) found that the reaction of potential targets was crucial. If disclosers detected listener rejection or lack of interest upon initially raising the issue, this stymied their future willingness to discuss what had been a pivotal life experience for them. Furthermore, Yeschke (1987) illustrated how acceptance is important in encouraging self-disclosure in the often stressful context of interrogations, giving the following advice to interrogators: 'Even if dealing with so called rag bottom, puke, scum bag type interviewees, select a positive accepting attitude' (p. 41).

Contextual factors

Warmth and privacy

A 'warm' environment has been found to encourage self-disclosure, so that if there are soft seats, gentle lighting, pleasant décor and potted plants in an office, a client is more likely to open up. This finding is interesting, since interrogation sessions stereotypically take place in 'cold' environments (bare walls, bright lights, etc). Presumably, the willingness of the person to self-disclose is an important factor in determining the type of environment for the interaction. A warm environment is likely to improve our mood and it has been shown that we are more expansive in our use of disclosure when in a positive rather than negative mood (Forgas, 2011). One piece of research (Jensen, 1996) also found that background classical music had an effect upon the choice of topics for disclosure, and promoted self-expression among undergraduates, but more research is needed to chart the exact effects of different types of music upon various people across diverse settings.

In terms of privacy, Solano and Dunnam (1985) showed that self-disclosure was greater in dyads than in triads, which in turn was greater than in a four-person group. They further found that this reduction applied regardless of the gender of the interactors and concluded that there may well be a linear decrease in self-disclosure as group size increases. Likewise, a study reported by Derlega *et al.* (1993) found that when student subjects were informed that their interaction with another subject (a confederate of the experimenter) was being video-recorded for later showing to an introductory psychology class, their depth of self-disclosures stayed at a superficial level, regardless of the intimacy of disclosures of the confederate subject. However, when no mention was made of being videotaped, the level of intimacy of disclosure from the confederate subject was reciprocated by the 'true' subject. This study highlighted the importance of privacy for encouraging self-disclosure.

One interesting exception to the privacy norm lies in the phenomenon of TV chat or 'shock' shows, when people appear in front of what they know will be huge audiences and disclose sometimes excruciatingly embarrassing and often negative personal information (Peck, 1995). So, why do they do this? Orrego *et al.* (2000) in researching this area found four main motives:

1   a desire to remedy negative views about themselves or their group, and 'set the record straight';
2   a forum to enable them to hit back against those whom they feel have victimised them;
3   wanting '15 minutes of fame';
4   the opportunity to promote some business venture.

One variant of privacy is that of anonymous disclosure, sometimes achieved through the camouflage of an alternative identity or pseudonym. Anonymity occurs in a range of contexts, such as unsigned letters, leaks and whistle blowing in organisations, the church confessional, radio call-in shows, police confidential telephone lines and computer-based bulletin boards and chat rooms. In his review of this field, Scott (using the byline Anonymous, 1998) illustrated how the rapid expansion in communication technologies resulted in a concomitant increase in anonymous messages being sent.

Proximity

Johnson and Dabbs (1976) found that there was less intimate disclosure at close interpersonal distances (18 inches: 46 centimetres), and more tension felt by the discloser, than at a medium distance (36 inches: 91 centimetres). However, there is some evidence to suggest that it is males, but not females, who find close interpersonal distance a barrier to disclosure (Archer, 1979). A good example of distal disclosure is via the internet. In a study of disclosure in computer-mediated communication, Joinson (2001) found that visually anonymous individuals disclosed significantly more information about themselves than did those who could be seen. Anonymity usually results in deeper levels and greater honesty of disclosure – the safety of remaining 'hidden' allows the individual to express intimate information or true feelings more readily. In this way, confidential telephone helplines, such as the Samaritans, encourage people to discuss very personal problems without undue embarrassment. This is because the anonymity in such encounters facilitates the establishment of 'psychological proximity' (Hargie *et al.*, 2004). Studies of cyberspace relationships have shown that within a short time people quickly disclose personal problems, sexual preferences, etc. to their online partners (Whitty and Carr, 2006). The internet also allows people to present a new 'self' to the world without upsetting existing 'off-line' relationships. It can be very difficult for someone to make changes to existing aspects of self when the social environment stays the same. One's family, colleagues and friends may resist these new sides of self. Such problems do not occur in virtual relationships. However, a systematic review of research has shown that disclosure is not greater in online than in face-to-face relationships, since factors such as the specific mode of communication, the context of the interaction and the nature of the relationship all moderate the extent of disclosure (Nguyen *et al.*, 2012). Perhaps not surprisingly, it has also been found that individuals with a stronger disposition towards self-disclosure are more likely to use social network sites (Trepte and Reinecke, 2013).

Crisis and isolation

People are more likely to self-disclose in situations where they are undergoing some form of crisis, especially if this stress is shared by both participants. Thus, patients in a hospital ward who are awaiting operations generally disclose quite a lot to one another. If individuals are cut off from the rest of society they then tend to engage in more self-disclosure. For example, two prisoners sharing a cell often share a high degree of personal information. Indeed, for this reason the police sometimes place a stooge in a cell along with a prisoner from whom they want some information. Likewise, in cults, people are encouraged to disclose fully their most intimate details. As well as fostering a sense of bonding and belonging, this enables the cult leaders to exploit members' expressed weaknesses (Tourish and Wohlforth, 2000).

OVERVIEW

Self-disclosure is the cement that binds the bricks in any relationship edifice. Without it, relational structures are inherently unstable and prone to collapse. It is an important skill for professionals to be aware of, from two perspectives. First, they need to be mindful of the likely effects of any self-disclosures they may make upon the clients with whom they come into contact. Second, many professionals operate in contexts wherein it is vital that they are able to encourage clients to self-disclose freely, and so knowledge of factors that facilitate self-disclosure is very useful. Our impressions of other people can be totally wrong in many cases since we do not know what is 'going on inside them'. As Jourard (1964, p. 4) pointed out, 'Man, perhaps alone of all living forms, is capable of *being* one thing and *seeming* from his actions and talk to be something else'. The only method of attempting to overcome this problem, of finding out what people are really like, is to encourage them to talk about themselves openly and honestly. If we cannot facilitate others to self-disclose freely, then we will never really get to know them.

When giving and receiving self-disclosures Stewart and Logan (1998) argued that three factors are important:

1   *Emotional timing.* Is the person in the right frame of mind to receive your disclosure?
2   *Relevance timing.* Does the disclosure fit with the purpose and sequence of this conversation?
3   *Situational timing.* Is this environment suitable for discussion of this topic?

The general importance of self-disclosure in everyday interaction reflects the fundamental value of this skill in many professional contexts. It is therefore useful to conclude with an early quotation from Chaikin and Derlega (1976, p. 178), which neatly encapsulates the central role that this aspect has to play:

> The nature of the decisions concerning self-disclosure that a person makes will have great bearing on his life. They will help determine the number of friends he has and what they are like: they will influence whether the discloser is regarded as emotionally stable or maladjusted by others: they will affect his happiness and the satisfaction he gets out of life. To a large extent, a person's decisions regarding the amount, the type, and the timing of his self-disclosures to others will even affect the degree of his own self-knowledge and awareness.

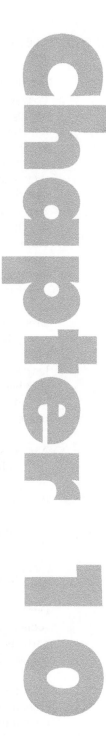

Chapter 10

Opening and closing interactions: the skills of set induction and closure

INTRODUCTION

S ET INDUCTION AND CLOSURE are the skills we employ to enter and exit social encounters. As summarised by Burgoon *et al.* (1996, p. 340), 'The first task for conversants is knowing how to start and stop interactions. Some conversations begin and end smoothly and effortlessly, others are difficult, uncomfortable, and problematic'. Firsts and lasts seem to be of special importance in life, and this is reflected in the host of words we have to describe these periods in interaction – beginning and ending, opening and closing, hello and goodbye, salutation and farewell, arrival and departure, introduction and conclusion, start and finish. In psychological terms, one of the reasons for this is that we are much more likely to remember what we encounter first (the *primacy effect*) and last (the *recency effect*) in any sequence. Events in between are less clearly recalled. Given that people are more likely to be influenced by what we said or did when they met us and just before they left us, we should give due consideration to how these interactional phases are handled. Not surprisingly, their role in the development and maintenance of relationships has been the subject of academic study for some considerable time (e.g. Roth, 1889).

Greetings and partings are therefore very important parameters within which social interaction takes place. They are structured, formalised sequences during which we have a greater opportunity to make important points or create an effective impact. Given their prevalence, Levinson (2006) referred to greetings and partings as 'strong universals' in interaction. Humans have developed elaborate meeting and leave-taking rituals to mark these occasions, and parents overtly teach their children to engage in appropriate behaviours at both stages ('Say hello…' 'Wave goodbye…'). As a result, infants from a very early age begin to use greeting behaviours, as shown by Degotardi (2011) in her analysis of how an 8-month-old infant was welcomed by other infants in a nursery school. The greeting auto-pilot kicks in when we meet those we know, even if we are just passing and do not intend to engage in conversation. As colleagues walk past one another they smile, engage in eye contact and make *adjacency pair* verbal responses where an utterance anticipates a related one from the other person (Schegloff, 2007), such as: 'Hi. How are you?' followed by the reply 'Good. And you?', and walk on. These responses are so much a part of our everyday lives that in fact we often only notice them when they are absent. Thus, if we meet a friend or colleague who does not engage in the process of salutation, or who leaves without any disengaging ritual, we become concerned. Indeed, if we cannot engage fully in greetings and partings, rules of interactional politeness deem that we provide some or all of: an apology ('Sorry…'), a justification ('…I can't stop now. I'm late for class…') and a relational continuity indicator ('…I'll phone you this evening').

Although in this chapter set induction and closure are discussed separately, these are complementary skills. There is truth in the old adage that to have a good ending you must first have a good beginning. The symbiotic relationship between the two can be exemplified by examining the behaviours initially identified by Kendon and Ferber (1973) as being associated with the three main phases of greetings and partings between friends:

A   *Distant phase.* When two friends are at a distance, but within sight, the behaviours displayed include hand waving, eyebrow flashing (raising both eyebrows briefly), smiling, head tossing and direct eye contact.

B   *Medium phase.* When the friends are at a closer, interim distance, they avoid eye contact, smile and engage in a range of grooming (self-touching) behaviours.

C   *Close phase.* At this stage the friends again engage in direct eye contact, smile, make appropriate verbalisations and may touch one another (shake hands, hug or kiss).

During greetings the sequence is ABC, while during partings the reverse sequence CBA, operates. At the greeting stage this signals the availability of the participants for interaction, whereas during parting it underlines the decreasing accessibility.

Greetings and partings are important relational events. Relationships have been conceptualised as mini-cultures with their own meanings, values, communication codes and traditions (Mittendorff *et al.*, 2006). Within them communicative symbols, often comprehensible only to those involved, are used as 'tie signs' to create feelings of 'we-ness'. As part of this, different groups develop their own special greeting and parting codes. For example, Steuten (2000) illustrated how bikers and rockers developed elaborate greeting rituals relevant to their type of group, which reflected their shared interests and helped to cement the bonds between members. In the military, members salute in a set style as they meet one another.

Opening and closing have been identified from a review of research studies in medicine as two of the 14 core skills that contribute to effective consultations (Lipkin, 1996). Interestingly, in the psychotherapeutic context, Flemmer *et al.* (1996) found that experienced therapists (with more than 16 years' experience) rated the opening phase as being significantly more important than did less experienced therapists. This suggests that over time the import of the skill of set induction becomes even more apparent.

SET INDUCTION

Anyone familiar with the world of athletics will be aware of the instructions given to competitors before a race – 'On your marks. Get set. Go!' By telling the athletes to get set, the starter is preparing them for the final signal, and allowing them to become both mentally and physically ready for the impending take-off. This simple example is a good introduction to the skill of set induction. Set induction was a term coined by psychologists to describe what occurs when 'an organism is usually prepared at any moment for the stimuli it is going to receive and the responses it is going to make' (Woodworth and Marquis, 1949, p. 298). In other words, it establishes in the individual a state of readiness, involves gaining attention and arousing motivation, as well as providing guidelines about what is to follow.

It is a skill that is widely used, in various forms, in interaction. At a simple level it may involve two people discussing local gossip, where, to stimulate the listener's attention, they may use phrases such as: 'Have you heard the latest...' At another level, on television and at the cinema, there are 'trailers' advertising forthcoming attractions in an exciting and dramatic fashion to arouse interest in what is to follow. Indeed, television programmes usually contain a fair degree of set induction in themselves, employing appropriate introductory music and accompanying action to stimulate the viewer.

The term set has many applications in our everyday lives. For example, how a table is set reveals quite a lot about the forthcoming meal – how many people will be eating, how many courses there are and how formal the behaviour of the diners is likely to be. Other uses of the term set include 'It's a set-up', 'Are you all set?' and 'Is the alarm set?' In all of these instances, preparation for some form of activity to follow is the central theme, and this is the main thrust of the skill of set induction.

In relation to social interaction, the induction of an appropriate set can be defined as *the initial strategy employed to establish a frame of reference, deliberately designed to facilitate the development of a communicative link between the expectations of the participants and the realities of the situation.* Set induction can therefore be a long, or a short, process depending upon the context of the interaction.

Purposes of set induction

Set induction involves more than simply giving a brief introduction at the beginning of a social encounter. It may involve a large number of different

---

Box 10.1 Goals of set induction

The main goals served by the skill of set induction are to:

1 induce in participants a state of readiness appropriate to the task to follow, through establishing rapport, arousing motivation and gaining attention
2 establish links with previous encounters (during follow-up sessions)
3 ascertain the expectations of participants
4 discover the extent of participants' knowledge of the topic to be discussed
5 indicate to, or negotiate with, participants' reasonable objectives for the encounter
6 explain what one's functions are, and what limitations may accompany these functions

---

activities, appropriate to the situation in which set is to be induced. The generic goals of the skill are shown in Box 10.1. However, the specific functions need to be tailored to the demands of the prevailing situation, and so varying techniques are employed to achieve them. Thus, a helper uses different behaviours to open a counselling session, from a professor introducing a lecture to a large university class. The process can take a large variety of forms both between and within contexts. The set used is influenced by, amongst other things, the subject matter to be discussed, amount of time available, time of day, length of time since the last meeting, location of the encounter and personality, experience and cultural background of those involved. Such factors should be borne in mind when evaluating the main techniques for inducing set. There is even some research to suggest that the approach used in greetings is influenced by the individual's testosterone level. In an interesting experimental study of greeting behaviour, Dabbs *et al.* (2001) discovered that high-testosterone males and females entered the room more quickly, were more business-like and forward in their manner, focused directly on the other person and displayed less nervousness. In comparison, low-testosterone individuals were more responsive, attentive and friendly, but also more tense and nervous.

During professional encounters set usually progresses through the four phases of:

Meeting → Greeting → Seating → Treating

At the meeting stage the initial *perceptions* gleaned of one another are very important. Greetings represent the *social* phase of welcome and salutation. During the seating stage the professional must demonstrate a *motivation* to become involved with the client. Finally, 'treating' represents the transition to the *cognitive* or substantive business to be transacted. These stages do not always progress in a linear fashion, but rather they overlap and are inter-dependent. However, it is useful in terms of analysis to examine each separately.

Perceptual set

How we perceive others upon first meeting plays a crucial role in social interaction (Weger *et al.*, 2014). The human brain is a predictive organ – it attempts to work out what to expect next. As noted by Tskhay *et al.* (2014, p. 901), 'Researchers have demonstrated that, within seconds of seeing people, individuals instantly and effortlessly perceive various characteristics from others' appearances'. Thus, during social encounters we search out and evaluate cues that may enable us to predict with accuracy how others will behave towards us (Pillet-Shore, 2011). Often these are what Cokely (2007) refers to as 'metanotative qualities', that is, noncontent characteristics of the interlocutor's presentation that influence our impression. We appraise both *static* cues, such as the interlocutor's dress, height and body shape, and *dynamic* cues in terms of verbal and nonverbal behaviour (Cafaro *et al.*, 2012).

Research on first impressions shows that the initial judgements we make upon meeting others are crucially important in influencing how we react to them and interpret their responses (Demarais and White, 2005; Ambady and Skowronski, 2008; Frauendorfer and Mast, 2015). For example, in their review of the facial domain, Sparko and Zebrowitz (2011, p. 243) concluded that 'First impressions from faces are made rapidly and they have significant social consequences, influencing stereotypes, expectations, and behavior toward others'. They are important because: 'The first impressions that occur in initial interactions can influence not only whether further contact is sought but also the trajectory of relationship development' (Sprecher *et al.*, 2013, pp. 497–498). There is now a considerable volume of research into the accuracy of first impressions (Wood, 2013). Those who score highly in terms of accuracy of first impressions tend to be more socially skilled and popular with peers, experience lower levels of loneliness, depression and anxiety, have higher quality of personal relationships and achieve more senior positions and higher salaries at work. In their review of this area, Hall and Andrzejewski (2008, p. 98) concluded: 'A large amount of research shows that it is good to be able to draw accurate inferences about people based on first impressions'. This is not really surprising, as accuracy of first impressions enables the individual to respond appropriately at the outset to different people, and to make informed decisions in a range of situations (e.g. Should I ask this person for a date? Should I appoint this person to this position?).

A fascinating recurring finding from research into first impressions is that we are often accurate in some of the snap judgements we make about others upon meeting them for the first time. What is referred to as 'zero-acquaintance' research, where individuals who have just met and have not interacted evaluate one another, has shown high levels of accuracy between judgements of personality and actual inventory scores of personality (Kenny and West, 2008). Likewise, there has also been research showing the potency of what is known as 'thin slices', or very short video segments, of behaviour in judging eventual outcomes (Eisenkraft, 2013). Curhan and Pentland (2007) illustrated how when people are shown such 'thin slices' of an interaction (ranging in different studies from between 6 seconds and 3 minutes), and especially of the opening sequence, they can make remarkably accurate judgements about how the encounter will progress. This has been found in diverse contexts, including, *inter alia*, marital relationships (e.g. whether a couple will divorce), employment interview decisions, sales and negotiation outcomes, poker winners and losers, criminal trial deliberations and ratings of professional competence. As noted by Pentland (2007, p. 192) we 'use these "thin slice" characterizations of others to quite accurately judge prospects for friendship, work relationship, negotiation, marital prospects, and so forth'.

These studies also show that we make evaluations of others at a very early stage and based upon minimal evidence. Thus, parents should carefully choose the names of their offspring, as a range of judgements are made based upon a person's first name (Mateos, 2014); well-known names are perceived more positively than unusual ones, so that, for example, hiring decisions favour people with more common names (Cotton *et al.*, 2008). However, while first impressions can be accurate, they can also be inaccurate (Gray, 2008; Vernon *et al.*, 2014). Thus, Willis and Todorov (2006) demonstrated that, after as little as one-tenth of a second, we have made inferences based upon the facial appearance of the interlocutor, and we then tend to become anchored on this initial judgement. Our early perceptions influence our expectations, and this in turn shapes our behaviour. Initial perceptions also impact upon subsequent processing, since we tend to adapt any conflicting information to make it fit more easily with our existing cognitive frame (Adler *et al.*, 2013b). This is part of a process known as *selective distortion*, wherein we assimilate new material in such a way as to make it compatible with our established beliefs (Orbe and Bruess, 2005). Distortion can take the form of the *halo effect*, whereby if our initial perceptions are positive, we then tend to view the person's future behaviour in a benevolent light. The corollary is the *horn effect*, where we form an early adverse opinion and then perceive the individual's future behaviour through this negative lens.

But why should first impressions be so important in social life? Some theorists argue that there is an evolutionary basis underpinning our seemingly visceral habit of making instant decisions based upon initial impressions. Schaller (2008) argued that many aspects of human cognition evolved as a result of their contribution to our social and physical well-being. One such aspect is the capacity to judge others rapidly. For our distant ancestors this was often crucial. For example, upon meeting others they had to answer questions such as: Is this person likely to cause me serious harm? Does the person appear to be carrying a potentially life-threatening and contagious disease? So, it is argued, the ability to make what could be life-saving decisions was learned and then evolved as society developed. We may be less worried today about whether someone will cause us bodily harm or be carrying a deadly disease, but we still need to ascertain whether the other person is likely to be a friend or foe. Thus we may ask questions such as: Is this person trustworthy? On a more positive note, since time immemorial humans, upon first meeting potential partners, have also asked themselves a question such as: Does this person seem suitable as a romantic partner?

But, like all aspects of interpersonal communication, impression formation is a two-way street. Lamb (1988) illustrated how:

> Infants develop fear of strangers at between seven and eight months, when they begin to make the distinction between who they know and who they do not. We never outgrow this uncertainty about people outside our established circle. As adults we worry about the first impressions we make, finding ourselves at the mercy of someone who is bound to form judgments on the basis of very little genuine knowledge about us.
>
> (p. 103)

We know that others are assessing us when we meet, and so we attempt to manage the impressions of ourselves that we convey to them (Pillet-Shore, 2011). Research shows that we can consciously manage the impressions we make on others. Human *et al.* (2012) found that, when subjects were given specific instructions to make a good impression and to 'put your best face forward', they actually did make more positive impressions on others than a control group of subjects not given these motivational instructions.

It is therefore clear that initial perceptions matter a great deal. There is considerable wisdom in the aphorism, 'You don't get a second chance to make a first impression'. Our perceptual set is determined by both the environment and the participants.

The nature of the environment

People organise their physical spaces to make statements about their identity. As a result, we form impressions of individuals based on how they organise their spaces. We make judgements based on 'behavioural residue', which refers to 'the traces left in the environment by behavioral acts' (Graham *et al.*, 2011, p. 775). A very tidy office with everything exactly in order and spotlessly clean, with a set of designer tea cups placed neatly on a separate table, is one form of behavioural residue, while an office with irregular piles of paper and dusty books everywhere, with stained coffee mugs here and there, is a very different residue. This residue provides information about the person occupying that space, and so we make inferences about the individual accordingly (Gosling *et al.*, 2008). Gosling *et al.* (2005a, b) carried out studies in which they had observers make judgements about the personality traits of the occupants of 94 offices and 83 student bedrooms. They found that observers could make reasonably accurate evaluations based solely on environmental cues.

Thus, the nature of the environment affects initial impressions. Dittmar (1992) carried out a study in which she filmed a young male and a young female individually in a relatively affluent and in a fairly impoverished environment. She found that, when filmed in the wealthy environment, the actors were rated as more intelligent, successful, educated and in control of their lives than when in the impoverished context, whereas when in the latter they were rated as warmer, friendlier and more self-expressive. Interestingly, close proximity to stigmatised others seems to increase the likelihood of the stigma 'rubbing off' on oneself. Thus, Hebl and Mannix (2003) found that, when a male job applicant was photographed sitting next to an overweight female, the applicant was stigmatised, even when the raters were informed that there was no social relationship between the two individuals.

People also arrange their spaces in order to help them to achieve their interactive goals. When we enter a room for the first time, the layout of tables, chairs and other furnishings is translated into a set of expectancies about the format for the interaction (for a full discussion of these aspects of nonverbal communication, see Chapter 3). For example, a table and upright chairs usually convey an impression of a business-like environment, whereas a coffee table and easy chairs suggest a more social or conversational type of interaction. Thus, someone attending a selection interview may be somewhat taken aback if confronted with the latter type of setting, since this is contrary to expectations.

Personal features of the participants

It has been found that important decisions, such as whether or not to offer someone a job, are affected by initial impressions of the candidate gleaned by the interviewer (Swider *et al.*, 2011; Barrick *et al.*, 2012). These impressions are influenced by a range of factors, including the body features, dress and age of the other person.

Body features

The features of height and body size were discussed in Chapter 3. Here, we will focus upon attractiveness. We are judged on level of attractiveness from childhood (Hawley *et al.*, 2007), so that, from as early as 4 years of age, children have learned the norms of attractiveness (Swami and Furnham, 2007a) and show a preference for physically attractive others. The importance of appearance is abundantly evident in both the amount and variety of artefacts sold annually, such as designer clothes, false nails, cosmetics, expensive shoes, cosmetic surgery and so forth. Studies have shown that there is a good reason for this. For example, in their review of research in relation to the use of make-up Guéguen and Jacob (2011, p. 284) found that, 'cosmetics enhance the perception of physical attractiveness and other feminine traits of women'. More generally, Zebrowitz and Montepare (2008, p. 176) concluded: 'People with more attractive faces are perceived as more likable, outgoing, and socially competent as well as higher in sexual responsiveness, social power, intelligence, and health'. We are bombarded every day with images of attractiveness in newspapers, magazines, the internet, cinema and TV. The media industry is well aware that beauty is popular and so sells well. Ugly film or pop stars are very much an exception. Furthermore, judgements of beauty are becoming more universally consistent. In their review of research in this field, Little and Perett (2002, p. 28) concluded:

'Across many studies it has been found that there is a high degree of agreement from individuals within a particular culture, and high agreement between individuals from different cultures'.

Medisauskaite *et al.* (2014, p. 21) point out that, 'The bias towards physically attractive people is well documented within the scientific literature'. In a large-scale meta-analysis of over 900 separate studies, Langlois *et al.* (2000) confirmed that 'attractiveness is a significant advantage for both children and adults in almost every domain of judgment' (p. 404). It is now well documented that we 'associate positive attributes with the physically attractive and negative attributes with the physically unattractive' (Petroshius and Newell, 2015, p. 16). Equating beauty with goodness has become known as the *physical attractiveness bias*, wherein pulchritudinous people are seen as more personable, popular, friendly, intelligent, persuasive, happy, interesting, confident and outgoing (Wilson and Nias, 1999; Harris and Garris, 2008; Patry, 2008). They receive higher academic grades, are more likely to be approached for help by strangers, have more dates and are less likely to be found guilty in court. They are also more likely to be trusted with secrets, have their work assessed favourably and be selected for jobs (Swami and Furnham, 2007b). Physically attractive politicians are more likely to be elected (Milazzo and Mattes, 2016). As summarised by Myers (2008, p. 390) 'there is now a file cabinet full of research studies showing that appearance *does* matter. The consistency and pervasiveness of this effect is astonishing. Good looks are a great asset.' It would therefore seem that expenditure on attractiveness enhancement measures can be money well spent.

It has been shown that unattractive, when compared to attractive, females are regarded as more deceptive and are less likely to be believed when making a claim of sexual harassment (Seiter and Dunn, 2001). In their research review of the area, Lindell and Lindell (2014, p. 768) conclude that, 'Humans are exquisitely sensitive to beauty: it plays a primary role in impression formation and influences subsequent judgements, favouring the beautiful'. In line with the 'what is beautiful is good' or 'beauty is good' stereotype (Callan *et al.*, 2007), attractive people tend to be responded to more positively, receiving more eye contact, more smiles, closer bodily proximity and greater body accessibility (openness of arms and legs) than those rated as being unattractive. By acting in a positive way towards attractive individuals, the latter in turn are more likely to reciprocate this positivity. This creates a *self-fulfilling prophecy*, wherein a belief leads directly to its fulfilment (Jussim, 2012). As explained by Aronson *et al.* (2007, p. 67), 'People have an expectation about what another person is like, which influences how they act towards that person, which causes that person to behave consistently with people's original expectations, making the expectations come true'.

The benefits of attractiveness can be striking. One Australian study showed that more attractive males earned an average salary of $81,750 compared to $49,600 for men of below-average looks (Borland and Leigh, 2014). Furthermore, it has been found that CEOs who are more facially attractive receive 'beauty premiums', in terms both of higher personal remuneration and better stock returns for their corporations (Halford and Hsu, 2013). Mehrabian and Blum (1997) derived several factors to account for ratings of physical attraction by both males and females from photographs of young adults of both sexes; the main ones were *masculinity* (determined by features to do with strength, larger chest, broader chin), *femininity* (based upon larger and rounder eyes, make-up, longer hair), *self-care* (suggested by shapely figure, well groomed, well-fitting clothes) and *pleasantness* (based upon perceptions of friendliness, happiness, babyish features).

Burnham and Phelan (2000) argued that some aspects of attractiveness are universal because they have a biological foundation. Clear skin is favoured because it is a sign of health, while physical symmetry is viewed as the ideal and so is desirable. In general, facial attractiveness and body weight seem to be the two key determining features in ratings of physical attraction, for both males and females (Swami *et al.*, 2007b). In relation to the latter aspect, in their research in this area Sabia and Rees (2012) found that overweight females in the USA earned substantially less per hour than their slimmer counterparts. Likewise, Roehling *et al.* (2008, p. 392) showed how, 'Research indicates that overweight job applicants and employees are stereotypically viewed as being less conscientious, less agreeable, less emotionally stable, and less extraverted than their "normal-weight" counterparts'.

Ratings of attractiveness also seem to be influenced by a range of impinging factors. For example, one study found that hungry males preferred females with a higher body weight, while satiated males rated those with a lower body weight as more attractive (Swami and Tovée, 2006). Another study, into female ratings of attractiveness in males, discovered that their preferences changed across the menstrual cycle (Penton-Voak and Perrett, 2000). When presented with a choice of faces varying in masculinity and femininity, females preferred the masculine face during the follicular (fertile) phase of the cycle (days 6–14) but not at other times. Many of these judgements about attractiveness are, of course, subconscious but they nevertheless influence the way in which we respond.

However, decisions about interpersonal attractiveness are not just skin deep and involve more than mere physical features. Rather, there are three types of attractiveness: physical, social and task (Burgoon and Bacue, 2003). Physical attractiveness encompasses facial and body features. Social attractiveness refers to how well the individual communicates interpersonally in terms of factors such as friendliness, warmth and humour. Ratings of task attractiveness are related to how appealing individuals are as work partners. A physically less attractive professional may be successful and popular with clients by adopting a pleasant, helpful interactive style (social attractiveness) together with a skilled, expert approach (task attractiveness).

Dress

People are frequently evaluated on the basis of their mode of dress. This was aptly expressed by William Shakespeare in *Hamlet*: 'the apparel oft proclaims the man'. One reason for this is that the style of dress which one adopts is often a sign of the image one wishes to project or the group to which one belongs (Howlett *et al.*, 2013). In social encounters we carefully select what clothes to wear, whether to have a tattoo or piercing, and so on. We do so to communicate a message to others about who we are and so we are judged on these aspects of our appearance. It is often said that you should pay very careful attention to your appearance because everyone else will. Others make all kinds of assumptions about us based upon how we are dressed, and react accordingly. Indeed, one study showed that subjects could make accurate judgements about the age, income and gender of individuals, based solely upon a photograph of their shoes (Gillath *et al.*, 2012). Several studies have shown that people are more inclined to take orders from, accept the lead given by, and comply with requests made by someone in authority wearing an appropriate uniform or 'high-status' clothing. As expressed by Smith and Mackie (2007, p. 374), 'Medical doctors wear white lab coats and sling stethoscopes around their necks; police officers, firefighters, and paramedics wear uniforms and identification badges. These symbols are usually enough to activate the norm of obedience to authority.'

One survey of patients in the USA showed that some 76 per cent preferred doctors to wear a white coat, compared to under 5 per cent who favoured casual dress; in addition, perceptions of dress correlated significantly with ratings of trust and confidence in the physician (Rehman *et al.*, 2005). These findings were confirmed in a study of patients by Chung *et al.* (2012, p. 389), who pointed out, 'Our results are also consistent with other studies, reporting higher scores in trustworthiness and confidence ratings for doctors wearing the white coat'. Numerous research studies have been conducted into determining the effects of dress, and physical attractiveness, upon evaluations of counsellors. In summarising the findings from these studies, Kleinke (1986) noted that counsellors who dress formally enough to portray an impression of competence and whose attire is in style, rather than old-fashioned, are preferred to those who dress very formally and are consequently seen as 'stuffy' or unapproachable. Likewise, more physically attractive counsellors are preferred.

In the corporate setting, Karl *et al.* (2013) reviewed studies which show that the way in which a person dresses affects others' impressions of that individual's credibility, intelligence, competence, status, professionalism, sociability, efficiency, honesty and reliability. In their workplace study they found evidence to support the aphorism that 'you are what you wear', so that workers felt more competent when wearing either business casual or formal business attire. Respondents also felt that uniforms had a positive effect on customer perceptions of service quality, and that a range of features, such as unconventional hair style or colouring, tattoos, facial piercing and clothes with tears or rips, had a negative effect. The adverse impact of these latter aspects of appearance has been corroborated in other studies (e.g. Johnson *et al.*, 2014; McElroy *et al.*, 2014). Research also shows that customers make judgements about a company and the service it provides based upon the attire and adornments of employees. In many service sectors, managers make decisions about how employees should dress, and so organisations are judged upon the image presented by their workforce. Those in sectors such as financial services and public administration are subject to more conservative expectations over how they dress for the office (Adler *et al.*, 2012). As far as colour is concerned, there is a maxim, 'the darker the suit, the greater the authority' (Greenleaf, 1998). There is also evidence of a 'red effect', in that females wearing red are viewed by both males and females as being more sexually receptive and having greater sexual intent (Johnson *et al.*, 2014); hence the derivation of terms such as 'scarlet women' and 'red-light district'. In employment interview settings, dressing in red has been shown to have a negative effect on hiring decisions (Maier *et al.,* 2013).

Interestingly, there is evidence of a causal relationship between dress and displays of attractiveness. Lõhmus *et al.* (2009) carried out a study in which they photographed the faces of 25 women wearing clothes that the females themselves regarded as attractive, unattractive or comfortable. They then had these facial photographs (the clothes were not visible) rated by males and significant differences emerged. The results showed that the men rated the faces of the females wearing attractive clothes most highly, followed by those wearing the comfortable clothes, while those wearing the unattractive clothes were rated as least attractive. The effects of their feelings about their attire seemed to have a direct impact upon the emotions of the females; this affected their facial expressions, which in turn influenced the way in which they were evaluated by males.

For women, dress choices at work are more complex and possible interpretations more varied than with men (Hamilton, 2014). In employment interviews, Forsythe (1990) found that female job applicants received more favourable hiring recommendations from experienced male and female business personnel when they were wearing more masculine clothing (e.g. a dark navy suit) than when wearing distinctly feminine attire (e.g. a soft beige dress). In their review of this area, Whetzel and McDaniel (1999, p. 222) concluded: 'interviewers' reactions to job candidates are strongly influenced by style of dress and grooming. Persons judged to be attractive or appropriately groomed or attired received higher ratings than those judged to be inappropriately dressed or unattractive'. Appropriateness, though, will depend ultimately upon the type of profession and the corresponding image cultivated. Three broad categories for females have been identified (Wallach, 1986; Larson, 2013):

1   *Corporate.* The corporate woman wants to be seen as competent, rational and objective (e.g. banker, accountant, lawyer), and so dresses more formally, for example, wearing suits in grey or blue colours. Women wearing a jacket rather than a dress or skirt and blouse tend to be perceived as more powerful (Temple and Loewen, 1993).

2   *Communicator.* This woman wants to project an image of warmth, sincerity and approachability (e.g. personnel, marketing, teaching, social work, media), and so dresses in a practical, relaxed style.

3   *Creative.* Here the image is one of flair, originality and innovation (e.g. musician, artist, writer, fashion designer, advertising), involving dramatic colours and exaggerated design.

Age

Initial judgements of others are also influenced by age (Ryan *et al.*, 2007). Generally, older, more mature professionals are likely to be viewed as having greater experience and are seen as more desirable when stable leadership is required, while younger professionals are perceived as having a more up-to-date knowledge base and being more suited to situations where change has to be implemented (Spisak *et al.*, 2014). In terms of gender, males tend be more positively evaluated if they are regarded as being competent, assertive and rational, whereas females are viewed more positively if they portray traits such as gentleness, warmth and tact (Hargie, 2006b).

These are the main facets of perceptual set linked to personal attributes. However, as our evaluations of individuals are influenced by a wide array of features, such as height (see Chapter 3), whether a male has facial hair or is clean-shaven (attitudes here vary across time; see van der Land and Muntinga, 2014) and whether or not glasses are worn. In relation to the latter aspect, research shows that people wearing glasses tend to be rated as being more intelligent, honest and of higher status than those not wearing them (Guéguen, 2015). In terms of hair, Mannes (2013) found that men with shaved heads were rated as more dominant, taller and stronger, compared to those with full heads of hair or with hair loss. Such aspects all come together to influence the judgements we make of others. Although it is also true that first impressions can be deceptive, they are also often accurate, and this is why most of us judge a book to some extent by its cover.

Social set

Greetings have been shown to be ubiquitous across time and cultures (Tessonneau, 2005; Bowe and Martin, 2007). Before proceeding with the main business of the interaction, it is desirable to employ a number of social techniques. These serve to humanise the encounter, and often facilitate the achievement of the core task objectives. Indeed, one of the difficulties with telephone communication is what has been labelled the *coffee and biscuits problem* (Hargie *et al.*, 2004). In most business meetings, the first thing that happens is that refreshments are wheeled in. The process of getting to know one another then begins, as the participants engage in the universal shared human activity of drinking coffee and eating biscuits. As well as being a sign of basic civility, this has a deeper level of significance. In a sense, coffee can help to lubricate the business machine. Before progressing to the main task, it enables each side to make judgements about the likely formality of the occasion, and how personable and amenable the other is. On the telephone this cannot happen and so the social opportunities are lost.

What is known as *sociality communication* has been the focus of research attention across a range of contexts, and has been shown to be central to effective interaction (Koermer and Kilbane, 2008). Sociality communication refers to behaviour that facilitates smooth co-operative interaction. It incorporates four separate dimensions (Koermer and McCroskey, 2006):

1 *courtesies* involve friendly greetings and a polite approach;
2 *pleasantries* relate to small talk on aspects such as the weather or current events;
3 *sociabilities* include jokes, and disclosures pertaining to gossip;
4 *privacies* are deeper disclosures about oneself.

Social set incorporates the first two of these dimensions and can also include elements of the third. The fourth dimension comes into play as relationships develop (see Chapter 9).

The induction of an appropriate social set is an important preliminary to the more substantive issues to follow, in that it serves to establish a good, amicable working relationship between the participants at the beginning of the interaction. Three techniques are employed here: receptivity, nontask comments and the provision of creature comforts.

Receptivity

The way that professionals receive their clients is of considerable importance. Robinson (1998) argued that the first stage is to negotiate a *participation framework* where both sides communicate their availability (or otherwise) to become involved. This is followed by an *engagement framework*, where they move on to mutually collaborative communication. In the doctor–patient context, Robinson charted how degree of willingness to be involved was signalled nonverbally by the doctor, from an extreme of not looking at the patient, through eye gaze but not body asymmetry, and on to full engagement with the upper and lower torso and feet oriented towards the patient. Research by Tallman *et al.* (2007) has shown that doctors who receive higher ratings of patient satisfaction devote time and effort to the greeting stage. As discussed in Chapter 5, when the doctor begins the interaction with an open question there is significantly greater engagement from patients than when the encounter is opened with a closed question. Similarly, in paediatric encounters the degree of involvement of children is influenced by the physician's first question. This can be directed to the child (e.g. 'Right, Colin, how can I help you today?'), parent (e.g. 'So what can we do for Colin today?') or open to either (e.g. 'How can I help you today?'). When the opening query is directed to the child, there is a greater likelihood of the child becoming more actively involved in the consultation (Stivers, 2001).

The use of social reinforcement techniques (handshake, smile, welcoming remarks, tone of voice and eye contact) is important at the outset, since they serve to make the other person feel more at ease and responsive (Bonnet and McAlexander, 2013). While some form of nonverbal greeting ritual is universal across countries and cultures, considerable variations have been charted in the exact form that this takes (Axtell, 1999; Migge, 2005). Indeed, some countries may or may not use some parts of the greeting ritual. For example, Germans have fewer conversational routines during opening and closing phases, and are much less likely to engage in polite conversation – to the extent that there is no German term for 'small talk' (House, 2005). Greetings across cultures range from Maori nose rubbing, Tibetan tribesmen sticking out their tongues at one another, Eskimos banging their hand on the other person's head or shoulders and East African tribes spitting at each other's feet. These behaviours all serve the same function – that of forming a human bond. They can also have important benefits.

Studies by Allday and Pakurar (2007) and Allday *et al.* (2011) found that the use of teacher greetings at the start of lessons both enhanced initial task engagement and increased the amount of time spent by pupils in on-task behaviours. Similarly, Brown and Sulzerazaroff (1994), in a study of bank tellers, demonstrated how words of greeting, a smile and direct eye contact were all significantly correlated with ratings of customer satisfaction. In the counselling context, smiles and facial signals of interest by the counsellor have been shown to be important in engaging clients at the outset (Sharpley *et al.*, 2006). The importance of smiling was also evidenced in an experimental study by Monahan (1998), who found that the effect existed even at a subconscious level. Subjects shown slides at a subliminal level of a person smiling gave increased ratings of the person's likeability and attractiveness.

Another important aspect of receptivity is the use of the client's name. This leads to a more favourable evaluation of the speaker and has been shown to be important in the professional context (Hargie *et al.*, 2004). Whether formal or first names are used is a matter for sensitive judgement or negotiation. One major survey of patients in the USA revealed that the majority wanted physicians to greet them with a handshake and to use their first name, and preferred the doctor to introduce themselves using both first and last names (Makoul *et al.*, 2007). They also wanted the physician to smile and be warm, attentive, friendly and calm. Thus, Kahn (2008, p. 1988) developed the following checklist for doctors to follow in their initial meeting with patients in hospital:

1   Ask permission to enter the room; wait for an answer.
2   Introduce yourself, showing ID badge.
3   Shake hands (wear glove if needed).
4   Sit down. Smile if appropriate.
5   Briefly explain your role on the team.
6   Ask the patient how he or she is feeling about being in the hospital.

An important aspect here is how greeting behaviours are employed. Let us consider for a moment just one common greeting procedure – the handshake. This is a very long-established human ritual, as illustrated by the fact that, on an Assyrian relief from Nimrud, dating from around 850 BC, the Assyrian king Shalmaneser III is depicted shaking hands with the king of Babylon, Marduk-zakir-shumi (Cohen, 2001). While this depiction is of the traditional 'horizontal hands' handshake, there are a number of variants, such as the 'fist bump' and the 'high five'. The standard handshake is almost always enacted with the right hand, whereas the other variants can be performed with either hand. The standard handshake remains the norm in formal encounters. A recurring aspect is that it is usually initiated by the person of higher status (Webster, 1984). However, the formal handshake itself is not a unitary behaviour, but, as illustrated by Astrom and Thorell (1996) takes many forms (see Box 10.2 for the main ones). In a Swedish study, Astrom and Thorell investigated the effects of handshakes and associated behaviour (e.g. direction of eye gaze) upon the rather eclectic mix of therapists, car salesmen and clergymen – all selected because they were professional groups who regularly engage in hand shaking. It was found that a strong handshake was

Box 10.2 Handshake variations

The other person:

- clasps your hand more weakly than 'normal'
- clasps your hand more strongly than 'normal'
- retains your hand longer than 'normal'
- releases your hand immediately after touching it
- pulls your hand towards him or her
- pumps your hand up and down several times
- performs pumping and clenching movements
- proffers only the fingers
- proffers the whole hand in a sort of thumb grip
- rejects your hand
- grasps your hand with both of his or hers
- clasps your hand from above
- clasps your hand from below
- clasps your hand with his or her palm turned downwards
- clasps your hand with his or her palm turned upwards

clearly associated with ratings of extraversion and a weak one with introversion. The most satisfying greeting behaviour was direct eye gaze, while a weak handshake was rated as the least satisfying.

This latter finding confirmed other research showing that a limp, wet, 'dead fish' handshake is disliked and rated negatively, whereas a firm handshake is viewed positively (Astrom, 1994). This result was also confirmed in a detailed study by Chaplin *et al.* (2000), who noted that the handshake has historically been seen as a male greeting behaviour. They studied the handshake in relation to gender, personality and first impressions. Four trained coders shook hands twice with college undergraduates, and rated each handshake on a 5-point scale along eight dimensions:

1   strength (weak–strong)
2   temperature (cold–warm)
3   dryness (damp–dry)
4   completeness of grip (very incomplete–full)
5   duration (brief–long)
6   vigour (low–high)
7   texture (soft–rough)
8   eye contact (none–direct).

These ratings were then correlated with the other variables. Among the main significant findings to emerge were that five of the above variables (strength, duration, completeness of grip, vigour and eye contact) combined to constitute the 'firm handshake', and male handshakes were firmer than females. Those with firm handshakes were more extraverted, and less shy and neurotic, and also created better first impressions. Chaplin *et al.* highlighted the significance of these findings for females in professional contexts, where 'giving a firm hand-shake may provide an effective initial form of self-promotion for women that does not have the costs associated with other less subtle forms of assertive self-promotion' (p. 117). This was corroborated in a study of employment interviews by Stewart *et al.* (2008), where a strong relationship was found between the quality of the handshake by candidates and hiring decisions. A firm handshake by females was shown to be especially important.

The handshake has also been shown to have persuasive qualities. Guéguen (2013) carried out a study of a door-to-door transaction, where a request was made to householders to donate money to a humanitarian organisation. The experimental condition was that, in half of the cases, the volunteer began with a handshake before making the request, while in the other half no handshake was employed. Results showed a statistically significant difference between con-ditions, with householders showing a very high percentage compliance to the request in the handshaking condition (96 per cent) compared to the no hand-shaking condition (53 per cent).

Gender differences have also been noted in greeting rituals. Thus, the eyebrow flash is used more often by men, and is rated more positively when used with members of the opposite sex, and as a greeting with people we know (Martin, 1997; Noller, 2005). In a study of 152 greeting dyads at Kansas City International Airport, Greenbaum and Rosenfeld (1980) found that bodily con-tact was observed in 126 (83 per cent) of the greetings. The types of contact observed were

- mutual lip kiss
- face kiss
- mutual face contact, excluding kiss
- handshake
- handholding
- hand to upper body (touching the face, neck, arm, shoulder or back)
- embrace.

Female greeting behaviour was very similar with both males and females, whereas males used markedly different greetings with females as opposed to males. Male same-sex dyads had a significantly higher frequency of handshak-ing, whereas dyads containing a female had significantly more mutual lip kisses and embraces. Indeed, males have been shown to be less approving of a male, than a female, friend kissing them when greeting (Felmlee *et al.*, 2012). In another study, females were shown to smile more and have closer interpersonal proximity during greetings (Astrom, 1994).

Nontask comments

A seemingly universal way of opening interaction involves what is known as the 'empty question' regarding the other's well-being. An example is the formal, and slightly ridiculous, 'How do you do?' Variants on this theme proliferate. For example, in inner-city Belfast it is 'How's about you?', often reduced to ''bout ye?' In their analysis of *phatic communion*, or small talk, Coupland *et al.* (1992) highlighted how this type of HAY (How are you?) question serves to signal recognition for and acknowledgement of the other person, but is not expected to produce any self-revelations from the respondent. They used the following joke to illustrate this.

> *A:* How are you?
> *B:* I have bursitis; my nose is itching; I worry about my future; and my uncle is wearing a dress these days.

But, although this type of question is in a sense redundant, it is nevertheless expected as a curtain raiser for the business to follow. To employ another metaphor, nontask comments are employed to 'break the ice' in social encounters and serve as a preliminary to the exchange of information at a more substantive level. Statements relating to the weather or noncontroversial current affairs are quite common social openers, as are comments relating to the specific situation (e.g. 'Sorry about the mess. We're having some renovations carried out…'). This form of opening is also important in the health care setting (Stein *et al.*, 2005). As discussed by Holli and Beto (2014), while the opening exchange can be time consuming for a busy professional, it is an important part of the consultation and should not be ignored. Interestingly, in the medical setting the HAY question, when posed by a physician, can be interpreted by patients either as a casual ice breaker, or a request for them to provide details of their medical condition (Rindstedt, 2014).

While nontask comments are useful in a range of situations, they need to be used judiciously. An early note of caution was sounded by the eminent psychiatrist Sullivan (1954), who warned against the use of nontask comments (which he termed *social hokum*) in the psychiatric interview. He argued that in this particular context it was more important to get into substantive issues as soon as possible. Also in the clinical context Morrison (2008) supported this perspective when he advised against small talk, noting: 'In most cases your patient has come for treatment because of troubling problems. Comments about the weather, baseball, or television shows may seem at best a distraction, or at worst an expression of unconcern on your part.' Similarly, Millar and Gallagher (1997, p. 392) cautioned that in selection interviews: 'Although non-task comments may help to reduce anxiety levels of nervous applicants, it is equally possible that the use of social chit-chat may introduce unwanted variations into the procedures'. Thus, nontask comments need to be appropriate to context.

Provision of 'creature comforts'

Creature comforts refer to those items used to make someone feel more at ease. These include a soft or 'easy' chair, an offer of tea or coffee, and reasonable lighting and temperature in the room. All of these are important for rapport building. This is clearly demonstrated by the fact that they are often taken away in situations where an individual is being subjected to stress, such as in severe interrogation sessions. In some settings professionals have little control over the physical location of the encounter and so have to try to compensate for the dearth of creature comforts by optimising their use of interpersonal skills.

Motivational set

A key function of set induction is to gain attention and arouse motivation at the beginning of an interaction. The way individuals perceive and assimilate information is affected by their initial motivation to attend. To maximise client involvement, the professional must both be motivated and be motivating. Thus, the two core methods used to induce motivational set are showing personal commitment and dramatic techniques.

Showing personal commitment

A pre-requisite to the successful motivation of others is that we are self-motivated by showing enthusiasm and commitment for the task ourselves (Wentzel and Brophy, 2014). In the service sector, employers use the technique of *mystery shopper*, whereby an assessor pretending to be a client visits the service area, to check whether staff are showing sufficient motivation when they meet clients (Hargie and Tourish, 2009). A professional who seems unprepared, uninterested, rushed or nervous is most unlikely to inspire confidence in, or be able to motivate, customers or clients. The best gospel preachers display evangelical zeal in their performance. Good counsellors adopt a caring style. Successful lawyers exude confidence and expertise. Looking and sounding the part are key aspects of motivational set. To engage clients fully, professionals must show concern, commitment, enthusiasm, interest, attention and expertise.

Dramatic techniques

In many situations, particularly in learning environments, it is very important to gain the attention of participants at the outset, so that the task may proceed as smoothly as possible. All good entertainers know the value of beginning a performance with a 'flash-bang' to grab the attention of the audience immediately – indeed, Munter (2000) used the term *grabbers* to describe such techniques. The following four dramatic techniques can be employed to engage motivational set.

1   *Novel stimuli.* These are effective attention-gaining devices. Magicians have long recognised the power of rabbits being pulled from hats. Producers of TV news programmes, aware of the value of stories involving violence in obtaining the attention of viewers, have a maxim regarding opening items of 'If it bleeds, it leads'. They also use 'teasers' to trail upcoming items, since it has been found that viewers pay more attention to news stories

that have been teased and to commercials immediately following the teaser (Cameron *et al.*, 1991; Wittebols, 2004). The implications of these results are fairly obvious. There are many aids (diagrammatic, real objects, audio-visual recordings, etc.) that can be used in order to arouse motivation. By focusing on any of these at the outset, the learning environment can be enhanced.

A word of caution is needed here, however, in that to be effective in the longer term the novel stimulus must be related to the task in hand. Otherwise this technique will be seen as gimmickry and all it will achieve is literally novelty value. In addition, it has been shown that the use of teasers can lead radio listeners to form premature judgements about culpability in relation to threatening stories (rape, murder, etc.). Dolinski and Kofta (2001) carried out an experiment whereby university students either heard stories as a whole, or as a headline followed by a break (the typical 'more on that story after this short break' approach) and then the full story. They found that listeners were consistently more likely to attribute culpability to the central person (e.g. a male arrested for suspected rape, or a hospital doctor who misdiagnosed a ruptured appendix as inflammation of the ovary, after which a patient died) when the story was teased. It seems that we make judgements based on the initial information available and these then become resistant to change (see the discussion later in the chapter on *need for closure*). Dolinski and Kofta (2001, p. 255) concluded that, 'newspaper readers, radio listeners, and TV viewers should be aware that they are prone to make biased moral judgments on the basis of information provided in the headline part of the message'.

2   *An intriguing problem.* Employed at the beginning of an interaction sequence, this can engage listeners' interest immediately, and hold it for a long time if they are required to solve the problem. This technique is equally applicable whether the problem posed is a technical or a social one. Furthermore, it does not really matter whether or not the problem has a correct solution. The idea here is to establish immediate involvement and participation at a cognitive or practical level. The use of case histories can be particularly relevant in this respect. Here, a tutor presents details of a particularly difficult case, and asks trainees how they would have dealt with it.

3   *A provocative statement.* This method of inducing set must be carefully thought out, since the object of the exercise is to provoke comment, rather than aggression, on the part of the listener. With very sensitive topics or volatile audiences, caution should be exercised.

4   *Behaviour change.* The adoption of unexpected, or unusual, behaviour can be a powerful method for gaining attention. This needs to depart from the normal behaviour pattern to be most effective. For example, a lecturer may sit with the audience or move about the room without speaking in order to grab attention. All humans have a basic cognitive structure that strives to accommodate new information of an unexpected nature. It is, therefore, the element of behavioural surprise that is central to the efficacy of this method, since it stimulates the individual's attentiveness.

Cognitive set

The main purpose of many encounters involves dealing with substantive issues of fact. Before proceeding to these issues, however, it is important to check that the terms of reference are clearly understood at the outset. In order to achieve this objective, it is necessary to ensure that all parties are in clear agreement as to the nature and objectives of the ensuing interaction. In other words, it is important to induce an appropriate cognitive set in participants, so that they are mentally prepared in terms of the background to, and likely progression of, the main business to follow. As Millar and Tracey (2009, p. 89), in their analysis of interviewing, noted: 'the interviewer must indicate what the objectives are, propose ideas about how the interview will proceed, and give an indication of the structure, content and duration of the interview'.

The functions of cognitive set can be summarised as the process of informing participants where they have been, what stage they are now at and where they are going. This involves five main components: providing prior instructions, reviewing previous information, ascertaining expectations, outlining functions and goal setting.

Prior instructions

It has long been known that prior instructions, such as techniques to use in solving a problem or special items to be aware of, help to improve performance. In an early study in this field, Reid *et al.* (1960) found that serial learning was speeded up by providing instructions to subjects about how to approach the learning task. In reviewing research into prior instructions, Turk (1985) concluded that telling individuals what they will hear actually biases them to perceive what they have been encouraged to expect, regardless of what message they actually receive. As Turk put it, 'Telling people what they are about to perceive will radically affect what they do perceive' (p. 76). Park and Kraus (1992) had a group of subjects ask one question each to a person they did not know. They found that, when the questioners were instructed to obtain as much information as possible about traits of the respondent such as intelligence, honesty, truthfulness and dependability, they were able to do so successfully. Park and Kraus concluded that it is possible to 'obtain a greater amount of verbal information relevant to difficult-to-judge dimensions when instructed to do so' (p. 445). On the basis of their results they recommended that personnel officers and selectors at employment interviews should be instructed in advance to search for specific information about candidates.

Even subtle aspects of prior instructions can have an impact. Thus, Song and Schwarz (2010) found that the font used in written instructions affected how an exercise described was perceived. In one experiment involving a physical exercise, when the easy-to-read Arial font was used subjects estimated that the task would take 8.2 minutes to complete, whereas when the difficult-to-read Mistral font was employed for the same set of instructions the anticipated time was 15.1 minutes. Respondents also viewed the task as being more difficult when

Box 10.3 Comparing instructions in Arial and Mistral fonts

Standing upright, hold a stick horizontally with both hands, keeping the palms down. Let the stick rest against the front of your thighs.
Now, with your good arm, push the injured arm out to the side and raise it up as far as you can, while keeping your elbows straight.
Hold this position for 5 seconds. Repeat the exercise ten times.

Standing upright, hold a stick horizontally with both hands, keeping the palms down. Let the stick rest against the front of your thighs.
Now, with your good arm, push the injured arm out to the side and raise it up as far as you can, while keeping your elbows straight.
Hold this position for 5 seconds. Repeat the exercise ten times.

Mistral was used as opposed to Arial. As a result, they were more willing to incorporate the exercise into their everyday routine when the easy-to-read font was employed. However, this effect can be mitigated by telling those subjects given the Mistral version that the instructions may be difficult to read owing to the font used. When this caveat is added to the prior instructions, the differential effect of the fonts is eliminated. It seems that the difficulty is then attributed to the font rather than the exercise *per se* (for a comparison of the two fonts, see Box 10.3, where the first set of instructions is given in Arial and then replicated in Mistral, using the same font size).

Finally, Miller *et al.* (2001) found that our reactions to others in need can be mediated by prior instructions. In a meta-analysis of research studies in this field they found that subjects responded much more sympathetically and empathically when asked either to put themselves in the other person's situation or to try hard to imagine how that person was actually feeling. Conversely, when asked only to focus objectively on the person's behaviour or the facts of the situation, feelings of empathy and sympathy were greatly reduced.

Reviewing previous information

It is important to ascertain the extent of knowledge participants may have regarding the subject to be discussed. This enables decisions to be made about the appropriate level for any ensuing explanations and whether or not to encourage contributions. These points are pertinent when addressing a new topic for the first time. The process of linking what is already known with the new material to follow has been shown to be an effective teaching procedure for facilitating the understanding and retention by pupils of new information (Burden and Byrd, 2012; Coe *et al.*, 2014).

In many interpersonal transactions, one encounter is influenced by decisions made and commitments undertaken in the previous meeting. Again, it is important to establish that all parties are in agreement as to the main points arising from prior interactions and the implications of these for the present discussion. If there is disagreement, or confusion, at this stage it is unlikely that the current encounter will be fruitful. This problem is formally overcome in many business settings, where minutes of meetings are taken. The minutes from a previous meeting are reviewed, and agreed at the outset, before the main agenda items for the current meeting are discussed. This ensures that all participants are in agreement about what has gone before, and have therefore a common frame of reference for the forthcoming meeting. In addition, agenda items are usually circulated prior to the meeting, and this in itself is a form of cognitive set, allowing individuals to prepare themselves for the areas to be discussed.

Dealing with expectations

Rahnev *et al.* (2011, p. 10,741) have demonstrated how, in general, 'Perceptual decisions are almost always informed and heavily biased by our prior expectations'. Rutledge *et al.* (2014) discovered that expectations can determine level of happiness in that, if we receive a reward that is more than we expected, our level of happiness increases, whereas if it is lower than we expected, then happiness levels drop. In the social domain, Snyder and Stukas (2007, p. 363) noted that, 'When people meet and interact with new acquaintances, they often use expectations about what these other people will be like to guide their interactions'. In this way, we approach social encounters with certain explicit or implicit expectations, which we expect to have fulfilled (Hamilton, 2005). If expectations are unrealistic, or misplaced, it is important to discover this and make it clear at a very early stage. Otherwise the conversation may proceed for quite some time before these become explicit. This may result in frustration, embarrassment or even anger, if people feel their time has been wasted. It can also result in the discussion proceeding at dual purposes, and even terminating, with both parties reading the situation along different, yet parallel, lines. By ascertaining the immediate goals of those involved, such problems can be overcome. This can be achieved simply by asking what others expect from the present encounter. Once goals are clarified, behaviour is more easily understood.

The process of *priming* is important here, as there is now considerable research to show that how we have been primed to receive information does indeed influence our judgements (Weisbuch *et al.*, 2008). The effect was borne out in a classic study by Kelley (1950), who found that when subjects were told to expect a 'warm' or 'cold' instructor they developed a positive or negative mental set respectively. This influenced both their evaluations of instructors and the way in which they interacted with them. More recently, Singh *et al.* (1997) and Fiske *et al.* (2007) confirmed the importance of 'warm' and 'cold' as central traits, which, once ascribed to someone, trigger other positive or negative evaluations respectively.

This is linked to the *interpersonal expectancy effect,* also known as the *Pygmalion effect* (Karakowsky *et al.*, 2012). This refers to the way in which our expectations of others influence how we perceive and respond to them, and how this in turn affects the way they respond to us (Harris and Garris, 2008).

In the words of Baker (1994, p. 38), 'Expectations are self-fulfilling prophesies. What we expect of people is often what we get.' Hanna and Wilson (1998, p. 102) gave as an example, 'if you are subconsciously looking for evidence that another person is angry with you, you are likely to find that evidence in the person's behavior'. This process is known as the *perceptual confirmation effect* (Willard *et al.*, 2012). In one classic study in the USA, researchers selected pupils at random and informed their teachers that these children had been identified as 'late bloomers' who would soon show marked improvements in their academic performance. Follow-up analyses revealed that these children had indeed out-performed their peers. This was attributed to the increased attention and reward they had received from teachers based upon the primed expectations (Rosenthal and Jacobson, 1992). A range of follow-up studies confirmed how teacher expectations directly impact upon pupil performance (Rubie-Davies *et al.*, 2006; Stronge *et al.*, 2011). This effect has also been shown to be prevalent in a range of other social contexts (Rosenthal, 2006). If we are set to perceive others in either a positive or negative light our behaviour towards them is likely to provoke the response we expected. As aptly summarised by Pratkanis (2007, p. 23), 'expectations guide interpretations and perceptions to create a picture of reality that is congruent with expectations'.

The corollary of the Pygmalion effect is the *Galatea effect*, which refers to the expectations we hold of ourselves, and the fact that we are likely to realise these self-expectations (Karakowsky *et al.*, 2012). In analysing this area, Kirsch (1999) distinguished between two types of expectancy:

1   *Stimulus expectancy* refers to our anticipations with regard to aspects of the external environment. For example, if I expect people of a certain race to be aggressive, when I interact with individuals of that race I am more likely to perceive their behaviour as aggressive regardless of whether it really is or not.

2   *Response expectancy* relates to one's anticipated responses in a situation. Thus, if I believe that I am really going to enjoy spending time with a particular individual, then when I am with that person I am more likely to behave in a way consistent with this expectation (smiling, laughing, paying attention to the other person, etc.). In fact, this example is very pertinent, since there is considerable research to show that people tend to behave in such a way as to ensure that their emotional expectations are confirmed (Catanzaro and Mearns, 1999).

Another distinction is between expectation-congruent (*assimilation effect*) stimuli that confirm what we had thought, and expectation-discrepant (*contrast effect*) stimuli that are contrary (Tormala and Petty, 2007). How the latter are perceived is crucial in shaping final opinions about the experience. The strength of expectations is central here. People spend months or years planning and looking forward to great occasions in their lives, such as wedding ceremonies or holidays. The anticipation of success and enjoyment is very high, and this in turn is likely to lead to expectation-discrepant (negative) experiences being filtered out of the occasion itself.

Outlining functions

This involves explaining one's professional job role and functions. If someone holds false expectations, as was discussed in the previous section, it is crucial to make this clear, and to point out what can and cannot be done within the limitation of professional parameters. Once this has been achieved the interaction should flow more smoothly, with both participants aware of their respective roles. This does not always occur. One study of doctor–patient interactions in a US hospital (Santen *et al.*, 2008), revealed that in 82 per cent of consultations physicians introduced themselves as a doctor and only in 7 per cent of cases did they identify themselves as a resident (in training). Also in this study, in 64 per cent of instances attending (supervising) physicians introduced themselves as a doctor, with only 6 per cent stating that they were in fact the supervising physician. Patients felt that it was very important for them to know the level of training of their doctor, yet most stated that they were unaware of this. Although the residents may fear a loss of perceived status (and the supervising physician may be sensitive to this), the patient has a right to know the stage of training of those responsible for their care.

Nelson-Jones (2014) used the term *structuring* to refer to the process by which professionals make clients aware of one another's roles, and argued that a key juncture for outlining functions is at the contracting phase of the initial session. At this stage the professional often has to answer the implicit or explicit client question, 'How are you going to help me?' Counsellors answer this question in different ways, depending upon their theoretical perspectives. A useful general approach is to respond to this question by emphasising that the role involves helping and supporting people as they sort out their problems and reach eventual personal decisions, rather than offering instant solutions.

Goal setting

As discussed in Chapter 2, goals are at the very epicentre of interaction. They provide direction for action and serve as an interpretation filter through which the behaviour of others is judged. A key goal in new or relatively unfamiliar contexts is that of *uncertainty reduction* or *uncertainty management* (Knobloch, 2010). When encountering new situations: 'We want to know what is expected of us, what the rules of the interaction are, what others think of us, what relationship we will have with them, and so on' (Hargie, 2006b, p. 42). Experienced professionals develop *cognitive schemas* to enable them to deal swiftly and efficiently with a range of persons and situations (see Chapter 2). These schemas, developed after repeated exposure to the same situation, are cognitive structures containing knowledge and information about how to behave in a particular context. They contain *scripts* that are readily enacted – for example, the same greeting ritual is often implemented automatically with every client. As shown by Balcetis (2008), we tend to be *cognitive misers*, using established schemas to guide our behaviour across different people and settings. However, for trainee professionals who have not acquired relevant schemas, interaction is much more difficult and uncertain.

Likewise, for clients the visit to a professional may be one in which no schema or script exists. Again, uncertainty will be high and so the stage of goal setting is crucial in helping the client to understand better what the interaction entails (Hargie *et al.*, 2009). Thus, in the medical field, orientation statements by the physician that explain to the patient the sequence and purpose of forthcoming activities that will be carried out are important (Stein *et al.*, 2005), as these have been shown to facilitate both the communication process and health-related outcomes (Robinson and Stivers, 2001). In the workplace, newly hired employees have been shown to use a range of techniques to decrease their uncertainty (Clampitt, 2013). At times of major change the information needs of all employees are heightened. If the organisation itself does not effectively deal with such uncertainty, the grapevine goes into overdrive and rumours proliferate (Meehan, 2013). Interestingly, one exception here is that police interrogators deliberately increase uncertainty when they imply to suspects that they know a lot more about their activities than they are being told, thereby keeping the suspect off-balance and so more vulnerable to 'cracking' under the pressure. This technique, whereby detectives exaggerate to suspects the evidence they have about them, is known as *maximisation* (Klaver *et al.*, 2008). However, the reduction of uncertainty should usually be a core goal of the opening phase of interaction. If it is not dealt with, the cognitive space of individuals is occupied with attempts to reduce it, often at the expense of what would be more profitable activities.

In many contexts it is not feasible for the professional simply to state the goals (e.g. in person-centred counselling, where the client is encouraged to help to set the agenda and decide what should be discussed). However, in those situations where it is appropriate, it is helpful to state clearly the goals for the interaction, and the stages that are likely to be involved in pursuit of these goals. This can be a useful method for structuring the encounter. For example, the ability of teachers to structure lesson material in a logical, coherent fashion has long been known to be a feature of effective teaching (Rosenshine, 1971; Coe *et al.*, 2014). There are other situations where it is desirable to structure interaction by providing guidelines about what is to be discussed and the stages through which the discussion will proceed. In the medical context, Cohen-Cole (1991, p. 53) pointed out that 'effective interviews begin with an explicit statement or acknowledgement of goals. Sometimes these may need to be negotiated between the doctor and the patient if there are some differences in objectives.' Kurtz *et al.* (1998) also highlighted the importance of the *screening* process, whereby the doctor checks and confirms the list of problems raised by the patient, giving as an example 'So that's headaches and tiredness. Is there anything else you'd like to discuss today?' (p. 23).

The importance of negotiating the agenda has been recognised in the counselling context. Lang and van der Molen (1990, p. 93) noted that as early as possible in the helping interview 'the helper is advised to inform the client straightaway about his way of working, and then see if the client agrees with that, or whether he has other expectations'. Similarly, in the negotiation context, the stage of formulating an agenda is essential to success. One side cannot simply decide upon the goals of the encounter and impose them on the other, but rather the first act of the negotiation drama is that of deciding the nature and structure of play (see Chapter 13).

Goal setting allows participants to prepare themselves fully. They will then be mentally prepared for the topics to be discussed, and be thinking about possible contributions they may be able to make. It also means that the individual feels less uncertain and more secure in the situation, knowing in advance what the purpose of the interaction is, what the main themes are likely to be, how the sequence of discussion should proceed and the anticipated duration of the interaction.

Overview of set induction

In *The Republic* Plato argued, 'The beginning is the most important part of the work'. This also holds for interpersonal encounters. Pillet-Shore (2011, p. 73) noted how, 'As the gateway to personal social relationships, introductions are critical to sustaining everyday social life'. In the interviewing context, the opening is critical, since it shapes perceptions of self, the other person and the situation (Stewart and Cash, 2013). Set induction is, therefore, a very important process – hence the expressions 'well begun is half done' and 'start off as you intend to go on'. It will vary in length, form and elaborateness depending on the context of the interaction. *Perceptual set* refers to the effects of the initial impression formed by people based upon the nature of the environment and the personal attributes of the interlocutors. *Social set* is the process of welcoming people, providing creature comforts and generally making them feel settled. *Motivational set* is concerned with showing personal commitment and encouraging clients to participate fully. *Cognitive set* involves establishing expectations and outlining goals for the interaction.

The acronym STEP can be used to describe the four main stages of the skill of set induction, as people step into a relationship.

1   *Start.* This involves welcoming others, settling them down and gaining attention.
2   *Transact.* Here, expectations are ascertained, and the functions of the participants outlined. Any links with previous encounters should be made.
3   *Evaluate.* An analysis is then carried out of the relationship between the expectations of the participants and the realities of the present situation. Any discrepancies must be clarified before the interaction can progress fruitfully.
4   *Progress.* This stage marks the end of the beginning, when the interaction moves on to the main body of the business to be conducted. It involves finalising and agreeing the goals for, and the nature, content and duration of, the forthcoming interaction.

CLOSURE

As mentioned earlier, closure is the parallel side to set induction. However, there are also differences between the two. First, in social encounters, while we may think about how we should welcome someone, we seldom give much thought to how we will disengage from that person (unless the relationship is not going well and we want to extricate ourselves from it). Generally, closure is more of an impromptu event – it just happens. But in professional contexts more care and attention needs to be paid to the closing phase. In his analysis of interviewing Stewart (2009, pp. 191–192) pointed out:

> Too often the closing is seen by both parties as merely a stopping point or way of saying goodbye, an unimportant appendage to the interview. The closing, however, is as important as the opening. An abrupt, brief, seemingly uncaring closing may destroy the relationship.

A second major difference, as noted by Goffman (1972), one of the first academics to study this field seriously, is that they are what he termed 'access rituals' in that 'greetings mark a transition to increased access and farewells to a state of decreased access' (p. 79). The fact that access is literally being closed down means that the ending of the encounter has to be managed in such a way that the relationship is maintained and no one feels a sense of being rejected. Burgoon *et al.* (1996, p. 343) noted that, 'It would be very efficient to end conversations by just walking away. But social norms call for balancing efficiency with appropriateness.' In fact, these norms are learned at an early age. First (1994) illustrated how 'The Leaving Game' is one of the first examples of dramatic play enacted by children (on average at the age of 2.3 years). In this game, the child shows knowledge of the ramifications of parting, by giving the twin instructions to the role-playing other: 'I'm leaving. You cry.'

In their review of the area, Bowe and Martin (2007, p. 69) noted that, 'A short and abrupt farewell seems to devalue the interaction in some way'. Indeed, abrupt closures usually indicate personal or relational dysfunction. For example, one study compared 24 autistic individuals with a group of 24 nonautistic persons matched for chronological and mental age (Hobson and Lee, 1996). It was found that the autistic individuals were less likely to engage in greeting and parting behaviours. More generally, abrupt closures occur for a variety of reasons, including:

- *ending an undesired interaction* (e.g. the rejection of unwanted sexual advances);
- *testing affinity* (e.g. to see if the other person will come after you as you walk away);
- *when frustration reaches a certain point* ('This is hopeless, I'm leaving');
- *avoiding possible conflict*. If discussion is becoming over-heated it may be better to leave rather than risk verbal or physical abuse;
- *demonstrating power and status*. Those with higher status can terminate interactions suddenly – they see their time as more important than anyone else's and so may decide unilaterally how it is used; for example, in her study of closure patterns in primary care visits, West (2006) found that it was the doctor who initiated the closure.

The nonverbal behaviours used in these abrupt endings range through breaking off all eye contact, stopping talking altogether, to the extreme of turning one's back and walking away. Verbal statements fall into three main types:

1   *rejection remarks*, that indicate you do not want the conversation to continue ('Would you please go away?'; 'Clear off');
2   *departure injunctions*, that are a sign of higher status and power ('Off you go now.'; 'I'm stopping it there. Go and work on it');
3   *exasperation exits*, that show you feel any further communication is a waste of time ('This is going nowhere. I've had enough'; 'I can't take any more of this').

In linguistic terminology, closure has been defined as a final speech turn that is recognised as such by both parties, involving: 'the simultaneous arrival of the conversationalists at a point where one speaker's completion will not occasion another speaker's talk, and that will not be heard as some speaker's silence' (Schegloff and Sacks, 1973, p. 295). This is achieved through 'a set of regularly occurring behaviors that provide a normative, mutually agreed-upon process for terminating interactions' (Kellerman *et al.*, 1991, p. 392). These behaviours, in turn, serve to consolidate the information, concerns, issues and agreements reached (Stewart and Cash, 2013). They also shift the perspective from the present to the future. Thus, *closure involves directing attention to the termination of an encounter, highlighting the main issues discussed, making arrangements for future meetings, and ending the interaction in such a way that the relationship is maintained.*

The expression 'need for closure' (NFC) has entered the everyday lexicon, in relation to ending a particular episode – such as an argument between colleagues, the completion of a work project or agreeing a divorce settlement. It is also widely employed to refer to the process of coming to terms with the loss of a loved one. This is especially so where there are problems surrounding the death, and indeed, the NFC is particularly strong where the deceased's remains have not been located. In this latter context, the term refers to the strongly felt human need to go through a process that will lead to acceptance of the loss. Understanding exactly how and why someone died and being able to go through the normal rituals associated with burial are all involved in this process of 'putting it all to rest' as part of final closure. This psychological phenomenon in many ways underscores and reflects the importance of closure more generally in human relationships.

There has been a considerable amount of research into the psychological phenomenon of NFC, which has been defined as 'a motivated need for certainty' (McKay *et al.*, 2006, p. 422). More specifically, it can be conceptualised as 'a desire for a firm answer to a question, and as an aversion toward ambiguity' (Chirumbolo and Leone, 2008, p. 1280). There are individual differences in the degree to which different people need to have issues sorted out and wrapped up quickly. Some can handle large amounts of uncertainty and try to put off making decisions for as long as possible, while others like to have things cut and dried and want decisions made as swiftly as is feasible. As shown by Mannetti *et al.* (2002), motivation for closure ranges along a continuum from a high need to secure closure at one end to a strong desire to avoid closure at the other. Related dimensions here are the concepts of *seizing* and *freezing*, in that those individuals with a high NFC seize upon early information to make judgements and then freeze their decision at that point, closing their minds to any further relevant information (Kruglanski, 2004). They use a process of *perceptual accentuation* so that in effect they see what they want to see (Orbe and Bruess, 2005). The *confirmation bias* also comes into play as the person with high NFC actively seeks data that confirms the early decision and filters out contradictory stimuli (Mojzisch *et al.*, 2008). Thus, in the courtroom context, Honess and Charman (2002, p. 74) have shown how 'once jurors have made up their mind, they stop thinking about the evidence too hard'.

Individuals with a high NFC are more rigid in their style of thinking and are generally 'cognitively impatient' – they do not want to think about things for long periods. Those with a low NFC are happier to accept that life may involve multiple interpretations and conflicting opinions, and will more readily suspend judgement and postpone decisions (Neale and Fragale, 2006). The *Need for Closure Scale* (Neuberg *et al.*, 1997) includes items such as 'I tend to put off making important decisions until the last possible minute' and 'I'd rather know bad news than stay in a state of uncertainty'.

However, the situational context is an important moderating variable here, so that as the costs of not making a decision escalate, the NFC increases accordingly (Richter and Kruglanski, 2004). For example, if your child is gravely ill and you have to make a decision about agreeing to what could be life-saving surgery, this decision is likely to be expedited regardless of degree of personal NFC. Linked to NFC is the *ability to achieve closure* (AAC) in that, regardless of level of NFC, some individuals do not know how to effect closure while others can do so readily (Kossowska and Bar-Tal, 2013). The *Ability to Achieve Closure Scale* (Bar-Tal and Kossowska, 2010) includes items such as: 'Sometimes, my doubts over making decisions irritate me' and 'I tend to postpone important decisions to the last moment and even then I have problems making them'.

The concepts of NFC and AAC have relevance both for interactional set and closure. Those with a high NFC are more heavily influenced by first impressions as they search for aspects to seize upon in terms of decision making. They desire clearly structured interactions with transparent goals, and readily accept the need to bring an encounter to an end in a neat and tidy manner. On the other hand, individuals with a low NFC are less likely to make judgements based upon initial information. They prefer interactions that are loosely structured with less clear-cut goals, and they can be difficult to persuade that it is time to terminate an interaction. As a result, with this type of person, closure can be more prolonged and messier. AAC also plays a central role, in that in order to achieve effective closure in social encounters we need to know how and in what ways this can best be achieved.

PURPOSES OF CLOSURE

The main goals of closure are shown in Box 10.4. Not all of these are relevant in every context, since to be effective, the closure must reflect the tone, tenor and overall purpose of the encounter. In addition, closure, like set induction, depends upon a range of variables, including location, time available, the type of

---

Box 10.4 Goals of closure

The main goals served by the skill of closure are to:

1 signal that the interaction is about to end
2 summarise substantive issues covered and agreements reached
3 consolidate any new material introduced in the session
4 assess the effectiveness of the interaction
5 motivate participants to carry out certain courses of action
6 provide links with future events
7 give participants a sense of achievement
8 establish commitment to the future of the relationship
9 formally mark the final termination of the encounter

---

people involved and the anticipated duration of separation. As with set induction, closure also progresses through four inter-related and overlapping sequential stages, in this case:

$$\text{Retreating} \rightarrow \text{Reviewing} \rightarrow \text{Reinforcing} \rightarrow \text{Re-bonding}$$

The retreating phase involves efforts to influence the *perceptions* of others in such a way that they fully realise that you are in the process of leaving. The stage of reviewing relates to *cognitive* issues pertaining to the substantive business conducted, when decisions taken are summarised. Third, clients should be reinforced or *motivated* to carry out certain actions. Finally, re-bonding refers to the *social* dimension of ensuring that a good rapport is maintained as leave taking occurs.

Perceptual closure

The first stage of closure is that of indicating to the client that it is time to close. This necessitates the use of closure indicators and markers to signal that the end of the interaction is approaching. These *preclosing behaviours* and *final closure markers* have been shown to occur in telephone conversations as well as in face-to-face encounters (Placencia, 1997). A wide range of behaviours has been identified within both categories (Wolvin and Coakley, 1996; West, 2006).

Preclosing

This involves the use of verbal and nonverbal behaviours to signal to clients that the time has come to start winding up, and help to steer the discussion gently and smoothly into the final termination. Bolden (2008, pp. 100–101) highlighted how 'the sequence of preclosing moves...used to initiate leave-taking creates a structural space where unaddressed issues can be raised, ensuring that the

---

Box 10.5 Nonverbal closure indicators

- Breaking eye contact and looking away from the other person
- Looking at a watch or mobile device
- Taking out car keys
- Gathering papers/belongings together
- Increased movement while speaking
- Changing seated posture to a more raised position
- Forward lean of 30° or more from previous position
- Placing both hands on the arms of the chair in a way that would assist standing up
- Explosive hand movements on the thighs or desk
- Smiling
- Nodding the head rapidly
- Orientating one's posture and feet towards the exit

---

closing is collaboratively achieved'. Closing indicators include elongated and emphasised words such as 'Soooo...' 'Oookaay'. In a study of telephone conversations, Bangerter *et al.* (2004) found that 'Okay' and 'All right' were the two most frequently used preclosing terms. These closure indicators can be followed by more direct phrases: 'In the last few minutes that we have...' 'We're coming to the end of our session...' Another tactic here is that of *projection*, where the other person is portrayed as the one really wanting or needing to terminate the interaction, owing to fatigue, other commitments, etc. ('You have worked very hard. I'm sure you've had enough for today'; 'I know how busy you are so I don't want to take up any more of your time'). Accompanying nonverbal signals that reinforce the preclosing message have been identified (e.g. O'Leary and Gallois, 1999), and these are summarised in Box 10.5.

This step of preparing the client for closure is very important. In the context of interviewing, Stewart and Cash (2013) illustrated how a hasty or insensitive close can linger in the mind of the interviewee and so serve to undo the relationship established in the interview itself. Using preclosing to shade into the final parting ritual is therefore well advised. Clients also make closing indicators when they feel that the time has come to end an interaction, and professionals need to be sensitive to these. In certain areas, such as selling and negotiating, this is a key to success. For example, in the former context clients emit buying signals to convey that they are ready to close. These include receptive verbalisations such as 'It looks really nice', body language including approving nods and smiles, physical actions such as handling the sales item possessively and acceptance-indicative questions such as 'Do you have it in blue?' (Hargie *et al.*, 2004).

Closure markers

These are used to mark and underscore the final ending of the encounter. They take three forms:

1   *formal markers*, usually used in business contexts – 'It was nice to meet you'; 'Goodbye';
2   *informal markers* used with friends and colleagues – 'Cheers'; 'See you later'; 'Bye'; 'All the best';
3   *departure announcements* – 'I've got to go now'; 'Right, I'm off'.

Likewise, accompanying nonverbal markers occur along a continuum of formality – at the formal end is the handshake, while at the informal side there may be not much more than a smile. In between there are waves, kisses and hugs. More formal parting rituals tend to occur with people of higher status, with those who are not kith and kin and in business encounters. The duration and intensity of closure markers are also greater when the period of anticipated separation is longer.

The success of closure indicators and markers is dependent upon the client. Those low in NFC or AAC may ignore closure attempts, and very direct methods may then be required (opening the door, walking slowly out of the office, etc.). Indeed, Kellerman *et al.* (1991) reported that, although much research has focused upon mutually negotiated leave taking, in fact some 45 per cent of all conversations have unilaterally desired endings. They found that when ending an encounter which the other side does not want to close, the most common tactic was the use of external and uncontrollable events, such as third-party entrances. For example, where it is known that a particular client will be difficult to get to leave, an *orchestrated intervention* can be arranged. Examples of this include the secretary coming in to announce your next urgent appointment, a colleague arriving to accompany you to a meeting or someone calling on the telephone at a prearranged time.

Cognitive closure

As defined by Millar and Tracey (2009, p. 94), cognitive closure is 'a means of seeking agreement that the main themes of the communication have been accurately received and understood'. It involves three main strategies: summarisation, checking out and continuity links.

Summarisation

Summaries offer both sides the opportunity to ensure that they are in agreement about the meaning of what has been discussed. There is now a considerable body of research across a wide range of professional contexts, including community pharmacy (Hargie *et al.*, 2000), university lecturing (Saunders and Saunders, 1993), medicine (Tallman *et al.*, 2007), psychotherapy (Flemmer *et al.*, 1996), physiotherapy (Adams *et al.*, 1994) and negotiating (Rackham, 2007), to attest to the fact that professionals see summarisation as a key part of their role. Interestingly, however, actual practice often differs from the ideal. Thus, in the above studies, university lecturers often closed lectures abruptly, claiming to have 'run out of time', doctors frequently ended the consultation with the writing and handing over of a prescription and pharmacists had brief closing statements (e.g. 'Go and see your doctor if it persists'). Time and effort therefore need to be allowed for summarisation.

Research has shown that an explicit concluding summary increases the listener's comprehension (Cruz, 1998). It should certainly take place at the end of an interaction, but in longer encounters *intermittent summaries*, or *spaced reviews*, can be used periodically. In essence, summaries are important at three points:

1   *At the end of discussion on a particular issue or topic.* Where there has been a detailed, involved or protracted exchange it is useful to provide a summary of what has been covered. Such transitional reviews help to map out the contours of the relational terrain. They enable both sides to reflect, and hopefully agree, on what was covered. In certain types of encounter (e.g. educational or medical) this also serves the purpose of consolidating learning, by cementing core material in the listener's memory. Another important function is that they enable the professional to bring that part of the discussion to a rational end, and progress on to the next topic.

2   *At the end of the session.* At the parting stage, the summary should scan back over the main features of the interaction. The key issues that emerged should be crystallised and linked to previous sessions and to future encounters. On the perceptual side, a session summary is also a very potent closure indicator, signalling that the interaction is now ending. For this reason, they were termed *historicising acts* by Albert and Kessler (1976), since they treat the session as something that is now in the past. Part of this may also involve *contingency planning*. This involves giving advice to the client about coping with unexpected events, what to do if things do not work out according to plan and when and how to seek help if required. Kurtz *et al.* (1998) emphasised the importance of this part of closure, which they referred to as *safety netting*.

3   *At the final termination of the professional relationship.* The summary at this stage must range back over all previous meetings, putting what has been covered into a final perspective. This is one of the most difficult periods of professional communication. Final endings of relationships are never easy. Once human bonds have been formed, we do not like to break them (Fine and Harvey, 2005). The impact upon clients of final termination has long been recognised within psychoanalytic theory (Ferraro and Garella, 1997). In his analysis of the psychoanalytic context, Schubert (2000) highlighted how clients at this 'mourning' stage of the loss of the relationship can experience separation anxiety and depressive affects. An important function of final summarisation is what is known in relational communication theory as *grave dressing* (Solomon and Theiss, 2013). The relationship is dead but its 'grave', or memory, should be presented in a positive light. The relationship is thereby portrayed as having been worthwhile and not a waste of time. Thus, the summary at this juncture should give emphasis to client achievements.

Checking out

This is the process whereby the professional ensures that the client fully understands what has been covered, and that both parties are in agreement about what has been decided. One of the identified weaknesses of health professionals is that they do not always check that patients fully comprehend the information they have been given (Dickson *et al.*, 1997). Indeed, studies have shown that, when filling prescriptions, community pharmacists are often asked by patients to re-explain what the doctor has already told them about how to use the prescribed medication (Morrow *et al.*, 1993). They had not understood, but this lack of comprehension was not picked up by the doctor.

Checks can be made in two ways. First, the professional can ask questions to test for understanding of the material covered. As discussed in Chapter 5, questions are widely used across every profession. However, while they are expected and accepted by pupils in classrooms or students in seminars, feedback questions need to be used with care in other contexts. It is not normal practice in social exchanges to 'test' others – it can be taken as a sign of being seen as somewhat slow or stupid. As explained in Chapter 8, a useful tactic is for the professional to accept responsibility for any failure in understanding, by prefacing such questions with statements like, 'I don't know if I explained that very clearly, could I just ask you...?' Questions can also be used to ascertain how the client feels about how the session went. This type of summative evaluation can provide very useful feedback for future encounters.

Second, the client can be invited to ask questions. Norms of professional–client interaction mean that clients often neither expect nor are encouraged to ask questions (see Chapter 5). This means that time, thought and effort may be needed to facilitate clients as they formulate relevant questions. One exception to this rule is in the employment interview, where there is a definite 'invite questions' stage, when candidates are asked, 'Is there anything you would like to ask us?' Here, interviewees are well advised to prepare informed questions and to ask these in an appropriate manner (Millar and Tracey, 2006).

Care also needs to be taken with this tactic of inviting questions. One problem is that the client may take the opportunity to introduce new material at this juncture. Those with a low NFC are particularly prone to this tactic. In their oft-quoted study of doctor–patient consultations, Byrne and Long (1976) termed this the *by the way...syndrome*, later referred to in the counselling context as the *door handle phenomenon* (Lang and van der Molen, 1990). In the latter context, an extreme example of this is where a client, standing at the door and about to leave, lobs an interactional hand grenade back into the room in the form of a controversial statement (e.g. 'I've been thinking a lot lately about suicide...'). The door handle phenomenon causes problems for the professional in making a decision as to whether to continue with the encounter (not easy when appointments have been booked), or arrange to discuss the issue at a later time.

White *et al.* (1997) carried out a detailed study of audio recordings of doctor–patient encounters. They found that new problems were introduced by patients at the end of the consultation in 23 per cent of cases. They termed

---

Box 10.6 Techniques for circumventing the interrupted closure

1   Orient the client at the beginning of the session (see the section on cognitive set) and continue this throughout the encounter, explaining what is going to happen next at each stage
2   Explicitly ask clients to state *all* of their concerns early in the encounter, and secure their agreement on the identified list. Heritage *et al.* (2007) found that, after the initial patient opening phase, the question, 'Is there something else you want to address in the visit today?' was especially effective in eliciting additional concerns at the outset of doctor–patient consultations. By comparison the question, 'Is there anything else you want to address in the visit today?' was ineffective
3   Address psychosocial and emotional as well as task concerns
4   Allow the person to talk freely and without interruptions
5   Do not invite questions during the final closing phase. A common reason for the 'by the way' interjections in the White *et al.* study was the tendency for doctors to finish with the 'Anything else?' question. This raises new expectations in the client's mind and may negate the closing ritual
6   When new issues are raised at the end, it is generally best to defer exploration of these to a future visit, rather than engage in a hurried discussion at the end

---

such instances *interrupted closures*, which they defined as occurring when, 'an attempt by one person to shift from present problems to a future orientation was not followed by a corresponding shift on the part of the other' (p. 159). To circumvent such problems they recommended a number of procedures. When combined with other findings (e.g. Park, 2013), it is possible to formulate six main strategies to help prevent interrupted closures (Box 10.6).

Continuity links

Most animals have greeting rituals, some of which are very elaborate. Indeed, nesting birds have greeting displays each time one of them returns to the nest with food. Chimpanzees are most similar to humans in that they touch hands, hug and kiss when they meet. However, in his analysis of greetings and partings, Lamb (1988, p. 103) noted that there is no ritual of parting among other animals, since, 'they presumably do not have any conception of the future of their relationships and therefore do not need to reassure each other that there will be such a future or that the past has been worthwhile'. For humans, however, the sense of temporal and relational continuity means that endings of interactions are seen as important. Bridges must be built at this stage to carry the interactors over to their next encounter. As Albert and Kessler (1978) show, the notion of continuity is reflected in the parting expressions used in many languages: 'See you later', 'Au revoir', 'Auf wiedersehen', 'Hasta la vista'. As summarised by Bolden (2008, p. 99), 'Leave-taking serves to project possible future encounters, and is, thereby, a practice for maintaining a continuous relationship across periods of separation'. Knapp *et al.* (1973) termed this stage of closure *futurism*.

In professional contexts, continuity links include reference to how the work covered in the current encounter will be carried on at the next one. In formal business meetings one aspect of futurism is the very simple task of agreeing or noting the date of the next meeting. At the same time, however, a good chairperson should relate the business transacted in the present meeting to the agenda for the next one. Relational bonds also need to be consolidated at this stage, in the form of social comments about future meetings (e.g. 'I look forward to seeing you again next week').

Motivational closure

Three principal methods are employed to effect motivational closure: motivational exhortations, thought-provoking aphorisms and interim tasks.

Motivational exhortations

In many interactions, an important function of this stage of closing is that of minimising the phenomenon of *cognitive dissonance*, initially identified by Festinger (1957), and widely researched since (Cooper, 2007). When individuals have made decisions, they often experience doubts and anxiety – or dissonance – about whether their decision was the right one. The more important the decision, the greater will be the dissonance, or discomfort. Eventually, dissonance is overcome in one of two ways, either by convincing oneself that the decision is indeed a good one and embracing it warmly, or alternatively by abandoning the decision and reverting to the former state of affairs. Motivational exhortations are useful in helping to persuade clients that they have made the correct decision. For example, Hargie *et al.* (2004) illustrated how such exhortations (e.g. 'This is the best deal in the store – and you'll get years of enjoyment from it') are of importance for salespeople in ensuring that clients stay committed to a buying decision. Likewise, after an initial counselling encounter, a client may experience dissonance about whether the decision to seek help and reveal personal details to a stranger was justified. Here, again, motivating exhortations can be used to reassure clients about the efficacy of their decision, and so encourage them to return for another session ('You have taken the first step towards resolving this by coming here today...').

Another function of these exhortations is to secure maximum commitment from clients. They are used ubiquitously by sports coaches during 'pep' talks before their players go out to perform. Sometimes the imagery used can be quite violent – and indeed unprintable here! Expressions used include: 'Go out and kill them'; 'Give them hell'; 'You have one chance. Don't blow it or you'll regret it for the rest of your life.' The purpose here is to ensure that the sportspeople are fully geed up to give of their utmost.

In their meta-analysis of research on motivational interviewing, Hettema *et al.* (2005) illustrated how securing *commitment* from clients to carry out a course of action is crucial. If this commitment is not there, then the behaviour is unlikely to follow. For example, research has shown that there is no point in explaining to clients the methods that they can employ to stop existing behaviour (such as smoking or drinking) unless they are fully committed to stopping (Gaume *et al.*, 2008). There is little advantage in knowing how to do something that you have no intention of doing. It is therefore important to secure overt client statements of high commitment to change. As noted by Miller and Rollnick (2013, p. 161), 'Commitment language signals the likelihood of action'. Saying 'I will' indicates significantly greater commitment than 'I might'. Thus, time is most gainfully spent in these contexts at gearing motivational exhortations towards maximum commitment. Once a person has fully and irrevocably decided upon a course of action, the means will usually be found to effect it (for further discussion on commitment, see Chapter 12).

Thought-provoking aphorisms

In certain types of situation, it is useful to end an interaction with a succinct and apt statement that encourages listeners to reflect upon the main theme covered. These can be self-produced or quotations from the great and the good. This strategy is very common in public presentations. Let us take two recent examples from the radio programme *Thought for Today*. Here, the presenter has a 2- or 3-minute slot in which to cover a topical issue. One speaker, discussing the issue of animal rights, finished with, 'When you're dying for a big steak, remember that a cow just did', while another talking about third-world poverty ended, 'Live simply so that others can simply live'. This strategy is also relevant in other contexts. Interviewers can use it to motivate clients to continue (or change) a certain course of action.

Interim tasks

Homework and assignments have a familiar ring for students. Although not always welcomed, they serve the important purpose of making them think more about the subject in between classes. This technique is used in many settings to motivate clients to carry out tasks relating to the issue under consideration after the interaction has ended. In therapy, clients may be encouraged to try out new techniques that have been discussed. In training, tasks are geared towards the process of optimising transfer from the training environment to the actual organisational setting. To effect maximum motivation, the task set should be one that is challenging but also manageable.

Social closure

If an interaction has been successful, the leave taking is marked by mixed emotions – happiness with the encounter coupled with sadness at its ending. As aptly expressed by Juliet to Romeo in Shakespeare's *Romeo and Juliet*, this means that 'Parting is such sweet sorrow'. One function of social closure is to underline a feel-good factor in terms of the relationship. How we leave an interaction influences our attitudes to it. If it ends on a relational high, we depart feeling that it has been an enjoyable and worthwhile venture. We are then more likely to contact the person again if required. Social closure encompasses both task and nontask elements.

Task rewards

These are used to underline for clients that they have achieved something of worth, and that this is recognised and valued (for a full discussion of the role of rewards, see Chapter 4). Task rewards can be employed to reward the person individually using 'you' language ('You achieved a lot today. Well done'; 'Your work is really paying dividends. I wish everyone would put in as much effort as you'). Alternatively, they can emphasise the sense of 'working together' using 'we' language ('This was a good meeting. We work well together'; 'That's great. I think we've nearly cracked it'). Where the interaction has involved a group, then whole-group rewards are appropriate. Thus, teachers and lecturers may reward an entire class for their work, or a chairperson in concluding a meeting can point out how well the members worked together. This technique helps to foster a sense of team spirit.

Like summaries, task rewards are important at three stages.

1   *At significant points within a session.* When a major part of the work has been completed, statements such as 'We are really getting somewhere' provide participants with a feeling that something is being achieved and encourage further effort. Rewards may also include a 'time out' ('I think we deserve a break and a coffee') to mark such successes. Negotiators often signal and celebrate interim agreements on particular points in this way.
2   *At the end of a session.* Here, the client should be rewarded for major efforts made during the encounter.
3   *At the termination of the relationship.* As discussed above, 'grave dressing' is important as the final curtain falls, and so clients must be rewarded for the efforts they made and everything they achieved during the professional relationship.

Nontask comments

The final part of closure should emphasise the human moment. The main business is over, tasks have been completed and it is time to acknowledge the client as a person. So, personal or welfare aspects of leave taking enter the discourse at this point. These fall into five main types:

1   *The 'expression of gratitude' phase,* as the name suggests, involves thanking the person for his or her time and efforts ('Thanks for coming along'; 'I appreciate you giving up your time').
2   *Social closing niceties.* Here, we owe a considerable debt to the weather and traffic in formulating comments such as, 'Oh dear it's really pouring down. Good thing you brought your umbrella'; 'Hope you get home before the rush hour'.
3   *Reference to generic or specific social events.* This is commonplace – ranging from the ubiquitous 'Have a nice day' in the USA service sector, to more tailored generalities ('Have a good weekend'), or mention of specific occasions ('Enjoy the wedding').
4   *Reference to future meetings.* These occur during continuity links ('Look forward to seeing you again next week').
5   *Well-wishing comments.* These are statements of concern regarding the other person's well-being ('Look after yourself'; 'Take care now').

At final termination, such statements not only reward the client, they also underline the finality of the occasion – 'It was a pleasure working with you. If you need to talk with me at any time in the future, you know where I am.' These statements should of course be accompanied by appropriate nonverbal reinforcers (see Chapter 4).

Overview of closure

In *Julius Caesar,* Shakespeare summarised the over-arching functions of closure:

> If we do meet again, why, we shall smile;
> If not, why then, this parting was well made.

Closure serves both to leave participants feeling satisfied with an encounter and happy to re-engage with one another as and when required. While introductions can be prepared, closures usually cannot. This is because the termination has to be directly related to the interaction that has gone before. However, knowing the stages through which closure progresses can greatly facilitate the implementation of the process. *Perceptual closure* is used initially to signal that the encounter is entering end-zone, and then to mark the final exchange. *Cognitive closure* allows agreements to be ratified regarding the main issues discussed and decisions made, as well as establishing links with the next meeting. *Motivational closure* is employed to encourage clients to continue to consider, and work on, issues further. Finally, *social closure* cements the relational bonds that have been established. It is important to remember that the closure is the last contact between interlocutors and so the one they are most likely to remember. The advice of Millar and Tracey (2009, p. 94) in their review of interviewing is pertinent here: 'it is important to plan and allocate time for ending the interview as both a business transaction and a social encounter'. Efforts made at this juncture can have very significant import, both on the impact of the current encounter and for the future of the relationship itself.

OVERVIEW

Greeting and parting skills represent the ties that bind interaction. Arrivals and departures are ubiquitous. Across countries and cultures people wish each other a good morning, afternoon, evening or night. We have all been taught the basics of these skills as part of the socialisation process, and so we often take them for granted. So much so, indeed, that we then proceed to ignore them by jumping quickly into and out of social encounters. As Irving and Hazlett (1999, pp. 264–265) noted, the busy professional 'often feels that he or she is pressed for time and it is these very important elements at the beginning and end that are often rushed or overlooked'. But a cheap and clipped hello and goodbye is no substitute for a sincere, focused welcome, and a warm, thoughtful parting. Due to the primacy and recency effects, much of what we do at these two junctures remains imprinted upon the minds of those with whom we interact. Time and effort spent at the opening and closing phases should therefore be regarded as a key investment towards the effectiveness of relationships.

Chapter 11

Standing up for yourself: the skill of assertiveness

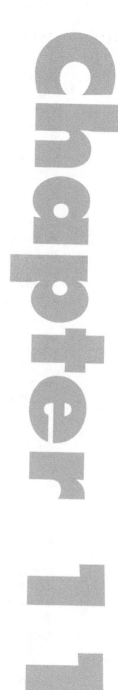

INTRODUCTION

OUR GOALS, NEEDS, INTERESTS and interpretations of fairness and equity rarely fit neatly with those of others and this puts us on a possible collision course with them. If we feel that they are not treating us justly, are taking unfair advantage of us or are ignoring our rights, we become annoyed. This annoyance, if not resolved, can grow and fester. So, we have to decide how to address and attempt to deal with the perceived inequities or injustices. Decisions have to be made about how, when and where to confront others about the behaviour that has caused us to feel aggrieved. This is a delicate balancing act. Saying nothing means that nothing will change. Being very confrontational can result in a boomerang effect in the form of retaliatory aggression from the interlocutor. The best response is to be skilfully assertive. This is one reason why the ability to be assertive has been shown to be related to feelings of psychological well-being and self-esteem (Sarkova *et al.*, 2103). But it is not easy, and indeed, in their research in this area Ames and Wazlawek (2014, p. 775) conclude that 'One of the great challenges of social life is being appropriately assertive'.

Assertiveness is an area of study with a long history. It dates back to the pioneering work in the field of behaviour therapy by Salter (1949) and Wolpe (1958), highlighting the fact that certain individuals in society had specific problems in standing up for their rights. As a result, the skill of assertiveness was introduced during therapy in an attempt to help such people function more effectively in their everyday lives. Since then, the skill has attracted enormous interest, reflecting the importance of this aspect of social interaction across many areas. As noted by McCartan and Hargie (2004a, p. 707), 'The contribution of assertiveness to communication competence is now widely recognized'. A huge volume of research has been conducted, and assertion training (AT) programmes are widespread.

Professionals must possess the ability to be assertive, and so AT programmes proliferate in this area. This is because a key feature of assertiveness is that it is an aspect of interpersonal communication that can be developed and improved. Thus, Pardeck *et al.* (1991), in a study of postgraduate students in the USA, found a significant and positive correlation between age and assertiveness. This may be because older people have gained more life experience, including of situations where they have to stand up for themselves, and so have learned how to be more assertive. As McKay *et al.* (2009, p. 125) pointed out, 'Assertiveness is a skill you can acquire, not a personality trait that some people are born with and others not'. It is a skill that is of importance when dealing with family, friends, peers, superiors and subordinates. It is pertinent to interactions between different groups of professionals, especially where differences of power and status exist, and it is of relevance to interactions between professionals and clients (Back and Back, 2005).

Early definitions of assertiveness were fairly all-embracing in terms of interactional skills. Lazarus (1971), for example, regarded assertiveness as comprising four main components, namely the ability to:

1 refuse requests
2 ask for favours and make requests
3 express positive and negative feelings
4 initiate, continue and terminate general conversations.

This conceptualisation of assertiveness is very broad, encompassing almost all forms of human interaction. Indeed, as Kelly (1982, p. 172) pointed out: 'the terms "assertion training" and "social skills training" were often used in interchangeable fashion; it was not recognized that assertiveness represents one specific kind of interpersonal competency'. It would seem that training in this field was introduced and found to be beneficial before the concept of assertiveness was defined with any precision. Dissatisfaction with this state of affairs led to a more focused study of assertion, based specifically upon the theme of standing up for one's rights in a sensitive, competent manner.

While differing meanings of assertion proliferate, useful definitions of assertive behaviour can be found in two of the influential texts in this area. Thus, Lange and Jakubowski (1976, p. 38) stated that, 'assertion involves standing up for personal rights and expressing thoughts, feelings and beliefs in direct, honest, and appropriate ways which respect the rights of other people'. More recently, Alberti and Emmons (2008, p. 8) posited that, 'Assertiveness enables us to act in our own best interests, to stand up for ourselves without undue anxiety, to exercise personal rights without denying the rights of others, and to express our feelings ... honestly and comfortably'. Both of these

---

Box 11.1 Negative and positive assertion

Negative, or *conflict, assertion* comprises six main components:

1 making reasonable requests
2 refusing unwanted or unreasonable requests
3 asking others to change their behaviour
4 giving personal opinions, even if unpopular
5 expressing disagreement or negative feelings
6 responding to criticism from others

Positive assertion also involves six main aspects:

1 expressing positive feelings
2 responding to positive feelings expressed by others
3 giving compliments
4 accepting compliments gracefully
5 admitting mistakes or personal shortcomings
6 initiating and sustaining interactions

---

definitions emphasise an important component of assertion, namely respect for the rights of other people. The skilled individual must therefore achieve a balance between defending personal rights while not infringing the rights of others.

Assertiveness can be conceptualised as comprising two broad response classes, one negative and the other positive (Box 11.1). However, most research and training efforts have been devoted to the negative, or conflict, components, since this is the aspect of assertion that many people find particularly difficult to put into practice.

PURPOSES OF ASSERTIVENESS

The skill of assertion helps us to achieve nine main interpersonal goals (Box 11.2). Most of these relate to the ability of the individual to respond effectively in an assertive manner. However, linked to the behavioural repertoire are functions to do with protection of personal rights (no. 1) and respect for the rights of others (no. 5), as well as the development of feelings of confidence (no. 8) and self-efficacy in being able to respond in a self-protecting fashion (no. 9). The type of assertiveness used can determine the extent to which each of these goals is fulfilled, and so knowledge of types of assertiveness is of importance during social encounters. Furthermore, personal and contextual factors also play a crucial role in determining the effectiveness of assertive responses.

Box 11.2 Goals of assertiveness

The main goals served by the skill of assertiveness are to:

1 protect one's personal rights
2 withstand unreasonable requests
3 make reasonable requests
4 deal effectively with unreasonable refusals
5 recognise the personal rights of others
6 change the behaviour of others
7 avoid unnecessary conflicts
8 communicate one's real position on any issue confidently
9 develop and maintain a personal sense of self-efficacy

SEQUENTIAL STAGES IN ASSERTIVENESS

A sequence of stages is involved in the decision-making process with regard to whether or not to implement an assertive approach (Figure 11.1).

Self-focus

First, the individual must engage in self-focused attention. This process of self-focus involves monitoring and evaluating the behaviour of self and others (Panayiotou *et al.*, 2007). Without an awareness of the nuances of interpersonal communication, success in assertion, or indeed in any interpersonal skill, is unlikely. As will be seen later in the chapter, at one extreme some (unassertive) people are often unaware that they are being treated woefully, while at the other there are those (aggressive) who have no idea of how obnoxious they appear to others. As I have emphasised throughout this book, skill necessitates acute perceptual acumen.

Knowledge of rights

Given that the individual has a good awareness of the behavior of self and others, the next pre-requisite is knowledge of personal rights. In order to protect our rights we must first know what they are. It is not always clear in many situations exactly what one's rights are, and it is therefore sometimes necessary to consult with others in order to gauge their views about whether personal rights have been infringed. This process of consultation is termed *reality testing*, which may involve asking other people either for advice about what exactly your rights are (e.g. 'Has he the right to ask me to do that?'), or about their perceptions of your behaviour (e.g. 'Have I upset you in some way?'; 'Do you mind doing this?'). There is evidence to indicate that assertive

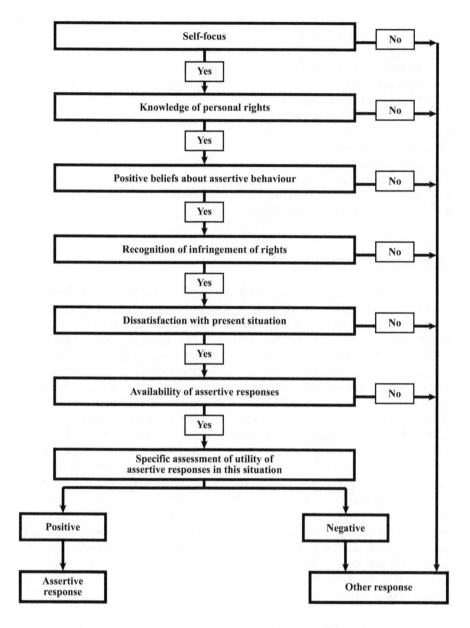

Figure 11.1 Sequential model of the assertion decision-making process.

individuals may have a greater awareness of what their job role actually entails. In a study of social workers, Rabin and Zelner (1992) found that assertiveness in the work setting was significantly and positively correlated to both role clarity and job satisfaction. Knowing the parameters of one's job facilitates the protection of personal rights, which may in turn contribute to increased happiness in the work environment (Back and Back, 2005).

In terms of actual rights, Zuker (1983) produced a general Assertive Bill of Rights for individuals, which included the right to:

- be treated with respect
- have and express personal feelings and opinions
- be listened to and taken seriously
- set one's own priorities
- say *no* without feeling guilty
- ask for what one wants
- get what one pays for
- make mistakes
- assert oneself even though it may inconvenience others
- choose not to assert oneself.

Positive beliefs about assertion

Our beliefs about assertive behaviour are very important. As expressed by Mnookin *et al.* (1996, p. 221), 'Assertiveness also presupposes the self-esteem or belief that one's interests are valid and that it is legitimate to satisfy them'. Arnes (2008) has shown that *assertive expectancies* are crucial in determining the extent to which an individual pursues an assertive response. He found that, based upon their expectations, people 'show dramatically different assertiveness due to different assumptions about behavioral consequences' (p. 1,541). Take someone who believes that one should always do what one's superiors say or negative consequences will accrue. Before this person could effectively be assertive, this belief would have to be replaced with a new one, for example, that it is always valid to ask for a good reason if requested to do anything that seems unreasonable. Piccinin *et al.* (1998) carried out a study with undergraduates on their ability to criticise others. They found that high as opposed to low assertives reported more confidence in their ability to criticise the behaviour of others effectively, believed that this was more likely to produce positive outcomes and were less worried about the possible negative consequences of doing so. Piccinin *et al.* identified five behaviours as being associated with quality of criticism. These can be illustrated with examples relating to a work situation where one person is too cold.

- '*I*'- *language* (e.g. 'I see the window is wide open...' rather than 'You have left the window wide open...');
- clearly *specifying the problem* ('I can't work because I'm freezing' rather than 'It's cold');
- showing *empathy* ('I know you like fresh air');
- *bi-directionality*, or 'roundedness' ('You are hardy and could survive an arctic expedition, but it's just too cold for me in here');
- suggesting *explicit change* ('Please close the window').

Interestingly, using these criteria Piccinin *et al.* found no difference between high and low assertives on quality of responses. This result confirmed earlier research that a crucial determinant of assertion is motivation to act rather than lack of understanding of how to be assertive.

Those who are very socially anxious are more likely to be nonassertive, as they have a strong desire to make a good impression but also doubt their ability to achieve this desired state (Hoffmann and DiBartolo, 2014). Thus, Sarkova *et al.* (2013) discovered that the more anxiety people experienced in situations that required assertiveness, the more likely they were to avoid those situations. This was confirmed in a study by Gudleski and Shean (2000), which found that depressed individuals rated themselves lower than nondepressed people on assertiveness, but significantly higher on measures of submissiveness and the need to please others. Anderson (1997) also found that those who experienced most anxiety were least assertive in terms of both verbal and nonverbal behaviours. In addition, research shows that outgoing individuals high in the trait of extraversion are more assertive than shyer people who are high in introversion, and that those higher in the trait of agreeableness are less assertive (Kammrath *et al.*, 2015).

These research findings illustrate how changes in beliefs and expectations may well be a pre-requisite for changes in assertive behaviour. The process of *cognitive restructuring* is important for people with inappropriate beliefs (Barber *et al.*, 2015). Such restructuring includes changes in *self-instructions*, those covert behaviour-guiding self-statements we employ when making decisions about which responses to carry out. A greater number of negative self-statements has been shown to be linked to lower social self-efficacy (Rudy *et al.*, 2013). Nonassertive individuals have a higher frequency of negative self-talk and a greater belief that their behaviour will lead to negative consequences. Thus, submissive individuals use self-statements such as 'She will not like me if I refuse', rather than 'I have the right to refuse'.

In terms of intrapersonal dialogue, there would also seem to be a difference in the use of self-reinforcements, with nonassertive people again being more negative in their self-evaluations of performance. Submissive people are more likely to think, 'I sounded terrible, stuttering and stammering. She is probably laughing at me now.' Assertive individuals, on the other hand, tend to be more positive (e.g. 'I'm glad I said no. She is not likely to bother me again'). In reviewing research in this field, Rakos (1991) illustrated how nonassertive individuals emit roughly equal numbers of positive and negative self-statements in conflict situations whereas assertive people generate about twice as many positive as negative self-statements. He concluded that 'direct training in autonomous self-instruction, apart from any other intervention, has resulted in significant gains in assertiveness' (p. 53). However, a note of caution is required here, in that positive self-statements may actually be detrimental for people with low self-esteem. In terms of the concept of *latitudes of acceptance*, we are more likely to accept messages that are close to our own attitudes and beliefs and reject those that are not. Thus, if those with low self-esteem are required to attempt to adopt self-statements that do not match their own self-view they are more likely to reject them, and this in turn will reinforce their original sense of low self-efficacy (Wood *et al.*, 2009).

Recognition of infringement of rights

In order to be assertive, the individual has to recognise that personal rights have been infringed. One study found that nonassertive people tend to need more time to perceive and assimilate information and make decisions about how to respond, and concluded, 'If individuals fall behind at this early step in the process of asserting themselves, then they may be more likely to miss opportunities to be assertive' (Collins *et al.*, 2000, p. 931). Thus, by the time submissive individuals realise that their rights have indeed been violated, it is probably too late to rectify the situation. To quote the title of this Collins *et al.* article, it is a case of 'Those who hesitate lose'. Submissive individuals are also more likely to perceive the behaviour of others inaccurately by, for example, perceiving unreasonable requests as being reasonable. Such people are viewed as 'easy touches' in terms of borrowing items from them, getting them to do extra work, etc., since they are always ready to be helpful. There comes a time when being helpful turns into being used, and we need not only to be able to draw the line between these two, but also actually to learn to perceive the behaviour of others more accurately, in order to distinguish reasonable and unreasonable requests. Indeed, on occasions friends or colleagues will point out to us that our rights are being infringed when we have accepted unreasonable behaviour as reasonable.

Dissatisfaction with present situation

A driving force in the employment of assertive responses is dissatisfaction with the existing state of affairs. Two core features in determining whether or not we will be assertive are the importance of the issue, and the strength of negative feeling. These are related, in that with more important issues we are likely to feel more dissatisfied or aggrieved when our rights are negated. Thus, affect is crucial in assertiveness. For example, when standing in line outside a theatre we may notice someone jumping the queue, but if it is a warm evening and we are chatting happily with our attractive new date, our mood may be such that we think 'what the heck' and ignore it. Alternatively, if we have had to wait for a long time in the pouring rain and have become annoyed, we may then challenge the line jumper assertively.

Availability of assertive responses

In order to be assertive, we must first be aware of what the available response alternatives are, and have learned how to use them. Much of this chapter is devoted to an analysis of assertive response components and their likely effects.

Assessment of response utility

Before we invoke an assertive response, we should assess the utility of so doing. Indeed, from their research in this area, Kammrath *et al.* (2015, p. 622) concluded that 'the most interpersonally effective person is one who is capable of engaging in either assertive or unassertive behavior, depending on the situation'. If we decide that assertion is a legitimate response in this context, and that it will produce a long-term positive benefit for the relationship (as opposed to merely a short-term behaviour change), then we are likely to choose this alternative. However, assertion is not always the most appropriate choice, since the effectiveness of an assertive response depends upon its situational appropriateness (Ryan et al., 2006). Following a detailed research investigation, Eisler et al. (1975, p. 339) concluded that:

> an individual who is assertive in one interpersonal context may not be assertive in a different interpersonal environment. Furthermore, some individuals may have no difficulty responding with negative assertions but may be unable to respond when the situation requires positive expressions.

The old description of a person who is 'a lion inside the home and a lamb outside' is an example of this. Few individuals are assertive across all contexts. Most find it easier to assert themselves in some situations than in others.

Certain professional groups, such as nurses, have been shown to have difficulty in being assertive, partly because of the caring aspect of their job role but also because nursing is a predominantly female profession (McCartan and Hargie, 2004a; Okuyama et al., 2014). Likewise, different types of assertiveness are more appropriate in some settings than in others. Cianni-Surridge and Horan (1983) found this to be the case in the job interview. They had 276 employers rate the efficacy of 16 'frequently advocated assertive job-seeking behaviours' in terms of whether or not each would enhance the applicant's chances of being offered employment. They found that some behaviours were advantageous and some disadvantageous. Thus, for example: 'Following an interview, an applicant writes you a letter thanking you for interviewing him/her and expressing his/her continued interest in the position' was regarded by 54 employers as greatly enhancing, by 176 as enhancing, by 46 as having no effect and by 0 as diminishing or greatly diminishing job prospects. On the other hand: 'An applicant feels his/her interview with you went poorly. He/she requests a second interview with another interviewer' was regarded by 44 employers as greatly diminishing, by 100 as diminishing, by 119 as having no effect, by 10 as enhancing and by 3 as greatly enhancing job prospects.

From working with a range of professional groups, I have ascertained a number of contexts in which it is more difficult to be assertive. These include:

- in someone else's home or office;
- in a strange country or sub-culture;
- when alone as opposed to with friends or colleagues;
- with superiors at work;
- with other professionals of higher status and power;
- when promoted to a position of authority over those who were formerly friends and colleagues;
- with the elderly;

- with the seriously or terminally ill and their relatives;
- with those in poverty or in severe social deprivation;
- with friends or close work colleagues;
- with members of the opposite sex;
- with those who are disabled; Glueckauf and Quittner (1992) in a Canadian study found that people confined to wheelchairs who received AT made significant increases in assertive responses and decreases in passive responses during a role-play test as compared to a control group who received no AT.

The utility of assertion in the above situations is more likely to be negatively evaluated. In addition, there are at least three broad contexts in which it may be more skilled to be nonassertive.

1 Interacting with a highly sensitive individual. If by being assertive someone is liable to burst into floods of tears, or physically attack you, it may be wise to be nonassertive, especially if the encounter is a one-off. Thus, in the example used earlier, if the queue jumper is a huge, inebriated male, uttering expletives and waving a knife, we may justifiably decide that there is a negative utility for an assertive response.

2 Seeing that someone is in a difficult situation. If you are in a busy restaurant and know that a new waitress has just been employed, you are more likely to overlook certain issues, such as someone who came in later being served before you. Here it is appropriate to be nonassertive, since personal rights are not deliberately being denied, and to be assertive may cause undue stress to the other person. Equally, if the interlocutor is from a different culture, and may not fully understand the norms of the present situation, you may decide not to adopt an assertive stance (issues of culture are discussed later in the chapter).

3 Manipulating others. Some females may deliberately employ a helpless style in order to achieve their goals, for example to encourage a male to change a flat tyre on their car. Equally, males may do likewise. If stopped by police following a minor traffic misdemeanour it is usually wise to be nonassertive ('I'm terribly sorry officer, but I've just bought this car...'), since such behaviour is more likely to achieve positive benefits.

STYLES OF RESPONDING

In order to understand fully the concept of assertiveness, it is necessary to distinguish this style of responding from two other approaches, namely nonassertion and aggression.

Nonassertion

Nonassertive responses involve expressing oneself in such a self-effacing, apologetic manner that one's thoughts, feelings and rights can easily be ignored. In this 'cap in hand' style, the person:

- hesitates and prevaricates
- speaks softly
- looks away
- tends to fidget nervously
- avoids issues
- agrees regardless of personal feelings
- does not express opinions
- values self below others
- lacks confidence
- suffers personal hurt to avoid any chance of hurting others.

The objective here is to appease others and avoid conflict at any cost. This can be described as the 'Uriah Heep' style, as epitomised in Charles Dickens' *David Copperfield,* in which Uriah explains how he was brought up: 'to be umble to this person, and umble to that; and to pull our caps off here, and to make bows there; and always to know our place, and abase ourselves before our betters'. Nonassertive individuals:

- tend to avoid public attention;
- use minimal self-disclosure or remain silent so as not to receive criticism for what they say;
- are modest and self-deprecating;
- use self-handicapping strategies whereby they underestimate potential future achievements so as to avoid negative evaluation if they fail;
- if they have to engage with others, prefer to play a passive, friendly and very agreeable role.

Assertion

Assertive responses involve standing up for oneself, yet taking the other person into consideration. The assertive style involves:

- answering spontaneously
- speaking with a conversational yet firm tone and volume
- looking at the other person
- addressing the main issue
- openly and confidently expressing personal feelings and opinions
- valuing oneself equal to others
- being prepared to listen to the other's point of view
- hurting neither oneself nor others.

The objective here is to try to ensure fair play for everyone. Perhaps not surprisingly, Karagözoğlu *et al.* (2007) found that there was a positive correlation between assertion and self-esteem. As mentioned earlier, people with low self-esteem find assertiveness problematic. Lightsey and Barnes (2007, p. 32) concluded that assertiveness is 'incompatible with or inversely related to many negative psychological symptoms', such as anxiety, depression and low self-esteem. Assertive individuals have also been found to be high in the constructive trait of *argumentativeness*, which is the tendency to present and defend one's position while also challenging opposing views, whereas *verbal aggressiveness* is a destructive trait that involves a tendency to focus one's attacks upon the other person's self-concept (Johnson *et al.*, 2007; Avtgis *et al.*, 2008). A key aspect of assertion is taking cognisance of the interlocutor's point of view (Sanchez, 2001).

Aggression

Aggression has been defined as, 'the delivery of an aversive stimulus from one person to another, with intent to harm and with an expectation of causing such harm, when the other person is motivated to escape or avoid the stimulus' (Geen, 2001, p. 3). These aversive stimuli involve more than just physical violence since, in social situations, verbal aggression is more prevalent. Verbal aggression has been defined as 'behavior that attacks an individual's self-concept in order to deliver psychological pain' (Myers and Bryant, 2008, p. 268). Such behaviours include attacks on one's ability, character or appearance, name calling, profanity, the use of demands, blunt directives and threats – all of which violate the rights of the other person. Using this style, the aggressor:

- interrupts and answers before the other is finished speaking;
- talks loudly and abrasively;
- glares at the other person;
- speaks 'past' the issue (accusing, blaming, demeaning);
- vehemently and arrogantly states feelings and opinions in a dogmatic fashion;
- values self above others;
- hurts others to avoid personal hurt.

The objective is to win, regardless of the other person. It may involve belittling others through the tactic of *downward comparison*, whereby an attempt is made to demean the achievements of those with whom one may be compared (Stets and Burke, 2014). This form of direct aggression is also known as *blasting*, which involves derogating others to make oneself appear superior (Guadagno and Cialdini, 2007). A variation of this tactic is a straight verbal attack on the other person.

Comparing the three styles

These three response styles can be exemplified in relation to a situation in which you are asked for the loan of a book which you do not wish to lend:

1   'Um...How long would you need it for? It's just that...ah...I might need it for an assignment. But...if it wasn't for long...' (nonassertion);

2   'I'm sorry. I'd like to help you out, but I bought this book so I would always have it to refer to, so I never lend it to anyone.' (assertion);

3   'No. Why don't you buy your own damn books!?' (aggression).

Although some psychoanalytic perspectives conceptualise assertiveness and aggression as distinct entities belonging to two different types of motivational system (Fosshage, 1998), most theorists see these response classes as differing in intensity rather than in kind (McCartan, 2001). In this sense, they are regarded as points on the same continuum of:

Nonassertion → Assertion → Aggression

Assertiveness forms the mid-point of this continuum, and is usually the most appropriate response. In reviewing research, Ames and Wazlawek (2014, p. 776) concluded that 'up to a point, pushing harder can bring rewards, but beyond a certain level, increasing assertiveness can entail mounting social costs, implying an inverted-U shape with some middle range of assertiveness often seen as optimal'. Aggressive individuals tend to be viewed as intransigent, coercive, overbearing and lacking in self-control. They may initially get their own way by brow-beating and creating fear in others, but they are usually disliked and avoided. Alternatively, this style may provoke a similar response from others, with the danger that the verbal aggression may escalate and lead to physical aggression. Nonassertive individuals, on the other hand, are often viewed as weak, 'mealy-mouthed' creatures who can be easily manipulated, and as a result frequently express dissatisfaction with their lives, owing to a failure to attain personal goals. They are less likely to inspire confidence in others or may even be seen as incompetent. Assertive people, however, tend to feel more in control of their lives, derive more satisfaction from their relationships and achieve their goals more often. They also obtain more respect from, and inspire confidence in, those with whom they interact since they tend to be viewed as strong characters who are not easily swayed.

This is evident at an early stage, so that in junior high school, Windschitl (2001) found that assertive pupils were more likely to voice their views, make suggestions and give directives to peers. Less assertive pupils, in turn, tended to acquiesce to these directives. Leaper (2000) linked the continuum of assertive–nonassertive to that of affiliative–nonaffiliative (Figure 11.2). This produces four styles of behaviour. Those who are assertive and affiliative are *collaborative* individuals who only use assertion when necessary, but place a high value on having good relationships with others. On the other hand, assertive individuals who are nonaffiliative do not care about being friendly, and use assertive skills to *control* others and get their own way. Nonassertive people who are affiliative are *obliging* by nature and like to fit in and do what others want. Finally, those who are both nonassertive and nonaffiliative tend to *withdraw* from interaction with others and like to keep themselves to themselves.

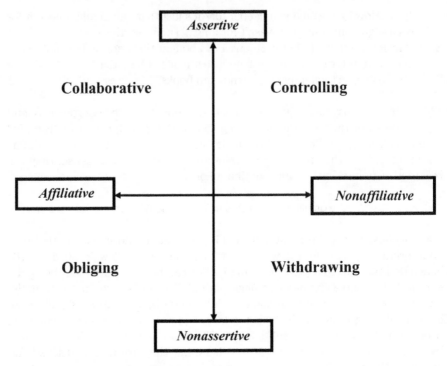

Figure 11.2 The assertion–affiliation matrix.

Several research studies have verified the behavioural responses associated with these three styles. An early investigation by Rose and Tryon (1979) found that assertive behaviour was clearly associated with:

- louder voice (68 decibel (dB) level was viewed as nonassertive; 76 dB level was the assertive ideal; 84 dB level was towards the aggressive end of the continuum);
- reduced response latency (pauses of 16 seconds before responding were seen as nonassertive, whereas pauses of 3–4 seconds were viewed as assertive);
- greater use of gestures (although increased gestures coupled with approach behaviour were seen as aggressive);
- increased vocal inflection.

The relationship between amplitude of voice and perceptions of dominance (high amplitude) and submissiveness (low amplitude) was confirmed in a later study by Tusing and Dillard (2000). They postulated the reason for this relationship as being that, 'during the course of evolutionary history, certain vocal cues became associated with dominance because they served as markers of organisms' aggressive potential' (p. 164). In other words, a loud bark was a signal of a deep bite. Hughes *et al.* (2014) confirmed these findings in a study in which both males and females who were asked to speak in such a way as to appear more dominant to others successfully achieved this by raising the pitch and volume of their voice.

McFall *et al.* (1982), in a detailed research investigation, identified what they termed *assertive body movements*, the most salient being hands, arms and overall body cues. The nonverbal behaviour of assertive individuals was controlled, smooth and purposive, whereas nonassertive people displayed shifty, shaky and fidgety body activity. Furthermore, Kolotkin *et al.* (1983) found that duration of eye contact was greater for assertive, as opposed to nonassertive, individuals. They also found that the use of smiles helps to convey that a response is meant to be assertive rather than aggressive. Interestingly, however, there is a relationship between laughter and dominance, in that submissive people laugh much more at the humour of dominant individuals than vice versa (Provine, 2000).

Types of aggression

Although most texts on assertion differentiate between three styles of responding, some theorists have made a distinction between different types of aggression (Spector, 2012). Buss and Perry (1992) developed an Aggression Inventory which contains four factors, or sub-divisions, of aggression. These are outlined below, with examples of actual items from the Inventory.

1   *Physical aggression*: 'Given enough provocation, I may hit another person'; 'If I have to resort to violence to protect my rights, I will'.
2   *Verbal aggression*: 'I tell my friends openly when I disagree with them'; 'When people annoy me I may tell them what I think of them'.
3   *Anger*: 'I sometimes feel like a powder keg ready to explode'; 'Sometimes I fly off the handle for no good reason'.
4   *Hostility*: 'I am sometimes eaten up with jealousy'; 'When people are especially nice, I wonder what they want'.

The relationship between these elements is that they each represent different dimensions of aggression: physical and verbal responses represent the instrumental or behavioural components; anger is the emotional or affective aspect; and hostility the cognitive element.

Another common distinction is that between open, direct aggression and passive, indirect aggression. Del Greco (1983) argued that these two types combine with nonassertion and assertion to form the two continua of coerciveness and directness, as shown in Figure 11.3. The passive, or indirect, aggressive style of responding seems to embrace a range of behaviours, including sulking, using emotional blackmail (such as crying in order to get your own way), pouting and being subtly manipulative. Del Greco developed an inventory to measure all four response styles. Indirect, or passive, aggressive items include: 'When I am asked for my preference I pretend I don't have one, but then I convince my friends of the advantages of my hidden preferences' and 'When my friend asks me for my opinion I state that I have none, then I proceed to make my true preference seem

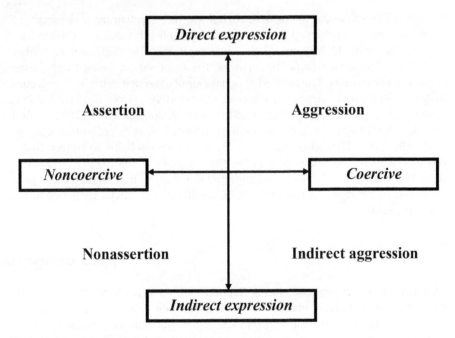

Figure 11.3 Four styles of responding.

the most attractive'. This type of Machiavellian approach is one clear example of indirect aggression. Another example is the *deflected aggression* scenario, where, for example, a person slams drawers and doors shut while refusing to discuss the reason for so doing.

The four response styles can be illustrated with reference to alternative ways of responding to someone smoking in a 'No Smoking' area:

1   'Hey, you, there's no smoking allowed in this area. Either put out or get out!' (aggressive);
2   'Excuse me, but do you realise that this is a No Smoking area? Cigarette smoke affects me quite badly, so I'd be grateful if you would not smoke here.' (assertive);
3   Not mentioning your discomfort, and hoping that someone else will confront the smoker. (nonassertive);
4   Coughing loudly and vigorously waving a hand towards the smoker as if to fan the smoke away. (indirectly aggressive).

Once again, assertiveness is regarded as the optimum approach. While it is possible to be skilfully manipulative, there is always the danger of being found out, with resulting negative consequences. Similarly, in the case of passive aggression, as in (4) above, this can also lead to a negative evaluation, or may simply be ignored by the interlocutor.

In research into consumers' verbal behaviour following a failure of service, a distinction has been made between aggression and resort-to-aggression styles

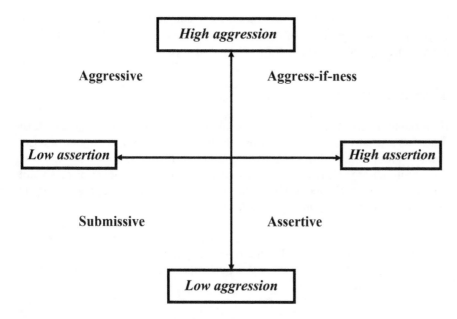

Figure 11.4 The aggression–assertion matrix.

(Richins, 1983; Swanson and McIntyre, 1998). As shown in Figure 11.4, aggressive individuals are high on aggression but low on assertion – they do not use the assertive approach at all. By comparison, individuals who are high on both assertion and aggression may employ an assertive style initially but are prepared to resort to aggression if necessary (I have termed this the 'aggress-if-ness' style) to get what they want.

TYPES OF ASSERTIVENESS

There are five key types of assertive behaviour: (1) basic assertion; (2) empathic assertion; (3) escalating assertion; (4) confrontive assertion; and (5) I-language assertion.

Basic assertion

This involves a simple expression of standing up for personal rights, beliefs, feelings or opinions. For example, when interrupted, a basic assertive response would be: 'Excuse me, I would like to finish what I was saying'.

Empathic assertion

This type of assertion conveys sensitivity to the interlocutor, by including a statement that conveys some recognition of the other person's situation or feelings before making the assertive statement. An example of an empathic assertive response to an interruption would be: 'I know you are keen to get your views across, but I would like to finish what I was saying'.

Escalating assertion

Here the individual begins by making a minimally assertive response, and, if the other person fails to respond to this, gradually escalates the degree of assertiveness employed. As Rakos (2006) pointed out, if your assertion attempts are repeatedly ignored, it may be necessary to escalate to the level of reasonable threats or actions. Someone visited at home by a 'pushy' salesperson may use escalating assertive responses as follows:

1   'No, I've decided that I don't wish to purchase any of these products.'
2   'No, as I've already said, I'm not buying any of them.'
3   'Look, I've told you twice that the answer is no. I'm going to have to ask you to leave now.'

Confrontive assertion

This is used when someone does not do what had been previously agreed. It involves clearly reminding the person what was agreed, contrasting this with what actually happened and then firmly stating what the other person must now do. For example: 'You said you would have the report finished by Tuesday. It is now Thursday and you still haven't produced it. I want you to have it completed by 4.00 p.m. today.'

I-language assertion

Here the speaker objectively describes the behaviour of the interlocutor, how this affects the speaker's life or feelings and why the other person should change this behaviour. In the case of being interrupted, an I-language assertive response would be: 'This is the fourth time you've interrupted me in the past few minutes. This makes me feel that you aren't interested in what I am saying, and I feel a bit hurt and annoyed. I would like you to let me finish what I want to say.' However, this statement also contains *you-language*, which tends to be perceived as blaming or accusing the other person and can result in defensive reactions. Compare the following two utterances.

1   'You are annoying me because you never pay for your fair share of these expenses.'
2   'I feel annoyed because I believe that I am paying more than my fair share of these expenses.'

Statement (2) is much less accusatory than (1) and therefore is less likely to provoke a hostile response. However, there is a danger, especially if overused, of

I-language being perceived as selfish, self-centred and unconcerned with the other person. Indeed, I-language statements do not seem to be characteristic of most everyday conversations (Gervasio, 1987). For these reasons, the use of *we-language* can be an effective alternative. We-language helps to convey the impression of partnership in, and joint responsibility for, any problems to be discussed. Continuing with the above exemplar, the we-language response would be:

3   'We need to talk about how we are both contributing to the payment of these expenses. It is important that neither of us feels annoyed about the present arrangement.'

Direct and indirect assertion

Linehan and Egan (1979) distinguished between direct and indirect styles of assertiveness. They argued that a direct, basic assertive style may not always be most effective, and that a more ambiguous, indirect style of response can be more appropriate. Let us look at an example of these two styles as a response to the question: 'Could you lend me that DVD you bought yesterday?'

    Direct: 'No, I never lend my DVDs to anyone.'
    Indirect: 'Oh, you mean *The Oceans* – You know, I'm still trying to get a chance to sit down and watch it myself. I usually take ages with a new DVD.'

Here the direct approach may be seen as brusque or even offensive. In the indirect approach, however, there has been no refusal and so the interlocutor may reply by attempting to obtain a commitment about borrowing the DVD in the future. However, the direct style can be less abrasive if it is coupled with an embellishment to turn it into a complex-direct style and so soften the impact of direct assertion. We will examine such embellishments later in the chapter. Some theorists suggest that little white lies may be used here, but caution is required as not only does this pose an ethical dilemma, it can backfire if the lie is later unveiled. At the same time, as mentioned in Chapter 9, deception occurs in around one-quarter of all conversations. Niikura (1999a), in a study of assertiveness across four cultures, found that the option of 'making an excuse' (a euphemism for telling a lie) when having to turn down a request from a senior colleague was very popular in all cultures.

    The goal is to lessen the impact of the refusal and so maintain the relationship. Thus, using the complex-direct approach, a response (whether truthful or not) to the above question would be:

    Complex-direct: 'I know you would look after it really well, but I've recently had two DVDs that I loaned damaged, so I've just had to make the general decision never to lend my DVDs to anyone again. That way I hope no one will feel personally offended.'

There is consistent evidence to show that standard, direct assertion is viewed as being as effective as, and more socially desirable than, aggressive behaviour, and more socially competent but distinctly less likeable than nonassertion (Wilson and Gallois, 1993; Hadfield and Hasson, 2010). It seems that assertiveness is evaluated positively in theory, but when faced with the practical reality is rated less favourably than nonassertion (McCartan and Hargie, 2004a). As expressed by Dickson *et al.* (1997, p. 131), 'One interesting research finding, however, is that while people tend to respect assertive individuals, they often do not like to have to deal with assertive responses'. For example, Harwood *et al.* (1997) carried out a study in which subjects evaluated conversations between a bystander and the driver following a car accident. They found that an assertive style of response from the bystander was perceived to be more competent but less kind and less respectful than a nonassertive style.

Equally, we may not like to be in the company of those who are continually assertive. In a review of research on complaining, Kowalski (1996) concluded that people who complain frequently are viewed more negatively than those who seldom do so. A similar dislike for assertion emerged in a Slovakian study, where Bugelova (2000) found an assertive style was perceived as unbecoming or impolite, and regarded as a hindrance to friendship. In fact, in their review of this phenomenon, Buslig and Burgoon (2000, p. 193) noted, 'submissive behavior is often ineffective for reaching instrumental goals, but perceived more positively in terms of interpersonal impressions'. We like, and probably have more empathy for, nonassertive people. Thus, assertion needs to be used sensitively.

Assertiveness can provoke a number of adverse reactions. This is especially the case if we make a change in style from submissiveness to assertiveness. It is useful to be aware of some of the possible negative reactions of others. Alberti and Emmons (2008) identified five main ones:

1   *Back-biting.* For example, making statements *sotto voce*, which the assertee ensures are overheard by the asserter ('Who does she think she is?'; 'All of a sudden he's now Mr Bigfellow').
2   *Aggression.* Others may try to negate the assertion by using threatening or hostile behaviour in an attempt to regain dominance. They may also use the tactic of *strategic umbrage* whereby they apparently take offence at the assertiveness of the interlocutor (Ames and Wazlawek, 2014). This may involve apologetic sarcasm ('I'm so terribly, terribly, sorry. How unforgivably rude of me even to think of asking you').
3   *Over-apologising.* Apologies can also be genuine. Some people may feel they have caused offence and as a result apologise profusely. In such instances reassurance by the asserter is needed, showing that the apology is accepted and the deed now in the past.
4   *Emotionality.* When someone who was formerly submissive becomes assertive, the recipient may react by becoming emotional. This can include temper tantrums, huffing or guilt-based accusations ('You don't love me any more'; 'You've become very selfish. Can't you think of me at all?').

In extreme cases, when the new behaviour signals a potential change in the relational power balance, it can also result in assertee psychosomatic reactions (headaches, stomach pains, feeling weak). Again, an assertive response is required to deal with these.

5   *Revenge seeking*. The assertion may apparently be accepted but the person retains hidden resentment and a desire to 'get their own back'.

Protective assertion

Assertiveness is an important skill when one is coming under pressure from others (Dryden and Constantinou, 2004). This is particularly important in areas such as drug abuse and safe sex. Thus, assertion has been shown to be related to a lower incidence of alcohol abuse (Epstein *et al.*, 2000), reductions in the regularity and quantity of alcohol, cocaine and heroin consumption (Torrecillas *et al.*, 2000) and greater condom use to prevent sexually transmitted disease (Zamboni *et al.*, 2000). Three specific types of protective assertion skills were identified by Fry (1983), as forms of verbal defence to be used against manipulation, nagging or rudeness:

1   *Broken record*. Here the person simply makes an assertive statement, and keeps repeating it (analogous to the needle sticking on a broken vinyl record) until it is accepted by the other person. For example, to repeated pleas for a loan the individual may just keep using the refusal assertion response: 'No, I'm not going to give you any money'.

2   *Fogging*. Using this tactic the person verbally accepts negative criticism but clearly has no intention of changing behaviour. The strategy here is that eventually the initiator will become tired of getting no real response to the criticisms and eventually give up. An example of a fogging sequence is:

     A: 'You always look down in the dumps.'
     B: 'Yes, I probably do.'
     A: 'Could you not try to look a bit happier?'
     B: 'I suppose I could.'
     A: 'If you did, you would be a bit more pleasant to work with.'
     B: 'Yes, I'm sure you're right.'

3   *Metalevel assertion*. As the name suggests, this involves an attempt to widen the perspective rather than sticking to a specific issue. One example of this approach, of moving from the particular to the general, would be where someone involved in an argument with a colleague says, 'We obviously are not going to agree about this, and I think this is typical of what is happening to our whole working relationship'.

COMPONENTS OF ASSERTIVENESS

In order to execute assertiveness skills effectively, three central components need to be mastered, namely content, process and nonverbal responses.

Content

The actual content of an assertive response should include both an expression of rights and a statement placing this within the context of socially responsible and appropriate behaviour. Several accompanying elaboration components, or embellishments, have been identified (Linehan and Egan, 1979; Rakos, 2006). Box 11.3 presents a summary of these in relation to an assertive response to the refusal of an invitation. These content statements can obviously be combined to soften the assertion, and distinguish the response from aggression. They serve the important purpose of protecting mutual face and so maintaining the relationship: the asserter achieves the desired personal goal, but at the same time shows concern for the face needs of the assertee (Edwards and Bello, 2001). However, a note of caution was sounded by Rakos, who showed how these embellishments are likely to be more consistent with a female than a male approach to, and expectations of, assertion.

One situation that can be difficult to cope with assertively is that of embarrassment. In their discussion of strategies for handling embarrassing predicaments, Cupach and Metts (1990) identified four main types of content responses.

Box 11.3 Elaboration components in assertion statements

Using the example of a refusal to an invitation from a colleague to go to the bar at lunchtime, the elaborations are:

- a short *delay*, or brief *filled pause* ('Ahh'), before responding, so that the refusal is not seen as abrupt or brusque
- an *expression of appreciation or praise* for the kindness and thoughtfulness of the other person in making the offer ('It's really nice of you to ask'). The power of praise in conflict assertion was aptly noted by Mark Twain: 'I think a compliment ought always to precede a complaint, where one is possible, because it softens resentment and insures for the complaint a courteous and gentle reception'
- a *cushioning* of the way the refusal itself is expressed, usually through an expression of regret at not being able to accept ('Much as I'd like to come, I'm afraid I won't be able to')
- an *explanation* for the necessity to assert oneself ('I have work to finish off during the lunch break')
- showing *empathy* for the other person's situation ('I know you had been looking forward to it')
- a short *apology* for any resulting consequence ('I'm sorry if you are on your own over lunch')
- an attempt to identify a mutually acceptable *compromise* ('I haven't time to go out to the bar, but how about just having a quick bite in the canteen?')

---

1   *Apology.* Hargie *et al.* (2010) reviewed the extensive corpus of research on apology across a wide array of academic areas. They found that apologies range in complexity, depending upon the severity of the transgression. They can involve any or all of: a basic statement of apology ('I'm so sorry'), an admission of responsibility ('It was entirely my fault'), a denial of intent ('It was an accident'), a direct plea to be pardoned ('Please forgive me'), an explanation ('I wasn't looking where I was going'), self-castigation ('I'm so clumsy'), a declaration of regret or remorse ('I feel terrible about this'), an attempt at remediation or reparation (e.g. offering to replace a spilled drink) and a promise of future forbearance ('I'll be more careful in the future'). Research shows that complex apologies, involving a greater number of these sub-elements, tend to have more beneficial effects in terms of reducing detrimental consequences, such as anger or a negative evaluation of the transgressor, and increasing positive outcomes such as empathy and liking for the transgressor.

2   *Accounts.* Stapleton and Hargie (2011) have shown how it is possible to negate face-threatening events through the use of strategic accounts. These can be either in the form of an *excuse*, which expresses denial of responsibility for an untoward act without negating its severity ('I know it is a mess, but it was an accident'); or a *justification*, which expresses responsibility for the untoward act but denies the pejorative nature of the consequences ('Yes, I did spill it, but there's no real harm done').

3   *Humour.* A joke can be one of the most effective methods for dealing with embarrassment, since it can convert a potential loss of social approval into a positive gain. In this sense, 'a well formed joke, especially one reflecting on the unintentional incompetence of the transgressor, can express remorse, guilt, and embarrassment as an apology would without unduly lowering the individual's status vis-à-vis others who are present' (Cupach and Metts, 1990, p. 329).

4   *Avoidance.* This strategy would include not mentioning sensitive topics to particular people, quickly changing an embarrassing topic, staying silent or simply leaving the room.

Obviously, two or more of these can be used at the same time. Thus an assertive response might involve giving an excuse, apologising and offering restitution, while at the same time employing appropriate humour.

In her analysis of tactics used by those who are held publicly responsible for an event that has been evaluated negatively, Schutz (1998) identified six possible response strategies:

1   *Denial.* This is summarised by the 'It never happened' response. The veracity and motives of those who claim that it did are then called into question.

2   *Reframing.* Here the essence is 'It was not like that'. The approach is to present the event in a new 'frame' – it did occur, but it was not nearly as bad as portrayed.

3   *Dissociation*. This is the 'I was not to blame' strategy. The event did occur but the person did not cause it. It was someone else's fault. One variation of this is in the use of pronominals to associate or dissociate oneself with what happened – here Schutz gave the example of supporters of sports teams when talking about victories saying, '*We* won', but when defeated saying '*They* lost'.

4   *Justification*. The nub of this approach is 'It was the only thing to do'. Responsibility is accepted but the argument is that nothing else could have been done, or even that the response averted potentially more damaging events and so the public should be grateful.

5   *Excuses*. The typical statement here is 'I could not prevent it'. The main excuse tends to be that of extenuating or extraordinary circumstances – that no one could have foreseen the event.

6   *Concessions, apologies and remediation*. The response here is 'I accept full responsibility and wish to do whatever I can to compensate'. As Schutz illustrated, when remediation is offered as well as an apology the impact is more positive in terms of public perceptions of the perpetrator's image.

Rose and Tryon (1979) made another important distinction between three general types of assertion content, which can be exemplified in relation to complaining about a meal in a restaurant, as follows:

1   *Description of the behaviour* – 'Excuse me, this meal is cold'.

2   *Description of behaviour plus indication of your noncompliance* – 'Excuse me, this meal is cold. I couldn't eat it'.

3   *Description, noncompliance, plus request for behaviour change* – 'Excuse me, this meal is cold. I couldn't eat it. Could you please replace it?'

Rose and Tryon found that ratings of assertiveness increased as individuals moved from simply giving a description, through to using all the above three types of content.

Process

The way in which assertive responses are carried out is crucial to their success (Townend, 2007). Thus the correct *timing* of vocalisations and nonverbal responses is vital. Although a slight delay is important in refusing a genuine invitation (Holman, 2000), assertive responses should be given without long hesitations. On occasions, we may have our rights infringed because we are unsure about whether they actually have been violated. If we later discover this to be the case then it is necessary to reconstruct the situation in which the infringement occurred ('Yesterday you asked me to do X. I have since discovered that it is not my job to do X. I would therefore be grateful if you would not ask me to do this again').

Stimulus control skills are also important. These refer to manipulations of the environment, or other people, to make the assertive response more successful. For example:

- asking someone to come to your room where you will feel more in charge, rather than discussing an issue in the corridor. Humans, like all animals, are territorial and our sense of *place* is very important to how we respond (Dixon and Durrheim, 2004). We feel more comfortable in our own lairs, with familiar sights, sounds and smells. Conversely we are more uncomfortable when on someone else's patch. To borrow a sporting analogy, it is always harder to get a result when playing away from home. Thus, it is easier to be assertive when we are on our own ground;
- requesting that you seek the opinion of another person to help settle the matter, when you already know that the views of this third person concur with your own;
- simply asking for time to think over a request, which allows you to reflect upon the ramifications thereof.

The use of *reinforcement* (see Chapter 4) is also important, for three reasons. First, rewarding another person is actually a positive use of assertion; someone who has performed a task well has the right to expect reward. Second, the reward can help to minimise any negative feelings resulting from the assertion. Third, it encourages the interlocutor to behave appropriately towards you in the future.

Nonverbal responses

The final component of assertiveness relates to the nonverbal behaviour of the asserter. The main nonverbal assertive behaviours are: medium levels of eye contact; avoidance of inappropriate facial expressions; smooth use of gestures while speaking, yet inconspicuous while listening; upright posture; direct body orientation; medium interpersonal distance; and appropriate paralinguistics (short response latency, medium response length, good fluency, medium volume and inflection, increased firmness).

PERSONAL AND CONTEXTUAL FACTORS

Three key factors that influence the degree, nature and effectiveness of assertion are gender, culture and the assertee.

Gender

Assertiveness tends to be viewed as more appropriate when employed by males rather than females. Indeed, research reveals that males have significantly higher scores than females on tests of assertiveness (Sigler *et al.*, 2008). Kahn (1981, p. 349), in an early review of this area, suggested that:

People expect women to behave unassertively. Women may not only accept this judgment ... but ... may avoid behaviors that do not fit 'the feminine role' and when they do engage in 'masculine assertiveness', they are likely to encounter disbelief or even hostility.

Over a quarter of a century later, in their review of the literature on gender differences in behaviour in organisations, Guadagno and Cialdini (2007, p. 485) showed that not much had changed, concluding that, 'assertiveness in a man is seen as a gender "appropriate" behavior, whereas an assertive woman is seen as violating gender-based expectations for behavior and may be thought of in a derogatory manner'. Thus, Amanatullah and Tinsley (2013) found that in the business world women who are assertive suffer from a *social backlash effect*, including perceptions of decreased likeability and of being too masculine. They tend to be judged as lower in social attractiveness and competence than males who use similar behaviours (Rakos, 2006).

Some feminist writers have argued that the entire concept of assertion is androcentric (male-centred) and imbued with demeaning portrayals of women for being 'weak' in this area (Cameron, 1994; Crawford, 1995). Despite such views, the main perspective within the feminist movement tends to be that this is a skill that women should possess (Rakos, 2006). Thus, females have consistently been advised to undertake AT (LaFrance and Harris, 2004). Likewise, several assertiveness books have been written specifically for women (e.g. Dickson, 2012). This is not surprising, given that females consistently report difficulties in being assertive. Indeed, the plethora of written material and self-help texts specifically designed for women and the popularity of women's AT programmes is in itself a form of evidence that females feel they need more help in this field. One reason for this is that the most successful style for females seems to be one where they are perceived to be both competent and nice (Rudman and Glick, 2001) – not always an easy combination to sustain in conflict situations.

One specific problem faced by females is that of sexual assertiveness, defined as 'the ability to communicate sexual needs and to initiate desired sexual behavior with a partner' (Brassard *et al.*, 2015, p. 112). To address this issue, Loshek and Terrell (2015) developed the *Sexual Assertiveness Questionnaire* for women. This measures the following three factors relating to sexual activity, with actual scale items given in parentheses:

1   communication about sexual initiation and satisfaction ('I approach my partner for sex when I desire it');
2   refusal of unwanted sex ('It is easy for me to say no if I don't want to have sex');
3   sexual history communication ('I ask my partners whether they have ever had a sexually transmitted infection/disease').

In relation to sexual assertiveness, Morokoff *et al.* (1997) found that:

- the greater a woman's sexual experience, the more likely she was to initiate sex;
- the anticipation of a negative partner response reduced the level of assertiveness in refusing a sexual advance or requesting barrier precautions;
- feelings of self-efficacy about how to use condoms were related to self-reported ability to refuse a sexual advance.

Also in this domain, Livingstone *et al.* (2007) demonstrated a significant link between low sexual assertiveness and subsequent sexual victimisation.

Some research has been carried out to ascertain whether gender differences in assertiveness emerge at an early age. One study of 4–6-year-olds in eastern USA found no difference in assertive behaviour between boys and girls (Beneson *et al.*, 1998). However, confounding variables here included the facts that the study focused upon almost exclusively white, middle/upper-class children, the girls were in the presence of friends, and they knew the boys. All of these factors facilitate assertion displays. In contrast, Leman *et al.* (2011) found differences in assertiveness among 7-year-old children in England, in that boy pairs were more assertive towards one another than girl pairs, while boys were more assertive in cross-gender pairs. Leaper (2000) analysed the assertion and affiliation behaviours of European American and Latin American girls and boys (mean age 48 months) and their parents in their own homes. Each child played individually with either mother or father, with a feminine-stereotyped toy (foods and plates) and a masculine-stereotyped toy (track and cars). It was found that fathers were more assertive (e.g. giving directions, disagreeing) than mothers who, in turn, were more affiliative (e.g. praising, asking for the child's opinion). Furthermore, in general, children were more assertive than their mothers but less assertive than their fathers. Leaper argued that this latter finding may reflect the mother's willingness to let the child take control, but that it could also lead to a learned stereotype of women as being less powerful than men. Differences also emerged in relation to the play settings, in that the toy food scenario produced higher levels of both assertion and affiliation – in other words, it was a more collaborative encounter (Figure 11.2).

Leaper argued that gender-typed play scenarios mean that girls learn to cooperate from an early age, whereas boys learn to compete. Another finding was that both fathers and mothers demonstrated less assertion than their sons, but not their daughters, in the toy track condition, while no such difference emerged in the food play. Leaper summarised these findings as showing a pattern of children being presented with role models of assertive fathers and affiliative mothers, and of boys but not girls being encouraged to be assertive and take control in masculine-stereotyped activities. Overall, this study illustrated how gender differences in assertion can be shaped by a combination of parental role models and reward for differential activities in stereotyped play activities.

Lewis and Gallois (1984) found that both males and females were more assertive towards those of the same gender; that expression of negative feeling was more acceptable from a member of the opposite sex; and that aggressive encounters were more prevalent in same-sex dyads. In another study, Nix *et al.* (1983) concluded that assertiveness is a masculine sex-role characteristic. They found that females achieving high masculinity scores in the Bem Sex Role Inventory scored significantly higher on measures of assertiveness than those high in femininity. This finding is consistent with general trends wherein masculine sex-role characteristics tend to be attributed to assertive individuals; masculine or androgynous females are more likely to be assertive than feminine women; masculinity and conflict assertiveness are positively correlated; and, direct assertiveness tends to be viewed as masculine (McCartan and Hargie, 2004b).

It has been suggested that, when dealing with disputes, males are more likely to operate on a 'one-up, one-down' basis, and so direct confrontation literally gives them the opportunity to achieve one-upmanship. Similarly, the *fight-or-flight response*, whereby the individual reacts to threats from others either by attacking the source of the threat or fleeing from it, has been portrayed as a male dilemma (Aronson *et al.*, 2007). Females, on the other hand, prefer a relational route to conflict resolution; they see the option of openly confronting the other person as leading to likely retaliation and harmful for the overall relationship (Lundgren and Rudawsky, 2000; Dindia and Canary, 2006). Accordingly, it has been argued that they develop a *tend-and-befriend response* as an alternative to fight or flight. That is, they prefer nurturing activities that protect themselves and their loved ones (tending) and the development of strong social networks (befriending) to buffer the effects of threat.

Research shows that, across the world, males use more direct aggression than females. However, females are more likely than males to be indirectly aggressive in terms of the derogation of others, especially other physically attractive females (Vaillancourt, 2013). Among females, this type of indirect or 'relational' aggression, often involving negative comments about appearance or sexual fidelity, has become a major form of bullying, and especially on social media (Catanzaro, 2011). Owens *et al.* (2000) carried out a study in Australia on the effects of peer indirect aggression on teenage girls. They discovered that victims suffered a wide range of psychological effects, including loss of self-esteem, anxiety and depression. This in turn led to a range of ideas about how to escape the pain, ranging from a desire to leave the school to thoughts of suicide. The most vulnerable girls were those who had few friends, were new to the school or lacked assertiveness. Some responded by retaliating against the perpetrator. This is interesting, given that another study found that training in physical self-defence actually served to increase women's self-reported levels of assertiveness (Weitlauf *et al.*, 2000).

Wood (2009) identified differences between what is regarded as typical masculine and feminine nonverbal behaviour, in that females are expected to smile more, disengage eye contact if someone stares (males hold eye contact), show interest in others (males try to show confidence and control) and interact in such a way as to be nice to others (while males interact in such a way as to impress others). Again, these female-typical behaviours of being nice, smiling, avoiding prolonged gaze and showing interest rather than confidence or control mean that females can find it more difficult to communicate in an assertive style. In terms of gender differences in language use, a meta-analysis of research studies by Leaper and Ayres (2007) found that males were significantly more likely to use assertive speech while females were significantly more likely to employ affiliative language patterns. In a later meta-analysis, Leaper and Robnett (2011) illustrated how females were more likely to employ a tentative language style (expressing uncertainty, using more hedges and tag questions), which tends to be linked with lack of assertion.

In their review of research studies of language and gender, Mulac *et al.* (2001) found a number of main difference effects, as shown in Box 11.4. These differences indicate why females may find it more difficult to be assertive, and why in work contexts they often consciously consider in depth those factors that may influence the nature and type of assertion that they should employ (Pfafman and McEwan, 2014). The male-preferred style reflects shorter, more directive, self-opinionated and explicit language use. Expressions of direct assertiveness will therefore not be so problematic. On the other hand, the preferred female style of longer and more indirect sentences, coupled with greater expressed uncertainty and qualification, does not lend itself so easily to assertion.

In reviewing the field of gender differences in language use, Mulac (2006) posed the question as to whether men and women really use language

---

Box 11.4 Gender differences in language

Males tend to make greater use of:

- references to quantity ('20 foot high', 'weighed at least a ton')
- judgemental adjectives (giving personal evaluations – 'That's stupid')
- directives (telling another what to do – 'Put it over there')
- locatives (indicate the position/location of objects – 'to the right of...')
- elliptical sentences (short or one-word sentences in which either the subject or predicate is understood, e.g. 'Awesome!' 'Great idea')
- self-referenced statements ('My view is...')

Females tend to use more:

- intensive adverbs ('terribly', 'so', 'really')
- dependent clauses to qualify the primary meaning (e.g. 'I am Communications Manager, which involves a host of responsibilities...')
- reference to emotions ('cheerful', 'angry')
- sentences of greater mean length
- sentence initial adverbials ('Due to the lighting, the room seems...')
- uncertainty verbs ('It seems to be...', 'I might be able to...')
- hedges ('sort of...' 'a bit like...')
- negations (statements of what something is not 'It is not a very deep shade of blue')
- oppositions ('He looks happy yet also sad')
- questions and tag questions

differently. His answer was 'an unrestrained "Yes!" – meaningful differences in language behavior do exist. This conclusion is supported by a substantial number of empirical investigations of actual male–female language use conducted in a variety of communication contexts' (p. 223). At the same time, he also noted that these differences should be read as *gender-indicative tendencies,* since both genders can and do display the same language features.

Indeed, questions have been raised regarding the validity of much of the research into gender differences in language since it often ignores the fine nuances of communication (Cameron, 2009). For example, context is very important; while, overall, women or men may have a higher mean differential level of production of certain linguistic features, their usage varies according to situation (LaFrance and Harris, 2004; Palomares, 2009b). As shown by Leaper and Smith (2004, p. 993), 'Although the pattern of gender differences in the use of language tends to be consistent when differences are reported, many studies find no significant differences'. In addition, specific individuals can and do use gender-opposite language styles. Thus, the relationship between gender and assertiveness is both complex and complicated, and as Leaper (2014, p. 62) has shown, 'the magnitude and direction of gender differences in the use of language are moderated by contextual variables'.

Three general, and in many ways complementary, explanations have been put forward to explain gender differences in language (Leaper and Ayres, 2007):

1. The *biological* perspective purports that gender differences were shaped by evolutionary necessities, wherein males were required to be assertive and aggressive (e.g. as hunters or warriors) while females were affiliative and nurturing, especially in terms of child rearing (Marchbank and Letherby, 2014). This approach emphasises gender differences in brain functioning and organisation (Andersen, 2006). Thus, girls usually develop language earlier than boys, and achieve higher scores on verbal production measures. However, while biological influences may impact upon some aspects of language production, most analysts would now accept that social factors play a prominent role in gender variations in language use (Halpern, 2000).

2. In the *social constructionist* approach, gender is viewed as being socially engineered (Burr, 2015). Here it is argued that females and males will behave similarly if they are placed in the same circumstances, with equal authority, and required to play the same roles. For example, in a university context both male and female students evaluated a female speaker more favourably when using an assertive as opposed to a tentative style of speech (Hawkes *et al.*, 1996). It is further posited that we can decide who we want to be in terms of gender identity, but at the same time we are also subjected to external situational and cultural demands and pressures to conform to certain expectations (Kimmel, 2004a). This approach highlights the demand characteristics of the specific context as playing a key role in language variation. In particular, it accords considerable relevance to the role of structural power (Marchbank and Letherby, 2014). It points to the higher power and status of males in society as an important

influence on gender variations in behaviour (Leaper and Robnett, 2011). This perspective is therefore linked to the *gender-as-power* perspective, where differences in male and female language use are purported to reflect the relative dominance and submissiveness of the two genders.

3　　The *social developmental* paradigm gives central importance to the cumulative impact of cognitive learning, practice and experience over time. This approach is also referred to as *gender as culture*, or the *two-cultures hypothesis*. It argues that boys and girls to a large extent inhabit different 'worlds' at the formative stage of development (up to 15 years old). As a result of their repeated exposure to the same gender in-group, they adopt a specific type of either 'masculine' or 'feminine' language usage. For example, boys and girls engage in very different games (Wood, 2009). Boys play games that usually involve large numbers, are competitive, grounded in doing something, and emphasise achievement – the notion of being the most valuable player is highly regarded. Communication is used primarily to attract attention and assert one's ideas. By contrast, girls play games involving smaller groups, such as house or school, where the goals are less clear-cut, and so negotiations have to take place about who does what. Communication is used to develop and sustain relationships, by ensuring that everyone is included. Opportunities for learning are central in terms of knowledge, expectations and skills, so that gender-differentiated experiences are more likely to result in increased feelings of self-efficacy in the gender-specific role. Likewise, responses and roles that are regarded as having greater relevance to one's own gender become more salient than those perceived to belong to the other gender. Thus, Martin and Ruble (2004, p. 67) argued that children quickly become 'gender detectives who search for cues about gender – who should or should not engage in a particular activity, who can play with whom, and why girls and boys are different'.

Overall, there is no clear picture as to the exact nature of the relationship between the effects of different types of assertiveness, the situation in which they are employed and the gender of asserter and assertee. One problem here, as with all studies in the field of assertion, is that different investigators use differing measurements and methodologies. For example, subjects may be asked to respond to written, audio or video vignettes of assertiveness, engage in role plays, complete one of the large numbers of self-report assertion scales that now exist or be confronted with an experimentally contrived assertive encounter they believe to be real. Ratings of assertion may be made by the subjects themselves, by those with whom they have interacted or by trained observers. These variations make comparisons between studies very difficult.

The final compounding factor is that the role of women in society has changed rapidly in recent years. Indeed, in terms of gender stereotypes we have gone through a 'transitional era' (Wood, 2007). In traditional fairy tales, portrayals of females were typically either of 'submissive/beautiful' (e.g. Cinderella, Snow White, Goldilocks) or 'aggressive/ugly' (ugly sisters, wicked witch, evil stepmother). Similarly, in films familiar storylines were of a bold, dashing knight in shining armour winning the hand of the shy fair maiden, or of a tough galloping cowboy in a white hat rescuing the defenceless damsel in distress. These stereotypes persisted for quite some time. For example, when the cult TV series *Star Trek* began in the late 1960s, its futuristic interpretation of advanced human civilisation had only one female member as part of the elite group on the bridge of the *Enterprise*, and she was in essence a glorified telephonist who rarely got 'beamed' anywhere. This has changed. The females on the programme are now centrally involved in the hard action, including as captain. The concept of 'ladette culture', replete with loud, hard-drinking, self-directed, often sexually predatory, females, has also affected gender image and expectations. Furthermore, female entrants to the traditional professions (medicine, pharmacy, law, etc.) now often outnumber males, and within many Protestant churches there are female clergy. All such changes influence the attitudes of both males and females to assertive behaviour by the latter.

In a fascinating longitudinal meta-analysis of 385 studies dating from the 1920s to the 1990s, Twenge (1998) charted changes in assertiveness across these eight decades. She found no consistent changes in male scores over this period. However, female assertion scores mirrored their social status and roles at each era, showing an increase before and during the Second World War (1928–1945), a decrease post-war (1945–1967) and an increase thereafter. Interestingly, she also found a positive correlation between assertion scores and overall figures for educational attainment for women. This suggests that 'getting on' in society involves 'standing up' for one's rights. It also indicates that female assertive behaviour changes according to shifting societal expectations, whereas male assertion remains constant.

Cultural background

As discussed in Chapter 2, the context within which responses are employed is important. For example, a sub-culture of people with certain strong religious beliefs may actually eschew assertiveness as a valid *modus operandi* and follow maxims of submissiveness. For such groups, AT would not be either relevant or appropriate. In this way, some Christians may be guided by the following verses from Matthew 5 in the Bible: 'Blessed are the meek: for they will inherit the earth'; 'If anyone slaps you on the right cheek, turn to them the other cheek also'; and 'Give to the one who asks you, and do not turn away from the one who wants to borrow from you'.

One of the most researched aspects of culture is that of individualism versus collectivism (Hagger *et al.*, 2014). The difference between the two cultural styles, as highlighted in Box 11.5, was neatly summarised by Morris *et al.* (2001, p. 100) in the example that, 'Brazilians display stronger intentions to do what is expected of them, whereas North Americans display a stronger intention to do what they personally desire'. Likewise, Libby and Eibach (2007) noted that the differing positive and negative cultural expectations from assertive responses was encapsulated in the saying in Western cultures, 'The squeaky wheel gets the grease' and in Eastern cultures, 'The nail that stands up gets pounded down'.

Box 11.5 Individualist and collectivist cultural differences	
Important in individualist cultures	Important in collectivist cultures
Needs	Duties
Rights	Norms
Concern for self ('I' orientation)	Concern for group ('we' orientation)
Being successful	Being accepted
Innovation	Respect for tradition
Equality	Given role
Privacy	Sharing
Competition	Co-operation
Informality	Formality
Directness	Indirectness
Being up-front	Protecting face
Assertion	Nonassertion

In this way, 'American parents try to raise their children to be independent, self-reliant, and assertive (a "cut above the rest"), whereas Japanese children are raised to fit into their groups and community' (Kassin *et al.*, 2011, p. 67). In individualist cultures such as North America (Canada and the USA) and some European countries (e.g. Norway and the UK), the emphasis tends to be upon the self as an independent entity with needs, wants and goals that are legitimate to pursue individually. As such, standing up for one's rights seems perfectly valid and, indeed, natural. In collectivist cultures, individual rights are subordinate to those of the group and so assertion is not so appropriate (Lee and Ciftci, 2014). Thus, in many Eastern countries (e.g. China, Japan, Korea) and in Latin America (e.g. Brazil, Mexico), the emphasis is more upon an interdependent self, and in Hispanic culture there is a high level of respect for and obedience towards those in authority (Shrestha and Menzel, 2014).

It should be noted that the difference between these two cultural styles is not as neat as it may at first seem (Feng and Wilson, 2012). Thus, collectivist cultures differ in the ways in which they maintain intergroup relations and avoid conflicts. Latin Americans achieve this through open, warm, expressive, emotional displays. On the other hand, the Chinese tradition of *jen* and the Japanese one of *amae* emphasise the maintenance of harmony through a more passive, respectful and less overtly emotional approach in their dealings with one another. In addition, as Hargie (2006b) illustrated, aspects of collectivism can be found in individual cultures and vice versa, so that, 'at different times, in varying situations, and with different people, we may adopt either an individualistic or a more collective style of communicating' (p. 63). In this way, an individual's own position on the individualist–collectivist continuum often plays a more influential role in determining responses than the individualist–collectivist norms of the national or cultural group to which the person belongs (Rubin and Morrison, 2014). However, it is also clear that cultural differences make attempts to employ assertive behaviour with people from different sub-cultures fraught with difficulty. In particular, assertive responses are not appropriate where values of humility, tolerance or subservience are prevalent.

Minority ethnic groups in the USA with a strong sense of separate identity, such as the Mexican, Japanese and Chinese communities, tend to report being less assertive than Whites. These sub-cultures also emphasise deference to elders and in particular parents, so that any form of assertion from child to parent is likely to be frowned upon. This again is different from the norm for Caucasians, where open disagreement and negotiated decisions are acceptable between parents and children. In a similar vein, in some cultures and sub-cultures (such as Muslim communities), assertion may be associated with a macho male role model, with females being expected to play an acquiescent or subservient role.

There is evidence to indicate that cultural differences in assertion may be cognitively based, emanating from cultural values and norms rather than from assertive behaviour deficits, since in role-play situations people from these cultures are able to behave as assertively as Whites. For example, Sue *et al.* (1990) found that second-generation Chinese-American female undergraduates were as assertive as Caucasian females on scores on the Rathus Assertiveness Scale and on role-play tests with either an Asian or a Caucasian experimenter. The only significant difference between the groups was that the Chinese-Americans scored higher on the Fear of Negative Evaluation Scale. It could therefore be the case that in real-life encounters such apprehension of disapproval from others may result in Chinese-American females being less assertive. As Sue *et al.* put it, 'Chinese-Americans are able to demonstrate assertiveness in laboratory settings, but do they inhibit this response in other situations?' (p. 161).

Hastings (2000a) investigated the behaviour of Asian Indian postgraduate students in the USA. She found that this cultural group disliked the American norm of extensive use of talk and their expression of direct, forceful opinions. The US students were perceived as pushy, verbally aggressive and showing a lack of respect for superiors (their professors). Indian culture places a very high value on acceptance, self-suppression and concern for the feelings of others. Hindu religion regards the role occupied by an individual as having been designated by God, and as such it has to be respected. The Indians in this study perceived the 'recipients' of their behaviour not to be just those immediately involved, but also their family and wider community that might eventually find out what had been said. Their decisions about assertive responses were guided by these factors. It was not the case that they did not know how to use assertive behaviours, but rather they believed that these were not culturally acceptable.

One study compared assertive responses of African American, Hispanic and European American high school students (Yager and Rotheram-Borus, 2000). It was found that assertive responses were more frequent among European Americans, while aggressive and expressive responses were more common in the Hispanic and African American groups. Yager and Rotheram-Borus argued that these response patterns could be misperceived by the out-group and thus be a potential source of cross-ethnic conflicts. Differences also emerged in a cross-cultural investigation of assertion in low-income 'thirty-something' women in the USA (Yoshioka, 2000). Here, African Americans, Hispanic Americans and Caucasians all agreed about appropriate assertive responses towards other females and towards children. However, in relation to assertion with males, the Hispanic group differed from the other two in that they were more affiliative in their reaction to male aggression.

Niikura (1999a, b) carried out an investigation which compared the responses of white-collar workers in the USA, Japan, Malaysia and the Philippines. Similarities were found between workers in Japan, Malaysia and the Philippines in terms of the psychological bonds they felt to relationships with superiors. The Japanese and Malaysians showed a much higher reluctance to refuse an annoying request from a friend directly. By contrast, the Americans were more likely to turn down unwanted requests from either superiors or friends directly. The Japanese respondents differed from the other groups in their reluctance to ask questions in a public forum. In Japan there is a sense of shame attached to asking questions about matters one does not understand and, indeed, it is regarded as a sign of over-assertiveness to ask questions. The Japanese, Malaysian and Filippino subjects placed greater importance on group solidarity and respect for senior members of staff than did the Americans. Niikura (1999b, p. 697) speculated that, 'the differences between the Asian and the U.S. perceptions of assertiveness in interpersonal relations and the conflicting views of how to maintain group harmony would be sources of misunderstanding and friction when such people interact'.

In the study by Leaper (2000) of parent–child interactions described earlier, it was found that there were higher levels of both assertion and affiliation in Latin American than European American families. While Leaper pointed out that this finding of collaborativeness or *familism* was consistent with other reports of Latino families, he also noted that care is needed in interpreting such findings, since other variables, including parent education and age, socioeconomic status, religion and family size, impact upon behaviour patterns. For example, Mexican-descent parents with higher education levels have been shown to hold more gender-egalitarian attitudes (Leaper and Valin, 1996). Furthermore, in his review of this area Rakos (1991, p. 13) concluded that, 'studies with diverse cultural groups generally find the normative level of self-reported assertive behavior generally approaches that of white Americans as the group's sociocultural similarity to mainstream American norms and values increases'.

Research shows that individuals use cultural expertise when choosing style of assertion. Thus, a study in Germany of the manner in which Turkish immigrants handled conflict situations found that the preferred style varied depending upon the interlocutor (Klinger and Bierbraver, 2001). When dealing with someone from the Turkish community a more indirect, nonconfrontational approach, typical of this cultural group, was usually employed. However, when dealing with a German a more direct, instrumental style, again in keeping with the norms of this target group, was used.

The above results present an opaque image of the relationship between cultural group and appropriate assertion. While it is clear that culture is a very important variable in the assertion equation, no hard-and-fast guidelines can be offered about how best to respond in any particular cultural context. Thus, Cheng and Chun (2008) found that the nature of the request in terms of degree of reasonableness was an important factor in distinguishing differences between Caucasian American and Chinese adults. While there was no difference between the two groups in relation to rejection of very reasonable or very unreasonable requests, the Caucasian Americans were significantly more likely than the Chinese to reject requests of moderate legitimacy. As Yoshioka (2000) in her review of this area pointed out, a key dimension of AT for sub-cultural groups is that of *message matching*. This involves a careful assessment of both situation and assertee to decide how best to match the specific message being delivered, and whether a sub-cultural or mainstream cultural response is most appropriate.

The assertee

A key aspect of assertion is the target person. From the above reviews, it is clear that the gender and cultural background of the assertee are core determinants of the effectiveness of assertive responses. However, the assertion level of the interlocutor is also important. In two early studies, Gormally (1982) found that assertive behaviour was rated more favourably by assertive individuals, while Kern (1982) discovered that low assertive subjects reacted negatively to assertive behaviour, whereas high assertive subjects generally devalued nonassertive behaviour. These findings suggest that decisions about when and how to apply assertion should be moderated by the assertive nature of the recipient.

Thus, the relationship with the interlocutor is of vital import in deciding how to be assertive. An interesting dimension of relationships was explored by Dickson *et al.* (2009) in relation to teasing behaviour (banter). They illustrated how teasing can be interpreted as either playfulness/joking or as derogation/aggression, since it usually has both friendly and hostile components. Between friends it is normally the former purpose that is served by banter and the humour is therefore two-way. In other contexts there would seem to be a dominance or control function prevalent, since high-status people can tease low-status people, but not usually vice versa. Banter has been shown to be a common feature of relationships between work colleagues, and, when used appropriately, to contribute to the process of relational development. Alberts (1992) pointed out that decisions about how to react to teasing behaviour are made on the basis of four main elements: the perceived goal of the teaser; background knowledge of and relationship with this person; the context in which the tease is employed; and the paralinguistic tone with which it is delivered. Where banter is used as a form of sarcasm, or 'put down', it is necessary to indicate assertively that such behaviour is unacceptable. This needs to be done skilfully to avoid accusations of not being able to take a joke.

Lewis and Gallois (1984) investigated the influence of friendship on assertiveness. They found that certain types of negative assertions (expression of anger, or difference of opinion) were more acceptable when made by friends as opposed to strangers. However, refusal of a request from a friend was perceived to be less socially skilled and more hurtful than refusal from a stranger. As a result, they recommended that with strangers it is 'wise to refrain from assertively expressing a difference of opinion or negative feelings, at least until the relationship is well established' (p. 366).

OVERVIEW

The three response styles reviewed in this chapter can be explained succinctly as follows:

1   aggressive – *talking at* others
2   assertive – *talking with* others
3   submissive – *talking little to* others.

Assertiveness is a very important social skill both in professional contexts and in everyday interactions. We feel hurt, aggrieved and upset if our rights have been violated. While, as explained in this chapter, assertiveness is not always the optimal response in every situation, it is essential to be able to employ this skill if other tactics fail. Yet, some individuals find it very difficult to be assertive. This is often related to upbringing, in that they may have been raised under a very strict regime by parents where they were seen and not heard, and learned in school that the quiet child who did as it was told was most approved of by the teacher. It can then be difficult in later life to overcome this residue of parental and educational upbringing. As summarised by Paterson (2000, p. 209):

> Assertiveness skills can be difficult to learn. Many of us grow up without learning to use them effectively. As well, assertiveness goes against our temptations. Sometimes we want to push other people to do our bidding. Sometimes we are desperately afraid of conflict. Assertiveness may mean holding back from our automatic ways of doing things.

One common pitfall is that individuals move from prolonged nonassertion straight into aggression, feeling they can no longer put up with being used, taken for granted or having their rights ignored. But such a sudden, and unexpected, explosion of anger is not the best approach, and indeed can destroy relationships. It is therefore important to employ assertiveness at an early stage, and in a skilled manner that recognises the rights of the other while also protecting one's own rights. This includes the use of embellishments to soften the impact of the assertive response. Research evidence has clearly shown that assertion skills are not innate – they are learned and can be improved. Once they are acquired, it becomes easier to stand up for oneself, to say 'no' without undue concern, to make reasonable requests and to regard oneself as equal to others. Our self-confidence and sense of self-worth are improved accordingly.

Chapter 12

Using your influence: the skill of persuasion

INTRODUCTION

PERSUASION AND INFLUENCE are omnipresent in human society (Dillard, 2010). As noted by Moons *et al.* (2009, p. 44), 'Persuasion is a pervasive and crucial component of social life'. We meet these change agents many times every day, and in different guises. Indeed, Forgas and Williams (2001, p. 7) noted that:

> The sophisticated ability of humans to influence, and be influenced by, each other is probably one of the cornerstones of the evolutionary success of our species, and the foundation of the increasingly complex forms of social organization we have been able to develop.

Consumers are exposed to an unending stream of commercial messages daily (on websites, TV, radio and newspaper adverts and billboard posters), all aimed at encouraging the target to adopt a service, idea or product (Larson, 2013). At this level, the persuasion attempt is directed towards the masses. Consequently, a vast volume of literature has been produced in this field, with research into the effects of TV and radio advertising, health promotion campaigns, posters, public relations interventions, and so on, attracting enormous interest (Jowett and O'Donnell, 2015).

However, in recent years there has been a growth of interest in influence and persuasion at the interpersonal level (Woodward and Denton, 2014). The main reason for this is the recognition that almost all exchanges between people involve some element of influence (Benoit and Benoit, 2008). As shown by Erb and Bohner (2007), influence is an integral part of human interaction. Even in the most informal encounters, such as when friends meet to 'hang out' together, they behave in such a way as to communicate liking for one another (through smiles, eye contact and verbal following). While these behaviours may be carried out without the goal consciously in mind, the purpose is clearly to influence the other person to maintain the friendship. In the work situation, persuasion is also endemic. Indeed, Mortensen (2008, p. 3) concluded that, 'Regardless of our actual job title, we all persuade – we all sell – for a living'.

Given the ubiquity and pervasiveness of influence in the social milieu, it is not surprising that, 'A long history of research has examined the methods we use to attempt to change someone's attitudes or behavior or to strengthen already established attitudes or behaviors' (Afifi, 2006, p. 53). Thus, Pratkanis (2007) identified a total of 125 tactics that we use to influence one another. These tactics have been found to be effective across a wide range of diverse social contexts (Levine, 2006). Knowledge of these is important, since it has been shown that 'Individuals vary greatly in their ability to use such tactics. Research findings indicate that such differences are related to success in a wide variety of occupations' (Baron and Markman, 2000, p. 109). This chapter navigates the large and complex terrain of persuasion, and identifies the central components thereof.

In terms of definition, while the terms influence and persuasion are often viewed as synonyms and used interchangeably, in fact there are four main differences between the two processes.

1   *Conscious awareness*. While it has been shown that a great deal of influence takes place at a subconscious level (Hogan and Speakman, 2006; Jarrett, 2008), persuasion attempts are carried out with clear and deliberate intent. For example, a film star who wears a certain brand of T-shirt on a TV show may *influence* young people to purchase a similar product, without consciously intending to do so. However, if the same film star had agreed to appear in a TV advert to promote this brand of T-shirt, then it would have been quite clear that a *persuasion* attempt was being made. Given this aspect of intentionality, interpersonal persuasion has been defined as, 'the conscious manipulation of face-to-face communication to induce others to take action' (Robbins and Hunsaker, 2014, p. 339). Taking this line of thought further, persuasion always involves influence, but influence does not always involve persuasion. This distinction was recognised by Hybels and Weaver (2011), who defined persuasion as the process that occurs when one person influences the values, beliefs, attitudes or behaviour of another.

2   *Resistance*. There is now considerable evidence to show that once people have made up their minds they become very resistant to change, even when it would be profitable, logical or socially desirable to do so (Chen *et al.*, 2013). Therefore, persuasion is required to effect change. Knowles and Riner (2007) identified overcoming resistance as a key defining feature of the process, noting that: 'Persuasion is only required when people feel "I don't like it!", "I don't believe it!", or "I won't do it!"… All persuasion, therefore is implicitly aimed at resistance.' Likewise, Sanders and Fitch (2001) highlighted that persuasion is influence when there is resistance, whereas

influence *per se*, 'is achieved by offering inducements that make it expedient or self-interested in the moment for that particular target person to do what is being asked, given his or her existing convictions and dispositions' (p. 263). They also made the important point that, 'not everything is a *persuadable*' (p. 268). Persuadable actions are those that are not obligatory, and as such there may well be resistance to what is being suggested. In a similar vein, Johnston (1994, p. 7) defined persuasion as, 'a voluntary change in beliefs, attitudes and/or behaviors'.

3   *Direction*. When we say that a persuasion attempt is being made, we usually assume that this process is one-way. Indeed, if both sides are simultaneously engaging in persuasive attempts, the interaction is usually a negotiation of some form. By contrast, interpersonal influence is a reciprocal process (Hsiung and Bagozzi, 2003). Thus, in a social encounter where person A is trying to persuade person B, both A and B will be concurrently engaged in a process of ongoing mutual influence.

4   *Success*. A final difference between the two terms is that persuasion is successful influence. As O'Keefe (2002, p. 3) pointed out, 'the notion of success is embedded in the concept of persuasion'. Thus, it does not make sense to say, 'I persuaded them to do it but they didn't'. However, it is possible to say, 'I influenced them but they still didn't do it'. Here, the person is indicating a shift or softening in attitude, but a failure at the behavioural level. In this way, influencing is often incremental, leading to eventual change, whereas persuasion usually refers to a specific change attempt. When parents perceive someone to be a 'bad influence' on their child, they believe that over a period of time this person will effect negative changes and that their son or daughter will eventually be led astray.

A distinction has also been made between 'hard' and 'gentle' persuasion. Pratkanis (2001) illustrated how in democratic societies *deliberative persuasion* is central. This involves debate, discussion, deliberation, argument and analysis – the process is two-way. By contrast, in authoritarian or autocratic regimes, leaders assume they know what others should think or want, and persuasion in the form of propaganda is employed to convince them that this is the case. In this latter form of *dictatorial persuasion*, communication is one-way and debate or dissent is discouraged. Deliberative persuasion has been shown to have the benefits of stimulating creative problem solving, fostering relationships and trust between individuals and developing greater consent for and commitment to what are regarded as group decisions. Dictatorial persuasion, on the other hand, results in an over-reliance on the leader to make decisions and give guidance, and a reduction in individual initiative. Members also have much less commitment to decisions imposed upon them to which they feel no sense of ownership. It also leads to hostility and distrust, making long-term group effort and relationships difficult to sustain. These findings have obvious ramifications for organisations, in that employees will respond more favourably to deliberative than dictatorial forms of persuasion.

PURPOSES OF PERSUASION

As shown by Johnston (1994), the goal of persuasion can take many forms. To take but five examples, it may include:

1   the elimination of an existing belief (e.g. that smoking is not bad for one's health);
2   a change in strength of an existing belief (from the position above to one where it is accepted that smoking can be bad for one's health);
3   the creation of a new belief (moving further from 2 above to believing that smoking is definitely bad for one's health);
4   a change in intentions to carry out an action (saying 'I now definitely intend to stop smoking');
5   a change in actual behaviour (stopping smoking).

In general terms, the six main goals of persuasion are shown in Box 12.1.

THE PERSUASION PROCESS

Figure 12.1 illustrates how the process of persuasion involves one person, the influencing 'agent', attempting to alter the beliefs, feelings, knowledge or behaviour of another, the 'target'. This has four main outcomes:

1   *Instant success.* It can be immediately effective, resulting in the intended changes to the target's beliefs, feelings, knowledge or behaviour.
2   *No change.* The target may simply reject the persuasion attempt and continue with the current response.
3   *Increased resistance.* There may not only be no change, but the target may also become very resistant to any future persuasion attempts from this agent. This process is referred to as the *boomerang effect*, which occurs when a persuasion attempt produces the opposite effect to the one originally anticipated (Byrne, 2009). For example, a flawed effort to persuade can backfire by strengthening the original position rather than changing it. As pointed out earlier, some degree of resistance by the target is a common feature of persuasion and ways of overcoming this must be formulated by the agent to ensure success (Knowles *et al.*, 2001). It should also be noted that resistance can take many forms. There are seven main resistance strategies used by targets to oppose persuasion attempts (Saucier *et al.*, 2014). These are:

(a)   showing *negative affect*, such as anger or other negative emotions;
(b)   using *counter arguments* to rebut the attempted persuasion;
(c)   *generating ideas* to reinforce and confirm one's current attitudes;
(d)   *assertion of confidence* by stating that nothing will alter one's views;
(e)   employing *source derogation tactics* to insult or dismiss the agent;
(f)   engaging in *social validation* by thinking about others who share one's views;
(g)   applying *selective exposure* by withdrawing from the encounter.

Box 12.1 The six main purposes of persuasion

The main goals served by the skill of persuasion are to achieve:

1 *Adoption.* Here the aim is to encourage targets to develop new responses – that is, to persuade them to *start doing or believing something.* Thus, a doctor may encourage an overweight individual to begin a diet or start an exercise regime, and to accept that weight loss will lead to better health

2 *Continuance.* The objective here is to encourage targets to *keep doing or believing something* at their current level of commitment. For example, if a sports team is top of their league, the main goal of persuasion would be maintenance of performance. Likewise, one goal of a priest should be to encourage devout members of his parish to maintain their faith

3 *Improvement.* The objective here is to get targets to perform at a higher level than at present. In other words, to get them to *do something better or have an increased level of belief.* The former is a common key goal of most educationalists. Thus, one reason teachers give their students detailed feedback on coursework is so that their next assignment may improve accordingly

4 *Deterrence.* Conversely, the objective may be to persuade targets not to develop a particular behaviour, so that they *do not start doing or believing something.* Indeed, this is the aim of many health education campaigns geared towards young people – to encourage them not to take up activities such as smoking, drug taking or drink driving, and not to form the view that such activities are 'cool'

5 *Discontinuance.* In this instance the goal is to get targets to desist from a current response – to persuade them to *stop doing or believing something.* This can often be the most difficult task for the persuader. Once behaviour patterns and beliefs have been learned they become resistant to change. For example, before new patterns of working can be introduced in an organisation, old practices have to be stopped. This can often be the most difficult aspect of such change. Humans are creatures of habit, and it is hard to 'unlearn' habituated patterns of behaviour and established belief systems

6 *Reduction.* Where it is deemed that targets may not be able to cease a certain action completely, the goal may be to encourage them to cut down and *do it less or believe it less strongly.* For example, it would be preferable if someone smoked 10 cigarettes a day rather than 20, or drank 3 pints of beer as opposed to 6

Likewise, in the work context, Yukl (2013) identified six main resistance strategies that are made to counter unwelcome persuasion requests:

(a) overt refusal to carry out the request;
(b) explanations or excuses as to why the request cannot be complied with

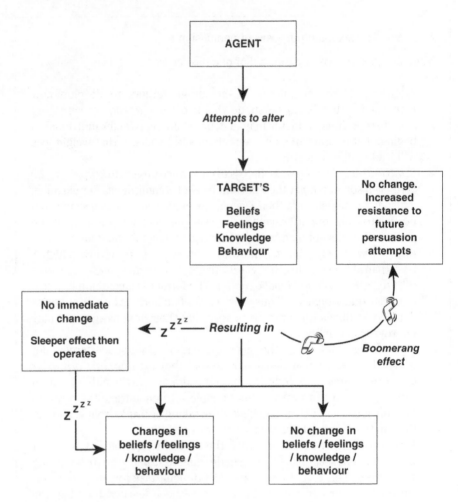

Figure 12.1 Persuasive communication: process and outcomes.

(c)   attempts to encourage the agent to alter or withdraw the request;
(d)   appeals to a higher authority to have the request removed;
(e)   delays in responding so that the requested action is not carried out;
(f)   pretending to comply while secretly attempting to sabotage the assignment.

4   *Delayed success.* There may be a time delay before the attempt proves successful. Here, a phenomenon known as, the *sleeper effect* occurs. As described by Allen and Stiff (1998, p. 176), 'The term *sleeper* derives from an expectation that the long-term effect is larger than the short-term effect in some manner (the effect is asleep but awakes to be effective later)'. Thus, a target may initially reject a persuasion attempt and yet some weeks or months later begin to accept it. In their meta-analysis of research studies, Allen and Stiff confirmed the existence of the sleeper effect.

This process often involves a separation or 'dissociation' between source and message (Foos *et al.*, 2015). For example, a message from a low-credibility source is likely to be rejected at the outset. With the passage of time, however, the message is further processed and also becomes de-coupled from its original source. The message content itself is remembered and becomes important – the source is now irrelevant. The target begins to say things like, 'I've changed my mind on that' or 'It's not quite so clear-cut as I used to think'. The sleeper effect is more potent when the target only discovers that the message is from a low-credibility source after having received the message (Kassin *et al.*, 2011). It can also be more powerful when people believe that their defence against a persuasion attempt was weak. In such cases, there is evidence that they then become less certain of their initial views, and demonstrate an increased vulnerability to later persuasion attempts (Tormala *et al.*, 2006).

Another important aspect to note here is that, even if persuasion attempts are not immediately successful in effecting actual changes in behaviour, they can still have a number of useful benefits. For example, Ohme (2001) itemised five positive effects of media influence attempts:

1   A clearer perception of reality. Thus, although many still smoke, most citizens of Western countries (including smokers) are now aware of the health risks associated with smoking as a result of media campaigns.
2   An increased awareness of the issue in general, and a possible enhanced receptivity to future messages on this topic. If you are a heavy drinker, messages about possible liver damage may not stop you drinking immediately, but could make you listen more carefully to such messages in the future.
3   Self-initiated information seeking about the topic – the wish to know more about it. Opportunities to read articles or watch TV programmes about the topic may be more likely to be taken once an initial interest has been stirred.
4   The stimulation of issue-related discussions with significant others. There can be an increased desire to ascertain what family, friends and work colleagues think of the issue.
5   The reinforcement of existing positive behaviour. For instance, health information messages about the importance of regular exercise reward those who currently take such exercise and encourage them to continue.

While the first four of these may not produce instant results, they can contribute to a 'slow burn' effect, resulting in later behavioural change.

Targets can also be encouraged to become more resistant to persuasion messages. There are two main methods whereby this can be achieved: forewarning and inoculation.

Forewarning

This refers to 'a strategy based on the simple assumption that warning people of an impending influence appeal enhances their vigilance and ability to resist it'

(Scheibe *et al.*, 2014, p. 273). As part of the strategy, the target audience is usually given information about the person or message they are about to encounter. The forewarning can come from (1) the speaker, or (2) someone who introduces this person, and so takes one of two forms, respectively:

1   *A persuasion intent statement.* This tells the target that a persuasion attempt is about to be made (e.g. 'I am going to present evidence to support the view that all drugs should be decriminalised').

2   *A topic and position statement.* This informs the target about the issue about to be presented and where the speaker stands on this (e.g. 'I now wish to introduce Jo Singh, a well-known supporter of animal rights, who hopes to convince you of the view that not only is it unethical to kill animals for food, but that as the dairy and related industries also involve considerable cruelty, you should adopt a vegan lifestyle').

In a meta-analysis of research in this field, the main conclusion reached by Benoit (1998, p. 146) was that: 'Forewarning an audience to expect a persuasive message tends to make that message less persuasive…regardless of type of warning'. However, Benoit found that to be effective the warning must come before the persuasion attempt. A message will not lose its persuasiveness if the warning is given after it has been delivered. Thus, it is not the information *per se* that affects persuasiveness, it is the forewarning. In this sense, prevention is essential. It appears that when targets are forewarned they adopt a less receptive frame of mind and become more resistant to the perceived 'interference'. In their meta-analysis of research, Wood and Quinn (2003) found forewarning to be an effective technique, showing how there is truth in the saying that to be forewarned is to be forearmed. For people who have to address an audience that has been forewarned, Benoit (1998) recommended the following five compensatory techniques in attempting to overcome such resistance:

1   be introduced by a credible third person;

2   stress a lack of personal bias on the issue;

3   ask the audience to keep an open mind;

4   emphasise that both sides of the argument have been given due consideration;

5   state that the target's best interests were considered – not just the speaker's.

Four 'reverse-psychology' approaches can also be employed in attempting to overcome resistance:

1   *Co-opting.* This is a method for attempting to minimise rejection by openly acknowledging it in advance (e.g. by saying, 'Your first reaction is likely to be to reject what I am about to say'). As expressed by Knowles and Linn (2004, p. 138), 'One of the ways to turn resistance against itself is to acknowledge it'. In such instances an appeal for *suppression* is useful. Here, the target audience is asked to suppress the instinctive denial response (e.g. 'I would like you to try to avoid the natural impulse

of immediately rejecting what I am about to say to you. Please hear me out and then make a judgement about what I have said').

2 *Ironic effect.* It is possible to get targets to do what you want by telling them to do the opposite. If I say to you, 'Don't think of a white bear', you will find it difficult not to think of a white bear. In this way, 'thought suppression can actually increase the thoughts one wishes to suppress instead of subsiding them' (Soetens *et al.*, 2006, p. 656). One common example of this is that people on a diet who try not to think about food often begin to think much more about food. This process is therefore also known as the *rebound effect*. The ironic effect seems to be caused by the interplay of two related cognitive processes (Byrne and Hart, 2009). This dual-process system involves, first, an intentional operating process, which consciously attempts to locate thoughts unrelated to the suppressed ones. Second, and simultaneously, an unconscious monitoring process tests whether the operating system is functioning effectively. If the monitoring system encounters thoughts inconsistent with the intended ones, it prompts the intentional operating process to ensure that these are replaced by appropriate thoughts. However, it is argued, the intentional operating system can fail due to increased cognitive load caused by fatigue, stress and emotional factors, and so the monitoring process filters the inappropriate thoughts into consciousness, making them highly accessible. They then can have a strong impact upon emotions, behaviour, and even dreams (Kozak *et al.*, 2007).

3 *Paradoxical suggestion.* This involves making a suggestion about the target person's future behaviour, but then indicating that perhaps it would be expecting too much and that the person might not be up to the task just yet (e.g. 'I am not sure you have reached the point where you feel you could do this. I'm worried about asking too much of you'). The rationale here is that when we are told that we may not be able to do something, paradoxically we often experience a stronger desire to do it (Knowles and Linn, 2004). This is a motivational technique in that the goal is to challenge the target indirectly to react to the perceived weakness by 'showing' the agent that the apparent lack of faith in the person's ability is misplaced. The target then becomes motivated to complete the suggested behaviour. This strategy should be employed when a relationship has been established, so that the stated lack of belief in the target's ability is seen in a caring light. However, with people of low self-esteem or low self-efficacy this approach needs to be used with care, as they may take the apparent lack of belief in their capability as a confirmation of their low level of worth or ability.

4 *Alternative-choice double-bind.* Using this technique, the agent devises 'creative' choices aimed at ensuring that targets carry out actions to which they may be initially resistant (Erickson and Rossi, 1975). For example, if a parent knows a child will resist going to bed, alternative choices can be introduced by saying to the child, 'Would you rather put on your pyjamas first or brush your teeth first?' The child is given a choice and has a desire to be the decision maker, but is in a double-bind in that both outcomes lead towards bed time. Similarly, a salesperson may say to a customer, 'Would you prefer the blue or the red?' Here, the offer is dual-positive, in that both alternatives lead subtly in the direction of a sale.

Reverse-psychology techniques are often employed in the therapeutic context (Sharf, 2016). However, while such techniques can be powerful, they are not without difficulties. The main problems are that they do not always work, and they are manipulative and indeed deceitful (Knowles and Riner, 2007). The target may take the agent's suggestions at face value and so act in the way opposite to that intended, or may refuse to participate at all. For reverse psychology to work, the agent must both have no moral qualms about engaging in subterfuge, and be fairly certain that the target will react as anticipated.

Inoculation

This is a stronger form of forewarning as it actively prepares targets to refute the messages that will be received (Dainton and Zelley, 2015). Research findings show inoculation to be an effective tactic for stimulating resistance (Parker et al., 2016). Inoculation messages can be affective or cognitive (Ivanov et al., 2009a). Emotional inoculation messages consist of 'affect-laden words, anecdotes, and opinionated statements' whereas cognitive inoculation messages are objective in tone with 'verifiable, falsifiable information, such as statistics, facts, and research findings' (Peau et al., 2001, p. 217). Inoculation attempts consist of two main components, *threat* (targets the affective level) and *refutational pre-emption* (targets the cognitive level). The effectiveness of these two mechanisms in inoculation has been well documented in a wide range of research studies (Pfau et al., 2009). The main aspects of each are:

- *Threat*. This involves warning targets about the imminent attack upon their attitudes or beliefs. All inoculation attempts have been shown to include threat, which in turn acts as a wake-up call for resistance. Thus, the objective is to mobilise targets to realise that their beliefs are about to be challenged, and to motivate them to pay attention to ways of dealing with it. This is the *anticipatory warning* stage of inoculation, when the emotions are stirred and the target is motivated towards action.
- *Refutational pre-emption*. Here, the likely future arguments with which the target will be faced are detailed, and counter-arguments are provided to refute each of these. This is the *anticipatory coping* stage, and it is at the epicentre of inoculation. The success of inoculation is affected by two main processes – delay and decay. Delay refers to the time it takes the target to generate counter-arguments with which to resist the message, while decay relates to the extent to which these arguments lose their force over time (Ivanov et al., 2009b). Techniques that reduce delay and protect against decay are therefore important in maximising the effectiveness of inoculation. Thus, it has been shown that the more effort that targets devote to the development of counter-arguments to possible future challenges, by engaging in what has been termed *cognitive work*, the greater is their resistance to later counter-persuasion attempts (Pfau et al., 2001). Another useful antidote to delay and decay is the technique of *rote learning*. Many religions and cults get members to rote learn sets

of beliefs, prayers and key statements so that they become embedded in their psyche, and as such very resistant to change. As part of this process, it is possible to get individuals to rote learn refutational arguments against future counter-messages.

A related tactic here is that of *anchoring*, which involves connecting the forthcoming new message to an already-established belief or set of values. It then becomes difficult to change one without the other. For example, a Roman Catholic priest discovers that a student in his parish will later hear a lecture from a pro-choice speaker on the rights of women to decide what to do with their own bodies. He may then attempt to 'anchor' the student by connecting the belief (1) that good and devout Catholics value the sanctity and sacredness of all life, to (2) an opposition to the future message in support of abortion.

Another form of pre-emption has been termed *stealing thunder*, which involves disclosing incriminating evidence about oneself or one's client, rather than have this revealed by someone else. For instance, defence lawyers in court will tell the jury negative facts about their client rather than giving the prosecuting attorney the opportunity to capitalise on this later. This gives the impression of openness and honesty. It also inoculates the target and so draws much of the poison from the sting of the potentially harmful detail. In their analysis of this phenomenon, Williams and Dolnik (2001) pointed out that stealing thunder is part of the process of *dissuasion*, which involves persuading people not to be swayed by something that could otherwise be influential. Their review of research concluded that: 'Stealing thunder has been shown to be an effective method of minimizing the impact of damaging information in a variety of different contexts' (p. 228).

STEPS TO SUCCESSFUL PERSUASION

Several *stage theories* have been put forward to explain the persuasion process (Weinstein and Sandman, 2002). These conceptualise a range of stages or steps that need to be gone through for the overall process to be successful. The most widely employed of these is the *transtheoretical model of change* initially developed by Prochaska and DiClemente (1992). This envisages five main stages.

1   *Precontemplation*. Here the person is not thinking about changing current behaviour or starting a new behaviour. There is no intention to change.
2   *Contemplation*. At this stage the person has been made aware of the issue and thought about the process of change, but is still ambivalent. No decision has been made about whether or not to act. Part of the person may want to change while another part does not. Change is always difficult (and even frightening), and so it does not happen without psychological upheaval.
3   *Preparing*. If the person decides that the benefits of change outweigh the costs, a decision is made to change. Preparations then have to be made to cope with this. Strategies need to be formulated about when, where and how the new response will be carried out. It may also involve publicly informing others about the intention to change.

4   *Action*. This is the implementation phase, when the person is actively involved in an overt attempt to carry out the behaviour. Others may need to be reminded that the new pattern of behaviour has deliberately been adopted, and is not an aberration.

5   *Maintenance*. Once a change has been made there is then the challenge of maintaining it. Behaviour change may meet with resistance from significant others and the person has to deal with this – to the extent of even altering friendship patterns.

A sequential model of the five stages is shown in Figure 12.2. Here it can be seen that the main outcomes of either behaviour change or no behaviour change are dependent upon whether or not there is progression through each stage. It is also

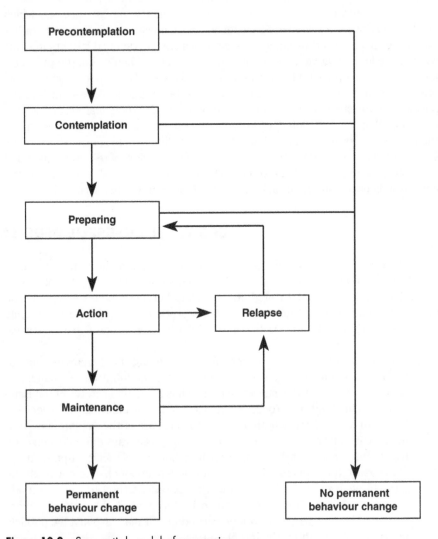

Figure 12.2 Sequential model of persuasion.

acknowledged that, even after the response has been implemented, relapse can take place. Where relapse occurs the individual either again prepares for action, or reverts to the former response pattern and abandons the new one. As explained in Chapter 10, after making an important decision individuals are affected by the process of *cognitive dissonance*, as doubts and anxiety are experienced about whether the decision was correct (Aronson *et al.*, 2007). This dissonance is eventually resolved in one of two ways. People can either become convinced that the decision was correct and so stay with it, or alternatively decide that a wrong decision was made and relapse to the former state of affairs. For effective persuasion, the target must be convinced in the long term about the rectitude of the decision taken. This is related to what is termed *regulatory fit* in the persuasion literature: when a message 'fits' with an individual's personal orientation then it is more likely to be assimilated and accepted (Petrou *et al.*, 2015). In this way, 'Persuasive messages are more effective when they are custom-tailored to reflect the interests and concerns of the intended audience' (Hirsh *et al.*, 2012, p. 578).

A more fine-grained 12-step sequential analysis of persuasion was presented by McGuire (1981), involving:

1 exposure to the message
2 attending to the message
3 becoming interested in it
4 understanding it
5 learning how to process and use it
6 yielding to it
7 memorising it
8 retrieving it when required
9 using it when making decisions
10 executing these decisions
11 reinforcing these actions
12 consolidating the decision based upon the success of the actions.

While each of these stages is important, they can be collapsed into five main steps (Figure 12.3). First, the message must be attended to if it is to have any

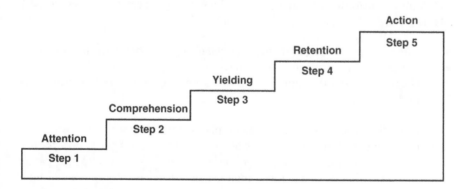

Figure 12.3 Five steps to successful persuasion.

impact. A message that is perceived to have a high level of direct relevance is more effective since, 'this enhanced personal relevance promotes greater attention, elaboration, message processing, and, ultimately, persuasion' (Noar *et al.*, 2009, p.113). Relevance therefore results in a higher degree of involvement by targets, and this has been shown to be a key factor in persuasion (Braverman, 2008). Those who are more actively involved pay more attention to the messages being delivered. However, as summarised by Buller and Hall (1998, p. 155) in their review of research into this stage:

> attention to persuasive messages is far from guaranteed; it is unstable, fickle, and capricious. Persuasive messages compete for receivers' consideration with other messages, environmental cues, and internal responses. As a result some messages receive detailed examination, whereas others remain ignored or only partially processed.

Buller and Hall investigated two types of distraction.

1   *Communication-irrelevant distractions*. These are stimuli extraneous to the interactive process that shift attention away from the speaker (e.g. intrusive noise). These lessen the power of persuasive appeals.
2   *Communication-relevant distractions*. This refers to stimuli intrinsic to the communication process (e.g. speaker attributes). When the distraction focuses upon positive aspects (e.g. attractiveness) persuasion is enhanced. However if attention is paid to negative features (e.g. poor speech pattern) persuasibility diminishes.

The second step in the model shown in Figure 12.3 is that the target person must fully understand what is being said. The importance of message delivery in ensuring comprehension will be discussed in more depth later in the chapter. Third, the message must be accepted, in that the person has to yield to it. This is at the heart of persuasion, and much of this chapter is concerned with techniques whereby acceptance can be encouraged. Fourth, the target has to retain or remember the message. Finally, the acid test is whether the person carries out the action and implements the recommended response. As discussed in Chapter 2, attitudes encompass three elements, often referred to as the 'ABC' of attitudes:

•   Affect – one's feeling and emotions regarding the object of the attitude.
•   Behaviour – how one actually behaves towards the other.
•   Cognitions – the thoughts, beliefs and knowledge one has concerning that under focus.

Long-term changes in behaviour usually necessitate changes in the other two aspects. An important distinction has been made between *private acceptance*, which produces attitude change, and *public compliance*, where the person complies with what is being recommended but does not really change inner beliefs or feelings (Hargie *et al.*, 2004). Retention and implementation of new responses are dependent on private acceptance.

COGNITIVE ROUTES TO PERSUASION

Dual-process models of persuasion posit the existence of two cognitive routes in the processing of persuasive messages. The *elaboration likelihood model* (Petty and Cacioppo, 1986) identified these as:

1   *Central route.* Here the target is aware that a persuasion attempt is being made, and consciously examines the advantages and disadvantages thereof before a final decision is taken (Griffin *et al.*, 2014). The *cognitive-response model* (Wright, 1980) demonstrated how individuals using this rational approach relate incoming material to existing knowledge and beliefs. For a persuasion attempt to be successful the message must receive a favourable evaluation during this cognitive elaboration process.

2   *Peripheral route.* In this case, information tends to be processed at a subconscious level, and the target is not aware that a persuasion attempt is being made. There is scant analysis or scrutiny of message content, and the response is more intuitive. The emotional state of the target is important, since, as shown in Box 12.2, it has been found that people in a happy or positive mood are less likely to process messages systematically via the central route than are those in a sad or negative state (Mitchell, 2000). Thus, establishing a 'feel-good' sense in the target encourages peripheral processing.

For example, a television advert may sell a particular brand of car by presenting details of its price and features and systematically comparing these to those of its rivals (central route strategy). An alternative approach would be to show lots of very attractive people having great fun as they drive the car past charming locations in bright sunshine under a blue cloudless sky, with a popular soundtrack playing in the background, and ending with a shot of the car and

---

Box 12.2 Negative and positive mood and persuasion

Negative mood is associated with:

- central processing of information
- a cognitive, systematic style of argument processing
- more time spent on the evaluation of persuasive appeals
- stronger arguments being more successful than weaker ones

Positive mood is associated with:

- peripheral processing of persuasion attempts
- a passive, less rational approach to the evaluation of information
- much more rapid processing of incoming information
- no differential being made between weak and strong arguments

---

a voice-over stating: 'It's out there' (peripheral route strategy). The latter is an attempt to plant a subconscious association between the car, being happy and being part of the beautiful people 'set'. If this were processed centrally the viewer would be asking questions such as: 'What does it mean to say that it's out there?' or 'How does buying this car bring with it a guarantee that I will be driving it with a beautiful young person sitting beside me?' However, the fact is that most TV adverts are not centrally processed, but rather are dealt with through the peripheral route. They are successful because they hit us at the more vulnerable subconscious level.

Message processing is moderated by a range of factors, including the cognitive ability and motivation of the target (O'Keefe, 2006). To take an example, there is a greater likelihood that those who have undergone third-level education will centrally evaluate the arguments being presented by a politician, while those with a basic education may be more influenced by a feeling of whether or not they like this person. However, if the better-educated target has no interest whatsoever in politics, then the likelihood of peripheral processing is increased. An important difference between the two routes is that attitudes formed via the central route are more persistent over time and more resistant to change (Haugtvedt and Petty, 1992). This is because the individual has thought through the process and made a conscious decision that is then likely to influence behaviour directly over a prolonged period. The inclusion in a message of rhetorical questions phrased in a leading manner (see Chapter 5) encourages greater engagement by the target. This, in turn, increases the likelihood of an elaborated consideration of the arguments, leading to greater resistance to opposing arguments (Blankenship and Craig, 2006). An example of this strategy would be the insertion of a rhetorical question such as the following into an argument encouraging greater government spending in the university sector: 'Wouldn't you agree therefore that money spent on higher education is a valuable investment that will have many positive benefits for society?'

Attempts to change attitudes that have been formed as a result of a cognitive elaboration process are more easily resisted, as the counter-arguments will have already been given consideration. By contrast, decisions taken via the peripheral route have been made without careful thought, and so are more vulnerable to counter-arguments. As noted by Quine et al. (2002, p. 176), '"central route" processing produces attitudes that have temporal persistence and are predictive of behaviour and resistant to change, while peripheral route processing is typified by absence of argument scrutiny and produces only temporary attitude change'.

Having said this, it must also be noted that the peripheral route is ubiquitous in human encounters. Cialdini (2007) argued that the fixed-action patterns that guide the behaviour of most animals also occur in humans. In other words, our behaviour becomes hard-wired and we respond without thinking. We do not have the time or cognitive space to analyse and evaluate the hundreds of persuasion attempts that impinge upon us every day. As a result we make short-cut decisions to save time and energy. These decisions are, in turn, guided by a set of core processes, or *heuristics* (Burger, 2007), that directly influence our behaviour and are for the most part based upon valid reasoning. Such behaviour-guiding templates are the keys that can unlock the doors to persuasibility in others. To use another metaphor, they are the triggers that fire compliance behaviours. As such, people can be manipulated by their use. For example, the aphorism that 'you get what you pay for' is usually true. The more you pay for a car, a hotel room or a watch, the better it is likely to be. Thus, we expect to pay more for the best. Knowing that this is the case, a sharp operator may take advantage of the 'more-expensive-is-best' short-circuit process in potential buyers by inflating the price of goods to make them appear to be of higher quality.

In interpersonal encounters much of what persuades us is processed peripherally. For example, we do not usually consciously rate others on their level of attractiveness, and are not aware on a moment-by-moment basis whether another person is smiling, is humorous, stands close to us, uses our first name, praises us, and so on. These behaviours are processed via the peripheral route, but they all affect the outcome of persuasion attempts. Likewise, if we go to the bar with someone and the person buys us a drink, we do not usually consciously think that we are in debt to this person and must reciprocate. Rather, we naturally feel this pressure and so the likelihood is that the reciprocation auto-pilot kicks in and we buy the next round. Indeed, if we become aware that a direct attempt is being made to persuade us to do something, we begin to process information centrally. Then we may become suspicious of the smiles and praise we are receiving or wonder why this person is offering us something with no obligation. Under such circumstances a compliance attempt is likely to boomerang.

PERSUASION PROOFS

The study of persuasion has a long tradition. The classical era of scholarship in this field ran from 500 BC to AD 300 and included notable scholars such as Plato, Aristotle and Cicero. It was the Greek philosopher Aristotle who provided the first detailed analysis of persuasion. He identified three main persuasion categories

1   *Ethos*: here the credibility of the persuader is highlighted.
2   *Logos*: here the rationality of the message is focused upon.
3   *Pathos*: this involves appeals to the emotions of the target.

These are now known respectively as *personal proofs, logical proofs* and *emotional proofs*, although it should be realised that they are not functionally discrete categories as there are areas of overlap between them, and they are inter-linked. During persuasion attempts, techniques from each area can be used in combination, and indeed Aristotle believed that the most effective appeals contain a balanced mix of the three. However, for the purposes of analysis it is useful to examine each separately.

Personal proofs

One of the most important components in the persuasion equation is the nature of the agent. In order to be persuaded we first have to be convinced of the *bona fides* of the person who is trying to persuade us. There are four main determinants of personal proof: power, the relationship, attractiveness and humour.

Power

The association between power and persuasion has been clearly established (Schulze and Pishwa, 2015). In their review of interpersonal power, which they define as 'having the discretion and the means to asymmetrically enforce one's will over others' (p. 139), Sturm and Antonakis (2015) demonstrate how its importance in shaping the behaviour of others has long been recognised. 'It is clear that power is a core determinant for gaining compliance in many contexts' (Robertson, 2013). Tourish and Wohlforth (2000, p. 23) illustrated how, 'human behavior is driven by an impulse to *conform to authority*'. It is therefore hardly surprising that agents are likely to use any power they possess to ensure such conformity. What is termed 'the iron law of power' means that people with greater power tend to use it as and when required to get their own way (Hargie *et al.*, 2004). Thus, while power may not be the first shot fired in a battle of wills, it will be brought into play at some stage to ensure compliance (Bendahan *et al.*, 2014). Given its importance, it is not surprising that we are influenced by the power of the source. But how, and in what ways, are we influenced?

This question can best be answered by examining the classic delineation of types of power initially identified by French and Raven (1959), that then became the accepted standard in the field (Raven, 1992). This includes six forms of power. The first three of these (legitimate, reward and coercive) emanate from the ability of the agent to determine and control the target person's outcomes. The last three (information, referent and expert) are purely to do with influence and here the target makes a willing decision to co-operate.

Legitimate power

In essence, the bases of this power are rights and duties. Some people, by virtue of their position, have a legitimate right to request certain types of compliance from others, who in turn have a duty to comply. The power resides in the position. The holder of the power is *in authority*. Thus, a police office has considerable power over citizens. If requested by an officer in uniform to move our car we are much more likely to comply than if asked by someone dressed in casual clothes. But the power only remains while the person is performing the job, so that when the officer is off duty, or retired, this is relinquished. Legitimate power is attached to the role, not the person. It is also limited to the functions of the role. For instance, the security guard in the building where we work may legitimately ask us for identification, but has no power to request that we work overtime. In addition, this is a two-way street. Both managers and subordinates wield legitimate power. While the former has the authority to direct and control the latter as they perform their job, the latter can insist that set procedures be carried out by the former in accordance with statutory requirements (e.g. appraisal interviews). Indeed, the introduction of initiatives such as the Patients' Charter, Citizens' Charter and Bill of Rights has empowered those who formerly had little such formal, legitimate authority. Interestingly, people often excuse their behaviour on the basis that someone with legitimate power told them to carry it out. The ultimate example of this was the defence plea of the Nazi leaders at the Nuremberg war crime trials following the Second World War: 'I was only following orders'.

Reward power

Those who have control over the administration of rewards wield considerable power. As discussed in Chapter 4, the impact of reinforcement upon performance is both far-reaching and ubiquitous. This is learned from a very early age. Young children soon realise that parents have control over valued resources, and that they often have to carry out certain tasks in order to receive these. They also quickly learn that they, too, have similar power over parents and so begin to trade rewards (e.g. 'If I get an A-grade will you buy me a bicycle?'). Throughout life, those who are the controllers of the rewards that we seek have power over us. Thus, lecturers have reward power over students, as do employers over employees. However, again this is a two-way process. Employees can reward their employer by working harder, and students their professors by turning up for class and appearing motivated. Social rewards such as praise are potent forms of power (see Chapter 4).

Coercive power

Those who are able to administer punishments also have considerable power. To continue with the earlier example, police officers possess this form of power, and we are therefore likely to obey their request, for example, to move our car from a restricted parking zone. We know that if we do not we are likely to receive a fine. There is a symbiotic relationship between reward and coercive power. Usually someone who can reward us can *ipso facto* also punish us (e.g. by withholding the rewards). Thus, parents can both reward their children (e.g. by allowing them to say up late to watch a TV programme) and punish them (e.g. by sending them to bed early). However, we tend to like those who reward us and dislike those who threaten or punish us. It is therefore wise to remember the advice proffered by Machiavelli in *The Prince*, written in 1514, that those in power should 'delegate to others the enactment of unpopular measures and keep in their own hands the distribution of favours' (Bull, 1961, p. 106). One reason for this is that the norm of exchange means that those who have been punished are likely to seek retribution, while those who have been rewarded seek to reciprocate the favours they have received.

Information power

Here, the content of the message is the basis of the power. Those who are 'in the know' are in a privileged position. The holders of information that is 'inside', 'top secret' and 'classified' have considerable power – they can keep this secret or share it with others. Indeed, bribery and blackmail are based upon the fact that someone has access to information that s/he knows someone else either wishes to find out or to remain hidden, respectively. Some managers adopt a policy where they inform employees purely on a 'need-to-know' basis. In other words, they only tell them what they need to know to do their job. The problem here is that staff also have access to vital information (e.g. that a piece of production equipment is about to malfunction) and they may retaliate by withholding this from management who adopt this approach. Research consistently shows that employees value managers who share as much information with them as they can (Hargie et al., 2004). If information is power, then this power should be used benignly within organisations.

Information can be powerful in another way. If I want you to stop smoking, I could give you some material to read that clearly documents the dangers of this practice. This may then persuade you to change your attitude towards smoking. Where the information is perceived to be objective and accurate and includes statistical details (e.g. the percentage of smokers compared to non-smokers who contract serious illnesses), its potency is heightened (Allen et al., 2000). Furthermore, the amount of information used in persuasive messages is important, and, here, more is better. As shown by Tormala and Petty (2007, p. 17), the 'numerosity effect, whereby presenting more persuasive information leads to more persuasion, is quite pervasive'.

Referent power

This relates to the power of the reference group. Our behaviour is shaped to a considerable extent by our wish to belong to, and be accepted by, certain groups of people (Haslam and Reicher, 2008). As summarised by Dillard et al. (2007, p. 467), 'It is well established that individuals often look to others to determine how to behave and what opinions to hold'. Thus, we are likely to adopt the response patterns of those we identify with, like, and to whose group we aspire. The widely used marketing technique of product endorsement by well-known and popular personalities is a good example of the use of referent power as a tool of influence. In many cases the celebrity has no real knowledge of or insight into the product being endorsed, but this does not negatively impact upon the power of the message. Sorenson et al. (2001) used the term *misplaced authority* to refer to the use of celebrities to endorse specialised products in this way. One example is when an actor who plays the role of a doctor in a TV series is used to advertise and recommend a medical product. The actor has no actual medical expertise or authority but an implicit or inferred link is planted in the target's mind.

In a similar vein, hotels and restaurants often have signed photographs of great and good clients prominently displayed. The implication is that to be in such an establishment is to be in with the 'in crowd'. Salespeople use another form of reference power termed *ubiquity technique* when they tell a target that lots of relevant and significant others are now using a particular item. Research has shown that this process of using *social proof* to validate the acceptability of a product or behaviour by dint of the fact that it is used by significant others is a highly effective compliance-gaining technique (Cialdini, 2007). Thus, sports stars are paid fortunes just to wear or use a certain product, as the producers know this will trigger enormous referent group sales from those who wish to emulate their hero. This became known as the *wannabe phenomenon*, after the thousands of teenage girls who wanted to be like the pop star Madonna (Hargie *et al.*, 2004).

Among teenagers, referent power in the form of peer pressure is particularly potent. As mentioned in Chapter 9, at this age the need to be accepted by peers is at its strongest, and so certain types of fashion simply *must* be followed. When this is compounded by the fact that the attachment to referent media symbols (music, sports and film stars) is at a high level, the potential for manipulation is huge. Managers of male pop music stars have long realised the value of this human phenomenon. A few planted female fans beginning to scream at a concert sets the example for the rest so that a cacophony of screaming soon ensues. As expressed by Cialdini (2007, p. 116), 'one means we use to determine what is correct is to find out what other people think is correct...We view a behaviour as more correct in a given situation to the degree that we see others performing it'. Interestingly, to pursue our example, this means that the young females then have a high level of involvement in the occasion and so do not evaluate it critically through the central route (e.g. they do not study the extent to which the singers are singing in tune). Peripheral processing is dominant as they enjoy their heightened emotionality, and rate the concert to be a great success. All of this in turn leads to increased merchandising sales (CDs, T-shirts, posters, etc.).

Referent power is most potent under two conditions. First, if we are *uncertain* about how to behave in a situation we follow the 'herd instinct' by looking to members of our reference group for guidance, and copying what they do. This is summed up in the well-known aphorism, 'Monkey see, monkey do'. Second, we are more likely to be influenced by *similar* others. For example, if a female teenager goes to a party where all the females are dancing in a group, while the males are sitting round a table, she is more likely to join the dancing group. This is part of the wider process of *conformity* in groups, given that: 'Social influence implies a pressure towards conformity with individual or group beliefs and behaviors' (Vishwanath, 2006, p. 325). While this will be discussed in more depth in Chapter 14, it is worth noting here that when we are in the presence of others, there is strong overt or covert pressure to agree with the views of the majority, and follow group norms. As noted by Ho and McLeod (2008, p. 193), in relation to the *spiral of silence theory*, 'individuals, driven largely by the fear of isolation, scrutinize their environment to evaluate the climate of opinion'. Two needs guide our behaviour in such circumstances – the need to be accepted and the need to know what is the right thing to do (Aronson *et al.*, 2007). These are powerful determinants in shaping our attitudes and behaviour.

In a classic study in this field, Sherif (1936) used the *autokinetic phenomenon* (where a tiny bulb in a pitch-black room appears to move if stared at for a few minutes) to study conformity. The bulb does not actually move, since this is an illusion caused by neural processes and unconscious eye movements. Sherif asked small groups of subjects to estimate the distance the bulb had moved. Interestingly, two things happened. First, after some discussion, each group eventually came to an agreement about the movement distance. Second, different groups differed widely in their estimates. Furthermore, once an estimate had been agreed upon it became internalised and resistant to change. Consequently, when a member from a group with a previously 'socially anchored' score was placed in a new group, the person persisted with the estimate developed in their initial group. In this way, the reference group score was internalised and influenced future behaviour. The fact that the subjects had participated in formulating the norm meant that they were more committed to the decision. A fascinating real-life variant of Sherif's experiment occurred in the Republic of Ireland in the 1980s when some people became convinced that statues outside churches were moving. This 'movement' was caused by the *autokinetic phenomenon*, but huge crowds gathered each evening and the massed throng convinced one another that a miracle was being witnessed.

In a second famous study on conformity, Asch (1952) developed a system wherein subjects were required to choose publicly which one of three lines matched a reference or 'target' line in length (Figure 12.4). The task was very simple, so that when it was completed individually few subjects made any errors of judgement. However, by placing a naïve subject next to last in a line of confederates who all concurred on an incorrect choice of line, the pressure to conform could be measured. Asch found that only 25 per cent of subjects did not conform at all to the incorrect majority, while 33 per cent conformed on more than half of the trials. Some 5 per cent conformed on all the blatantly incorrect decisions. When interviewed later, those who conformed admitted that they disagreed with the others but felt under pressure to concur. As aptly described in an earlier paper by Asch (1940, p. 455), what occurred represented, 'a change in the object

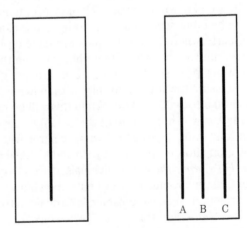

Figure 12.4   The Asch experiment: the subject's task was to state publicly which line on the right matched the reference line on the left.

of judgment, rather than in the judgment of the object'. In other words, the decision was not internalised, and so subjects demonstrated public compliance but
not private acceptance. This was confirmed in a neat reversal of the study procedures, in which Asch ran experiments where there was only one confederate
who made the clearly incorrect decision on each trial. In these instances, the
group of naïve subjects strongly affirmed the correctness of their decision and
treated the single deviating confederate with bemusement and scorn. Likewise,
in yet another variation Asch had the experimenter inform the naïve subjects
that as they had arrived late for the experiment they would have to write down
their answers rather than speak them aloud. In this experimental condition, the
subjects did not conform to the group norms, thus showing that the normative
pressures were social rather than informational.

Expert power

We live in the age of 'the expert'. In courtrooms, on TV screens and in newspapers, expert sources are used to give a definitive perspective on issues. This is
because people who are perceived to be experts, in that they have specialised
knowledge or technical skill, have high persuasive power. Here the basis of
the power is the extent to which the agent is seen as *an authority*. As shown
in Box 12.3, this type of power is conveyed by what are known as the 'three
Ts' – titles, threads and trappings.

The acid test of expert power is credibility. In his review of research in
this field, Pratkanis (2007, p. 31) concluded, 'the advice "be credible" should
be heeded by all who seek to persuade'. Indeed, Clampitt (2013, p. 160) noted
that 'every message has a credibility tag attached to it that determines, to a
large extent, how that message will be treated'. If the source of the message
is regarded as lacking in credibility, then it will have little persuasive power.
Thus, Schutz (1998) showed how attacks upon the credibility of a source who
has negatively evaluated someone can serve to weaken the force of the criticism. Gass and Seiter (2014) identified three important features of credibility.
First, it is a *perceptual phenomenon* – it is the target who decides whether a
particular source is credible or not; the same person may be regarded as credible by one target and not credible by another. Second, it is *situational*, in that
a person may be regarded as credible in one context but not in another. Third, it
is *dynamic* in that perceptions of credibility can change over time; someone we
once perceived to be highly credible may eventually seem less so.

Judgements of credibility are based upon two factors, competence and
trustworthiness. We judge competence based upon the extent to which people
'know their stuff'. If we go to a store to buy a computer system and the assistant
keeps admitting insufficient knowledge of the technical details of the equipment
and continually seeks advice from someone in the office, we will not see that person as being an expert, and so that individual's advice will carry little power. Part
of this is to do with confidence, in two senses. First, we need to be confident in
the person's expertise. Second, the agent must behave in a confident manner. We
would never be taken in by a 'no-confidence trickster'. The counter-balance to

---

Box 12.3 The three Ts of expert power

1 *Titles* are ubiquitous across all societies (e.g. Queen, Chief, President, Emperor). Powerful people use them to set themselves apart from others. The power of titles is illustrated by the way they are sought and used. Schoolchildren are introduced to them from an early age (Principal, Vice Principal, etc.) and they acquire importance thereafter. In the UK, the Honours system dispenses a huge range of titles every year (Lord, Lady, Sir, Member of the British Empire, etc.). These carry no monetary value but the social cachet attached means that there is no shortage of people eager to accept them. Similarly, employees often work much longer hours for little or no more money just by being given a designated title such as Unit Co-ordinator. In organisations, titles often reflect both the job level and expertise of the individual (e.g. Chief Technician). Because we are so accustomed to the role of titles we give respect to those who hold important ones. Thus a Professor of Nuclear Physics is perceived as having a high level of expertise in this field, and so will be more influential when speaking on this topic

2 *Threads* refer to the specialised clothes worn by experts to set them apart from others. Examples abound, from the fire officer's uniform, to the vicar's black robes and white dog collar, to the 'power' suits worn by business people. While some of these clothes may be functional, for the most part their purpose is that of clearly setting the expert apart from the general populace

3 *Trappings* are all the paraphernalia used to convey specialised knowledge or know-how. This encompasses framed certificates on the wall, specialist books on shelves or sophisticated pieces of equipment. For example, for the layperson a visit to the dentist entails an encounter with a baffling array of all kinds of strange apparatus, including a special chair, unusual lights and various implements for probing, drilling, filling and extracting. All of these combine to convey the impression of a high level of expertness

---

competence is trust. If someone is perceived to be highly competent but untrustworthy, that person's credibility rating drops dramatically. Trust has been shown to be central to successful outcomes in interpersonal encounters involving persuasion attempts, such as buyer–seller dyads (Andersen and Kumar, 2006). Trust may be based on our previous experience of the source, upon what others have told us about the person, or upon perceived neutrality. In relation to the latter, we will place more trust in a colleague who tells us that her new *Nevercrash* computer is superb, than in a highly competent salesperson in the *Nevercrash* store who gives us the same story. The former has no personal stake in selling the message and so is more credible.

Thus, in terms of expert power, we give less credence to those whom we regard as honest if they are incompetent, and tend to have lower trust in those with a vested interest regardless of their level of expertise. One highly influential event is when people argue against their own interest. For example, in the following statements we are more likely to be influenced by A than B.

A: 'I'm a meat eater myself, but I have read the research and it does show that a vegetarian diet is better for your health.'

B: 'As a committed vegetarian I have read the research and it shows that a vegetarian diet is better for your health.'

Staying with the vegetarian theme, on one occasion I was at a conference and went to the local dining area for an evening meal. Looking for vegetarian food, I tried a few restaurants without much luck. I then visited an Italian restaurant, where after I had explained my requirements, the owner said she could certainly cater for me but she would recommend the Spanish restaurant in the same complex as it had a good variety of choice for vegetarians. I explained that I had been there but the waitress I had spoken to had told me they did not really do much in the way of vegetarian food. The owner said that was untrue as she knew the range of food and would recommend it. Her demeanour was most helpful and she was knowledgeable about vegetarian cuisine, but she was also arguing against her own interest in terms of losing my business. The result was that I ended up staying in her restaurant for the meal. My trust in her had increased as a result of her perceived lack of bias.

A meta-analytic review has shown that testimonial evidence is an effective influencing technique (Kim *et al.*, 2012). This involves the use of statements by experts that support the speaker's message. A good example is the fact that in this book scholarly sources have been regularly cited to back up arguments. For this effect to be impactful, the supporting source must have high credibility and the evidence cited has to be believable. Interestingly, when people are in the middle of a discussion, the introduction of testimonial evidence serves to make the impact of this technique even more powerful (Reinhard, 1998). Thus, it is useful to have relevant sources to refer to during discussions.

The relationship

We are much more likely to be influenced by those with whom we have developed a close relationship. In fact, the link between interpersonal relationships and the persuasion process is the focus of one of the best-selling popular self-help books in this field (having sold over 16 million copies): *How to Win Friends and Influence People,* by Dale Carnegie. It has long been known that the more similar people are, the greater will be their liking for one another – this is termed the *law of attraction* (Byrne, 1971). Indeed, the phenomenon of *homophily* has been found to be of central importance in the communication process (Wolvin and Coakley, 1996). Homophily refers to the extent to which people share significant similarity in terms of aspects such as age, dress, appearance, cultural background, religion, political outlook, educational level, social status, habits, interests, beliefs, values and attitudes. Just as birds of a feather flock together, so people who perceive they share significant commonalities tend to form bonds more readily. In highlighting the potency of similarity as an influencing weapon, Cialdini (2014, p. 162) noted, 'those who want us to like them so that we will comply with them can accomplish that purpose by appearing similar to us in a wide variety of ways'. Part of this involves communication accommodation, whereby in order to enhance relational development we adapt our behaviours to converge with, or become similar to, those of the interlocutor (Hargie, 2014). The opposite of homophily is *heterophily*, where individuals have major differences across these dimensions. In essence, the greater the heterophily, the more difficult the influence process becomes.

In a meta-analysis of studies in the field, Miller *et al.* (2001) found that perceived similarity to another was associated with strong feelings of sympathy or empathy for that person if he was in a difficult situation. However, this was moderated by whether or not the person was thought to be responsible for the predicament. Thus, if an individual's need for help (e.g. money) is regarded as being due to external causes (e.g. being burgled), levels of sympathy and empathy are significantly higher than if the cause seems to be personal (e.g. spending too much on drink, drugs or gambling).

In addition to similarity, relational liking is improved by six other main factors.

1   Increased contact under positive circumstances. As we get to know people our liking for them tends to increase, providing this takes place within a conducive context. Even a few minutes of initial relational communication with a stranger prior to that person making a persuasion attempt can significantly increase the success rate (Burger, 2007).

2   Physical attractiveness. Beautiful people tend to be liked better than unattractive ones. This is discussed further below.

3   Association with success. Successful people act as a form of social magnet that attracts others. It is as if we are drawn to them in the hope that some of their glitter will rub off on us. We might be able to share in their success or be seen to be successful just by being with them. So powerful is this drive that people visit wax museums to look at and be photographed beside waxwork models of famous people.

4   Praise. We tend to like people who give us valued social rewards (see Chapter 4).

5   Use of less formal name. There is a whole psychology to the use of names, whether titles (Professor), formal address (Mr, Mrs), first name, pet name or nickname. As relationships deepen, forms of address become less formal. Spouses rarely address one another by title, and more often use pet names (e.g. honey, sweetheart). Salespeople are usually trained to get on first-name terms with clients as soon as possible to deepen the relationship. At the other end of the continuum, there is the process of *de-humanisation*. When individuals are not to be treated as humans the labels attributed to them reflect this. Thus, terrorists use derogatory terms such as 'legitimate target', 'collaborator' or 'traitor' for those they plan to murder.

6   Eating together. As discussed by Hargie *et al.* (2004), food and drink are essential for human survival and we have an innate drive to seek and protect our sources of sustenance. Although food and drink are plentiful in the Western world, the instinct remains. This means that we usually choose to eat, 'have a cuppa' or go for a drink with people that we like and trust. The ubiquitous business breakfasts and lunches therefore serve a very useful function as part of the process of influence. They help to cement the bonds between people and thereby lubricate the flow of commerce.

As Hargie *et al.* (2000) found, the existence of a good relationship allows for the expression of negative emotions from professional to client (e.g. anxiety, frustration). For example, a patient who is trying to move away from drug abuse, and who perceives the health professional as someone who genuinely cares, is more likely to accept statements such as, 'Look, what you are doing to yourself and your family is just awful. You are harming yourself and causing a great deal of grief to everyone who cares about you.' Indeed, when expressed in the context of a positive relationship, such statements of negative affect have been shown to be related to greater adherence to the advice and direction offered. This is because the communication of genuine concern is likely to be reciprocated by the wish of the target person to sustain the balance of the relationship, and so comply. The forceful delivery of negative messages from a liked and respected agent also serves to heighten the person's awareness of the gravity of the behaviour.

Attractiveness

As discussed in Chapter 10, there is now an abundance of research to show that good-looking people are both well regarded and persuasive (Brooks *et al.*, 2014; Petroshius and Newell, 2015). They have greater credibility, and are perceived to be higher in expertise, trustworthiness and likeability. Thus, physically attractive fund-raisers obtain more donations and attractive politicians more votes than their less attractive counterparts (Goodman-Delahunty and Howes, 2016). For individuals to optimise their persuasiveness they should therefore maximise their attractiveness (Reinhard *et al.*, 2006). It is also the case that initial judgements of physical attractiveness are moderated by psychological, sociological, relational and contextual influences (Duck, 1995). Features such as sense of humour, similarity to the other person, attentiveness, competence and sensitivity all affect overall ratings of attractiveness. These aspects can be employed by an influencing agent to make full use of the power of attraction.

Humour

Meyer (2000, p. 328) pointed out that, 'Use of humor clearly enhances one's leadership and persuasive influence because of the nearly universal admiration of this skill (in moderation – overuse of humor can lower credibility)'. Of course, to be effective the humour has to be appropriate to the target (Riesch, 2014) and suitable

---

Box 12.4 Advantages of humour in persuasion

Humour can facilitate persuasion by:

- building rapport and making the target more favourably disposed towards the agent – we like people who make us laugh and are therefore more likely to be influenced by them
- encouraging the target to attend more closely to the message – humour is engaging and increases our attentiveness
- producing in the target a feeling of relaxation and related increased receptivity to the message
- increasing retention by making the message more memorable
- filling cognitive space – if we are laughing, we are not thinking of counter-arguments
- encouraging peripheral rather than central processing of the message. The feel-good factor inculcated by humour is in itself persuasive

---

for the context (Spielmann, 2014). It should also be affiliative and pro-social, since humour that is used to demean others is dysfunctional for relational development (Wanzer *et al.*, 2010). Furthermore, sarcastic wits are regarded as influential but not popular, while clowning wits are seen as popular but not influential (Foot, 1997). Appropriate humour has been found to be a key determinant of interpersonal attraction (Cann *et al.*, 1997). For instance, one study of dating behaviour in college students found that a good sense of humour was rated by both males and females as the most important feature of a member of the opposite sex (Buss, 1988). Humour facilitates persuasion in a number of ways (Foot and McCreaddie, 2006; Skalski *et al.*, 2009), and these are summarised in Box 12.4. A meta-analysis of research in the field of advertising revealed that humour significantly enhances attention, positive emotions and recall (Eisend, 2009). Likewise, the use of humour by professionals has been found to be effective across a wide range of settings, including health care, education, sales and management (Campbell *et al.*, 2001; Bergeron and Vachon, 2008; Hughes and Avey, 2009; Wanzer *et al.*, 2010).

Logical proofs

Appeals to reason and logic, involving carefully constructed and forcefully delivered arguments, with clear premises leading to logical conclusions, are very persuasive. This section examines five logical proofs that can be used to convince others of the rationality of one's position: message delivery, case study, sidedness, request size and reciprocation.

Message delivery

In terms of delivery of arguments, these are more persuasive when there is a *powerful* speech style, wherein the person speaks in a firm, authoritative, tone and uses intensifiers – words or phrases that magnify the potency of what is being communicated (e.g. 'definitely', 'absolutely', 'I can say without a shadow of doubt...'). By contrast, a *powerless* style is characterised by five main features:

1   hesitations ('um...'; 'ah...');
2   hedges or qualifiers ('I sort of think...'; 'It might possibly be...');
3   disclaimers ('I don't have any real knowledge of this area, however...'; 'I might be wrong, but...');
4   tag questions ('...don't you think?'; '...isn't it?') and statements made with a questioning intonation;
5   lower voice volume.

In a review of the area, Durik *et al.* (2008) concluded: 'that messages with hedges led to less persuasion, more negative perceptions of the source, and weaker evaluations of the argument'. In their meta-analytic review of research in this area, Burrell and Koper (1998) found that a powerful speech pattern was perceived to be more credible and persuasive. Likewise, in their analysis of this field, Holtgraves and Lasky (1999, p. 196) concluded: 'a speaker who uses powerless language will be perceived as less assertive, competent, credible, authoritative, and in general evaluated less favorably than a speaker who uses powerful language'. If uncertainty has to be expressed, a powerful style should employ *authoritative doubt*, which underlines that the dubiety is from a vantage point of expertise (e.g. 'I know the literature very well and the evidence is just not clear on that...'). A powerless style accepts the blame for the uncertainty ('I'm not very well experienced in this...'). However, Holtgraves and Lasky also noted that speech power forms a continuum from low to high, so that degree of powerlessness may be important in determining impact. In other words, the occasional hesitation, hedge, tag question or lowered voice may have no impact on persuasiveness, but a high number of each will.

While early work in this field suggested that there was a gender difference in that males used a more powerful speech style, whereas females tended to employ powerless speech, later studies refuted this (McFadyen, 1996). What seems to be the case is that females may choose to use powerless speech more often if they see this as being in line with the cultural norm or feminine style they wish to portray (Hargie, 2006b).

A related element of language intensity is the extent to which the message contains emotionality and specificity. In terms of the former it can be delivered along a continuum from mild (e.g. 'I am annoyed) to high emotional intensity (e.g. 'I am furious'). Hamilton and Hunter (1998a), in a review of research into this aspect, found that stress was a moderating variable on the effects of emotional intensity. Relaxed targets are more persuadable as a result of the increased stress/arousal from high-intensity messages, whereas with highly stressed receivers the added stress from the emotionality causes a boomerang effect. With regard to intensity, this again forms a continuum from low ('A few of them came and they stayed for a little while') to high specificity ('Nine of then came and they stayed for 45 minutes'). More specific messages possess greater clarity and this in turn increases the power of the message.

Another aspect of message delivery, as highlighted by Bull and Feldman (2011) in their analysis of the importance of rhetoric in political persuasion, is the use of three-part lists ('we must fight, fight and fight again') and contrasts ('the dark night we have lived through with this government will be transformed into a bright new dawn'). In political speeches these have been shown to attract audience applause – a good indicator of approval and acceptance. The former tactic is part of the *repetition strategy*, whereby the speaker 'stays on message' to ensure that it gets through and people remember it. The power of three-part repetition was recognised by Lewis Carroll in *The Hunting of the Snark*, when he has the Bellman say:

> ...I have said it thrice:
> What I tell you three times is true.

Repetition of arguments has been shown to be effective in increasing their persuasive power (Moons *et al.*, 2009). This has long been known, as illustrated by the quotation from Hugh Latimer, the Bishop of Worcester and Protestant martyr during the reign of Queen Mary I of England, who in 1549 stated, 'The drop of rain maketh a hole in the stone, not by violence but by oft falling'. Statements heard more than once tend to be rated as more valid than those heard for the first time – an effect known as the *illusion of truth*. As shown by Song and Schwarz (2010, p. 111), in their review of research, 'the mere repetition of a statement facilitates its perception as true'. One reason for this is that, having heard the statement in the past, when we hear it again we experience a 'feeling of familiarity' with it, which in turn serves to increase its perceived validity. Indeed, the Nazi propaganda minister Joseph Goebbels demonstrated the potency of repetition when he argued that if you told a lie often enough people would believe it to be the truth. He claimed that: 'It would not be impossible to prove with sufficient repetition and psychological understanding of the people concerned that a square is in fact a circle' (cited in Baillargeon, 2007, p. 19). This is related to the *mere exposure effect*, wherein the more frequently we encounter an unfamiliar stimulus, the more favourably we begin to evaluate it (Gass and Seiter, 2014). One hypothesised reason for this effect is *perceptual fluency*, which purports that positive feelings are generated by repetition of a message due to the fact that the more we are exposed to a stimulus, the easier it becomes for us to process and assimilate it. Thus, it is common to hear people say that they did not like something at first but that after a while 'it grew on them'.

The use of *metaphor* has been shown to be important in message delivery (Tourish and Hargie, 2012). This term is derived from the Greek words for over (*meta*) and carry (*pherein*), and so the term indicates that an example from one area is carried over to another. For instance, a salesperson may say that the product being sold is 'like gold dust', to indicate that it has a range of positive properties, such as being rare, very valuable and highly sought after. Sopory and Dillard (2002) carried out a meta-analytic review of research into the use of metaphors (this subsumed analogies, similes and personification), as compared to literal language, in persuasion. Their conclusion was that, 'Theorists since Aristotle have proposed that metaphor could be fruitfully used for persuasion.

The meta-analytic summary of existing empirical studies affirms this supposition regarding metaphor's suasory effectiveness over literal counterparts' (p. 413). They found that the persuasive power of metaphors was greatest when they were novel, easily understood by the target, used early in the message, single and not extended.

However, a word of caution is required here. Metaphors must be used skilfully, and care needs to be exercised if using them in a negative fashion. One linguistic form that is widely employed by public speakers is that of *rebuttal analogy*. This occurs when a speaker uses an analogy as part of an attack on the position of an opponent. For example, an opposition politician might attack the government's policy on health by saying: 'They have done too little too late. *What they are doing is the equivalent of giving a patient an aspirin to treat stomach cancer.*' The part in italics is an example of rebuttal analogy. Its purpose is to rebut the other side's arguments by showing them to be ridiculous or absurd. But research has found that this form of message delivery needs to be used with caution, as it often causes a boomerang effect (Whaley and Wagner, 2000). Those who use it are rated as more impolite and less likeable. Furthermore, when compared to nonanalogy equivalents, it prompts the target person to formulate more counter-arguments to the message, and to remember fewer of the arguments put forward by the speaker. With partisan listeners, such as at a party political conference, rebuttal analogy, especially when humorous, can be acceptable to the audience. But even here the analogy should not be too insidious, especially if it is likely to be reported by the media to neutral observers (to whom it may seem like a 'smart-ass' comment). Overall, the research findings advise against the use of this tactic. It would be better for our hypothetical politician to reword the above example as follows: 'They have done too little too late. *They have failed so many seriously ill people in our society, who need and deserve to receive the best possible treatment. Their record is truly shameful*'.

Another question is whether a speaker should have a clear and explicit conclusion at the end of an argument or leave this implicit and allow the audience to draw it out for themselves (see Chapter 10 for more information on closure skills). The evidence here is clear: 'messages with explicit conclusions are more persuasive than those with implicit conclusions' (O'Keefe, 2006, p. 334). In a meta-analysis of research in this field, Cruz (1998, p. 228) explained why this is the case:

> The more explicit the conclusions to a persuasive message, the better the conclusion is comprehended. Greater conclusion comprehension produces perceptions that the source of the message advocates a more extreme position. Finally, perceptions that the source holds a more extreme position produces more attitude change.

Case study

What is known as *the power of exemplary narrative*, or, to put it more simply, the power of purposive story telling, has been shown to be effective in persuasive communication (Pinnington, 2001). From childhood we are nurtured on a diet of

'Once upon a time...' stories, and as adults the inner child in us responds reflexively and positively to case studies about actual people and events. One reason for the success of this tactic is that, 'the vividness and psychological closeness of a single case study is often more relevant to an individual than are scientific data' (Ohme, 2001, p. 314). While, as mentioned earlier, statistics can heighten the power of evidence, they may appear to be cold and detached, and we can get lost in the detail. Moreover, the oft-quoted remark by Mark Twain that 'There are lies, damned lies and statistics' means that we are often suspicious of statistics. The fact that academics frequently engage in the intellectual equivalent of arm wrestling over the validity of one another's statistical methods does not help.

On the other hand, we can readily identify with, and indeed enjoy, human-interest stories (Larson, 2013). The agent can use such tales to persuade the audience about the importance of the message being delivered. In terms of effectiveness, it does not seem to matter whether the narrative is fictional or true. This technique has a long history. For example, the early Christian church found that 'the medieval exemplum' (a brief story used to illustrate a particular moral point) was a much more effective tactic for conversion than subtle and learned sermons about doctrine (Scanlon, 1994). As discussed by Pinnington (2001), preachers were therefore encouraged to use relevant examples in order to persuade more easily. This is also shown in the Bible, where Christ made forceful use of 'the parable', which was a case study in the form of a moral tale.

A key feature of the potency of persuasive narrative is the extent to which the target becomes engaged with the story. Thus, the phenomenon of *absorption* (also known as *transportation*) is important, wherein the 'message recipient is cognitively and affectively invested in a narrative' (Slater and Rouner, 2002, p. 179). This means that the story should be well told and be of interest to the listeners. In terms of cognitive processing, successful narratives tend to be assimilated through the peripheral as opposed to the central route. Those who are engrossed in a story are less likely to employ counter-arguments and are more affected by the emotional part of the message. In this way, narrative messages have been shown to be more effective than statistical ones (Weber *et al.*, 2006; DeWit *et al.*, 2008).

Given its effectiveness, it is not surprising that the case study tactic can be found in the practice of a wide spectrum of persuaders (Hoeken and Hustinx, 2007), such as advertisers, politicians and insurance salespeople. Of course it is not an either/or decision with regard to statistics and case studies. In a major study involving 1,270 participants and 15 different messages, Allen *et al.* (2000) found that a combination of statistics and narrative produced the most potent influencing message. Likewise, in two reviews of the area, Gass and Seiter (2009, p. 160) concluded that, 'The best advice we can offer is to combine the two', while Kim *et al.* (2012, p. 67) found that, 'Research indicates that a combination of statistical and narrative evidence is the most persuasive message'.

Sidedness

An important decision is whether to use one-sided or two-sided arguments. In other words, should the disadvantages of what is being recommended also be presented? In general, studies show that two-sided messages are more effective (Cornelis *et al.*, 2014). However, there are some caveats. Research findings indicate that one-sided messages are best with those who already support the view being expressed. Accordingly, at party political conferences, the leader should present a partisan perspective, designed to boost the faithful. Equally, it would be unusual for a clergyman to stand up in church and express doubts about the existence of God. When preaching to the converted it is best to target the message in a single direction. One-sided messages are also better with those of a lower IQ, who may become confused if presented with seemingly contradictory arguments. What is known as *attribute framing*, where certain aspects are emphasised, is important in accentuating advantages. For example, consumers are more likely to buy beef that is labelled as 75 per cent lean as opposed to beef labelled as 25 per cent fat (Pratkanis, 2007).

Two-sided arguments are more appropriate with those with a higher IQ. Thus, in a study of college students, Feng and Burleson (2008) found that arguments were rated as more effective when they not only presented the efficacy and feasibility of the advised action, but also addressed its potential limitations. Since intelligent people are well capable of formulating counter-arguments, it is best to recognise openly that there are two sides to an argument, rather than attempt to 'insult their intelligence'. It is also better to present the disadvantages as well as advantages to those who are initially opposed to the message, who have heard an opposing perspective earlier, or who will hear one later. In all these instances, of course, while the opposing perspective should be recognised it should also be countered. The evidence here is quite clear (Allen, 1998; O'Keefe, 2006). The most effective approach is a refutational two-sided presentation, where there is recognition of the opposing point of view but a clear refutation of it. This is much more effective than either not mentioning the opposing arguments at all, or, even worse, using a nonrefutational two-sided presentation where the counter-perspective is highlighted, but not undermined.

Request size

Two alternatives exist in relation to the scale of request made in persuasion attempts. The first is *foot-in-the-door* (FITD), where a small first request is made, and if acceded to, this is followed by a slightly larger request, and so on. For example, a manager who wants an employee to cover three extra shifts could use the FITD approach to explain that there were severe staffing problems that required urgent cover, and initially ask for the employee to cover one extra shift. If the person agrees to this, the manager could gratefully accept this and thank the employee, but then ask if it would be possible for the employee to cover two shifts, as this would be an even greater help. Once accepted, a 'final' request to cover three shifts could be made. This technique, of asking for a very small amount and gradually increasing it, has been found to be effective. Thus a famous study by Cialdini and Schroeder (1976) illustrated how donations to charities increase when the agent adds the term 'even a penny will help' when making the request. More recent research has confirmed the utility of this 'legitimisation of paltry favours' effect when making requests for donations

(Shearman and Yoo, 2007; Takada and Levine, 2007). However, two mediating factors seem important here (Andrews *et al.*, 2008). First, the request must be made face to face. Second, the request is more successful if it is for an immediate monetary donation, as opposed to a pledge from the target to donate.

The second tactic is known as *door-in-the-face* (DITF), where a very large initial (and usually unacceptable) request is made, and once it has been rejected, a much more reasonable one follows. To continue with the above example, using DITF the manager would explain the severe staffing problems and ask the employee to work an extra shift every day that week, knowing this request would probably be refused. The manager could then ask if the employee could cover four or even three shifts. Now the target request seems much more reasonable – and in fact the manager has made two concessions from the first request.

Both FITD and DITF, which are termed *sequencing requests*, have been shown to be successful tactics when used skilfully (Dillard and Knobloch, 2011; Guéguen *et al.*, 2015). Their effectiveness depends upon circumstances. For example, a cult is unlikely to be successful if it has a DITF strategy of stopping passers-by in the street and asking them to join their group, explaining that this will involve giving all of their money to the cult, breaking all contacts with family and friends, wearing strange clothes, accepting new and seemingly weird beliefs and rituals, living a frugal existence and having to recruit strangers. Rather, a FITD strategy is more usual. In their text on cults, Tourish and Wohlforth (2000) termed this tactic the *spiral of escalating commitment*. Here, potential recruits are initially invited to attend an evening meeting to hear more about the group. This is then followed by an increased level of request, such as participation in a weekend conference. In this way, the potential member is slowly 'sucked in' and the level of request escalates gradually, until the person has become a fully-fledged cult participant.

One explanation for the success of FITD is *self-perception theory* (Johnston, 1994). This purports that we make inferences about our attitudes, values and beliefs based upon how we behave. When we carry out an action we infer that we did so because we are the type of person who would perform such an act. In other words, our overt behaviour is seen as reflecting our inner 'self'. Then, when we are asked to perform a slightly larger action in the same vein, we wish to portray a consistent self and so we also accede to this request. Meta-analytic reviews of FITD have shown it to be effective (Dillard *et al.*, 1984; Fern *et al.*, 1986; Pascual and Guéguen, 2005), provided that the conditions listed in Box 12.5 are met.

DITF is also known as *reciprocation of concessions*. The rationale here is that the target feels bad about having made the initial refusal. Furthermore, the agent has now made a concession in request size and so the target is under pressure to reciprocate. Compliance with the later request serves both to reciprocate the agent's concession and to make the target feel personally better. DITF also seems to benefit from *perceptual contrast*, wherein the second request is judged in the context of the initial one, and in comparison is perceived to be smaller than it really is. Many stores use the DITF tactic in this way by placing very expensive items at the entrance, so that when customers

---

Box 12.5 Foot-in-the-door conditions

For the foot-in-the door tactic to be successful, the following conditions must be met:

- *The cause should be pro-social.* If the request is made for purely selfish reasons it can be much more easily resisted; if it is in some way antisocial then it can be rejected with impunity
- *No incentive should be given for carrying out the initial request.* If a reward is given, this may change the interpreted reason for the action (e.g. 'I did it purely for the money'). This, in turn, can make refusal easier to subsequent requests, especially if there is no concomitant increase in the scale of the reward
- *The follow-up requests should be related to the initial one.* A later request is more easily rejected by the target without any fear of appearing to be inconsistent if it is unrelated to the issue or theme of the first one
- *There should not be a huge discrepancy between each subsequent request.* If the disparity is too large, the request may be more easily rejected as being 'unreasonable'

---

then encounter comparatively cheaper ones further into the shop these appear to be more reasonably priced than if they had been viewed without the contrast effect. Successive research reviews have confirmed the effectiveness of DITF (O'Keefe and Hale, 1998, 2001; Turner *et al.*, 2007; Feeley *et al.*, 2012). However, they also show that for DITF to be successful the conditions listed in Box 12.6 must be met.

A related tactic here is known as *foot-in-the-mouth* (FITM) (Howard, 1990). This occurs when, before making a request of the target, the agent asks the HAY ('How are you?') question. The purpose here is to get the reply, 'Good'. Having given this reply, the target then feels under internal pressure to stay consistent with this expressed positive mood (Dillard and Knobloch, 2011). In the case of a request to help a charity, the target also then feels a sense of obligation to try to help less fortunate others who are not feeling so good. For both reasons, the person is more likely to accede to the request. However, Dolinski *et al.* (2001) carried out experiments to show that it is the establishment of initial dialogue with the target prior to making the request that may be crucial during influence attempts. They argue that, in relation to FITM, it may well be the effect of having an interaction with the agent that is the important element of this technique.

Guéguen *et al.* (2015) found that the combination of two other techniques worked in an additive fashion. The first is the *pique technique,* where a request to a passer-by for an unusual sum of money (e.g. 37 cents) increases compliance. It is hypothesised that the request for the strange amount works in two ways: first by creating a legitimisation effect, whereby the target rationalises that it

---

Box 12.6 Door-in-the-face conditions

For the door-in-the-face tactic to be successful the following conditions must be met:

- *The same agent must make both requests.* If a different person makes the second request, the effect disappears. For example, a student arranges to see the Faculty Dean and asks for a large donation to the students' end-of-term party. This is refused. Later, another student also arranges a meeting with the Dean and asks for a smaller sum. Here, no real concession has been made, as it has become a different interaction with new rules. Furthermore, how many more such requests are liable to be made? The effect has been at best compromised and at worst destroyed
- *The beneficiary should be the same for both requests.* If the recipient is different in the second request the effect is lost. For example, if the agent requests a large sum from the target for one charity initially, and then follows this up by asking for a smaller sum for a different charity, again the concession 'rules' have changed
- *The requests need to be delivered face to face.* When the request is made by telephone the likelihood of success is much weaker. One reason for this is that research has shown that it is easier to refuse requests when they are mediated as opposed to when made in person (Hargie *et al.*, 2004)
- *There is no time delay between the requests.* If there is a delay the power of the effect diminishes. There is truth in the maxim that 'Time changes everything'. When making the second request at a later time, the initial scenario has to be reconstructed and may be difficult to recreate, and the pressure to reciprocate has eased for the target
- *The requests should be pro-social.* As with foot-in-the-door, purely selfish or antisocial requests can be readily rejected

---

must be needed for a specific purpose, and second by disrupting the target's normal request refusal script. The second is the *disrupt-then-reframe* (DTR) technique, wherein unusual phrasing is used in the first part of a message (the disrupt), followed by a reason to comply (the reframe). An example of DTR would be a shopkeeper saying to a customer who is looking at a product, 'They are 400 cents, that's 4 dollars (*disrupt*) … It's a bargain (*reframe*).' A meta-analysis of DTR studies shows that this is an effective technique (Carpenter and Boster, 2009). One reason that it works is because the reframe acts as a legitimisation, providing a reason for the agent to comply. In the Guéguen *et al.* (2015) real-world study, passers-by gave most money to the experimenter's confederate when a pique request, which also served as a disrupt, was used, immediately followed by a reframe: 'Hello, can you spare 37 cents, please? That would help me a lot.'

Reciprocation

In our interactions with others there seems to be a need for balance between what we give and what we receive. For example, Chapter 9 highlighted how in social situations when one person discloses to another, the recipient then feels under pressure to make a reciprocal disclosure. Cialdini (2014, p. 53), in noting that, 'one of the most widespread and basic norms of human cultures is embodied in the rule for reciprocation', identified three main characteristics of this phenomenon:

1   The expectation of reciprocity is such a potent facet of the human condition that it often supercedes other factors that may influence compliance.
2   The rule applies even to uninvited first favours. Hence companies offer customers free samples or free trials, so that the recipient then feels under an obligation to return the favour.
3   To relieve ourselves of any lingering feeling of indebtedness we may actually return more to the giver than we received.

Reciprocity can be used in two ways, First, by *pre-giving* and so placing the target in the position of indebtedness. Then, when a favour is sought in return it is more likely that the target will comply. If not, debt reminders can be invoked, such as 'I did that for you…You owe me.' Favours also increase liking and gratitude, which, in turn, can influence compliance (Goei and Boster, 2005). A favour has been shown to be most effective when it is used with a stranger; the target attributes it to benevolent intentions rather than an ulterior motive on the part of the agent; the target feels that a high level of benefit has been received; the agent is perceived to have made a significant sacrifice in making it; and, the subsequent persuasion attempt is regarded as pro-social rather than antisocial (Goei *et al.*, 2007). Second, a *promise* can be made that if the target performs a certain action, this will be rewarded by a reciprocal event at a later time. Colloquially this is known as 'you scratch my back and I'll scratch yours'. For example, a manager may say to a member of staff, 'If you successfully achieve this target I will recommend you for a performance bonus'.

Promises work best when there is a close and trusting relationship between people. There is then less danger of what is known as the *low-ball technique*, where someone gets another to do something by making a promise with no intention of keeping it. For example, in a classic study in Iowa, USA, Pallak *et al.* (1980) investigated methods to persuade natural gas consumers to conserve their usage. They began by just asking a sample of domestic users to be fuel-conscious. This had absolutely no effect when usage figures were measured. They then contacted a new sample but this time informed them that those who agreed to take part would later be named in newspaper articles as model citizens. The effect was immediate. Within a month participants had made significant reductions in gas consumption. Then the researchers contacted them to say that it was not going to be possible to publicise their names after all. What happened to energy usage now? Well, interestingly, it continued to drop even more. Although they had been low-balled into the initial behaviour, once established, the new response became resistant to change. There are clear ethical problems about using the low-ball technique but, as this study illustrated, it certainly can be effective.

However, failure to reciprocate often has negative consequences. Research in the business context has shown that, in both the public and private sectors, employees can have a sense that the efforts they make for the organisation may well not be reciprocated, and that explicit or implicit assurances given by senior management might not be adhered to. For example, changes that impact negatively upon employees may be made to pension schemes, medical insurance or sickness entitlements, and downsizing schemes are readily introduced even when there is no real economic necessity. Research reviewed by Belmi and Pfeffer (2015) shows that such experiences have negative implications for the organisation, in that when employees perceive that management has failed to deliver what was promised, they reciprocate by becoming less productive, less committed and more likely to leave.

Emotional proofs

Emotions have been shown to be a very powerful force in driving and shaping human thoughts and behaviour. Appeals to the heart are as successful in effecting influence as appeals to the head (Andersen and Kumar, 2006; Timmers and van der Wijst, 2007). In their review of research in this field, Dillard and Peck (2001, p. 38) concluded, 'there is a great deal of evidence that affect plays a significant role in the process of opinion change'. There are literally thousands of terms to describe affective states (Hargie, 2006b). However, as discussed in Chapter 3, there are six main categories of emotion – sadness, happiness, surprise, disgust, anger and fear. Each contains a large number of sub-categories (e.g. sadness subsumes, *inter alia*, embarrassment, chagrin, guilt, shame, distress and depression). Given the power and ubiquity of emotions in our lives, they are potent persuasion tools.

The *dual-systems approach* argues that emotions fall into one of two categories. Energetic arousal is seen as positive affect, and experienced as exuberance and vigour. Tense arousal is viewed as negative affect, experienced as anxiety and nervousness. These are in turn linked to two underlying physiological behaviour-guiding systems.

1   The *behaviour approach system* is triggered by cues of reward and escape from punishment. Activation of the behaviour approach system leads to the experience of positive affect.
2   The *behaviour inhibition system* is triggered by cues of punishment and nonreward. Activation of the behaviour inhibition system leads to the experience of negative affect.

The discrete-emotions approach purports that negative emotions arise from a situation where the environment is hindering the achievement of the individual's goals, while positive emotions arise from a situation where the environment facilitates the individual's goals. As discussed earlier, this in turn impacts upon the way in which persuasion attempts are processed (Box 12.2). It is therefore important to examine how both negative and positive emotions can be invoked to 'move' people to act in certain ways.

Threat/fear

As a core emotion, threatening messages that heighten our sense of fear can be very effective in changing attitudes and behaviour (Joffe, 2008). The *protection motivation model* has shown that there are four main pre-requisites for fear to be successful as a weapon of influence (Sutton, 1982).

1   The likelihood and consequences of the threatened outcome must be severe enough to *really frighten* the target. The threat appraisal must be high so that it is perceived as noxious and real and the target must feel vulnerable (Ruiter *et al.*, 2014). This can be difficult to achieve, since the psychological phenomenon of *unrealistic optimism* means that most people believe they are less likely than the average to suffer from negative experiences in life and more likely to experience the positive aspects (Chambers, 2008). For example, others are seen as being more likely to get heart disease or cancer than oneself. Young people in particular are often immune to health messages – they believe that it is old people who get sick. For health educators this sense of invulnerability is difficult to overcome in terms of fear induction. Another phenomenon that is relevant here is the *third-person effect*, whereby people believe that media messages have the greatest effect not on them (first person), or people like them (second person), but on 'others' (third person) (Sun *et al.*, 2008). A consequence of this is that if people believe they are less likely to be influenced by media messages they may become more passive, less critical consumers, and so more susceptible to persuasion attempts (Chapin, 2008).
    While a sense of vulnerability is essential to the effectiveness of fear appeals, more generally it makes targets susceptible to persuasive messages. Contrary to popular beliefs, research on cults has shown that, while about one-third of the people who join these bodies are psychologically disturbed, the remaining two-thirds are normal (Tourish and Wohlforth, 2000). However, the latter are more vulnerable to recruitment when they have just undergone a personal trauma, such as bereavement, divorce, job loss or serious illness. Vulnerability is also high when the individual is experiencing a major change of circumstance. For example, young adults who have left home to go to college are often unsettled and confused. Their social anchors have been drawn up and they find they are afloat in a new world having to fend for themselves, often for the first time. Their support network is not at hand, and levels of uncertainty and insecurity can be high. As a result, many cults, religions and various other bodies (sporting, political, etc.), specifically target the college fresher population, seeing this as fertile fishing ground. Furthermore, as intelligent (and often energetic, attractive and articulate) individuals, once such students join a group they can be great emissaries to further its cause.

2   In relation to fear appeals, the second pre-requisite is that there must be *specific recommendations* about how to prevent or remove the danger. The steps needed to remove the threat must be clear and unambiguous. This has been shown to be a key component in the effectiveness of fear appeals (Ruiter *et al.*, 2014).

3   The perceived *response efficacy* has to be high. In other words, the target must believe that what is being recommended will be *effective* in circumventing or overcoming the threat. The remedial actions should be shown to work. In their meta-analysis of research studies, Peters *et al.* (2013) found that for fear appeals to be effective, threat and response efficacy levels must both be high.

4   The target needs to be *willing to take action* to remove the threat. There should be a high level of *coping appraisal and self-efficacy* so that the target is confident about being able to implement the recommended behaviours. Thus, Rimal (2002) showed that a crucial determining factor in the success of fear appeals was how highly individuals rated their own ability to carry out the recommended actions. If the target feels able to implement and maintain these, then fear messages are more likely to be successful.

If all four factors are operative, then threat/fear is a potent tool for persuasion. If one or more is absent, then the power of the message is reduced accordingly. Let us use the example of alcohol intake. People may accept that being a very heavy drinker is detrimental to health and carries a much higher risk of illness and earlier mortality. They may agree that if they drank less or stopped drinking altogether they would have a drastically reduced rate of risk. However, they may also believe that they need to drink and just could not give it up. Here the power of the threat/fear message begins to dissipate. The target may then either respond with feelings of hopelessness ('I'm going to die anyway so I might as well enjoy my drink'), or reject the threat ('There is no real evidence to show any causal link between alcohol intake and ill health').

Much of the early work on threat and fear appeals was carried out in the field of health, and indeed, the *health belief model* emphasised the above four points, as well as a fifth aspect of *cue to action* (Rutter and Quine, 2002). Here, a specific event triggers the entire process. To continue with our example, a friend who drank heavily dies of cirrhosis of the liver and this then makes you think seriously about the dangers of your own drinking. The *parallel response model* (Leventhal, 1970) and the *extended parallel process model* (Witte, 1992) illustrate how people cope with fear messages by responding at one of two levels:

1   *Danger control.* Threat evaluation initially takes place at this level, so that the target is motivated to take action to reduce the danger. Here the person responds in such a way as to reduce the danger that causes the fear. If the recommended course of action is perceived to be effective and viable, the recommendations are likely to be implemented. Thus, the person would cut down, or eliminate, alcohol. In other words, the fear message is accepted and acted upon. However, if the evaluation of the efficacy of, or ability to implement, the suggested action is negative, then the person will respond at the fear control level.

2   *Fear control.* If the danger cannot be averted the target then takes steps to control or reduce internal feelings of fear. Here the person avoids the negative messages that arouse fear. Heavy drinkers responding at this level would avoid newspaper articles or TV programmes that highlight the risks of heavy alcohol intake. They may also make a distinction between *general beliefs* ('Heavy drinking is harmful to health') and *personal beliefs* that either minimise the degree of risk ('I don't really drink that much') or emphasise personal immunity ('Drinking never causes me any problems. I'm built for it'). They may also engage in rationalisations such as generalising from the particular ('I know a man who drank heavily all his life and he lived to be over 80 years old'), or accentuating the positive ('Taking a drink actually improves my well-being, by helping me to relax').

In a meta-analysis of research into fear arousal and persuasion, Mongeau (1998, p. 65) concluded, 'Overall, increasing the amount of fear-arousing content in a persuasive message is likely to generate greater attitude and behavior change'. However he also found that the use of this tactic was not always successful. Fear is more effective with older subjects (i.e. with adults as opposed to school children), and with low-anxiety individuals. With highly anxious people it may backfire, so that the heightened anxiety induced by an intense fear scenario can inhibit attention and increase distraction. This in turn reduces comprehension, or results in the message either being ignored completely or rejected. Such defensive responses are more common among those who are most at risk from the threat (Van't Riet and Ruiter, 2013). Thus, if people already have very high levels of fear about a subject, attempting to increase this even further has been shown to be counter-productive (Muthusamy *et al.*, 2009) and may well cause a boomerang effect. For example, Emery *et al.* (2014) illustrated how health promotion campaigns that use fear appeals may boomerang with some targets because they raise the stress levels in an already anxious individual, who then responds by actually performing the targeted behaviour (e.g. smoking or drinking) to reduce this increased anxiety. The reactions of the target therefore need to be carefully and constantly monitored. The objective is to encourage change, not instil panic and an accompanying 'flight' reaction (where the target just wants to escape from the threatening message).

One interesting extension of the fear tactic is the effect of what is known as *fear-then-relief* (FTR) upon compliance. A series of studies has shown that, when fear is instilled in people and is then suddenly removed, compliance with requests increases (Dolinski, 2007). In one study, while a jaywalker was crossing a road, a police whistle was blown. The jaywalker then turned round and was relieved to discover there was in fact no police officer present. These subjects were then asked to complete a questionnaire, as were jaywalkers who did not hear a whistle, and a control group of pedestrians who were not jaywalkers. The results showed that the FTR group more frequently acceded to the questionnaire completion request. This technique seems to work for two reasons (Perloff, 2008). First, the relief experienced upon removal of the threat is reinforcing. This enhanced positive emotional mood is then associated with the subsequent request, thereby increasing the likelihood of acquiescence. Second, the sudden relief from anxiety means that the target is in a cognitive state of temporary mindlessness, being still distracted by the danger that was nearly experienced. This means that the target is less attentive to the request (and less likely to engage in central route processing of it) and so more susceptible.

Moral appeals

Part of the socialisation process in all societies is that individuals are taught the difference between what is right and what is wrong. Behaviour that is upright, ethical and honest is viewed positively by others and encouraged, while that which is underhand, immoral and deceitful is disapproved of and discouraged. These societal norms play a powerful role in the development of a personal moral code that in turn shapes our behaviour. Most people are therefore susceptible to appeals to conscience, in the form of reminders that we have a duty to 'do the right thing', and that if we do not fulfil our moral obligations we will feel bad about ourselves. Thus, inducing 'anticipated guilt', where the person is persuaded that by pursuing a course of action later feelings of guilt will be experienced, can move the individual to act in such a way as to prevent the guilt occurring (Lindsey, 2005). Few people like to be left feeling guilty, regretful or ashamed, or to be the subject of opprobrium from significant others, and so messages that target the moral domain can be persuasive (Antonetti and Baines, 2015).

An important aspect here, as summarised by Dillard and Peck (2001, p. 42), is that 'Guilt may prompt efforts to redress the failure, but only if the transgression can be remedied'. In other words, inducing a sense of guilt is useful in moving someone to act, only if the person can do so in such a way as to right the wrong. If the misdemeanour is irreversible or not salvageable, then all that a moral appeal will do at best is to make the target feel very bad (Chang, 2014). Furthermore, induced guilt does not always produce the desired result. In his review of the area, O'Keefe (2006) noted that guilt may backfire, in that it may cause the target not to change behaviour in line with previous attitudes and beliefs, but instead to change those attitudes and beliefs to be consistent with the new behaviour. O'Keefe also illustrated that, while more explicit guilt appeals do effect greater guilt, less explicit guilt appeals are actually more effective in changing behaviour. The reason for this seems to be that more explicit guilt appeals can evoke resentment or anger in the target, and this tempers the success of the appeal.

Moral appeals take a number of forms, as shown in Box 12.7. Although these can be effective tactics, there are also drawbacks to their use and so this strategy needs to be treated with some caution (Hargie et al., 2004). Since we do not like to be made to feel guilty, we tend to dislike the person who has caused this to occur, and we are then more likely to avoid that person in future. This is especially true when what we have done cannot be easily remedied. Another finding is that an accusation of being uncaring results in the target being more likely to accede to a second moral appeal, providing the follow-up one is made by a different person. This is because the target then wishes to show that he or she is not uncaring and so the accusation was unfounded. For example, you pass

---

Box 12.7 Types of moral appeal

- *Duty calls.* These remind people that they have a moral obligation, or responsibility, to carry out certain actions. For example, parents may be told that it is their duty to provide for their child. In fact, insurance companies use this technique to sell life policies. The person who dies obviously will not benefit financially from the policy, but it is argued that that person has a duty to his or her family to provide for them in the event of their death
- *Altruism exhortations.* These are direct attempts to trigger a caring or altruistic response in the target person, who has no obligation to help and will receive no tangible benefit from giving assistance. Many charities operate at this level, when they appeal to the population to help others less fortunate than them. Likewise beggars may ask you to give them money 'out of the kindness of your heart'
- *Social esteem precepts.* Here, social norms are invoked to underline the probability that the reaction of others to a response will either be negative ('You will be shunned if you do that') or positive ('You will be well thought of if you do this'). Most of us care about the reactions of others, and so the danger of being ostracised on the one hand, or the likelihood of recognition and social approval on the other, is a powerful force
- *Self-feeling injunctions.* The concept of self-regard is an important force in driving behaviour. For example, people who donate anonymously to charities do not receive social esteem, but they do have a reward in the form of positive self-feeling. This means that individuals can be influenced by appeals at this level, cast in either a negative manner ('You will find it very difficult to live with yourself if you do not do this') or in a positive frame ('You will feel good if you do this')
- *Altercasting appeals.* This involves encouraging others to 'step outside themselves' and examine their behaviour objectively. The individual is then asked to consider the view that either only a bad, uncaring person would continue with the present behaviour, or that a good and caring person would carry out the recommended action. For example, a heavy gambler whose family was suffering and in severe debt could be asked, 'Wouldn't you agree that anyone who cared anything for their family would try to stop this?'

---

a charity collector shaking a tin in the street without donating, and the person calls after you, 'I can see that you really care about those a lot less fortunate than yourself. I wouldn't like to have to rely on you for help.' A few streets later you encounter another charity collector waving a tin. There is now an increased probability that you will donate.

Scarcity value

While this aspect of persuasion is sometimes included within logical proofs (e.g. Hargie *et al.*, 2004), there is also a strong element of emotionality involved and so it can also be incorporated within emotional proofs. The scarcity principle operates on the basis that, once the availability of something is restricted, it becomes more valuable and desirable (Lee *et al.*, 2014). Items that are hard to get tend to have more value and appeal. There is a perfectly good rationale here – our experience tells us that the best things in life are often in scarce supply. The phenomenon of an increased desire for what is scarce is part of what is known as *reactance theory* (Brehm, 1966), which explains how, when access to something is denied, or when restrictions are placed upon an item or activity, our freedom of choice is threatened. This results in the phenomenon of reactance, which refers to the reaction we have to the imposition of restrictions on our freedom. Such reaction involves a combination of anger and negative cognitions, such as counter-arguing and source derogation (Rains and Turner, 2007). The degree of reactance experienced is a factor of both how much the person values a particular freedom and the extent of the perceived threat to that freedom (Byrne and Hart, 2009).

When we are threatened by something being denied to us, we react to this threat by experiencing an increased desire for the restricted item. Indeed, the more restricted an item, the greater tends to be its appeal. This process first occurs in children at around the age of 2 years, when temper tantrums are often the order of the day if a much-wanted toy, snack or activity is not immediately forthcoming. One early study showed that when children at this age were offered access to toys of parallel attractiveness, if one was unavailable (behind a Plexiglas barrier) this was the one upon which most attention was focused (Brehm and Weintraub, 1977). Likewise, if teenagers are told by parents not to date a certain person, their desire to be with the forbidden individual is often heightened. Although the best things in life may be free, we only fully appreciate them if they become less available. In fact, we expect to pay more for the better things in life. We know that the best house, suit or computer costs more. Shops that sell 'rare artefacts' or 'precious gems' do not 'stack 'em high and sell 'em cheap'. A key implication of this is that we can persuade others to do something by convincing them that there is scarcity value attached to it. For example, people pay exorbitant fees to join clubs that market themselves as 'exclusive'.

Reactance can be reduced by the *evoking freedom* technique (Guéguen *et al.*, 2015). Here, the agent makes a request but adds the caveat that the person has the freedom to refuse. Having been given this 'increased' freedom, people feel more in control and less under duress, with the result that they become more acquiescent. Likewise *acknowledging resistance* increases compliance. By simply saying, 'I know you might not want to, but...' before making the request, the agent can increase the number of people who comply. It seems that the act of openly acknowledging and accepting the target's feelings of resistance serves to reduce this resistance. For example, in one study the number of subjects who gave to an experimenter requesting money for a parking meter increased from 58 per cent to 91 per cent by including the 'I know you might not want to, but...' preface (Knowles and Riner, 2007). Similarly, what is known as *the power of 'Yes'* helps to reduce reactance. Here, the agent avoids saying 'No' but rather says 'Yes', and then adds a caveat. For instance, if a 17-year-old girl asks her mother if she can host a party in the family home for all her friends, rather than replying 'No, you cannot!' it is better for the mother to say something like: 'Yes, you can, if you buy all of the food and drink, your father and I act as security and you cover the costs for a professional cleaning company to come in the next day'. Finally, inoculating targets by warning them of the likelihood that they will experience reactance to health messages has been shown to be effective in reducing such reactance (Richards and Banas, 2015); in this study the use of inoculation to prepare targets for health campaign messages designed to reduce alcohol consumption resulted in reduced reactance and lower intention to drink alcohol.

There are three important factors attached to scarcity value:

1   Resources attain an even greater value when they are seen to be *newly scarce*. This holds both for items that were once plentiful but have now become rare, and for recently discovered or invented items that are not yet widely available. Salespeople are able to sell more easily things that are brand new, but still hard to get hold of. Indeed, the price of an item usually remains high so long as it is scarce, but tends to drop as availability increases.

2   If we have to *compete* for the scarce resource it attains even greater attraction in our eyes. It is for this reason that auctioneers are delighted when two or more people begin to bid seriously for the same object. The winner is then likely to pay well above the odds to secure it.

3   *Losses are more influential than gains*. Gain and loss appeals take the form of a 2×2 matrix, where the outcome is described either as desirable or undesirable, and the likelihood of attaining it is portrayed either as more likely or less likely (O'Keefe and Jensen, 2009). Scarcity value is increased where the outcome is seen as highly desirable but the likelihood of achieving it is less likely. Research shows that messages are more effective when scarcity benefits can be presented not as gains but as preventable losses (Pratkanis, 2007). What is known as *prospect theory* (Tversky and Kahneman, 1981) shows that people are more concerned with minimising losses than maximising gains. There has been shown to be truth in the maxim that 'a penny lost is valued more highly than a penny earned' (Rasmussen and Newland, 2008, p. 157). Thus, the prospect of something becoming scarce as a result of losing it motivates us more than the thought of gaining something of equal value. For example, smokers are influenced more when told by a physician how many years of life they are likely to lose if they do not quit, as opposed to how many years they will gain if they give up (Cialdini, 2014), and that if they do not stop smoking their lungs will not heal, than if they stop their lungs will heal (Ohme, 2001). Similarly, anti-drug ads targeted at adolescents have been shown to be more effective when the message is framed in terms of loss, rather than gain, language (Cho and Boster, 2008).

However, this is mediated by the degree of risk involved. People are often willing to select a risky option to prevent losses but are generally less willing to choose risky options to secure gains. This means that gain language may be more effective than loss language for promoting illness *prevention* behaviours perceived to be only minimally risky to carry out. However, with health *detection* behaviours associated with a higher degree of risk, loss-framed messages may be more effective. This was confirmed in a meta-analysis of research into health prevention behaviours by Gallagher and Updegraff (2012), who found that gain-framed messages were significantly more likely than loss-framed messages to promote illness prevention behaviour, especially in relation to smoking cessation, skin cancer prevention and physical activity.

Consistency and commitment

A powerful human drive is the desire to be regarded as *consistent*. We have a need to show others that we mean what we say and will do what we promise. This means that, once we have made a public declaration of *commitment* to a course of action we are more likely to rate it highly and continue with it. A ubiquitous strategy in many organisations and institutions is to get people to make such a declaration. Its potency is reinforced if the person also makes the declaration in writing. Examples of the successful use of this tactic include 'I am an alcoholic...' declarations made at Alcoholics Anonymous gatherings, personal testimonies or confessions by members of religious denominations and statements of devotion to one another made by couples during the marriage ceremony. At another level, performers know that if they can get the audience actively involved (e.g. by clapping, laughing, cheering, chanting or singing along), their level of perceived enjoyment will increase accordingly. This tactic has been aptly termed the *clap trap* (Huczynski, 1996). Involvement increases enjoyment and so reduces the likelihood of central processing. Such a strategy is used at mass rallies (witness the 'Sieg Heil' roars and Nazi salutes during Hitler's speeches), in religious services, the armed forces and in the best classrooms. Involvement in synchronised group activities, such as marching, chanting and singing, has been shown to enhance group bonding and loyalty (Wiltermuth and Heath, 2009).

Thus, the twin pillars of consistency and commitment can be used to shape and direct the behaviour of others. The principle of *retrospective rationality* means that once people perform a certain behaviour or publicly state a point of view they are then more likely to infer in retrospect that they really believe in what they said or did (Iyengar and Brockner, 2001). One example of this is the technique known as *counter-attitudinal advocacy* (CAA), which is the act of arguing for or acting upon a position that is contrary to one's original point of view. So doing can result in modifications to one's original perspective, and a shift towards the other viewpoint. This occurs for two reasons. First, individuals have a desire to portray a consistent sense of self. Consequently, when they publicly espouse an opinion that runs counter to their beliefs, to maintain this consistency their attitudes tend to move in the direction of the public utterances. This phenomenon is part of what is known as the *saying is believing effect* (Beukeboom, 2014). Second, the cognitive processes involved in CAA can lead to a positive reappraisal of the arguments involved (Hamilton and Hunter, 1998b). A meta-analysis of research studies has shown CAA to be an effective persuasion method (Kim *et al.*, 2014).

In reviewing this area Cialdini (2014, p. 101) concluded, 'Commitments are most effective when they are active, public, effortful, and viewed as internally motivated (uncoerced)'. They are also more impactful when the decision taken is final. It is useful to examine these commitment aspects of persuasion in further depth.

1   *Public declaration*. When a statement is made publicly the commitment to it is greater. The presence of others has a significant impact – we like to be seen as true to our word. Those who change their mind or renege on what they said are generally perceived as fickle, weak or untrustworthy. Consequently, oaths of allegiance made in public are a key element in the initiation ceremonies of many bodies. Once you have publicly sworn undying allegiance to a cause it becomes more difficult to retract. For example, Islamic suicide bombers usually record a video statement before they go on their mission. This is a very public declaration, as the tape may be seen by millions of people. Having made such a declaration, it then becomes extremely difficult to recant. In fact, members of terrorist organisations who become disillusioned about their organisation may turn informer rather than face the opprobrium of being seen to go back on their publicly sworn oath. More generally, the media love to expose public figures who have broken promises or shown inconsistency, and relish stories involving crooked cops, unfrocked vicars or corrupt politicians. Where someone is inconsistent, the use of *induced hypocrisy* is a powerful force. As noted by Stone *et al.* (1997), this occurs when an individual is:

(a)   reminded of having publicly espoused a personal position;
(b)   confronted with evidence of having failed to live up to this position.

When both of these events occur, the effect of induced hypocrisy is powerful. The individual experiences cognitive dissonance and is motivated to be more consistent in future. Having been shown to have broken our word, and as such to be hypocritical, we then have a renewed determination to 'put this right'. This is particularly marked in individuals who are high in the psychological trait of *preference for consistency* (Sénémeaud *et al.*, 2014).

2   *Implementation intentions*. An important distinction has been made between *goal intentions*, where the individual makes a basic, general commitment to a particular action ('I intend to do X'), and *implementation intentions*, which involve detailed planning about when, where and

exactly how 'X' will be carried out (Gollwitzer, 1999). Research across a wide range of fields has shown that individuals who plan at the implementation level are much more likely to carry out the stated behaviour (Rutter and Quine, 2002).

3   *Level of initial commitment.* The more actively involved individuals are in the public declaration process, the more binding their commitment becomes. One way of ensuring that people stay committed to the message they have recently been persuaded to adopt is to get them to proselytise about it. This is a tactic that is used by many religions and cults. In the high street of most major cities, we meet individuals selling a message either on an individual basis or, as with 'manic street preachers', to all and sundry. Having to 'sell' the message means that it becomes cognitively embedded and resistant to change. It is more difficult to reject later that which you have publicly and vehemently espoused. If individuals have to make sacrifices as part of their commitment they are more likely to 'bond' with the behaviour. Thus, many bodies have initiation ceremonies or 'rites of passage' where the initiate may have to endure humiliations before becoming a fully fledged member. Likewise, terrorist leaders recognise the importance of getting volunteers involved in an early 'mission', especially one where targets are killed. The volunteer is then literally 'bloodied' and more likely to aver the worth of the cause. People also rate the strength and depth of their belief or attitude based upon the extent of effort they have shown to it in the past. Thus, if you decided to become a vegetarian 6 months ago but since then have lapsed and eaten flesh at least once a week, you are likely to rate your commitment to vegetarianism lower than if you had never eaten flesh since.

4   *Voluntary act.* If the behaviour has been freely chosen the individual is more committed to it. There is now a huge volume of research to show that freedom of choice is a central factor in the influence equation. In reviewing this area, Iyengar and Brockner (2001, p. 16) concluded, 'The provision of choice seems inherently linked with intrinsic motivation, perceived control and personal commitment'. If we can argue that a public commitment was made as a result of threat or duress, then we do not feel the need to stick to it (Kim *et al.*, 2014). For example, some American prisoners of war held by communists in the Korean and Vietnam conflicts made public statements in favour of their captors and against US policy. Interestingly, some stayed committed to what they had said and remained there after the war, while others argued they had been forced by physical or psychological torture to say what they had, and never personally believed in what they were told to say. The reaction of others is similarly mediated by the extent to which they perceive the declaration to have been coerced or voluntary.

Snyder and Omoto (2001) identified five key motivations for the phenomenon of *volunteerism*, where individuals volunteer to give of their time in the service of others; such volunteerism is crucial for the

---

Box 12.8 Motivations for volunteerism

1 A general personal system of values and beliefs that includes a felt humanitarian obligation to help others. Self-centred, materialistic egotists who believe that 'it's a jungle out there' and that only the fittest will survive are less likely to become volunteers

2 Specific concern for or interest in the target group to whom the voluntary work is directed. For example, a committed Christian in the developed world may be motivated to go and give practical help to other fellow Christians in the third world

3 A desire to develop a greater understanding of the field in which one will be working. This is the rationale behind work placement programmes. The person can spend some time in the type of environment that s/he feels s/he wishes to work in, and gain first-hand insight into what is involved

4 As part of personal development. This may include the motivation to feel a sense of challenge, e.g. volunteering to become a member of the crew of a lifeboat. It may also be a wish to enlarge one's social network, by meeting other volunteers who are of the same age and likely to hold similar attitudes and beliefs

5 A need to enhance one's self-esteem and feel better about one's self. Thus, someone who earns a high salary in a very competitive but not socially satisfying job may stay in the job to earn money but at the same time become involved in charity activities in his or her spare time

---

survival of many organisations (Haski-Leventhal and Bargal, 2008). As shown in Box 12.8, the first two motivations are other-centred and the last three self-focused. Those who want to encourage others to volunteer need to take cognisance of these different motivations. For example, if producing a publicity video aimed at recruitment, as many of these motivations as possible should be targeted. As expressed by Snyder and Omoto (2001, p. 295), 'Rather that adopt a *one size fits all* approach to volunteer recruitment and training, organizations may be better served by creating advertisements and recruitment materials that differentially speak to the different motivations'.

5 *Incentives*. In their review of research in CAA, Kim *et al.* (2014) found that attitude change is highest when a small incentive is offered. People who are highly paid to carry out the CAA activity can claim they did it for the money rather than because they really believed in it. However, someone who receives a very small reward cannot use this justification and so is more likely to rationalise the CAA as reflecting personal attitudes.

6 *Involvement in message construction*. In terms of CAA, people are more likely to internalise the attitudes being espoused by a message if they have

been actively involved in its construction (Preiss and Allen, 1998). If they have formulated the message, and its core hypotheses and conclusions, they will more readily 'own' it and publicly support it. On the other hand, if they are given the message and simply asked to present it they can more readily disown it.

7   *Finality.* We are heavily influenced by commitments that are irrevocable. If there is a possibility that we can change our minds, the alternatives may linger and eventually influence our behaviour. However, if the deed is final, we are more likely to become convinced of its worth. For example, once you have signed the legal contract to sell your house you are more likely to believe that you have made the correct decision. Likewise, some in society argue that because divorce is possible it encourages less of a commitment to marriage.

Commitment to a cause is particularly strong amongst vociferous minority groups, who maintain their attitudes by using three techniques (Wojciszke, 2001):

1   *Increasing their belief in the subjective validity of their own attitude and the invalidity of opposing perspectives.* This serves to increase the difference between ingroup and outgroup. The minority believe that their views represent the only rational or logical possibility. Those who hold an opposing view are not thinking straight, do not know the full facts and so must be put right or are just biased against the minority.

2   *Over-estimating the amount of social support for one's position.* The minority group convinces itself that it has huge support for its views. This is part of what is known as the *false consensus effect*, where we believe (erroneously) that our beliefs or behaviours are more prevalent than is actually the case.

3   *Belief in the moral superiority of one's position.* Not only does the minority group see its perspective as valid, members also believe that they hold the high moral ground. A good example of this is those militant minority groups who claim to have God on their side, and so are fighting for a 'just cause' or 'holy war'.

These three perspectives are part of the phenomenon of groupthink (see Chapter 14).

Self-prophecy

The *self-prophecy effect*, also termed the *question–behaviour effect*, occurs when we are asked to predict our future performance. As summarised by Spangenberg *et al.* (2012, p. 211), 'Answering a question about performance of a behavior influences the probability of a person performing a target action in the future'. Having made a public prediction, we feel under pressure to live up to this. This is explained in terms of cognitive dissonance theory; our public espousal of a predicted behaviour creates inner pressure for us to achieve our self-prediction and so maintain a positive self-view, and causes cognitive discomfort, or dissonance, if we fail to meet our predicted goal. There is considerable evidence to support the potency of this form of self-prophecy in guiding future behaviour. In their review of research in this field, Spangenberg and Greenwald (2001, p. 52) concluded:

> several researchers have shown in multiple contexts that predicting one's own behavior can induce subsequent action consistent with the prediction, yet different than would otherwise have been observed...its robustness – regarding both the magnitude of the effect size and the variety of contexts in which it has been observed – is compelling.

As a university professor, I have become very aware of how asking final-year students to predict their degree classification, or dissertation grade, produces remarkably accurate results. In fact, during supervision of their dissertations, students, without overtly realising its effect, return to their initial self-prophecy by asking questions such as, 'Is the literature review at first-class standard?' and 'What do I need to do to make sure this is upper second?' One problem with self-prophecy, of course, is that it can be negative as well as positive. Those involved in the therapeutic professions have to deal with clients with poor self-esteem and low expectations of self-efficacy. They, too, are likely to match their projected level of negative performance. As part of the process of goal setting, therapists must therefore encourage clients to be as positive as possible in their prophecies, while staying within realistic parameters.

A related perspective here is the *theory of planned behaviour*. As mentioned in Chapter 2, this purports that a person's responses can be predicted from his or her behavioural intentions, since, 'the best predictor of behaviour is the person's intention to perform the behaviour' (Rutter and Quine, 2002, p. 11). Thus, if a self-prophecy is framed in terms of behavioural intentions, the likelihood of the prophecy being realised is strengthened. The theory of planned behaviour further argues that intentions are determined by three main factors (Thompson-Leduc *et al.*, 2015):

1   *Attitude to the behaviour.* This is based upon one's beliefs about the consequences (e.g. 'Taking drugs would adversely affect my health') and related emotional evaluations thereof (e.g. 'It would be wrong to risk my health').

2   *Subjective norms*, in the form of perceived social pressure to carry out the behaviour (e.g. 'My parents would be very sad if they heard that I was taking drugs'), moderated by the individual's desire to comply with this pressure (e.g. 'I respect my parents and do not want to let them down').

3   *Perceived behavioural control.* This refers to one's perceptions about the level of difficulty associated with performing the behaviour, and related obstacles one would face in carrying it out.

In relation to the above example, a student may believe that obtaining a first-class degree would be very beneficial (attitude to the behaviour), and positively acclaimed by family and friends (subjective norms), but that it is just beyond her ability level or would require more work than she is prepared to expend (perceived behavioural control). The student is therefore more likely to predict the more achievable, yet still personally and socially laudable, upper second, and gear her work schedule accordingly.

OVERVIEW

From the review of research presented in this chapter it is clear that the field of influence and persuasion is a multi-faceted and complex area. These are different but overlapping constructs, both of which are concerned with ways in which we can shape or change the attitudes, beliefs and actions of others. The success or failure of persuasion attempts is determined by a range of often inter-locking elements. We must be aware that targets may be resistant to change and so we need to understand the causes of such resistance and strategies that can be used to overcome it. For example, Rogers (2003) famously demonstrated how different people respond in differing ways to innovation. Some people want to be first to have a new gizmo, and warmly embrace all novel developments whether in technology, procedures or processes. Their motto tends to be 'off with the old and on with the new'. Such individuals are termed *innovators*. At the other end of the scale are those who are extremely reluctant to change their ways at all, and do not want to adopt new approaches or even adapt to them. Their mantra is 'I like things just as they are'. This group of people are called *laggards*. In between the two ends of the continuum, some will react more swiftly than others to change, and as such are more amenable to persuasion.

There is growing evidence to show that persuasion is 'additive' in that the most persuasive messages use a combination of tactics (Kim *et al.*, 2012). However, there is no set of fixed guidelines or magic formula with regard to persuasion, and attempts to persuade others can have delayed success, can fail, and indeed, can boomerang, with the target becoming even more resistant to change. Failure is more likely if targets are forewarned and inoculated against persuasion attempts. It is therefore necessary to consider the target, the situation in which the interaction is taking place and the way in which the persuasion attempt is made. Like all communication, this is a two-way process and so the target must make an evaluation of the agent in considering how to respond. This chapter has followed Aristotle's template for analysing persuasion, in terms of *ethos* (personal proofs), *logos* (logical proofs) and *pathos* (emotional proofs). A knowledge of each of the sub-elements of these areas, as summarised in Box 12.9, provides detailed insight into the fascinating world of persuasion.

Box 12.9 Summary of the main persuasion tactics

Personal proofs

- Muster all the *power* you have to good effect
- Develop a good *relationship* with the target
- Make yourself as *attractive* as possible
- Use appropriate *humour*

Logical proofs

- Deliver the message in a *confident and authoritative* manner
- Try to get the target to *argue against his or her own position*
- Back up your arguments with *case studies* as well as *hard evidence*
- Give *two-sided arguments with intelligent people*, but refute the counter-arguments
- Have a *consistent sliding scale of sequential request*, either low gradating to high or vice versa
- Invoke the norm of *reciprocation*

Emotional proofs

- Employ *threat/fear*, especially with older and less anxious subjects
- Introduce *moral appeals* to make the person feel guilty
- Emphasise the *scarcity value* of the item
- Get a public declaration of *commitment*, to which the target will then want to be *consistent*
- Ask the target to make a *self-prophecy* about his or her performance, as this will then tend to guide the target's behaviour

Chapter 13

Working things out together: the skill of negotiating

INTRODUCTION

IN THEIR ANALYSIS OF THE FIELD, Lewicki *et al.* (2007, p. v) pointed out that, 'negotiation is not only common, it is also essential to living an effective and satisfying life. We all need things – resources, information, cooperation and support from others. Others have those needs as well, sometimes compatible with ours sometimes not.' This means that we inevitably have to enter into regular exchanges of give and take with others. In this sense, 'Negotiation is a ubiquitous social activity that occurs when individuals do not have identical interests but nevertheless must rely upon others to reach their goals' (Kong *et al.*, 2014, p. 1236). While initially we may think of negotiations in the context of resolving employer–trade union wage disagreements, international disagreements or hostage situations, in fact we all have to negotiate on a day-to-day basis. It may take place in the context of, for example, agreeing where to eat, what movie to see, what time adolescents should be home on a night out, whose turn it is to walk the dog, where to go on holiday, or more formally, the sale and purchase of houses and cars.

In the work setting we have to negotiate continually with colleagues, managers, clients, suppliers, and so on. Yet, despite the huge volume of literature on the topic, many practitioners receive little or no instruction or training in this dimension of practice (Gates, 2006). Furthermore, this is a skill that has to be learned (Taylor *et al.*, 2008). From a developmental perspective, research findings show that, as children mature, their capacity for complex negotiation routines becomes more refined and developed (Green and Rechis, 2006; Kenward *et al.*, 2015). Very young children are totally egocentric. They want what they want and they want it *now*. Learning that others also have needs and wants is an important part of the maturation process, and essential for negotiation. Thus, research has shown that most children at the age of 3–4 years behave in a very selfish fashion and want to receive more than their peers (Sheskin *et al.*, 2014), but by the age of 7–8 years they have learned the importance of egalitarianism when dealing with others (Fehr *et al.*, 2008).

A main reason why negotiation plays an important role in our everyday lives is that conflict is part of social existence (Zhang *et al.*, 2014). Finnegan and Hackley (2008, p. 7) pointed out that, 'Negotiation and nonviolent action are arguably the two best methods humanity has developed for engaging constructively with conflict. Both have played central roles in helping manage or resolve seemingly intractable conflicts.' Conflict is not always negative and – at least in moderation – may actually be productive. An element of competition can start the flow of creative juices, increase the motivation of all parties and produce improved end results. As summarised by Paramasivam (2007, p. 92), 'Well-managed disagreement boosts productivity, reduces stress, sparks creativity, enhances working relationships and benefits workplace diversity'. The secret is to deal with it at optimal levels to ensure that it has positive effects. When conflict remains unresolved the results may be very damaging. Failure to ameliorate disputes can have a range of dysfunctional consequences, including unresolved and lingering resentment, relationship breakdown, financial loss, and even violence or the threat of violence. Negotiating is a more positive alternative that has a very important contribution to make to conflict management (Thompson, 2014).

But what exactly does negotiation entail, and how can we perform this process more effectively? This chapter attempts to answer these questions by charting the core features of negotiation and delineating the key skills and strategies required for successful outcomes.

DEFINITION OF NEGOTIATION

Negotiation has been conceptualised in many ways (see Morley, 2006), as, for example:

- a *game* in which both sides carry out strategic moves (such as making offers);
- an *economic forum* in which resources are exchanged;
- a *cognitive information-processing exercise* in which individuals have to use a range of intra- and interpersonal processes to make decisions;
- a *form of reflexive social action* in which people are concerned with the interpretation of messages and meanings in particular social and historical contexts.

In general terms, for negotiation to occur there has to be some incompatibility of interest, both sides must be interested in seeking a settlement and the process usually involves exchanging concessions in order to reach agreement. The term 'negotiation' has been defined in a variety of ways. Some definitions emphasise the importance of communicating with and eventually influencing the other side. In this sense, 'Negotiation is a highly interdependent process in which each party continuously incorporates information from the other party to develop responses that might lead to resolution of the conflict at hand' (Weingart *et al.*, 1999, p. 367). The notion of exchange was underscored by Robbins and Hunsaker (2014, p. 356), who defined negotiation as: 'a process in which two or more parties exchange goods or services and attempt to agree upon the exchange rate for them'.

As well as emphasising the relationship element and the search for mutual benefit, negotiation has been viewed as 'an attempt by two parties to change the terms and conditions of their relationship in a situation in which it is to their mutual benefit to do so or in which it is impossible to quit the relationship' (Whitney, 1990, p. 77). This definition highlights the fact that often people have no alternative but to negotiate with one another. Parents and their young children negotiate (often passionately) about many issues, but neither can just walk away from the relationship. Similarly, it is difficult for professionals not to negotiate with one another, or with clients, if they are to execute their duties effectively. In large organisations, sub-divisions have to negotiate regularly if the firm is to thrive. For example, the sales, production and delivery departments must co-ordinate their actions and agree a joint schedule. There is no point in salespeople winning sales that production cannot meet, or agreeing deadlines that delivery cannot make. Likewise, work colleagues have to negotiate about tasks, duties and responsibilities.

The issue of truth telling was raised by Morley (1981, p. 86), who defined negotiation as, 'an exercise in which parties struggle to exploit asymmetries of interest and power, each knowing that the other may disguise or misrepresent their real position'. Research has shown that deceit is widespread, with negotiators often giving misleading information about, *inter alia*, their resources, interests, position, alternatives and deadlines (Barry and Rehel, 2014; Fleck *et al.*, 2014). At the same time, each side knows that the other is likely to be economical with the truth by concealing or distorting their real situation (Olekalns *et al.*, 2014). The reason for this is that: 'There are very few negotiating situations where you can afford to be completely open and honest without risking being exploited by the other side' (Mills, 1991, p. 2). Continuing with this theme, Morley (1981) viewed negotiation as a type of 'incomplete antagonism' or 'precarious partnership' that allows each participant the opportunity to manipulate perceptions of common interest while endeavouring to achieve private goals. As we will see later in the chapter, effective negotiators build a relationship of trust with the other side so that there is much less suspicion of deceit.

Although the terms 'negotiating' and 'bargaining' are often used synonymously, distinctions have been made between them. While parties may enter negotiation with no intention of reaching a settlement (e.g. it may be in their interests to prolong a dispute so as to achieve a better final outcome), when they bargain it is their firm intention to make a deal. In this way, when we bargain we negotiate for agreement. Thus, bargaining has been defined as 'an operative desire to clarify, ameliorate, adjust or settle the dispute or situation' (Lall, 1966, p. 31).

In reviewing definitional issues, Thompson (1990) identified five defining features of negotiation:

1 There is a conflict of interest on at least one issue.
2 The parties are involved in a voluntary relationship, where communication is emphasised and no one is coerced into being at the negotiation.
3 The interaction is concerned with the division or exchange of resources and intermediate solutions or compromises are possible.
4 Discussion centres upon the sequential presentation of offers, evaluation of these and subsequent concessions and counter-offers.
5 Offers and proposals do not determine outcomes until agreed upon by both parties.

However, this process does not always run smoothly. One reason is that there is a balance to be struck, since negotiation is 'a mixed-motive task, one in which individuals strive to balance individual and joint gain' (Olekalns and Adair, 2013, p. 5). In this regard, Mnookin *et al.* (1996) noted three core tensions.

1 maximising one's own personal profit while at the same time attempting to ensure equity and a fair deal for both sides;
2 standing up for one's own position, yet showing concern for the interests and needs of the other side;
3 personal interests versus clients' interests. For example, a social worker has to negotiate on behalf of clients and get the best deal possible for them, but is also a government employee who needs to demonstrate to line managers an ability to stay within budgetary limits.

In relation to the last point, many people negotiate on behalf of others and not just for personal gain (Mnookin and Susskind, 1999). For example, when you buy a car, the salesperson is acting on behalf of the auto retailer and the car manufacturer, while you may be representing your entire family who will use the vehicle. Indeed, many professionals have jobs in which negotiating on behalf of others is central to their work (agents, lawyers, politicians, union officials, etc.). Research has shown that such 'accountable negotiators' work hard to achieve the expectations of those whom they represent, to avoid loss of status or respect (Peng *et al.*, 2015).

GOALS OF NEGOTIATION

As shown in Box 13.1, negotiation serves a number of very important purposes. In essence, it involves engaging in a structured and reasonably formal process during which each side should be given the opportunity to put forward their arguments, and also show a willingness to listen to the views of the other parties involved. The eventual goal is to engage in give and take in order to agree a mutually beneficial compromise position that will be acceptable to all those involved.

Box 13.1 Purposes of negotiation

To enable people to engage in a process in which parties:

1   present a sequence of arguments to support their case
2   state their preferences
3   recognise and acknowledge what the other side see as important
4   try to achieve an in-depth understanding of all the issues
5   ascertain areas of agreement and disagreement
6   enter into a series of offers and bids relating to personal targets
7   seek out options to overcome areas of disagreement
8   engage in a process of mutual concession making
9   formally agree and ratify a final deal that is acceptable to both sides, and that can be successfully implemented

NEGOTIATING STRATEGIES

The main decisions to be made during a negotiation encounter can be interpreted in terms of a negotiating decision tree (Figure 13.1). The first decision is whether or not to enter into negotiation at all. Malhotra and Bazerman (2007, p. 282) advised that a decision not to negotiate should occur:

> when the costs of negotiation exceed the amount you stand to gain… when negotiation would send the wrong signal to the other party, when the potential harm to the relationship exceeds the expected value from the negotiation, when negotiating is culturally inappropriate, or when your BATNA [best alternative to negotiated agreement] beats the other side's best possible offer.

If a decision is taken not to negotiate, then the latter, BATNA, should already have been formulated. Ury (2007, p. 58) describes a BATNA, or what he also refers to as a plan B, as the best course of action to protect your interests in the event that you cannot reach agreement with the other side. Thompson (2014) pointed out that a BATNA is a fact of life rather than something that a negotiator wishes for. This is because negotiations can and do fail, and each party is then left with their BATNA (Figure 13.1). Conlon et al. (2014, p. 328) point out that, 'a negotiator's BATNA determines what a negotiator will do if an agreement is not reached'; they also review research to show that negotiators with higher-value BATNAs achieve better deals than those with lower-value ones. A strong BATNA can be disclosed to the other side as a negotiating tactic to encourage them to agree a deal.

Two aspects of the BATNA are important. First, the opposing side may try to moderate your perceptions of your BATNA in a negative fashion. In other words, they may attempt to persuade you that your BATNA is actually worse

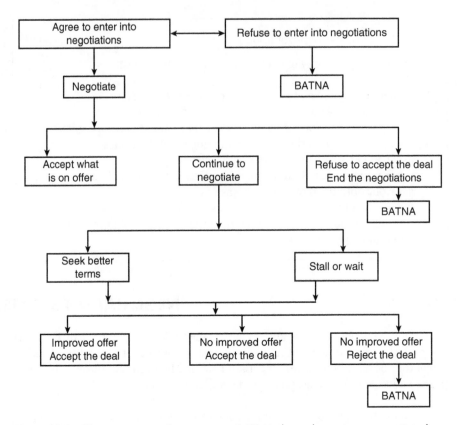

Figure 13.1 The negotiation decision tree. BATNA, best alternative to negotiated agreement.

than you had thought. It is therefore important to work out your BATNA carefully and objectively, and not to deviate from your belief in this, whatever the counter-arguments. Second, you should attempt to ascertain what the other side's BATNA is, and be aware that they may not tell the truth about this. In his review of the area, Wong (2014, p. 78) concluded that, 'Knowledge of opponent BATNAs is probably the most important information negotiators can have in a negotiation'.

If negotiation begins, it may be either a short or long process, depending upon how things progress. Indeed, 'time-outs' are often an important part of the scenario, where both sides leave to consult privately with relevant colleagues. These time-outs can be very useful to provide each side with the time, space and distance to take a 'helicopter view' of what is happening. To adapt a well-known analogy, during time-outs the solidity of the wood on offer can be separated from the shape of the trees surrounding the deal.

Another possibility is that of stalling, during which one side may engage in *avoidance negotiation*, which is defined as 'an effort to defeat negotiation by mimicking its purpose' (Wallihan, 1998, p. 267). This may be part of what is an overall avoidance strategy, where one side withdraws from any active engagement in negotiation (Taylor, 2002). It can also take the form of *demand avoidance,* where one side prefers the status quo but is under pressure to be 'seen' to be negotiating. This can be part of *opportunistic avoidance,* where eventual agreement is not ruled out, but one side knows that a delay in reaching settlement is to their benefit. This is also referred to as *false negotiation,* which 'occurs when a party gains more by stalling the negotiations until an external change takes place that improves its position considerably' (Glozman *et al.,* 2015, p. 671). For example, a strike may be very costly for a manufacturer, and so the trade union may hope to get a better eventual deal for its members by holding up negotiations and allowing the strike to continue. Wallihan illustrated how nations, before they declare war on their neighbours, need to be seen to have 'tried to reason' with them, and so negotiate for a time before declaring their opponents to be 'intransigent', 'aggressive' or 'insulting'.

In essence, there are four main negotiation strategies (Hargie *et al.,* 2004):

1   *Unilateral concession.* Here, one side simply yields to the demands of the other. Bingham (2007, p. 113) aptly summarised the advantages and disadvantages of just giving in:

> This strategy makes sense if you may be wrong, if you are in a weak position, if you want something in the future, and if you want to preserve the relationship. However, it may be a mistake if you believe you are right, the issue is important, and the other is unethical.

The person who unilaterally concedes often feels aggrieved and resentful at the outcome. It is therefore not a viable long-term strategy.

2   *Individual gain.* Here, one party is interested only in how best to maximise its share, with no thought whatsoever for the other side. There is no concern as to whether others do well or badly, just an all-encompassing focus upon self. In one-off negotiations this may work, but the other side will feel alienated, and if further negotiations are required then this approach may well backfire.

3   *Competition.* This usually occurs in what is known as *distributive bargaining,* where both parties attempt to obtain a higher share of the distribution of benefits than the other. Competition is also more likely in *zero-sum* payoff situations, so called because the total sum involved in the negotiation equals zero and a gain to one person is a direct loss to the other. For example, if I ask for a pay increase of 8 per cent and the company offers me 2 per cent, then if I accept, the company will have benefited by 6 per cent and I have lost by the same amount. As a result, this is also referred to as win–lose negotiation. It is, of course, possible to reach a compromise by finding some common ground between the initial offers through distributive bargaining – for example, in agreeing to split the difference at a pay increase of 5 per cent. A danger with competition is that the whole negotiation edifice may collapse if neither side is willing to concede what they perceive to be defeat (or surrender), and so it becomes *lose–lose* negotiation. As Lax and Sebenius (2006, p. 8) concluded,

'the aggressive win–lose negotiator gets a better deal some of the time. But he or she may damage relationships in the process, may overlook more creative agreements, and may even precipitate a deadlock, thereby causing promising discussions to break down.' In a meta-analysis of research into *distributive* bargaining, Hüffmeier *et al.* (2014) found that the use of hard-line negotiation strategies resulted in higher economic outcomes, whereas softer strategies produced better socioemotional outcomes. In particular, hard-line negotiators achieved larger economic benefits in circumstances in which they were instructed to maximise outcomes, the opposing party was male, negotiation was face to face, and they were aware of the bargaining range within which a settlement was possible.

4   *Co-operation.* In this strategy, negotiation is viewed as a form of problem-solving exercise, with the goal of achieving the best possible deal for both sides. The emphasis is upon *integrative bargaining*, in the context of a variable-sum payoff in which both sides can benefit from the deal. This transforms the negotiation into a *win–win* encounter, or what is known as a *mutual gains approach* (Movius *et al.*, 2006). Unlike distributive bargaining, where the focus is upon how to 'cut up the cake', with each intent upon getting the bigger share (or even the whole lot), the possibility of both producing a bigger cake is acknowledged when co-operation is countenanced (Kong *et al.*, 2014). As summarised by Tomlinson and Lewicki (2015, p. 86), an integrative approach is 'best suited for not only reaching an agreement (as opposed to impasse), but also for ensuring that the resulting agreement will fulfill its purpose, continue in force, and facilitate subsequent agreements'. The concept of justice is very important for successful negotiations; each side should feel that the agreed deal is fair and equitable (Druckman and Wagner, 2016). Conditions favouring a win–win approach are outlined in Box 13.2. A word of caution is warranted here, since someone who is very co-operative may experience internal pressures to compromise and so may be vulnerable to manipulation by a competitive and deceptive opponent (Murray, 1990). Also, effective negotiators are able to employ co-operative and competitive behaviours, as and if required, at different points within a negotiation (Haselhuhn *et al.* 2014). This is important since negotiators have to 'cooperate to ensure that the supply of resources available for exchange is as large as possible and to compete to ensure that they are able to claim an acceptable share of these resources for themselves' (Neale and Fragale, 2006, p. 32).

Four possible outcomes can emanate from these negotiating strategies.

1   There may simply be *no agreement* and negotiation breaks down.
2   There may be a *victory for one side over the other*. In negotiation parlance, and following the work in this area by the Italian economist Vilfredo Pareto, *Pareto superior* agreements occur when the outcome creates added benefits to one party without incurring losses for the other. *Pareto inferior* agreements occur when one side ends up worse off.

Box 13.2 The seven rules for 'win–win' negotiations

1 Have a main goal of achieving an outcome that maximises the outcome for both sides
2 Do not view negotiation as simply getting the best for yourself. Likewise, do not see it as a contest in which you have to beat the other side. These strategies are likely to result in conflict and lessen the benefits for everyone
3 Remain flexible and do not adopt an entrenched position. Remember, there are many routes to Success City in negotiations
4 Develop a good relationship with the other party, founded on mutual trust
5 Foster the capacity to distinguish the people from the problem – overcoming the latter should be seen as a joint venture
6 Investigate the needs that may be driving demands – often demands can be adapted in ways that still satisfy the underlying needs
7 Approach the task on the basis of logic and reason, rather than being swept along on a tide of emotion

---

3 A *compromise solution* connecting the two offers may be agreed.
4 An *integrative agreement* can occur in which both sides achieve higher joint benefits than in the compromise. Such *Pareto optimal* agreements occur where both sides achieve the best possible gains and the benefits to one side cannot be improved without reducing the gains to the other.

A widely used, if somewhat contrived, example that illustrates the difference between these approaches is that of two sisters arguing over who should have an orange. If negotiation breaks down, neither gets the orange. In unilateral concession, one sister would just give the orange to the other, and in the individual gain approach one sister would try to get the entire orange. In the competitive strategy, a compromise could be reached whereby they agree to divide it in half and distribute the halves equally. However, using the co-operative mode, following discussion they discover that one sister wants the orange to squeeze for juice, while the other just wants the peel for a cake she is baking. As a result, they reach an integrative agreement where one sister gets all of the peel and the other gets all of the juice. Both benefit more than in any of the other strategies. A more realistic example would be where a salesperson offers a corporate buyer a product at a discount of 4 per cent per unit for 500 units. The buyer in return initially asks for a discount of 10 per cent per unit. In relation to the above four strategies:

1 Negotiation may break down and no sale is made.
2 The seller agrees to the higher discount of 10 per cent, or the buyer agrees to the 4 per cent offer.

3   They split the difference at a discount of 7 per cent.
4   They work out a new deal wherein the company buyer agrees to take not just 500 but 10,000 units of the new product over a set period, if a discount of 10 per cent is agreed. In other words, both sides benefit.

There are three main reasons why integrative agreements are the most effective negotiating outcome (Pruitt, 1990; Roloff, 2014).

1   They are likely to be more stable, whereas compromises are often unsatisfactory to one or both parties, leading to issues not being fully resolved and thus re-surfacing in the future.
2   Since they are mutually beneficial, they help to develop the relationship between the two parties. This, in turn, facilitates communication and problem solving in later encounters. An important feature in negotiation is what is known as the *response in kind* (Griessmair *et al.*, 2015). This refers to the norm of reciprocity, whereby if we receive something positive from another person we feel obliged to reciprocate by giving something positive back (see Chapter 12 for more information on reciprocation). Alternatively, if we receive negative feedback from others we are likely to return it in kind. Integrative behaviour is likely to beget integrative responses from the other side. In contrast, as Watkins (2006, p. 11) cautioned, 'Driving deals that are too favourable for you can leave counterparts bitter, disinclined to energetically implement agreements, and looking for payback next time'.
3   Where aspirations are high and both sides are loath to concede, compromise may simply not be possible and an integrative approach, which allows both sides to gain, will be the best solution.

STAGES IN THE NEGOTIATION PROCESS

Negotiations have been conceptualised as typically progressing through, and characterised by, five sequential stages: pre-negotiation, opening, exploration, bargaining and settlement.

The pre-negotiation stage

Before meeting face to face, time and effort should be devoted to preparing for the encounter. Time devoted to planning is time well spent, and so negotiators should never short-change themselves on making ready. Indeed, preparation is often regarded as the most important part of negotiation (Simons and Tripp, 2007). Thus, Cairns (1996, p. 64), citing the maxim 'Failing to prepare is preparing to fail', cautioned negotiators to 'ignore it at their cost'. Rackham (2007) investigated differences in the planning strategies of skilled and average negotiators. As well as interviewing negotiators about their planning techniques, actual planning sessions were observed and recorded. There were actually no differences in amount of planning time *per se*. Rather, it was what they did with the time that mattered. Skilled negotiators considered a much wider range of possible outcomes and options – 5.1 per issue, as opposed to 2.6 for average negotiators – and gave over three times as much attention to areas of common ground.

The key elements of the pre-negotiation stage are: the formulation of realistic goals, identification of key issues, information gathering, deciding upon the type of negotiation to pursue, and the formulation of an agenda for the negotiation.

Formulating realistic goals

To adapt an old maxim: 'If you don't know where you are going, how will you know what direction to take and whether you have arrived?' Before entering into negotiations it is essential to be fully aware of your goals (Roloff and Jordan, 1992). Indeed, as shown in Figure 13.1, the first decision to be made is whether or not to enter into negotiations at all. For example, the other side may be seen to be completely inflexible and impossible to deal with, your demands may simply not be negotiable or the goals may be achievable in some other way. If negotiation seems the best option, decisions need to be made about resistance and target points.

The *resistance point* is the bottom line beyond which you decide that a deal will not be done. It has also been termed the *reservation price* (Carnevale and Pruitt, 1992) and the *minimum necessary share* (Morley, 2006). It is also sometimes called the 'walk-away' point, for obvious reasons. Related to this is the *target point* or *target range*. This is also known as the *level of aspiration* (Hüffmeier et al., 2014). It is the ideal point that you hope to attain. The goal of negotiation may be viewed in terms of achieving an exact amount (target point) or as settling somewhere between an upper and lower limit (target range). Rackham (2007) found that skilled negotiators were significantly more likely to plan in terms of a settlement *range* (e.g. 'I'd like 6 per cent discount but would settle for 2 per cent minimum'), whereas average negotiators planned around a fixed *point* (e.g. 'I want to get 6 per cent discount'). It has also been shown that negotiators obtain better results if they focus their efforts upon achieving their target point rather than concentrating upon not going below their resistance point (Galinsky et al., 2002).

In terms of gender, research indicates that males tend to set higher target points than females, and so achieve higher gains, and that females are more likely to settle once their resistance point is met (Olekalns and Smith, 2012). One suggested reason for this is that women may moderate material benefits to ensure positive relational outcomes (Kray and Babcock, 2006). Females prefer a co-operative strategy and may do less well than males when negotiating in competitive or distributive encounters (Niederle and Vesterlund, 2008; Hüffmeier *et al.*, 2014). There is also evidence that norms and social role expectations of gender behaviour can serve to make negotiating more difficult for females (Stuhlmacher and Linnabery, 2013), so that women who negotiate assertively may be negatively labelled by males (e.g. as 'ball breakers')

(Babcock and Laschever, 2008). Similarly, females who make higher demands tend to be evaluated more negatively than males who negotiate at the same level (Bowles *et al.*, 2007). Another gender difference here is that males tend to retaliate to what they perceive to be threats to their status, whereas females are more likely to retaliate to threats to their tangible resources (Geniole *et al.*, 2015). Indeed, there is evidence that when women are negotiating for personal rewards in a context in which they are aware of what others have received, they are as aggressive as males (Douglas and Miller, 2015). In their meta-analysis of research, Mazei *et al.* (2015, p. 85) concluded that 'gender differences in negotiations are contextually bound and can be subject to change'. While they found that males in general achieved better economic outcomes than females, these differences were reduced when the situation had low role incongruity for females, when they had previous negotiation experience, were given information about the bargaining range or were negotiating on behalf of someone else.

It is important to remember that the other party has target and resistance points. Deals will be struck somewhere between the two sets of resistance points, and so this is known as the 'settlement range'. It is also referred to as the zone of possible agreement (ZOPA). If there is no ZOPA, in that the resistance points are hopelessly far apart, then negotiations will break down (Haselhuhn, 2015). In the example given in Figure 13.2, the buyer would ideally wish to purchase 550 units at the agreed price, whereas the seller wants to sell 650 at this price. The respective resistance points, which represent the worst deals for each side, are 600 for the buyer and 500 for the seller, and so this is the ZOPA within which any eventual settlement will occur. One of the first things an experienced negotiator attempts to do is to ascertain the target and resistance points of the other side, so a deal can be made that is closer to the opponent's resistance point.

Identifying key issues

When examining issues, a guiding principle is to be as flexible and open as possible. Try not to conceptualise the process as a single-issue debate. Think

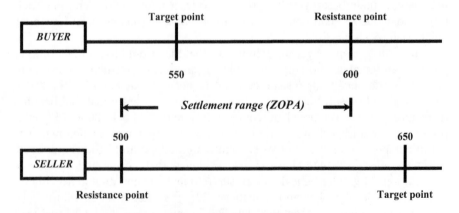

Figure 13.2 Example of target and resistance points in negotiation.

laterally to identify everything that might be important. Once the main issues have been identified, they should then be prioritised. Which are absolutely essential and which are more peripheral? How, in what ways, and to what extent are issues linked? In essence, as much information as possible should be gathered about all aspects of the negotiation. Negotiators have been shown to differ in their degree of self-monitoring. High self-monitors are more occupied with situational norms, the impression they create and how they are being reacted to by others (Griffin and Bone, 2014). They then adjust their performance accordingly. Low self-monitors are guided in their behaviour to a greater extent by internal thoughts and feelings. Jordan and Roloff (1997), in an analysis of written pre-negotiation plans, discovered that those of high self-monitors were not only more elaborate than low self-monitors, but that this type of negotiator subsequently achieved a higher percentage of initial profit goals.

Gathering information

Forewarned is definitely forearmed when negotiating. It is vital that all members are fully apprised of their own team's perspectives on all of the key issues. The arguments in favour, and likely counter-arguments and how these can be overcome, should all be worked out in advance. Metaplanning is also important, in that party A should try to see the planning world through the eyes of party B. It is useful to consider realistically how much they know about your position. Do they have an accurate picture of your true BATNA? Similarly, as much information as possible should be gleaned about the other side's likely position on each issue. As advised by Davies (1998, p. 128), 'You need to know as much as you can about your opposite number: who they are, what they want, how they are likely to act and react'. It is also beneficial to know something about the interactive style of the other party. Do they tend to play hardball or are they likely to be more co-operative?

This process of information gathering allows areas of potential agreement and conflict to be formulated. Staking out common ground shared by both sides is always important, as it enables the negotiation to be built upon a solid foundation of early joint agreement. However, likely areas of disagreement should also be identified, together with possible proposals for overcoming them. This includes an analysis of what and how much you can concede, and the concessions you may realistically seek from the other side in return.

Deciding upon the type of negotiation to pursue

The next phase is the decision about how to 'play' the negotiation. Cultural background is a factor here, since it can affect how negotiators conceptualise the process and behave during actual negotiations (Gelfand and Brett, 2004; Adair et al., 2013). Salacuse (1998), in an investigation involving 310 negotiators from North America, Latin America and Europe, across professions such as law, engineering, accounting, the military, teaching and marketing, identified a range of factors that are affected by culture (Box 13.3). Some studies

---

Box 13.3 Some variations in negotiations across cultures

Factor	Cultural response range
Communication style	Indirect ....Direct
Aspirations	Individualist ....Collectivist
Protocol	Informal ....Formal
Goal	Task ....Relationship
Negotiator selection	Experience/ability ....Status/position
Attitude to negotiation	Win–win ....Win–lose
Persuasion preference	Logic/reason ....Affective/emotional
Attitude to time	High/clock-driven ....Low/events-driven
Team structure	Consensus ....Leader-dominated
Risk taking	High/risk-tolerant ....Low/risk-averse
Nature of agreements	Explicit ....Implicit

---

have found that the Japanese are much more amenable to win–win encounters than are the Russians (LePoole, 1991), and more likely to adapt tactics in line with the other party when involved in intercultural integrative negotiations (Adair *et al.*, 2001). By contrast, Russians tend to have an aggressive style of negotiating (Balykina, 2015). However, Salacuse (1998) also found that professional and occupational culture was as important as national culture in determining negotiation behaviour. Thus, in a study of negotiators in Costa Rica, Ogliastri and Quintanilla (2016) found that some had an emotional and expressive style while others adopted a formal, rational style. Likewise, Metcalf *et al.* (2007) in an investigation involving 1,000 business people across four countries (Finland, Turkey, USA and Mexico) found differences in approach between negotiators from the same country, and also considerable similarities in negotiation styles across countries. They concluded that, rather than depending upon pre-set cultural stereotypes, negotiators should take cognisance of the individual attitudes of the other party. A similar conclusion was reached by Movius *et al.* (2006, p. 390) in their detailed investigation of cultural differences in negotiation: 'it is a mistake to assume that all individuals from a culture have the same personality or background…it is also a mistake to ascribe difficulties or uncertainties that emerge during negotiations to "the unique culture" of a given country'.

Formulating an agenda

Following on from the above considerations, a proposed agenda for the negotiation can be drawn up, to include the items that you wish to discuss and the preferred order. Of course, the other side will have its own ideas about what should be discussed and when. An important element here may be the actual location for the negotiations. In some settings this may not be a problem – for example, in sales negotiations, the salesperson usually visits the buyer. There is an advantage to negotiating on your own 'home ground', where you will tend to feel more relaxed and the opposition may be less settled (Mills, 1991). There can also be benefits in visiting the other person's patch to gain some insight into where s/he is coming from (e.g. status in the organisation and the nature of the operation). Negotiations may, of course, take place at a neutral location so that neither side feels disadvantaged. This is often the case in political negotiations, where much of the dispute is about territory.

Flexibility is important in relation to how issues are to be addressed. Rackham (2007) found that average negotiators tended to use sequence planning, where each issue had to be dealt with in turn (i.e. issue 1 → issue 2 → issue 3 → issue 4). The problem is that the other side may wish to discuss issue 4 first. More successful negotiators therefore simply planned in terms of key issues, which they would then be willing to discuss in any order. The term *mono-chronicity* refers to the tendency to deal with information one issue at a time, while *polychronicity* relates to the capacity to deal with many different issues simultaneously (Turner and Reinsch, 2007). Brett *et al.* (1998) found that negotiators high in polychronicity were more effective. They discovered that joint gains (win–win encounters) were influenced by three key factors: 'a value for information sharing, an ability to deal with multiple issues simultaneously, and the motivation to keep on improving the option on the table' (p. 78).

Having said all the above about the importance of preparation, flexibility must be the key, as things do not always go according to plan. Indeed, Wilson *et al.* (2001, p. 305) described negotiation as, 'a complex planning environment'. It may sometimes be necessary to formulate multiple goals in circumstances where there are only fuzzy criteria for ordering priorities. Again, while pre-planning is essential, initial decisions typically have to be revisited and revised when the negotiation gets under way.

The opening stage

As discussed in Chapter 10, the opening phase of any interaction is of key importance, and negotiation is no exception. During the initial meeting, decisions are made about how co-operative or competitive the other party is likely to be, and whether the social relationship will be conducive to the task in hand (Kolb and Porter, 2015). As the ideal is the development of a win–win framework, the general advice here is to be co-operative and courteous, but also well organised (Scott, 1988). As discussed earlier, negotiators often respond in kind to each other's use of strategies and tactics (Brett *et al.*, 1998). The process where the approach adopted by one side causes the other to reciprocate is also known as *entrainment*. Thus, if one party seems frosty and adopts a rather belligerent opening stance, it is likely that the other will follow suit (Taylor, 2002). On the other hand, a more co-operative and amenable initial approach is also likely to be responded to in kind (Weingart *et al.*, 1999). This can be facilitated by the use of 'we' language to indicate joint responsibility for the process (e.g. 'We seem to agree that our main joint concerns are...'). Several factors are central to the establishment of a good negotiating rapport (Berry, 1996; Kolb and Porter, 2015):

- paying attention to and allowing time for opening rituals such as personal introductions;
- verbally and nonverbally displaying signs of receptivity and enthusiasm;
- ascertaining what issues the other side regards as important and giving recognition to these;
- portraying any identified difficulties as problems to be solved jointly;
- avoiding point scoring or cheap one-upmanship ploys to gain an early advantage; these can backfire and cause problems for the entire relationship.

The final act of the opening phase is usually the ratification of an agreed agenda, endorsed by all those present.

The exploration stage

Here, parties begin to examine one another's positions. This allows each side to become familiar with the main proposals being put forward by the other. If these are in complete symmetry and harmony, then an agreement may be possible without further negotiation. If there are areas of disagreement, then these should be fully identified and clarified. Party A can only hope to satisfy the demands of party B, and vice versa, by ascertaining exactly what these are. An important aspect at this stage is probing in depth beyond the expressed surface-level demands, to explore the needs that may underpin these. What people say they want may not always be what they really need, and following concerted discussion and sharing of perspectives, this often becomes clear. In addition, the needs may be capable of being met in ways other than expressed in the initial demands. But this realisation usually takes some time and so the exploration stage should not be rushed. Indeed, later breakdowns in the negotiation process can often be traced back to a lack of time devoted to initial exploration and clarification of demands, wants and needs.

The goal here is to achieve a panoramic view of the other side and chart the full topography of their needs terrain. The contours of the peaceful valleys where areas of agreement lie, and of the rugged hills of dispute that will have to be climbed, should then be carefully drawn. In addition, ways in which both sides can help one another to climb these hills should be identified. It is important to remember that the purpose is not to begin bargaining at this juncture. The main goal relates to the exploration and clarification of core areas of each other's position. It has been shown that an in-depth understanding of the precise nature of the outcome gains that can be made by the other side, rather than just an awareness of their interests, leads to more effective negotiation (Moran and Ritov, 2007). Central to all of this is the skill of listening (Finnegan and Hackley, 2008). As explained in Chapter 7, this involves paying attention to the other person's verbal and nonverbal messages, to the slant or emphasis they put on what the individual says, as well as listening to what is not being said. In her analysis of hostage situations, Dunne (2001, p. 15) pointed out that, 'The best negotiators are good listeners'. If the auguries are good following exploration, then the parties can move on to the next stage, that of bargaining.

The bargaining stage

Once a decision has been made to move from initial explorations to more substantive bargaining, two main processes come into play, making proposals and concession making.

Making proposals

The opening proposals must be clearly stated. Both parties should fully understand precisely what the other is proposing. The generally accepted rule here is that the initial proposal should be high (if you are selling) or low (if buying), but realistically so. For instance, if you apply for a job where the percentage performance bonus is negotiable, and you learn that the average executive in a similar post receives a 4 per cent bonus, it would be inappropriate to ask for a bonus of 20 per cent. Initial bids should not be so high or low that they appear to be lacking in credibility, are seen as nonsensical or the person making them is regarded as highly avaricious. Outrageous opening proposals can quickly lead to a 'take it or leave it' position and negotiation breakdown (Gatchalian, 2000). The first offer should also be stated in a confident manner. If a high/low bid is made in an apologetic fashion it is immediately undermined. It is important to avoid 'one-down' statements such as 'I think this is probably far too much to ask for, but...' Realistically high/low opening gambits presented in an assertive fashion serve a number of important functions, in that they:

- influence the opposition's estimate of your target and resistance points and can in turn move their target point more favourably in your direction;
- provide information about the other side's goals; careful scrutiny of their reaction allows insight into their target and resistance points (Do they seem stunned at one end of the reaction scale or overly happy at the other?);
- allow 'generous' concessions to be made if necessary;
- make the eventual settlement, with your concessions, appear more appealing to the other side.

Another decision here is whether or not to make the first proposal. Is it better to get in first or to play a waiting game so that your bid can take advantage of the knowledge gleaned from the other side's opening shot? It seems that there are advantages and disadvantages in both strategies, and so a decision about this issue needs to be based on the specific nature of the negotiation. The advantages are that the side that goes first:

- is proactive, and the second party then becomes reactive and may be more on the defensive;
- sets the initial rate; there is evidence from distributive negotiation that if the seller makes the initial offer, the settlement price is higher than if the buyer makes the initial offer (Magee et al., 2007);
- can make the other side revise their target point in the light of the initial demand. Studies show that the other side may 'anchor' around the level of the opening offer and fail to moderate their counterproposal back towards their own target (Maaravi et al., 2014); the eventual settlement is then more favourable for the party making the first proposal (Carnevale and De Dreu, 2006).

Some of the disadvantages, on the other hand, are that the side that opens may:

- not bid at a sufficiently high (or low) level and so be at an immediate disadvantage;
- be put on the defensive by the other party if they begin to probe the initial offer;
- have to make the first concession after the other party has made a counter-proposal.

Concession making

When both sides have made their opening pitches, the process moves on to one of trying to formulate mutually acceptable compromises in which each side moves towards the other's position. Positional bargaining has been described by Fisher et al. (2011) as happening when each side adopts their own position and argues for this, but also makes concessions in order to secure a compromise. A concession is a change in the level of demand made by party A in the direction of party B's interests that reduces the level of benefit for A (Hargie et al., 2004). Concessions lead to *position loss*, which can be interpreted as a willingness to compromise and be co-operative. They are an essential part of the process, since a failure to offer any concessions tends to create a perception of not negotiating 'in good faith', which in turn can lead to a breakdown of the process (Hüffmeier et al., 2014). However, if too many are conceded too quickly, this can result in *image loss*, where the person is viewed as someone who is weak and easily manipulated. Interestingly, Morris et al. (1999) discovered that negotiators often attribute the bargaining behaviour of the other party to personality and personal predispositions (e.g. disagreeableness, truculence) rather than to the circumstances of the negotiation with which they are confronted. Such misperception can evoke a more hostile response, if a lack of willingness to compromise is attributed to the other party being seen as an obstinate or greedy individual, as opposed to being interpreted as due to the fact that the organisation to which the person belongs has given strict guidelines about what can and cannot be negotiated.

A core dimension of negotiation is the ability to persuade the opposition to make concessions. Pruitt (1981) identified four main tactics in this regard:

1   *Promote a friendly atmosphere.* The goal here is to develop a socia-
    ble relationship between bargainers that is conducive to 'give and take'.
    Friends will not want the negotiation to spoil or destroy their relation-
    ship and so are willing to forgo economic benefits so as to reduce conflict
    and possible negative relational outcomes (McGinn, 2006). For example,
    Halpern (1994) found that buyers offered higher opening amounts and
    sellers made lower initial demands when dealing with friends as opposed
    to strangers. Interestingly, this bias to co-operate can have a down side.
    Friends can actually lose out on a better deal for both sides, owing to the
    fact that they wish to avoid the appearance of being awkward. A relational
    bias towards affiliation means they are liable to settle for the first mutually
    acceptable solution to emerge, when more debate and discussion about
    all the alternatives might have produced a higher, Pareto optimal, result
    (Jeffries and Reed, 2000).

2   *Impose time pressures.* This is a common tactic used in attempts to influ-
    ence others. For example, companies offer bargain discount rates – but
    only for a set time period; time-share salespeople offer a 'special price'
    which will be withdrawn if the prospective buyer leaves without signing
    a contract; and, in hostage negotiation, threats may be made to execute
    hostages at a set time if demands are not met.

3   *Increase the impression of firmness.* This may involve making small con-
    cessions but few of them as a way of seeking reciprocal concessions from
    the other side. Firmness can be enhanced through emphasising that there
    are specific reasons for the concessions, such as:

    •   emphasising that this is a one-off event ('Just this once and just for
        you – do not tell anyone else I gave you it at this price');
    •   stating that the concession is based on special circumstances ('There
        is a new model coming in next month so I want to sell off this one');
    •   seeking a reciprocal concession. This may involve *logrolling* – that
        is, trading off pairs of issues that differ in importance to both parties.
        For example, a car dealer may agree to offer a longer warranty
        (at small personal cost) rather than reduce the price of the car, while
        the customer values this service and sees it as adequate compen-
        sation for no price reduction. Experienced negotiators have been
        shown to use logrolling more often and more effectively than novice
        negotiators (Loewenstein and Thompson, 2006).

4   *Reduce the opponent's resistance to making concessions* by using a
    range of techniques, including:

    •   Face-saving devices. These make it easier for the other side to con-
        cede without appearing to lose or be weak. Maintaining and saving
        face is very important in conflict situations (Zhang *et al.*, 2014). This
        can involve some of the techniques discussed in 3 above in relation to
        perceptions of firmness (e.g. explaining that you understand the con-
        cession will only be a 'one-off'). This is important since, 'Sensitivity

to the other side's face does more than head off resistance: it lays the groundwork for trust' (Kolb and Williams, 2007, p. 211).

- Highlighting the benefits of the deal. For example, the head of a university department may use the argument with senior management that if more staff were allocated to the department the research profile would improve, in turn bringing in more money and greater prestige for the university. Kennedy (1998) termed this tactic 'Sell Cheap, Get Famous', a title derived from the entertainment industry, where actors can be persuaded to lower their fee on the promise that the film will make them famous and open the door to untold fame and fortune. The persuasive benefits of logical arguments are fully discussed in Chapter 12.

- 'Salami slicing'. This is so called on the basis that if you request a whole salami from someone the person may well refuse. However, if you ask for just one slice you are more likely to succeed. If you keep getting more small slices you end up with most of the salami.

- Threats. While these can force concessions, they are not usually recommended since they are viewed as hostile and so are dysfunctional for the relationship between the two parties (Putnam and Roloff, 1992). The threatened side is likely to counter with threats of equal force; will not be committed to any settlement achieved; and will feel resentful, attempting to seek revenge where possible. Research findings clearly show that threats are associated with less successful outcomes (Olekalns and Smith, 2001). As Fisher (2001, p. 77) put it, 'making threats is a particularly expensive and dangerous way of trying to exert influence'. If threats are used these should be portrayed as emanating from a third party (e.g. 'There is no way my union members would accept that. If I go back and put it to them I know they will want to go on strike').

- *Fait accompli.* Under certain conditions a pre-emptive strike may force the other side's hand. Terrorists may set off a large bomb explosion so that they are then seen to be negotiating from a position of strength (with the threat potential of further such bombs also ever present). A spouse may buy a new dining-room suite and have it delivered, arguing that it can be sent back within 10 days if the partner so desires.

- Power. As discussed in Chapter 12, power is an important factor in interpersonal relationships. In negotiations power is 'the ability to control consequences, to achieve one's goals, and particularly to get others to serve one's goals, even against their own preference' (Nelson et al., 2015, p. 2). People who control resources have been found to have a definite advantage in negotiations (Cai et al., 2001; Magee et al., 2007; Sturm and Antonakis, 2015). This is because 'powerful negotiators tend to end up with the larger share of the pie' (Van Kleef et al., 2006, p. 559). An extreme example is that a shop owner is unlikely to cede to a polite request to give all the money in the cash register to a stranger, whereas if the stranger is wielding a handgun then the request is likely to be acceded to. In this case the gun represents greater power. Imbalances of power have a marked influence upon negotiating encounters, in that those who have power will tend to use it and so be less open to making concessions or listening to counter-arguments. Thus, Kipnis and Schmidt (1990, p. 49) found that:

The more one-sided the power relationship at work, the more likely managers are to demand, get angry and insist with people who work for them, and the more likely they are to act humble and flatter when they are persuading their bosses.

However, it is hardly surprising that people are happier with the outcomes of bargaining encounters when both sides have equal power (Mastenbroek, 1989). People tend to be unhappy if they feel they have been 'forced' to reach a settlement. As pointed out by Korobkin (2007, p. 255), 'Before attempting to employ bargaining power, the negotiator must carefully compare the gains that might be achieved to the increased risk of impasse today and the costs of angering, alienating, or reducing trust among potential future trading partners'.

Garko (1992) carried out an investigation into the influencing strategies employed by physician executives (those carrying out managerial roles) when attempting to gain compliance from superiors. They found that, with superiors who interacted in an attractive fashion (were attentive, friendly, relaxed), reason was used most frequently. On the other hand, with superiors who interacted in an unattractive style, assertiveness, bargaining, coalition formation with others and reference to higher authority were more likely to be used. Thus, it would seem that with people of higher power or status, the negotiating tactics of subordinates are influenced by the interactive approach of the former.

Concessions are an integral part of negotiations. Where differences exist, without concessions there can be no mutual agreement. It is important, though, that concession making is guided by the pointers shown in Box 13.4.

The settlement stage

Catching the settlement moment is a key aspect of negotiation. There comes a time when the other side is receptive and a deal can be struck. If this is missed, problems can arise. When a settlement attempt is made too early the other party can feel pressurised and resentful. Conversely, if the opportunity is missed, further issues may then be raised and more concessions sought by the opposition. The closing stage is important in all interactions (see Chapter 10), including negotiation. At some stage there comes a point beyond which it is not possible to

Box 13.4 Pointers for making concessions

Bargainers should:

- not concede too readily
- make concessions as small as possible
- monitor the number and rate of concession making
- link concessions to an image of firmness

Bargainers should not:

- concede too soon in the negotiations
- make the first main concession
- make unilateral concessions
- make large initial concessions – this is likely to give an impression of weakness
- concede without due consideration of the positive and negative consequences for both parties
- always engage in reciprocal concessions. A concession by the other side may be justified in its own right – it may bring that party's bid down to what is a reasonable level

concede any further. The secret is to convince the opposition that in all honesty this point has been reached and any deal must be struck at this limit. A number of elements are crucial to agreeing a settlement (e.g. Cairns, 1996; Kennedy, 1998).

Trial closure

Here, one side behaves as if a deal has been agreed and so is moving beyond this to the fine-grained implementation issues. It includes what are known as 'assumptive questions', where the assumption of a deal is inferred in the question. An example would be, 'Do you intend to pay by cheque or credit transfer?' Linked to this is what is termed 'summary closure'. This involves providing a summary of what the other side has gained in the way of concessions, what the benefits are for them of the deal as it stands and outlining the potential dangers of failing to agree this deal. Negotiators should scan for settlement indicators from the other side. Positive signals include *implementation questions* (e.g. 'You can definitely deliver at that price?'), *confirmatory statements* (e.g. 'That seems like a reasonable deal') and *nonverbal responses* (smiling, head nods and receptive facial expressions).

Split the difference

As mentioned earlier, this is quite common in sales negotiations as a way of reaching agreement. It is fine in a basic one-off negotiation for a single item, but where issues are more complex it is not always applicable. In addition, if one side has already conceded a considerable amount and the other has conceded little, then the 'difference' is not just what is left.

Celebrate success

Both sides need to feel that the agreement has been a good one from their point of view. This cements the relationship and facilitates future encounters. It also helps to ensure that the deal will not unravel, but will actually be implemented. Celebrations may include smiles, handshakes and hugs; breaking open the bubbly; or having a meal out together.

Document the agreement

In formal negotiations, agreements are typically enshrined in a written legal contract, although the actual drafting and signing may take place at a later date (Guirdham, 2002). Settlements that cannot be enforced are of little value. It is important, therefore, that all parties are agreed on the exact terms of the deal. Time spent jointly reviewing and agreeing the precise nature of what has been negotiated can avoid difficulties at a later date. For example, the ongoing confusions and uncertainties amongst political parties that have plagued subsequent development in Northern Ireland in the aftermath of the Belfast Agreement can be traced back to areas of the settlement that were left (deliberately) vague. Thus, one party to this Agreement later used the interesting semantic argument that, while what was negotiated was an (interim) *agreement* it was not a (final) *settlement* (of the political dispute). Paying attention to detail and ensuring that this is contained in the written documentation can pay dividends when it comes to implementing the resolution. It is worth spending time discussing how, and in what ways, the deal will actually be implemented in practice. Who will do what, when will it be done and how is it to be carried out? Also, what are the ramifications if what has been agreed is not implemented? What penalties and costs will be incurred by either side?

NEGOTIATING SKILLS

There is general agreement that negotiation is a higher-order skill, involving a range of other sub-skills (Taylor, 2002; Kesting and Smolinski, 2007). As expressed by Lewicki (1997, p. 265), 'effective negotiation is not a single skill; rather it is a complex collection of elements that entail aspects of strategizing, advocacy, communication, persuasion, and cognitive packaging and repackaging of information'. Similarly, McRae (1998, p. 2) likened negotiation to 'a symphony orchestra of skills. Each instrument (subskill) must be used together with all the others in a harmonious and congruent manner. If one instrument (subskill) is off, the whole orchestra will be off.'

While there is consensus in most texts about what good negotiators should do, and a host of laboratory studies have been conducted in this area, there is not a great deal of empirical research into the behaviour of negotiators in real encounters. The main reason for this is that conducting such research necessitates obtaining the agreement of both parties to the negotiation, and this is obviously difficult to arrange – especially given the delicate nature of such encounters. One major empirical study was carried out by Rackham (2007), in which the author studied 48 successful negotiators over a total of 102 separate negotiating sessions, and compared their behaviour with that of a similar number of average negotiators. Rackham used three criteria to select the effective negotiators, namely they should: (1) be regarded as successful by both sides; (2) have a consistent record of significant success over time; and (3) have a low incidence of implementation failures – they should reach agreements that work. It was found that skilled negotiators showed significant differences to average negotiators on a range of behaviours. These, and other key negotiating behaviours, will now be reviewed.

Leadership

Many negotiations take place between groups. Indeed, even if only two individuals engage face to face, they will be reporting to and liaising with a range of others. This means that the skilled negotiator must have the capacity to organise and co-ordinate a group of individuals. Each group in a negotiation is rarely a homogeneous entity. Many groups suffer from divisions and disagreements between members. A minority may not concur with the majority view as to the way ahead. Intra-group disharmony has to be dealt with in such a way that it does not jeopardise the negotiation effort and outcomes (Wood, 2001). There should be a designated leader – someone who is both a recognised content expert in the field within which the negotiation is taking place, and who has successful experience of bargaining. This individual, who should have skills in consensus building, will then co-ordinate and direct the team effort in preparing for, conducting and evaluating the effectiveness of the bargaining encounters (see Chapter 14 for more information on leadership skills).

Empathising and problem solving

It is clear that the ability to be empathic is a characteristic of effective negotiators (Lax and Sebenius, 2006; Martinovski *et al.*, 2007). The capacity to empathise by seeing the world through the eyes of the other person is very important. People are unlikely to accept your view of their situation readily, but rather need to be reassured that you appreciate their perspective. Thus, efforts should be made to understand where the other side is coming from and to communicate this understanding overtly (Davis, 2015). It is said that in negotiation the cheapest (and often most warmly received) concession that you can make is to show that you are paying attention to what the other side is saying. You need to ascertain what their concerns are and why they have these. Why might they accept or reject your proposals? Linked to this, when presenting a proposal, skilled negotiators frame this as a problem to be solved. The golden rule is to 'Present your proposals as solutions to problems. State the problem before you give your answer' (Morley, 2006, p. 413). Bald proposals are often seen as selfish moves and as the other side listens they formulate counter-arguments as a way of obstructing these. When cast as a joint problem with a suggested solution, the listening perspective changes and the encounter becomes more co-operative.

Controlling emotionality

While negotiation is often regarded as a logical process, emotions are an important part of the process (Olekalns and Druckman, 2014; Martinovski, 2015). The most effective negotiators are those who, as well as being able to think logically, can understand and control their emotions (Fisher and Shapiro, 2006). As shown by Adler *et al.* (1998), the two most intense emotions in negotiation are fear and anger. The former may be caused by anxieties such as the deal falling through, being told untruths, losing out unnecessarily or not achieving all that one should. The development of a good trusting relationship helps to reduce such fear-arousing thoughts. While expressions of anger tend to produce higher concessions from the other side than displays of other emotions (Adam and Brett, 2015), high levels of anger have been shown to be destructive to the negotiation process (Taylor, 2002), and so must be controlled. The recipient of anger may harbour resentment and a desire for retaliation, which can take covert forms such as spreading rumours about the other side to damage their reputation (Wang *et al.*, 2012). The expression of anger can be directed towards the offer (e.g. 'That offer is ridiculous'), or targeted directly at the other person (e.g. 'You are being ridiculous'). Where the anger is focused upon the offer, the other side is more likely to make larger concessions, but when it is directed at the person the other side tends to concede less (Van Kleef *et al.*, 2008). Those who display anger also suffer a loss of image, in that the other person forms negative impressions of them, expresses lower levels of satisfaction with the negotiation and is disinclined to interact with them in the future (Van Kleef *et al.*, 2006). Anger can be caused by one side:

- being found to have given misleading or untrue information;
- insisting on discussing unimportant details;
- not listening to what the other has to say;
- making unreasonable or excessive demands;
- being rude or overtly aggressive;
- querying the other person's ability or authority to negotiate;
- over-stepping their authority;
- going over the other person's head to deal with his or her superior.

While expressing concern for the feelings of the other party is important in all negotiations, in crisis situations, 'detecting and controlling emotional arousal is one of the primary concerns of negotiators' (Rogan and Hammer, 1995, p. 554). More generally, Liu (2014, p. 12) has demonstrated how, 'The essence of successful crisis negotiation is effective communication'. As a result, in these contexts (e.g. suicide attempts, criminal barricades, hostage taking or prison revolts) the tactics used include:

- communicating empathy and concern for the other;
- using an encouraging and agreeing style to calm the other person;
- making appeals to the person ('Please, please do not hurt anyone');
- giving frequent reassurance;
- protecting and saving the perpetrator's face;
- slowing the pace of negotiation;
- emphasising that the interaction is one of problem solving (as opposed to crisis).

Rackham (2007) identified two negative emotional facets of negotiation that can be dysfunctional for the process, and so need to be curbed: irritators and defend/attack spirals.

Irritators

As the name suggests, irritators are words or phrases used by one side that irritate, annoy or offend the other. Examples include:

- 'unreasonable demand' (this is doubly irritating – the proposal may have been put forward as being perfectly reasonable, and the term 'demand' suggests aggression);
- 'very fair offer' (again, this is annoying, as it is up to the other side to decide what is fair and what is not);
- 'you are being unhelpful' (such an accusation is likely to cause problems for the relationship as it is an attack on the other party's interactive style).

Rackham (2007) found that less skilled negotiators used five times as many irritators as skilled ones. Often these irritators are used without too much conscious thought. When caught up in the emotional heat of the occasion, they can slip out. Thus, negotiators need to take care with their forms of expression. There is little point in describing an offer as a 'good deal' if the other side does not think it is.

Defend/attack spirals

This occurs when one side accuses or attacks the other and this is responded to in kind, leading to a spiral of retaliation, with the result that emotions become heated and the entire relationship begins to disintegrate. As summarised by Lytle et al. (1999, p. 32):

the reality is that negotiations, especially in the dispute context, often become ugly and difficult...parties may find themselves drawn to respond to threats with counter-threats, escalating the negotiations to a standoff from which it is difficult or embarrassing to retreat.

For example:

A: 'You don't seem to want to resolve this, as you keep raising objections to every reasonable proposal we make. We may have to pull out of these talks.'

B: 'On the contrary, you have done everything to prevent an agreement and we are the ones who have had to deal with your ridiculous demands. So don't try to threaten us, as we may be ahead of you out of the door.'

A: 'You think that we're the problem? I don't believe I'm hearing this.'

B: 'That's exactly been the problem. You just don't listen.'

Given the potential relationship damage that can emanate from such encounters, not surprisingly Rackham (2007) found that skilled negotiators were significantly less likely to get entangled in emotional defend/attack spirals.

Building trust

Trust is at the heart of successful relationships (Korsgaard *et al.*, 2014), and so has been shown to be a central feature in negotiations (Lewicki and Polin, 2013; Kong *et al.*, 2014). It has been defined as, 'the extent to which a person is confident in, and willing to act on the basis of, the words, actions, and decisions of another' (McAllister, 1995, p. 25). We rarely develop or maintain positive relationships with people of whom we are suspicious or wary. As shown by Alon and Brett (2007), the outcome of a negotiation is highly dependent on a relationship of trust. It can be divided into three separate components (Jeffries and Reed, 2000):

1   *Cognitive trust* refers to the extent to which we believe someone has sound technical know-how or a solid knowledge base.
2   *Affective trust* is rooted in the degree of emotional feeling of attachment, and of mutual care and concern for one another's well-being, that exists.
3   *Organisational trust* encompasses both intra-organisational (the extent to which staff trust others in their own organisation), and inter-organisational (the degree to which staff in two corporations trust one another) dimensions.

Where all three types of trust are present at high levels, negotiations are enhanced. The skill of self-disclosure is central to relationship development and trust (see Chapter 9). Rackham (2007) termed this 'giving internal information'. His results showed that effective negotiators used this skill more than average negotiators, especially in relation to their feelings about the way the negotiation was progressing. He pointed out that, 'This revelation may or may not be genuine, but it gives the other party a feeling of security because such things as motives appear to be explicit and above board' (p. 180). As a result, the use of self-disclosure is likely to contribute to the establishment of trust in the negotiator. This technique can also serve as an alternative to disagreeing, e.g.:

- 'I'm very worried that we seem to be so far apart on this'.
- 'I'm uncertain how to react to what you've just said. I like most of it, but I feel some doubts'.

Providing focus

A key aspect of negotiation is the ability to keep the discussion focused on the main issues at hand. Two sub-skills are important here: questioning and behaviour labelling.

Questioning

Given the fundamental importance of this skill in social encounters (see Chapter 5), it is not surprising that questioning is central to effective negotiation (Lewicki et al., 2014; Thompson, 2014). Rackham (2007) found that skilled negotiators asked over twice as many questions as average negotiators. Questions serve several important functions in negotiations (Miles, 2013). A primary purpose is to gather detailed information about the other side and their aspirations. In their analysis of the use of questions in negotiations, Kolb and Porter (2015, p. 152) point out that, 'The more we know about the other's concerns, the more likely it is that we can propose ideas that meet our mutual needs'. Questions also allow the questioner to control the focus and flow of the interaction since the opposition has to answer the questions and in so doing has less space for contemplation. This, in turn, gives one's own side a breathing space to reflect on the current state of affairs. Finally, questions can act as an alternative to an overt statement of disagreement. Compare the following statements by a trade union official when negotiating a pay deal with a corporation:

A: 'No. Our members would never accept that proposal.'
B: 'You know our members fairly well. How do you think they would react to this proposal?'

The approach used in B is much less abrasive and more likely to produce a receptive response.

Behaviour labelling

Skilled negotiators have been shown to signal in advance more often the behaviour they are about to use, by labelling it (Rackham, 2007). For example, rather than asking a question outright (e.g. 'How many can it produce per day?') they are more likely to announce it in advance (e.g. by saying 'Can I *ask you a question*? How many can it produce per day?'). Other examples of behaviour labelling include:

- 'I would like to *make a proposal...*'
- 'I would like to *listen* to your concerns...'
- 'Could I *suggest a compromise* here...'
- 'If I could just *explain* to you why we see this as so important...'

Rackham found that skilled negotiators used five times as many instances of behaviour labelling as their average counterparts. This process of labelling is beneficial in that it reflects a formal and rational approach to bargaining, and subtly puts pressure on opponents to reciprocate in a logical fashion (Morley, 2006). Since it flags the behaviour that is about to follow, it provides focus, reduces ambiguity and clarifies the purpose of the next comment. It also helps to ensure that the negotiation is conducted at a moderate pace. Part of this labelling process involves the acknowledgement of *joint progress* (e.g. 'We are getting on really well here...'). Effective negotiators are twice as likely to make statements labelling joint progress as their less effective counterparts (McRae, 1998).

However, one behaviour which average negotiators were more likely to label was that of expressing disagreement. By comparison, the skilled negotiators gave reasons which in themselves were expressions of disagreement, but tried to avoid overt statement of dissent. Rackham argued that the order in which our thought processes occur involves deciding that an argument is unacceptable and then assembling the reasons to show why. He posited that average negotiators follow this tendency overtly, whereas those who are more skilled are able to stifle this initial impulse. When one side has put forward an argument it is likely that a blunt statement of disagreement will increase their antagonism and aggression and make them less likely to give in. Indeed, Dunne (2001, p. 15) illustrated how in hostage contexts the general advice is that 'the negotiator should never reply "no" to any question posed by the kidnapper'. The calm presentation of counter-arguments, without a public statement of negation, encourages logical debate, such that the eventual acceptance of alternative proposals then involves much less loss of face. It is therefore a useful general rule always to give reasons before (or as an alternative to) expressing disagreement. Furthermore, what has been termed *process labelling* has been shown to be effective in resolving disagreements (Lytle *et al.*, 1999). This involves openly stating and recognising that both sides simply cannot agree about an issue, and that it may be more productive to move on to discuss other aspects first and return to the contentious issue later.

Testing understanding and summarising

As discussed earlier in the chapter, it is crucial for both parties in a negotiation to be fully cognisant with what has been discussed and agreed. It is not unusual for a negotiation to end with each side holding differing views about what has been agreed. A primary concern among less skilled negotiators is to achieve agreement, and so they tend to ignore rather than confront areas of potential ambiguity or misunderstanding. Rackham (2007) found that, to circumvent such confusion, skilled negotiators checked for agreement on all of the issues to ensure that the deal could be fully ratified and implemented. Thus, they used summaries at the end of key points in the negotiation, to check that both sides were in full agreement about precisely what had been decided. A linked skill here was that of reflection, and indeed, this skill has been shown to have a number of advantages in encounters where clarification of communication is important (see Chapter 6). Reflective statement helps to portray concern for the other side. Examples of reflections in negotiating include:

- 'So delivery times are crucial for you'.
- 'In essence you are saying that if we can move on volume you could move on price'.
- 'You are clearly concerned about this'.

Reasoned argument

As explained in Chapter 12, the use of logic can be very persuasive. In negotiations, the image of rationality is desirable. Rackham (2007) identified two aspects that should be avoided to ensure that arguments are used to maximum effect: retaliatory counter-proposals and argument dilution.

Retaliatory counter-proposals

A mistake made by inexperienced negotiators is to respond to a proposal with an immediate counter-proposal, e.g.:

> A: 'We will offer you a discount of 10 per cent per unit providing we are your sole supplier for the next 12 months'.
> B: 'Well, what we want is for you to pay all delivery costs and guarantee delivery times'.

Here, while delivery and guarantees may be important to B, these could have been addressed after responding to A's initial proposal. Rackham found that skilled negotiators used about 50 per cent fewer counter-proposals than average negotiators. Counter-proposals are not recommended in negotiation, for three reasons.

1   They muddy the waters. One side has put forward a proposal and suddenly a different one is introduced by the opposition. Which should be discussed? One at a time? Both together? In some instances the first side retaliates to the counter-proposal by introducing a third proposal and this immediately throws the entire process completely out of kilter.
2   They are annoying. One side has made what they regard as a valid proposal and they want this to be fully considered. A counter-proposal completely

ignores their bid, and so they in turn are less likely to treat this with respect or consideration.

3   They are regarded as blocking tactics rather than serious proposals *per se*, and so counter-proposals tend to get lost in the negotiation mists that follow. Arguments then begin to become emotional rather than logical.

Argument dilution

Less skilled negotiators tend to give more reasons to justify their bids. This is not good practice, since the more reasons that are proffered, the better chance the opposition has of finding and highlighting a weakness in at least one of them. This then puts the first party on the back foot. Rackham argued that this is because weaker arguments tend to dilute stronger ones. Interestingly, he also found that an unexpectedly high proportion of skilled negotiators had little formal higher education and suggested that graduates, having been steeped in a culture of devising numerous reasons to defend and justify a case, then suffer from the dilution effect in negotiation encounters. Skilled negotiators tend to put forward one reason at a time and only introduce another reason if they are in danger of losing ground.

OVERVIEW

This chapter has examined the nature of negotiation and charted its defining features. The relationship between negotiating and bargaining has been explained. There is a burgeoning literature in this field that has identified a range of strategies and skills central to effectiveness. The alternative strategies of negotiation were charted and the likely outcomes of each discussed. The typical process of negotiation was outlined and the role of concession making therein highlighted, and tactics for producing concessions from the other party itemised. Finally, the key skills employed by effective negotiators were discussed in concert with the behaviours that they tend not to employ.

In the mind of the layperson, negotiation is often perceived as a game of hardball played by tough-minded, hard-boiled, aggressive individuals. Here, the objective is seen as winning at all costs and, if the other party is singed in the process, well, then, they should avoid the heat of the negotiating kitchen in future. But this win–lose perspective is both short-sighted and mistaken. The focus in negotiation should not be on who gets the spoils but rather on how to improve the spoils for both parties. The objective is not victory for one side, but for both. To achieve such win–win outcomes the following points need to be borne in mind:

- view negotiation in a co-operative frame;
- try to develop a good relationship and a sense of mutual trust;
- identify all of the issues at the outset;
- these issues should be re-interpreted as necessary;

- never lose sight of the total picture when single issues are being discussed;
- be flexible as to how your goals are to be achieved;
- identify and highlight areas of agreement and common interest;
- begin with these to establish initial rapport;
- build a relationship of trust;
- show a concern for partnership through the use of 'we' language;
- listen carefully to and empathise with the other side;
- use questions to understand their perspective and slow the pace;
- overtly recognise and acknowledge what they see as important;
- think laterally about new options that might be introduced to overcome disagreements;
- treat differences as challenges to be overcome;
- stay rational and avoid emotionality;
- separate the people from the problem – be kind to the former and work hard on the latter;
- use gentle persuasion techniques rather than threats, anger or coercion;
- formally review, agree and ratify the final settlement.

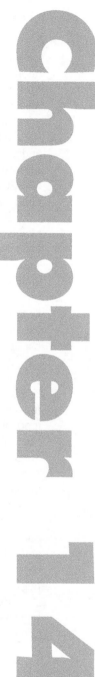

Chapter 14

Working with others: skills of participating in and leading small groups

INTRODUCTION

G ROUPS HAVE ALWAYS BEEN an integral part of the human experience. Group living is universal across cultures and societies. In terms of evolution, the ability to work as a group facilitated human development by enabling us to fulfil basic needs such as protection and defence, food seeking and child rearing. Groups also contribute to the satisfaction of psychological needs such as support, information and self-esteem. Not only do groups make it easier for us to complete a wide array of tasks, they also provide a sense of identity (Corey *et al.*, 2014). As summarised by Levine (2013, p. 1): 'In order to understand human behavior, it is essential to understand the critical role that groups play in people's lives'. If individuals are asked to write about or explain who they are, it is not long before they begin to anchor a sense of self in some particularly salient group membership/s. We are born into a social group (the family) and, as we develop, come to play a more active part in an increasing number and range of other groups. Growing out from the family, children find themselves in playgroups, school classes, sports teams, youth groups, and so on. In later life these are replaced by a host of other groups, such as student societies, work teams, drama groups, choirs, golf clubs, leisure classes, trade union committees, parent–teacher associations and political party executives, to mention just a few of the myriad possibilities.

Increasingly, the contemporary workplace is structured to optimise the dynamic potential of small groups, especially when moulded into teams (Levi, 2013). Such teams require skilled leadership. As shown by Tourish *et al.* (2007, p. 5): 'Effective leadership is increasingly recognised as an important factor in determining the ability of organisations to achieve their aims and objectives. Many organisations are therefore investing a great deal of time and money on various forms of leadership development'. Indeed, Peshawaria (2011) points out that some $60 billion is spent annually on leadership training, most of which is devoted to developing the skills of individual leaders. Focusing upon health-care delivery, Northouse and Northouse (1998) made the point that many functions that were previously performed by an individual both in community and acute care settings are now team-based. This is perhaps particularly true of mental health care, where Yalom and Leszcz (2005) identified a wide diversity of group involvement.

Shifting the setting from the workplace to the community, again groups play a prominent role. They may include volunteer, civic or church groups that meet the needs of different sections of the community, and in different ways. The phenomenal rise in popularity of various forms of self-help group can be included here. In this regard, Napier and Gershenfeld (2004) highlighted the growth of self-help groups that had been set up to help members deal with problems including, *inter alia*, bereavement, illness, marital breakdown, poor self-esteem and gender issues. They estimated some half a million variants in the USA alone, with a collective membership of approximately six million people.

Different attempts have been made to impose order on the wide variety of groups that exist by developing a typology of categories (e.g. Lickel *et al.*, 2006; Spencer-Rodgers *et al.*, 2007). Much of this work relates to the functional significance of groups for the individual. Johnson *et al.* (2006) identified three main motivational drivers for group membership. First the desire for *affiliation* – the need to belong and feel a sense of connectedness with others. These needs are met through membership of small, intimate groups such as family or friends. A second drive is the need for *achievement*, in terms of feeling a sense of competence, success and mastery. Such needs are met through, for example, membership of sports teams or established business corporations. The third type of motivation relates to *identity* needs, in terms of maintaining and enhancing one's sense of self-identity. Individuals can meet these needs through membership of political parties, church congregations or supporters' clubs. Of course, these needs are not mutually exclusive, so membership of particular groups can help to satisfy more than one type of need.

Perhaps the most common distinction here is that between *task* and *process* alternatives. These have also been referred to as the *task* and *social* (Fujishin, 2013), or *task* and *relationship* (Northouse, 2013), dimensions of groups. This distinction is also portrayed as a continuum of communication with *content* messages at one extreme and *process* messages at the other. The former are primarily concerned with substantive issues, quality of decisions reached, amount of output, etc. In task groups, such as committees or boards of directors' meetings, most of the interaction is at this level. Process messages, by contrast, address relational matters, the internal workings of the group and the well-being of its members. Process groups rely strongly upon such contact: examples include those delivering a therapeutic service. However, most groups share elements of both; it is the relative proportion that serves to locate them at some point on a task–process continuum. *Midrange groups* are those where

---

Box 14.1 Common types of small group

1 *Family* – this is our first group
2 *Friendship/leisure* – meet needs for affiliation, emotional expression and relaxation
3 *Work* – facilitate productivity
4 *Self-help/action* – mobilise individual and community support for courses of action
5 *Training/therapy groups* – promote personal awareness and growth
6 *Spiritual* – meet transcendental needs
7 *Laboratory/focus* – short-term groups whose purpose is to provide research data

---

content and process exchanges are roughly balanced. A more differentiated list of group types can be found in Box 14.1.

While many of the communication skills that form part of dyadic interaction are also used when people get together in groups, there are added complexities associated with the latter. It is with such factors that this chapter is concerned. The starting point is a consideration of what exactly is meant by 'a group', and a number of basic features associated with the concept. This will be developed further by concentrating upon the characteristics and skills associated with a rather special and particularly important position within the group – that of leader.

DEFINING FEATURES OF A GROUP

Devising a formal definition of 'group' is more difficult than it might initially appear. It is fairly self-evident that a group necessarily involves a plurality of individuals – but how many? While four or five people would probably be acceptable, would 40 or 50 – and what about 4,000 or 5,000? Is a group the same as a gathering, a crowd or a mob? What about an audience, is it necessarily a group? Can a group be thought of as any social category – e.g. all Portuguese women over 2 metres tall? Have groups special characteristics and qualities that set them apart from other social aggregates? Indeed, does the word 'group' refer to a specific entity at all? For example, in an early treatise on the subject, Cartwright and Zander (1968) concluded that it merely marks an area of study whose boundaries are altogether blurred and uncertain. More recently, Levine (2013) pointed out that many scholars have moved away from attempting to draw a definitive distinction between 'groups' and 'non-groups', but instead now focus upon the characteristics of 'groupness'.

One common distinction is that between *small groups* and larger collectives. This chapter is concerned with the former. Describing a group in this way suggests that quite a precise numeric specification should be possible. However, while figures can be found suggesting membership of from 2–5 at the lower end to 15–20 at the upper, there is little agreement on precise numbers, leading many to abandon attempts to define small groups purely in terms of size *per se*. Size alone does not seem to be what really counts. Rather, the telling factor is its ability to facilitate or inhibit other interactive processes. Gamble and Gamble (2012) argued that the optimal size for a task group is the smallest number of people capable of effectively completing the assigned task. The multinational corporation Amazon agrees and operates a two-pizza rule, stipulating that no group meeting should involve more people than could be fed on two pizzas. A number of significant features of what exactly constitutes a small group have been teased out by, for example, Johnson and Johnson (2013) and Levine and Hogg (2009), and these will now be considered.

Interaction

To belong to a group, members must be able to interact with others who are also part of the collective. Until relatively recently the importance of face-to-face interaction was stressed. This requirement was conspicuous in the definition by one of the early authorities in this field, George Homans (1950, p. 1), who defined a group as 'a number of people who communicate with one another often over a span of time, and who are few enough so that each person is able to communicate with all the others, not at secondhand, through other people, but face-to-face'. Face-to-face communication is, of course, more media-rich than alternative forms. This characteristic also forms the basis of the distinction between primary and secondary groups, first drawn by Cooley (1929). Primary groups are typified by the potential for close and frequent face-to-face association. But do people have to be in each other's presence for 'groupness' to occur? What about those who regularly keep in contact via the internet? It is now accepted that virtual groups, who make use of technologically mediated interaction, should not be denied group status on that count alone. However, in this text the focus is specifically upon face-to-face communication.

Influence

Not only should members interact but they should be subjected to mutual influence in the process. Each must be able, to some extent, to make a difference to the way that others think, feel and behave and be influenced in return. Indeed, this is one of the most important stipulations of groupness (Levine, 2013). In this way, as noted by Wheelan (2005, p. 121), 'group members and the group create a mutual influence system'.

Shared goal/s or common interest/s

The fact that groups are typically formed for some identifiable purpose and that those who belong share at least one common goal has long been regarded as an essential characteristic (Hare, 1976). Furthermore, having a common goal, vision and sense of mission have been shown to be very important sources of influence in focusing the group's energies and shaping its processes and procedures (Hare and O'Neill, 2000). Thus Rothwell (2016, p. 32) defined a group as 'a human communication system composed of three or more individuals, interacting for the achievement of some common goal(s), who influence and are influenced by each other'. Indeed, Larson (2010) illustrated how effective groups produce 'synergy', which refers to the gains in performance outputs that accrue when individuals work as a cohesive group as compared to the same number of individuals working on their own. In the case of a formal group, its goal is often reflected in the name (e.g. Eastham Branch of the Animal Rights Movement; Eastham Photographic Society; Eastham Miners' Welfare). Interestingly, when a group's goal has been attained (or rendered obsolete), members may channel their energies in other directions, thereby ensuring the continued existence of the group. Eastham Miners' Welfare may still meet to have a drink and play snooker even though the Eastham coal pit has long since closed. New goals can come to dominate group activities. In other cases, the achievement of the group goal or goals results in the group's demise.

Apart from acting to maintain the group and direct its activities, goals also influence the development of particular structures and procedures within it. Such considerations will be dealt with more fully in a later section of the chapter.

Inter-dependence

In addition to interacting with and influencing each other, the inter-dependence of group members is often highlighted as a core defining feature of a small group (Platow *et al.*, 2012). Members share a common fate. If the group fails to achieve the set goal no member is successful. Thus events that affect one person will have a bearing on the rest of the group and group outcomes will affect each individual member.

Shared group identity

Another important feature is the requirement that members see themselves as belonging to a group: that they share a sense of group identity. This type of more subjective criterion involves the concept of people's self-categorisations. As such, a group exists to the extent that two or more individuals consider themselves as belonging to the same social category. The corresponding perceptions of non-group members are also important. Members must be seen by outsiders to belong to this collective. As expressed by Hogg (2004, p. 203), 'Groups exist by virtue of there being outgroups. For a collection of people to be a group, there must, logically, be other people who are not in the group.' The concept of entitativity is of importance in this regard. Entitativity refers to the perception that a collection of individuals actually constitutes a separate entity or group, and so are high in 'groupiness' (Kurebayashi *et al.*, 2012). There is a continuum here, in that groups may be more or less entitative. Thus, intimacy groups, such as family, will be perceived as being very high in entitativity, while loose aggregations, such as individuals standing on a railway platform, will be seen as very low in entitativity.

Shared social structure

When individuals join a group they begin to function in terms of a system of expectations that shapes what they do as members and their contribution to the collective. They start to take on a role and abide by a set of norms that specify appropriate conduct. They will also slot into a particular status structure, according to which prestige and a sense of value are bestowed. These pivotal elements of group structure will be returned to shortly.

Various definitions combine sets of these key characteristics. For example, Johnson and Johnson (2013, pp. 7–8) defined a small group as: 'two or more individuals in face-to-face interaction who are aware of their positive interdependence as they strive to achieve mutual goals, aware of their membership in the group, and aware of the others who belong to the group'. Along similar lines, Beebe and Masterson (2014) delineated small-group communication as interaction amongst a small number of individuals who have a feeling of belonging to the group, share a common purpose and influence one another to ensure that their goals are achieved.

WHY DO PEOPLE JOIN GROUPS?

As discussed earlier, a common explanation as to why people join groups is that we rely upon group membership to achieve goals and satisfy certain needs that would be either more difficult or impossible to satisfy alone. In particular, groups help us to achieve material, interpersonal and informational needs.

Material needs

It can be advantageous for individuals to pool and share their various resources in order to complete a task more efficiently. Each will differ in the knowledge, skills and physical attributes as well as possible technical expertise to be contributed. As mentioned earlier, the evolutionary perspective is that the gregarious nature of *Homo sapiens* stems from the advantages of working together in groups. Trade union and co-operative movements are among the examples of aggregates that are formed to further the material well-being of members. The group can directly provide advantages or be indirectly instrumental in bringing them about. For instance, a person may join the local golf club to avail of the related business contacts that come with membership. In this way, we become attracted to a group on account of the sorts of activities in which participants engage and the outcomes that they achieve. This attraction is strongest when those outcomes coincide with what we want for ourselves and when membership is believed to enhance our opportunities for success.

Interpersonal needs

By their very nature, to be successfully met, these require some form of group contact. Individuals on their own cannot satisfy them. Such needs, according to Schutz (1955) in a seminal work, may be for varying degrees of:

1   *inclusion* – to want to belong or feel part of a social entity;
2   *control* – to dominate or be controlled;
3   *affection* – at the extremes, to love (and be loved), or hate.

Argyle (1995) also proposed that much of interpersonal behaviour is in response to social drives for affiliation, dominance, dependency, ego-identity or aggression. But, of course, being able to dominate depends upon one or more others who are prepared to be submissive. Likewise, it is impossible to be dependent if there is no one to depend upon. The sense of identity that membership affords has already been mentioned and is among the advantages of being part of a collective. In sum, we gravitate towards groups whose members we find attractive, and where we feel that we will be accepted and well received.

Information needs

While we may not have to join a group in order to gain knowledge of aspects of our physical environment, it is only through association with others that we come to an understanding of the social world that we inhabit and, indeed, of ourselves. As discussed in Chapter 9, social comparison is an important phenomenon. According to *social comparison theory*, individuals make judgements about the quality of their abilities, or accuracy and justifiability of beliefs and opinions, by watching others perform similar tasks, or listening to what they have to say on relevant topics (Suls and Wheeler, 2012). By so doing you gradually create an impression of yourself, including your strengths and weaknesses. For example, it is only possible to decide if you are a good, average or weak student by comparing your marks with others on the course. Feelings of self-worth are heightened when the individual compares favourably with others on tasks valued by other members and diminished when the opposite is the case.

Social comparison processes can have pronounced effects for the group as well. A common finding is that groups of people often take more extreme decisions than individuals on their own. In this way, following discussion, members of a group are likely to decide upon a more extreme decision than if they had acted alone. One explanation for this *risky shift* or *group polarisation* effect makes use of social comparison (Kugler *et al.*, 2012). This is because members obtain insights into the stances taken by others in the group in relation to the issue as it is discussed. Being seen to be 'middle of the road', or 'sitting on the fence', tends to be unattractive, so initial positions are shifted to be more extreme in the direction of the prevailing pole. Another aspect here is that the riskier decision is not the responsibility of any one individual – there is collective accountability. As a result, the group as a whole decides upon a riskier, or more polarised, position than would any single member acting alone, as this person would then have sole responsibility for the outcome.

To conclude this line of thought, to be a loner is not only to be denied potential material benefit and fellowship, but also an understanding of ourselves and our social worlds. It is not surprising that small groups are so prevalent.

HOW ARE GROUPS ORDERED AND REGULATED?

Given that groups are made up of individuals, each with particular, and often contrasting, personalities, opinions and preferences, it seems reasonable to ask how they manage to become sufficiently organised and co-ordinated for goals to be pursued efficiently and effectively. Order within the group is made possible through the creation of structure in respect of *norms*, *roles* and *status*, and the related processes of *conformity* and *cohesion*.

Norms

The emergence of norms is of crucial importance in regulating the activities of members. As groups evolve, regularities of operation begin to emerge that reflect the creation of expectations on the part of members. The most common of these are *performance norms*, whereby new members are given explicit or implicit messages about what the group regard as acceptable standards of behaviour, in terms of work levels, outputs, attitude to punctuality, dress code, and so on (Robbins and Judge, 2013). Norms can be defined as:

> behaviours, attitudes, and perceptions that are approved of by the group and expected – and, in fact, often demanded – of its members. Such socially established and shared beliefs regarding what is normal, correct, true, moral and good generally have powerful effects on the thoughts and actions of group members.
>
> (Baron and Kerr, 2003, p. 6)

Thus, it is not only overt performance that is subject to a normative influence, but also the characteristic perceptions, thoughts and feelings that members entertain.

Napier and Gershenfeld (2004) teased out four main types of norm, differing in levels of formality and explicitness.

1   *Documented.* These sets of prescriptions are explicit and written down in a formal code of conduct. They are typically communicated directly to those in the group, together with the consequences of violation. Examples would include receiving a contract of employment once one has taken up a new post, or giving a newcomer the members' Handbook of Rules and Regulations governing club activities.

2   *Explicit.* Here the norm is drawn to the attention of members, but the expectations would not typically be codified or documented. As such they

are slightly less formal, but certainly not to be disregarded. Thus, a CEO addressing new employees at an induction session states, 'We like our male executives to present the right image for the company, wearing a smart suit, collar and tie'. Although this form of dress code may not be written into the contract of employment, the newcomers are very likely to take cognisance of this advice.

3   *Implicit.* In this instance, requirements are not stated directly but have to be assimilated more discreetly by watching what established members do and following their example. It is often only when a violation occurs that one becomes conscious of the existence of the norm. For example, some years ago a friend of mine was undertaking a teacher training course. On his first day of teaching practise at a very formal school he did not realise that in the staff room it was the norm that everyone sat in a particular chair. He broke this implicit norm by sitting in an available seat, but was quickly told by another member of staff, 'Mr Davies always sits there'.

4   *Invisible.* Here the norms are so tightly woven into the fabric of group life that they can no longer be identified as separate threads: they have become virtually invisible. No one is aware of them but everyone simply and automatically acts in accordance. These 'rules' sometimes have to do with standards of politeness or decorum, such as acknowledging the presence of another.

Not all aspects of group life are governed to the same extent by norms. Those most stringently subjected to this type of influence include activities:

*   directly concerned with the achievement of group goals and the satisfaction of members' needs, especially the needs of the most powerful in the group;
*   commonly associated with group membership by those both within and outside the group;
*   amenable to public scrutiny; thus, strict norms govern the physical examination of a patient, but not the colour of underwear the doctor should wear while conducting it!

Apart from facilitating goal achievement, norms serve to increase regularity and predictability in the operation of the group (Hogg and Reid, 2006). Members can determine, with reasonable accuracy, what is likely to happen in most situations. This sets down guidelines as to the nature and extent of their own involvement. For the individual they also provide a clear picture of social reality together with a firm sense of belonging (Oyserman *et al.*, 2006). Personal needs for status and esteem can also be satisfied through the operation of norms. Many of the tacit rules of everyday conversation are intended to avoid causing offence or embarrassment in public. A further advantage of having certain actions norm-governed is that it obviates the necessity of frequently having to rely upon personal influence. It can be pointed out, for example, that new recruits to the military are expected to behave in a deferential manner to *all* commanding officers: it is not just me – it is the system, the way things are done around here.

Regardless of how they are communicated, whether in writing or by disapproving look, norms are decidedly *prescriptive*. They stipulate what should and should not be done. Members, to a greater or lesser extent, are required to comply. Furthermore, the fact that certain norms have to do with the maintenance and integrity of the group must not be overlooked. There is a *proscriptive* element involving evaluation, in that those who contravene norms can be labelled 'bad' or morally flawed and deserving of punishment by the rest of the members, which may even take the form of exclusion from the group. This is reflected in the disapprobation associated with pejorative terms such as 'traitor', 'shirker', 'deserter', 'scab', etc., often levelled at those who violate the norms of particular groups.

Roles

Norms apply to all group members, although not necessarily to the same extent. In any group, however, it would be highly undesirable for everyone to act in *exactly* the same way. A committee where all members acted as secretary would get very little work done (although anything that was done would be well documented!). Against a backdrop of shared norms, it is important that individuals take on different tasks for the group to make the most of its resources and maximise productivity. A differentiation of functions is required. Specific sets of expectations concerning the behaviour of those in particular positions in the group are referred to as *roles*. Particular roles that evolve are a function of a number of determinants, including the nature of the specific group and its tasks. Nevertheless, it would seem that there are certain roles that typify small-group interaction (Forsyth, 2010). Some of these were identified and labelled in an important piece of early work by Benne and Sheats (1948), and confirmed by Mudrack and Farrell (1995). This encompassed three categories of role:

1   *Task roles* (e.g. information giver, information seeker, opinion giver, opinion seeker, evaluator-critic, energiser). These contribute to the ability of the group to accomplish its objective successfully.
2   *Relationship-building and maintenance roles* (e.g. encourager, harmoniser, compromiser, follower, gatekeeper). Here the focus is upon promoting good internal relations, a strong sense of solidarity and a congenial social atmosphere.
3   *Individual roles* (e.g. aggressor, blocker, recognition seeker, playboy, dominator). Unlike the previous two categories, these tend to be self-serving and dysfunctional to the smooth and successful operation of the group.

Additionally, some groups have a member who tends to be much more reticent than the rest, who interacts minimally with others and fails to participate fully in group activities. This individual is commonly labelled an *isolate* and, indeed, in larger groups can go unnoticed. The fact that such individuals do not become fully involved does not mean that they have nothing to offer, as tactful handling by an adroit leader can often demonstrate. When a group is dogged by set-back and failure it is not uncommon for some member to be singled out as the cause and accused of not 'pulling your weight' or 'letting the group down'. This poor unfortunate becomes the scapegoat. By 'identifying' the source of failure, members can have their flagging beliefs in the worth of the group reaffirmed and redouble their efforts to achieve the goal. The projection of unacceptable personal feelings or tendencies upon the scapegoat can also mitigate feelings of guilt among others.

In many respects a role can only be properly understood in terms of how it relates to others in a system or network. For example, to grasp fully what a teacher does requires some understanding of pupils, classroom assistant, school principal, etc. Likewise, nurses operate in a context of patients, doctors, consultants, and so on. Furthermore, we all play a number of roles, although not necessarily in the same situation. A teacher may also be a mother, daughter, wife, captain of the local ladies' hockey team, joker of the evening art class. This can on occasion lead to *role conflict,* when the demands of one are incompatible with those of another. Given that members do not invariably slip smoothly into well-moulded roles in the first place, it is small wonder that problems often arise to disrupt group life. Some of these, it has been suggested (Burton and Dimbleby, 2006), stem from differences between the:

- *perceived role* – what the recipient understands is required;
- *expected role* – what others in the group expect;
- *enacted role* – what the person actually does.

When a member is no longer sure what his or her role demands or expectations are, that person is said to be in a state of *role confusion*.

Status

Roles also reflect status differences that exist between various positions in the group. Status refers to the evaluation of a position in terms of the importance or prestige associated with it. Most groups are hierarchically organised in this respect, with high-status positions affording greater opportunities to exercise social power and influence. Although status and power are usually closely associated, this need not necessarily be the case. Thus, members of the British monarchy are often portrayed as having very high status but relatively little power. As shall be seen in the following section, one facet of intra-group communication has to do with the acknowledgement and confirmation of status differences. This frequently operates at a covert level; for example, the chairperson *directs* the secretary while the secretary *advises* the chairperson.

Conformity

Despite what has just been said about norms, roles and status, none of these would make much contribution to ordering and structuring group functioning if members disregarded them. So members must conform: there have to be pressures on them to fit in. The origins of these influences may be internal. From an informational point of view, it can be personally comforting for members to be able to enjoy a feeling of certitude derived from accepted group norms. People like to be part of a shared sense of social reality. However, as explained by *social identity theory*, a group can also provide members with a social identity – it becomes tied up in their sense of who they are: its ways are their ways (Ellemers and Haslam, 2012). Members then comply because they have accepted a particular group-based self-categorisation.

On the other hand, external pressures in the form of positive and negative group sanctions may be brought to bear to force compliance (Wit, 2006). Tourish *et al.* (2009) charted the types of pressures employed by many companies to effect the conformity of employees to corporate norms and practices. New entrants are given mentors to shape appropriate behaviour. Praise and other forms of reward are bestowed for behaving appropriately, criticism or ridicule for failing to do so. Rewards are often allocated to teams rather than individuals, and so peer pressure to behave in such a way as to achieve set goals is intensified. Extreme cases of recalcitrance may result in boycott or, indeed, expulsion.

But conformity to the commonly held views and practices of the majority can also have advantages for the group. It tends to increase efficiency, facilitate group maintenance, reduce uncertainty or confusion among members and project a strong group image to others. Factors that promote conformity (Napier and Gershenfeld, 2004) include:

- an extreme norm
- strong pressure to conform
- member self-doubt
- a large group
- reinforcement of appropriate behaviour
- members' need to self-ingratiate
- a strong sense of group identity.

Under circumstances where a number of these factors apply, the forces generated to conform to the ways of the group should never be under-estimated. They can lead to young people dressing in strange ways and sporting peculiar haircuts. More seriously, drug abuse and antisocial behaviour may be promoted. In the extreme, examples of soldiers, paramilitary groups and street gangs behaving with unbelievable brutality towards victims have been attributed to pressures to abide by the ways of the group. Destructiveness can also be turned in on the group itself. This is common in cults, where pressures for conformity can be enormous (Lalich, 2004). For example, in March 1997, 39 men and women belonging to the Heaven's Gate cult committed group suicide in San Diego, California, in the belief that their souls would make contact with a spacecraft that they believed was flying in the tail of a passing comet. The spacecraft was to be their passport to paradise.

Cohesion

Cohesiveness refers to the degree of mutual attraction among those who belong to the group. It can be thought of as the bonding agent that holds the group together, and so is a key ingredient of group success (Drescher *et al.*, 2012). Some groups are tight-knit, cohesive teams while others are comprised of individuals who have a weak sense of affiliation to fellow members or the work of the group. A number of advantages of belonging to a cohesive group have been identified (Johnson and Johnson, 2013). The main ones are listed in Box 14.2. A key distinction here is between task cohesion – commitment to the goals, tasks and activities of the group – and social cohesion – attraction towards and liking amongst group members. Both are necessary for success. As shown by Sullivan and Feltz (2005), a sports team that is high on social cohesion will enjoy their get-togethers, but if they are low on task cohesion in terms of how they operate as a functional unit, then they will not win many games.

One common problem in groups is that of *social loafing*. This refers to the phenomenon whereby individuals demonstrate a sizeable decrease in individual effort when working as part of a group as opposed to when working alone (Ying *et al.*, 2014). As shown by van Dick *et al.* (2009, p. 233), 'An enormous number of empirical studies have been carried out for over more than three decades which repeatedly demonstrated that, when working in groups, individuals typically fall short of their usual performance shown when working alone'. Part of the problem here is that of *free riding*, where individuals think they can reduce their personal effort as this will be compensated for by the group as a whole. Although there can be a variety of reasons as to why an individual engages in free riding (Hall and Buzwell, 2013), it is most likely to occur where the group member believes the reduced effort is unlikely to be detected. Hargie *et al.* (2004) identified a range of measures to reduce loafing and free riding. These include incorporating individual contributions as part of the overall team task,

---

Box 14.2 Advantages of group cohesion

Cohesive groups are typified by:

1 ease of goal setting
2 commitment to goal attainment
3 heightened productivity
4 reduced absenteeism
5 willingness of members to endure greater hardships and difficulties
6 increased morale and satisfaction
7 resolute defence against external criticism or attack
8 participants listening to and accommodating other members
9 less anger and tension
10 greater mutual support

encouraging maximum involvement and participation in the group process by all members, ensuring that the task and the group are as interesting as possible, and fostering a strong sense of group identity and loyalty.

However, pressures against dissent within a group can result in less desirable outcomes through flawed decision making. One of these tendencies is *groupthink* (Janis, 1982, 2007), which is brought about by a strong internal dynamic to conform to the suggested group position prematurely. Groupthink is a beguiling seducer – but the consequences can be dysfunctional for those falling under its spell. Groupthink is exemplified by a mad dash to reach consensus and avoid potential differences of opinion and internal conflict. The group vigorously supports a course of action, and actively discourages any dissenting opinions. There is no real critical scrutiny of alternative options, or of the possible negatives of the consensus view. Several reviews of groupthink and studies investigating conditions under which it flourishes have been carried out (e.g. Esser, 1998; Henningsen *et al.*, 2006; Rose, 2011). It tends to be fostered under conditions where:

- levels of cohesiveness are high;
- there are time pressures to reach a decision;
- the group is in crisis;
- minority dissent is stifled;
- the group is under external threat;
- there is a sense of group infallibility or moral superiority;
- the group is insulated from outside influence;
- there is a very dominant leader who vigorously champions a specific option to the denigration of others.

Groupthink is often endemic in groups that operate on the margins of society, such as cults (Tourish, 2013) and terrorist groups (Tsintsadze-Maass and Maass, 2014), but also affects mainstream decision making. The financial crisis of 2008 has been attributed to groupthink by key groups, particularly in the banking sector (Bénabou, 2013; Tourish, 2013). Likewise, the decision by the Bush administration and Western allies to go to war on Iraq in 2003 was a classic example of faulty political decision making attributed to groupthink (Schafer and Crichlow, 2010). One main justification for the war was that Iraq had amassed weapons of mass destruction. As later became evident, no such weapons existed. However, following the passenger airline attacks by terrorists in the USA on 9/11 and the subsequent declaration of the retaliatory 'war on terror' by President George W. Bush, there were intense pressures on Bush and his advisers to strike back. In terms of the decision to wage war on Iraq, Badie (2010) explained how groupthink resulted in the Bush administration formulating policy based on incomplete and inconclusive evidence. They disregarded warnings about potential errors in their deliberations and felt that they held the moral high ground. The presence of groupthink was confirmed by the Senate Report (2004) into the war, one of its conclusions being that:

The Intelligence Community (IC) suffered from a collective presumption that Iraq had an active and growing weapons of mass destruction (WMD) program. This 'group think' dynamic led Intelligence Community analysts, collectors and managers to both interpret ambiguous evidence as conclusively indicative of a WMD program as well as ignore or minimize evidence that Iraq did not have active and expanding weapons of mass destruction programs. This presumption was so strong that formalized IC mechanisms established to challenge assumptions and group think were not utilized.

(p. 18)

The consequences of groupthink in this instance were huge. While there is debate about the exact figure, the war and its aftermath led to the deaths of at least 100,000 Iraqis and made refugees of some two million (Johnson, 2014). The financial cost was also enormous, since for the USA alone this amounted to at least three trillion dollars, and this sum could increase significantly owing to continuing interest payments on loans, costs of caring for wounded veterans, and so on (Stiglitz and Bilmes, 2008). The war also contributed to considerable and ongoing instability, not just in Iraq but in the entire Middle East region.

However, Kramer and Dougherty (2013) argue that we should define groupthink in terms of a defective communication process rather than a negative outcome. This is because some decisions taken under conditions that could be construed as groupthink can be effective. A context where groupthink is particularly strong is within terrorist groups (Tsintsadze-Maass and Maass, 2014). Terrorist cells consist of a closed homogeneous group of fanatical individuals who meet in secret, insulated from the rest of society, under threat from government authorities, with leaders who are dogmatic and autocratic. They fervently espouse homogeneous values and a set course of action, refuse to consider other alternatives, demand uniformity of conviction, believe in the morality of their actions, discourage and censor dissent and punish (often lethally) any member who espouses an opposing view. They therefore take decisions under groupthink circumstances, and yet may succeed in achieving short-term terrorist goals (bombings, shootings, kidnappings, etc.). However, there are questions about the lasting success of such actions, since terrorist groups almost always fail to achieve their long-term goals and indeed often implode (Tsintsadze-Maass and Maass, 2014; Hargie and Irving, 2016). The more enduring consequences of groupthink are therefore negative.

In the modern business world, many organisations operate on the basis of largely discrete self-functioning teams comprising 4 to 12 individuals. The team is tasked to work on a specific time-framed project. These self-directed groups have a leader with a strong sense of focus, operate independently of the larger corporation, usually generate considerable commitment from members and are under time pressure to complete their task (Bikfalvi et al., 2014). All of this increases the possibility of groupthink among members (Sims and Sauser, 2013). Hargie et al. (2004) recommended steps that can be taken to help organisations avoid such groupthink (Box 14.3).

Box 14.3 Avoiding groupthink

Groupthink is less likely to beset group decision making when:

1 tasks are established that involve everyone
2 clear performance goals are set for the group
3 individual contributions are capable of being identified, evaluated and rewarded
4 the expression of minority opinion and a dissenting voice is encouraged and rewarded, not punished or ignored
5 the leader refrains from expressing a particular stance in relation to the issue, especially at an early stage in the discussion
6 the expression of a range of viewpoints is promoted
7 each member is given responsibility for critically examining views put forward
8 four questions are posed of any major decision: What is wrong with it? How can it be improved? What other possibilities have not been considered? What is the contingency plan if it fails?
9 sub-groups, each with its own chairperson, are assigned the task of independently developing solutions
10 independent parties are brought in from outside the group, from time to time, to review the group deliberations
11 one member is given the role of 'devil's advocate'
12 after arriving at a decision, a 'second chance' meeting is held during which all members, including the leader, express residual concerns and uncertainties
13 members are made aware of the insidious dangers of groupthink

In sum, through the establishment and operation of norms, status and roles, together with pressures to act accordingly, regular and predictable patterns of activity come to characterise much of group life. For many, this process evolves through identifiable stages as the group changes from being little more than a gathering of relative strangers, at initial meetings, to become eventually a properly functioning unit. This raises the question as to how groups develop over time.

GROUP FORMATION

Various models have been formulated to explain the process of group formation. The most widely cited is that proposed by Tuckman (1965), who conceptualised groups as evolving through fixed, progressive stages. He identified four such stages, later extended to become five (Tuckman and Jensen, 1977), based upon reviews of over 50 investigations of groups. These stages are forming, storming, norming, performing and adjourning.

- *Forming.* Initially group life is characterised by a good deal of uncertainty and confusion. Individuals are essentially strangers and there is a need to get to know one another both at a social level but also in terms of who does what. A clear picture of group goals and how they can best be achieved is often missing. This tends to increase the dependence of members on a leader if one is present. Despite the uncertainty at this forming stage, there can be a good deal of optimism in the group and, in this 'honeymoon' period, little explicit conflict.

- *Storming.* This second stage is typified by negative emotion stemming from conflict and disagreement. Initial individual uncertainty over what to do and how to do it now gives way to individuals' attempts to impose their interpretations on the group. Cliques and temporary sub-groups can form as those with shared views or agendas come together. Since there is a poorly formed role structure individuals disagree over who should be doing what. Members may feel aggrieved that others have suddenly begun to do the tasks that they had hoped to undertake. Lacking a recognised status structure, there can also be resentment and hostility over what are seen as illegitimate attempts by some to impose authority on others. It is therefore not surprising that a recurring theme in the literature is the importance for the group of dealing with emotional issues (Egolf and Chester, 2013).

- *Norming.* Assuming that the group makes it through to the calmer waters of this next stage, we now find conflict ebbing as a growing consensus, unity of purpose and shared sense of identity begin to take hold. Group structures become established, differentiating member roles, norms and status. Members now begin to form a clearer vision of the group, what it is about and where they, as well as others, fit in. While conflict may not be banished for good, at least the group is better prepared to handle it.

- *Performing.* Now members are in a position to begin to work together more efficiently and productively to achieve goals. They synchronise efforts and harmonise contributions, co-operating with one another to meet challenges, solve problems, reach decisions and implement agreed strategies.

- *Adjourning.* Finally, most groups reach the adjourning phase when specific goals are achieved and there is nothing left to do. Indeed, a set lifespan may have been envisaged when the group was created, and that time has now arrived. Alternatively, the end may come when members leave through lack of continued commitment. Once more, there may be a marked emotional dimension to what takes place during this valedictory phase. If strong social cohesion has been created members will have developed friendships. As shown in Chapter 10, closure is difficult, and so a deep sense of loss, loneliness and grief can develop at the prospect of social bonds being broken as participants go their separate ways. This can be partly mitigated by vows to remain in contact, plans for reunions, etc. Additionally, much talk at this time is usually devoted to *grave dressing* – reflecting back on how good the group was and what it accomplished.

But do all groups go through these same stages? If so, do they invariably follow the same sequence? Is progress always as ordered as suggested by the above model? For many who have reflected upon group development, the answers to these questions are 'No'. Doubt has been cast on this predictable, linear, fixed-progression sequence view of group development, with no cognisance paid to the possibility of regression or fluctuation between stages or of the group becoming stuck at a particular stage (Wittnebel and Boone, 2013). Worchel (1994) purported that a group moves through re-emerging cycles during its existence. He identified six stages:

1   discontent – the individual has minimal engagement with the group;
2   a precipitating event brings members together;
3   group identification is created and forces to conform are established;
4   the group agrees goals and strategies to enhance productivity;
5   individuation – the achievement of goals is associated with a growing focus by members upon personal needs;
6   disintegration – as members' contributions become more self-serving, conflict and division increase, leading to decay and group disintegration. Disintegration produces discontent – and another cycle commences.

For others, group life is typified by efforts to cope with recurring themes or issues. From a psychodynamic stance, these centre on unconscious assumptions that create an emotional climate and influence members to satisfy unconscious needs and control anxiety (Bion, 2003; Agazarian, 2012). Three basic assumptions concern:

1   *dependency* – the search for someone to take control of, protect and steer the group;
2   *fight/flight* – united effort to repel or evade attack from within or outside the group and thereby control anxiety;
3   *pairing* – bringing pairs of members together, subconsciously motivated by the desire to create a solution to the difficulties of the group.

TEAMS

Teams are a special type of group formed to complete tasks, such as in the workplace. Many organisations have responded to ever-present pressures to increase quality production in a more efficient way by turning to teams as core operational units charged with delivering success (Levi, 2013). This strategic move has often been associated with a flattening of the organisational hierarchy, reducing status differentials and devolving power to lower levels. There is good evidence that more is achieved by having staff pool their efforts in well-managed, self-directed and committed units of this type rather than either striving on their own or being at odds with others (O'Hair et al., 2011; West, 2012).

But what sets teams apart from the types of small group that have already been explored? When embedded in an organisational setting, Drucker (2007) pointed to issues such as task inter-dependence amongst members, a shared

---

Box 14.4 How to spot an effective team

Effective teams have:

- specific task objectives that are clearly understood and accepted by all members
- a high level of ownership of and commitment to group tasks
- a great deal of mutual trust, care and respect among members
- a culture of inclusivity
- strong support within the unit
- a firm sense of collective accountability
- quality communication that is honest and open, with participants feeling listened to and understood
- self-control, self-motivation and self-direction
- interaction and socialising outside of the strict work setting
- conflicts accepted and worked through
- an emphasis upon positive, constructive feedback to members
- a strong sense of collective success or failure and a reliance upon all members to create and maintain an acceptable image
- members whose skills, knowledge and abilities complement each other and enhance the group

---

sense of being an intact social entity and being seen as a group by others as being crucial. Teams usually achieve more than would the same number of individuals working alone. The most effective teams are cohesive, develop their own ways of doing things and are largely self-managing (Gallie *et al.*, 2012). The main characteristics of effective teams are outlined in Box 14.4.

INTRA-GROUP COMMUNICATION

Cattell (1951, p. 163) coined the term 'group syntality', which, he argued, 'defines for the group precisely what personality does for the individual'. The syntality or 'personality' of the group is shaped by the context in which the group operates, the nature of the individual members and the interplay between them. Effective intragroup communication has been shown to be a critical element in group functioning (Silberstang and London, 2009). Regardless of how groups develop and the stages through which this occurs, communication amongst members is the growth hormone that makes it happen. It is a necessary pre-requisite for the emergence and perpetuation of norms and roles, conformity and coherence, and for the achievement of outcomes. Frey (1999) pointed to both the constitutive and functional nature of the phenomenon: groups emerge through communication and it is through it that they achieve their objectives. At the same time, the communication process is heavily influenced in turn by the internal structures that are created, as will be seen in the next section.

The importance of communication in the group cannot therefore be over-estimated. Communication makes it possible for those belonging to the group to organise themselves, pool resources and through co-operative action solve common difficulties or reach a desired goal (Galanes and Adams, 2012). Two types of communication are important for groups. These have been referred to as *content* and *process* dimensions, or alternatively, as *task* and *socioemotional* (also referred to as *person-focused* or *relational*) communication. Task communication, as the name suggests, concerns substantive group activities and typically operates in accordance with reason and logic. On the other hand, socioemotional communication is concerned with the formation and maintenance of caring and harmonious relationships between members. This does not mean that each communicative act must be either task or relational in function (Burke *et al.*, 2006). It is not a question of 'either–or'. While discussing how to solve a task issue, members will also be forming impressions of where they stand in relation to the others in terms of respect, liking, attitudes, and so on.

Interaction processes

In his seminal work into interaction in small groups, Bales (1950, 1970) teased out task and socioemotional aspects of group communication using a system that he developed, known as *Interaction Process Analysis*. He found that specific contributions of participants to small-group interaction could be analysed and categorised within one of 12 distinct categories (Box 14.5). Six of these

---

Box 14.5 Interaction process analysis categories

Socioemotional: positive

1 Shows solidarity, supports, rewards
2 Shows tension release, jokes, laughs, defuses
3 Agrees, shows passive acceptance, concurs, complies

Task: neutral

4 Gives suggestions, directions, implying autonomy for the other
5 Gives opinion, evaluation, analysis; expresses wishes and feelings
6 Gives orientation, information, clarification, confirmation
7 Asks for orientation, information, clarification, confirmation
8 Asks for opinion, evaluation, analysis; expresses wishes and feelings
9 Asks for suggestions, directions, implying autonomy for the other

Socioemotional: negative

10 Disagrees, shows passive rejection, acts formally, withholds help
11 Shows tension, asks for help, withdraws
12 Shows antagonism, undermines other's status, defends or asserts self

---

are concerned with task functions. Of these, three involve giving suggestions and directions, giving opinions and points of view and giving orientation and information. These are mirrored in three further task functions, this time with a focus upon asking for (rather than giving) suggestions, opinions or orientation. The remaining six categories relate to socioemotional reactions, with a symmetry between the positive and negative. The three positives are: showing solidarity and support; showing tension release (e.g. joking, laughing); and showing agreement or acceptance. The final three categories, also in the socioemotional area, but negative in character, are: disagreeing or rejecting; showing tension, asking for help or withdrawing; and showing antagonism.

By analysing the communication between members in this way, interesting insights can be gained into the type of group and how it operates. It can be established, for example, whether most of what takes place is concerned with task or relational issues, and, if the latter, the type of relationships that seem to predominate in the group. Different sorts of difficulty are detectable. A group sometimes struggles to achieve a compromise between task and socioemotional concerns. As it devotes all of its energies to completing the task, disagreements and friction may be experienced amongst members. This places a demand upon the group to pay greater heed to relational needs or risk becoming dysfunctional or even fragmented. However, if the balance tips too much towards relational matters, the task may not get done, hence a need for readjustment. At the level of the individual, the extent and nature of the contribution of members, reflecting the roles taken up, can also be profiled through observation systems such as Interaction Process Analysis. Schermuly and Scholl (2012), in discussing their own Discussion Coding System for groups, point out that, while the Interaction Process Analysis is not without flaws, it 'has had the strongest influence of all existing coding systems on small group research' (p. 15).

A common finding to emerge from this sort of detailed observation and analysis is that some members participate markedly more than others in discussion. This seems to be a function of several factors, including:

1   Position and status in the group – high-status members, particularly group leaders, tend to contribute extensively.
2   Knowledge – those with relevant information are frequently vociferous and indeed may be encouraged to be so by other group members.
3   Personality – extraverts, almost by definition, are more communicative than their introverted colleagues. There is some evidence to suggest that individuals have their characteristic levels of participation across groups, although these are not immutable.
4   Physical location – those centrally located in the group frequently take a more active part.
5   Group size – differences between members in the amount of contribution to group interaction increase in relation to increases in overall group size. In addition, the potential for dissensus becomes greater as the group size increases beyond ten members (Klimek et al., 2008). One reason for this is that the complexity of inter-relationships increases in line with group

size. Rosengren (2000) identified the following formula to chart the number of dyadic relationships (R) in a group, as a factor of the number of members (n):

$$R = \frac{n\,(n-1)}{2}$$

Thus, a group of $n = 6$ people would have $6 \times 5 \div 2 = 15$ separate potential two-way relationships between members. However, as the group size grows, the number of potential relationships increases dramatically, such that a group of 12 people will involve 66 possible two-way relationships.

As well as quantitative differences existing between high and low participants, contrasts in the typical form of their communications have been identified. While high participators tend to provide information, give opinions and make suggestions, low participators, when they do contribute, are more likely to ask questions or express agreement. The target of such communication is also different. Low contributors tend to direct contributions to individual members, but high contributors are more inclined to address their remarks to the group. This is frequently associated with attempts to exert influence and exercise power. Those who contribute most are also likely to be the recipients of frequent messages from others.

Communication networks

As participants interact with one another, regularities begin to emerge in the form of identifiable patterns of communication. Restrictions on member access that may develop as group structures emerge help to shape such networks. Researchers have investigated the effects of these patterns, or communication networks, on a number of variables, including group efficiency and member satisfaction. In early experiments carried out by Bavelas (1950), five subjects were given a number of cards, each containing several symbols. Their task was to identify the symbol common to each member's card. Since the subjects were located in separate booths, channels of communication between them could be carefully controlled by the experimenter, creating the four networks outlined in Figure 14.1.

In each of the four diagrams in Figure 14.1, the circles represent particular group members and the adjoining lines are available channels of communication. Thus in the circle arrangement, for example, (a) and (b) could communicate but not (a) and (e) – at least not directly. Beyond the rather special circumstances of the experiments conducted by Bavelas, it should be appreciated that members in other group situations do not necessarily have to occupy the particular spatial relationship to each other depicted in the diagrams in Figure 14.1 for that specific network to pertain. It is rather the pattern of communication channels in each case that is the telling feature. In other words, people may be physically sitting in a circle but typify a wheel communication network as they direct their contributions for the most part to some one member who in turn reciprocates.

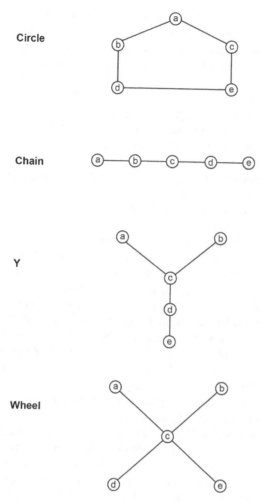

Figure 14.1 Communication networks.

This person becomes the hub in the wheel through which communication is channelled to the rest of the group.

Networks differ in two important respects:

1 *connectivity* – the number of channels available to members in the network;
2 *centrality* – the extent to which a member is tied or connected to other members; this is a function of the number of channels from a given position to each other position.

The circle in Figure 14.1 contains five channels and is therefore a more highly connected structure than any of the others. It is also the least centralised structure, followed by the chain, Y and wheel, in order. With the wheel it can be seen that one person (c) can communicate directly with a total of four others.

Results from a number of research studies found that these networks have a significant impact on group efficiency and member satisfaction (Wilke and Wit, 2001). Group productivity (in terms of the number of tasks completed) and efficiency (measured by time taken to complete each and the number of messages needed) improved with increases in group centrality. The wheel was, therefore, more productive and efficient, followed by the Y, the chain and the circle. The likelihood of emerging as group leader was directly related to the centrality of the person's position in the arrangement. The increased productivity and efficiency of more centralised structures are mainly due to organisational and informational factors – it is easier to control what takes place without at the same time overwhelming the key person with information. As tasks become more complex, though, this may not be so. Highly centralised networks may be less, rather than more, effective due to the unreasonable data-processing demands placed upon the individual at 'the hub'.

However, most everyday tasks that groups face are much less straight-forward than those set in the laboratory by researchers such as Bavelas (Hollingshead and Poole, 2012). While more centrally organised groups tend to be higher in productivity and efficiency (especially when dealing with simple problems), members frequently manifest low morale and express little satisfaction with group activities. Subjects operating in the circle typically express much greater satisfaction with their involvement in the group than those in the wheel, in spite of the fact that they may not, collectively, achieve as much. This is most likely a result of the greater independence of action enjoyed by members in the former.

As well as more elaborate tasks being tackled in naturally operating groups, the communication channels between members are not limited in the contrived fashion described by Bavelas, nor are they unchanging. Networks are typically completely connected, in principle, with each individual free to communicate with every other. In practice, however, those patterns that actually emerge frequently resemble one of the more restricted configurations already examined. A range of factors, including the roles being played by different individuals, may serve to reduce the number and sequence of channels typically used. Physical arrangements determining visual accessibility of certain members to others may also play a part (Johnson and Johnson, 2013). The likelihood of initiation of conversation, for instance, depends upon those individuals being able to engage in eye contact. What the group is essentially about will also dictate the most accommodating network for the task. A completely connected pattern typified by openness and high connectivity would best suit a therapy group. The wheel, by contrast, would better serve the purposes of one where the intention is for one member to disseminate information to the others in a limited space of time.

Having considered the defining characteristics of groups, some of the reasons for their existence, the mechanisms by which they become ordered and regulated and the types and patterns of communication between members, the next step is to examine a particularly influential position within the group – that of leader – and the characteristics and skills associated with leadership.

LEADERS AND LEADERSHIP

The related topics of *leader* and *leadership* are amongst the most widely explored in the fields of group structure and dynamics and, indeed, of larger social aggregates (Rumsey, 2013). However, there is considerable debate on a range of issues to do with why certain members become leader: the exceptional qualities (if any) that set them apart, their early experiences of playing leadership roles, the special nature of their contribution to collective life, even the defining features of leadership itself (Haslam *et al.*, 2011; Northouse, 2013). One thing is agreed, however, and that is that all of these matters are centrally important in shaping groups, their functioning and effectiveness. Providing neatly manicured definitions of 'leader' and 'leadership' is not an easy task. Alternatives abound for each. Furthermore, while the terms are related, they should not be confused. The former pre-dates the latter. From the dawn of history, scholars have been fascinated by the powers bestowed upon certain individuals to govern the lives of others. In the Chinese book of wisdom *Tao Te King*, dating from 600 BC, it was written that most leaders are despised, some leaders are feared, few leaders are praised and the very good leader is never noticed.

A *leader* refers to a person who occupies a certain high-status position and fulfils an associated role in the group. That person, according to Galanes and Adams (2012), may be leader by dint of:

- exerting a positive influence on the group to achieve its goal

and/or

- being placed in a position to lead (e.g. chairperson, supervisor, co-ordinator)

and/or

- being perceived by the other members as the leader.

In some situations a *designated* leader may be formally appointed to organise the group. While carrying the title of leader confers legitimate power, the respect and acceptance of the membership still have to be earned. When accepted in this way, having a designated leader can be a tremendously facilitative resource, acting as a catalyst to organise and regulate activities, syphon off internal tensions, assuage potential power struggles and maximise productivity. But not all leaders are put in place in this formal way. Others emerge from within the group to take on a leadership role. It is often they (the 'power behind the throne'), rather than the titular head, who wield the real power and to whom the rest look for guidance and support. One big advantage that *emergent* leaders have is that they are known to members, have risen to the top through association with them and are regarded as 'one of us'. Issues of acceptance, allegiance and respect are therefore less likely to surface.

Not all leaders provide leadership. Neither does the fact that a group lacks a conspicuous leader mean that leadership is lacking. All members can make a contribution in this direction and, in effective groups, members share responsibility for leadership skills. For this reason, the study of 'followership', which emphasises the process of reciprocal influence between leaders and followers, has attracted growing interest (Tourish, 2014). So what exactly is leadership? Concurring with Baker (2001, p. 475), most would agree that, 'We all know what leadership is until someone asks us to define it specifically'. The word 'leadership' did not appear in the English language until about 1800 and as such is much more recent than 'leader'. Since then, there have almost been as many definitional variants as there are contributors who have proffered a meaning for the term. Northouse (2013, p. 5) defined leadership as, 'a process whereby an individual influences a group of individuals to achieve a common goal', and drawing upon a classificatory scheme proposed by Bass (1990), he further identified several foci amongst available sets of definitions.

- *Leadership as group process.* The emphasis here is upon the leader at the centre of the group operation and as catalyst for change. The mechanisms through which influence comes to be channelled in this way, and the relationship between leader and follower, have also been a topic of enquiry. After all, leaders can only adopt and continue to fulfil their role with the consent of followers. From this point of view, leadership can be thought of as the process of being accepted by group members as the leader (Lord and Brown, 2004).
- *Leadership as personality.* Here the focus is upon the unique complement of personality traits and personal qualities that enable one member to attain a dominant position and exercise influence over the rest. This issue will be returned to shortly.
- *Leadership as power.* Those who have taken this line accentuate the issue of power at the heart of leadership and how it is handled in the relationship with followers (Iszatt-White and Saunders, 2014). Is it concentrated in the personification of an authoritarian tyrant or distributed in a more egalitarian fashion? In the world of the modern organisation, Tourish (2013) has shown how traditional practices of top-down leadership can become dysfunctional. Rather, it must be recognised that the workforce is the fulcrum for change in creative partnership with the person 'at the top'. Issues of power can be further extended by introducing political and ideological dimensions into thinking about leadership.
- *Leadership as goal achievement.* The importance of goals to the formation and functioning of groups has found its way into attempts to distil the essence of leadership (Haslam *et al.*, 2011; Huber, 2014). After all, if goals figure prominently in group life, if success is measured in terms of goal output and if leadership is to have any real significance as a group-based concept, then it must in some way serve to facilitate goal achievement. Indeed, this perspective was underlined in the definition of leadership proffered by Northouse earlier.

THEORIES OF LEADERSHIP

Fascination with the role of leader has not merely been confined to the investigations of social scientists. Although not studied extensively and scientifically until the second half of the twentieth century, leadership has intrigued philosophers and historians for much longer. But, even restricted to the social sciences, a range of theories and perspectives has been advanced to account for why or how leaders emerge and with what effects. As expressed by Gessner *et al.* (1999, p. xiii), 'Leadership theories are like fingerprints: everyone has them and no two are alike'. A comprehensive review of alternatives is well beyond the reach of this chapter, but it is useful to examine several of the better known.

Trait approach

What is proposed here is that leaders possess certain personality traits and capacities that set them apart from the rest and make it possible for them to lead. Without this unique advantage, any attempt to fill this role is doomed to failure. In its earliest form, it was furthermore believed that these crucial predispositions were innate – that leaders were born, not made. Proponents of this *Great Person* (invariably *Man*) *Theory* pointed to colossal heroic figures as 'proof' of their views. Alexander the Great was an even greater leader than his father Philip II. From Biblical times there is a long tradition of chosen ones having the hand of God placed upon them and a divine right to rule conferred. Indeed, Machiavelli in the early sixteenth century provoked the wrath of the Church by audaciously setting out a set of principles by which a commoner could *learn* to exert the influence of leadership.

The belief that leadership is inborn would receive little contemporary support from serious social scientists. This still leaves open the possibility that predisposing attributes can be acquired, perhaps early in life. Considerable research effort has been devoted to their identification and isolation. At best a handful of weak associations have emerged, with leaders tending to be taller, more attractive, healthy, intelligent, confident, extraverted and having a greater desire for dominance (Hogg and Vaughan, 2008). However, an extensive and frequently cited review by Stogdill (1974) failed to unearth a distinct set of general qualities or abilities of leadership. Indeed, while Alexander the Great, Mahatma Gandhi, Winston Churchill and Nelson Mandela all share the accolade of having been major global leaders, it is probably their differences that impress rather than their similarities. If given a battery of personality tests, would a common leadership factor emerge?

That said, however, Rowitz (2014) identified five recurring traits in studies of admired leaders: honesty, being forward-looking, an ability to inspire others, competence and intelligence. It is widely acknowledged, however, that such traits operate at the level of preconditions and are not in themselves sufficient for success (Van Yperen and Van de Vliert, 2001). Yet, interest in this line of research keeps being rekindled. In the mid-1970s, House (1976) reintroduced the notion of the charismatic leader, originally mooted by Weber (1947). Such charismatic leaders are perceived as being strong, eloquent and effective; they articulate appealing visions and express a strong belief that members can accomplish the stated objectives (Wilderom *et al.*, 2012). Several alternate versions of this theory now exist. While inconsistencies and ambiguities persist (Yukl, 2013), their major impact has been in addressing the behavioural manifestations of charismatic leadership rather than weeding out underlying personality factors *per se*. Also, the fact that leaders can lose charisma poses questions for a strict personality-based explanation.

Situation approach

If we cannot explain why certain people come to prominence through concentrating upon those individuals and charting their personalities, then perhaps we can do so by shifting the direction of enquiry to the circumstances of their rise to power. In its most extreme form, the situational approach attributes leadership not to the person, but to the particular demands of the situation. This perspective purports that there are no universally important traits of leadership, nor is it the case that a person who becomes leader in one situation will do so in another. For example, Winston Churchill scarcely covered himself in glory during his military service in the First World War, but the perilous situation that Britain faced when he became Prime Minister during the later world conflict made him an ideal person to lead the nation on that occasion. Once circumstances changed, with the advent of peace, however, he lost power at the next general election. But should the individual not be factored into the equation in some way? His or her unique contribution, in whatever form that may take, is still important. Churchill coming to power when he did was a feature of both the situation faced and the special qualities that he could bring to tackling it.

Contingency approach

Theories that can be listed here have in common the assumption that effective leadership is a function of situational variables, including task demands and the approach adopted by the leader in tackling them. Perhaps the best known is that proposed by Fiedler (1967, 1986). Using a variety of group situations, ranging from sports groups through to military and industrial settings, Fiedler's starting point was that some leaders were more committed to the nature or structure of the task and reaching a goal. Others were more oriented to achieving good personal relationships within the group. He concluded that it was unusual to find individuals who were equally orientated to both group socioemotional needs and task completion.

Turning attention to the situational context, there are three important factors:

1   the relationship between leader and members
2   the degree to which the task is clearly structured
3   the amount of power enjoyed by the leader to reward and punish members.

Fiedler found evidence that the type of leader required in order for group performance to be enhanced was contingent upon the nature of the situation defined in terms of these three factors. For instance, task-oriented leaders appear to be most effective when they are on very good terms with group members, the task is clearly structured and they are in a powerful position within the group. Such leaders are also effective when on poor terms with group members, the task is ambiguous and they have limited power. However, it would appear that when moderate relationships exist between leader and group members, when the task is reasonably clear and when the leader has an intermediate position of influence, the leader who emphasises good relationships within the group is the most effective at achieving member participation and productivity. Effectiveness therefore depends upon a proper match between elements of the situation and the type of leadership provided.

While much research has been produced in broad support of Fiedler's findings, criticisms have also been levelled. One source stems from the fact that the theory provides little explanation about the patterns of relationship between personal and situational variables (Northouse, 2013). Another major criticism is that group performance is measured in terms of task or goal completion. But output is only one measure of a group's value. Group members' satisfaction may be equally important, yet not contribute to the achievement of the extrinsic goal. It will be recalled from earlier in the chapter that the most satisfied members do not necessarily belong to the most productive groups. Furthermore, the validity of the instrument used to measure leadership orientation (task vs. relation) has also been brought into question (Fiedler, 1993).

Transformational approach

As part of a more recent way of thinking about the topic, 'transformational leadership' can be traced back to the work of Burns (1978). He focused upon the relationship between leaders and followers and distinguished between its *transactional* and *transformational* characterisations.

- *Transactional leadership* concentrates upon the exchange nature of the leader–follower relationship. Each makes a contribution in return for some reciprocating input from the other party. Leaders provide expertise and direction, followers contribute effort and compliance. Leaders dispense rewards, followers meet their production targets. This attitude has typified much traditional thinking.

- *Transformational leadership* focuses on the process by which the leader engages with members in such a way as to raise to new heights the levels of motivation, aspiration and commitment of the whole group. As part of this approach, a new way of thinking and feeling is brought about such that the greater good of the collective takes precedence over the separate needs of individuals, creating a different set of moral values that they all share. Mahatma Gandhi is a good example of this type of leader. He did much more than merely offer political direction to the Indian people in exchange for their recognition and support. Rather, he offered them a new vision of independence to which they could aspire, together with a sense of hope, belief and commitment to its achievement.

The early contribution by Burns (1978) has since been extended, perhaps most noticeably by Bass and his co-workers (Bass, 1985, 1996; Bass and Riggio, 2006; Conger and Riggio, 2007). Leaders who provide this sort of transformational influence are thought to raise members to new levels of accomplishment by:

1   heightening their conscientiousness about actual and potential goals;
2   having them promote the greater interests of the group over narrow personal agendas;
3   bringing attention to bear upon higher-order needs.

Transformational leadership is therefore provided when the leader induces members to see beyond their own limited personal interests, to recognise and embrace the mission of the group. Followers, in turn, tend to respond with a sense of trust, loyalty and mutual respect towards the leader and are sufficiently motivated to accomplish more than they would have initially thought possible. As a corollary, they experience conditions conducive to the maximisation of their full potential. According to Bass (1985), four factors lie behind this effect.

1   *Charisma or idealised influence.* As noted by Amernic *et al.* (2007, p. 1841), 'Charisma is assumed to be an important component of transformational leadership'. However, Bass (1996) proposed that charisma was a necessary but not sufficient condition of transformational leadership – a leader could be charismatic but not necessarily transformational. For him, it was important that the transformational leader be someone that the rest can look up to and wish to emulate, capable of commanding confidence, allegiance and unwavering loyalty and encapsulating a vision to be shared by all. On the other hand, it has been noted that there are key differences between these two concepts (Yukl, 2013). Thus, it is argued, a leader can be transformational but not charismatic. In this way, whereas transformational leaders exist in most organisations, charismatic leaders are the exception.
2   *Inspirational motivation.* This factor is about instilling a strong sense of will to achieve for the good of the group. It is created through developing ownership of a collective vision of the group and what it is going to achieve, together with an appreciation of the part that the individual member has to play in bringing this to fruition. Team spirit and collaboration for the good of the organisation are important. Emotion, dynamism and symbolism are often tools at the disposal of the transformational leader in this regard.
3   *Intellectual stimulation.* It should not be thought, however, that transformational leadership is merely a more sophisticated way of brainwashing followers to do the bidding of the leader – but now with a smile. When truly implemented, this approach stimulates followers to challenge their

established ways of thinking, evaluating and reacting, as well as challenging those of the leader and the organisation. Members should be both encouraged and facilitated to consider innovative approaches for tackling problems and bringing these to the attention of the group.

4   *Individualised consideration.* Transformational leaders should also be capable of dealing with members on an individual basis, listening to their concerns, acknowledging their needs and taking an interest in their personal development.

The transformational approach to explaining leadership can rightly claim a number of advantages. It offers a broader perspective than some of the alternatives and not only emphasises the relationship between leader and follower, but also introduces a moral dimension to the process. In addition to a certain intuitive appeal, a considerable body of supportive empirical research for this form of leadership has now been generated, particularly in organisations, showing that it is associated with the perceived effectiveness of leaders, higher levels of performance, reduced turnover rates, greater productivity, lower employee stress and burnout and increased satisfaction (Robbins and Judge, 2014).

However, concerns have also been raised about this approach (Tourish, 2013). There is a tendency to assume that certain traits and personal qualities set transformational leaders apart, but we know little about what precisely these are. It is unclear why some leaders employ a transformational approach while others do not. Similarly, we have little understanding of the underlying psychological processes employed by transformational leaders to influence followers to achieve higher levels of performance (Avolio *et al.*, 2009). Concomitantly, there has been a lack of research into the contextual determinants of effective transformational leadership. For example, this approach has been shown to be particularly difficult to implement within public-sector organisations, where policy makers rather than leaders transform the context, and the extent of leadership discretion is constricted by central government (Currie and Lockett, 2007). Furthermore, the primary level of analysis tends to be pitched at the dyad, between the leader and individual followers, rather than at the organisation. Tourish and Pinnington (2002) also drew attention to the inordinate levels of power necessitated by transformational leadership, the lack of associated checks and balances and the misconception and mishandling of dissent amongst followers, as problematic areas. They argued that, in the context of corporate management, this form of leadership may mean that, 'the leader may be able to impose his or her vision on recalcitrant followers, however erroneous it is. The edge of a cliff might seem the starting point of an adventurous new journey' (p. 152).

Behavioural approach

The final approach to be considered here shifts the focus from the traits and aptitudes that may set leaders apart, and places it upon how leaders actually conduct themselves when providing leadership in different situations. What do effective leaders do that their ineffective counterparts fail to, and vice versa?

Here, performance can be analysed at different levels, from the broad examination of styles of leadership to the fine-grained identification of skills and actions that express them.

Leadership styles

Style generally can be thought of as the characteristic manner in which someone handles an interactive episode (Dickson, 2006). Leadership style has been defined as 'the combination of traits, skills, and behaviors leaders use as they interact with followers' (Lussier and Achua, 2010, p. 70). The style of the leader has important implications for team performance. Organisational leaders who display 'destructive' leadership styles have been shown to have a range of very negative effects upon the workforce. Schyns and Schilling (2013, p. 141) defined destructive leadership as the process whereby 'the activities, experiences and/or relationships of an individual or the members of a group are repeatedly influenced by their supervisor in a way that is perceived as hostile and/or obstructive'. In a review of research, they found that this leadership approach resulted in dislike for and resistance to the leader, negative attitudes to the job and the organisation as a whole, increased intention to leave, and heightened personal and occupational stress. Not surprisingly, therefore, destructive leadership has also been shown to be dysfunctional for the organisation as a whole (Sheard et al., 2013). By contrast, positive leadership style has been linked to higher levels of: job satisfaction (Lam and O'Higgins, 2012); organisational commitment and evaluation of leader competence (DuBrin, 2013); enjoyment (Fox et al., 2000); creativity (Sosik et al., 2000); and mental health (Gardiner and Tiggemann, 1999).

It has already been shown that leaders can be mainly task-oriented or relation-oriented. But perhaps the best-known variants of style are those initially developed by Lewin et al. (1939). In what is now considered a classical study involving groups of juvenile boys in a recreational youth centre, they investigated three style types:

1   *Autocratic* – the leader was totally authoritarian, directing, giving orders and making all decisions.
2   *Democratic* – the leader encouraged participation, helped group members to interact and consulted them when taking decisions.
3   *Laissez-faire* – the leader more or less left the boys to get on with it.

The results revealed that members were more dependent on the leader and lacking in co-operation with their peers when led by an autocratic leader. When the leaders adopted a democratic approach, the same boys showed more initiative and responsibility for the progress of the group and were friendlier towards one another, even when the leader left the room. In the laissez-faire, or leaderless, group the boys lacked interest in their tasks and failed to complete successfully any that had been set. Aggressive acts were more frequent under autocratic and laissez-faire leaders. Finally, it was found that the democratic leader was the most liked and the autocratic leader the least so. Transferred to a 'real-life' working environment, Packard and Kauppi (1999) found that those who recorded their immediate supervisor's style as democratic, rather than autocratic or laissez-faire, also reported that they enjoyed greater support, reduced work pressure and greater job satisfaction, while Skogstad *et al.* (2007) showed that the laissez-faire style was correlated with increased conflict between workers and greater role ambiguity.

Muczyk and Reimann (1987) suggested that such styles actually involve two separate dimensions.

1 *Autocratic–democratic*. This charts the extent to which leaders allow members to become actively involved in the decision-making process.
2 *Permissive–directive*. This determines the degree to which leaders tell members what to do.

When these two dimensions are put together, four possibilities exist.

1 *Directive autocrat* – members are permitted little autonomy in organising their work and the leader makes all significant decisions.
2 *Permissive autocrat* – members have considerable autonomy in organising their work, but the leader makes all significant decisions.
3 *Directive democrat* – members are permitted little autonomy in organising their work but are actively involved in the decision-making process.
4 *Permissive democrat* – members have considerable autonomy in organising their work and are actively involved in the decision-making process.

Related to these four options, *participative* and *directive* styles are two further contrasting possibilities that derive from the same underlying issues of the management of power and members' involvement (Somech, 2005; Lorinkova *et al.*, 2013).

- *Participative leaders* share power with members, empower them by actively involving them in decision making and seeking their views and suggestions, and take their views into account rather than trying to impose personal opinions.
- *Directive leaders* give instructions, clarify regulations, make their preferences known and seek to influence others to their way of thinking when reaching decisions. Two sub-components of this style were identified by Peterson (1997):
  - *Outcome directiveness* has to do with advancing a solution favoured by the leader.
  - *Process directiveness* concerns the degree to which steps taken to reach an outcome (but not the outcome itself) are shaped by the leader. In the study undertaken by Peterson this element emerged as a significant predictor of the quality of both decisions reached by groups and the processes they used.

A much more elaborate system for identifying leadership styles and one of the most popular was first introduced in the 1960s by Blake and Mouton (1964). Since then it has undergone several revisions (Blake and Mouton, 1985; Blake and McCanse, 1991). According to this model a range of leadership patterns can be plotted on a managerial grid formed from the intersection of two basic dimensions:

1   *Concern for people* relates to the leader's commitment to members, their levels of satisfaction, working conditions, sense of being valued and their feeling of belonging to a community. It also involves showing empathy and concern for their welfare and putting their needs to the fore (Holt and Marques, 2012). This type of person is epitomised by what is termed the 'servant-leader', who has a high desire to serve others (Andersen, 2009).
2   *Concern for production* has to do with the leader's dedication to the task in terms of achieving organisational goals, maximising quality output and getting results (Power *et al.*, 2013).

Each of these dimensions can be plotted on an axis and scored from low to high on a nine-point scale. Various styles can be identified in the resulting matrix, characterised by a combination of a certain level of concern for people on the one hand, and for production on the other. Five principal styles to emerge are as follows:

1   *Impoverished management* – low on concern for people and production. This person simply goes through the motions but provides no meaningful influence (similar to the laissez-faire leader, already mentioned).
2   *Country club management* – high concern for people but low for production. Here leaders concentrate narrowly on relationships within the workforce and the needs of its members, to the neglect of output.
3   *Middle-of-the-road management* – medium concern for people and for production. In this case, a balance is struck between relational and task matters.
4   *Produce or perish* – low concern for people but high concern for production. This is also referred to as the *authority–compliance style*, where members' concerns only count to the extent that they may hamper output. Achievement and the processes that promote it are all important.
5   *Team leadership* – high on people and high on production. This style integrates the importance of both factors. Members are treated as important, their ideas and contributions valued and their active involvement encouraged. A team environment is created, based on respect and trust. This boosts morale and satisfaction, and so promotes high-level production.

While the 'team leader' would appear to win the best style award, there is concern that this potent combination of high production coupled with high care for people may not be pertinent to all situations. The maturity of the group (i.e. whether newly formed or existing) can have a major influence on optimal leadership style. The best style for a newly formed group, for instance, may be one where task issues are promoted over those of group members. While leaders are thought to have a preferred style and a fallback alternative when this customary approach fails, *opportunism* describes a person who makes use of any combination of these five styles as circumstances require.

It is not only in relation to the work of Blake and Mouton, and their leadership grid, that questions are raised as to which style is best. While democratic, participative options have much to commend them and fit neatly into a broader Western political ideology, no one style is 'right' or 'best' (Power *et al.*, 2013). Indeed, Müller and Turner (2007) showed that the effectiveness of leadership styles is dependent on the type of work project involved. Napier and Gershenfeld (2004, p. 207) contended that, 'it is the ability of leaders to first identify the most appropriate behavioral response called for in a particular situation and then to actually use it as needed that separates those who are successful from the rest'.

Groups under directive leadership have been criticised for being prone to flawed decision making. However, Lorinkova *et al.* (2013) found that teams led by leaders with a directive style initially outperformed those led by leaders with a participative style, although the participative groups showed greater performance improvement over time. In a study by Kahai *et al.* (1997), the degree of structure of the task also played a part. With moderately structured tasks, participative leadership was conducive to proposing solutions, but this advantage was lost as the level of structure increased. Likewise, gender has been found to be related to ideal leadership style, with females preferring a more relational and democratic approach (Trinidad and Normore, 2005; Snaebjornsson and Edvardsson, 2013). However, Gardiner and Tiggemann (1999) discovered that it was only in female-dominated industries that females were more interpersonally oriented than males. The cultural background of participants should also be taken into account, since different cultures have contrasting perspectives on leadership and what it means (Chokker *et al.*, 2008; Dorfman *et al.*, 2012).

In sum, Hargie *et al.* (2004) listed a set of fourfold considerations that are central to decisions about which leadership style may be most effective, namely the:

1   task faced by the group
2   nature, abilities and characteristics of the members
3   past history of the group and its members
4   pressures and demands of the external environment.

Leadership skills

Leaders are required to fulfil a wide range of functions, thereby making considerable demands on the complement of skills, competencies and tactics that they must have at their disposal. Being a potent agent of influence, building successful teams, making effective presentations, negotiating and bargaining, selecting and appraising are just some of the sets of skills that managers must possess. In his review of research into leadership skills in organisations, Yukl (2012) divided the leader's activities into four main categories:

1   *Task actions.* These involve achieving work-related goals and targets in the most effective and efficient way. This encompasses four main skills.

- *Planning* involves making decisions about operational activities, assigning task responsibilities, scheduling activities, setting objectives and organising resources.
- *Clarifying* includes explaining team and individual objectives, work roles and responsibilities, communicating targets, timetables and deadlines, setting appropriate goals and related performance standards and ensuring that corporate regulations, policies and procedures are understood.
- *Monitoring* comprises checking operational activities to ensure that the work schedule is progressing effectively, that members are completing their assigned tasks on schedule and identifying any problems.
- *Problem solving* then necessitates taking steps to resolve identified work-related difficulties.

2   *Relational actions.* These are used to develop positive relationships with members, promote identification with the workplace and ensure commitment to the organisation's goals. This involves four core skills.

- *Supporting* people by building conducive relationships, fostering a feeling of being part of a team, showing empathy and positive regard, listening, and helping staff to cope with periods of stress in their lives.
- *Developing* members by showing an interest in and concern for their personal and career development, providing training opportunities, coaching them in their work and encouraging them to take on new roles, such as mentoring new recruits.
- *Recognising* achievement by giving rewards to staff as acknowledgement for significant performance. This can take various forms, including praise, employee-of-the-month award or a pay increase or bonus.
- *Empowering* members by not only regularly consulting them in the decision-making process and taking cognisance of their views, but also delegating relevant power and authority to them to take actions.

3   *Change-oriented actions.* This category includes encouraging innovation, ensuring acceptance of change initiatives and fostering collective learning. This again involves four central skills.

- *Advocating change,* by explaining to members exactly why change is required, overcoming any resistance and persuading them to embrace the change.
- *Envisioning change,* through articulating a clear and positive vision of what can be attained by the team as a result of the change.

- *Encouraging innovation* by creating a climate that enables team members proactively to suggest change and innovation.
- *Facilitating collective learning* through encouraging people to work collaboratively, accept joint responsibility and learn together from failures as well as successes.

4   *External actions.* These are concerned with building a network of external contacts and effectively promoting and defending the interests of the organisation in the external world. There are three key skills here.

- *Networking* includes attending relevant meetings and conferences, joining and becoming an office bearer of pertinent associations and maintaining useful outside contacts.
- *External monitoring* involves 'environmental scanning' in terms of scrutinising information regarding events that may be either a threat to or an opportunity for the organisation.
- *Representing* comprises being an ambassador both for one's own department when dealing with more senior managers and for the organisation when communicating with external stakeholders.

Gentry *et al.* (2009) carried out a major study involving almost 15,000 managers, in which they compared changes in the perceived importance of key managerial skills over the previous 15 years. Two of the most dramatic changes were that the significance of 'relationship' and 'time management' skills in management had increased in significance. This is not surprising. Leaders are much more accessible now as a result of mobile technology and so they have a greater need to manage their time efficiently. But remote communications also carry the risk of reduced opportunities for face-to-face interaction, and so concerted efforts need to be made to ensure that this medium of communication is not ignored. As Blanchard (2010, p. 89) pointed out, 'Leadership is not something you do to people, but something you do with people'. However, despite a number of empirical investigations into leadership skills and competencies (e.g. Deschamps, 2005; Marta *et al.*, 2005; Mumford *et al.*, 2007; Gentry *et al.*, 2009; McCallum and O'Connell, 2009), the majority of contributions to this literature are based upon conceptual analysis and experiential insights, rather than systematic research.

Providing inclusive leadership is undoubtedly a multi-faceted process (Hollander, 2009). In the workplace, meetings are typically valued by members of staff, especially when they provide an opportunity for face-to-face contact with immediate and senior management (Hargie, 2007). For the workforce, they offer an important avenue into the decision-making process. People, in turn, are more likely to comply with decisions reached under circumstances affording some level of ownership (Deetz and Brown, 2004). One of the common functions expected of leaders by most groups, therefore, involves taking charge of discussions (Adams and Galanes, 2008). Several publications (e.g. Hanna and Wilson, 1998; Hargie *et al.* 2004; Wilson, 2004; Adams and Galanes, 2008; Yukl, 2012; Johnson and Johnson, 2013) have teased out taxonomies of skills and tactics involved in this activity. These sources will be drawn upon in the following outline of the major requirements demanded of those leading group discussions. Additionally, most of the skills already covered in this book have relevance when applied to this role. The key skills involved are preparing, opening the discussion, structuring and guiding discussion, managing conflict, regulating participation and closing.

Preparing

The work of leading a productive discussion doubtlessly begins in advance of members coming together. Tasks to be taken on board by (or on behalf of) the leader include:

- researching the issue/s fully, if knowledge is lacking;
- identifying the purpose of the meeting and formulating an agenda, if appropriate; in formal meetings, this may be distributed in advance for agreement by members;
- selecting a suitable location and making all necessary physical arrangements, including seating, equipment, materials, refreshments, and so on;
- choosing when it is best to hold the meeting and how long it should last;
- deciding who should be present, including particular people not part of the group who may be usefully invited on account of their relevant expertise.

Opening the discussion

Much of the relevance here has already been covered in relation to set induction in Chapter 10. Many of the ways of effecting perceptual, social, cognitive and motivational sets discussed there can be tailored to this particular situation. Briefly, the leader should:

- *Introduce all present.* If members are meeting for the first time, it is particularly important that time be taken to ensure that each is known to the rest and that all begin to feel at ease with the company. Ice-breaking chitchat can help people to relax and assuage primary tension before moving on to meaningful discussion of more substantive issues.
- *Identify roles.* Where people have been brought along for a particular reason, this should be made known. Alternatively, the leader may invite a participant to take on a special role, e.g. secretary, observer, devil's advocate.
- *Establish the agreed aim of the meeting and what it is designed to accomplish.*
- *Agree the procedures to follow.* Where an agenda has been drawn up, the leader may want to agree the order in which items are taken. Additionally, the 'ground rules' to be followed as well as strategic steps to achieve the goal may need to be dealt with. If the task in hand is essentially to solve a problem, it may be prudent to suggest:

1   spending some time analysing the problem and its causes;
2   agreeing the criteria that an acceptable solution would have to meet;
3   brainstorming possible solutions;
4   critically evaluating suggestions;
5   selecting an agreed option;
6   considering implementation issues.

- *Direct a clear question at the group.* This is a way of getting the discussion going and focusing the group's attention on the first of the issues to be tackled.

Structuring and guiding discussion

Once the discussion has been initiated, the leader plays an important role in keeping it on target. Here a judicious balance has to be struck between, at one extreme, letting the discussion run amok and at the other perpetrating a slow strangulation by forcing it into a straitjacket of the leader's choosing. The style of leadership selected (e.g. directive vs. participative) will influence how this delicate task is carried out. Structuring and guiding the discussion can be achieved in different ways:

- *Be alert to digression.* When members raise a peripheral issue, point out that this may be an interesting debate for another occasion, but right now it would divert the group from its goal in the limited time set aside to achieve it.
- *Clarify.* It is essential that participants fully appreciate what is happening, what their roles are and what is expected of them. In addition, where it is felt that an issue that has been raised by a member has not been fully grasped or been misunderstood, the leader may clarify or invite the person who made it to do so.
- *Elaborate.* Certain contributions may be thought more worthy of having greater attention paid to them than others. Here the leader can elaborate directly by offering further information or encourage extended discussion by using techniques such as probing questions (see Chapter 5) and paraphrases (see Chapter 6).
- *Summarise.* In addition, it is useful for the leader to provide transitional summaries at the end of each phase of the meeting or discussion before introducing the next issue. These act as signposts, reminding members where they have been, where they are now and where they are going. This can be a very effective way of guiding the discourse.

Managing conflict

Conflict during discussion is sometimes mistakenly regarded as invariably destructive and to be avoided at all costs. While it may heighten tension in the group and challenge the skill of the leader in dealing with it, having members express different views and opinions can be to the advantage of the group outcome. This form of 'good conflict' (Cragan *et al.*, 2009) can help to circumvent the perils of groupthink, as described earlier in the chapter. It is the controlling and harnessing of conflict that is important. Tactics to consider include:

- *Focusing on issues, not on personalities.* When conflict becomes personalised it tends to shift from being potentially productive to very counter-productive. In this form, internal group relations will suffer. The leader should ensure that disagreements do not become personal.
- *Make all contributors feel that their suggestions have at least some merit.* The leader should avoid creating a situation of 'winners' and 'losers', or having some stakeholders feel sidelined or humiliated. Ways of giving face to those whose line of argument is ultimately not taken up should be found. Likewise all should feel that they have received a 'fair hearing'.
- *Highlight broader areas of agreement.* If discussion reaches loggerheads, taking the group back to a point where all were in agreement on some broader matter can ease tension.
- *Emphasise 'we' and 'us'.* It is an oft-quoted mantra that: 'There is no "I" in team'. Constantly re-establishing a sense of group unity prevents factionalism and damaged morale. Another well-known expression is that TEAM stands for *together everyone achieves more*. Even in a situation where views of one member or faction prevail over those of another, the contribution of all to the quality of the decision reached by the group should be stressed.

Regulating participation

The following set of tactics addresses the task of conducting the discussion so that everyone has an opportunity to contribute, thereby ensuring an orderly meeting:

- *Encourage contributions.* Here some of the techniques of reinforcement, discussed in Chapter 4, can be employed. Members who feel rewarded for their contributions, or who see others being rewarded, are more likely to contribute further. In particular, the leader should pay special attention to the more reticent member who may have an important input to make but may only be prepared to do so if directly invited in a tactful way. It is a mistake, though, to assume that the leader must comment on each contribution received. Frequently a more useful response is simply silence, or inviting the group or individual members to respond, if none is immediately forthcoming.
- *Discourage contributions.* On the other hand, the garrulous member has to be prevented from monopolising the proceedings. Decisions as to how much one person is permitted to hog the floor should take cognisance of the value of that person's input. It may be necessary to thank some diplomatically for their commitment to the discussion while reminding them

that they have already spoken twice on the issue while others still have not been heard, and that it is important to be inclusive.

- *Prevent over-talk.* While all members should be encouraged to contribute to the discussion, if they all insist on doing so at the same time then the effect will be lost. Regulating contributions by bringing individuals in and out of the conversation at particular times is something that effective chairpersons are particularly skilled at doing. Much of this can be conducted nonverbally.

Closing

A good deal of what was said in Chapter 10 on closure is directly applicable here. In drawing the discussion to a close, the leader should:

- ensure that there is general agreement on the decision/s taken and that no remaining doubt or confusion exists;
- identify any outstanding business still to be finalised;
- establish how the outcome of the meeting is to be taken forward. If certain members have been tasked with doing specific things, this should be re-established. It is always advisable to have this committed to paper, in the form of a minute, as quickly as possible;
- deal with any residual tension that may exist, perhaps from an earlier disagreement. It may be sufficient to mention the contribution of a member still 'smarting', without of course appearing to patronise that person. Taking time personally to have a few informal words before leaving may also be appreciated;
- thank all for their efforts in achieving the aims of the discussion.

OVERVIEW

This chapter has been concerned with small groups, how they operate and the manner in which leaders emerge and leadership is exercised within them. Groups, in this sense, can be thought of as involving a plurality of individuals who influence each other in the course of interaction and share a relationship of inter-dependence in pursuit of some common goal or goals. Members also characteristically develop a sense of belonging to this particular social entity. People come together to form groups to satisfy needs which may be interpersonal, informational or material. In so doing they become part of an ordered and regulated system which evolves through the establishment of norms, or commonly expected and accepted ways of perceiving, thinking, feeling and acting; the enactment of roles including that of leader; and the creation of identifiable forms and patterns of communication between members.

Additionally, leadership has been highlighted as virtually synonymous with the act of influencing others in a range of group contexts. However, it is important to bear in mind the distinction between leadership and leader. While specific individuals may occupy the position of leader, acts of leadership can be manifested by any group member. Theories of leadership offer contrasting explanations about the emergence of leaders and their functioning. Focusing on the actual performance of leaders, their behaviour can be examined on two levels: leadership styles at the macro level and leadership skills and tactics at the micro level. While different styles have been suggested, the three most commonly mentioned are autocratic, democratic and laissez-faire.

Underlying dimensions for these and other stylistic variants have to do with the extent to which the leader takes all important decisions single-handedly; directs what subordinates should do and denies them autonomy; and concentrates on group task or relational issues. Finally, it was emphasised that the skills involved in leading group discussions are crucial to effective leadership. The core skills involved were analysed within the categories of opening the discussion, structuring and guiding discussion, managing conflict, regulating participation and closing.

Chapter 15

Concluding comments

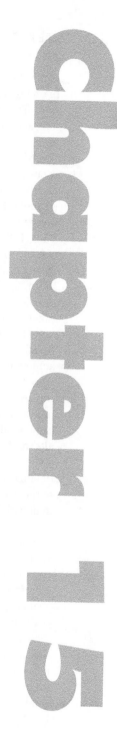

HUMANS SEEM TO HAVE an innate predisposition to commune with one another. Our ability to develop sophisticated methods for communicating both within and between generations is the core dimension that separates us from all other species. The research reviewed in Chapter 1 showed that, the better able we are to communicate, the more successful we will be in all walks of life. Skilled interpersonal communication is central to almost everything we do (Egan, 2014). An increased knowledge and comprehension of communication enables us to understand and adapt our own behaviour to situational demands, as well as providing us with deeper insights into the responses of others.

This book has been concerned with an examination of the central components of interpersonal communication, namely the skills that individuals employ in order to achieve their goals in social encounters. The theory behind the skills approach to the study of interpersonal behaviour, as outlined in Chapters 1 and 2, has provided a key conceptual framework that has been successfully applied across numerous settings and in a wide range of research studies.

Thus, there is a solid theoretical base underpinning the skills perspective. In his historical overview of this field, Argyle (1999, p. 142) noted, 'One of the implications of looking at social behaviour as a social skill was the likelihood that it could be trained'. This proved to be the case, and there has been an enormous explosion of interest in communication skills training. When individuals receive systematic skills tuition, their social performance has been shown to improve (Hargie, 2006b). Not surprisingly, there has been a concomitant and exponential growth in publications pertaining to interpersonal skills, within a variety of social and professional contexts. As evidenced by the references in this text, research in this field has been voluminous.

This book has not offered a cook-book approach to the study of interpersonal interaction. Some criticisms of the skills approach are based upon the mistaken assumption that it offers a narrow, reductionist analysis to the study of human behaviour (Sanders, 2003; Salmon and Young, 2011). As Hargie (2006c), in his rebuttal of such criticisms has shown, this is far from the case. Rather, the skills perspective recognises that interpersonal communication is a complex and often strange phenomenon, which, on occasion, can become dysfunctional and cause immense difficulties in terms of human relationships (Spitzberg and Cupach, 2007; Vangelista and Hampel, 2010). It also acknowledges that there are no 'right' or 'wrong' ways to communicate with others (Hargie *et al.*, 2010; Clarke, 2013). One aspect emphasised throughout the book is that most skills have a 'happy medium' in terms of usage. For example, someone who bombards us with questions, continually self-discloses or reinforces every single thing we say or do would not be regarded as skilled. In this sense, a measured combination of skills is required.

Indeed, two important elements of goals were highlighted by Shah and Kruglanski (2000). The first is that of *multifinality*, wherein any one means of achieving a goal may serve more than one purpose. For example, a negotiator who demonstrates an interest in and pays attention to the other side may achieve the twin goals of (1) building a good relationship and (2) making the chances of a successful negotiation more likely. The second is *equifinality*, whereby the same goal can be attained in a variety of equally effective ways. Thus, there are alternative approaches that can be employed in any particular interactive episode to achieve a desired outcome, and it is up to the individual to select what is deemed to be the most appropriate mix. Such selection, however, demands an extensive knowledge of the range of alternatives available and their likely effects in any given context. It is at this level that the present book has been geared.

The model of the interpersonal process outlined in Chapter 2 provides a conceptual framework, which can be used as a basis for making such strategic decisions. Awareness of the skills covered, and of their behavioural determinants, as presented in the remaining chapters, will contribute to the increased understanding of the process of interpersonal communication. These furnish the reader with a language with which to study, and interpret, this process more fully. Fiske (2000, p. 77) pointed out that, for the most part: 'people do not know how they coordinate, plan, construct their action, or interpret each other's action'. While for much of the time we operate at this subconscious level, it is necessary to have insight into, and understanding of, the skills and strategies that underpin human intercourse. Such knowledge enables us to operate swiftly and effectively without always having to think consciously about what we should do. When problems arise it also allows us to analyse possible underlying reasons, and make alternative responses.

COMMUNICATION ETHICS

Before ending this text, we must consider the role of communication ethics. Ethics can be defined as 'the principles, norms, and standards of conduct governing an individual or group' (Treviño and Nelson, 2011, p. 17). It is important to have high ethical principles and standards when communicating with others. When people have information, they can use it for good or ill. It is the same with interpersonal skills. It is possible to use the information contained in this book in ethical or unethical ways. For example, the influencing techniques reviewed in Chapter 12 could be used in a manipulative and Machiavellian manner to get others to do what we want. Alternatively, they can be employed for the greater good of everyone. In the business world there have long been criticisms of the lack of communication ethics (Hargie *et al.*, 2004). The ethical manager is seen as being something akin to the Yeti. Several people claim to have seen one in the distance, there is some circumstantial, though not very convincing, evidence that one exists, but no one has actually encountered the beast face to face, and we would be rather taken aback if we saw it in all its glory.

But it is clear that in the end an unethical style of operating will be costly both for relational and more material goals (Clampitt, 2013). For this reason, all professional bodies have strict codes of ethics to which members are required to adhere. For example, the ethical code of the International Association of Business Communicators (2015) stipulates that members should communicate in ways that are not only legal but also ethical, truthful, accurate and fair, and that show respect and mutual understanding as well as sensitivity to cultural values and beliefs. A detailed code for communication professionals, put forward by Montgomery *et al.* (2001), included the following guidelines.

Treat others justly

The principle of justice involves recognising and respecting the rights and dues of others. While in principle the norm of justice would be accepted by many, in practice it is more difficult to operationalise. For example, is it just to earn significantly more than others? In communication terms, in group discussions it is just that everyone's views should be heard. But what if they disagree with our views and if their perspective is accepted they could benefit at our expense? The answer is that we should treat others as we would wish to be treated – with justice. There is a growing literature in the field of interpersonal justice, which refers to, 'the degree to which people are treated with politeness, dignity and respect' (Colquitt *et al.*, 2001, p. 427). We expect to receive consideration and fairness in interactions and react negatively if we perceive this not to be the case (Holtz and Harold, 2013). Being subjected to aggressive, bullying or demeaning behaviour is a breach of this moral principle. As discussed in Chapter 11, a 'soft' form of assertiveness is the best policy. Here the rights of both sides are protected equally, and there is concern for the relationship. Norms of justice also dictate that we should not keep people in the dark about information that may impact upon them. Managers within organisations should show respect for employees by treating them as having a *right to know* what is going on, rather than only telling them what they *need to know*. While it is not always possible to treat all staff *equally*, they should all be treated *justly*.

In organisations there are two types of justice. Distributive justice involves ensuring equity in the allocation of duties, rewards and resources for all employees. Procedural justice relates to fairness in the procedures and processes employed when making decisions about the distribution of task and rewards. This involves ensuring that the related formal organisational procedures are fair and equitable. But it also necessitates interactional justice, in terms of how managers communicate with employees as they make and implement decisions. For example, they should not spend a greater amount of time communicating with certain 'favourites', or give them more encouragement to apply for rewards. Leader–member exchange theory purports that, because leaders have restricted amounts of personal and functional resources, they have to be selective about how these are distributed (Dulebohn et al., 2012). This selective distribution and perceived differential treatment then impact upon the quality of the leader–member exchange. As shown by Ferris et al. (2012), there is a link between perceived interpersonal injustice and workplace deviance. Employees who believe they have not been treated justly seek revenge by engaging in negative behaviours such as reducing their output, withholding important information and being less co-operative. They also experience negative emotional states such as anger, stress and resentment. There should therefore be justice in terms of both the allocation of tasks and rewards and in the procedures used to decide upon their distribution.

Tell the truth

As discussed in Chapter 9, harmless white lies (like telling someone their new suit is lovely when you really don't like it) can sometimes be conducive to relationships, but as deceit increases, the potential for dysfunctional outcomes escalates. Honesty is usually the best policy, and it is better to be open rather than evasive. While many politicians are skilled at prevarication and obfuscation, they are often not respected or trusted. Where it is simply not possible to tell the truth, it may be advisable to follow the old adage: 'Whatever you say, say nothing'. In other words, respond in such a way as not to disclose a secret you had promised to keep, unnecessarily hurt someone by being brutally frank, and so on. As discussed in Chapter 9, equivocation is often a useful alternative to a blunt truth or a lie. However, while there will be occasions when obfuscation can be acceptable, it should not be one's everyday *modus operandi*. While euphemisms can play a useful, and indeed sympathetic, role in communication (e.g. saying that someone has 'passed away' rather than 'died'), they can also distort reality. Thus, organisations employ euphemisms for laying off staff, such as 'downsizing', 'rightsizing' or 'delayering', but these do not camouflage the harsh reality of job losses. The over-use of such terms often leads to a decrease in trust in the communicator.

Do not harm others

The *nonmaleficence* (literally 'do no harm') *principle* refers to the tenet that your communication should not deliberately harm others, but rather that you should treat them with dignity and respect. The autonomy of others should be recognised and their independent decisions encouraged. Using interpersonal skills in a devious fashion (e.g. persuading people to act against their best interests) is not good practice. Spreading false and malicious rumours about an acquaintance or colleague is a breach of this moral code. Selling others something they don't need at an inflated price is another example of how this tenet can be broken. In practice, of course, nonmaleficence can pose difficulties. For example, at a disciplinary hearing it is necessary and ethical to tell the truth about the behaviour of the appellant, even though this may be hurtful or harmful for that person. The key factor here is that the *intention* is not to cause harm.

Another potential form of harm is that caused by gossip. In general terms it is wrong to listen to rumours and certainly wrong to spread them. However, the grapevine tends to grow prolifically in most social environments. Gossip is usually much 'juicier' that the true story and so more enticing. Indeed, the communication of rumours seems to be an endemic component of the human condition (Kimmel, 2004b). As a result, the temptation is to join the rumour club. Another reason why this is a potent channel is that the information delivered along the grapevine has been shown to be accurate about 80 per cent of the time (Karathanos and Auriemmo, 1999). It is also a very swift form of communication. However, while some rumours are harmless, others can be hurtful or harmful. When rumours are about uncorroborated issues that could be injurious to individuals or the organisation, then it is wrong to engage in this activity.

Act professionally at all times

Professional behaviour involves behaving with integrity and acting in such a way as to inspire confidence in and respect from others. For example, we need to listen carefully, respond in a manner that is apposite to the other person's emotional needs, be assertive but not aggressive, accept responsibility for our mistakes and avoid the use of inappropriate humour. Professional behaviour involves respecting information that is given in private by treating it confidentially. It also encompasses attending professional development courses to update and improve one's competence. An important ethical issue for professionals is that of *whistleblowing*. This takes place when information about immoral, illegal or illegitimate corporate practices is disclosed, even though this may be detrimental to the organisation in which the whistleblower is employed. The opposite of whistleblowing is *swallowing the whistle,* when an employee remains silent about a troubling ethical issue. In general, whistleblowing occurs when internal attempts to resolve the problem have been rejected (Miceli *et al.*, 2008). This means that organisations should have in place rigorous procedures to encourage employees to report what they perceive to be instances of wrongdoing and to protect them when they do so (Vandekerckhove and Lewis, 2012).

Treat others as equals

In both professional–client and manager–employee encounters there is asymmetry, in that the former often has knowledge and status that the latter does not possess. This can cause *dysfunctional discordance* in the relationship (Morrow and Hargie, 2001). The concept of *concordance* is therefore important as a way of trying to achieve greater balance, whereby interactions are conceived as a meeting between equals. It is possible to behave in a power-crazed fashion, by, for example, asking all of the questions and only rewarding responses that suit your intentions for the other person. This is not good practice. Rather, it is better to empower others to participate as fully as possible. Explain to them what your goals are throughout the interaction, and check these for agreement. Concordance necessitates adopting a more reflective than directive style.

OVERVIEW

Success in most walks of life is predicated on communicative ability. As shown in this book, we now know a great deal about the key constituents of effective social performance. The areas selected for inclusion were: nonverbal communication, reinforcement, questioning, reflecting, listening, explanation, self-disclosure, set induction, closure, assertiveness, influencing, negotiating and group interaction. It is recognised that this selection is not exhaustive, since other specialised skills may be employed in particular settings. Nevertheless, these represent core behavioural elements of skilled interpersonal communication. For this reason, practising professionals need to have a sound working knowledge of them. They also need to use these skills in a responsible, ethical way.

In the final analysis, improvements in performance necessitate practical action. In other words, it is only by converting knowledge of skills into actual behaviour that increments in social competence can occur. This may necessitate changes in existing behavioural repertoire, and this is not always easily achieved. The most difficult part of learning new responses is often the unlearning of old ones. Thus, it is essential to experiment with various social techniques in order to develop, refine, maintain or extend one's existing repertoire of skills. Once a wide repertoire has been developed, the individual thereby becomes a more effective communicator with the ability to adjust and adapt to varying social situations.

Bibliography

Aarts, H. and Elliott, A. (2012a) Preface, in H. Aarts and A. Elliott (eds) *Goal-directed Behavior*. New York: Taylor and Francis.

Aarts, H. and Elliott, A. (2012b) (eds) *Goal-directed Behavior*. New York: Taylor and Francis.

Achinstein, P. (1983) *The Nature of Explanation*. Oxford: Oxford University Press.

Adair, W., Okumura, T. and Brett, J. (2001) Negotiation behaviour when cultures collide: The United States and Japan, *Journal of Applied Psychology*, 86, 371–385.

Adair, W., Taylor, M., Chu, J. *et al.* (2013) Effective influence in negotiation, *International Studies of Management and Organization*, 43, 6–25.

Adam, H. and Brett, J. (2015) Context matters: The social effects of anger in cooperative, balanced, and competitive negotiation situations, *Journal of Experimental Social Psychology*, 61, 44–58.

Adams, K. and Galanes, G. (2008) *Communicating in Groups: Applications and Skills*, 7th edition. Boston, MA: McGraw-Hill.

Adams, N., Bell, J., Saunders, C. and Whittington, D. (1994) *Communication Skills in Physiotherapist–Patient Interactions*. Jordanstown: University of Ulster Monograph.

Adams, R. and Kleck, R. (2003) Perceived gaze direction and the processing of facial displays of emotion, *Psychological Science*, 14, 644–647.

Adams, R., Hess, U. and Kleck, R. (2015) The intersection of gender-related facial appearance and facial displays of emotion, *Emotion Review*, 7, 5–13.

Adler, R. and Proctor, R. (2014) *Looking Out, Looking In*, 14th edition. Belmont, CA: Wadsworth, Cengage Learning.

Adler, R., Rosen, B. and Silverstein, E. (1998) Emotions in negotiation: How to manage fear and anger, *Negotiation Journal*, 14, 161–179.

Adler, R., Elmhorst, J. and Lucas, K. (2012) *Communicating at Work: Strategies for Success in Business and the Professions*, 11th edition. Boston, MA: McGraw-Hill.

Adler, R., Rodman, G. and du Pre, A. (2013a) *Understanding Human Communication*, 12th edition. New York: Oxford University Press.

Adler, R., Rosenfeld, L. and Proctor, R. (2013b) *Interplay: The Process of Interpersonal Communication*, 12th edition. New York: Oxford University Press.

Adler, T. (1993) Congressional staffers witness miracle of touch, *APA Monitor*, Feb, 12–13.

Afifi, T. and Steuber, K. (2009) The revelation risk model (RRM): Factors that predict the revelation of secrets and the strategies used to reveal them, *Communication Monographs*, 76, 144–176.

Afifi, T., Caughlin, J. and Afifi, W. (2007) The dark side (and light side) of avoidance and secrets, in B. Sitzberg and W. Cupach (eds) *The Dark Side of Interpersonal Communication*. Mahwah, NJ: Lawrence Erlbaum.

Afifi, W. (2006) Nonverbal communication, in B. Whaley and W. Samter (eds) *Explaining Communication: Contemporary Theories and Exemplars*. Mahwah, NJ: Lawrence Erlbaum.

Afifi, W. and Caughlin, J. (2006) A close look at revealing secrets and some consequences that follow, *Communication Research*, 33, 467–488.

Afifi, W. and Guerrero, L. (2000) Motivations underlying topic avoidance in close relationships, in S. Petronio (ed.) *Balancing the Secrets of Private Disclosures*. Mahwah, NJ: Lawrence Erlbaum.

Afifi, W. and Johnson, M. (2005) The nature and function of tie-signs, in V. Manusov (ed.) *The Sourcebook of Nonverbal Measures: Going Beyond Words*. Mahwah, NJ: Lawrence Erlbaum.

Agazarian, Y. (2012) Systems-centered group psychotherapy: A theory of living human systems and its systems-centered practice, *Group*, 36, 19–36.

Ajzen, I. (1991) The theory of planned behaviour, *Organizational Behavior and Human Decision Processes*, 50, 179–211.

Akande, A. (1997) Determinants of personal space among South African students, *Journal of Psychology*, 131, 569–571.

Alavinia, P. and Sameei, A. (2012) Potential bonds between extroversion/introversion and Iranian EFL learners' listening comprehension ability, *English Language Teaching*, 5, 19–30.

Alavosius, M., Adams, A., Ahern, D. and Follick, M. (2000) Behavioural approaches to organisational safety, in J. Austin and J. Carr (eds) *Handbook of Applied Behaviour Analysis*. Reno, NV: Context Press.

Albarracin, D., Johnson, B. and Zanna, M. (2005) *The Handbook of Attitudes*. London: Routledge.

Albert, S. and Kessler, S. (1976) Processes for ending social encounters: The conceptual archaeology of a temporal place, *Journal of the Theory of Social Behaviour*, 6, 147–170.

Albert, S. and Kessler, S. (1978) Ending social encounters, *Journal of Experimental Social Psychology*, 14, 541–553.

Alberti, R. and Emmons, M. (2008) *Your Perfect Right: Assertiveness and Equality in Your Life and Relationships*, 9th edition. Atascadero, CA: Impact.

Alberts, J.K. (1992) An inferential/strategic explanation for the social organisation of teases, *Journal of Language and Social Psychology*, 11, 153–178.

Ali, M. and Levine, T. (2008) The language of truthful and deceptive denials and confessions, *Communication Reports*, 21, 82–91.

Alibali, M. and Nathan, M. (2012) Embodiment in mathematics teaching and learning: Evidence from learners' and teachers' gestures, *Journal of the Learning Sciences*, 21, 247–286.

Alibali, M., Nathan, M., Wolfgram, M. *et al.* (2014) How teachers link ideas in mathematics instruction using speech and gesture: A corpus analysis, *Cognition and Instruction*, 32, 65–100.

Allday, R. and Pakurar, K. (2007) Effects of teacher greetings on student on-task behaviour, *Journal of Applied Behavior Analysis*, 40, 317–320.

Allday, R., Bush, M., Ticknor, N. and Walker, L. (2011) Using teacher greetings to increase speed to task engagement, *Journal of Applied Behavior Analysis*, 44, 393–396.

Allen, J., Waitzkin, H. and Stoeckle, J. (1979) Physicians' stereotypes about female health illness: A study of patients' sex and the information process during medical interviews, *Women and Health*, 4, 135–146.

Allen, K. and Stokes, T. (1987) Use of escape and reward in the management of young children during dental treatment, *Journal of Applied Behavior Analysis*, 20, 381–389.

Allen, M. (1998) Comparing the effectiveness of one- and two-sided messages, in M. Allen and R. Preiss (eds) *Persuasion: Advances through Meta-analysis*. Cresskill, NJ: Hampton Press.

Allen, M. and Stiff, J. (1998) An analysis of the sleeper effect, in M. Allen and R. Preiss (eds) *Persuasion: Advances through Meta-analysis*. Cresskill, NJ: Hampton Press.

Allen, M., Bruflat, R., Fucilla, R., Kramer, M., McKellips, S., Ryan, D. and Spiegelhoff, M. (2000) Testing the persuasiveness of evidence: Combining narrative and statistical forms, *Communication Research Reports*, 17, 331–336.

Allen, M., Timmerman, L., Ksobiech, K., Valde, K., Gallagher, E., Hookham, L., Bradford, L. and Emmers-Sommer, T. (2008) Persons living with HIV: Disclosure to sexual partners, *Communication Research Reports*, 25, 192–199.

Allwinn, S. (1991) Seeking information: Contextual influences on question formulation, *Journal of Language and Social Interaction*, 10, 169–184.

Alon, I. and Brett, J. (2007) Perceptions of time and their impact on negotiations in the Arabic-speaking Islamic world, *Negotiation Journal*, 23, 55–73.

Altman, I. (1977) The communication of interpersonal attitudes: An ecological approach, in T. Houston (ed.) *Foundations of Interpersonal Attraction*. London: Academic Press.

Altman, I. and Taylor, D. (1973) *Social Penetration: The Development of Interpersonal Relationships*. New York: Holt, Rinehart and Winston.

Alvesson, M. and Sveningsson, S. (2003) Managers doing leadership: The extra-ordinarization of the mundane, *Human Relations*, 56, 1435–1459.

Amanatullah, E. and Tinsley, C. (2013) Punishing female negotiators for asserting too much…or not enough: Exploring why advocacy moderates backlash against assertive female negotiators, *Organizational Behavior and Human Decision Processes*, 120, 110–122.

Ambady, N. and Skowronski, J. (eds) (2008) *First Impressions*. New York: Guilford.

Amernic, J., Craig, R. and Tourish, D. (2007) The transformational leader as *pedagogue, physician, architect, commander*, and *saint*: Five root metaphors in Jack Welch's letters to stockholders of General Electric, *Human Relations*, 60, 1839–1872.

Ames, D. (2008) Assertiveness expectancies: How hard people push depends on the consequences they predict, *Journal of Personality and Social Psychology*, 95, 1541–1557.

Ames, D. and Wazlawek, A. (2014) Pushing in the dark: Causes and consequences of limited self-awareness for interpersonal assertiveness, *Personality and Social Psychology Bulletin*, 40, 775–790.

Amiot, C., Blanchard, C. and Gaudreau, P. (2007) The self in change: A longitudinal investigation of coping and self-determination processes, *Self and Identity*, 7, 204–224.

Andersen, J. (2009) When a servant-leader comes knocking…, *Leadership and Organization Development Journal*, 30, 4–15.

Andersen, P. (2005) The touch avoidance measure, in V. Manusov (ed.) *The Sourcebook of Nonverbal Measures: Going Beyond Words*. Mahwah, NJ: Lawrence Erlbaum.

Andersen, P. (2006) The evolution of biological sex differences in communication, in K. Dindia and D. Canary (eds) *Sex Differences and Similarities in Communication*, 2nd edition. New York: Lawrence Erlbaum.

Andersen, P. (2008) *Nonverbal Communication: Forms and Functions*. Long Grove, IL: Waveland Press.

Andersen, P. (2011) Tactile traditions: Cultural differences and similarities in haptic communication, in M. Hertenstein and S. Weiss (eds) *The Handbook of Touch: Neuroscience, Behavioral, and Applied Perspectives*. New York: Springer Publications.

Andersen, P. and Andersen, J. (2005) Measurements of perceived nonverbal immediacy, in V. Manusov (ed.) *The Sourcebook of Nonverbal Measures: Going Beyond Words*. Mahwah, NJ: Lawrence Erlbaum.

Andersen, P. and Kumar, R. (2006) Emotions, trust and relationship development in business relationships: A conceptual model for buyer–seller dyads, *Industrial Marketing Management*, 35, 522–535.

Andersen, P., Gannon, J. and Lalchik, J. (2013) Poxemic and haptic interaction: The closeness continuum, in J. Hall and M. Knapp (eds) *Nonverbal Communication*. Berlin: Walter de Gruyter.

Andersen, P., Guerrero, L. and Jones, S. (2006) Nonverbal behaviour in intimate interactions and intimate relationships, in V. Manusov and M. Patterson (eds) *The Sage Handbook of Nonverbal Communication*. Thousand Oaks, CA: Sage.

Anderson, R. (1997) Anxiety or ignorance: The determinants of interpersonal skill display, *Dissertation Abstracts International: The Sciences and Engineering*, 57 (9–B), 5959.

Andrews, K., Carpenter, C., Shaw, A. and Boster, F. (2008) The legitimization of paltry favors effect: A review and meta-analysis, *Communication Reports*, 21, 59–69.

Andriessen, E. and Drenth, P. (1998) Leadership: Theories and models, in P. Drenth, H. Thierry and C. de Wolff (eds) *A Handbook of Work and Organizational Psychology, Volume 4: Organizational Psychology*. Hove: Psychology Press.

Anonymous (1998) To reveal or not to reveal: A theoretical model of anonymous communication, *Communication Theory*, 8, 381–407.

Ansfield, M. (2007) Smiling when distressed: When a smile is a frown turned upside down, *Personality and Social Psychology Bulletin*, 33, 763–775.

Anthony, A. (2008) Baby P stepfather rape case raises questions over impact on child witnesses. *The Observer*, 3 May (http://www.guardian.co.uk/society/2009/may/03/child-witnesses-baby-p-stepfather) (accessed 2 December 2009).

Antonakis, J., Fenley, M. and Liechti, S. (2012) Learning charisma: Transform yourself into the person others want to follow, *Harvard Business Review*, 90, 127–130.

Antonetti, P. and Baines, P. (2015) Guilt in marketing research: An elicitation–consumption perspective and research agenda, *International Journal of Management Reviews*, 17, 333–335.

Aoki, H. (2011) Some functions of speaker head nods, in C. Goodwin, C. LeBaron and J. Streeck (eds) *Embodied Interaction: Language and Body in the Material World*. Cambridge: Cambridge University Press.

App, B., McIntosh, D., Reed, C. and Hertenstein, M. (2011) Nonverbal channel use in communication of emotion: How may depend on why. *Emotion*, 11, 603–617.

Aranguren, M. and Tonnelat, S. (2014) Emotional transactions in the Paris subway: Combining naturalistic videotaping, objective facial coding and sequential analysis in the study of nonverbal emotional behaviour, *Journal of Nonverbal Behavior*, 38, 495–521.

Arasaratnam, L. (2014) Ten years of research in intercultural communication competence (2003–2013): A retrospective, *Journal of Intercultural Communication*, 35 (http://immi.se/intercultural/) (accessed 19 August 2014).

Archer, R. (1979) Role of personality and the social situation, in G. Chelune (ed.) *Self-disclosure*. San Francisco: Jossey-Bass.

Argyle, M. (1983) *The Psychology of Interpersonal Behaviour*, 4th edition. Harmondsworth: Penguin.

Argyle, M. (1988) *Bodily Communication*, 2nd edition. New York: Methuen.

Argyle, M. (1995) Social skills, in N. Mackintosh and A. Colman (eds) *Learning and Skills*. London: Longman.

Argyle, M. (1999). Why I study social skills. *The Psychologist*, 12, 142.

Argyle, M. and Cook, M. (1976) *Gaze and Mutual Gaze*. Cambridge: Cambridge University Press.

Argyle, M. and Dean, J. (1965) Eye-contact, distance and affilation, *Sociometry*, 28, 289–304.

Argyle, M., Furnham, A. and Graham, J. (1981) *Social Situations*. Cambridge: Cambridge University Press.

Arnes, D. (2008) Assertiveness expectancies: How hard people push depends on the consequences they predict, *Journal of Personality and Social Psychology*, 95, 1541–1557.

Arnold, E. and Boggs, K. (2016) *Interpersonal Relationships: Professional Communication Skills for Nurses*, 7th edition. St Louis, MI: Elsevier.

Aron, A., Mashek, D. and Aron, E. (2004) Closeness as including other in the self, in D. Mashek and A. Aron (eds) *Handbook of Closeness and Intimacy*. Mahwah, NJ: Lawrence Erlbaum.

Aron, A., Mashek, D., McLaughlin-Volpe, T., Wright, S., Lewandowski, G. and Aron, E. (2006) Including close others in the cognitive structure of the self, in M. Baldwin (ed.) *Interpersonal Cognition*. New York: Guilford.

Aronson, E. (2007) The evolution of cognitive dissonance theory: A personal appraisal, in A. Pratkanis (ed.) *The Science of Social Influence: Advances and Future Progress*. New York: Psychology Press.

Aronson, E. (2008) *The Social Animal*, 10th edition. New York: WH Freeman.

Aronson, E., Wilson, T. and Akert, R. (2007) *Social Psychology*, 6th edition. Upper Saddle River, NJ: Pearson.

Arundale, R. (2013) Conceptualizing 'interaction' in interpersonal pragmatics: Implications for understanding and research, *Journal of Pragmatics*, 58, 12–26.

Asai, A. and Barnlund, D. (1998) Boundaries of the unconscious private and public self in Japanese and Americans: A cross-cultural comparison, *International Journal of Intercultural Relations*, 22, 431–452.

Asante, M., Miike, Y. and Yin, J. (2014) *The Global Intercultural Communication Reader*, 2nd edition. New York: Routledge.

Asch, S. (1940) Studies in the principles of judgments and attitudes: II. Determination of judgments by group and by ego standards, *Journal of Social Psychology*, 12, 433–465.

Asch, S. (1952) *Social Psychology*. Englewood Cliffs: Prentice Hall.

Ashkanasy, N., Ayoko, O. and Jehn, K. (2014) Understanding the physical environment of workand employee behavior: An affective events perspective, *Journal of Organizational Behavior*, 35, 1169–1184.

Ashley, L., Duberley, J., Sommerlad, H. and Scholarios, D. (2015) *A Qualitative Evaluation of Non-Educational Barriers to the Elite Professions*. London: Social Mobility and Child Poverty Commission.

Ashley, L., O'Connor, D. and Jones, F. (2013) A randomized trial of written emotional disclosure interventions in school teachers: Controlling for positive expectancies and effects on health and job satisfaction, *Psychology, Health and Medicine*, 18, 588–600.

Ashmore, R. and Banks, D. (2001) Patterns of self-disclosure among mental health nursing student, *Nurse Education Today*, 21, 48–57.

Astrom, J. (1994) Introductory greeting behaviour: A laboratory investigation of approaching and closing salutation phases, *Perceptual and Motor Skills*, 79, 863–897.

Astrom, J. and Thorell, L. (1996) Greeting behaviour and psychogenic need: Interviews on experiences of therapists, clergymen and car salesmen, *Perceptual and Motor Skills*, 83, 939–956.

Audet, C. and Everall, R. (2010) Therapist self-dislosure and the therapeutic relationship: A phenomenological study from the client perspective, *British Journal of Guidance and Counselling*, 38, 327–342.

Auerswald, M. (1974) Differential reinforcing power of restatement and interpretation on client production of affect, *Journal of Counseling Psychology*, 21, 9–14.

Augoustinos, M., Walker, I. and Donaghue, N. (2014) *Social Cognition: An Integrated Introduction*, 3rd edition. Thousand Oaks, CA: Sage.

Austin, J. and Carr, J. (eds) (2000) *Handbook of Applied Behavior Analysis*. Reno, NV: Context Press.

Avolio, B., Walumbwa, F. and Weber, T. (2009) Leadership: Current theories, research, and future directions, *Annual Review of Psychology*, 60, 421–449.

Avtgis, T., Rancer, A., Kanjeva, P. and Chory, R. (2008) Argumentative and aggressive communication in Bulgaria: Testing for conceptual and methodological equivalence, *Journal of Intercultural Communication Research*, 37, 17–245.

Axtell, R. (1999) Initiating interaction: Greetings and beckonings across the world, in L. Guerrero, J. DeVito and M. Hecht (eds) *The Nonverbal Communication Reader: Classic and Contemporary Readings Disclosures*, 2nd edition. Prospect Heights, IL: Waveland.

Ayduk, Ö, Gyurak, A., Akinola, M. and Mendes, W. (2013) Consistency over flattery: Self-verification processes revealed in implicit and behavioral responses to feedback, *Social Psychological and Personality Science*, 4, 538–545.

Babcock, L. and Laschever, S. (2008) *Why Women Don't Ask: The High Cost of Avoiding Negotiation – and Positive Strategies for Change*. London: Paitkus.

Back, K. and Back, K. (2005) *Assertiveness at Work: A Practical Guide to Handling Awkward Situations*, 3rd edition. London: McGraw-Hill.

Baddeley, A., Eysenck, M. and Anderson, M. (2009) *Memory*. Hove: Psychology Press.

Badie, D. (2010) Groupthink, Iraq, and the war on terror: Explaining US policy shift toward Iraq, *Foreign Policy Analysis*, 6, 277–296.

Bagozzi, R. and Verbeke, W. (2014) Biomarketing: An emerging paradigm linking neuroscience, endocrinology, and genetics to buyer–seller behavior, in L. Moutinho, E. Bigné and A. Manrai (eds) *The Routledge Companion to the Future of Marketing*. Abingdon, Oxon: Routledge.

Bagwell, C. and Schmidt, M. (2011) *Friendships in Childhood and Adolescence*. New York: Guilford Press.

Baillargeon, N. (2007) *A Short Course in Intellectual Self-defense: Find Your Inner Chomsky*. New York: Seven Stories Press.

Baker, H., Crockett, R., Uus, K., Bamford, J. and Marteau, T. (2007) Why don't health professionals check patient understanding? A questionnaire-based study, *Psychology, Health and Medicine*, 12, 380–385.

Baker, R. (2001) The nature of leadership, *Human Relations*, 54, 469–494.

Baker, W. (1994) *Networking Smart: How to Build Relationships for Personal and Organizational Success.* New York: McGraw-Hill.

Bakker-Pieper, A. and de Vries, R. (2013) The incremental validity of communication styles over personality traits for leader outcomes, *Human Performance*, 26, 1–19.

Bakx, A., Koopman, M., de Kruijf, J. and den Brok, P. (2015) Primary school pupils' views of characteristics of good primary school teachers: An exploratory, open approach for investigating pupils' perceptions, *Teachers and Teaching: Theory and Practice*, 21, 543–564.

Balachandra, L., Bordone, R., Menkel-Meadow, C., Ringstrom, P. and Sarath, E. (2005) Improvisation and negotiation: Expecting the unexpected, *Negotiation Journal*, 21, 415–423.

Balcetis, E. (2008) Where the motivation resides and self-deception hides: How motivated cognition accomplishes self-deception, *Social and Personality Psychology Compass*, 2, 361–381.

Baldwin, M. (ed.) (2000) *The Use of Self in Therapy*, 2nd edition. New York: The Haworth Press.

Bales, R. (1950) *Interaction Process Analysis: A Method for the Study of Small Groups.* Cambridge, MA: Addison-Wesley.

Bales, R. (1970) *Personality and Interpersonal Behavior.* New York: Holt, Rinehart and Winston.

Balykina, G. (2015) Intercultural aspect of Russian business negotiation practices, *Social Science Research Network* (http://ssrn.com/abstract=2577188) (accessed 19 August 2015).

Balzer Riley, J. (2012) *Communication in Nursing*, 7th edition. St Louis, MO: Elsevier Mosby.

Bambacas, M. and Patrickson, M. (2008) Interpersonal communication skills that enhance organisational commitment, *Journal of Communication Management*, 12, 51–72.

Bandura, A. (1986) *Social Foundations of Thought and Action: A Social Cognitive Theory.* Englewood Cliffs, NJ: Prentice-Hall.

Bandura, A. (1989) Self-regulation of motivation and action through internal standards and goal systems, in L. Pervin (ed.) *Goal Concepts in Personality and Social Psychology*. Hillsdale, NJ: Lawrence Erlbaum.

Bandura, A. (1997) *Self-efficacy: The Exercise of Control.* New York: WH Freeman.

Bandura, A. (2006) *Psychological Modeling: Conflicting Theories.* Piscataway, NJ: Aldine Transaction.

Bangerter, A. (2000) Self-presentation: Conversational implications of self-presentational goals in research interviews, *Journal of Language and Social Psychology,* 19, 436–462.

Bangerter, A., Clark, H. and Katz, A. (2004) Navigating joint projects in telephone conversations, *Discourse Processes*, 37, 1–23.

Banse, R. and Scherer, K.R. (1996) Acoustic profiles in vocal emotion expression, *Journal of Personality and Social Psychology*, 70, 614–636.

Bänziger, T., Patel, S. and Schere, K. (2014) The role of perceived voice and speech characteristics in vocal emotion communication, *Journal of Nonverbal Behavior*, 38, 31–52.

Barber, K., Donegan, E., Ouimet, A. and Radomsky, A. (2015) Cognitive restructuring, in I. Milosevic and R. McCabe (eds) *Phobias: The Psychology of Irrational Fear*. Santa Barbara, CA: Greenwood.

Bargh, J. (2005) Bypassing the will: Towards demystifying behavioral priming effects, in R. Hassin, J. Uleman and J. Bargh (eds) *The New Unconscious*. Oxford, UK: Oxford University Press.

Baron, R. and Byrne, D. (2000) *Social psychology*, 9th edition. Boston: Allyn and Bacon.

Baron, R. and Kerr, N. (2003) *Group Process, Group Decision, Group Action*, 2nd edition. Buckingham: Open University Press.

Baron, R. and Markman, G. (2000) Beyond social capital: How social skills can enhance entrepreneurs' success, *Academy of Management Executive*, 14, 106–116.

Baron, R., Cowan, G., Ganz, R. and McDonald, M. (1974) Interaction of locus of control and type of reinforcement feedback: Considerations of external validity, *Journal of Personality and Social Psychology*, 30, 285–292.

Barrett, L., Mesquita, B. and Gendron, M. (2011) Emotion perception in context, *Current Directions in Psychological Science*, 20, 286–290.

Barrick, M., Dustin, S., Giluk, T. *et al.* (2012) Candidate characteristics driving initial impressions during rapport building: Implications for employment interview validity, *Journal of Occupational and Organizational Psychology*, 85, 330–352.

Barry, B. and Rehel, E. (2014) Lies, damn lies, and negotiation: An interdisciplinary analysis of the nature and consequences of deception at the bargaining table, in O. Ayoko, N. Ashkanasy and K. Jehn (eds) *Handbook of Research in Conflict Management*. Cheltenham, Gloucestershire: Edward Elgar.

Bar-Tal, Y. and Kossowska, M. (2010) The efficacy at fulfilling need for closure: The concept and its measurement, in J. Villanueva (ed.) *Personality Traits: Classification, Effects and Changes*. New York: Nova Publishers.

Barwise, P. and Meehan, S. (2008) So you think you're a good listener, *Harvard Business Review*, 88, 22.

Bass, B. (1985) *Leadership and Performance Beyond Expectations*. New York: Free Press.

Bass, B. (1990) *Bass and Stogdill's Handbook of Leadership: A Survey of Theory and Research*. New York: Free Press.

Bass, B. (1996) *A New Paradigm of Leadership: An Inquiry Into Transformational Leadership*. Alexandria, VA: US Army Research Institute for the Behavioral and Social Sciences.

Bass, B. and Riggio, R. (2006) *Transformational Leadership*, 2nd edition. Mahwah, NJ: Lawrence Erlbaum.

Bassnett, S. (2007) Well, it's a matter of, um, plain speaking, *The Times Higher Education*, 21/28 December, p. 20.

Baum, L. (2013) *American Courts: Process and Policy*, 7th edition. Boston, MA: Wadsworth, Cengage Learning.

Bavelas, A. (1950) Communication patterns in task-oriented groups, *Journal of the Acoustical Society of America*, 22, 725–30.

Bavelas, J. and Chovil, N. (2006) Nonverbal and verbal communication: Hand gestures and facial displays as part of language use in face-to-face dialogue, in V. Manusov and M. Patterson (eds) *The Sage Handbook of Nonverbal Communication*. Thousand Oaks, CA: Sage.

Bavelas, J., Gerwing, J. and Healing, S. (2014) Hand and facial gestures in conversational interaction, in T. Holtgraves (ed.) *The Oxford Handbook of Language and Social Psychology*. Oxford: Oxford University Press.

Baxter, L. and Sahlstein, E. (2000) Some possible directions for future research, in S. Petronio (ed.) *Balancing the Secrets of Private Disclosures*. Mahwah, NJ: Lawrence Erlbaum.

Baxter, J., Boon, J. and Marley, C. (2006) Interrogative pressure and responses to minimally leading questions, *Personality and Individual Differences*, 40, 87–98.

Bayat, M. (2011) Clarifying issues regarding the use of praise with young children, *Topics in Early Childhood Special Education*, 31, 121–128.

Beagrie, S. (2007) How to...speak in public, *Occupational Health*, 59, 26.

Beall, M., Gill-Rosier, J., Tate, J. and Matten, A. (2008) State of the context: Listening in education, *International Journal of Listening*, 22, 123–132.

Beattie, G. (2004) *Visible Thought: The New Psychology of Body Language*. Hove: Routledge.

Beaumeister, R. (1999) The nature and structure of the self, in R. Beaumeister (ed.) *The Self in Social Psychology*. Philadelphia, PA: Psychology Press.

Beaver, D. (2005) Nobody knows you're nervous: How to conquer those public speaking jitters, *ABA Banking Journal*, 96, 60.

Beaver, D. (2006) They don't like my accent, *ABA Banking Journal*, 98, 49.

Beaver, D. (2007) With visual aids, more is less, *ABA Banking Journal*, 99, 61.

Beck, C. (1999) *Managerial Communication: Bridging Theory and Practice*. Upper Saddle River, NJ: Prentice-Hall.

Bedwell, W., Fiore, S. and Salas, E. (2014) Developing the future workforce: An approach for integrating interpersonal skills into the MBA classroom, *Academy of Management Learning and Education*, 13, 171–186.

Beebe, S. and Masterson, J. (2014) *Communication in Small Groups: Principles and Practice*, 11th edition. Boston: Pearson Education.

Beebe, S., Beebe, S. and Redmond, M. (2014) *Interpersonal Communication: Relating to Others*, 7th edition. Boston: Pearson Education.

Beezer, R. (1956) Research on methods of interviewing foreign informants, George Washington University, *Human RRO Technical Reports*, no. 30.

Beharry, E. (1976) The effect of interviewing style upon self-disclosure in a dyadic interaction, *Dissertation Abstracts International*, 36, 4677B.

Beier, E. and Young, D. (1998) *The Silent Language of Psychotherapy*. New York: Aldine De Guyter.

Bell, C. (1806) *Essays on the Anatomy of Expression in Painting*. London: J. Murray.

Bell, R. and Healey, J. (1992) Idiomatic communication and interpersonal solidarity in friends' relational cultures, *Human Communication Research*, 18, 307–335.

Belmi, P. and Pfeffer, J. (2015) How 'organization' can weaken the norm of reciprocity: The effects of attributions for favors and a calculative mindset, *Academy of Management Discoveries*, 1, 35–55.

Bénabou, R. (2013) Groupthink: Collective delusions in organizations and markets, *Review of Economic Studies*, 80, 429–462.

Bendahan, S., Zehnder, C., Pralong, F. and Antonakis, J. (2014) Leader corruption depends on power and testosterone, *The Leadership Quarterly*, 26, 101–122.

Beneson, J., Aikins-Ford, S. and Apostoleris, N. (1998) Girls' assertion in the presence of boys, *Small Group Research*, 29, 198–211.

Benjamin, A. (2001) *The Helping Interview with Case Illustrations*, 4th edition. Boston: Houghton Mifflin.

Benn, A., Jones, G. and Rosenfield, S. (2008) Analysis of instructional consultants' questions and alternatives to questions during the problem identification interview, *Journal of Educational and Psychological Consultation*, 18, 54–80.

Benne, K. and Sheats, P. (1948) Functional roles of group members, *Journal of Social Issues*, 4, 41–49.

Bennis, W. and Townsend, R. (2005) *Reinventing Leadership: Strategies to Empower the Organization*. New York: Harper Collins.

Benoit, W. (1998) Forewarning and persuasion, in M. Allen and R. Preiss (eds) *Persuasion: Advances through Meta-analysis*. Cresskill, NJ: Hampton Press.

Benoit, W. (2015) *Accounts, Excuses, and Apologies*, 2nd edition: *Image Repair Theory and Research*. Albany, NY: State University of New York Press.

Benoit, W. and Benoit, P. (2008) *Persuasive Messages: The Process of Influence*. Malden, MA: Blackwell.

Bensing, J., Rimondini, M. and Visser, A. (2013) What patients want. *Patient Education and Counseling*, 90, 287–290.

Bente, G., Donaghy, W. and Suwelack, D. (1998) Sex differences in body movement and visual attention: An integrated analysis of movement and gaze in mixed-sex dyads, *Journal of Nonverbal Behavior*, 22, 31–58.

Berger, C. (1994) Power, dominance and social interaction, in M. Knapp and G. Miller (eds) *Handbook of Interpersonal Communication*, 2nd edition. Beverly Hills, CA: Sage.

Berger, C. (1995) A plan-based approach to strategic communication, in D. Hewes (ed.) *The Cognitive Basis of Interpersonal Communication*. Hillsdale, NJ: Lawrence Erlbaum.

Berger, C. (2000) Goal detection and efficiency: Neglected aspects of message production, *Communication Theory*, 10, 135–138.

Berger, C. (2002) Goals and knowledge structures in social interaction, in M. Knapp and J. Daly (eds) *Handbook of Interpersonal Communication*, 3rd edition. Thousand Oaks, California: Sage.

Berger, C., Roloff, M. and Roskos-Ewoldsen D. (eds) (2010) *The Handbook of Communication Science*. Thousand Oaks, CA: Sage.

Berger, J. (2005) Ignorance is bliss? Ethical considerations in therapeutic non-disclosure, *Cancer Investigation*, 1, 94–98.

Bergeron, J. and Vachon, M. (2008) The effects of humour usage by financial advisors in sales encounters, *International Journal of Bank Marketing*, 26, 376–398.

Berlew, D. (1990) How to increase your influence, in I. Asherman and S. Asherman (eds) *The Negotiating Sourcebook*. Amherst, MA: Human Resource Development Press.

Bernard, H. (2006) *Research Methods in Anthropology: Qualitative and Quantitative Approaches*. Lanham, MD: AltaMira Press.

Bernieri, F. (2005) The expression of rapport, in V. Manusov (ed.) *The Sourcebook of Nonverbal Measures: Going Beyond Words*. Mahwah, NJ: Lawrence Erlbaum.

Berry, W. (1996) *Negotiating in the Age of Integrity: A Complete Guide to Negotiating Win/Win in Business*. London: Nicolas Brealey.

Beukeboom, C. (2009) When words feel right: How affective expressions of listeners change a speaker's language use, *European Journal of Social Psychology*, 39, 747–756.

Beukeboom, C. (2014) Mechanisms of linguistic bias: How words reflect and maintain stereotypic expectancies, in J. Laszlo, J. Forgas and O. Vincze (eds) *Social Cognition and Communication*. New York: Psychology Press.

Bhattacharya, J. and Isen, A. (2008) On inferring demand for health care in the presence of anchoring, acquiescence, and selection biases, NBER Working Paper No. W13865 (http://ssrn.com/abstract=1106591) (accessed 2 December 2009).

Bikfalvi, A., Jäger, A. and Lay, G. (2014) The incidence and diffusion of team-work in manufacturing – evidences from a Pan-European survey, *Journal of Organizational Change Management*, 27, 206–231.

Billing, M. (2001) Arguing, in W. Robinson and H. Giles (eds) *The Handbook of Language and Social Psychology*. Chichester: John Wiley.

Bingham, L. (2007) Avoiding negotiation: Strategy and practice, in A. Schneider and C. Honeyman (eds) *The Negotiator's Fieldbook: The Desk Reference for the Experienced Negotiator*. Chicago, IL: American Bar Association.

Bion, W. (2003) *Learning from Experience*. London: Karnac.

Birdwhistell, R. (1970) *Kinesics and Context*. Philadelphia: University of Pennsylvania Press.

Birnholtz, J., Hancock, J., Smith, M. and Reynolds, L. (2012) Understanding una-vailability in a world of constant connection, *Interactions*, 19, 32–35.

Bitar, G., Kimball, T., Bermúdez, J. and Drew, C. (2014) Therapist self-disclosure and culturally competent care with Mexican–American court mandated clients: A phenomenological study, *Contemporary Family Therapy*, 36, 417–425.

Blake, B. and McCanse, A. (1991) *Leadership Dilemmas – Grid Solutions*. Houston: Gulf Publishing.

Blake, R. and Mouton, J. (1964) *The Managerial Grid: The Key to Leadership Excellence*. Houston, TX: Gulf Publishing.

Blake, R. and Mouton, J. (1985) *The Managerial Grid III*, Houston, TX: Gulf Publishing.

Blanchard, K. (2010) *Leading at a Higher Level.* Upper Saddle River, NJ: FT Press.

Blando, J. (2011) *Counseling Older Adults.* New York: Routledge.

Blankenship, K. and Craig, T. (2006) Rhetorical question use and resistance to persuasion: An attitude strength analysis, *Language and Social Psychology*, 25, 111–128.

Bless, H. (2001) The consequences of mood on the processing of social information, in A. Tesser and N. Schwarz (eds) *Blackwell Handbook of Social Psychology: Intraindividual Processes*. Malden, MA: Blackwell.

Bless, H., Bohner, G., Hild, T. and Schwarz, N. (1992) Asking difficult questions: Task complexity increases the impact of response, *European Journal of Social Psychology*, 22, 309–312.

Bloch, C. (1996) Emotions and discourse, *Text*, 16, 323–341.

Blonna, R. and Water, D. (2005) *Health Counseling: A Microskills Approach.* Sudbury, MA: Jones and Bartlett.

Blundel, R. (1998) *Effective Business Communication: Principles and Practice for the Information Age.* London: Prentice-Hall.

Bochner, D. (2000) *The Therapist's Use of Self in Family Therapy.* Northvale, NJ: Jason Aronson.

Boddy, J., Carvier, A. and Rowley, K. (1986) Effects of positive and negative verbal reinforcement on performance as a function of extroversion–introversion: Some tests of Gray's theory, *Personality and Individual Differences*, 7, 81–88.

Bodie, G. (2010) A racing heart, rattling knees, and ruminative thoughts: Defining, explaining, and treating public speaking anxiety, *Communication Education*, 59, 70–105.

Bodie, G. (2011) The understudied nature of listening in interpersonal communication, *International Journal of Listening*, 25, 1–9.

Bodie, G. (2012) Listening as positive communication, in T. Socha and M. Pitts (eds), *The Positive Side of Interpersonal Communication*. New York: Peter Lang.

Bodie, G. (2013) Issues in the measurement of listening, *Communication Research Reports*, 30, 76–84.

Bodie, G. and Jones, S. (2012) The nature of supportive listening II: The role of verbal person centeredness and nonverbal immediacy, *Western Journal of Communication*, 76, 250–269.

Bodie G., St. Cyr, K., Pence, M., Rold, M. and Honeycutt, J. (2012) Listening competence in initial interactions I: Distinguishing between what listening is and what listeners do, *The International Journal of Listening*, 26, 1–28.

Bodie, G., Gearhart, C., Denham, J. and Vickery, A. (2013) The temporal stability and situational contingency of active-empathic listening, *Western Journal of Communication*, 77, 113–138.

Bodie, G., Vickery, A. and Gearhart, C. (2013) The nature of supportive listening, I: Exploring the relation between supportive listeners and supportive people, *International Journal of Listening*, 27, 39–49.

Bodie, G., Jones, S., Vickery, A., Hatcher, L. and Cannava, K. (2014) Examining the construct validity of enacted support: A multitrait–multimethod analysis of three perspectives for judging immediacy and listening behaviors, *Communication Monographs*, 81, 495–523.

Bohner, G. and Dickel, N. (2011) Attitudes and attitude change, *Annual Review of Psychology*, 62, 391–417.

Bolden, G. (2008) Reopening Russian conversations: The discourse particle *-to* and the negotiation of interpersonal accountability in closings, *Human Communication Research*, 34, 99–136.

Bolden, G. (2009) Beyond answering: Repeat-prefaced responses in conversation, *Communication Monographs*, 76, 121–143.

Bolden, G. and Robinson, J. (2011) Soliciting accounts with *why*-interrogatives in conversation, *Journal of Communication*, 61, 94–119.

Bolton, R. (1986) *People Skills: How to Assert Yourself, Listen to Others, and Resolve Conflicts*. Sydney, Australia: Simon and Schuster.

Bond, G., Malloy, D., Arias, E. *et al.* (2005) Lie-biased decision making in prison, *Communication Reports*, 18, 9–19.

Bond, C., Levine, T. and Hartwig, M. (2015) New findings in non-verbal lie detection, in P. Granhag, A. Vrij and B. Verschuere (eds) *Detecting Deception: Current Challenges and Cognitive Approaches*. Chichester: Wiley.

Bonnet, J. and McAlexander, B. (2013) First impressions and the reference encounter: The influence of affect and clothing on librarian approachability, *The Journal of Academic Librarianship*, 39, 335–346.

Boore, J. (1979) *Prescription for Recovery*. London: RCN.

Borisoff, D. and Merrill, L. (1991) Gender issues and listening, in D. Borisoff and M. Purdy (eds) *Listening in Everyday Life*. Lanham, MD: University of America Press.

Borisoff, D. and Purdy, M. (1991a) What is listening? in D. Borisoff and M. Purdy (eds) *Listening in Everyday Life*, Lanham, MD: University of America Press.

Borisoff, D. and Purdy, M. (eds) (1991b) *Listening in Everyday Life*. Lanham, MD: University of America Press.

Borland, J. and Leigh, A. (2014) Unpacking the beauty premium. What channels does it operate through, and has it changed over time? *Economic Record*, 90, 17–32.

Bostrom, R. (1990) *Listening Behavior: Measurement and Applications*. New York: Guilford.

Bostrom, R. (1996) Memory, cognitive processing and the process of 'listening': A reply to Thomas and Levine, *Human Communication Research*, 23, 298–305.

Bostrom, R. (2006) The process of listening, in O. Hargie (ed.) *The Handbook of Communication Skills*, 3rd edition. London: Routledge.

Bostrom, R. (2011) Rethinking conceptual approaches to the study of 'listening', *International Journal of Listening*, 25, 10–26.

Boudreau, J., Cassell, E. and Fuks, A. (2009) Preparing medical students to become attentive listeners, *Medical Teacher*, 31, 22–29.

Bousfield, D. (2008) *Impoliteness in Interaction*. Amsterdam: John Benjamins.

Bowe, H. and Martin, K. (2007) *Communication Across Cultures: Mutual Understanding in a Global World*. Cambridge: Cambridge University Press.

Bowles, P. and Sharman, S. (2014) A review of the impact of different types of leading interview questions on child and adult witnesses with intellectual disabilities, *Psychiatry, Psychology and Law*, 21, 205–217.

Bowles, H., Babcock, L. and Lai, L. (2007) Social incentives for gender differences in the propensity to initiate negotiations: Sometimes it does hurt to ask, *Organizational Behavior and Human Decision Processes*, 103, 84–103.

Bowman, B., Punyanunt-Carter, N., Cheah, T., Watson, W. and Rubin, R. (2007) Does listening to Mozart affect listening ability? *International Journal of Listening*, 21, 124–139.

Boyas, J., Wind, L. and Kang, S. (2012) Exploring the relationship between employment-based social capital, job stress, burnout, and intent to leave among child protection workers: An age-based path analysis model, *Children and Youth Services Review*, 34, 50–62.

Bradbury, A. (2010) *Successful Presentation Skills*, 4th edition. London: Kogan Page.

Brammer, L. and MacDonald, G. (2003) *The Helping Relationship: Process and Skills*, 8th edition. Boston: Pearson Education.

Brammer, L., Shostrom, E. and Abrego, P. (1989) *Therapeutic Psychology: Fundamentals of Counselling and Psychotherapy*. Englewood Cliffs, NJ: Prentice-Hall.

Brashers, D., Goldsmith, D. and Hsieh, E. (2002) Information seeking and avoiding in health contexts, *Human Communication Research*, 28, 258–271.

Brassard, A., Dupuy, E., Bergeron, S. and Shaver, P. (2015) Attachment insecurities and women's sexual function and satisfaction: The mediating roles of sexual self-esteem, sexual anxiety, and sexual assertiveness, *The Journal of Sex Research*, 52, 110–119.

Brataas, H., Thorsnes, S. and Hargie, O. (2009) Cancer nurses narrating after conversations with cancer outpatients. How do nurses' roles and patients' perspectives appear in the nurses' narratives? *Scandinavian Journal of Caring Sciences*, 23, 767–774.

Brataas, H., Thorsnes, S. and Hargie, O. (2010) Themes and goals in cancer outpatient–cancer nurse consultations, *European Journal of Cancer Care*, 19, 184–191.

Braun, M. and Bryan, A. (2006) Female waist-to-hip and male waist-to-shoulder ratios as determinants of romantic partner desirability, *Journal of Social and Personal Relationships*, 23, 805–819.

Braverman, J. (2008) Testimonials versus informational persuasive messages: The moderating effect of delivery mode and personal involvement, *Communication Research*, 35, 666–694.

Breakwell, G., Hammond, S., Fife-Schaw, C. and Smith, J. (eds) (2006) *Research Methods in Psychology*, 3rd edition. London: Sage.

Brehm, J. (1966) *A Theory of Psychological Reactance*. New York: Academic Press.

Brehm, J. and Weintraub, M. (1977) Physical barriers and psychological reactance: Two-year-olds' responses to threats to freedom, *Journal of Personality and Social Psychology*, 35, 830–836.

Brehm, S., Miller, R., Perlman, D. and Campbell, S. (2006) *Intimate Relationships*, 3rd edition. New York: McGraw-Hill.

Brett, J., Shapiro, L. and Lytle, A. (1998) Breaking the bonds of reciprocity in negotiation, *Academy of Management Journal*, 41, 410–424.

Brett, J., Adair, W., Lempereur, A., Okumura, T., Shikhirev, P., Tinsley, C. and Lytle, A. (1998) Culture and joint gains in negotiation, *Negotiation Journal*, 14, 61–86.

Brewer, N., Chapman, G., Schwartz, J. and Bergus, G. (2007) The influence of irrelevant anchors on the judgments and choices of doctors and patients, *Medical Decision Making*, 27, 203–211.

Brey, E. and Shutts, K. (2015) Children use nonverbal cues to make inferences about social power, *Child Development*, 86, 276–286.

Brodsky, S., Hooper, N., Tipper, D. and Yates, S. (1999) Attorney invasion of witness space, *Law and Psychology Review*, 23, 49–68.

Brody, S. (2013) Entering night country: Reflections on self-disclosure and vulnerability, *Psychoanalytic Dialogues: The International Journal of Relational Perspectives*, 23, 45–58.

Brohan, E., Henderson, C., Wheat, K. *et al.* (2012) Systematic review of beliefs, behaviours and influencing factors associated with disclosure of a mental health problem in the workplace, *BMC Psychiatry*, 12, 11 (http://www.biomedcentral.com/1471-244X/12/11) (accessed 28 June 2014).

Bronson, P. and Merryman, A. (2009) *NurtureShock: New Thinking about Children*. New York: Twelve, Hatchett Book Group.

Brooks, A., Huang, L., Kearney, S. and Murray, F. (2014) Investors prefer entrepreneurial ventures pitched by attractive men, *Proceedings of the National Academy of Sciences*, 111, 4427–4431.

Brooks, W. and Heath, R. (1993) *Speech Communication*. Dubuque, IA: WC Brown.

Brophy, J. (1981) Teacher praise: A functional analysis, *Review of Educational Research*, 51, 5–32.

Brown, C. and Sulzerazaroff, B. (1994) An assessment of the relationship between customer satisfaction and service friendliness, *Journal of Organizational Behavior Management*, 14, 55–75.

Brown, E. (1997) Self-disclosure, social anxiety, and symptomatology in rape victim-survivors: The effects of cognitive and emotional processing, *Dissertation Abstracts International: The Sciences and Engineering*, 57 (10-B), 6559.

Brown, G. (2006) Explaining, in O. Hargie (ed.) *The Handbook of Communication Skills*, 3rd edition. London: Routledge.

Brown, G. and Armstrong, S. (1989) Explaining and explanations, in E. Wragg (ed.) *Classroom Teaching Skills*, 2nd edition. London: Croom Helm.

Brown, G. and Bakhtar, M. (1988) Styles of lecturing: A study and its implications, *Research Papers in Education*, 3, 131–153.

Brown, G. and Edmunds, S. (2009) Lectures, in J. Dent and R. Harden (eds) *A Practical Guide for Medical Teachers*. Amsterdam: Elsevier.

Brown, G., Harris, L. and Harnett, J. (2013) Teacher beliefs about feedback within an assessment for learning environment: Endorsement of improved learning over student well-being, *Teaching and Teacher Education*, 28, 968–978.

Brown, H. (1996) Themes in experimental research on groups from the 1930s to the 1990s, in M. Wetherell (ed.) *Identities, Groups and Social Issues*. London: Sage in association with the Open University.

Brown, P. and Levinson, S. (1978) Universals in language usage: Politeness phenomena, in E. Goody (ed.) *Questions and Politeness: Strategies in Social Interaction*. Oxford: Basil Blackwell.

Brown, T., Boyle, M., Williams, B. *et al.* (2010) Listening styles of undergraduate health students, *Education for Health*, 23 (http://www.educationfor-health.net/temp/EducHealth233424-2407671_064116.pdf) (accessed 16 September 2014).

Brownell, J. (2012) *Listening: Attitudes, Principles, and Skills*, 8th edition. Boston: Allyn and Bacon.

Bruce, V. and Young, A. (2012) *Face Perception*. London: Psychology Press.

Brummelman, E., Thomaes, S., de Castro, B. *et al.* (2014a) 'That's not just beautiful – that's incredibly beautiful!' The adverse impact of inflated praise on children with low self-esteem, *Psychological Science*, 25, 728–735.

Brummelman, E., Thomaes, S., Overbeek, G. *et al.* (2014b) On feeding those hungry for praise: Person praise backfires in children with low self-esteem, *Journal of Experimental Psychology: General*, 143, 9–14.

Brummelman, E., Thomaes, S., Nelemans, S. *et al.* (2015) Origins of narcissism in children, *Proceedings of the National Academy of Sciences*, 112, 3659–3662.

Bruner, J., Goodnow, J. and Austin, G. (1956) *A Study of Thinking*. New York: Wiley.

Bryon, K., Terranova, S. and Nowicki, S. (2007) Nonverbal emotion recognition and salespersons: Linking ability to perceive and actual success, *Journal of Applied Social Psychology*, 37, 2600–2619.

Buck, R. (1994) Facial and emotional functions in facial expression and communication: The readout hypothesis, *Biological Psychology*, 38, 95–115.

Buck, R. and Miller, M. (2015) Beyond facial expression: Spatial distance as a factor in the communication of discrete emotions, in A. Kostić and D. Chadee (eds) *The Social Psychology of Nonverbal Communication*. New York: Palgrave Macmillan.

Buckmann, W. (1997) Adherence: A matter of self-efficacy and power, *Journal of Advanced Nursing*, 26, 132–137.

Buckwalter, A. (1983) *Interviews and Interrogations*. Stoneham: Butterworth.

Bugelova, T. (2000) Comparative analysis of communication skills of university students and median level executives in relation to career orientation, *Studia Psychologica*, 42, 273–277.

Bull, G. (1961) *Machiavelli: The Prince* (translated by G. Bull). Harmondsworth: Penguin.

Bull, P. (2002) *Communication under the Microscope: The Theory and Practice of Microanalysis*. London: Routledge.

Bull, P. (2003) *The Microanalysis of Political Communication: Claptrap and Ambiguity*. London: Routledge.

Bull, P. (2006) What is skilled interpersonal communication? in M.B. Hinner (ed.) *Freiberger Beitraege zur interkulturellen und Wirtschaftskommunikation: A Forum for General and Intercultural Business*, Vol. 3, 93–113. Frankfurt am Main, Germany: Peter Lang.

Bull, P. (2011) What makes a successful politician? The social skills of politics, in A. Weinberg (ed.) *The Psychology of Politicians*. Cambridge: Cambridge University Press.

Bull, P. (2013) The role of adversarial discourse in political opposition: Prime Minister's questions and the British phone-hacking scandal, *Language and Dialogue*, 3, 254–272.

Bull, P. and Feldman, O. (2011) Invitations to affiliative audience responses in Japanese political speeches, *Journal of Language and Social Psychology*, 30, 158–176.

Bull, P. and Feldman, O. (2012) Theory and practice in political discourse research, in R. Sun (ed.) *Grounding Social Sciences in Cognitive Sciences*. Cambridge, MA: MIT Press.

Bull, P. and Frederikson, L. (1995) Nonverbal communication, in M. Argyle and A. Colman (eds) *Social Psychology*. London: Longman.

Buller, D. (2005) Methods for measuring speech rate, in V. Manusov (ed.) *The Sourcebook of Nonverbal Measures: Going Beyond Words*. Mahwah, NJ: Lawrence Erlbaum.

Buller, D. and Burgoon, J. (1996) Interpersonal deception theory, *Communication Theory*, 6, 203–242.

Buller, D. and Burgoon, B. (1998) Emotional expression in the deception process, in P. Anderson and L. Guerrero (eds) *Handbook of Communication and Emotion: Research, Theory, Applications, and Contexts*. San Diego: Academic Press.

Buller, D. and Hall, J. (1998) The effects of distraction during persuasion, in M. Allen and R. Preiss (eds) *Persuasion: Advances through Meta-analysis*. Cresskill, NJ: Hampton Press.

Burden, P. and Byrd, D. (2012) *Methods for Effective Teaching: Meeting the Needs of All Students*, 6th edition. Boston, MA: Pearson.

Burger, J. (2007) Fleeting attraction and compliance with requests, in A. Pratkanis (ed.) *The Science of Social Influence: Advances and Future Progress*. New York: Psychology Press.

Burgoon, J. (1980) Nonverbal communication in the 1970s: An overview, in D. Nimmo (ed.) *Communication Yearbook 4*. New Brunswick, NJ: Transaction Publishers.

Burgoon, J. (1995) Cross-cultural and intercultural applications of expectancy violation theory, in R. L. Wiseman (ed.) *Intercultural Communication Theory*. Thousand Oak, CA: Sage.

Burgoon, J. (2005) Measuring nonverbal indicators of deceit, in V. Manusov (ed.) *The Sourcebook of Nonverbal Measures: Going Beyond Words*. Mahwah, NJ: Lawrence Erlbaum.

Burgoon, J. and Bacue, A. (2003) Nonverbal communication skills, in J. Greene and B. Burleson (eds) *Handbook of Communication and Social Interaction Skills*, Mahwah, NJ: Lawrence Erlbaum.

Burgoon, J. and Dunbar, N. (2006) Nonverbal expressions of dominance and power in human relationships, in V. Manusov and M. Patterson (eds) *The Sage Handbook of Nonverbal Communication*. Thousand Oaks, CA: Sage.

Burgoon, J. and Langer, E. (1995) Language, fallacies, and mindlessness–mindfulness in social interaction, in B. Burleson (ed.) *Communication Yearbook 18*. Thousand Oaks, CA: Sage.

Burgoon, J. and Levine, T. (2010) Advances in deception detection, in S. Smith and S. Wilson (eds) *New Directions in Interpersonal Communication Research*. Thousand Oaks, CA: Sage.

Burgoon, J., Birk, T. and Pfau, M. (1990) Nonverbal behaviors, persuasion, and credibility, *Human Communication Research*, 17, 140–169.

Burgoon, J., Walther, J. and Baesler, E. (1992) Interpretations, evaluations, and consequences of interpersonal touch, *Human Communication Research*, 19, 237–263.

Burgoon, J., Buller, D. and Woodall, W. (1996) *Nonverbal Communication: The Unspoken Dialogue*. New York: McGraw-Hill.

Burgoon, J., Guerrero, L. and Floyd, K. (2010) *Nonverbal Communication*. Boston, MA: Allyn and Bacon.

Burgoon, J., Guerrero, L. and Manusov, V. (2011) Nonverbal signals, in M. Knapp and J. Daly (eds) *The Sage Handook of Interpersonal Communication*, 4th edition. Thousand Oaks, CA: Sage.

Burgoon, J., Proudfoot, J., Schuetzler, R. and Wilson, D. (2014) Patterns of nonverbal behavior associated with truth and deception: Illustrations from three experiments, *Journal of Nonverbal Behavior*, 38, 325–354.

Burkard, A., Knox, S., Groen, M., Perez, M. and Hess, S. (2006) European American therapist self-disclosure in cross-cultural counselling, *Journal of Counseling Psychology*, 50, 324–332.

Burke, C., Stagl, K., Klein, C., Goodwin, G., Salas, E. and Halpin, S. (2006) What type of leadership behaviors are functional in teams? A meta-analysis, *The Leadership Quarterly*, 17, 288–307.

Burke, T., Woszidlo, A. and Segrin, C. (2013) The intergenerational transmission of social skills and psychosocial problems among parents and their young adult children, *Journal of Family Communication*, 13, 77–91.

Burkitt, I. (2014) *Emotions and Social Relations*. London: Sage.

Burleson, B. (2003) Emotional support skill, in J. Greene and B. Burleson (eds) *Handbook of Communication and Interaction Skills*. Mahwah, NJ: Lawrence Erlbaum.

Burleson, B. (2007) Constructivism: A general theory of communication skill, in B. Whaley and W. Samter (eds) *Explaining Communication: Contemporary Theories and Exemplars*. Mahwah, NJ: Lawrence Erlbaum.

Burleson, B. (2008) What counts as effective emotional support? Explorations of individual and situational differences, in M. Motley (ed.) *Studies in Applied Interpersonal Communication*. Thousand Oaks, CA: Sage.

Burleson, B. (2010a) The nature of interpersonal communication: A message centered approach, in C. Berger, M. Roloff and D. Roskos-Ewoldsen (eds) *The Handbook of Communication Science*. Thousand Oaks, CA: Sage.

Burleson, B. (2010b) Explaining recipient responses to supportive messages: Development and tests of a dual-process theory, in S. Smith and S. Wilson (eds) *New Directions in Interpersonal Communication Research*. Thousand Oaks, CA: Sage.

Burleson, B. (2011) A constructivist approach to listening, *International Journal of Listening*, 25, 27–46.

Burley-Allen, M. (1995) *Listening: The Forgotten Skill*. New York: Wiley.

Burnett, P. and Mandel, V. (2010) Praise and feedback in the primary classroom: Teachers' and students' perspectives, *Australian Journal of Educational and Developmental Psychology*, 10, 145–154.

Burnham, T. and Phelan, J. (2000) *Mean Genes: From Sex to Money to Food: Taming Our Primal Instincts*. Cambridge, MA: Perseus Books.

Burns, J. (1978) *Leadership*. New York: Harper and Row.

Burr, V. (2015) *Social Constructionism*, 3rd edition. Hove: Routledge.

Burrell, N. and Koper, R. (1998) The efficacy of powerful/powerless language on attitudes and source credibility, in M. Allen and R. Preiss (eds) *Persuasion: Advances through Meta-analysis*. Cresskill, NJ: Hampton Press.

Burton, G. and Dimbleby, R. (2006) *Between Ourselves: An Introduction to Interpersonal Communication*. London: Hodder Education.

Buslig, A. and Burgoon, J. (2000) Aggressiveness in privacy-seeking behavior, in S. Petronio (ed.) *Balancing the Secrets of Private Disclosures*. Mahwah, NJ: Lawrence Erlbaum.

Buss, A. (1983) Social rewards and personality, *Journal of Personality and Social Psychology*, 44, 553–563.

Buss, A. and Perry, M. (1992) The aggression questionnaire, *Journal of Personality and Social Psychology*, 63, 452–459.

Buss, D. (1988) The evolution of human intersexual competition: Tactics of mate attraction, *Journal of Personality and Social Psychology*, 54, 616–628.

Butler, J., Pryor, B. and Grieder, M. (1998) Impression formation as a function of male baldness, *Perceptual and Motor Skills*, 86, 347–350.

Buttny, R. and Morris, G. (2001) Accounting, in W. Robinson and H. Giles (eds) *The New Handbook of Language and Social Psychology*. Chichester: Wiley.

Byrne, D. (1971) *The Attraction Paradigm*. New York: Academic Press.

Byrne, S. (2009) Media literacy interventions: What makes them boom or boomerang? *Communication Education*, 58, 1–14.

Byrne, S. and Hart, P. (2009) The boomerang effect: A synthesis of findings and a preliminary theoretical framework, in C. Beck (ed.) *Communication Yearbook 33*. New York: Routledge.

Byrne, P. and Long, B. (1976) *Doctors Talking to Patients*. London: HMSO.

Cafaro, A., Vilhjálmsson, H., Bickmore, T. *et al.* (2012) First impressions: Users' judgments of virtual agents' personality and interpersonal attitude in first encounters, *Intelligent Virtual Agents: Lecture Notes in Computer Science*, 7502, 67–80.

Cai, D., Wilson, S. and Drake, L. (2001) Culture in the context of intercultural negotiation: Individualism-collectivism and paths to integrative agreements, *Human Communication Research*, 26, 591–617.

Cairns, L. (1996) *Negotiating Skills in the Workplace: A Practical Handbook.* London: Pluto Press.

Cairns, L. (2006) Reinforcement, in O. Hargie (ed.) *The Handbook of Communication Skills*, 3rd edition. London: Routledge.

Calder, A., Rhodes, G., Johnson, M. and Haxby, J. (eds) (2011) *The Oxford Handbook of Face Perception.* Oxford: Oxford University Press.

Caliendo, T. (2004) A proposed solution to jury confusion in patent infringement cases involving means-plus-function claims, *Brigham Young University Law Review*, 1, 209–234.

Callan, M., Powell, N. and Ellard, J. (2007) The consequences of victim physical attractiveness on reactions to injustice: The role of observers' belief in a just world, *Social Justice Research*, 20, 433–456.

Cameron, D. (1994) Verbal hygiene for women: Linguistics misapplied? *Applied Linguistics*, 15, 382–398.

Cameron, D. (2000) *Good to Talk? Living and Working in a Communication Culture.* London: Sage.

Cameron, D. (2009) A language in common, *The Psychologist*, 22, 578–580.

Cameron, J. and Pierce, W. (1994) Reinforcement, reward and intrinsic motivation: A meta-analysis, *Review of Educational Research*, 64, 363–423.

Cameron, J. and Pierce, W. (1996) The debate about rewards and intrinsic motivation: Protests and accusations do not alter the results, *Review of Educational Research*, 66, 39–51.

Cameron, H. and Xu, X. (2011) Representational gesture, pointing gesture, and memory recall of preschool children, *Journal of Nonverbal Behavior*, 35, 155–171.

Cameron, G., Schleuder, J. and Thorson, E. (1991) The role of news teasers in processing TV news and commercials, *Communication Research*, 18, 667–684.

Campbell, K., Martin, M. and Wanzer, M. (2001) Employee perceptions of manager humor orientation, and assertiveness, responsiveness, approach/avoidance strategies, and satisfaction, *Communication Research Reports*, 18, 67–74.

Campbell, R., Benson, P., Wallace, S., Doesbergh, S. and Coleman, M. (1999) More about brows: How poses that change brow position affect perceptions of gender, *Perception*, 28, 489–504.

Cann, A., Calhoun, L. and Banks, J. (1997) On the role of humour appreciation in interpersonal attraction: It's no joking matter, *Text*, 10, 77–89.

Cannell, C.F., Oksenberg, L. and Converse, J.M. (1977) Striving for response accuracy: Experiments in new interviewing techniques, *Journal of Marketing Research*, 14, 306–321.

Cappella, J. and Schreiber, D. (2006) The interaction management function of nonverbal cues: Theory and research about mutual behavioural influence in face-to-face settings, in V. Manusov and M. Patterson (eds) *The Sage Handbook of Nonverbal Communication.* Thousand Oaks, CA: Sage.

Capstick, J. (2005) Pupil and staff perceptions of rewards at a pupil referral unit, *Emotional and Behavioural Difficulties*, 10, 95–117.

Carducci, B. (2015) *Psychology of Personality: Viewpoints, Research, and Applications*, 3rd edition. Malden, MA: Wiley.

Caris-Verhallen, W., Kerkstra, A. and Bensing, J. (1999) Nonverbal behaviour in nurse–elderly patient communication, *Journal of Advanced Nursing*, 29, 808–818.

Carlson, L., Feldman-Stewart, D., Tishelman, C. and Brundage M. (2005) Patient–professional communication research in cancer: An integrative review of research methods in the context of a conceptual framework, *Psycho-Oncology*, 14, 812–828.

Carmichael, C., Tsai, F., Smith, S., Caprariello, P. and Reis, H. (2007) The self and intimate relationships, in C. Sedikides and S. Spencer (eds) *The Self*. New York: Psychology Press.

Carnevale, P. and De Dreu, C. (2006) Motive: The negotiator's raison d'être, in L. Thompson (ed.) *Negotiation Theory and Research*. New York: Taylor and Francis.

Carnevale, P. and Pruitt, D. (1992) Negotiation and mediation, *Annual Review of Psychology*, 43, 531–582.

Carpiac-Claver, M. and Levy-Storms, L. (2007) In a manner of speaking: Communication between nurse aides and older adults in long-term care settings, *Health Communication*, 22, 59–67.

Carpenter, C. and Boster, F. (2009) A meta-analysis of the effectiveness of the disrupt-then-reframe compliance gaining technique, *Communication Reports*, 22, 55–62.

Carter, K. (1990) Teacher's knowledge and learning to teach, in W. Houston (ed.), *Handbook of Research on Teacher Education*. New York: Macmillan.

Carter, S. and Sanna, L. (2006) Are we as good as we think? Observers' perceptions of indirect self-presentation as a social influence tactic, *Social Influence*, 1, 185–207.

Cartwright, D. and Zander, A. (1968) *Group Dynamics*, 3rd edition. New York: Harper and Row.

Carver, C. and Scheier, M. (1999) Themes and issues in the self-regulation of behavior, in R. Wyer (ed.) *Advances in Social Cognition*. Mahwah, NJ: Lawrence Erlbaum.

Carver, C. and Scheier, M. (2000) On the structure of behavioral self-regulation, in M. Boekaerts, P. Pintrich and M. Zeidner (eds) *Handbook of Self-regulation*. San Diego, CA: Academic Press.

Case, A. and Paxson, C. (2008) Stature and status: Height, ability, and labor market outcomes, *Journal of Political Economy*, 116, 499–532.

Case, A., Paxson, C. and Islam, M. (2009) Making sense of the labour market height premium: Evidence from the British Household Panel Survey, *Economics Letters*, 102, 174–176.

Castonquay, L. and Beutler, L. (eds) (2005) *Principles of Therapeutic Change that Work*. New York: Oxford University Press.

Catanzaro, M. (2011) Indirect aggression, bullying and female teen victimization: A literature review, *Pastoral Care in Education: An International Journal of Personal, Social and Emotional Development*, 29, 83–101.

Catanzaro, S. and Mearns, J. (1999) Mood-related expectancy, emotional experience, and coping behavior, in I. Kirsch (ed.) *How Expectations Shape Experience*. Washington, DC: American Psychological Association.

Cattell, R. (1951) New concepts for measuring leadership, in terms of group syntality, *Human Relations*, 4, 161–184.

Caughlin, J. and Scott, A. (2010) Toward a communication theory of the demand/withdraw pattern of interaction in interpersonal relationships, in S. Smith and S. Wilson (eds) *New Directions in Interpersonal Communication Research*. Thousand Oaks, CA: Sage.

Cavanaugh, B. (2013) Performance feedback and teachers' use of praise and opportunities to respond: A review of the literature, *Education and Treatment of Children*, 36, 111–136.

Cayanus, J. and Martin, M. (2008) Teacher self-disclosure: Amount, relevance, and negativity, *Communication Quarterly*, 56, 325–341.

Cayanus, J., Martin, M. and Goodboy, A. (2009) The relation between teacher self-disclosure and student motives to communicate, *Communication Research Reports*, 26, 105–111.

CBI (2012) *Learning to Grow: What Employers Need from Education and Skills. Education and Skills Survey 2012*. London: Confederation of British Industry.

Chaikin, A. and Derlega, V. (1976) Self-disclosure, in J. Thibaut, J. Spence and R. Carson (eds) *Contemporary Topics in Social Psychology*. Morristown, NJ: General Learning Press.

Chakrabarti, B. and Baron-Cohen, S. (2008) The biology of mind-reading, in N. Ambady and J. Skowronski (eds) *First Impressions*. New York: Guilford.

Chambers, J. (2008) Explaining false uniqueness: Why we are both better and worse than others, *Social and Personality Psychology Compass*, 2, 878–894.

Chang, C. (2014) Guilt regulation: The relative effects of altruistic versus egoistic appeals for charity advertising, *Journal of Advertising*, 43, 211–227.

Channa, R. and Siddiqi, M. (2008) What do patients want from their psychiatrist? A cross-sectional questionnaire based exploratory study from Karachi, *BMC Psychiatry*, 8, 14 (http://www.pubmedcentral.nih.gov/picrender.fcgi?artid=2275251andblobtype=pdf) (accessed 2 March 2015).

Chapin, J. (2008) Third-person perception and racism, *International Journal of Communication*, 2, 100–107.

Chaplin, W., Phillips, J., Brown, J., Clanton, N. and Stein, J. (2000) Handshaking, gender, personality, and first impressions, *Journal of Personality and Social Psychology*, 79, 110–117.

Charrow, R.P. and Charrow, V. (1979) Making legal language understandable: A psycholinguistic study of jury instructions, *Columbia Law Review*, 79, 1306.

Chartrand, T. and Lakin, J. (2013) The antecedents and consequences of human behavioral mimicry, *Annual Review of Psychology*, 64, 285–308.

Chelune, G. (1976) The self-disclosure situations survey: A new approach to measuring self-disclosure, *JCSAS Catalog of Selected Documents in Psychology* 6, (ms. no. 1367), 111–112.

Chen, F., Minson, J., Schöne, M. and Heinrichs, M. (2013) In the eye of the beholder: Eye contact increases resistance to persuasion, *Psychological Science*, 24, 2254–2261.

Chen, S., Fitzsimons, G. and Andersen, S. (2007) Automaticity in close relationships, in J. Bargh (ed.) *Social Psychology and the Unconscious: The Automaticity of Higher Mental Processes*. New York: Psychology Press.

Cheng, C. and Chun, W. (2008) Cultural differences and similarities in request rejection: A situational approach, *Journal of Cross-Cultural Psychology*, 39, 745–764.

Chesebro, J. (2014) *Professional Communication at Work: Interpersonal Strategies for Career Success*. New York: Routledge.

Chesner, S. and Beaumeister, R. (1985) Effects of therapist's disclosure of religious beliefs on the intimacy of client self-disclosure, *Journal of Social and Clinical Psychology*, 3, 97–105.

Chirumbolo, A. and Leone, L. (2008) Individual differences in need for closure and voting behaviour, *Personality and Individual Differences*, 44, 1279–1288.

Cho, H. and Boster, F. (2008) Effects of gain versus loss frame antidrug ads on adolescents, *Journal of Communication*, 58, 428–446.

Cho, H., Reimer, T. and McComas, K. (2015) *The SAGE Handbook of Risk Communication*. Thousand Oaks, CA: Sage.

Chokker, J., Brodbeck, F. and House, R. (eds) (2008) *Culture and Leadership across the World*. New York: Taylor and Francis.

Christenfeld, N. (1995) Does it hurt to say um? *Journal of Nonverbal Behavior*, 19, 171–186.

Christian J., Turner, R., Holt, N. *et al*. (2014) Does intergenerational contact reduce ageism: When and how contact interventions actually work? *Journal of Arts and Humanities*, 3, 1–15.

Chu, J. (2014) *When Boys Become Boys: Development, Relationships, and Masculinity*. New York: New York University Press.

Chua, A. (2011) *The Battle Hymn of the Tiger Mother*. London: Bloomsbury.

Chui, H., Hill, C., Ain, S. *et al*. (2014) Training undergraduate students to use challenges, *The Counseling Psychologist*, 42, 758–777.

Chung, H., Lee, H., Chang, D. *et al*. (2012) Doctor's attire influences perceived empathy in the patient–doctor relationship, *Patient Education and Counseling*, 89, 387–391.

Church, R., Kelly, S. and Lynch, K. (1999) Immediate memory for mismatched speech and representational gesture across development, *Journal of Nonverbal Behavior*, 24, 151–74.

Cialdini, R. (2007) *Influence: The Psychology of Persuasion*. New York: HarperCollins.

Cialdini, R. (2014) *Influence: Science and Practice*, 5th edition. Harlow: Pearson Education.

Cialdini, R. and Schroeder, D. (1976) Increasing compliance by legitimizing paltry contributions: When even a penny helps, *Journal of Personality and Social Psychology*, 34, 599–604.

Cialdini, R., Wosinska, W., Barrett, D., Butner, J. and Gornik-Durose, M. (2001) The differential impact of two social influence principles on individualists and collectivists in Poland and the United States, in W. Wosinska, R. Cialdini, D. Barrett and J. Reykowski (eds) *The Practice of Social Influence in Multiple Cultures*. Mahwah, NJ: Lawrence Erlbaum.

Cianni-Surridge, M. and Horan, J. (1983) On the wisdom of assertive jobseeking behavior, *Journal of Counseling Psychology*, 30, 209–214.

Cipani, E. and Schock, K. (2011) *Functional Behavioral Assessment, Diagnosis, and Treatment: A Complete System for Education and Mental Health Settings*, 2nd edition. New York: Springer.

Clampitt, P. (2013) *Communicating for Managerial Effectiveness: Problems, Strategies, Solutions*, 5th edition. Thousand Oaks, CA: Sage.

Clark, H. (2012) Wordless questions, wordless answers, in J. de Ruiter (ed.) *Questions: Formal, Functional and Interactional Perspectives*. Cambridge: Cambridge University Press.

Clark, H. and Fox Tree, J. (2002) Using 'uh' and 'um' in spontaneous speech, *Cognition*, 84, 73–111.

Clarke, J. (2013) Interviewing forensic clients, in J. Clarke and P. Wilson (eds) *Forensic Psychology in Practice: A Practitioner's Handbook*. Basingstoke: Palgrave MacMillan.

Clore, G. and Byrne, D. (1974) A reinforcement-affect model of attraction, in T. Huston (ed.) *Perspectives on Interpersonal Attraction*. New York: Academic Press.

Coco, A., Ingoglia, S. and Lundqvist, L. (2014) The assessment of susceptibility to emotional contagion: A contribution to the Italian adaptation of the emotional contagion scale, *Journal of Nonverbal Behavior*, 38, 67–87.

Cody, M. and McLaughlin, M. (1988) Accounts on trial: Oral arguments in traffic court, in C. Antakis (ed.) *Analysing Everyday Explanations: A Casebook of Methods*. London: Sage.

Coe, R., Aloisi, C., Higgins, S. and Lee Elliot Major, L. (2014) *What Makes Great Teaching? Review of the Underpinning Research*. The Sutton Trust (http://www.suttontrust.com/researcharchive/great-teaching/) (accessed 11 November 2014).

Cohen, R. (2001) The great tradition: The spread of diplomacy in the ancient world, *Diplomacy and Statecraft*, 12, 23–38.

Cohen-Cole, S. (1991) *The Medical Interview: The Three-function Approach*. St. Louis, MO: Mosby-Yearbook.

Cohen-Cole, S. and Bird, J. (1991) Function 1: Gathering data to understand the patient, in S. Cohen-Cole (ed.) *The Medical Interview: The Three-Function Approach*. St. Louis, MO: Mosby-Yearbook.

Cokely, D. (2007) Metanotative qualities: How accurately are they conveyed by interpreters? in D. Cokely (ed.) *Challenging Sign Language Teachers and Interpreters: The Reflector Revisited*. Burtonsville, MD: Sign Media.

Coleman, E., Brown, A. and Rivkin, I. (1997) The effects of instructional explanations on learning from scientific texts, *The Journal of the Learning Sciences*, 6, 347–365.

Collins, L., Powell, J. and Oliver, P. (2000) Those who hesitate lose: The relationship between assertiveness and response latency, *Perceptual and Motor Skills,* 90, 931–943.

Colquitt, J., Conlon, D., Wesson, M., Porter, C. and Ng, K. (2001) Justice in the millennium: A meta-analytic review of 25 years of organizational justice research, *Journal of Applied Psychology,* 86, 425–445.

Comadena, M., Hunt, S. and Simonds, C. (2007) The effects of teacher clarity, nonverbal immediacy, and caring on student motivation, affective and cognitive learning, *Communication Research Reports,* 24, 241–248.

Conger, J. and Riggio, R. (eds) (2007) *The Practice of Leadership: Developing the Next Generation of Leaders.* San Francisco: Jossey Bass.

Conlon, D., Connor, A. and Howett, M. (2009) A conceptual model of intentional comfort touch, *Journal of Holistic Nursing,* 27, 127–135.

Conlon, D., Pinkley, R. and Sawyer, J. (2014) Getting something out of nothing: Reaping or resisting the power of a phantom BATNA, in O. Ayoko, N. Ashkanasy and K. Jehn (eds) *Handbook of Conflict Management Research.* Cheltenham, Gloucestershire: Edward Elgar.

Connor, A. and Howett, M. (2009) A conceptual model of intentional comfort touch, *Journal of Holistic Nursing,* 27, 127–135.

Conway, A., Jarrold, C., Kane, M., Miyake, A. and Towse, J. (2007) *Variation in Working Memory.* New York: Oxford University Press.

Cook, E. (2009) *Ask Your Father: The Questions Children Ask and How to Answer Them.* London: Short Books.

Cook, M. (1970) Experiments on orientation and proxemics, *Human Relations,* 23, 61–76.

Cooks, L. (2000) Family secrets and the lie of identity, in S. Petronio (ed.) *Balancing the Secrets of Private Disclosures.* Mahwah, NJ: Lawrence Erlbaum.

Cooley, C. (1929) *Social Organization.* New York: Scribner.

Cooper, J. (2007) *Cognitive Dissonance: Fifty Years of a Classic Theory.* Thousand Oaks, CA: Sage.

Coover, G. and Murphy, S. (2000) The communicated self: Exploring the interaction between self and social context, *Human Communication Research,* 26, 125–147.

Corey, G. (2005) *Theory and Practice of Counselling and Psychotherapy,* 7th edition. Belmont, CA: Brooks/Cole–Thomson Learning.

Corey, M., Corey, G. and Corey, C. (2014) *Groups: Process and Practice,* 9th edition. Belmont, CA: Brooks/Cole, Cengage Learning.

Corey, S. (1940) The teachers out-talk the pupils, *School Review,* 48, 745–752.

Cormier, S., Nurius, P. and Osborn, C. (2008) *Interviewing and Change Strategies for Helpers: Fundamental Skills and Cognitive Behavioral Interventions,* 6th edition. Pacific Grove, CA: Brooks/Cole.

Cornelis, E., Cauberghe, V. and De Pelsmacker, P. (2014) Being healthy or looking good? The effectiveness of health versus appearance-focused arguments in two-sided messages, *Journal of Health Psychology,* 19, 1132–1142.

Corpus, J. and Lepper, M. (2007) The effects of person versus performance praise on children's motivation: Gender and age as moderating factors, *Educational Psychology,* 27, 1–22.

Corr, C. and Corr, D. (2013) *Death and Dying, Life and Living*. Belmont, CA: Wadsworth Cengage Learning.

Corts, D. and Pollio, H. (1999) Spontaneous production of figurative language and gesture in college lecturers, *Metaphor and Symbolic Activity*, 14, 81–100.

Cotton, J., O'Neill, B. and Griffin, A. (2008) The 'name game': Affective and hiring reactions to first names, *Journal of Managerial Psychology*, 23, 18–39.

Coupland, J., Coupland, N. and Grainger, K. (1991) Integrational discourse: Contextual variations of age and elderliness, *Ageing and Society*, 11, 189–208.

Coupland, J., Coupland, N. and Robinson, J. (1992) How are you? Negotiating phatic communion, *Language in Society*, 21, 207–230.

Cowan, N., Morey, C. and Chen, Z. (2007) The legend of the magical number seven, in S. Della Sala (ed.), *Tall Tales about the Brain: Separating Fact from Fiction*. Oxford: Oxford University Press.

Cragan, J., Wright, D. and Kasch, C. (2009) *Communication in Small Groups: Theory, Process, Skills*, 7th edition. Boston, MA: Wadsworth Cengage Learning.

Craighead, L., Wilcoxon, L., Heather, N., Craighead, W. and DeRosa, R. (1996) Effect of feedback on learning rate and cognitive distortions among women with bulimia, *Behavior Therapy*, 27, 551–563.

Crawford, M. (1995) Gender, age and the social evaluation of assertion, *Behavior Modification*, 12, 549–564.

Creswell, D., Lam, S., Stanton, A., Taylor, S., Bower, J. and Sherman, D. (2007) Does self-affirmation, cognitive processing, or discovery of meaning explain cancer-related health benefits of expressive writing? *Personality and Social Psychology Bulletin*, 33, 238–250.

Crusco, A. and Wetzel, C. (1984) The Midas touch: Effects of interpersonal touch on restaurant tipping, *Personality and Social Psychology Bulletin*, 10, 512–517.

Cruz, M. (1998) Explicit and implicit conclusions in persuasive messages, in M. Allen and R. Preiss (eds) *Persuasion: Advances through Meta-analysis*. Cresskill, NJ: Hampton Press.

Crystal, D. (1997) *The Cambridge Encyclopaedia of Language*, 2nd edition. New York: Cambridge University Press.

Cullen, J. and Parboteeah, P. (2010) *International Business: Strategy and the Multinational Company*. New York: Routledge.

Cupach, W. and Canary, D. (1997) *Competence in Interpersonal Conflict*. New York: McGraw-Hill.

Cupach, W. and Metts, S. (1990) Remedial processes in embarrassing predicaments, in J. Anderson (ed.) *Communication Yearbook 13*. Newbury Park: Sage.

Curhan, J. and Pentland, A. (2007) Thin slices of negotiation: Predicting outcomes from conversational dynamics within the first five minutes, *Journal of Applied Psychology*, 92, 802–811.

Currie, G. and Lockett, A. (2007) A critique of transformational leadership: Moral, professional and contingent dimensions of leadership within public services organizations, *Human Relations*, 60, 341–370.

Cutica, I. and Bucciarelli, M. (2015) Non-determinism in the uptake of gestural information, *Journal of Nonverbal Behavior*, 39, 289–315.

Dabbs, J. (1985) Temporal patterns of speech and gaze in social and intellectual conversation, in H. Giles and R. St Clair (eds) *Recent Advances in Language, Communication and Social Psychology.* London: Lawrence Erlbaum.

Dabbs, J., Bernieri, F., Strong, R., Campo, R. and Milun, R. (2001) Going on stage: Testosterone in greetings and meetings, *Journal of Research in Personality*, 35, 27–40.

Dael, N., Mortillaro, M. and Scherer, K. (2012) Emotion expression in body action and posture, *Emotion*, 12, 1085–1101.

D'Agostino, T. and Bylund, C. (2014) Nonverbal accommodation in health care communication, *Health Communication*, 29, 563–573.

Dainton, M. and Zelley, E. (2015) *Applying Communication Theory for Professional Life: A Practical Introduction.* Thousand Oaks, CA: Sage.

Daly, J., Kreiser, P. and Roghaar, L. (1994) Question-asking comfort: Explorations of the demography of communication in the eighth-grade classroom, *Communication Education*, 43, 27–41.

Daly, J., McCroskey, J., Ayres, J., Hopf, T. and Ayres, D. (eds) (1997) *Avoiding Communication: Shyness, Reticence and Communication Aprehension*, 2nd edition. Cresskill, NJ: Hampton Press.

Danish, S. and Hauer, A.L. (1973) *Helping Skills: A Basic Training Program.* New York: Behavioral Publications.

Darley, J. (2001) Social comparison motives in ongoing groups, in M. Hogg and S. Tindale (eds) *Blackwell Handbook of Social Psychology.* Malden, MA: Blackwell.

Darwin, C. (1872/1955) *The Expression of Emotions in Man and Animals.* London: John Murray.

Davidhizar, R. and Giger, J. (1997) When touch is not the best appproach, *Journal of Clinical Nursing*, 6, 203–206.

Davies, J. (1998) The art of negotiating, *Management Today*, Nov, 126–28.

Davis, J., Foley, A., Crigger, N. and Brannigan, M. (2008b) Healthcare and listening: A relationship for caring, *International Journal of Listening*, 22, 168–175.

Davis, J., Thompson, C., Foley, A., Bond, C. and DeWitt, J. (2008a) An examination of listening concepts in the healthcare context: Differences among nurses, physicians, and administrators, *International Journal of Listening*, 22, 152–167.

Davis, M. (2015) Empathy and prosocial behaviour, in D. Schroeder and W. Graziano (eds) *The Oxford Handbook of Prosocial Behavior.* Oxford: Oxford University Press.

Davitz, J. (1964) *The Communication of Emotional Meaning*, New York: McGraw-Hill.

Deci, E. and Ryan, R. (1985) *Intrinsic Motivation and Self-determination in Human Behavior.* New York: Plemun Pess.

Deci, E., Koestner, R. and Ryan, M. (1999) A meta-analytic review of experiments examining the effects of extrinsic rewards on intrinsic motivation, *Psychological Bulletin*, 125, 627–668.

Deen, D., Lu, W., Rothstein, D. *et al.* (2011) Asking questions: The effect of a brief intervention in community health centers on patient activation, *Patient Education and Counseling*, 84, 257–260.

Deetz, S. and Brown, D. (2004) Conceptualizing involvement, participation and workplace decision processes, in D. Tourish and O. Hargie (eds) *Key Issues in Organizational Communication*. London: Routledge.

Degotardi, S. (2011) From greetings to meetings: How infant peers welcome and accommodate a newcomer into their group, *The First Years Tga Tua Tuatahi: New Zealand Journal of Infant and Toddler Education*, 13, 29–33.

DeGrada, E., Kruglanski, A., Mannetti, L. and Pierro, A. (1999) Motivated cognition and group interaction: Need for closure affects the contents and processes of collective negotiations, *Journal of Experimental Social Psychology*, 35, 346–365.

Del Greco, L. (1983) The Del Greco assertive behavior inventory, *Journal of Behavioral Assessment*, 5, 49–63.

Demarais, A. and White, V. (2005) *First Impressions: What You Don't Know About How Others See You*. New York: Bantam.

deMayo, R. (1997) How to present at case conference, *Clinical Supervisor*, 16, 181–189.

Demetriou, H. and Wilson, E. (2008) A return to the use of emotion and reflection, *The Psychologist*, 21, 938–940.

Denes, A. (2102) Pillow talk: Exploring disclosures after sexual activity, *Western Journal of Communication*, 76, 91–108.

Den Hartog, D.N., House, R.J., Hanges, P.J. *et al.* (1999) Culture specific and cross-culturally generalizable implicit leadership theories: Are attributes of charismatic/transformational leadership universally endorsed? *Leadership Quarterly*, 10, 219–256.

DePaulo, B., Kashy, D., Kirkendol, S. and Wyer, M. (1996) Lying in everyday life, *Journal of Personality and Social Psychology*, 70, 779–795.

DePaulo, B., Lindsay, J., Malone, B. *et al.* (2003a) Cues to deception, *Psychological Bulletin*, 129, 74–118.

DePaulo, B., Wetzel, C., Sternglanz, R. and Walker Wilson, J. (2003b) Verbal and nonverbal dynamics of privacy, secrecy, and deceit, *Journal of Social Issues*, 59, 391–410.

Derevensky, J. and Leckerman, R. (1997) Teachers' differential use of praise and reinforcement practices, *Canadian Journal of School Psychology*, 13, 15–27.

Derlega, V. and Chaikin, A. (1975) *Sharing Intimacy: What We Reveal to Others and Why*. Englewood Cliffs, NJ: Prentice-Hall.

Derlega, V., Metts, S., Petronio, S. and Margulis, S. (1993) *Self-disclosure*. Newbury Park: Sage.

Derlega, V., Winstead, B. and Folk-Barron, L. (2000) Reasons for and against disclosing HIV-seropositive test results to an intimate partner: A functional perspective, in S. Petronio (ed.) *Balancing the Secrets of Private Disclosures*. Mahwah, NJ: Lawrence Erlbaum.

Derlega, V., Winstead, B., Mathews, A. and Braitman, A. (2008) Why does someone reveal highly personal information? Attributions for and against self-disclosure in close relationships, *Communication Research Reports*, 25, 115–130.

Derlega, V., Janda, L., Miranda, J. *et al.* (2014) How patients' self-disclosure about sickle cell pain episodes to significant others relates to living with sickle cell disease, *Pain Medicine*, 15, 1496–1507.

de Ruiter, J. (2012) Introduction: Questions are what they do, in J. de Ruiter (ed.) *Questions: Formal, Functional and Interactional Perspectives.* Cambridge: Cambridge University Press.

Deschamps, J. (2005) Different leadership skills for different innovation strategies, *Strategy and Leadership*, 33, 31–38.

DeVito, J. (2011) *Human Communication: The Basic Course*, 12th edition. Boston: Pearson Education.

DeVito, J. (2012) *50 Communication Strategies.* Bloomington, IN: iUniverse.

DeVito, J. (2013) *Essentials of Human Communication*, 8th edition. Boston: Pearson Education.

DeVito, J. (2016) *The Interpersonal Communication Book*, 14th edition. Harlow, Essex: Pearson Education.

de Vries, R., Bakker-Pieper, A., Konings, F. and Schouten, B. (2013) The Communication Styles Inventory (CSI): A six-dimensional behavioral model of communication styles and its relation with personality, *Commmunication Research*, 40, 506–532.

de Vries, R., Bakker-Pieper, A., Siberg, R., Gameren, K. and Vlug, M. (2009) The content and dimensionality of communication styles, *Communication Research*, 36, 178–206.

DeWit, J., Das, E. and Vet, R. (2008) What works best: Objective statistics or a personal testimonial? An assessment of the persuasive effects of different types of message evidence on risk perception, *Health Psychology*, 27, 110–115.

DiBiase, R. and Gunnoe, J. (2004) Gender and culture differences in touching behavior, *Journal of Social Psychology*, 144, 49–62.

Di Blasi, Z., Harkness, E., Ernst, E., Georgiou, A. and Kleijnen, J. (2001) Influence of context effects on health outcomes: A systematic review, *Lancet*, 357, 757–762.

Dickson, A. (2012) *A Woman in Your Own Right: Assertiveness and You.* London: Quartet Books.

Dickson, D. (1981) *Microcounselling: An Evaluative Study of a Programme*, unpublished PhD thesis. Ulster: Ulster Polytechnic.

Dickson, D. (1999) Barriers to communication, in A. Long (ed.) *Interaction for Practice in Community Nursing.* Houndsmills, Basingstoke: MacMillan.

Dickson, D. (2006) Reflecting, in O. Hargie (ed.) *The Handbook of Communication Skills*, 3rd edition. London: Routledge.

Dickson, D. and Hargie, O. (2006) Questioning, in O. Hargie (ed.) *The Handbook of Communication Skills*, 3rd edition. London: Routledge.

Dickson, D. and McCartan, P. (2005) Communication, skill and health care delivery, in D. Sines, F. Appleby and M. Frost (eds) *Community Health Care Nursing*, 3rd edition. Oxford: Blackwell Publishing.

Dickson, D., Hargie, O. and Morrow, N. (1997) *Communication Skills Training for Health Professionals*, 2nd edition. London: Chapman and Hall.

Dickson, D., Hargie, O. and Rainey, S. (2000) Communication and relational development between Catholic and Protestant students in Northern Ireland, *Australian Journal of Communication*, 27, 67–82.

Dickson, D., Hargie, O., O'Donnell, A. and McMullan, C. (2009) Adapting to difference: Organisational socialisation in the Northern Ireland workplace, *Shared Space*, 7, 33–52.

Dickson, D., Saunders, C. and Stringer, M. (1993) *Rewarding People: The Skill of Responding Positively*. London: Routledge.

Dieckmann, L. (2000) Private secrets and public disclosures: The case of battered women, in S. Petronio (ed.) *Balancing the Secrets of Private Disclosures*. Mahwah, NJ: Lawrence Erlbaum.

Dijkman, M., Harting, J. and van der Wal, M. (2014) Adoption of the Good Behaviour Game: An evidence-based intervention for the prevention of behaviour problems, *Health Education Journal*, 74, 168–182.

Dijksterhuis, A., Chartrand, T. and Aarts, H. (2007) Effects of priming and perception on social behaviour and goal pursuit, in J. Bargh (ed.) *Social Psychology and the Unconscious: The Automaticity of Higher Mental Processes*. New York: Psychology Press.

Dillard, J. (1990) The nature and substance of goals in tactical communication, in M. Cody and M. McLaughlin (eds) *The Psychology of Tactical Communication*. Cleveland, England: Multilingual Matters.

Dillard, J. (1998) The role of affect in communication, biology, and social relationships, in P. Andersen and L. Guerrero (eds) *Handbook of Communication and Emotion: Research, Theory, Applications, and Contexts*. San Diego, CA: Academic Press.

Dillard, J. (2008) Goals-plans-action theory of message production, in L. Baxter and D. Braithwaite (eds) *Engaging Theories in Interpersonal Communication: Multiple Perspectives*. Thousand Oaks, CA: Sage.

Dillard, J. (2010) Persuasion, in C. Berger, M. Roloff and D. Roskos-Ewoldsen (eds) *The Handbook of Communication Science*. Thousand Oaks, CA: Sage.

Dillard, J. and Knobloch, L. (2011) Interpersonal influence, in M. Knapp and J. Daly (eds) *The Sage Handbook of Interpersonal Communication*, 4th edition. Thousand Oaks, CA: Sage.

Dillard, J. and Peck, E. (2001) Persuasion and the structure of affect: Dual systems and discrete emotions as complementary models, *Human Communication Research*, 27, 38–68.

Dillard, J., Hunter, J. and Burgoon, M. (1984) Sequential-request strategies: Meta-analysis of foot-in-the-door and door-in-the-face, *Human Communication Research*, 10, 461–488.

Dillard, J., Shen, L. and Vail, R. (2007) Does perceived message effectiveness cause persuasion or vice versa? 17 consistent answers, *Human Communication Research*, 33, 467–488.

Dillon, J. (1982) The multidisciplinary study of questioning, *Journal of Educational Psychology*, 74, 147–165.

Dillon, J. (1988) The remedial status of student questioning, *Journal of Curriculum Studies*, 20, 197–210.

Dillon, J. (1990) *The Practice of Questioning*. London: Routledge.

Dillon, J. (1997) Questioning, in O. Hargie (ed.), *The Handbook of Communication Skills*, 2nd edition. London: Routledge.

Dillow, M., Dunleavy, K. and Weber, K. (2009) The impact of relational characteristics and reasons for topic avoidance on relational closeness, *Communication Quarterly*, 57, 205–223.

Dimbleby, R. and Burton, G. (1998) *More than Words: An Introduction to Communication*. London: Routledge.

Di Domenico, S., Quitasol, M. and Fournier, M. (2015) Ratings of conscientiousness from physical appearance predict undergraduate academic performance, *Journal of Nonverbal Behavior*, 39, 339–353.

Dindia, K. (2000) Sex differences in self-disclosure, reciprocity of self-disclosure, and self-disclosure and liking: Three meta-analyses reviewed, in S. Petronio (ed.) *Balancing the Secrets of Private Disclosures*. Mahwah, NJ: Lawrence Erlbaum.

Dindia, K. and Canary, D. (eds) (2006) *Sex Differences and Similarities in Communication*, 2nd edition. Mahwah, NJ: Lawrence Erlbaum.

Ding, D. (2006) An indirect style in business communication, *Journal of Business and Technical Communication*, 20, 87–100.

Dinsbach, A., Feij, J. and de Vries, R. (2007) The role of communication content in an ethnically diverse organization, *International Journal of Intercultural Relations*, 31, 725–745.

Dittmar, H. (1992) Perceived material wealth and first impressions, *British Journal of Social Psychology*, 31, 379–392.

Dixon, J. and Durrheim, K. (2004) Dislocating identity: Desegregation and the transformation of place, *Journal of Environmental Psychology*, 24, 455–473.

Dixson, B., Grimshaw, G., Linklater, W. and Dixson, A. (2011) Eye-tracking of men's preferences for waist-to-hip ratio and breast size of women, *Archives of Sexual Behavior*, 40, 43–50.

Dohrenwend, B. (1965) Some effects of open and closed questions on respondents' answers, *Human Organization*, 24, 175–184.

Dolgin, K. (1996) Parents' disclosure of their own concerns to their adolescent children, *Personal Relationships*, 3, 159–169.

Dolgin, K. and Berndt, N. (1997) Adolescents' perceptions of their parents' disclosure to them, *Journal of Adolescence*, 20, 431–441.

Dolgin, K. and Lindsay, K. (1999) Disclosure between college students and their siblings, *Journal of Family Psychology*, 13, 393–400.

Dolinski, D. (2007) Emotional see-saw, in A. Pratkanis (ed.) *The Science of Social Influence: Advances and Future Progress*. New York: Psychology Press.

Dolinski, D. and Kofta, M. (2001) Stay tuned: The role of the break in the message on attribution of culpability, in W. Wosinska, R. Cialdini, D. Barrett and J. Reykowski (eds) *The Practice of Social Influence in Multiple Cultures*. Mahwah, NJ: Lawrence Erlbaum.

Dolinski, D., Nawrat, M. and Rudak, I. (2001) Dialogue involvement as a social influence technique, *Personality and Social Psychology Bulletin*, 27, 1395–1406.

Donahoe, J. (2014) Evocation of behavioral change by the reinforcer is the critical event in both the classical and operant procedures, *International Journal of Comparative Psychology*, 27, 537–543.

Dorfman, P., Javidan, M., Hanges, P., Dastmalchian, A. and House, R. (2012) GLOBE: A twenty year journey into the intriguing world of culture and leadership, *Journal of World Business*, 47, 504–518.

Douglas, Y. and Miller, S. (2015) Availability bias can improve women's propensity to negotiate, *International Journal of Business Administration*, 6, 86–95.

Dovidio, J., Ellyson, S., Keating, C., Heltman, K. and Brown, C. (1988) The relationship of social power to visual displays of dominance between men and women, *Journal of Personality and Social Psychology*, 54, 233–242.

Dow, B. and Wood, J. (eds) (2006) *The Sage Handbook of Gender and Communication*. Thousand Oaks, CA: Sage.

Dowell, N. and Berman, J. (2013) Therapist nonverbal behavior and perceptions of empathy, alliance, and treatment credibility, *Journal of Psychotherapy Integration*, 2, 158–165.

Downing, J. and Garmon, C. (2002) A guide to implementing PowerPoint and overhead LCD projectors in communication classes, *American Journal of Communication*, 5(2) (http://www.acjournal.org/holdings/vol5/iss2/articles/guide.pdf) (accessed 2 December 2009).

Doyle, A. (2001) *A Study in Scarlet*. London: Penguin (first published 1887, Ward Lock).

Dozier, C., Iwata, B., Thomason-Sassi, J. *et al.* (2012) A comparison of two pairing procedures to establish praise as a reinforcer, *Journal of Applied Behavior Analysis*, 45, 721–735.

Drahota, A., Costall, A. and Reddy, V. (2008) The vocal communication of different kinds of smile, *Speech Communication*, 50, 278–287.

Draper, P. (2005) Patronizing speech to older patients: A literature review, *Reviews in Clinical Gerontology*, 15, 273–279.

Drescher, S., Burlingame, G. and Fuhriman, A. (2012) Cohesion: An odyssey in empirical understanding, *Small Group Research*, 43, 662–689.

Drucker, P. (2007) *Management: Tasks, Responsibilities, Practices*. Edison, NJ: Transaction.

Druckman, D. and Wagner, L. (2016) Justice and negotiation, *Annual Review of Psychology*, 67, 387–413.

Drummond, P. and Bailey, T. (2013) Eye contact evokes blushing independently of negative affect, *Journal of Nonverbal Behavior*, 37, 207–216.

Dryden, W. and Constantinou, D. (2004) *Assertiveness Step by Step*. London: Sheldon Press.

DuBrin, A. (2011) *Impression Management in the Workplace: Research, Theory and Practice*. New York: Routledge.

DuBrin, A. (2013) *Leadership: Research Findings, Practice, and Skills*, 7th edition. Mason, OH: Cengage Learning.

Duck, S. (1995) Repelling the study of attraction, *The Psychologist*, 8, 60–63.

Duck, S. (1999) Expressing meaning to others, in J. Stewart (ed.) *Bridges Not Walls*, 7th edition, Boston, MA: McGraw-Hill.

Duck, S. and McMahan, D. (2012) *The Basics of Communication: A Relational Perspective*, 2nd edition. Thousand Oaks, CA: Sage.

Duggan, A. and Bradshaw, Y. (2008) Mutual influence processes in physician–patient communication: An interaction adaptation perspective, *Communication Research Reports*, 25, 211–226.

Duggan, A. and Parrott, R. (2001) Physicians' nonverbal rapport building and patients' talk about the subjective component of illness, *Human Communication Research*, 27, 299–311.

Dulebohn, J., Bommer, W., Liden, R., Brouer, R. and Ferris, G. (2012) A meta-analysis of antecedents and consequences of leader–member exchange: Integrating the past with an eye toward the future, *Journal of Management*, 38, 1715–1759.

Dunbar, N. and Burgoon, J. (2005) Measuring nonverbal dominance, in V. Manusov (ed.) *The Sourcebook of Nonverbal Measures: Going Beyond Words*. Mahwah, NJ: Lawrence Erlbaum.

Duncan, L., Latimer, A., Pomery, E. *et al.* (2013) Testing messages to encourage discussion of clinical trials among cancer survivors and their physicians: Examining monitoring style and message detail, *Journal of Cancer Education*, 28, 119–126.

Duncan, S. and Fiske, D.W. (1977) *Face-to-face Interaction: Research, Methods and Theory*. Hillsdale, NJ: Lawrence Erlbaum.

Dunne, H. (2001) One wrong word and we lose him, *Daily Telegraph*, 29 October, p. 15.

Durik, M., Britt, A., Reynolds, R. and Storey, J. (2008) The effects of hedges in persuasive arguments: A nuanced analysis of language, *Journal of Language and Social Psychology*, 27, 217–234.

Durrant, J. and Ensom, R. (2012) Physical punishment of children: Lessons from 20 years of research, *Canadian Medical Association Journal*, 184, 1373–1377.

Dweck, C. (2007) The perils and promises of praise, *Educational Leadership*, 65, 34–39.

Ebesu-Hubbard, A., Tsuji, A., Williams, C. and Seatriz, V. (2003) Effects of touch on gratuities in same-sex and cross-gender interaction, *Journal of Applied Social Psychology*, 33, 2427–2438.

Edwards, A., Elwyn, G. and Mulley, A. (2002) Explaining risks: Turning numerical data into meaningful pictures, *British Medical Journal*, 324, 827–830.

Edwards, R. (2011) Listening and message interpretation, *International Journal of Listening*, 25, 47–65.

Edwards, R. and Bello, R. (2001) Interpretation of messages: The influence of equivocation, face concerns, and ego-involvement, *Human Communication Research*, 27, 597–631.

Egan, G. (2014) *The Skilled Helper: A Problem-Management and Opportunity Development Approach to Helping*, 10th edition. Belmont, CA: Brooks/Cole.

Eggen, P. and Kauchak, D. (2012) *Educational Psychology: Windows on Classrooms*, 9th edition. Upper Saddle River, NJ: Pearson.

Egolf, D. and Chester, S. (2013) *Forming, Storming, Norming, Performing: Successful Communication in Groups and Teams*, 3rd edition. Bloomington, IN: iUniverse.

Ehrlich, R., D'Augelli, A. and Danish, S. (1979) Comparative effectiveness of six counsel to verbal responses, *Journal of Counselling Psychology*, 26, 390–398.

Eisend, M. (2009) A meta-analysis of humor in advertising, *Journal of the Academy of Marketing Science*, 37, 191–203.

Eisenkraft, N. (2013) Accurate by way of aggregation: Should you trust your intuition-based first impressions? *Journal of Experimental Social Psychology*, 49, 277–279.

Eisler, R., Hersen, M., Miller, P. and Blanchard, D. (1975) Situational determinants of assertive behavior, *Journal of Consulting and Clinical Psychology*, 43, 330–340.

Ekman, P. (1985) *Telling Lies*. New York: Norton.

Ekman, P. (2009) Lie catching and microexpressions, in C. Martin (ed.) *The Philosophy of Deception*. Oxford: Oxford University Press.

Ekman, P. and Friesen, W. (1969) The repertoire of non-verbal behaviour: Categories, origins, usage and coding, *Semiotica*, 1, 49–98.

Ekman, P. and Friesen, W. (2003) *Unmasking the Face*. Cambridge, MA: Malor Books.

Ekman, P. and Keltner, D. (1997) Universal facial expressions of emotion, in U. Segerstrale and P. Molnar (eds) *Nonverbal Communication: Where Nature Meets Culture*. Mahwah, NJ: Lawrence Erlbaum.

Ekman, P. and O'Sullivan, M. (1991) Facial expression: Methods, means and mouses, in R. Feldman and B. Rime (eds) *Fundamentals of Nonverbal Behaviour*. Cambridge: Cambridge University Press.

Ekman, P. and Rosenberg, E. (eds) (2005) *What the Face Reveals*. New York: Oxford University Press.

Ekman, P., O'Sullivan, M., Friesen, W. and Scherer, K. (1991) Invited article: Face, voice and body in detecting deceit, *Journal of Nonverbal Behavior*, 15, 125–135.

Ellemers, N. and Haslam, S. (2012) Social identity theory, in P. Van Lange, A. Kruglanski and E. Higgins (eds) *Handbook of Theories of Social Psychology*: Vol. 2. London: Sage.

Elliott, A. (2014) *Concepts of the Self*. Cambridge: Polity Press.

Ellis, A. and Beattie, G. (1986) *The Psychology of Language and Communication*. London: Weidenfeld and Nicholson.

Ellis, K. (2000) Perceived teacher confirmation: The development and validation of an instrument and two studies of the relationship to cognitive and affective learning, *Human Communication Research*, 26, 264–292.

Ellison, C. and Firestone, I. (1974) Development of interpersonal trust as a function of self-esteem, target status and target style, *Journal of Personality and Social Psychology*, 29, 655–663.

Emery, S., Szczypk, G., Abri, E. *et al.* (2014) Are you scared yet? Evaluating fear appeal messages in tweets about the Tips campaign, *Journal of Communication*, 64, 278–295.

Emmons, R. (1989) The personal striving approach to personality, in L. Pervin (ed.) *Goal Concepts in Personality and Social Psychology*. Hillsdale, NJ: Lawrence Erlbaum.

Endres, J., Poggenpohl, C. and Erben, C. (1999) Repetitions, warnings and video: Cognitive and motivational components in preschool children's susceptibility, *Journal of Legal and Criminological Psychology*, 4, 129–149.

Engleberg, I. (2002) Presentations in everyday life: Linking audience interest and speaker eloquence, *American Journal of Communication*, 5 (http://ac-journal.org/journal/vol5/iss2/special/engleberg.pdf) (accessed 2 March 2015).

Engleberg, I. and Daly, J. (2006) *Presentations in Everyday Life: Strategies for Effective Speaking*, 2nd edition. Boston, MA: Allyn and Bacon.

Ennis, E., Vrij, A. and Chance, C. (2008) Individual differences and lying in everyday life, *Journal of Social and Personal Relationships*, 25, 105–118.

Epstein, J., Griffin, K. and Botvin, G. (2000) Role of general and specific competence skills in protecting inner-city adolescents from alcohol use, *Journal of Studies on Alcohol*, 61, 379–386.

Epstein, R., Warfel, R., Johnson, J., Smith, R. and McKinney, P. (2013) Which relationship skills count most? *Journal of Couple and Relationship Therapy: Innovations in Clinical and Educational Interventions*, 12, 297–313.

Erb, H. and Bohner, G. (2007) Social influence and persuasion: Recent theoretical developments and integrative agreements, in K. Fiedler (ed.) *Social Communication*. New York: Psychology Press.

Erceau, D. and Guéguen, N. (2007) Tactile contact and evaluation of the toucher, *The Journal of Social Psychology*, 147, 441–444.

Erickson, M. and Rossi, E. (1975) Varieties of double bind, *American Journal of Clinical Hypnosis*, 17, 143–147.

Erickson, T. and Mattson, M. (1981) From words to meaning: A semantic illusion, *Journal of Verbal Learning and Verbal Behavior*, 20, 540–551.

Esser, J. (1998) Alive and well after 25 years: A review of groupthink, *Organizational Behavior and Human Decision Processes*, 73, 116–141.

Fagan, D. (2014) Beyond 'excellent!' Uncovering the systematicity behind positive feedback turn construction in ESL classrooms, *Novitas-ROYAL (Research on Youth and Language)*, 8, 45–63.

Farber, B. (2003) Patient self-disclosure: A review of the research, *Journal of Clinical Psychology*, 59, 589–600.

Farber, B. (2006) *Self-disclosure in Psychotherapy*. New York: Guilford.

Farley, S. (2008) Attaining status at the expense of likeability: Pilfering power through conversational interruption, *Journal of Nonverbal Behavior*, 32, 241–260.

Farley, S. (2014) Nonverbal reactions to an attractive stranger: The role of mimicry in communicating preferred social distance, *Journal of Nonverbal Behavior*, 38, 195–208.

Farrington, C. (2011) Reconciling managers, doctors, and patients: The role of clear communication, *Journal of the Royal Society of Medicine*, 104, 231–236.

Faye, J. (2014) *The Nature of Scientific Thinking: On Interpretation, Explanation, and Understanding*. London: Palgrave Macmillan.

Feeley, T., Anker, A. and Aloe, A. (2012) The door-in-the-face persuasive message strategy: A meta-analysis of the first 35 years, *Communication Monographs*, 79, 316–343.

Feeney, J., Noller, P., Sheehan, G. and Peterson, C. (1999) Conflict issues and conflict strategies as contexts for nonverbal behaviour in close relationships, in P. Philippot, R. Feldman and E. Coats (eds) *The Social Context of Nonverbal Behavior*. Cambridge: Cambridge University Press.

Fehr, E., Bernhard, H. and Rockenbach, B. (2008) Egalitarianism in young children, *Nature*, 454, 1079–1083.

Feldman, R. (1985) *Social Psychology: Theories, Research and Applications*. New York: McGraw-Hill.

Feldman, R., Philippot, P. and Custrini, R. (1991) Social skills, psychopathology, and nonverbal behavior, in R. Feldman and B. Rime (eds) *Fundamentals of Nonverbal Behaviour*. Cambridge: Cambridge University Press.

Felmlee, D., Sweet, E. and Sinclair, H. (2012) Gender rules: Same- and cross-gender friendships norms, *Sex Roles*, 66, 518–529.

Feng, B. and Burleson, B. (2008) The effects of argument explicitness on responses to advice in supportive interactions, *Communication Research*, 35, 849–874.

Feng, H. and Wilson, S. (2012) Cultural variations in the reasons people provide avoidance support, *Journal of International and Intercultural Communication*, 5, 64–87.

Fern, E., Monroe, K. and Avila, R. (1986) Effectiveness of multiple request strategies: A synthesis of research results, *Journal of Marketing Research*, 23, 144–152.

Ferraro, F. and Garella, A. (1997) Termination as a psychoanalytic event, *International Journal of Psycho-Analysis*, 78, 27–41.

Ferris, D., Spence, J., Brown, D. and Heller, D. (2012) Interpersonal injustice and workplace deviance: The role of esteem threat, *Journal of Management*, 38, 1788–1811.

Festinger, L. (1957) *A Theory of Cognitive Dissonance*. Stanford: Stanford University Press.

Feyereisen, P. and Havard, I. (1999) Mental imagery and the production of hand gestures while speaking in younger and older adults, *Journal of Nonverbal Behavior*, 23, 153–171.

Fiedler, F. (1967) *A Theory of Leadership Effectiveness*. New York: McGraw-Hill.

Fiedler, F. (1986) The contribution of cognitive resources and leader behaviour to organizational performance, *Journal of Applied Social Psychology*, 16, 532–548.

Fiedler, F. (1993) The leadership situation and the black box in contingency theories, in M. Chemers and R. Ayman (eds) *Leadership, Theory and Research: Perspectives and Directions*. New York: Academic Press.

Fiedler, K. (1993) Constructive processes in person cognition, *British Journal of Social Psychology*, 32, 349–364.

Fiedler, K. (2007) Frontiers of research on social communication: Introduction and overview, in K. Fiedler (ed.) *Social Communication*. New York: Psychology Press.

Fiedler, K. and Bless, H. (2001) Social cognition, in M. Hewstone and W. Stroebe (eds) *Introduction to Social Psychology*, 3rd edition. Oxford: Blackwell.

Field, T. (2014) *Touch*, 2nd edition. Massachussetts: MIT Press.

Figley, C. (ed.) (2002) *Treating Compassion Fatigue*. New York: Brunner/Mazel.

Fine, M. and Harvey, J. (eds) (2005) *Handbook of Divorce and Relationship Dissolution*. Mahwah, NJ: Lawrence Erlbaum.

Finkenauer, C. and Hazam, H. (2000) Disclosure and secrecy in marriage: Do both contribute to marital satisfaction? *Journal of Social and Personal Relationships*, 17, 245–263.

Finkenauer, C., Frijns, T., Engels, R. and Kerkhof, P. (2005) Perceiving concealment in relationships between parents and adolescents: Links with parental behavior, *Personal Relationships*, 12, 387–406.

Finnegan, A. and Hackley, S. (2008) Negotiation and nonviolent action: Interacting in the world of conflict, *Negotiation Journal*, 24, 7–24.

First, E. (1994) The leaving game, or I'll play you and you play me: The emergence of dramatic role play in 2-year-olds, in A. Slade and D. Wolf (eds) *Children at Play: Clinical and Developmental Approaches to Meaning and Representation*. New York: Oxford University Press.

Firth, C. (2012) The role of metacognition in human social interactions, *Philosophical Translations of the Royal Society of Biological Sciences*, 367, 2213–2223.

Fishbach, A. and Ferguson, M. (2007) The goal construct in social psychology, in A. Kruglanski and E. Higgins (eds) *Social Psychology: Handbook of Basic Principles*, 2nd edition. New York: Guilford.

Fisher, C., Corrigan, O. and Henman, M. (1991) A study of community pharmacy practice, *Journal of Social and Administrative Pharmacy*, 8, 15–23.

Fisher, D. (1984) A conceptual analysis of self-disclosure, *Journal for the Theory of Social Behavior*, 14, 277–296.

Fisher, R. (2001) Negotiating power: Getting and using influence, in I. Asherman and S. Asherman (eds) *The Negotiating Sourcebook*, 2nd edition. Amherst, MA: Human Resource Development Press.

Fisher, R. and Shapiro, D. (2006) *Beyond Reason: Using Emotions as You Negotiate*. London: Random House.

Fisher, R., Ury, W. and Patton, B. (2011) *Getting to Yes: Negotiating an Agreement Without Giving In*. London: Random House.

Fisher, S. and Groce, S. (1990) Accounting practices in medical interviews, *Language in Society*, 19, 225–250.

Fiske, A. (2000) Complementarity theory: Why human social capacities evolved to require cultural complements, *Personality and Social Psychology Review*, 4, 76–94.

Fiske, J. (1990) *Introduction to Communication Studies*, 2nd edition. London: Routledge.

Fiske, S. and Berdahl, J. (2007) Social power, in A. Kruglanski and E. Higgins *Social Psychology: Handbook of Basic Principles*, 2nd edition. New York: Guilford.

Fiske, S. and Taylor, S. (2014) *Social Cognition: From Brains to Culture*, 2nd edition. Thousand Oaks, CA: Sage.

Fiske, S., Cuddy, S. and Glick, P. (2007) Universal dimensions of social cognition: Warmth and competence, *Trends in Cognitive Sciences*, 11, 77–83.

Fitzmaurice, S. and Purdy, K. (2015) Disfluent pausing effects on listener judgments of an ASL-English interpretation, *Journal of Interpretation*, 24, 1 (available at: http://digitalcommons.unf.edu/joi/vol24/iss1) (accessed 10 March 2015).

Fleck, D., Volkema, R., Pereira, S. *et al.* (2014) Neutralizing unethical negotiating tactics: An empirical investigation of approach selection and effectiveness, *Negotiation Journal*, 30, 23–48.

Flemmer, D., Sobelman, S., Flemmer, M. and Astrom, J. (1996) Attitudes and observations about nonverbal communication in the psychotherapeutic greeting situation, *Psychological Reports*, 78, 407–418.

Flintoff, J. (2001) Sayonara to ceremony, *Financial Times Weekend*, May 5–6, p. 1.

Floyd, K. (2006) An evolutionary approach to understanding nonverbal communication, in V. Manusov and M. Patterson (eds) *The Sage Handbook of Nonverbal Communication*. Thousand Oaks, CA: Sage.

Floyd, K. (2014) Empathic listening as an expression of interpersonal affection, *International Journal of Listening*, 28, 1–12.

Flynn, J., Valikoski, T. and Grau, J. (2008) Listening in the business context: Reviewing the state of research, *International Journal of Listening*, 22, 141–151.

Foley, M. and Duck, S. (2006) Relational communication, in O. Hargie (ed.) *The Handbook of Communication Skills*, 3rd edition. London: Routledge.

Foos, A., Keeling, K. and Keeling, D. (2015) Source misattribution for the sake of attitude change: A conceptualization of the role of social identity in inducing dissociative processing, in Robinson, L. (ed.) *Marketing Dynamism and Sustainability: Things Change, Things Stay the Same…* Heidelberg: Springer.

Foot, H. (1997) Humour and laughter, in O. Hargie (ed.) *The Handbook of Communication Skills*, 2nd edition. London: Routledge.

Foot, H. and McCreaddie, M. (2006) Humour and laughter, in O. Hargie (ed.) *The Handbook of Communication Skills*, 3rd edition. London: Routledge.

Ford, S. and Hall, A. (2004) Communication behaviours of skilled and less skilled oncologists: A validation study of the Medical Interaction Process System (MIPS), *Patient Education and Counseling*, 54, 275–282.

Forgas, J. (1994) Sad and guilty? Affective influences on the explanation of conflict in close relationships, *Journal of Personality and Social Psychology*, 66, 56–68.

Forgas, J. (2011) Affective influences on self-disclosure: Mood effects on the intimacy and reciprocity of disclosing personal information, *Journal of Personality and Social Psychology*, 100, 449–461.

Forgas, J. and Williams, K. (2001) Social influence: introduction and overview, in J. Forgas and K. Williams (eds) *Social Influence: Direct and Indirect Processes*. Philadelphia: Psychology Press.

Forrest, G. (2010) *Self-Disclosure in Psychotherapy and Recovery*. Lanham, MD: Aronson.

Forrester, D., Kershaw, S., Moss, H. and Hughes, L. (2008) Communication skills in child protection: How do social workers talk to parents? *Child and Family Social Work*, 13, 41–51.

Forrester, D., Westlake, D. and Glynn, G. (2012) Parental resistance and social worker skills: Towards a theory of motivational social work, *Child and Family Social Work*, 17, 118–129.

Forsyth, D. (2010) *Group Dynamics*, 5th edition. Belmont, CA: Wadsworth Cengage Learning.

Forsythe, S. (1990) Effect of applicant's clothing on interviewer's decision to hire, *Journal of Applied Social Psychology,* 20, 1579–1595.

Fosshage, J. (1998) On aggression: Its forms and functions, *Psychoanalytic Inquiry,* 18, 45–54.

Fowler, C. and Soliz, D. (2013) Communicative responses to the painful self-disclosures of familial and non-familial older adults, *The International Journal of Aging and Human Development*, 77, 163–188.

Fowler, F. and Mangione, T. (1990) *Standardised Survey Interviewing: Minimizing Interviewer-related Error.* Newbury Park, CA: Sage.

Fox, E., Lester, V., Russo, R., Bowles, R., Pichler, A. and Dutton, K. (2000) Facial expressions of emotion: Are angry faces detected more efficiently? *Cognition and Emotion*, 14, 61–92.

Fox, L., Rejeski, W. and Gauvin, L. (2000) Effects of leadership style and group dynamics on enjoyment of physical activity, *American Journal of Health Promotion,* 14, 277–283.

Francis, A. (2014) Locus of control, *Encyclopedia of Psychology and Religion,* pp. 1035–1036. New York: Springer.

Frank, M. and Svetieva, E. (2013) Deception, in D. Matsumoto, M. Frank and H. Hwang (eds) *Nonverbal Communication: Science and Applications.* Thousand Oaks, CA: Sage.

Frauendorfer, D. and Mast, M. (2015) The impact of nonverbal behavior in the job interview, in A. Kostic and D. Chadee (eds) *The Social Psychology of Nonverbal Communication*. Basingstoke: Palgrave Macmillan.

Freed, A. and Ehrlich, S. (2010) *Why do you Ask? The Function of Questions in Institutional Discourse*. New York: Oxford University Press.

Freeman, P., Rees, T. and Hardy, L. (2009) An intervention to increase social support and improve performance, *Journal of Applied Sport Psychology*, 21, 186–200.

Freeth, M., Foulsham, T. and Kingstone, A. (2013) What affects social attention? Social presence, eye contact and autistic traits, *PLoS ONE*, 8(1) (doi:10.1371/journal.pone.0053286) (accessed 4 February 2015).

French, J. and Raven, B. (1959) The bases of social power, in D. Cartwright (ed.) *Studies in Social Power*. Ann Arbor, MI: Institute for Social Research.

French, P. (1994) *Social Skills for Nursing Practice*, 2nd edition. London: Chapman and Hall.

Freshwater, D. (2003) *Counselling Skills for Nurses, Midwives and Health Visitors*. Maidenhead: Open University Press.

Freud, S. (1953) Fragment of an analysis of a case of hysteria. *Standard Edition of the Complete Psychological Works of Sigmund Freud, Volume 7*, pp. 7–122 (1st edition 1905). Translated and edited by James Strachey. London: Hogarth.

Frey, L. (1999) Introduction, in L. Frey, D. Gouran and M.S. Poole (eds) *The Handbook of Group Communication Theory and Research*. Thousand Oaks, CA: Sage.

Frick, R. (1992) *Interestingness*, British Journal of Psychology, 83, 113–128.

Fridlund, A. and Russell, J. (2006) The function of facial expressions: What's in a face? in V. Manusov and M. L. Patterson (eds) *The Sage Handbook of Nonverbal Communication*. Thousand Oaks, CA: Sage.

Friedman, H. (1979) The concept of skill in nonverbal communication: Implications for understanding social interaction, in R. Rosenthal (ed.) *Skill in Nonverbal Communication: Individual Differences*. Cambridge, MA: Oelgeschlager, Gunn and Hain.

Friesen, W. (1972) *Cultural Differences in Facial Expression: An Experimental Test of the Concept of Display Rules*, PhD thesis. San Francisco: University of California, San Francisco.

Friesen, W., Ekman, P. and Wallblatt, H. (1980) Measuring hand movements, *Journal of Nonverbal Behavior*, 4, 97–113.

Frijda, N. (2006) *The Laws of Emotion*. London: Routledge.

Fry, L. (1983) Women in society, in S. Spence and G. Shepherd (eds) *Developments in Social Skills Training*. London: Academic Press.

Fujishin, R. (2013) *Creating Effective Groups: The Art of Small Group Communication*, 3rd edition. Lanham, MD: Rowman and Littlefield.

Furnham, A., Lavancy, M. and McClellenad, A. (2001) Waist-to-hip ratio and facial attractiveness: A pilot study, *Personality and Individual Differences*, 30, 491–502.

Fussell, S. and Kreuz, R. (1998) Social and cognitive approaches to interpersonal communication: Introduction and overview, in S. Fussell and P. Kreuz (eds) *Social and Cognitive Approaches to Interpersonal Communication*. Mahwah, NJ: Lawrence Erlbaum.

Gable, J. (2007) *Counselling Skills for Dieticians*, 2nd edition. Oxford: Blackwell.

Gable, S. and Shean, G. (2000) Perceived social competence and depression, *Journal of Social and Personal Relationships*, 17, 139–150.

Gage, N., Belgard, M., Dell, D., Hiller, J., Rosenshine, B. and Unruh, W. (1968) *Explorations of the Teachers' Effectiveness in Explaining, Technical Report 4*. Stanford: Stanford University Centre for Research and Development in Teaching (http://www.eric.ed.gov/ERICDocs/data/ericdocs2sql/content_storage_01/0000019b/80/37/dc/58.pdf (accessed 3 December 2009).

Galanes, G. and Adams, K. (2012) *Effective Group Discussion: Theory and Practice*, 14th edition. Boston: McGraw-Hill.

Galinsky, A., Mussweiler, T. and Medvec, V. (2002) Disconnecting outcomes and evaluations: The role of negotiator focus, *Journal of Personality and Social Psychology*, 81, 1131–1140.

Gallagher, K. and Updegraff, J. (2012) Health message framing effects on attitudes, intentions, and behavior: A meta-analytic review, *Annals of Behavioral Medicine*, 43, 101–116.

Gallagher, M. (1987) *The Microskills Approach to Counsellor Training: A Study of Counsellor Personality, Attitudes and Skills*, unpublished D.Phil. thesis. Jordanstown: University of Ulster.

Gallagher, M. and Hargie, O. (1992) The relationship between counsellor interpersonal skills and core conditions of client-centred counselling, *Counselling Psychology Quarterly*, 5, 3–16.

Gallie, D., Zhou, Y., Felstead, A. and Green F. (2012) Teamwork, skill development and employee welfare, *British Journal of Industrial Relations*, 50, 23–46.

Gamble, T. and Gamble, M. (2012) *Communication Works*, 11th edition. New York: McGraw-Hill.

Gardiner, M. and Tiggemann, M. (1999) Gender differences in leadership style, job stress and mental health in male- and female-dominated industries, *Journal of Occupational and Organizational Psychology*, 72, 301–315.

Garko, M. (1992) Physician executives' use of influence strategies: Gaining compliance from superiors who communicate in attractive and unattractive styles, *Health Communication*, 4, 137–154.

Garland, E. and Howard, M. (2014) A transdiagnostic perspective on cognitive, affective, and neurobiological processes underlying human suffering, *Research on Social Work Practice*, 24, 142–151.

Garrison, M. and Bly, M. (1997) *Human Relations: Productive Approaches for the Workplace*. Boston: Allyn and Bacon.

Garven, S., Wood, J., Malpass, R. and Shaw, J. (1998) *More than Suggestion: Consequences of the Interview Techniques from the McMartin Preschool Case*. Paper presented at the American Psychology and Law Association Biennial Conference, Redondo Beach.

Gaskell, G., Wright, D. and O'Muircheartaigh, C. (1993) Reliability of surveys, *The Psychologist*, 11, 500–503.

Gass, R. and Seiter, J. (2009) Persuasion and compliance gaining, in W. Eadie (ed.) *21st Century Communication: A Reference Handbook*. Thousand Oaks, CA: Sage.

Gass, R. and Seiter, J. (2014) *Persuasion, Social Influence, and Compliance Gaining*. Boston, MA: Pearson/Allyn and Bacon.

Gatchalian, J. (2000) Principled negotiations – A key to successful collective bargaining, *Management Decision*, 36, 222–225.

Gates, S. (2006) Time to take negotiation seriously, *Industrial and Commercial Training*, 38, 238–241.

Gathercole, S. (2008) Working memory in the classroom, *The Psychologist*, 21, 382–385.

Gathercole, S., Pickering, S., Knight, C. and Stegmann, Z. (2004) Working memory skills and educational attainment: Evidence from national curriculum assessments at 7 and 14 years of age, *Applied Cognitive Psychology*, 18, 1–16.

Gaume, J., Gmel, G. and Daeppen, J. (2008) Brief alcohol interventions: Do counsellors' and patients' communication characteristics predict change? *Alcohol and Alcoholism*, 43, 62–69.

Gayle, B., Preiss, R. and Allen, M. (2006) How effective are teacher-initiated classroom questions in enhancing student learning? in B. Gayle, R. Preiss, N. Burrell and M. Allen (eds) *Classroom Communication and Instructional Processes: Advances through Meta-analysis.* Mahwah, NJ: Lawrence Erlbaum.

Gazdik, A. (2011) *Multiple Questions in French and Hungarian: A Lexical-Functional Analysis with Special Emphasis on the Syntax–Discourse Interface,* doctoral thesis. Paris, France: Université Paris Diderot (http://llf.linguist.jussieu.fr/llf/Gens/Gazdik/Thesis-final.pdf) (accessed 25 November 2014).

Gearhart, C. and Bodie, G. (2011) Active-empathic listening as a general social skill: Evidence from bivariate and canonical correlations, *Communication Reports*, 24, 86–98.

Gearhart, C., Denham, J. and Bodie, G. (2014) Listening as a goal-directed activity, *Western Journal of Communication*, 78, 668–684.

Gee, S., Gregory, M. and Pipe, M. (1999) What colour is your pet dinosaur? The impact of pre-interview training and question type on children's answers, *Journal of Legal and Criminological Psychology*, 4, 111–128.

Geen, R. (2001) *Human Aggression*, 2nd edition. Buckingham: Open University.

Geers, A. and Lassiter, G. (1999) Affective expectations and information gain: Evidence for assimilation and contrast effects in affective experience, *Journal of Experimental Social Psychology*, 35, 394–413.

Gelfand, M. and Brett, J. (2004) (eds) *Handbook of Negotiation and Culture.* Palo Alto, CA: Stanford University Press.

Gellatly, A. (1986) How can memory skills be improved? in A. Gellatly (ed.) *The Skilful Mind: An Introduction to Cognitive Psychology*. Milton Keynes: Open University.

Geniole, S., Cunningham, C. and Keyes, A. (2015) Costly retaliation is promoted by threats to resources in women and threats to status in men, *Aggressive Behavior*, 41, 515–525.

Gentry, W., Harris, L., Baker, B. and Leslie, J. (2009) Managerial skills: What has changed since the late 1980s, *Leadership and Organization Development Journal*, 29, 167–181.

Gervasio, A.H. (1987) Assertiveness techniques as speech acts, *Clinical Psychology Review*, 7, 105–119.

Gessner, M., Arnold, V. and Mobley, W. (1999) Introduction, in W. Mobley, M. Gessner and V. Arnold (eds) *Advances in Global Leadership, Volume 1*. Greenwich, CT: JAI Press.

Gesteland, R. (2012) *Cross-cultural Business Behavior: A Guide for Global Management*. Copenhagen: Copenhagen Business School Press.

Ghetti, S. and Goodman, G. (2001) Resisting distortion, *The Psychologist*, 14, 592–595.

Gibbs, R. and Bryant, G. (2008) Striving for optimal relevance when answering questions, *Cognition*, 106, 345–369.

Gibson, M. (2012) Opening up: Therapist self-disclosure in theory, research, and practice, *Clinical Social Work Journal*, 40, 287–296.

Gifford, R. (2013) Personality is encoded in, and decoded from, nonverbal behavior, in J. Hall and M. Knapp (eds) *Nonverbal Communication*. Berlin: Walter de Gruyter.

Gilbert, J., Boulter, C. and Rutherford, M. (1998) Models of explanations, Part 2: Whose voice? Whose ears? *International Journal of Science Education*, 20, 187–203.

Giles, H. and Le Poire, B.A. (2006) Introduction: The ubiquity and social meaningfulness of nonverbal communication, in V. Manusov and M. Patterson (eds) *The Sage Handbook of Nonverbal Communication*. Thousand Oaks, CA: Sage.

Giles, H. and Street, R. (1994) Communicator characteristics and behaviour, in M. Knapp and G. Miller (eds) *Handbook of Interpersonal Communication*, 2nd edition. Thousand Oaks, CA: Sage.

Gillath, O., Bahns, A., Ge, F. and Crandall, C. (2012) Shoes as a source of first impressions, *Journal of Research in Personality*, 46, 423–430.

Giordano, J. (2000) Effective communication and counseling with older adults, *International Journal of Aging and Human Development*, 51, 315–324.

Gleason, J. and Perlmann, R. (1985) Acquiring social variation in speech, in H. Giles and R. St Clair (eds) *Recent Advances in Language, Communication and Social Psychology*. London: Lawrence Erlbaum.

Glenberg, A., Schroeder, J. and Robinson, D. (1998) Averting the gaze disengages the environment and facilitates remembering, *Memory and Cognition*, 26, 651–658.

Glozman, E., Barak-Corren, N. and Yaniv, I. (2015) False negotiations: The art and science of not reaching an agreement, *Journal of Conflict Resolution*, 59, 671–697.

Glueckauf, R. and Quittner, A. (1992) Assertiveness training for disabled adults in wheelchairs: Self-report, role-play, and activity pattern outcomes, *Journal of Consulting and Clinical Psychology*, 60, 419–425.

Glynn, C. and Huge, M. (2008) Opinions as norms: Applying a return potential model to the study of communication behaviors, *Communication Research*, 34, 548–568.

Gnisci, A., Sergi, I., De Luca, E. and Errico, V. (2012) Does frequency of interruptions amplify the effect of various types of interruptions? Experimental evidence, *Journal of Nonverbal Behavior*, 36, 39–57.

Goby, V. and Lewis, J. (2000) The key role of listening in business: A study of the Singapore insurance industry, *Business Communication Quarterly*, 63, 41–51.

Goei, R. and Boster, F. (2005) The roles of obligation and gratitude in explaining the effectiveness of favors on compliance, *Communication Monographs*, 72, 284–300.

Goei, R., Roberto, A., Meyer, G. and Carlyle, K. (2007) The effects of favor and apology on compliance, *Communication Research*, 34, 575–595.

Goffman, E. (1959) *The Presentation of Self in Everyday Life*. Garden City, NY: Doubleday.

Goffman, E. (1972) *Relations in Public: Micro-studies of the Public Order*. Harmondsworth: Penguin.

Golchi, M. (2012) Listening anxiety and its relationship with listening strategy use and listening comprehension among Iranian IELTS learners, *International Journal of English Linguistics*, 2 (http://www.ccsenet.org/journal/index.php/ijel/article/view/17093/12699) (accessed 26 September 2014).

Golden, N. (1986) *Dress Right for Business.* New York: McGraw-Hill.

Goldin-Meadow, S. and Albali, M. (2013) Gesture's role in speaking, learning, and creating language, *Annual Review of Psychology*, 64, 257–283.

Goldman, M. (1980) Effect of eye-contact and distance on the verbal reinforcement of attitude, *Journal of Social Psychology*, 111, 73–78.

Goldstein, M., Schwade, J. and Bornstein, M. (2009) The value of vocalizing: Five-month-old infants associate their own noncry vocalizations with responses from caregivers, *Child Development*, 80, 636–644.

Gollwitzer, P. (1999) Implementation intentions: Strong effects of simple plans, *American Psychologist*, 54, 493–503.

Gómez, A., Morales, J., Huici, C., Gaviria, E. and Jiménez, J. (2007) When the world understands me...and my alignment with the group. From self-verification to verification of one's group identity, *International Journal of Psychology and Psychological Therapy*, 7, 213–236.

Gonzales, A., Hancock, J. and Pennebaker, J. (2010) Language style matching as a predictor of social dynamics in small groups, *Communication Research*, 37, 3–19.

Good, T. and Brophy, J. (2008) *Looking in Classrooms*, 10th edition. New York: Allyn and Bacon.

Goodman-Delahunty, J. and Howes, L. (2016) Social persuasion to develop rapport in high-stakes interviews: Qualitative analyses of Asian-Pacific practices, *Policing and Society: An International Journal of Research and Policy*, 26, 70–90.

Gordon, R., Druckman, D., Rozelle, R. and Baxter, J. (2006) Non-verbal behaviour as communication: Approaches, issues and research, in O. Hargie (ed.) *The Handbook of Communication Skills*, 3rd edition. London: Routledge.

Gormally, J. (1982) Evaluation of assertiveness: Effects of gender, rater involvement and level of assertiveness, *Behavior Therapy*, 13, 219–225.

Gosling, S., Craik, K., Martin, N. and Prior, M. (2005a) Material attributes of personal living spaces, *Home Cultures*, 2, 51–88.

Gosling, S., Craik, K., Martin, N. and Prior, M. (2005b) The Personal Living Space Cue Inventory: An analysis and evaluation, *Environment and Behavior*, 37, 683–705.

Gosling, S., Gaddis, S. and Vadzire, S. (2008) First impressions based on the environments we create and inhabit, in N. Ambady and J. Skowronski (eds) *First Impressions*. New York: Guilford.

Gouran, D. (1990) Introduction: Speech communication after seventy-five years, issues and prospects, in G. Phillips and J. Wood (eds) *Speech Communication: Essays to Commemorate the 75th Anniversary of the Speech Communication Association*, Carbondale, IL: Southern Illinois University Press.

Graff, M. (2007) Rise of the cyber-cheat, *The Psychologist*, 20, 678–679.

Graham, L., Sandy, C. and Gosling, S. (2011) Manifestations of individual differences in physical and virtual environments, in T. Chamorro-Premuzic, S. von Strumm and A. Furnham (eds) *The Wiley-Blackwell Handbook of Individual Differences*. Chichester: Wiley.

Graham, S., Huang, J., Clark, M. and Helgeson, V. (2008) The positives of negative emotions: Willingness to express negative emotions promotes relationships, *Personality and Social Psychology Bulletin*, 34, 394–406.

Granhag, P. and Vrij, A. (2007) Deception detection, in N. Brewer and K. Williams (eds) *Psychology and Law: An Empirical Perspective*. New York: Guilford.

Granhag, P., Vrij, A. and Verschuere, B. (2015) Introduction, in P. Granhag, A. Vrij and B. Verschuere (eds) *Detecting Deception: Current Challenges and Cognitive Approaches*. Chichester: Wiley.

Grant, L., Hindman, J. and Stronge, J. (2010) *Planning, Instruction, and Assessment: Effective Teaching Practices*. New York: Taylor and Francis.

Gray, B. (2003) Negotiating with your nemesis, *Negotiation Journal*, 19, 299–310.

Gray, H. (2008) To what extent, and under what conditions, are first impressions valid? in N. Ambady and J. Skowronski (eds) *First Impressions*. New York: Guilford.

Gray, H. and Ambady, N. (2006) Methods for the study of nonverbal communication, in V. Manusov and M. Patterson (eds) *The Sage Handbook of Nonverbal Communication*. Thousand Oaks, CA: Sage.

Grebelsky-Lichtman, T. (2014) Parental patterns of cooperation in parent–child interactions: The relationship between nonverbal and verbal communication, *Human Communication Research*, 40, 1–29.

Green, V. and Rechis, R. (2006) Children's cooperative and competitive interactions in limited resource situations: A literature review, *Applied Developmental Psychology*, 27, 42–59.

Greenbaum, P. and Rosenfeld, H. (1980) Varieties of touching in greetings: Sequential structure and sex-related differences, *Journal of Nonverbal Behavior*, 5, 13–25.

Greenberg, M.A. and Stone, A.A. (1992) Emotional disclosure about traumas and its relation to health: Effects of previous disclosure and trauma severity, *Journal of Personality and Social Psychology*, 63, 75–84.

Greene, J. (1995) An action-assembly perspective on verbal and nonverbal message production: A dancer's message unveiled, in D. Hewes (ed.) *The Cognitive Basis of Interpersonal Communication*. Hillsdale, NJ: Lawrence Erlbaum.

Greene, J. (2000) Evanescent mentation: An ameliorative conceptual foundation for research and theory on message production, *Communication Theory*, 10, 139–155.

Greene, K., Derlega, V. and Mathews, A. (2006) Self-disclosure in personal relationships, in A. Vangelista and D. Perlman (eds) *The Cambridge Handbook of Personal Relationships*. New York: Cambridge University Press.

Greenhill, N., Anderson, C., Avery, A. and Pilnick, A. (2011) Analysis of pharmacist–patient communication using the Calgary-Cambridge guide, *Patient Education and Counseling*, 83, 423–431.

Greenleaf, C. (1998) *Attention to Detail: A Gentleman's Guide to Professional Appearance and Conduct*. New York: Mass Market Press.

Greenspoon, J. (1955) The reinforcing effect of two spoken sounds on the frequency of two responses, *American Journal of Psychology*, 68, 409–416.

Gregg, A. (2007) When vying reveals lying: The timed antagonistic response alethiometer, *Applied Cognitive Psychology*, 21, 621–647.

Gregg, V. (1986) *Introduction to Human Memory*. London: Routledge and Kegan Paul.

Griessmair, M., Hippmann, P. and Gettinger, J. (2015) Emotions in e-negotiations, in B. Martinovski (ed.) *Emotion in Group Decision and Negotiation*. Dordrecht, Netherlands: Springer.

Griffin, C. and Bone, J. (2014) *Invitation to Human Communication Theory*. Boston, MA: Wadsworth, Cengage Learning.

Griffin, E., Ledbetter, A. and Sparks, G. (2014) *A First Look at Communication Theory*, 9th edition. New York: McGraw-Hill.

Griffin, K. (2016) *Fundamentals of Management*, 8th edition. Boston, MA: Cengage Learning.

Grigsby, J. and Weatherley, D. (1983) Gender and sex-role differences in intimacy of self-disclosure, *Psychological Reports*, 53, 891–897.

Groogan, S. (1999) Setting the scene, in A. Long (ed.) *Interaction for Practice in Community Nursing*. Basingstoke: MacMillan Press.

Guadagno, R. and Cialdini, R. (2007) Gender differences in impression management in organizations: A qualitative review, *Sex Roles*, 56, 483–494.

Gudjonsson, G. (1999) Police interviewing and disputed confessions, in A. Memon and R. Bull (eds) *Handbook of the Psychology of Interviewing*. Chichester: Wiley.

Gudjonsson, G. (2001) False confession, *The Psychologist*, 14, 588–591.

Gudleski, G. and Shean, G. (2000) Depressed and nondepressed students: Differences in interpersonal perceptions, *Journal of Psychology*, 134, 56–62.

Guéguen, N. (2010) The effect of a woman's incidental tactile contact on men's later behaviour, *Social Behavior and Personality: An International Journal*, 38, 257–266.

Guéguen, N. (2013) Handshaking and compliance with a request: A door-to-door setting, *Social Behavior and Personality: An International Journal*, 41, 1585–1588.

Guéguen, N. (2014) Effect of an interviewer's tactile contact on willingness to disclose voting choice, *Social Behavior and Personality: An International Journal*, 42, 1003–1006.

Guéguen, N. (2015) Effect of wearing eyeglasses on judgment of socioprofessional group membership, *Social Behavior and Personality: An International Journal*, 43, 661–666.

Guéguen, N. and Fisher-Lokou, J. (2003) Another evaluation of touch and helping behavior, *Psychological Reports*, 90, 267–269.

Guéguen, N. and Jacob, C. (2011) Enhanced female attractiveness with use of cosmetics and male tipping behavior in restaurants, *Journal of Cosmetic Science*, 62, 283–290.

Guéguen, N., Meineri, S., Pascual, A. and Girandola, F. (2015) The pique then reframe technique: Replication and extension of the pique technique, *Communication Research Reports*, 32, 143–148.

Guerrero, L. (2005) Observer ratings of nonverbal involvement and immediacy, in V. Manusov (ed.) *The Sourcebook of Nonverbal Measures: Going Beyond Words*. Mahwah, NJ: Lawrence Erlbaum.

Guerrero, L. and Floyd, K. (2006) *Nonverbal Communication in Close Relationships*. Mahwah, NJ: Lawrence Erlbaum.

Guerrero, L., Andersen, P. and Afifi, W. (2014) *Close Encounters: Communication in Relationships*, 4th edition. Thousand Oaks, CA: Sage.

Guffey, M. and Loewy, D. (2013) *Essentials of Business Communication*, 9th edition. Mason, OH: South-Western, Cengage Learning.

Guimond, S. and Massrieh, W. (2012) Intricate correlation between body posture, personality trait and incidence of body pain: A cross-referential study report. *PLoS ONE*, 7. (http://journals.plos.org/plosone/article?id=10.1371/journal.pone.0037450) (http://dx.doi.org/10.2139/ssrn.2357756) (accessed 1 June, 2016).

Guirdham, M. (2002) *Interactive Behaviour at Work*, 3rd edition. Harlow, Essex: Pearson.

Gunderson, E., Gripshover, S., Romero, C. *et al.* (2013) Parent praise to 1- to 3-year-olds predicts children's motivational frameworks 5 years later, *Child Development*, 84, 1526–1541.

Gunnery, S. and Hall, J. (2014) Reflections on historical trends and prospects in contemporary nonverbal research, *Journal of Nonverbal Behavior*, 38, 181–194.

Gupta, S. and Shukla, A. (1989) Verbal operant conditioning as a function of extraversion and reinforcement, *British Journal of Psychology*, 80, 39–44.

Gupton, T. and Le Bow, M. (1971) Behavior management in a large industrial firm, *Behavioral Therapy*, 2, 78–82.

Gureghian, J. (2013) *Vicarious Reinforcement Procedures: An Analysis of Stimulus Control and Potential Side Effects*, PhD thesis. Lawrence, KS: University of Kansas.

Haans, A., Bruijn, R. and Ijsselsteijn, W. (2014) A virtual Midas touch? Touch, compliance, and confederate bias in mediated communication, *Journal of Nonverbal Behavior*, 3, 301–311.

Haase, R.F. and Di Mattia, D. (1976) Spatial environment and verbal conditioning in a quasi-counseling interview, *Journal of Counseling Psychology*, 23, 414–421.

Hackman, M. and Johnston, C. (2013) *Leadership: A Communication Perspective*, 6th edition. Long Grove, IL: Waveland Press.

Hadfield, S. and Hasson, G. (2010) *How to be Assertive in Any Situation*. Harlow, Essex: Pearson Education.

Hagger, M., Rentzelas, P. and Koch, S. (2014) Evaluating group member behaviour under individualist and collectivist norms: A cross-cultural comparison, *Small Group Research*, 45, 217–228.

Hagihara, A., Tarumi, K. and Nobutomo K. (2006) Physicians' and patients' recognition of the level of the physician's explanation in medical encounters, *Health Communication*, 20, 101–104.

Hajek, C., Villagran, M. and Wittenberg-Lyles, E. (2007) The relationships among perceived physician accommodation, perceived outgroup typicality, and patient inclinations toward compliance, *Communication Research Reports*, 24, 293–302.

Halberstadt, A., Parker, A. and Castro, V. (2013) Nonverbal communication: Developmental perspectives, in J. Hall and M. Knapp (eds) *Nonverbal Communication*. Berlin: Walter de Gruyter.

Halford, J. and Hsu, H. (2013) Beauty is wealth: CEO appearance and shareholder value, *Social Science Research Network* (http://dx.doi.org/10.2139/ssrn.2357756) (accessed 10 March 2014).

Hall, D. and Buzwell, S. (2013) The problem of free-riding in group projects: Looking beyond social loafing as reason for non-contribution, *Active Learning in Higher Education*, 14, 37–49.

Hall, E. (1966) *The Hidden Dimension*. Garden City: Doubleday.

Hall, J. (1984) *Nonverbal Sex Differences: Communication Accuracy and Expressive Style*. Baltimore, MD: John Hopkins University.

Hall, J. (1996) Touch, status, and gender at professional meetings, *Journal of Nonverbal Psychology*, 20, 23–44.

Hall, J. (2006) Women's and men's nonverbal communication: Similarities, differences, stereotypes, and origins, in V. Manusov and M. Patterson (eds) *The Sage Handbook of Nonverbal Communication*. Thousand Oaks, CA: Sage.

Hall, J. (2011) Gender and status patterns in social touch, in M. Hertenstein and S. Weiss (eds) *The Handbook of Touch: Neuroscience, Behavioral, and Applied Perspectives*. New York: Springer Publications.

Hall, J. and Andrzejewski, S. (2008) Who draws accurate first impressions? Personal correlates of sensitivity to nonverbal cues, in N. Ambady and J. Skowronski (eds) *First Impressions*. New York: Guilford.

Hall, J., Mast, M. and Latu, I. (2015) The vertical dimension of social relations and accurate interpersonal perception: A meta-analysis, *Journal of Nonverbal Behavior*, 39, 131–163.

Halone, K. and Pecchioni, L. (2001) Relational listening: A grounded theoretical model, *Communication Reports*, 14, 59–71.

Halpern, D.F. (2000) *Sex Differences in Cognitive Abilities*, 3rd edition. Mahwah, NJ: Erlbaum.

Halpern, J. (1994) The effect of friendship on personal business transactions, *Journal of Conflict Resolution*, 38, 647–664.

Hamilton, C. (2014) *Communicating for Results: A Guide for Business and the Professions*, 10th edition. Boston, MA: Wadsworth.

Hamilton, D. (2005) *Social Cognition: Key Readings*. New York: Psychology Press.

Hamilton, M. and Hunter, J. (1998a) The effect of language intensity on receiver evaluations of message, in M. Allen and R. Preiss (eds) *Persuasion: Advances through Meta-analysis*. Cresskill, NJ: Hampton Press.

Hamilton, M. and Hunter, J. (1998b) A framework for understanding meta-analyses of persuasion, in M. Allen and R. Preiss (eds) *Persuasion: Advances through Meta-analysis*. Cresskill, NJ: Hampton Press.

Hamilton, W., Round, A. and Sharp, D. (1999) Effects on hospital attendance rates of giving patients a copy of their referral letter: Randomised control trial, *British Medical Journal*, 318, 1392–1395.

Hammen, C. (1997) *Depression*. Hove: Psychology Press.

Hample, D., Richards, A. and Skubisz, C. (2013) Blurting, *Communication Monographs*, 80, 503–532.

Hancil, S. and Hirst, D. (eds) (2013) *Prosody and Iconicity*. Amsterdam: John Benjamins.

Hancock, D. (2000) Impact of verbal praise on college students' time spent on homework, *The Journal of Educational Research*, 93, 384–89.

Hanna, M. and Wilson, G. (1998) *Communicating in Business and Professional Settings*, 4th edition. New York: McGraw-Hill.

Hanzal, A., Segrin, C. and Dorros, S. (2008) The role of marital status and age on men's and women's reactions to touch from a relational partner, *Journal of Nonverbal Behavior*, 32, 21–35.

Harbour, K., Evanovich, L., Sweigart, C. and Hughes, L. (2015) A brief review of effective teaching practices that maximize student engagement, *Preventing School Failure: Alternative Education for Children and Youth*, 59, 5–13.

Hardman, F. (2011) Promoting a dialogic pedagogy in English teaching, in J. Davison, C. Daly and J. Moss (eds) *Debates in English Teaching*. Abingdon, Oxon: Routledge.

Hardy, C. and van Leeuwen, S. (2004) Interviewing young children: Effects of probe structures and focus of rapport-building talk on the qualities of young children's eyewitness statements, *Canadian Journal of Behavioural Science*, 36, 155–165.

Hare, A.P. (1976) *Handbook of Small Group Research*. New York: Free Press.

Hare, L. and O'Neill, K. (2000) Effectiveness and efficiency in small group academic peer groups: A case study, *Small Group Research*, 31, 24–53.

Hargie, O. (1983) The importance of teacher questions in the classroom, in M. Stubbs and H. Hiller (eds) *Readings on Language, Schools and Classrooms*. London: Methuen.

Hargie, O. (2006a) Skill in theory: Communication as skilled performance, in O. Hargie (ed.) *The Handbook of Communication Skills*, 3rd edition. London: Routledge.

Hargie, O. (2006b) Training in communication skills: Research, theory and practice, in O. Hargie (ed.) *The Handbook of Communication Skills*, 3rd edition. London: Routledge.

Hargie, O. (2006c) Skill in practice: An operational model of communicative skilled performance, in O. Hargie (ed.) *The Handbook of Communication Skills*, 3rd edition. London: Routledge.

Hargie, O. (2007) Managing your communications: A key determinant of organizational success, in R. Karlsdottir (ed.) *Læring, Kommunikasjon og Ledesle i Organisasjoner*. Trondheim, Norway: Tapir Akademisk Forlag.

Hargie, O. (2009) Listening, in H. Reis and S. Sprecher (eds) *Encyclopedia of Human Relationships*. Thousand Oaks, CA: Sage.

Hargie, O. (2014) Communication accommodation in a divided society: Interaction patterns between Protestants and Catholics in Northern Ireland, *Studies in Communication Sciences*, 14, 78–85.

Hargie, O. and Irving, P. (2016) Crisis communication and terrorist attacks, in A. Schwarz, M. Seeger and C. Auer (eds) *Handbook of International Crisis Communication Research*. Chichester: Wiley-Blackwell.

Hargie, O. and Tourish, D. (1999) The psychology of interpersonal skill, in A. Memon and R. Bull (eds) *Handbook of the Psychology of Interviewing*. Chichester: Wiley.

Hargie, O. and Tourish, D. (eds) (2009) *Auditing Organizational Communication: A Handbook of Research, Theory and Practice*. London: Routledge.

Hargie, O., Boohan, M., McCoy, M. and Murphy, P. (2010) Current trends in communication skills training in UK schools of medicine, *Medical Teacher*, 32, 385–391.

Hargie, O., Brataas, H. and Thorsnes, S. (2009) Cancer patients' sensemaking of conversations with cancer nurses in outpatient clinics, *Australian Journal of Advanced Nursing*, 26, 70–78.

Hargie, O., Dickson, D. and Tourish, D. (2004) *Communication Skills for Effective Management*. Basingstoke: Palgrave Macmillan.

Hargie, O., Dickson, D., Mallett, J. and Stringer, M. (2008) Communicating social identity: A study of Catholics and Protestants in Northern Ireland, *Communication Research*, 35, 792–821.

Hargie, O., Morrow, N. and Woodman, C. (2000) Pharmacists' evaluation of key communication skills in practice, *Patient Education and Counseling*, 39, 61–70.

Hargie, O., Stapleton, K. and Tourish, D. (2010) Interpretations of CEO public apologies for the banking crisis: Attributions of credit, blame and responsibility, *Organization*, 17, 721–742.

Harper, J. (2004) Presentation skills, *Industrial and Commercial Training*, 36, 125–127.

Harper, M. and Welsh, D. (2007) Keeping quiet: Self-silencing and its association with relational and individual functioning among adolescent romantic couples, *Journal of Social and Personal Relationships*, 24, 99–116.

Harper, V. and Harper, E. (2006) Understanding student self-disclosure typology through blogging, *The Qualitative Report*, 11, 251–261.

Harrigan, J. (2005) Proxemics, kinesics and gaze, in J. Harrigan, R. Rosenthal and K. Scherer (eds) *The New Handbook of Methods in Nonverbal Behavioral Research*. Oxford: Oxford University Press.

Harris, J. (1973) Answering questions containing marked and unmarked adjectives and adverbs, *Journal of Experimental Psychology*, 97, 399–401.

Harris, M. and Garris, C. (2008) You never get a second chance to make a first impression: Behavioral consequences of first impressions, in N. Ambady and J. Skowronski (eds) *First Impressions*. New York: Guilford.

Harris, P. and Brown, B. (1998) The home and identity display: Interpreting resident territoriality from home exteriors, *Journal of Environmental Psychology*, 16, 187–203.

Harris, S., Dersch, C. and Mittal, M. (1999) Look who's talking: Measuring self-disclosure in MFT, *Contemporary Family Therapy*, 21, 405–415.

Hart, B. and Risley, T. (2003) The early catastrophe: The 30 million word gap, *American Educator*, 27, 4–9.

Hartley, P. (1999) *Interpersonal Communication*, 2nd edition. London: Routledge.

Hartley, P. and Chatterton, P. (2015) *Business Communication: Rethinking Your Professional Practice for the Post-digital Age*. London: Routledge.

Harwood, J., Ryan, E., Giles, H. and Tysoski, S. (1997) Evaluations of patronizing speech and three response styles in a non-service-providing context, *Journal of Applied Communication*, 25, 170–195.

Haselhuhn, M. (2015) Support theory in negotiation: How unpacking aspirations and alternatives can improve negotiation performance, *Journal of Behavioral Decision Making*, 28, 1–13.

Haselhuhn, M., Wong, E., Ormiston, M., Inesi, M. and Galinsky, A. (2014) Negotiating face-to-face: Men's facial structure predicts negotiation performance, *The Leadership Quarterly*, 25, 835–845.

Haski-Leventhal, D. and Bargal, D. (2008) The volunteer stages and transitions model: Organizational socialization of volunteers, *Human Relations*, 61, 67–102.

Haslam, S. and Reicher, S. (2008) Questioning the banality of evil, *The Psychologist*, 21, 16–19.

Haslam, S., Reicher, S. and Platow, M. (2011) *The New Psychology of Leadership*. Hove: Psychology Press.

Hasson, G. (2013) *Mindulness: Be Mindful. Live in the Moment*. Chichester: Capstone.

Hastings, S. (2000a) Asian Indian "self-suppression" and self-disclosure: Enactment and adaptation of cultural identity, *Journal of Language and Social Psychology*, 19, 85–109.

Hastings, S. (2000b) 'Egocasting' in the avoidance of dialogue: An intercultural perspective, in S. Petronio (ed.) *Balancing the Secrets of Private Disclosures*. Mahwah, NJ: Lawrence Erlbaum.

Hatfield, E., Cacioppo, J. and Rapson, R. (1994) *Emotional Contagion*. Cambridge: Cambridge University Press.

Hatfield, E., Carpenter, M. and Rapson, R. (2014) Emotional contagion as a precursor to collective emotions, in C. von Scheve and M. Salmela (eds) *Collective Emotions*. Oxford: Oxford University Press.

Hattie, J. and Timperley, H. (2007) The power of feedback, *Review of Educational Research*, 77, 81–112.

Hauch, V., Siegfried, L., Sporer, S., Michael, S. and Meissner, C. (2016) Does training improve the detection of deception? A meta-analysis, *Communication Research*, 43, 283–343.

Haugtvedt, C. and Petty, R. (1992) Personality and attitude change: Need for cognition moderates the persistence and resistance of persuasion, *Journal of Personality and Social Psychology*, 63, 308–319.

Hawkes, K., Edelman, H. and Dodd, D. (1996) Language style and evaluation of a female speaker, *Perceptual and Motor Skills,* 83, 80–82.

Hawkins, K. and Power, C. (1999) Gender differences in questions asked during small decision-making group discussions, *Small Group Research,* 30, 235–256.

Hawley, P., Johnson, S., Mize, J. and McNamara, K. (2007) Physical attractiveness in preschoolers: Relationships with power, status, aggression and social skills, *Journal of School Psychology*, 5, 499–521.

Hayashi, M. (2009) Marking a 'noticing of departure' in talk: Eh-prefaced turns in Japanese conversation, *Journal of Pragmatics*, 41, 2100–2129.

Hayashi, M., Raymond, G. and Sidnell, J. (2013) *Conversational Repair and Human Understanding*. Cambridge: Cambridge University Press.

Hayes, J. (2002) *Interpersonal Skills at Work*, 2nd edition. London: Routledge.

Heath, C. (1984) Talk and recipiency: Sequential organization in speech and body movement, in J.M. Atkinson and J. Heritage (eds) *Structures of Social Actions*. Cambridge: Cambridge University Press.

Heath, R. and Bryant, J. (2012) *Human Communication Theory and Research: Concepts, Contexts, and Challenges*, 2nd edition. Mahwah, NJ: Lawrence Erlbaum.

Heatherton, T., Krendl, A., Macrae, C. and Kelley, W. (2007) A social brain sciences approach to understanding self, in C. Sedikides and S. Spencer (eds) *The Self*. New York: Psychology Press.

Hebl, M. and Mannix, L. (2003) The weight of obesity in evaluating others: A mere proximity effect, *Personality and Social Psychology Bulletin*, 29, 28–38.

Heerey, E. and Crossley, H. (2013) Predictive and reactive mechanisms in smile reciprocity, *Psychological Science*, 24, 1446–1455.

Hehman, J., Corpuz, R. and Bugental, D. (2012) Patronizing speech to older adults, *Journal of Nonverbal Behavior*, 36, 249–261.

Heldner, M. and Edlund, J. (2010) Pauses, gaps and overlaps in conversations, *Phonetics*, 38, 555–568.

Heller, K. (2006) The cognitive psychology of circumstantial evidence, *Michigan Law Review*, 105 (http://ssrn.com/abstract=891695) (accessed 2 April 2015).

Heller, M. (1997) Posture as an interface between biology and culture, in U. Segerstrale and P. Molnar (eds) *Nonverbal Communication: Where Nature Meets Culture*. Mahwah, NJ: Lawrence Erlbaum.

Helminen, T., Pasanen, T. and Hietanen, J. (2016) Learning under your gaze: The mediating role of affective arousal between perceived direct gaze and memory performance, *Psychological Research*, 80, 159–171.

Helweg-Larsen, M., Cunningham, S., Carrico, A. and Pergram, A. (2004) To nod or not to nod: An observational study of nonverbal communication and status in female and male college students, *Psychology of Women Quarterly*, 28, 358–361.

Henderlong, J. and Lepper, M. (2002) The effects of praise on children's intrinsic motivation: A review and synthesis, *Psychological Bulletin*, 128, 774–795.

Henningsen, D., Henningsen, M., Eden, J. and Cruz, M. (2006) Examining the symptoms of groupthink and retrospective sensemaking, *Small Group Research*, 37, 36–64.

Henretty, J. and Levitt, H. (2010) The role of therapist self-disclosure in psychotherapy: A qualitative review, *Climnical Psychology Review*, 30, 63–77.

Henretty, J., Currier, J., Berman, J. and Levitt, H. (2014) The impact of counselor self-disclosure on clients: A meta-analytic review of experimental and quasi-experimental research, *Journal of Counseling Psychology*, 61, 191–207.

Henry, J. (2009) School pupils praised too much, says research, *Daily Telegraph*, 19 September (http://www.telegraph.co.uk/education/primary education/6209938/School-pupils-praised-too-much-says-research.html) (accessed 2 December 2009).

Henry, S., Fuhrel-Forbis, A., Rogers, M. and Eggly, S. (2012) Association between nonverbal communication during clinical interactions and outcomes: A systematic review and meta-analysis, *Patient Education and Counseling*, 86, 297–315.

Henry, S., Medway, F. and Scarbo, H. (1979) Sex and locus of control as determinants of children's responses to peer versus adult, *Journal of Educational Psychology*, 71, 604–612.

Hensley, W. and Cooper, R. (1987) Height and occupational success: A review and critique, *Psychological Reports*, 60, 843–849.

Heritage, J. (1998) Oh-prefaced responses to inquiry, *Language in Society*, 27, 291–334.

Heritage, J. and Raymond, R. (2012) Navigating epistemic landscapes: Acquiescence, agency and resitance in responses to polar questions, in J. de Ruiter (ed.) *Questions: Formal, Functional and Interactional Perspectives*. Cambridge: Cambridge University Press.

Heritage, J. and Robinson, J. (2006) The structure of patients' presenting concerns: Physicians' opening questions, *Health Communication*, 19, 89–102.

Heritage, J., Robinson, J., Elliott, M., Beckett, M. and Wilkes, M. (2007) Reducing patients' unmet concerns in primary care: The difference one word can make, *Journal of General Internal Medicine*, 22, 1429–1433.

Herndon, L., Brunner, T. and Rollins, J. (2006) The Glaucoma Research Foundation patient survey: Patient understanding of glaucoma and its treatment, *American Journal of Opthamology*, 141, S22–S28.

Hertenstein, M. (2011) The communicative functions of touch in adulthood, in M. Hertenstein and S. Weiss (eds) *The Handbook of Touch: Neuroscience, Behavioral, and Applied Perspectives*. New York: Springer Publications.

Hertenstein, M. and Keltner, D. (2011) Gender and the communication of emotion via touch, *Sex Roles*, 64, 70–80.

Hertenstein, M. and Weiss, S. (eds) (2011) *The Handbook of Touch: Neuroscience, Behavioral, and Applied Perspectives*. New York: Springer Publications.

Heslin, R. and Alper, T. (1983) Touch: A bonding gesture, in J. Wiemann and R. Harrison (eds) *Nonverbal Interaction*. London: Sage.

Hess, U., Adams, R. and Kleck, R. (2008) The role of facial expression in person perception, in N. Ambady and J. Skowronski (eds) *First Impressions*. New York: Guilford.

Hess, U., Philippot, P. and Blairy, S. (1999) Mimicry: Facts and fiction, in P. Philippot, R. Feldman and E. Coats (eds) *The Social Context of Nonverbal Behavior*. Cambridge: Cambridge University Press.

Hetsroni, A. (2007) Open or closed – This is the question: The influence of question format on the cultivation effect, *Communication Methods and Measures*, 1, 215–226.

Hettema, J., Steele, J. and Miller, W. (2005) Motivational interviewing, *Annual Review of Clinical Psychology*, 1, 91–111.

Hewes, D. (1995) Cognitive interpersonal communication research: Some thoughts on criteria, in B. Burleson (ed.) *Communication Yearbook 18*. Thousand Oaks, CA: Sage.

Hewes, D. and Planalp, S. (1987) The individual's place in communication science, in C. Berger and S. Chaffee (eds) *Handbook of Communication Science*. Newbury Park, CA: Sage.

Highlen, P. and Baccus, G. (1977) Effects of reflection of feeling and probe on client self-referenced affect, *Journal of Counseling Psychology*, 24, 440–443.

Highlen, P. and Nicholas, R. (1978) Effects of locus of control, instructions, and verbal conditioning on self-referenced affect in a counseling interview, *Journal of Counseling Psychology* 25, 177–183.

Hill, C. (1989) *Therapist Techniques and Client Outcomes*. Newbury Park, CA: Sage.

Hill, C. (1992) Research on therapist techniques in brief individual therapy: Implications for practitioners, *The Counseling Psychologist*, 20, 689–711.

Hill, C. (2014) *Helping Skills: Facilitating Exploration, Insight and Action*, 4th edition. Washington, DC: American Psychological Association.

Hill, C. and Gormally, J. (1977) Effects of reflection, restatement, probe and nonverbal behaviors on client affect, *Journal of Counseling Psychology*, 24, 92–97.

Hill, C., Helms, J., Tichenor, V., Spiegel, S., O'Grady, K. and Perry, E. (1988) Effects of therapist response modes in brief psychotherapy, *Journal of Counseling Psychology*, 35, 222–233.

Hiller, J., Fisher, G. and Kaess, W. (1969) A computer investigation of verbal characteristics of effective classroom lecturing, *American Educational Research Journal*, 6, 661–675.

Hind, C. (1997) *Communication Skills in Medicine*. London: BMJ Publishing Group.

Hinton, P. (2015) *The Perception of People: Integrating Cognition and Culture*, 2nd edition. London: Psychology Press.

Hirsh, J. (2009) Choosing the right tools to find the right people, *The Psychologist*, 22, 752–755.

Hirsh, J., Kang, S. and Bodenhausen, G. (2012) Personalized persuasion: Tailoring persuasive appeals to recipients' personality traits, *Psychological Science*, 23, 578–581.

Hirt, E., Lynn, S., Payne, D., Krackow, E. and McCrea, S. (1999) Expectations and memory: Inferring the past from what must have been, in I. Kirsch (ed.) *How Expectations Shape Experience*. Washington, DC: American Psychological Association.

Hitt, M., Ireland, R., Sirmon, D. and Trahms, C. (2011) Strategic entrepreneurship: Creating value for individuals, organizations, and society, *Academy of Management Perspectives*, 25, 57–75.

HMSO (1995) *Health Services Commissioner for England, for Scotland and for Wales, Annual Report for 1994–5*. London: HMSO.

Ho, S. and McLeod, D. (2008) Social-psychological influences on opinion expression in face-to-face and computer-mediated communication, *Communication Research*, 35, 190–207.

Hobson, R. and Lee, A. (1996) Hello and goodbye: A study of social engagement in autism, *Journal of Autism and Developmental Disorders*, 28, 117–127.

Hoeken, H. and Hustinx, L. (2007) The impact of exemplars on responsibility stereotypes in fund-raising letters, *Communication Research*, 34, 596–617.

Hoffman, R. (1995) Disclosure needs and motives after a near-death experience, *Journal of Near-Death Studies*, 13, 237–266.

Hofmann, S. and DiBartolo, P. (eds) (2014) *Social Anxiety: Clinical, Developmental, and Social Perspectives*. London: Elsevier.

Hofstede, G. (1980) *Culture's Consequences: International Differences in Work-related Values*. Beverly Hills, CA: Sage.

Hogan, K. and Speakman, J. (2006) *Covert Persuasion: Psychological Tactics and Tricks to Win the Game*. New York: Wiley.

Hogg, M. (2004) Social categorisation, depersonalization, and group behavior, in M. Brewer and M. Hewstone (eds) *Self and Social Identity*. Malden, MA: Blackwell.

Hogg, M. and Reid, S. (2006) Social identity, self-categorization, and the communication of group norms, *Communication Theory*, 16, 7–30.

Hogg, M. and Vaughn, G.M. (2008) *Social Psychology*, 5th edition. Harlow, Essex: Pearson Prentice Hall.

Hogwood, J., Campbell, T. and Butler, S. (2013) I wish I could tell you but I can't: Adolescents with perinatally acquired HIV and their dilemmas around self-disclosure, *Clinical Child Psychology and Psychiatry*, 18, 44–60.

Hollander, E. (2009) *Inclusive Leadership: The Essential Leader–Follower Relationship*. New York: Taylor and Francis.

Holler, J. and Wilkin, K. (2011) Co-speech gesture mimicry in the process of collaborative referring during face-to-face dialogue, *Journal of Nonverbal Behavior*, 35, 133–153.

Holli, B. and Beto, J. (2014) *Nutrition Counseling and Education Skills for Dietetics Professionals*, 6th edition. Baltimore, MD: Lippincott Williams and Wilkins.

Holliday, A., Hyde, M. and Kullman, J. (2010) *Intercultural Communication*, 2nd edition. London: Routledge.

Holliday, R. and Albon, A. (2004) Minimising misinformation effects in young children with cognitive interview mnemonics, *Applied Cognitive Psychology*, 18, 263–281.

Hollinger, L. and Buschmann, M. (1993) Factors influencing the perception of touch by elderly nursing home residents and their health caregivers, *International Journal of Nursing Studies*, 30, 445–461.

Hollingshead, A. and Poole, M. (eds) (2012) *Research Methods for Studying Groups and Teams: A Guide to Approaches, Tools, and Technologies*. New York: Taylor and Francis.

Holman, D. (2000) A dialogical approach to skill and skilled activity, *Human Relations*, 53, 957–980.

Holmes, J. and Stubbe, M. (2015) *Power and Politeness in the Workplace: A Sociolinguistic Analysis of Talk at Work*, 2nd edition. Abingdon, Oxon: Routledge.

Holt, S. and Marques, J. (2012) Empathy in leadership: Appropriate or misplaced? An empirical study on a topic that is asking for attention, *Journal of Business Ethics*, 105, 95–105.

Holtgraves, T. and Lasky, B. (1999) Linguistic power and persuasion, *Journal of Language and Social Psychology*, 18, 196–206.

Holtz, B. and Harold, C. (2013) Interpersonal justice and deviance: The moderating effects of interpersonal justice values and justice orientation, *Journal of Management*, 39, 339–365.

Homans, G. (1950) *The Human Group*. New York: Harcourt, Brace.

Honess, T. and Charman, E. (2002) Members of the jury – Guilty of incompetence? *The Psychologist*, 15, 72–75.

Honma, M. (2013) Hyper-volume of eye-contact perception and social anxiety traits, *Consciousness and Cognition*, 22, 167–173.

Hooper, C. (1995) A behavioral analysis of clinical performance discriminating novice from expert nurses, *Dissertation Abstracts International Section A: Humanities and Social Sciences* 56 (6-A), 2098.

Hopper, R., Bosma, J. and Ward, J. (1992) Dialogic teaching of medical terminology at the Cancer Information Service, *Journal of Language and Social Psychology*, 11, 63–74.

Horwitz, B. (2001) *Communication Apprehension: Origins and Management*. Albany, NY: Delmar.

Hosek, A. and Thompson, J. (2009) Communication privacy management and college instruction: Exploring the rules and boundaries that frame instructor private disclosures, *Communication Education*, 58, 327–349.

Hosman, L. and Siltanen, S. (2011) Hedges, tag questions, message processing, and persuasion, *Journal of Language and Social Psychology*, 30, 341–349.

Hostetter, A. (2011) When do gestures communicate? A meta-analysis, *Psychological Bulletin*, 137, 297–315.

Hostetter, A. and Skirving, C. (2011) The effect of visual vs. verbal stimuli on gesture production, *Journal of Nonverbal Behavior*, 35, 205–223.

Hough, M. (2006) *Counselling Skills and Theory*, 2nd edition. London: Hodder Arnold.

House, J. (2005) Politeness in Germany: Politeness in *Germany*? in L. Hickey and M. Stewart (eds) *Politeness in Europe*. Clevedon: Multilingual Matters.

House, R. (1976) A 1976 theory of charismatic leadership, in J. Hunt and L. Larson (eds) *Leadership: The Cutting Edge*. Carbondale: Southern Illinois University.

Houser, M. (2005) Are we violating their expectations? Instructor communication expectations of traditional and nontraditional students, *Communication Quarterly*, 53, 213–228.

Howard, D. (1990) The influence of verbal responses to common greetings on compliance behavior: The foot-in-the-mouth effect, *Journal of Applied Social Psychology*, 20, 1185–1196.

Howe, N., Aquan-Assee, J., Bukowski, W., Rinaldi, C. and Lehoux, P. (2000) Sibling self-disclosure in early adolescence, *Merrill Palmer Quarterly*, 46, 653–671.

Howlett, N., Pine, K., Orakçıoğlu, I. and Fletcher, B. (2013) The influence of clothing on first impressions: Rapid and positive responses to minor changes in male attire, *Journal of Fashion Marketing and Management*, 17, 38–48.

Hsiung, R. and Bagozzi, R. (2003) Validating the relationship qualities of influence and persuasion with the family social relations model, *Human Communication Research*, 29, 81–110.

Huber, D. (2014) *Leadership and Nursing Care Management*, 5th edition. St Louis, MO: Elsevier.

Huczynski, A. (1996) *Influencing Within Organizations*. London: Prentice Hall.

Hüffmeier, J., Freund, P., Zerres, A. *et al.* (2104) Being tough or being nice? A meta-analysis on the impact of hard- and softline strategies in distributive negotiations, *Journal of Management*, 40, 866–892.

Hughes, L. and Avey, J. (2009) Transforming with levity: Humor, leadership, and follower attitudes, *Leadership and Organizational Development Journal*, 30, 540–562.

Hughes, S., Mogilski, J. and Harrison, M. (2014) The perception and parameters of intentional voice manipulation, *Journal of Nonverbal Behavior*, 38, 107–127.

Human, L., Biesanz, J., Parisotto, K. and Dunn, E. (2012) Your best self helps reveal your true self: Positive self-presentation leads to more accurate personality impressions, *Social Psychological and Personality Science*, 3, 23–30.

Hummert, M. (2014) Age changes in facial morphology, emotional communication and age stereotyping, in P. Verhaeghen and C. Hertzog (eds) *The Oxford Handbook of Emotion, Social Cognition, and Problem Solving in Adulthood*. Oxford: Oxford University Press.

Hurley, C. and Frank, M. (2011) Executing facial control during deception situations, *Journal of Nonverbal Behavior*, 35, 119–131.

Huxley, A. (1954) *The Doors of Perception*. New York: Harper and Row.

Hybels, S. and Weaver, R. (2011) *Communicating Effectively*, 10th edition. New York: McGraw-Hill.

Imber, J. (2008) *Trusting Doctors: The Decline of Moral Authority in American Medicine*. Princeton, NJ: Princeton Press.

Imhof, M. (2010) Listening to voices and judging people, *International Journal of Listening*, 24, 19–33.

Inskipp, F. (2006) Generic skills, in C. Feltham and I. Horton (eds) *The Sage Handbook of Counselling and Psychotherapy*. London: Sage.

International Association of Business Communicators (2015) *Code of Ethics for Professional Communicators* (http://www.iabc.com/about/code.htm) (accessed 22 May 2015).

International Listening Association (2015) (http://www.listen.org/) (accessed 19 January 2015).

Irving, P. and Dickson, D. (2006) A re-conceptualization of Rogers' core conditions: Implications for research, practice and training, *International Journal for the Advancement of Counselling*, 28, 183–194.

Irving, P. and Hazlett, D. (1999) Communicating with challenging clients, in A. Long (ed.) *Interaction for Practice in Community Nursing*. Basingstoke: MacMillan.

Ishi, C., Ishiguro, H. and Hagita, N. (2014) Analysis of relationship between head motion events and speech in dialogue conversations, *Speech Communication*, 57, 233–243.

Iszatt-White, M. and Saunders, C. (2014) *Leadership*. Oxford: Oxford University Press.

Ivanov, B., Pfau, M. and Parker, K. (2009a) The attitude base as a moderator of the effectiveness of inoculation strategy, *Communication Monographs*, 76, 47–72.

Ivanov, B., Pfau, M. and Parker, K. (2009b) Can inoculation withstand multiple attacks? An examination of the effectiveness of the inoculation strategy compared to the supportive and restoration strategies, *Communication Research*, 36, 655–676.

Ivey, A., Ivey, M. and Zalaquett, C. (2012) *Essentials of Intentional Interviewing: Counseling in a Multicultural Society*, 2nd edition. Belmont, CA: Brooks/Cole, Cengage Learning.

Ivey, A., Ivey, M. and Zalaquett, C. (2014) *Intentional Interviewing and Counseling: Facilitating Client Development in a Multicultural Society*, 8th edition. Belmont, CA: Brooks/Cole, Cengage Learning.

Iyengar, S. and Brockner, J. (2001) Cultural differences in self and the impact of personal and social influences, in W. Wosinska, R. Cialdini, D. Barrett and J. Reykowski (eds) *The Practice of Social Influence in Multiple Cultures*. Mahwah, NJ: Lawrence Erlbaum.

Jack, R., Garrod, O., Yu, H., Caldara, R. and Schyns, P. (2012) Facial expressions of emotion are not culturally universal, *Proceedings of the National Academy of Sciences*, 109, 7241–7244.

Jackson, P., Skirrow, P. and Hare, D. (2012) Asperger through the looking glass: An exploratory study of self-understanding in people with Asperger's syndrome, *Journal of Autism and Developmental Disorders*, 42, 697–706.

Jacobs, C. and Coghlan, D. (2005) Sound from silence: On listening in organizational learning, *Human Relations*, 58, 115–138.

Jacobson, R. (1999) Personal space within two interaction conditions as a function of confederate age and gender differences, *Dissertation Abstracts International: Section B: The Sciences and Engineering*, 59(7-B), Jan, 3743.

Jagosh, J., Boudreau, J., Steinert, Y., McDonald, M. and Ingram, L. (2011) The importance of physician listening from the patients' perspective: Enhancing diagnosis, healing, and the doctor–patient relationship, *Patient Education and Counseling*, 85, 369–374.

Jalongo, M. (2010) Listening in early childhood: An interdisciplinary review of the literature, *International Journal of Listening*, 24, 1–18.

James, W. (1890) *Principles of Psychology*. Chicago: Encyclopaedia Britannica.

James, W. (1892) *Psychology: The Briefer Course*. New York: Henry Holt.

Janis, I. (1982) *Groupthink*, 2nd edition. Boston: Houghton-Mifflin.

Janis, I. (2007) Groupthink, in R. Vecchio (ed.) *Leadership: Understanding the Dynamics of Power and Influence in Organizations*. Notre Dame, IN: University of Notre Dame Press.

Janse, E. (2004) Word perception in fast speech: Artificially time-compressed vs. naturally produced fast speech, *Speech Communication*, 42, 155–173.

Janusik, L. (2007) Building listening theory: The validation of the conversational listening span, *Communication Studies*, 58, 139–156.

Jarrett, C. (2008) Mind wide open, *The Psychologist*, 21, 294–297.

Jeffries, K. and Reed, R. (2000) Trust and adaptation in relational contracting, *Academy of Management Review*, 25, 873–882.

Jensen, K. (1996) The effects of selected classical music on writing and talking about significant life events, *Dissertation Abstracts International: Humanities and Social Sciences*, 56 (12-A), 4602.

Jensen, M. (2014) *Smile as Feedback Expressions in Interpersonal Communication: A First Acquaintance Context*, Technical Report 2014.02: SSKKII-Publications (http://www.scciil.gu.se/digitalAssets/1484/1484333_smile_as_feedback---mikael-jensen.pdf) (accessed 10 March 2015).

Joffe, H. (2008) The power of visual material: Persuasion, emotion and identification, *Diogenes*, 217, 84–93.

John, O., Robins, R. and Pervin, L. (2008) *Handbook of Personality: Theory and Research*, 3rd edition. New York: Guilford.

Johnson, A. (ed.) (2014) *Wars in Peace: British Military Operations since 1991*. London: Royal United Services Institute.

Johnson, A., Becker, J., Wigley, S. *et al.* (2007) Reported argumentativeness and verbal aggressiveness levels: The influence of type of argument, *Communication Studies*, 58, 189–205.

Johnson, A., Crawford, M., Sherman, S. *et al.* (2006) A functional perspective on group memberships: Differential need fulfillment in a group typology, *Journal of Experimental Social Psychology*, 42, 707–719.

Johnson, C. and Dabbs, J. (1976) Self-disclosure in dyads as a function of distance and the subject–experimenter relationship, *Sociometry*, 39, 257–263.

Johnson, D. and Johnson, F. (2013) *Joining Together: Group Theory and Group Skills*, 11th edition. Upper Saddle River, NJ: Pearson Education.

Johnson, K., Lennon, S. and Rudd, N. (2014) Dress, body and self: Research in the social psychology of dress, *Fashion and Textiles*, 1, 20 (http://link.springer.com/article/10.1186/s40691-014-0020-7) (accessed 14 March 2015).

Johnson, S. and Bechler, C. (1998) Examining the relationship between listening effectiveness and leadership emergence: Perceptions, behaviors and recall, *Small Group Research,* 29, 452–471.

Johnston, D. (1994) *The Art and Science of Persuasion,* Boston: McGraw-Hill.

Johnston, L., Miles, L. and Macrae, C. (2010) Why are you smiling at me? Social functions of enjoyment and non-enjoyment smiles, *British Journal of Social Psychology,* 49, 107–127.

Joinson, A. (2001) Self-disclosure in computer-mediated communication: The role of self-awareness and visual anonymity, *European Journal of Social Psychology,* 31, 177–192.

Jones, S. (1999) Communicating with touch, in L. Guerrero, J. DeVito and M. Hecht (eds) *The Nonverbal Communication Reader: Classic and Contemporary Readings.* Prospect Heights, IL: Waveland Press.

Jones, S. (2005) The Touch Log Record: A behavioral communication measure, in V. Manusov (ed.) *The Sourcebook of Nonverbal Measures: Going Beyond Words.* Mahwah, NJ: Lawrence Erlbaum.

Jones, S. (2008) Nature and nurture in the development of social smiling, *Philosophical Psychology,* 21, 349–357.

Jones, S. (2011) Supportive listening, *International Journal of Listening,* 25, 85–103.

Jones, S., Collins, K. and Hong, H. (1991) An audience effect on smile production in 10 month old infants, *Psychological Science,* 2, 45–49.

Jones, W., Hobbs, S. and Hockenbury, D. (1982) Loneliness and social skill deficits, *Journal of Personality and Social Psychology,* 42, 682–689.

Jordan, J. (1998) Executive cognitive control in communication: Extending plan-based theory, *Human Communication Research,* 25, 5–38.

Jordan, J. and Roloff, M. (1997) Planning skills and negotiator accomplishment: The relationship between self-monitoring and plan generation, plan enhancement, and plan consequences, *Communication Research,* 24, 31–63.

Jost, K., Bryck, R., Vogel, E. and Mayr, U. (2011) Are old adults just like low working memory young adults? Filtering efficiency and age differences in visual working memory, *Cerebral Cortex,* 21, 1147–1154.

Jourard, S. (1961) Religious denomination and self-disclosure, *Psychological Bulletin,* 8, 446.

Jourard, S. (1964) *The Transparent Self.* New York: Van Nostrand Reinhold.

Jourard, S. (1966) An exploratory study of bodily accessibility, *British Journal of Social and Clinical Psychology,* 26, 235–242.

Jourard, S. (1971) *Self-disclosure.* New York: Wiley.

Jowett, G. and O'Donnell, V. (2015) *Propaganda and Persuasion.* Thousand Oaks, CA: Sage.

Jucks, R., Bromme, R. and Runde, A. (2007) Explaining with nonshared illustrations: How they constrain explanations, *Learning and Instruction,* 17, 204–218.

Jucks, R., Paus, E. and Bromme, R. (2012) Patients' medical knowledge and health counseling: What kind of information helps to make communication patient-centered? *Patient Education and Counseling,* 88, 177–183.

Judge, T. and Cable, D. (2004) The effect of physical height on workplace success and income: Preliminary test of a theoretical model, *Journal of Applied Psychology*, 89, 428–441.

Jussim, L. (2012) *Social Perception and Social Reality: Why Accuracy Dominates Bias and Self-fulfilling Prophecy*. Oxford: Oxford University Press.

Justine, A. and Howe, B. (1998) Player ability, coach feedback, and female adolescent athletes' perceived competence and satisfaction, *Journal of Sport and Exercise Psychology*, 20, 280–299.

Kagan, C. (2007) Interpersonal skills and reflection in regeneration practice, *Public Money and Management*, 27, 169–174.

Kagan, C. and Evans, J. (1995) *Professional Interpersonal Skills for Nurses*. London: Chapman and Hall.

Kagee, A. (2013) Training lay counsellors to provide psychosocial support to ART users: Successes and failures, *AIDS Care: Psychological and Sociomedical Aspects of AIDS/HIV*, 25, 496–502.

Kahai, S., Sosik, J. and Avolio, J. (1997) Effects of leadership style and problem structure on work group process and outcome in an electronic meeting system environment, *Personnel Psychology*, 50, 121–136.

Kahn, M. (2008) Etiquette-based medicine, *The New England Journal of Medicine*, 358, 1988–1999.

Kahn, R. and Cannell, C. (1957) *The Dynamics of Interviewing*. New York: Wiley.

Kahn, S. (1981) Issues in the assessment and training of assertiveness with women, in J. Wine and M. Smye (eds) *Social Competence*. New York: Guilford.

Kammrath, L., McCarthy, M., Cortes, K. and Friesen, C. (2015) Picking one's battles: How assertiveness and unassertiveness abilities are associated with extraversion and agreeableness, *Social Psychological and Personality Science*, 6, 622–629.

Kang, Y. (1998) Classroom context, teacher feedback and student self-effiacy, *Dissertation Abstracts International Section A: Humanities and Social Sciences*, 59(2-A), 0419.

Kappas, A., Hess, U. and Scherer, K. (1991) Voice and emotion, in R. Feldman and B. Rime (eds) *Fundamentals of Nonverbal Behaviour*, Cambridge: Cambridge University Press.

Karagözoğlu, S., Kahve, E., Koç Ö. and Adamişoğlu, D. (2007) Self esteem and assertiveness of final year Turkish university students, *Nurse Education Today*, 28, 641–649.

Karakowsky, L., DeGama, N. and McBey, K. (2012) Facilitating the Pygmalion effect: The overlooked role of subordinate perceptions of the leader, *Journal of Occupational and Organizational Psychology*, 85, 579–599.

Karathanos, P. and Auriemmo, A. (1999) Care and feeding of the organizational grapevine, *Industrial Management*, 41, 26–30.

Karl, K., Hall, L. and Peluchette, J. (2013) City employee perceptions of the impact of dress and appearance: You are what you wear, *Public Personnel Management*, 42, 452–470.

Kaspar, K. and Stelz, H. (2013) The paradoxical effect of praise and blame: Age-related differences, *Europe's Journal of Psychology*, 9(2). DOI: 10.5964/ejop.v9i2.540.

Kassin, S. and Gudjonsson, G. (2004) The psychology of confessions: A review of the literature and issues, *Psychological Science in the Public Interest*, 5, 33–67.

Kassin, S., Fein, S. and Markus, H. (2011) *Social Psychology*, 8th edition. Boston, MA: Houghton Mifflin.

Katz, D. and Stotland, E. (1959) A preliminary statement of a theory of attitude theory and change, in S. Koch (ed.) *Psychology: A Study of a Science, Vol. 3*. New York: McGraw-Hill.

Katz, M., Jacobson, T., Veledar, E. and Kripalani, S. (2007) Patient literacy and question-asking behavior during the medical encounter: A mixed-methods analysis, *Journal of General Internal Medicine*, 22, 782–786.

Kaya, N. and Erkip, F. (1999) Invasion of personal space under the condition of short-term crowding: A case study on an automatic teller machine, *Journal of Environmental Psychology*, 19, 183–189.

Kazdin, A. (2013) *Behavior Modification in Applied Settings*, 7th edition, Long Grove, IL: Waveland Press.

Keaton, S., Bodie, G. and Keteyian, R. (2015) Relational listening goals influence how people report talking about problems, *Communication Quarterly*, 63, 480–494.

Keats, D. (2000) *Interviewing: A Practical Guide for Students and Professionals*, Buckingham: Open University Press.

Kellerman, K., Reynolds, R. and Chen, J. (1991) Strategies of conversational retreat: When parting is not sweet sorrow, *Communication Monographs*, 58, 362–383.

Kellermann, K. (1992) Communication: Inherently strategic and primarily automatic, *Communication Monographs*, 59, 288–300.

Kelley, H. (1950) The warm–cold variable in first impressions of persons, *Journal of Personality*, 18, 431–439.

Kelley, H. and Thibaut, J. (1978) *Interpersonal Relations: A Theory of Interdependence*. New York: Wiley.

Kelly, A. and McKillop, K. (1996) Consequences of revealing personal secrets, *Psychological Bulletin*, 120, 450–465.

Kelly, F. and Daniels, J. (1997) The effects of praise versus encouragement on children's perceptions of teachers, *Individual Psychology*, 53, 331–341.

Kelly, J. (1982) *Social Skills Training: A Practical Guide for Interventions*. New York: Springer.

Kendon, A. (1967) Some functions of gaze direction in social interaction, *Acta Psychologica*, 26, 22–63.

Kendon, A. (1984) Some use of gestures, in D. Tannen and M. Saville-Troike (eds) *Perspectives on Silence*. Norwood, NJ: Ablex.

Kendon, A. and Ferber, A. (1973) A description of some human greetings, in R. Michael and J. Crook (eds) *Comparative Ecology and Behaviour of Primates*. London: Academic Press.

Kenman, L. (2007) Tone and style: Developing a neglected segment of business communication, *Business Communication Quarterly*, 70, 3005–3008.

Kennedy, G. (1998) *Kennedy on Negotiation*. Aldershot: Gower.

Kennedy, S., Hodgson, M., Edgett, L., Lamb, N. and Rempel, R. (2006) Subjective assessment of listening environments in university classrooms: Perceptions of students, *The Journal of the Acoustical Society of America*, 119, 299–309.

Kennedy, T., Timmons, E. and Noblin, C. (1971) Nonverbal maintenance of conditioned verbal behavior following interpretations, reflections and social reinforcers, *Journal of Personality and Social Psychology*, 20, 112–117.

Kennelly, K.J. and Mount, S.A. (1985) Perceived contingency of reinforcements, helplessness, locus of control and academic performance, *Psychology in the Schools*, 22, 465–469.

Kenny, D. and West, T. (2008) Zero acquaintance: Definitions, statistical model findings and process, in N. Ambady and J. Skowronski (eds) *First Impressions*. New York: Guilford.

Kenward, B., Hellmer, K., Winter, L. and Eriksson, M. (2015) Four-year-olds' strategic allocation of resources: Attempts to elicit reciprocation correlate negatively with spontaneous helping, *Cognition*, 136, 1–8.

Kern, J. (1982) Predicting the impact of assertive, empathic-assertive and non-assertive behavior: The assertiveness of the assertee, *Behavior Therapy*, 13, 486–498.

Kesting, P. and Smolinski, R. (2007) When negotiations become routine: Not reinventing the wheel while thinking outside the box, *Negotiation Journal*, 23, 419–438.

Kestler, J. (1982) *Questioning Techniques and Tactics*. Colorado Springs, CO: McGraw-Hill.

Khan, W. and Inamullah, H. (2011) Study of lower-order and higher-order questions at secondary level, *Asian Social Science*, 7, 149–157.

Kidd, C., White, K. and Aslin, R. (2011) Toddlers use of speech disfluencies to predict speakers' referential intentions, *Developmental Science*, 14, 925–934.

Kidwell, M. (2009) What happened? An epistemics of before and after in 'at-the-scene' police questioning, *Research on Language and Social Interaction*, 42, 20–41.

Kim, H. and Ko, D. (2007) Culture and self-expression, in C. Sedikides and S. Spencer (eds) *The Self*. New York: Psychology Press.

Kim, S., Allen, M., Gattoni, A. *et al.* (2012) Testing an additive model for the effectiveness of evidence on the persuasiveness of a message, *Social Influence*, 7, 65–77.

Kim, S., Allen, M., Preiss, R. and Peterson, B. (2014) Meta-analysis of counterattitudinal advocacy data: Evidence for an additive cues model, *Communication Quarterly*, 62, 607–620.

Kimble, P. and Bamford-Wade, A. (2013) The journey of discovering compassionate listening, *Journal of Holistic Nursing*, 31, 285–290.

Kimmel, A. (2004a) *Rumors and Rumor Control: A Manager's Guide to Understanding and Combatting Rumours*. Mahwah, NJ: Lawrence Erlbaum.

Kimmel, M. (2004b) *The Gendered Society*, 2nd edition. New York: Oxford University Press.

King, A. (1992) Comparison of self-questioning, summarizing and notetaking-review as strategies for learning from lectures, *American Educational Research Journal*, 29, 303–323.

King, P. and Behnke, R. (2004) Patterns of state anxiety in listening performance, *Southern Communication Journal*, 70, 72–80.

Kinzler, K. and DeJesus, J. (2013) Northern = smart and Southern = nice: The development of accent attitudes in the United States, *The Quarterly Journal of Experimental Psychology*, 66, 1146–1158.

Kinzler, K., Dupoux, E. and Spelke, E. (2007) The native language of social cognition, *Proceedings of the National Academy of Sciences*, 104, 12577–12580.

Kipling, R. (1902) The elephant child, in *Just-so Stories*. London: Macmillan.

Kipnis, D. and Schmidt, S. (1990) The language of persuasion, in I. Asherman and S. Asherman (eds) *The Negotiating Sourcebook*. Amherst, MA: Human Resource Development Press.

Kirsch, I. (1999) Response expectancy: An introduction, in I. Kirsch (ed.) *How Expectations Shape Experience*. Washington, DC: American Psychological Association.

Klakovich, M. and dela Cruz, F. (2006) Validating the Interpersonal Communication Assessment Scale, *Journal of Professional Nursing*, 22, 60–67.

Klaver, J., Lee, Z. and Rose, G. (2008) Effects of personality, interrogation techniques and plausibility in an experimental false confession paradigm, *Legal and Criminological Psychology*, 13, 71–88.

Kleinke, C. (1977) Compliance to requests made by gaze and touching experimenters in field settings, *Journal of Experimental Social Psychology*, 13, 218–223.

Kleinke, C. (1986) *Meeting and Understanding People*. New York: W.H. Freeman.

Klimek, P., Hanel, R. and Stefan Thurner, S. (2008) To how many politicians should government be left? *Physics and Society* (http://arxiv.org/PS_cache/arxiv/pdf/0804/0804.2202v1.pdf) (accessed 2 December 2009).

Klinger, E. and Bierbraver, G. (2001) Acculturation and conflict regulation of Turkish immigrants in Germany: A social influence perspective, in W. Wosinska, R. Cialdini, D. Barrett and J. Reykowski (eds) *The Practice of Social Influence in Multiple Cultures*. Mahwah, NJ: Lawrence Erlbaum.

Klinger, E., Barta, S. and Maxeiner, M. (1981) Current concerns: Assessing therapeutically relevant motivation, in P. Kendall and S. Hollon (eds) *Assessment Strategies for Cognitive Behavioral Interventions*. New York: Academic Press.

Klüver, J. and Klüver, C. (2007) *On Communication: An Interdisciplinary and Mathematical Approach*. Dordrecht, The Netherlands: Springer.

Knapp, M. (2013) Establishing a domain for the study of nonverbal phenomena: *e pluribus unum*, in J. Hall and M. Knapp (eds) *Nonverbal Communication*. Berlin: Walter de Gruyter.

Knapp, M. and Vangelisti, A. (2009) *Interpersonal Communication and Human Relationships*, 6th edition. Boston: Allyn and Bacon.

Knapp, M., Hall, J. and Horgan, T. (2014) *Nonverbal Communication in Human Interaction*, 8th edition. Boston, MA: Wadsworth, Cengage Learning.

Knapp, M., Hart, R., Friedrich, G. and Schulman, G. (1973) The rhetoric of goodbye: Verbal and nonverbal correlates of human leave-taking, *Speech Monographs*, 40, 182–198.

Knight, C. (2014) Students' attitudes towards and engagement in self-disclosure: Implications for supervision, *The Clinical Supervisor*, 33, 163–181.

Knobloch, L. (2010) Relational uncertainty and interpersonal communication, in S. Smith and S. Wilson (eds) *New Directions in Interpersonal Communication Research*. Thousand Oaks, CA: Sage.

Knowles, E. and Linn, J. (2004) Approach-avoidance model of persuasion: Alpha and omega strategies for change, in E. Knowles and J. Linn (eds) *Resistance and Persuasion*. Mahwah, NJ: Lawrence Erlbaum.

Knowles, E. and Riner, D. (2007) Omega approaches to persuasion: Overcoming resistance, in A. Pratkanis (ed.) *The Science of Social Influence: Advances and Future Progress*. New York: Psychology Press.

Knowles, E., Butler, S. and Linn, J. (2001) Increasing compliance by reducing resistance, in J. Forgas and K. Williams (eds) *Social Influence: Direct and Indirect Processes*. Philadelphia: Psychology Press.

Knowlton, S. and Berger, C. (1997) Message planning, communication failure and cognitive load: Further explorations of the Hierarchy principle, *Human Communication Research*, 24, 4–30.

Knox, S. and Hill, C. (2003) Therapist self-disclosure: Research-based suggestions for practitioners, *Journal of Clinical Psychology*, 59, 529–539.

Knox, S., Hess, S., Petersen, D. and Hill, C. (1997) A qualitative analysis of client perceptions of the effects of helpful therapist self-disclosure in long-term therapy, *Journal of Counseling Psychology*, 44, 274–283.

Ko, S., Judd, C. and Blair, I. (2006) What the voice reveals: Within- and between-category stereotyping on the basis of voice, *Personality and Social Psychology Bulletin*, 32, 806–819.

Koermer, C. and Kilbane, M. (2008) Physician sociality communication and its effect on patient satisfaction, *Communication Quarterly*, 56, 69–86.

Koermer, C. and McCroskey, L. (2006) Sociality communication: Its influence on customer loyalty with the service provider and service organization, *Communication Quarterly*, 54, 53–65.

Kohut, S., Riddell, R., Flora, D. and Oster, H. (2012) A longitudinal analysis of the development of infant facial expressions in response to acute pain: Immediate and regulatory expressions, *Pain*, 153, 2458–2465.

Kolb, D. and Porter, J. (2015) *Negotiating at Work: Turn Small Wins into Big Gains*. San Francisco, CA: Wiley.

Kolb, D. and Williams, J. (2007) Breakthrough bargaining, in R. Lewicki, B. Barry and D. Saunders (eds) *Negotiation: Readings, Exercise and Cases*, 5th edition. New York: McGraw-Hill.

Kolotkin, R., Wielkiewicz, R., Judd, B. and Weisler, S. (1983) Behavioral components of assertion: Comparison of univariate and multivariate assessment strategies, *Behavioral Assessment*, 6, 61–78.

Komaki, J. (1982) Managerial effectiveness: potential contributions of the behavioral approach, *Journal of Organizational Behavior Management*, 3, 71–83.

Kong, A., Law, S., Chimng, C. *et al.* (2015) A coding system with independent annotations of gesture forms and functions during verbal communication: Development of a database of speech and GEsture (DoSaGE), *Journal of Nonverbal Behavior*, 39, 93–111.

Kong, D., Dirks, K. and Ferrin, D. (2014) Interpersonal trust within negotiations: Meta-analytic evidence, critical contingencies, and directions for future research, *Academy of Management Journal*, 57, 1235–1255.

Koprowska, J. (2014) *Communication and Interpersonal Skills in Social Work*. London: Sage.

Korda, H. and Itani, Z. (2013) Harnessing social media for health promotion and behavior change, *Health Promotion Practice*, 14, 15–23.

Korda, M. (1975) *Power! How to Get It, How to Use It*. New York: Random.

Kormanik, M. and Rocco, T. (2009) Internal versus external control of reinforcement: A review of the locus of control construct, *Human Resource Development Review*, 8, 463–483.

Korobkin, R. (2007) On bargaining power, in A. Schneider and C. Honeyman (eds) *The Negotiator's Fieldbook: The Desk Reference for the Experienced Negotiator*. Chicago, IL: American Bar Association.

Korsgaard, M., Brower, H. and Lester, S. (2014) It isn't always mutual: A critical review of dyadic trust, *Journal of Management*, 41, 47–70.

Kortt, M. and Leigh, A. (2010) Does size matter in Australia? *Economic Record* (http://econrsss.anu.edu.au/~aleigh/pdf/BodySize.pdf) (accessed 2 December 2009).

Kossowska, M. and Bar-Tal, Y. (2013) Need for closure and heuristic information processing: The moderating role of the ability to achieve the need for closure, *British Journal of Psychology*, 104, 457–480.

Kowalski, R. (1996) Complaints and complaining: Functions, antecedents, and consequences, *Psychological Bulletin*, 119, 179–196.

Kowalski, R. (1999) Speaking the unspeakable: Self-disclosure and mental heath, in R. Kowalski and M. Leary (eds) *The Social Psychology of Emotional and Behavioral Problems*. Washington, DC: American Psychological Association.

Kozak, M., Sternglanz, R., Viswanathan, U. and Wegner, D. (2007) The role of thought suppression in building mental blocks, *Consciousness and Cognition*, 17, 1123–1130.

Krähenbühl, S. and Blades, M. (2006) The effect of interviewing techniques on young children's responses to questions, *Child: Care, Health and Development*, 32, 321–331.

Kramer, M. (2001) *Business Communication in Context*. Upper Saddle River, NJ: Prentice-Hall.

Kramer, M. and Dougherty, D. (2013) Groupthink as communication process, not outcome, *Communication and Social Change*, 1, 44–62.

Kramer, R. (1998) Revisiting the Bay of Pigs and Vietnam decisions 25 years later: How well does the groupthink hypothesis stand the test of time? *Organizational Behavior and Human Decision Processes*, 73, 236–271.

Krasnova, H., Spiekermann, S., Koroleva, K. and Hildebrand, T. (2010) Online social networks: Why we disclose, *Journal of Information Technology*, 25, 109–125.

Kraus, M. and Chen, T. (2013) Winning smile? Smile intensity, physical dominance, and fighter performance, *Emotion*, 13, 270–279.

Krause, R., Steimer, E., Sanger-Alt, C. and Wagner, G. (1989) Facial expression of schizophrenic patients and their interaction partners, *Psychiatry*, 52, 1–12.

Kray, L. and Babcock, L. (2006) Gender in negotiations: A motivated social cognitive analysis, in L. Thompson (ed.) *Negotiation Theory and Research*. New York: Taylor and Francis.

Kreiman, J. and Sidtis, D. (2011) *Foundations of Voice Studies: An Interdisciplinary Approach to Voice Production and Perception*. Chicester: Wiley-Blackwell.

Kreps, G. and Thornton, B. (1992) *Health Communication: Theory and Practice*. Prospect Heights, IL: Waveland Press.

Kret, M. and de Gelder, B. (2012) A review on sex differences in processing emotional signals, *Neuropsychologia*, 50, 1211–1221.

Kret, M., Pichon, S., Grèzes, J. and de Gelder, B. (2011) Similarities and differences in perceiving threat from dynamic faces and bodies: An fMRI study, *NeuroImage*, 54, 1755–1762.

Krueger, J. (2009) A componential model of situation effects, person effects, and situation-by-person interaction effects on social behavior, *Journal of Research in Personality*, 43, 127–136.

Kruglanski, A. (2004) *The Psychology of Closed Mindedness: Essays in Social Psychology*. New York: Psychology Press.

Krumhuber, E., Kappas, A. and Manstead, A. (2013) Effects of dynamic aspects of facial expressions: A review, *Emotion Review*, 5, 41–46.

Krumhuber, E., Likowski, K. and Weyers, P. (2014) Facial mimicry of spontaneous and deliberate Duchenne and non-Duchenne smiles, *Journal of Nonverbal Behavior*, 38, 1–11.

Kugler, T., Kausel, E. and Kocher, M. (2012) Are groups more rational than individuals? A review of interactive decision making in groups, *Cognitive Science*, 4, 471–482.

Kunda, Z. and Fong, G. (1993) Directional questions direct self-conceptions, *Journal of Experimental Social Psychology*, 29, 63–86.

Kupperbusch, C., Matsumoto, D., Kooken, K., Loewinger, S., Uchida, H., Wilson-Cohn, C. and Yrizarry, N. (1999) Cultural influences on nonverbal expressions of emotion, in P. Philippot., R. Feldman and E. Coats (eds) *The Social Context of Nonverbal Behavior*. Cambridge: Cambridge University Press.

Kurebayashi, K., Hoffman, L., Ryan, C. and Murayama, A. (2012) Japanese and American perceptions of group entitativity and autonomy: A multilevel analysis, *Journal of Cross-Cultural Psychology*, 43, 349–364.

Kurtz, S., Silverman, J. and Draper, J. (1998) *Teaching and Learning Communication Skills in Medicine*. Abingdon, Oxon: Radcliffe Medical Press.

LaFrance, M. (2011) *Lip Service: Smiles in Life, Death, Trust, Lies, Work, Memory, Sex, and Politics*. New York: W.W. Norton.

LaFrance, M. and Harris, J. (2004) Gender and verbal and nonverbal communication, in M. Paludi (ed.) *Praeger Guide to the Psychology of Gender*. Westport, CT: Greenwood Press.

Lakin, J. (2006) Automatic cognitive processes and nonverbal communication, in V. Manusov and M. Patterson (eds) *The SAGE Handbook of Nonverbal Communication*. Thousand Oaks, CA: Sage.

Lalich, J. (2004) *Bounded Choice: True Believers and Charismatic Cults*. Berkeley, CA: University of California Press.

Lall, A. (1966) *Modern International Negotiation: Principles and Practice*. New York: Columbia University Press.

Lam, C. and O'Higgins, E. (2012) Enhancing employee outcomes: The interrelated influences of managers' emotional intelligence and leadership style, *Leadership and Organization Development Journal*, 33, 149–174.

Lamb, M., Sternberg, K., Orbach, Y., Hershkowitz, I. and Esplin, P. (1999) Forensic interviews of children, in A. Memon and R. Bull (eds) *Handbook of the Psychology of Interviewing*. Chichester: Wiley.

Lamb, R. (1988) Greetings and partings, in P. Marsh (ed.) *Eye to Eye: Your Relationships and How They Work*. London: Sidgwick and Jackson.

Land, M. (1984) Combined effect of two teacher clarity variables on student achievement, *Journal of Experimental Education*, 50, 14–17.

Lang, G. and van der Molen, H. (1990) *Personal Conversations: Roles and Skills for Counsellors*. London: Routledge.

Lange, A. and Jakubowski, P. (1976) *Responsible Assertive Behavior*. Champaign, IL: Research Press.

Langer, E., Blank, A. and Chanowitz, B. (1978) The mindlessness of ostensibly thoughtful action, *Journal of Personality and Social Psychology*, 36, 635–642.

Langlois, J., Kalakanis, L., Rubenstein, A., Larson, A., Hallam, M. and Smoot, M. (2000) Maxims and myths of beauty: A meta-analytic and theoretical review, *Psychological Bulletin*, 126, 390–423.

Larson, C. (2013) *Persuasion: Reception and Responsibility*, 13th edition. Boston, MA: Wadsworth Cengage Learning.

Larson, J. (2010) *In Search of Synergy in Small Group Performance*. New York: Psychology Press.

Lasernal, C., Seih, Y. and Pennebaker, J. (2014) *Um . . . who like says you know*: Filler word use as a function of age, gender, and personality, *Journal of Language and Social Psychology*, 33, 328–338.

Lausberg, H., Zaidel, H., Cruz, R. and Ptito, A. (2007) Speech-independent production of communication gestures: Evidence from patients with complete callosal disconnection, *Neuropsychologia*, 45, 3092–3104.

Laver, J. and Hutcheson, S. (eds) (1972) *Communication in Face-to-Face Interaction*, Harmondsworth: Penguin.

Lawler, J. (2006) *Behind the Screens: Nursing, Somology and the Problem of the Body*. Sydney, Australia: Sydney University Press.

Lawrence, J. (2001) Does academic praise communicate stereotypic expectancies to Black students? *Dissertation Abstracts International: Section B: The Sciences and Engineering*, 61(10-B), May, 5622.

Lawyer, J. and Katz, N. (1985) *Communication and Conflict Management Skills*. Dubuque, IA: Kendall/Hunt.

Lax, D. and Sebenius, J. (2006) *3-D Negotiation: Powerful Tools to Change the Game in Your Most Important Deals*. Boston, MA: Harvard Business School Press.

Lazarus, A. (1971) *Behavior Therapy and Beyond*. New York: McGraw-Hill.

Lazowski, L. and Andersen, S. (1991) Self-disclosure and social perception: The impact of private, negative and extreme communications, in M. Booth-Butterfield (ed.) *Communication, Cognition and Anxiety*. Newbury Park: Sage.

Leakey, R. (1994) *The Origin of Mankind*. London: Weidenfeld and Nicolson.

Leaper, C. (2000) Gender, affiliation, assertion, and the interactive content of parent–child play, *Developmental Psychology*, 36, 381–393.

Leaper, C. (2014) Gender similarities and differences in language, in T. Holtgraves (ed.) *The Oxford Handbook of Language and Social Psychology*. Oxford: Oxford University Press.

Leaper, C. and Ayres, M. (2007) A meta-analytic review of gender variations in adults' language use: Talkativeness, affiliative speech, and assertive speech, *Personality and Social Psychology Review*, 11, 328–363.

Leaper, C. and Robnett, R. (2011) Women are more likely than men to use tentative language, aren't they? A meta-analysis testing for gender differences and moderators, *Psychology of Women Quarterly*, 35, 129–142.

Leaper, C. and Smith, T. (2004) A meta-analytic review of gender variations in children's language use: Talkativeness, affiliative speech, and assertive speech, *Developmental Psychology*, 40, 993–1027.

Leaper, C. and Valin, D. (1996) Predictors of Mexican-American mothers' and fathers' attitudes towards gender equality, *Hispanic Journal of Behavioral Sciences*, 18, 343–355.

Leary, M. (1996) *Self-presentation: Impression Management and Interpersonal Behavior*. Boulder, CO: Westview Press.

Leary, M. (2001) Towards a conceptualisation of interpersonal rejection, in M. Leary (ed.) *Interpersonal Rejection*. Oxford: Oxford University Press.

Lecheler, S., de Vreese, C. and Slothuus, R. (2009) Issue importance as a moderator of framing effects, *Communication Research*, 36, 400–425.

Lee, E. (2014) A therapist's self-disclosure and its impact on the therapy process in cross-cultural encounters: Disclosure of personal self, professional self, and/or cultural self? *Families in Society: The Journal of Contemporary Social Services*, 95, 15–23.

Lee, J. and Ciftci, A. (2014) Asian international students' socio-cultural adaptation: Influence of multicultural personality, assertiveness, academic self-efficacy, and social support, *International Journal of Intercultural Relations*, 38, 97–105.

Lee, S., Oh, S. and Jung, S. (2014) The effects of scarcity appeal on product evaluation: Consumers' cognitive resources and company reputation, *Social Behavior and Personality: An International Journal*, 42, 743–756.

Leman, P., Macedo, A., Bluschke, A. *et al.* (2011) The influence of gender and ethnicity on children's peer collaborations, *British Journal of Developmental Psychology*, 29, 131–137.

Leodoro, G. and Lynn, M. (2007) The effect of server posture on the tips of whites and blacks, *Journal of Applied Social Psychology*, 37, 201–209.

LePoire, B., Hallett, J. and Erlandson, K. (2000) An initial test of inconsistent nurturing as control theory: How partners of drug abusers assist their partners' sobriety, *Human Communication Research*, 26, 432–457.

LePoole, S. (1991) *Never Take No for an Answer: A guide to Successful Negotiating*. London: Kogan Page.

Leslie, J. and O'Reilly, M. (1999) *Behavior Analysis: Foundations and Applications to Psychology*. Amsterdam: Harwood Academic Publishers.

Lester, M. (2008) *McGraw-Hill's Essential ESL Grammar: A Handbook for Intermediate and Advanced ESL Students*. New York: McGraw-Hill.

Leventhal, H. (1970) Findings and theory in the study of fear communications, in L. Berkowitz (ed.) *Advances in Experimental Social Psychology Volume 5*. New York: Academic Press.

Levi, D. (2013) *Group Dynamics for Teams*, 4th edition. Thousand Oaks, CA: Sage.

Levine, J. (2013) Group processes: Introduction and Overview, in J. Levine (ed.) *Group Processes*. New York: Routledge.

Levine, J. and Hogg, A. (eds) (2009) *Encyclopedia of Group Processes and Intergroup Relations*. Thousand Oaks: Sage.

Levine, R. (2006) *The Power of Persuasion: How We're Bought and Sold*. Oxford: Oneworld Publications.

Levine, T. (2014) (ed.) *Encyclopedia of Deception*. Thousand Oaks, CA: Sage.

Levine, T. and McCornack, S. (2001) Behavioral adaptation, confidence, and heuristic-based explanations of the probing effect, *Human Communication Research*, 27, 471–502.

Levinson, S. (2006) Cognition at the heart of human interaction, *Discourse Studies*, 8, 85–93.

Levy, D. (1999) The last taboo, *Time*, June 28, p. 77.

Lewicki, R. (1997) Teaching negotiation and dispute resolution in Colleges of Business: The state of the practice, *Negotiation Journal*, 13, 253–269.

Lewicki, R. and Polin, B. (2013) Trust and negotiation, in M. Olekalns and W. Adair (eds) *Handbook of Research on Negotiation*, London: Edward Elgar.

Lewicki, R., Barry, B. and Saunders, D. (2014) *Negotiation: Readings, Exercise and Cases*, 7th edition. New York: McGraw-Hill.

Lewicki, R., Saunders, D., Minton, J. and Barry, B. (2007) Preface, in R. Lewicki, B. Barry and D. Saunders (eds) *Negotiation: Readings, Exercise and Cases*, 5th edition. New York: McGraw-Hill.

Lewin, K., Lippitt, R. and White, R. K. (1939) Patterns of aggressive behaviour in experimentally created social climates, *Journal of Social Psychology*, 10, 271–299.

Lewis, P. and Gallois, C. (1984) Disagreements, refusals, or negative feelings: Perception of negatively assertive messages from friends and strangers, *Behavior Therapy*, 15, 353–368.

Ley, P. (1988) *Communicating with Patients*, London: Chapman and Hall.

Leydon, G., Boulton, M., Moynihan, C., Jones, A., Mossman, J., Boudioni, M. and McPherson, K. (2000) Cancer patients' information needs and information seeking behaviour: In depth interview study, *British Medical Journal*, 320, 909–913.

Li, H., Chan, S., Mak, Y. and Lam, T. (2013) Effectiveness of a parental training programme in enhancing the parent–child relationship and reducing harsh parenting practices and parental stress in preparing children for their transition to primary school: A randomised controlled trial, *BMC Public Health*, 13, 1079 (http://www.biomedcentral.com/1471-2458/13/1079) (accessed 19 May 2016).

Liaw, S. (2004) Considerations for developing constructivist web-based learning, *International Journal of Instructional Media*, 31, 309–321.

Libby, L. and Eibach, R. (2007) How the self affects and reflects the content and subjective experience of autobiographical memory, in C. Sedikides and S. Spencer (eds) *The Self*. New York: Psychology Press.

Lickel, B., Rutchick, A., Hamilton, D. and Sherman, S. (2006) Intuitive theories of group types and relational principles, *Journal of Experimental Social Psychology*, 42, 28–39.

Lieberman, D. (2012) *Human Learning and Memory*. Cambridge: Cambridge University Press.

Lieberman, P. (1998) *Eve Spoke*: *Human Language and Human Evolution*. London: Picador.

Lievens, F. and Sackett, P. (2012) The validity of interpersonal skills assessment via situational judgment tests for predicting academic success and job performance, *Journal of Applied Psychology*, 97, 460–468.

Lightsey, O.R. and Barnes, P.W. (2007) Discrimination, attributional tendencies, generalized self-efficacy, and assertiveness as predictors of psychological distress among African Americans, *Journal of Black Psychology*, 33, 27–50.

Lin, A., Adolphs, R. and Rangel, A. (2012) Social and monetary reward learning engage overlapping neural substrates, *Social Cognitive and Affective Neuroscience*, 7, 274–281.

Lin, M., Harwood, J. and Hummert, M. (2008) Young adults' intergenerational communication schemas in Taiwan and the USA, *Journal of Language and Social Psychology*, 27, 28–50.

Lindell, A. and Lindell, K. (2014) Beauty captures the attention of the beholder, *Journal of Cognitive Psychology*, 26, 768–780.

Lindon, J. and Lindon, L. (2007) *Mastering Counselling Skills*, 2nd edition, Basingstoke: PalgraveMacMillan.

Lindsey, L. (2005) Anticipated guilt as behavioural motivation. An examination of appeals to help unknown others through bone marrow donation, *Human Communication Research*, 31, 453–481.

Linehan, M. and Egan, K. (1979) Assertion training for women, in A. Bellack and M. Hersen (eds) *Research and Practice in Social Skills Training*. New York: Plenum.

Lipkin, M. (1996) Physician–patient interaction in reproductive counseling, *Obstetrics and Gynecology*, 88, S31–S40.

Little, A. and Perett, D. (2002) Putting beauty back in the eye of the beholder, *The Psychologist*, 15, 28–32.

Little, A., Jones, B. and DeBruine, L. (2011) Facial attractiveness: Evolutionary based research, *Philosophical Transactions of the Royal Society B*, 366, 1638–1659.

Liu, J. (2014) Review of psychological study on crisis negotiation, *Cross-Cultural Communication*, 10, 12–16.

Livingstone, J., Testa, M. and VanZile-Tamsen, C. (2007) The reciprocal relationship between sexual victimization and sexual assertiveness, *Violence Against Women*, 13, 298–313.

Loewenstein, J. and Thompson, L. (2006) Learning to negotiate: Novice and experienced negotiators, in L. Thompson (ed.) *Negotiation Theory and Research*. New York: Taylor and Francis.

Loftus, E. (1975) Leading questions and the eyewitness report, *Cognitive Psychology*, 7, 560–572.

Loftus, E. (1982) Interrogating eyewitnesses – Good questions and bad, in R. Hogarth (ed.) *Question Framing and Response Consistency*. San Francisco: Jossey-Bass.

Loftus, E. (2001) Imagining the past, *The Psychologist*, 14, 584–587.

Loftus, E. (2006) Memory distortion: Problems solved and unsolved, in M. Garry and H. Hayne (eds) *Do Justice and Let the Sky Fall*. Mahwah, NJ: Lawrence Erlbaum.

Loftus, E. and Palmer, J. (1974) Reconstruction of automobile destruction: An example of the interaction between language and memory, *Journal of Verbal Learning and Verbal Behavior*, 13, 585–589.

Loftus, E. and Zanni, G. (1975) Eyewitness testimony: The influence of the wording of a question, *Bulletin of the Psychonomic Society*, 5, 86–88.

Lõhmus, M., Sundström, L. and Björklund, M. (2009) Dress for success: Human facial expressions are important signals of emotions, *Annales Zoologici Fennici*, 46, 75–80.

Long, K., Fortney, S. and Johnson, D. (2000) An observer measure of compulsive communication, *Communicaton Research Reports*, 17, 349–356.

Long, L. and Long, T. (1976) Influence of religious status and religious attire on interviewees, *Psychological Reports*, 39, 25–26.

Lord, R. and Brown, D. (2004) *Leadership Processes and Follower Self-identity*. Mahwah, NJ: Lawrence Erlbaum.

Lorinkova, N., Pearsall, M. and Sims, H. (2013) Examining the differential longitudinal performance of directive versus empowering leadership in teams, *Academy of Management Journal*, 56, 573–596.

Loshek, E. and Terrell, H. (2015) The development of the Sexual Assertiveness Questionnaire (SAQ): A comprehensive measure of sexual assertiveness for women, *The Journal of Sex Research*, 52, 1017–1027.

Loukusa, S., Ryder, N. and Leinonen, E. (2008) Answering questions and explaining answers: a study of Finnish-speaking children, *Journal of Psycholinguist Research*, 37, 219–241.

Luft, J. (1970) *Group Processes: An Introduction to Group Dynamics*. Palo Alto, CA: National Press Books.

Lundgren, D. and Rudawsky, D. (2000) Speaking one's mind or biting one's tongue: When do angered persons express or withhold feedback in transactions with male and female peers? *Social Psychology Quarterly*, 63, 253–263.

Lundqvist, L. and Dimberg, U. (1995) Facial expressions are contagious, *Journal of Psychophysiology*, 9, 203–211.

Lundsteen, S. (1971) *Listening: Its Impact on Reading and Other Language Acts*. New York: National Council of Teachers of English.

Lussier, R. and Achua, C. (2010) *Leadership: Theory, Application, and Skill Development*, 4th edition. Mason, OH: Cengage Learning.

Lytle, A., Brett, J. and Shapiro, D. (1999) The strategic use of interests, rights, and power to resolve disputes, *Negotiation Journal*, 15, 31–51.

Maag, J. (2003) *Behaviour Management: From Theoretical Implications to Practical Applications*, 2nd edition. Belmont, CA: Wadsworth.

Maaravi, Y., Pazy, A. and Ganzach, Y. (2014) Winning a battle but losing the war: On the drawbacks of using the anchoring tactic in distributive negotiations, *Judgment and Decision Making*, 9, 548–557.

MacLure, M. and Jones, L. (2009) *Becoming a Problem: How and Why Children Acquire a Reputation as 'Naughty' in the Earliest Years at School*. Economic and Social Research Council Report (http://www.esri.mmu.ac.uk/resprojects/reports/becomingaproblem.pdf) (accessed 2 October 2014).

Mader, T.F. and Mader, D.C. (1990) *Understanding One Another: Communicating Interpersonally*, 2nd edition. Madison: WCB Brown and Benchmark.

Maes, J., Weldy, T. and Icenogle, M. (1997) A managerial perspective: Oral communication competency is most important for business students in the workplace, *Journal of Business Communication*, 34, 67–80.

Maes, S. and Gebhardt, W. (2000) Self-regulation and health behaviour: The health behaviour goal model, in M. Boekaerts, P. Pintrich and M. Zeidner (eds) *Handbook of Self-regulation*. San Diego: Academic Press.

Magee, J., Galinsky, A. and Gruenfeld, D. (2007) Power, propensity to negotiate, and moving first in competitive interactions, *Personality and Social Psychology Bulletin*, 33, 200–212.

Maguire, P. (1985) Deficiencies in key interpersonal skills, in C. Kagan (ed.), *Interpersonal Skills in Nursing*. London: Croom Helm.

Maguire, P., Fairburn, S. and Fletcher, C. (1986) Consultation skills of young doctors, *British Medical Journal*, 292, 1573–1578.

Maier, M., Elliot, A., Lee, B. *et al.* (2013) The influence of red on impression formation in a job application context, *Motivation and Emotion*, 37, 389–401.

Maio, G. and Haddock, G. (2015) *The Psychology of Attitudes and Attitude Change*, 2nd edition. Thousand Oaks, CA: Sage.

Makoul, G., Zick, A. and Green, M. (2007) An evidence-based perspective on greetings in medical encounters, *Archives of Internal Medicine*, 167, 1172–1176.

Malhotra, D. and Bazerman, M. (2007) *Negotiation Genius: How to Overcome Obstacles and Achieve Brilliant Results at the Bargaining Table and Beyond*. New York: Bantam Dell.

Malone, B. and De Paulo, B. (2001) Measuring sensitivity to deception, in J. Hall and F. Bernieri (eds) *Interpersonal Sensitivity: Theory and Measurement*. Mahwah, NJ: Lawrence Erlbaum.

Maltby, J., Day, L. and Macaskill, A. (2013) *Personality, Individual Differences and Intelligence*, 3rd edition. Harlow, UK: Pearson Education.

Mann, S. and Robinson, A. (2009) Boredom in the lecture theatre: An investigation into the contributors, moderators and outcomes of boredom amongst university students, *British Educational Research Journal*, 35, 243–258.

Mannes, A. (2013) Shorn scalps and perceptions of male dominance, *Social Psychological and Personality Science*, 4, 198–205.

Mannetti, L., Pierro, A., Kruglanski, A., Taris, T. and Bezinovic, P. (2002) A cross-cultural study of the Need for Cognitive Closure Scale: Comparing its structure in Croatia, Italy, USA and The Netherlands, *British Journal of Social Psychology*, 41, 139–156.

Manthei, R. (1997) *Counselling: The Skills of Finding Solutions to Problems*. London: Routledge.

Manusov, V. and Patterson, M. (eds) (2006) *The Sage Handbook of Nonverbal Communication*. Thousand Oaks, CA: Sage.

Marchbank, J. and Letherby, G. (2014) *Introduction to Gender: Social Science Perspectives*, 2nd edition. Abingdon, Oxon: Routledge.

Margo, A. (1997) Why Barbie is perceived as beautiful, *Perceptual and Motor Skills*, 85, 363–374.

Margutti, P. (2006) 'Are you human beings?' Order and knowledge construction through questioning in primary classroom interaction, *Linguistics and Education*, 17, 313–346.

Marisi, D.Q. and Helmy, K. (1984) Intratask integration as a function of age and verbal praise, *Perceptual and Motor Skills*, 58, 936–939.

Markham, R. and Wang, L. (1996) Recognition of emotion by Chinese and Australian children, *Journal of Cross-Cultural Psychology*, 27, 616–643.

Marlowe, F. and Westman, A. (2001) Preferred waist-to-hip ratio and ecology, *Personality and Individual Differences*, 30, 481–489.

Marta, S., Leritz, L. and Mumford, M. (2005) Leadership skills and the group performance: Situational demands, behavioral requirements, and planning, *The Leadership Quarterly*, 16, 97–120.

Martin, C. and Ruble, D. (2004) Children's search for gender cues: Cognitive perspectives on gender development, *Current Direction in Psychological Science*, 13, 67–70.

Martin, D. (1997) Slaughtering a sacred cow: The eyebrow flash is not a universal social greeting, *Dissertation Abstracts International: The Sciences and Engineering*, 58 (5-B), 2751.

Martin, D. and Gayle, B. (2004) Humour works: Communication style and humour functions in manager/subordinate relationships, *Southern Communication Journal*, 69, 206–222.

Martin, G. and Pear, J. (2015) *Behavior Modification: What It Is and How to Do It*, 10th edition. Upper Saddle River, NJ: Pearson.

Martin, G., Carlson, N. and Buskist, W. (2013) *Psychology*, 5th edition. Harlow, Essex: Pearson.

Martin, J. (1970) *Explaining, Understanding and Teaching*. New York: McGraw-Hill.

Martinovski, B. (ed.) (2015) *Emotion in Group Decision and Negotiation*. Dordrecht, The Netherlands: Springer.

Martinovski, B., Traum, D. and Marcella, S. (2007) Rejection of empathy in negotiation, *Group Decision and Negotiation*, 16, 61–76.

Marulis, L. and Newman, S. (2010) The effects of vocabulary intervention on young children's word learning: A meta-analysis, *Review of Educational Research*, 80, 300–335.

Mastenbroek, W. (1989) *Negotiate*. Oxford: Basil Blackwell.

Masters, W. and Johnson, V. (1970) *Human Sexual Inadequacy*. Boston: Little, Brownand.

Mateos, P. (2014) *Names, Ethnicity and Populations: Tracing Identity in Space*. Berlin: Springer.

Mathews, A., Derlega, V. and Morrow, J. (2006) What is highly personal information and how is it related to self-disclosure decision-making? The perspective of college students, *Communication Research Reports*, 23, 85–92.

Matlin, M. and Stang, D. (1978) *The Pollyanna Principle: Selectivity in Language, Memory, and Thought*. Cambridge, MA: Schenkman.

Matsumoto, D. (2006) Culture and nonverbal behavior, in V. Manusov and M. Patterson (eds) *The Sage Handbook of Nonverbal Communication*. Thousand Oaks, CA: Sage.

Matsumoto, D. and Hwang, H. (2013a) Culture influences on nonverbal behavior, in D. Matsumoto, M. Frank and H. Hwang (eds) *Nonverbal Communication: Science and Applications*. Thousand Oaks, CA: Sage.

Matsumoto, D. and Hwang, H. (2013b) Cultural similarities and differences in emblematic gestures, *Journal of Nonverbal Behavior*, 37, 1–27.

Matsumoto, D. and Willingham, B. (2009) Spontaneous facial expressions of emotion of congenitally and noncongenitally blind individuals, *Journal of Personality and Social Psychology*, 96, 1–10.

Matsumoto, D., Frank, M. and Hwang, H. (2013) Reading people: Introduction to the world of nonverbal behavior, in D. Matsumoto, M. Frank and H. Hwang (eds) *Nonverbal Communication: Science and Applications*. Thousand Oaks, CA: Sage.

Matsushima, R., Shomi, K. and Kuhlman, D. (2000) Shyness in self-disclosure mediated by social skill, *Psychological Reports*, 86, 33–338.

Mayer, R. (2014) Multimedia instruction, in J. Spector, M. Merrill, J. Elen *et al.* (eds) *Handbook of Research on Educational Communications and Technology*. New York: Springer.

Mayer, R. and Jackson, J. (2005) The case for coherence in scientific explanations: Quantitative details can hurt qualitative learning, *Journal of Experimental Psychology*, 11, 13–18.

Mayer, R., Fennell, S., Farmer, L. and Campbell, J. (2004) A personalization effect in multimedia learning: Students learn better when words are in conversational style rather than formal style, *Journal of Educational Psychology*, 96, 389–395.

Mazei, J., Hüffmeier, J., Freund, P. *et al.* (2015) A meta-analysis on gender differences in negotiation outcomes and their moderators, *Psychological Bulletin*, 141, 85–104.

McAllister, D. (1995) Affect- and cognition-based trust as foundations for interpersonal cooperation in organizations, *Academy of Management Journal*, 38, 24–59.

McBride, M. and Wahl, S. (2005) 'To say or not to say': Management of privacy boundaries in the classroom, *Texas Speech Communication Journal*, 30, 8–22.

McCall, C., Blascovich, J., Young, A. and Persky, S. (2009) Proxemic behaviors as predictors of aggression towards Black (but not White) males in an immersive virtual environment, *Social Influence*, 34, 138–154.

McCallum, S. and O'Connell, D. (2009) Social capital and leadership development: Building stronger leadership through enhanced relational skills, *Leadership and Organization Development Journal*, 30, 152–166.

McCann, K. and McKenna, H. (1993) An examination of touch between nurses and elderly patients in a continuing care setting in Northern Ireland, *Journal of Advanced Nursing*, 18, 838–846.

McCartan, P. (2001) *The Identification and Analysis of Assertive Behaviours in Nurses,* unpublished PhD thesis. Jordanstown: University of Ulster.

McCartan, P. and Hargie, O. (2004a) Assertiveness and caring: Are they compatible? *Journal of Clinical Nursing*, 13, 707–713.

McCartan, P. and Hargie, O. (2004b) Effects of nurses' sex-role orientation on positive and negative assertion, *Nursing and Health Sciences*, 6, 45–49.

McCarthy, P. and Hatcher, C. (2002) *Presentation Skills: The Essential Guide for Students*. London: Sage.

McClave, E. (2000) Linguistic functions of head movements in the context of speech, *Journal of Pragmatics*, 32, 855–878.

McConnell, A. and Strain, L. (2007) Content and structure of the self-concept, in C. Sedikides and S. Spencer (eds) *The Self*. New York: Psychology Press.

McCroskey, J., Richmond, V. and McCroskey, L. (2006) Nonverbal communication in instructional contexts, in V. Manusov and M. Patterson (eds) *The Sage Handbook of Nonverbal Communication*. Thousand Oaks, CA: Sage.

McDaniel, R. (1994) *Scared Speechless: Public Speaking Step by Step*. Thousand Oaks, CA: Sage.

McDaniel, S., Beckman, H., Morse, D., Silberman, J., Seaburn, D. and Epstein R. (2007) Physician self-disclosure in primary care visits: Enough about you, what about me? *Archives of Internal Medicine*, 167, 1321–1326.

McElroy, J., Summers, J. and Moore, K. (2014) The effect of facial piercing on perceptions of job applicants, *Organizational Behavior and Human Decision Processes*, 125, 26–38.

McEwan, H. (1992) Teaching and the interpretation of texts, *Educational Theory*, 42, 59–68.

McFadyen, R. (1996) Gender, status and 'powerless' speech: Interactions of students and lecturers, *British Journal of Social Psychology*, 35, 353–367.

McFall, M., Winnett, R., Bordewick, M. and Bornstein, P. (1982) Nonverbal components in the communication of assertiveness, *Behavior Modification*, 6, 121–140.

McGinn, K. (2006) Relationships and negotiations in context, in L. Thompson (ed.) *Negotiation Theory and Research*. New York: Taylor and Francis.

McGuire, W.J. (1981) Theoretical foundations of campaigns, in R. Rice and W. Paisley (eds) *Public Communication Campaigns*. Newbury Park: Sage.

McInnes, A., Humphries, T., Hogg-Johnson, S. and Tannock, R. (2003) Listening comprehension and working memory are impaired in attention-deficit hyperactivity disorder irrespective of language impairment, *Journal of Abnormal Child Psychology*, 31, 427–443.

McKay, M., Davis, M. and Fanning, P. (2009) *Messages: The Communication Skills Book*. Oakland, CA: New Harbinger.

McKay, R., Langdon, R. and Coltheart, M. (2006) Need for closure, jumping to conclusions, and decisiveness in delusion-prone individuals, *The Journal of Nervous and Mental Disease*, 194, 422–426.

McKenna, K. and Bargh, J. (2000) Plan 9 from cyberspace: The implications of the internet for personality and social psychology, *Personality and Social Psychology Review*, 4, 57–75.

McLaughlin, M., Cody, M. and Read, S. (eds) (1992) *Explaining One's Self to Others*. Mahwah, NJ: Lawrence Erlbaum.

McLean, A. (2009) *Motivating Every Learner*. London: Sage.

McNeill, D. (2005) *Gesture and Thought*. Chicago: University of Chicago Press.

McRae, B. (1998) *Negotiating and Influencing Skills*. Thousand Oaks, CA: Sage.

McSherry, R. and Pearce, P. (2011) *Clinical Governance: A Guide to Implementation for Healthcare Professionals*, 3rd edition. Chichester: Wiley.

Medisauskaite, A., Kamau, C. and Endriulaitiene, A. (2014) Activation of the 'What is beautiful is good' stereotype during job candidate selection: What is the role of the recruiter's own characteristics? *European Work and Organizational Psychology in Practice*, 6, 6–25.

Meehan, A. (2013) *The Role of Internal Communication in the Management of Organizational Uncertainty*, unpublished PhD thesis. Jordanstown: University of Ulster.

Mehl, M., Vazire, S., Ramírez-Esparza, N., Slatcher, R. and Pennebaker, J. (2007) Are women really more talkative than men? *Science*, 317(5834), 82.

Mehrabian, A. (2007) *Nonverbal Communication*. Piscataway, NJ: Aldine Transaction.

Mehrabian, A. and Blum, J. (1997) Physical appearance, attraction, and the mediating role of emotions, *Current Psychology: Developmental, Learning, Personality, Social*, 16, 20–42.

Melamed, J. and Bozionelos, N. (1992) Managerial promotion and height, *Psychological Reports*, 71, 587–593.

Memon, A. and Bull, R. (eds) (1999) *Handbook of the Psychology of Interviewing*. Chichester: Wiley.

Menzel, K. and Carrell, L. (1994) The relationship between preparation and performance in public speaking, *Communication Education*, 43, 17–26.

Merbaum, M. (1963) The conditioning of affective self-references by three classes of generalized reinforcers, *Journal of Personality*, 31, 179–191.

Merrill, A. and Afifi, T. (2012) Examining the bidirectional nature of topic avoidance and relationship dissatisfaction: The moderating role of communication skills, *Communication Monographs*, 79, 499–521.

Messer, D. (1995) *The Development of Communication: From Social Interaction to Language*. Chichester: Wiley.

Metcalf, L., Bird, A., Peterson, M., Shankarmahesh, M. and Lituchy, T. (2007) Cultural influences in negotiations: A four country comparative analysis, *International Journal of Cross Cultural Management*, 7, 147–168.

Metts, S. and Cupach, W. (2008) Face theory, in L. Baxter and D. Braithwaite (eds) *Engaging Theories in Interpersonal Communication: Multiple Perspectives*. Thousand Oaks, CA: Sage.

Metts, S. and Mikucki, S. (2008) The emotional landscape of romantic relationship initiation, in S. Sprecher, A. Wenzel and J. Harvey (eds) *Handbook of Relationship Initiation*. New York: Psychology Press.

Meyer, J. (1997) Cognitive influences on the ability to address interaction goals, in J. Greene (ed.) *Message Production: Advances in Communication Theory*. Mahwah, NJ: Lawrence Erlbaum.

Meyer, J. (2000) Humor as a double-edged sword: Four functions of humor in communication, *Communication Theory,* 10, 310–331.

Meyer, W., Miggag, W. and Engler, U. (1986) Some effects of praise and blame on perceived ability and affect, *Social Cognition,* 4, 293–308.

Miceli, M., Near, J. and Dworkin, T. (2008) *Whistleblowing in Organisations*. New York: Routledge.

Michalak, J., Troje, N., Fischer, J., Vollmar, P., Heidenreich, T. and Schulte, D. (2009) Embodiment of sadness and depression – Gait patterns associated with dysphoric mood, *Psychosomatic Medicine*, 71, 580–587.

Miczo, N., Segrin, C. and Allspach, L. (2001) Relationship between nonverbal sensitivity, encoding, and relational satisfaction, *Communication Reports,* 14, 39–48.

Migge, B. (2005) Greeting and social change, in S. Muhleisen and B. Migge (eds) *Politeness and Face in Caribbean Creoles*. Amsterdam: John Benjamins.

Milakovich, J. (1999) Differences between therapists who touch and those who do not, in E. Smith, P. Clance and S. Imes (eds) *Touch in Psychotherapy: Theory, Research, and Practice*. New York: Guilford.

Milazzo, C. and Mattes, K. (2016) Looking good for election day: Does attractiveness predict electoral success in Britain? *The British Journal of Politics and International Relations*, DOI: 10.1111/1467-856X.12074.

Milburn, T. (1998) Psychology, negotiation and peace, *Applied Psychology and Preventive Psychology*, 7, 109–119.

Miles, E. (2013) Developing strategies for asking questions in negotiation, *Negotiation Journal*, 29, 383–412.

Millar, R. and Gallagher, M. (1997) The selection interview, in O. Hargie (ed.) *The Handbook of Communication Skills*, 2nd edition. London: Routledge.

Millar, R. and Gallagher, M. (2000) The interview approach, in O. Hargie and D. Tourish (eds) *Handbook of Communication Audits for Organisations*. London: Routledge.

Millar, R. and Tracey, A. (2006) The employment interview, in O. Hargie (ed.) *The Handbook of Communication Skills*, 3rd edition. London: Routledge.

Millar, R. and Tracey, A. (2009) The employment interview, in O. Hargie and D. Tourish (eds) *Auditing Organizational Communication: A Handbook of Research, Theory and Practice*. London: Routledge.

Millar, R., Crute, V. and Hargie, O. (1992) *Professional Interviewing*. London: Routledge.

Miller, A. and Hom, H. (1997) Conceptions of ability and the interpretation of praise, blame and material rewards, *The Journal of Experimental Education*, 65, 163–177.

Miller, G. (1956) The magic number seven, plus or minus two, *Psychological Review*, 63, 81–96.

Miller, K., Cooke, L., Tsang, J. and Morgan, F. (1992) Nature and impact of positive and boastful disclosures for women and men, *Human Communication Research*, 18, 364–369.

Miller, L. and Kenny, D. (1986) Reciprocity of self-disclosure at the individual and dyadic levels: A social relations analysis, *Journal of Personality and Social Psychology*, 50, 713–719.

Miller, L., Berg, J. and Archer, R. (1983) Openers: Individuals who elicit intimate self-disclosure, *Journal of Personality and Social Psychology*, 44, 1234–1244.

Miller, L., Cody, M. and McLaughlin, M. (1994) Situations and goals as fundamental constructs in interpersonal communication research, in M. Knapp and G. Miller (eds) *Handbook of Interpersonal Communication Skills*, 2nd edition. Thousand Oaks, CA: Sage.

Miller, P. (2000) *Nonverbal Communication in the Classroom*. New York: Miller and Associates.

Miller, P., Kozu, J. and Davis, A. (2001) Social influence, empathy, and prosocial behavior in cross-cultural perspective, in W. Wosinska, R. Cialdini, D. Barrett and J. Reykowski (eds) *The Practice of Social Influence in Multiple Cultures*. Mahwah, NJ: Lawrence Erlbaum.

Miller, S., Brody, D. and Summerton, J. (1988) Styles of coping with threat: Implications for health, *Journal of Personality and Social Psychology*, 54, 142048.

Miller, W. and Rollnick, S. (2013) *Motivational Interviewing: Helping People Change*, 3rd edition. New York: Guilford Press.

Mills, H. (1991) *Negotiate: The Art of Winning*. Aldershot: Gower.

Mills, M. (1983) Adolescents' self-disclosure in individual and group theme-centred modelling, reflecting and probing interviews, *Psychological Reports*, 53, 691–701.

Milne, R. (1999) Interviewing children with learning disabilities, in A. Memon and R. Bull (eds) *Handbook of the Psychology of Interviewing*. Chichester: Wiley.

Miltz, R. (1972) *Development and Evaluation of a Manual for Improving Teachers' Explanation, Technical Report 26*. Stanford: Stanford University Center for Research and Development in Teaching.

Mitchell, M. (2000) Able but not motivated: The relative effects of happy and sad mood on persuasive message processing, *Communication Monographs*, 67, 215–226.

Mitchell, M., Cropanzano, R. and Quisenberry, D. (2012) Social exchange theory, exchange resources, and interpersonal relationships: A modest resolution of theoretical difficulties, in K. Törnblom and A. Kazemi (eds) *Handbook of Social Resource Theory: Theoretical Extensions, Empirical Insights, and Social Applications*. New York: Springer.

Mittendorff, K., Geijsel, F., Hoeve, A., de Laat, M. and Nieuwenhuis, L. (2006) Communities of practice as stimulating forces for collective learning, *Journal of Workplace Learning*, 18, 298–312.

Mizes, J. (1985) The use of contingent reinforcement in the treatment of a conversion disorder: A multiple baseline study, *Journal of Behavior Therapy and Experimental Psychiatry*, 16, 341–345.

Mnookin, R. and Susskind, L. (eds) (1999) *Negotiating on Behalf of Others*. Thousand Oaks, CA: Sage.

Mnookin, R., Peppet, S. and Tulumello, A. (1996) The tension between empathy and assertiveness, *Negotiation Journal*, 12, 217–230.

Mogg, K., Millar, N. and Bradley, B. (2000) Biases in eye movements to threatening facial expressions in generalized anxiety disorder and depressive disorder, *Journal of Abnormal Psychology*, 109, 695–704.

Mojzisch, A., Schulz-Hardt, S., Kerschreiter, R. and Frey, D. (2008) Combined effects of knowledge about others' opinions and anticipation of group discussion on confirmatory information search, *Small Group Research*, 39, 203–223.

Mokros, H. and Aakhus, M. (2002) From information-seeking behavior to meaning engagement practice: Implications for communication theory and research, *Human Communication Research*, 28, 298–312.

Molinari, L., Mameli, C. and Gnisci, A. (2013) A sequential analysis of classroom discourse in Italian primary schools: The many faces of the IRF pattern, *British Journal of Educational Psychology*, 83, 414–430.

Monahan, J. (1998) I don't know it but I like you: The influence of nonconscious affect on person perception, *Human Communication Research*, 24, 480–500.

Monahan, D. (2014) Eye contact, in T. Levine (ed.) *Encyclopedia of Deception*. Thousand Oaks, CA: Sage.

Monarth, H. and Kase, L. (2007) *The Confident Speaker: Beat Your Nerves and Communicate at Your Best in Any Situation*. New York: McGraw-Hill.

Mondloch, C., Nelson, N. and Horner, M. (2013) Asymmetries of influence: Differential effects of body postures on perceptions of emotional facial expressions, *PLoS ONE*, 8(9), e73605.

Mongeau, P. (1998) Another look at fear-arousing persuasive appeals, in M. Allen and R. Preiss (eds) *Persuasion: Advances through Meta-analysis*. Cresskill, NJ: Hampton Press.

Montague, E., Chen, P., Xu, J. *et al.* (2013) Nonverbal interpersonal interactions in clinical encounters and patient perceptions of empathy, *Journal of Participatory Medicine*, 5 (http://www.jopm.org/evidence/research/2013/08/14/nonverbal-interpersonal-interactions-in-clinical-encounters-and-patient-perceptions-of-empathy/) (accessed 7 March 2015).

Montepare, J., Koff, E., Zaitchik, D. and Albert, M. (1999) The use of body movements and gestures as cues to emotions in younger and older adults, *Journal of Nonverbal Behavior*, 23, 133–152.

Montgomery, D., Wiesman, D. and DeCaro, P. (2001) Towards a code of ethics for organizational communication professional: A working proposal, *American Communication Journal* 5(1) (http://ac-journal.org/journal/vol5/iss1/special/montgomery.htm) (accessed 2 October 2014).

Moody, J., Stewart, B. and Bolt-Lee, C. (2002) Showcasing the skilled business graduate: Expanding the tool kit, *Business Communication Quarterly*, 65, 21–33.

Moon, Y. (2000) Intimate exchanges: Using computers to elicit self-disclosure from consumers, *Journal of Consumer Research*, 26, 323–339.

Moons, W., Mackie, D. and Garcia-Marques, T. (2009) The impact of repetition-induced familiarity on agreement with weak and strong arguments, *Journal of Personality and Social Psychology*, 96, 32–44.

Moore, K. (2005) Become a better communicator by keeping your mouth shut, *Journal for Quality and Participation*, 28, 8–10.

Moors, A. and De Houwer, J. (2007) What is automaticity? An analysis of its component features and their interrelations, in J. Bargh (ed.) *Social Psychology and the Unconscious: The Automaticity of Higher Mental Processes*. New York: Psychology Press.

Moran, S. and Ritov, I. (2007) Experience in integrative negotiations: What needs to be learned? *Journal of Experimental Social Psychology*, 43, 77–90.

Morgan, N. and Saxton, J. (2006) *Asking Better Questions*, 2nd edition. Markham, ON: Pembroke Publishers.

Morley, I. (1981) Negotiating and bargaining, in M. Argyle (ed.) *Social Skills and Work*. London: Methuen.

Morley, I. (2006) Negotiation and bargaining, in O. Hargie (ed.) *The Handbook of Communication Skills*, 3rd edition. London: Routledge.

Morley, I. and Hosking, D. (1986) The skills of leadership, in G. Debus and H. Schrioff (eds) *The Psychology of Work and Organization*. North Holland: Elsevier Science.

Morokoff, P., Quina, K., Harlow, L., Whitmire, L., Grimley, D., Gibson, P. and Burkholder, G. (1997) Sexual Assertiveness Scale (SAS) for women: Development and validation, *Journal of Personality and Social Psychology*, 73, 790–804.

Morris, M., Larrick, R. and Su, S. (1999) Misperceiving negotiation counterparts: When situationally determined bargaining behaviours are attributed to personality traits, *Journal of Personality and Social Psychology*, 77, 52–67.

Morris, M., Podolny, J. and Ariel, S. (2001) Culture, norms, and obligations: Cross-national differences in patterns of interpersonal norms and felt obligations toward coworkers, in W. Wosinska, R. Cialdini, D. Barrett and J. Reykowski (eds) *The Practice of Social Influence in Multiple Cultures*, Mahwah, NJ: Lawrence Erlbaum.

Morrison, E., Morris, P. and Bard, K. (2013) The stability of facial attractiveness: Is it what you've got or what you do with it? *Journal of Nonverbal Behavior*, 37, 59–67.

Morrison, J. (2008) *The First Interview*, 3rd edition. New York: Guilford.

Morrow, N. and Hargie, O. (2001) Effective communication, in K. Taylor and G. Harding (eds) *Pharmacy Practice*. London: Taylor and Francis.

Morrow, N., Hargie, O., Donnelly, H. and Woodman, C. (1993) Why do you ask? A study of questioning behaviour in community pharmacist–client consultations, *International Journal of Pharmacy Practice*, 2, 90–94.

Mortensen, K. (2008) *Persuasion I.Q.* New York: AMACOM.

Moskowitz, G. (2012) The representation and regulation of goals, in H. Aarts and A. Elliott (eds) *Goal-directed Behavior*. New York: Taylor and Francis.

Moskowitz, G. and Grant, H. (2009) *The Psychology of Goals*. New York: Guilford.

Motley, M. (1992) Mindfulness in solving communicators' dilemmas, *Communication Monographs*, 59, 306–313.

Movius, H., Matsuura, M., Yan, J. and Kim, D. (2006) Tailoring the mutual gains approach for negotiations with partners in Japan, China, and Korea, *Negotiation Journal*, 22, 389–435.

Moyers, T., Martin, T., Catley, D., Harris, K. and Ahluwalia, J. (2003) Assessing the integrity of motivational interviewing interventions: Reliability of the Motivational Interviewing Skills Code, *Behavioural and Cognitive Psychotherapy*, 31, 177–184.

Muczyk, J. and Reimann, B. (1987) The case of directive leadership, *Academy of Management Executive*, 1, 301–311.

Mudrack, P. and Farrell, G. (1995) An examination of functional role behaviour and its consequences for individuals in group settings, *Small Group Research*, 26, 542–571.

Mulac, A. (2006) The gender-linked language effect: Do language differences really make a difference? in K. Dindia and D. Canary (eds) *Sex Differences and Similarities in Communication*, 2nd edition. Mahwah, NJ: Lawrence Erlbaum.

Mulac, A., Bradac, J. and Gibbons, P. (2001) Empirical support for the gender-as-culture hypothesis: An intercultural analysis of male/female language differences, *Human Communication Research*, 27, 121–152.

Müller, R. and Turner, J. (2007) Matching the project manager's leadership style to project type, *International Journal of Project Management*, 25, 21–32.

Mumford, T., Campion, M. and Morgeson, F. (2007) The leadership skills strataplex: Leadership skill requirements across organizational levels, *The Leadership Quartlerly*, 18, 154–166.

Munro, I. and Randall, J. (2007) I don't know what I'm doing, how about you? Discourse and identity in practitioners dealing with the survivors of childhood sexual abuse, *Organization*, 14, 887–907.

Munter, M. (2000) *Guide to Managerial Communication*, 5th edition. Upper Saddle River, NJ: Prentice Hall.

Murray, J. (1990) Understanding competing theories of negotiation, in I. Asherman and S. Asherman (eds) *The Negotiating Sourcebook*. Amherst, MA: Human Resource Development Press.

Murtagh, L. (2014) The motivational paradox of feedback: Teacher and student perceptions, *Curriculum Journal*, 25, 516–541.

Muthusamy, N., Levine, T. and Weber, R. (2009) Scaring the already scared: Some problems with HIV/Aids fear appeals in Namibia, *Journal of Communication*, 59, 317–344.

Myers, D. (2008) *Social Psychology*, 9th edition. Boston: McGraw-Hill.

Myers, S. and Bryant, L.(2008) Emerging adult siblings' use of verbally aggressive messages as hurtful messages, *Communication Quarterly*, 56, 268–283.

Nagata, D., Nay, W. and Seidman, E. (1983) Nonverbal and verbal content behaviors in the prediction of interviewer effectiveness, *Journal of Counseling Psychology*, 30, 83–86.

Napier, R. and Gershenfeld, M. (2004) *Groups: Theory and Experience*, 7th edition. Boston, MA: Houghton Mifflin.

Neale, M. and Fragale, A. (2006) Social cognition, attribution, and perception in negotiation: The role of uncertainty in shaping negotiation processes and outcomes, in L. Thompson (ed.) *Negotiation Theory and Research*. New York: Taylor and Francis.

Nelson, N., Bronstein, I., Shacham, R. and Ben-Ari, R. (2015) The power to oblige: Power, gender, negotiation behaviors, and their consequences, *Negotiation and Conflict Management Research*, 8, 1–24.

Nelson, T. (ed.) (2009) *Handbook of Prejudice, Stereotyping and Discrimination*. Hove: Psychology Press.

Nelson-Gray, R., Haas, J., Romand, B., Herbert, J. and Herbert, D. (1989) Effects of open ended versus close ended questions on interviewees' problem related statements, *Perceptual and Motor Skills*, 69, 903–911.

Nelson-Jones, R. (1996) *Effective Thinking Skills*. London: Cassell.

Nelson-Jones, R. (2014) *Practical Counselling and Helping Skills*, 6th edition. London: Sage.

Neuberg, S., Judice, T. and West, S. (1997) What the Need for Closure Scale measures and what it does not: Toward differentiating among related epistemic motives, *Journal of Personality and Social Psychology*, 72, 1396–1412.

Newman, B. and Newman, P. (2007) *Theories of Human Development*. Mahwah, NJ: Lawrence Erlbaum.

Newton, M. (2002) *Savage Girls and Wild Boys: A History of Feral Children*, London: Faber.

Nguyen, M., Bin, Y. and Campbell, A. (2012) Comparing online and offline self-disclosure: A systematic review, *Cyberpsychology, Behavior, and Social Networking*, 15, 103–111.

Nicholas, L. (2008) *Introduction to Psychology*, 2nd edition. Cape Town, South Africa: Juta.

Nichols, R. (1947) Listening: Questions and problems, *Quarterly Journal of Speech*, 33, 83–86.

Niederle, N. and Vesterlund, L. (2008) Gender differences in competition, *Negotiation Journal*, 24, 447–463.

Niikura, R. (1999a) The psychological processes underlying Japanese assertive behavior: Comparison of Japanese with Americans, Malaysians and Filipinos, *International Journal of Intercultural Relations*, 23, 47–76.

Niikura, R. (1999b) Assertiveness among Japanese, Malaysian, Filipino, and U.S. white-collar workers, *The Journal of Social Psychology*, 139, 690–699.

Nix, J., Lohr, J. and Mosesso, L. (1983) The relationship of sex-role characteristics to self-report and role-play measures of assertiveness in women, *Behavioral Assessment*, 6, 89–93.

Noar, S., Harrington, N. and Aldrich, R. (2009) The role of message tailoring in the development of persuasive health communication messages, in C. Beck (ed.) *Communication Yearbook 33*. New York: Routledge.

Noller, P. (1980) Gaze in married couples, *Journal of Nonverbal Behavior*, 5, 115–129.

Noller, P. (2005) Behavioral coding of visual affect behavior, in V. Manuslov (ed.) *The Sourcebook of Nonverbal Measures: Going Beyond Words*. London, Routledge.

Northouse, L. and Northouse, P. (1998) *Health Communication: Strategies for Health Professionals*, 3rd edition. Englewood Cliffs, NJ: Prentice Hall.

Northouse, P. (2009) *Introduction to Leadership: Concepts and Practice.* Thousand Oaks, CA: Sage.

Northouse, P. (2013) *Leadership: Theory and Practice*, 6th edition. Thousand Oaks, CA: Sage.

Norton, R.W. (1983) *Communicator Style: Theory, Applications and Measures*. Beverly Hills, CA: Sage.

Nussbaum, J. and Coupland, J. (eds) (2004) *Handbook of Communication and Ageing Research*, 2nd edition. Mahwah, NJ: Lawrence Erlbaum.

Oakes, P., Haslam, A. and Turner, J. (1994) *Stereotypes and Social Reality*. Oxford: Blackwell.

O'Connor, D., Ashley, L., Jones, F. and Ferguson, E. (2014) Maladaptive rumination moderates the effects of written emotional disclosure on ambulatory blood pressure levels in females, *Health Psychology and Behavioral Medicine: An Open Access Journal*, 2, 1067–1077.

O'Connor, E. and Simms, C. (1990) Self-revelation and manipulation: The effects of sex and machiavellianism on self-disclosure, *Social Behaviour and Personality*, 18, 95–100.

Oettingen, G. and Gollwitzer, P. (2001) Goal setting and goal striving, in A. Tesser and N. Schwarz (eds), *Blackwell Handbook of Social Psychology: Intraindividual Processes*. Malden, MA: Blackwell.

Oettingen, G., Bulgarella, C., Henderson, M. and Gollwitzer, P. (2004) The self-regulation of goal pursuit, in R. Wright, J. Greenberg and S. Brehm (eds), *Motivational Analyses of Social Behavior*. Mahwah, NJ: Lawrence Erlbaum.

Office Angels (2000) *Forget Kissing…Everyone's Busy Telling!* London: Office Angels.

Office of the Health Services Commissioner (2008) *Annual Report*. Victoria, Australia (http://www.health.vic.gov.au/hsc/downloads/annrep08.pdf) (accessed 2 October 2014).

Ogliastri, E. and Quintanilla, C. (2016) Building cross-cultural negotiation prototypes in Latin American contexts from foreign executives' perceptions, *Journal of Business Research*, 69, 452–458.

Oguchi, T (*1991*) Goal-based analysis of willingness of self-disclosure, *Japanese Psychological Research*, 33, 180–187.

O'Hair, D., Friedrich, G. and Dixon, L. (2011) *Strategic Communication in Business and the Professions*, 7th edition. Boston, MA: Ally and Bacon.

Ohata, K. (2005) Auditory short-term memory in L2 listening comprehension processes, *Journal of Language and Learning*, 5, 21–28.

Ohme, R. (2001) Social influence in media: Culture and antismoking advertising, in W. Wosinska, R. Cialdini, D. Barrett and J. Reykowski (eds) *The Practice of Social Influence in Multiple Cultures*. Mahwah, NJ: Lawrence Erlbaum.

Okanda, M. and Itakura, S. (2008) Children in Asian cultures say yes to yes–no questions: Common and cultural differences between Vietnamese and Japanese children, *International Journal of Behavioral Development*, 32, 131–136.

O'Keefe, D. (2002) *Persuasion: Theory and Research*, 2nd edition. Thousand Oaks, CA: Sage.

O'Keefe, D. (2006) Persuasion, in O. Hargie (ed.) *The Handbook of Communication Skills*, 3rd edition. London: Routledge.

O'Keefe, D. and Hale, S. (1998) The door-in-the-face influence strategy: A random effects meta-analytic review, in M. Roloff (ed.) *Communication Yearbook 21*. Thousand Oaks, CA: Sage.

O'Keefe, D. and Hale, S. (2001) An odds-ratio-based meta-analysis of research on the door-in-the-face influence strategy, *Communication Reports*, 14, 31–38.

O'Keefe, D. and Jensen, J. (2009) The relative persuasiveness of gain-framed and loss-framed messages for encouraging disease detection behaviors: A meta-analytic review, *Journal of Communication*, 59, 296–316.

Okuyama, A., Wagner, C. and Bijnen, B. (2014) How we can enhance nurses' assertiveness: A literature review, *Journal of Nursing Care*, 3(5) (http://dx.doi.org/10.4172/2167-1168.1000194) (accessed 23 April 2015).

O'Leary, M. and Gallois, C. (1999) The last ten turns in conversations between strangers, in L. Guerrero, J. DeVito and M. Hecht (eds) *The Nonverbal Communication Reader: Classic and Contemporary Readings Disclosures*, 2nd edition. Prospect Heights, IL: Waveland.

Olekalns, M. and Adair, W. (2013) The complexity of negotiation: From the individual to the complex, and what lies between, in M. Olekalns and W. Adair (eds) *Handbook of Research on Negotiation*. London: Edward Elgar.

Olekalns, M. and Druckman, D. (2014) With feeling: How emotions shape negotiation, *Negotiation Journal*, 30, 455–478.

Olekalns, M. and Smith, P. (2001) Understanding optimal outcomes: The role of strategy sequences in competitive negotiations, *Human Communication Research*, 26, 527–557.

Olekalns, M. and Smith, P. (2012) Psychological aspects of negotiating strategies and processes, in D. Christie (ed.) *Encyclopedia of Peace Psychology*. Hoboken, NJ: Wiley Blackwell.

Olekalns, M., Horan, C. and Smith, P. (2014) Maybe it's right, maybe it's wrong: Structural and social determinants of deception in negotiation, *Journal of Business Ethics*, 122, 89–102.

Olivola, C., Eubanks, D. and Lovelace, J.B. (2014) The many (distinctive) faces of leadership: Inferring leadership domain from facial appearance, *The Leadership Quarterly*, 5, 817–834.

Omarzu, J. (2000) Disclosure decision model: Determining how and when individuals will self-disclose, *Personality and Social Psychology Review*, 4, 174–185.

Ong, L., de Haes, J., Hoos, A. and Lammes, F. (1995) Doctor–patient communication: A review of the literature, *Social Science and Medicine*, 40, 903–918.

Orbe, M. and Bruess, C. (2005) *Contemporary Issues in Interpersonal Communication*. Los Angeles: Roxbury.

Orlich, D., Harder, R., Callahan, R. *et al.* (2013) *Teaching Strategies: A Guide to Effective Instruction*, 10th edition. Belmont, CA: Wadworth Cengage Learning.

Orrego, V., Smith, S., Mitchell, M., Johnson, A., Yun, K. and Greenberg, B. (2000) Disclosure and privacy issues on television talk shows, in S. Petronio (ed.) *Balancing the Secrets of Private Disclosures*. Mahwah, NJ: Lawrence Erlbaum.

Oshima, S. (2014) Achieving consensus through professionalized head nods: The role of nodding in service encounters in Japan, *International Journal of Business Communication*, 51, 31–57.

Oskay-Özcelik, G., Lehmacher, W., Könsgen, D. *et al.* (2007) Breast cancer patients' expectations in respect of the physician–patient relationship and treatment management results of a survey of 617 patients, *Annals of Oncology*, 18, 479–484.

Osman, M. (2015) Does our unconscious rule? *The Psychologist*, 28, 114–117.

Ostrom, R., Serovich, J., Lim, J. and Mason, T. (2006) The role of stigma in reasons for HIV disclosure and non-disclosure to children, *AIDS Care*, 18, 60–65.

Owens, L., Slee, P. and Shute, R. (2000) It hurts a hell of a lot…The effects of indirect aggression on teenage girls, *School Psychology International*, 21, 359–376.

Oyserman, D., Brickman, D., Bybee, D. and Celious, A. (2006) Fitting in matters: Markers of in-group belonging and academic outcomes, *Psychological Science*, 17, 854–861.

Packard, S. and Kauppi, D. (1999) Rehabilitation agency leadership style: Impact on subordinates' job satisfaction, *Rehabilitation Counselling Bulletin*, 43, 5–11.

Pagliaro, M. (2011) *Exemplary Classroom Questioning: Practices to Promote Thinking and Learning*. Lanham, MD: Rowman and Littlefield.

Paivio, A. (1971) *Imagery and Verbal Processes*. New York: Holt.

Pallak, M., Cook, D. and Sullivan, J. (1980) Commitment and energy conservation, *Applied Social Psychology Journal*, 1, 235–253.

Palomares, N. (2008) Toward a theory of goal detection in social interaction: Effects of contextual ambiguity and tactical functionality on goal inferences and inference certainty, *Communication Research*, 35, 109–148.

Palomares, N. (2009a) Did you see it coming? Effects of the specificity and efficiency of goal pursuit on the accuracy and onset of goal detection in social interaction, *Communication Research*, 36, 538–560.

Palomares, N. (2009b) Women are sort of more tentative than men, aren't they? How men and women use tentative language differently, similarly, and counterstereotypically as a function of gender salience, *Communication Research*, 36, 475–509.

Panayiotou, G., Brown, R. and Vrana, S. (2007) Emotional dimensions as determinants of self-focused attention, *Cognition and Emotion*, 21, 982–998.

Papini, D., Farmer, F., Clark, S., Micka, J. and Barnett, J. (1990) Early adolescent age and gender differences in patterns of emotional self-disclosure to parents and friends, *Adolescence,* 25, 959–976.

Papousek, H., Jürgens, U. and Papousek, M. (2008) *Nonverbal Vocal Communication: Comparative and Developmental Approaches.* Cambridge: Cambridge University Press.

Paramasivam, S. (2007) Managing disagreement while managing not to disagree: Polite disagreement in negotiation discourse, *Journal of Intercultural Communication Research*, 36, 91–116.

Pardeck, J., Anderson, C., Gianino, E. and Miller, B. (1991) Assertiveness of social work students, *Psychological Reports*, 69, 589–590.

Park, B. and Kraus, S. (1992) Consensus in initial impressions as a function of verbal information, *Personality and Social Psychology Bulletin,* 182, 439–449.

Park, Y. (2013) Negotiating last-minute concerns in closing Korean medical encounters: The use of gaze, body and talk, *Social Science and Medicine,* 97, 176–191.

Parker, K., Rains, S. and Ivanov, B. (2016) Examining the 'blanket of protection' conferred by inoculation: The effects of inoculation messages on the cross-protection of related attitudes, *Communication Monographs*, 83, 49–68.

Parkinson, B. (2013) Contextualizing facial activity, *Emotion Review*, 5, 97–103.

Parrott, R., Duncan, V. and Duggan, A. (2000) Promoting patients' full and honest disclosure during conversations with health caregivers, in S. Petronio (ed.) *Balancing the Secrets of Private Disclosures*. Mahwah, NJ: Lawrence Erlbaum.

Parrott, R., Greene, K. and Parker, R. (1992) Negotiating child health care routines during paediatrician–parent conversations, *Journal of Language and Social Psychology,* 11, 35–46.

Pascual, A. and Guéguen, N. (2005) Foot-in-the-door and door-in-the-face: A comparative meta-analytic study, *Psychological Reports*, 96, 122–128.

Paterson, R. (2000) *The Assertiveness Workbook: How to Express Your Ideas and Stand Up for Yourself at Work and in Relationships*. Oakland: New Harbinger.

Pathak, A. (2001) Teaching and assessing multimedia-based oral presentations, *Business Communication Quarterly*, 64, 63–71.

Patry, M. (2008) Attractive but guilty: Deliberation and the physical attractiveness bias, *Psychological Reports*, 102, 727–733.

Patterson, M. (2014) Reflections on historical trends and prospects in contemporary nonverbal research, *Journal of Nonverbal Behavior*, 38, 171–180.

Pavitt, C. (2000) Answering questions requesting scientific explanations for communication, *Communication Theory*, 10, 379–404.

Pavlov, I. (1927) *Conditioned Reflexes.* New York: Dover Reprint.

Pawlikowska, T., Zhang, W., Griffiths, F. *et al.* (2012) Verbal and non-verbal behavior of doctors and patients in primary care consultations: How this relates to patient enablement, *Patient Education and Counseling*, 86, 70–76.

Pearson, J. and Nelson, P. (2000) *An Introduction to Human Communication: Understanding and Sharing*, 5th edition. Boston, MA: McGraw-Hill.

Pearson, J. and Spitzberg, B. (1987) *Interpersonal Communication: Concepts, Components, and Contexts*, 2nd edition. Madison, WI: WCB Brown and Benchmark.

Pearson, J., Nelson, P., Totsworth, S. and Harter, L. (2006) *Human Communication*, 2nd edition. Boston: McGraw-Hill.

Peau, M., Szabo, E., Anderson, J., Morrill, J., Zubric, J. and Wan, H. (2001) The role and impact of affect in the process of resistance to persuasion, *Human Communication Research*, 27, 216–252.

Peck, J. (1995) TV talk shows as therapeutic discourse: The ideological labor of the televised talking cure, *Communication Theory*, 5, 58–81.

Pemberton, J., Borrego J. and Sherman, S. (2013) Differential attention as a mechanism of change in Parent–Child Interaction Therapy: Support from time-series analysis, *Journal of Psychopathology and Behavioral Assessment*, 35, 35–44.

Penciner, R. (2013) Does Powerpoint enhance learning? *Canadian Journal of Emergency Medicine*, 15, 109–112.

Peng, A., Dunn, J. and Conlon, D. (2015) When vigilance prevails: The effect of regulatory focus and accountability on integrative negotiation outcomes, *Organizational Behavior and Human Decision Processes*, 126, 77–87.

Penman, D. and Burch, V. (2013) *Mindfulness for Health: A Practical Guide to Relieving Pain, Reducing Stress and Restoring Wellbeing*. London: Piatkus.

Penman, R. (2000) *Reconstructing Communicating: Looking to a Future*. Mahwah, NJ: Lawrence Erlbaum.

Pennebaker, J. and Francis, M. (1996) Cognitive, emotional, and language processes in disclosure, *Cognition and Emotion*, 10, 601–626.

Pentland, A. (2007) On the collective nature of human intelligence, *Adaptive Behavior*, 15, 189–198.

Penton-Voak, I. and Perrett, D. (2000) Female preference for male faces change cyclically: Further evidence, *Evolution and Human Behavior*, 21, 39–48.

Perloff, R. (2008) *The Dynamics of Persuasion: Communication and Attitudes in the 21st Century*, 3rd edition. Mahwah, NJ: Lawrence Erlbaum.

Perrett, D., Burt, D., Penton-Voak, I., Lee, K., Rowland, D. and Edwards, R. (1999) Symmetry and human facial attractiveness, *Evolution and Human Behavior*, 20, 295–307.

Perrott, E. (1982) *Effective Teaching*. London: Longman.

Pershing, J. (ed.) (2006) *Handbook of Human Performance Technology: Principles, Practice, Potential*. San Francisco: Pfeiffer.

Pervin, L. (1978) Definitions, measurements and classifications of stimuli, situations and environments, *Human Ecology*, 6, 71–105.

Peshawaria, R. (2011) The great training robbery: Why the $60 billion investment in leadership development is not working, *Forbes* (http://www.forbes.com/sites/rajeevpeshawaria/2011/11/01/the-great-training-robbery-2/) (accessed 2 May 2014).

Peters, G., Ruiter, R. and Kok, G. (2013) Threatening communication: A critical re-analysis and a revised meta-analytic test of fear appeal theory, *Health Psychology Review*, 7, S8–S31.

Peterson, R. (1997) A directive leadership style in group decision making can be both virtue and vice: Evidence from elite and experimental groups, *Journal of Personality and Social Psychology*, 72, 1107–1121.

Peterson, R. (2007) An exploratory study of listening practice relative to memory testing and lecture in business administration courses, *Business Communication Quarterly*, 70, 285–300.

Petrie, K., Booth, R., Pennebaker, J., Davison, K. and Thomas, M. (1995) Disclosure of trauma and immune response to a hepatitis B vaccination program, *Journal of Consulting and Clinical Psychology*, 63, 787–792.

Petronio, S. (2002) *Boundaries of Privacy: Dialectics of Disclosure*. Albany, NY: State University of New York Press.

Petronio, S. and Bantz, C. (1991) Controlling the ramifications of disclosure: 'Don't tell anybody but...', *Journal of Language and Social Psychology*, 10, 263–270.

Petroshius, S. and Newell, S. (2015) Beauty and the prince vs. beauty and the beast: An investigation of the effects of male and female communicators' physical attractiveness on evaluations of advertisements, in C. Noble (ed.) *Proceedings of the 1999 Academy of Marketing Science (AMS) Annual Conference*. Heidelberg: Springer.

Petrou, P., Demerouti, E. and Häfner, M. (2015) When fit matters more: The effect of regulatory fit on adaptation to change, *European Journal of Work and Organizational Psychology*, 24, 126–142.

Petty, R. and Cacioppo, J. (1986) *Communication and Persuasion: Central and Peripheral Routes to Attitude Change*. New York: Springer-Verlag.

Pezdek, K. and Banks, W. (eds) (1996) *The Recovered Memory/False Memory Debate*. San Diego: Academic Press.

Pfafman, T. and McEwan, B. (2014) Polite women at work: Negotiating professional identity through strategic assertiveness, *Women's Studies in Communication*, 37, 202–219.

Pfau, M., Semmler, S., Deatrick, L. *et al.* (2009) Nuances about the role and impact of affect in inoculation, *Communication Monographs*, 76, 73–98.

Pfau, M., Szabo, E., Anderson, J., Morrill, J., Zubric, J. and Wan, H. (2001) The role and impact of affect in the process of resistance to persuasion, *Human Communication Research*, 27, 216–252.

Philippot, P. and Feldman, R. (2005) *The Regulation of Emotion*. London: Routledge.

Phillips, E. (1978) *The Social Skills Basis of Psychopathology*. New York: Grune and Stratton.

Phillips, K., Rothbard, N. and Dumas, T. (2009) To disclose or not to disclose? Status distance and self-disclosure in diverse environments, *Academy of Management Review*, 34, 710–732.

Phillips, M. (1998) *All Must Have Prizes*. London: Time Warner Books

Phillips, L., Leventhal, H. and Leventhal, E. (2012) Physicians' communication of the common-sense self-regulation model results in greater reported adherence than physicians' use of interpersonal skills, *British Journal of Health Psychology*, 17, 244–257.

Piccinin, S., McCarrey, M., Fairweather, D., Vito, D. and Conrad, G. (1998) Impact of situational legitimacy and assertiveness-related anxiety/discomfort on motivation and ability to generate effective criticism responses, *Current Psychology: Developmental, Learning, Personality, Social*, 17, 75–92.

Pichler, P. and Coates, J. (eds) (2011) *Language and Gender: A Reader*, 2nd edition. Chichester: Wiley-Blackwell.

Pickering, M. (2006) The dance of dialogue, *The Psychologist*, 19, 734–737.

Pilkington, C. and Smith, K. (2000) Self-evaluation maintenance in a larger social context, *British Journal of Social Psychology*, 39, 213–229.

Pillet-Shore, D. (2011) Doing introductions: The work involved in meeting someone new, *Communication Monographs*, 78, 73–95.

Pinnington, A. (2001) Charles Handy: The exemplary guru, *Reason in Practice*, 1, 47–55.

Pipe, M., Lamb, M., Orbach, Y. and Cederborg, A. (eds) (2014) *Child Sexual Abuse: Disclosure, Delay, and Denial*. London: Routledge.

Pisacreta, J., Tincani, M., Connell, J. and Axelrod, S. (2011) Increasing teachers' use of a 1:1 praise to behavior correction ratio to decrease student disruption in general education classrooms, *Behavioral Interventions*, 26, 243–260.

Pitts, M. and Roberts, M. (1997) *Fairweather Eden*. London: Century.

Placencia, M. (1997) Opening up closings – The Ecuadorian way, *Text*, 17, 53–81.

Planalp, S. (1998) Communicating emotion in everyday life: Cues, channels and processes, in P. Andersen and L. Guerrero (eds) *Handbook of Communication and Emotion: Research, Theory, Applications, and Contexts*. San Diego: Academic Press.

Platow, M., Grace, D. and Smithson, M. (2012) Examining the preconditions for psychological group membership: Perceived social interdependence as the outcome of self-categorization, *Social Psychological and Personality Science*, 3, 5–13.

Plotnikoff, J. and Woolfson, R. (2009) *Measuring Up? Evaluating Implementation of Government Commitments to Young Witnesses in Criminal Proceedings*. Research Report: Nuffield Foundation and NSPCC (http://www.nspcc.org.uk/Inform/research/Findings/measuring_up_report_wdf66579.pdf) (accessed 2 December 2009).

Pomerantz, E. and Kempner, S. (2013) Mothers' daily person and process praise: Implications for children's theory of intelligence and motivation, *Developmental Psychology*, 49, 2040–2046.

Postmes, T., Baray, G., Haslam, A., Morton, T. and Swab, R. (2006) The dynamics of social and personal identity formation, in T. Postmes and P. Jetten (eds) *Individuality and the Group: Advances in Social Identity*. London: Sage.

Powell, G. and Graves, L. (2006) Gender and leadership: Perceptions and realities, in K. Dindia and D. Canary (eds) *Sex Differences and Similarities in Communication*, 2nd edition. Mahwah, NJ: Lawrence Erlbaum.

Powell, M. and Snow, P. (2007) Guide to questioning children during the free-narrative phase of an investigative interview, *Australian Psychologist*, 42, 57–65.

Powell, M., Fisher, R. and Wright, R. (2007) Investigative interviewing, in N. Brewer and K. Williams (eds) *Psychology and Law: An Empirical Perspective*. New York: Guilford.

Powell, W. (1968) Differential effectiveness of interviewer interventions in an experimental interview, *Journal of Consulting and Clinical Psychology*, 32, 210–15.

Power, J., Brotheridge, C., Blenkinsopp, J. *et al.* (2013) Acceptability of workplace bullying: A comparative study on six continents, *Journal of Business Research*, 66, 374–380.

Pratkanis, A. (2001) Propaganda and deliberative persuasion: The implications of Americanized mass media for established and emerging democracies, in W. Wosinska, R. Cialdini, D. Barrett and J. Reykowski (eds) *The Practice of Social Influence in Multiple Cultures*. Mahwah, NJ: Lawrence Erlbaum.

Pratkanis, A. (2007) Social influence analysis: An index of tactics, in A. Pratkanis (ed.) *The Science of Social Influence: Advances and Future Progress*. New York: Psychology Press.

Preiss, R. and Allen, M. (1998) Performing counterattitudinal advocacy: The persuasive impact of incentives, in M. Allen and R. Preiss (eds) *Persuasion: Advances through Meta-analysis*. Cresskill, NJ: Hampton Press.

Premack, D. (1965) Reinforcement theory, in D. Levine (ed.) *Nebraska Symposium on Motivation, Vol. 13*. Lincoln: University of Nebraska Press.

Preston, J. (2014) Be short, be simple and be human, *Sunday Telegraph Seven Magazine*, 23 March, 14–15.

Prkachin, K. (1997) The consistency of facial expressions of pain, in P. Ekman and E. Rosenberg (eds) *What the Face Reveals: Basic and Applied Studies of Spontaneous Expression Using the Facial Action Coding System (FACS)*. Oxford: Oxford University Press.

Prochaska, J. and DiClemente, C. (1992) Stages of change in the modification of problem behaviors, in M. Hersen, R. Eisler and P. Miller (eds) *Progress in Behavior Modification*. Sycamore, IL: Sycamore Press.

Proctor, R. and Dutta, A. (1995) *Skill Acquisition and Human Performance*. Thousand Oaks, CA: Sage.

Provine, R. (2000) *Laughter: A Scientific Investigation*. London: Penguin.

Prue, D. and Fairbank, J. (1981) Performance feedback in organizational behavior management: A review, *Journal of Organizational Behavior Management*, 3, 1–16.

Pruitt, D. (1981) *Negotiating Behavior*. New York: Academic Press.

Pruitt, D. (1990) Achieving integrative agreements, in I. Asherman and S. Asherman (eds) *The Negotiating Sourcebook*. Amherst, MA: Human Resource Development Press.

Pruitt, D. and Carnevale, P. (1993) *Negotiation in Social Conflict*. Buckingham: Open University Press.

Puce, A. (2013) Perception of nonverbal cues, in K. Ochsner and S. Kosslyn (eds) *The Oxford Handbook of Cognitive Neuroscience, Volume 1: Core Topics*. Oxford: Oxford University Press.

Putnam, L. and Roloff, M. (1992) Communication perspectives on negotiation, in L. Putnam and M. Roloff (eds) *Communication and Negotiation*. Newbury Park: Sage.

Quadflieg, S., Vermeulen, N. and Rossion, B. (2013) Differential reliance on the Duchenne marker during smile evaluations and person judgments, *Journal of Nonverbal Behavior*, 37, 69–77.

Quine, L., Rutter, D. and Arnold, L. (2002) Increasing cycle helmet use in school age cyclists: An intervention based on the theory of planned behaviour, in D. Rutter and L. Quine (eds) *Changing Health Behaviour*. Buckingham: Open University Press.

Quinlan, P. and Dyson, B. (2008) *Cognitive Psychology*. Harlow, Essex: Pearson Education.

Rabin, C. and Zelner, D. (1992) The role of assertiveness in clarifying roles and strengthening job satisfaction of social workers in multidisciplinary mental health settings, *British Journal of Social Work*, 22, 17–32.

Rackham, N. (1972) Controlled pace negotiation, *Industrial and Commercial Training*, 4, 266–275.

Rackham, N. (2007) The behavior of successful negotiators, in R. Lewicki, B. Barry and D. Saunders (eds) *Negotiation: Readings, Exercises, and Cases*, 5th edition. New York: McGraw-Hill/Irwin.

Rahnev, D., Lau, H. and de Lange, F. (2011) Prior expectation modulates the interaction between sensory and prefrontal regions in the human brain, *The Journal of Neuroscience*, 31, 10741–10748.

Rains, S. and Turner, M. (2007) Psychological reactance and persuasive health communication: A test and extension of the intertwined model, *Human Communication Research*, 33, 241–269.

Rakos, R. (1991) *Assertive Behavior: Theory, Research and Training*. London: Routledge.

Rakos, R. (2006) Asserting and confronting, in O. Hargie (ed.) *The Handbook of Communication Skills*, 3rd edition. London: Routledge.

Ransdell, S. and Gilroy, L. (2001) The effects of background music on word processed writing, *Computers in Human Behavior*, 17, 141–148.

Rasmussen, E. and Newland, M. (2008) Asymmetry of reinforcement and punishment in human choice, *Journal of the Experimental Analysis of Behavior*, 89, 157–167.

Ratanawongsa N., Karter, A., Parker, M. *et al.* (2013) Communication and medication refill adherence: The diabetes study of northern California, *JAMA Internal Medicine*, 173, 210–218.

Ratnayake, B. and Broderick, A. (2014) Auitobiographical episodes, semantic memories and branding, in L. Moutinho, E. Bigné and A. Manrai (eds) *The Routledge Companion to the Future of Marketing*. Abingdon, Oxon: Routledge.

Rautalinko, E. and Lisper, H. (2004) Effects of training reflective listening in a corporate setting, *Journal of Business and Psychology*, 18, 281–299.

Rauthmann, J. (2012) You say the party is dull, I say it is lively. A componential approach to how situations are perceived to disentangle perceiver, situation, and perceiver × situation variance, *Social Psychological and Personality Science*, 3, 519–528.

Rauthmann, J., Sherman, R., Nave, C. and Funder, D. (2015) Personality-driven situation experience, contact, and construal: How people's personality traits predict characteristics of their situations in daily life, *Journal of Research in Personality*, 55, 98–111.

Raven, B. (1992) A power/interaction model of interpersonal influence: French and Raven thirty years later, *Journal of Social Behavior and Personality*, 7, 217–244.

Raven, B. and Rubin, J.Z. (1983) *Social Psychology*, 2nd edition. New York: Wiley.

Raymond, G. (2003) Grammar and social organization: Yes/no interrogatives and the structure of responding, *American Sociological Review*, 68, 939–967.

Rebellon, C. (2006) Do adolescents engage in delinquency to attract the social attention of peers? An extension and longitudinal test of the social reinforcement hypothesis, *Journal of Research in Crime and Delinquency*, 43, 387–411.

Reed, L., Zeglen, K. and Schmidt, K. (2012) Facial expressions as honest signals of cooperative intent in a one-shot anonymous Prisoner's Dilemma game, *Evolution and Human Behavior*, 33, 200–209.

Rehling, D. (2008) Compassionate listening: A framework for listening to the seriously ill, *International Journal of Listening*, 22, 83–89.

Rehman, S., Nietert, P., Cope, D. and Kilpatrick, A. (2005) What to wear today? Effect of doctor's attire on the trust and confidence of patients, *The American Journal of Medicine*, 118, 1279–1286.

Rehman, U., Fallis, E. and Byers, E. (2013) Sexual satisfaction in heterosexual women, in D. Castaneda (ed.) *The Essential Handbook of Women's Sexuality*. Santa Barbara, CA: Praeger.

Reich, M., Leemans, C., Vermorken, J. *et al.* (2014) Best practices in the management of the psycho-oncologic aspects of head and neck cancer patients: Recommendations from the European Head and Neck Cancer Society Make Sense Campaign, *Annals of Oncology*, 25, 2115–2124.

Reid, D. and Parsons, M. (2000) Organisational behavioural management in human service settings, in J. Austin and J. Carr (eds) *Handbook of Applied Behaviour Analysis*. Reno, NV: Context Press.

Reid, L., Henneman, R. and Long, E. (1960) An experimental analysis of set: The effect of categorical instruction, *American Journal of Psychology*, 73, 568–572.

Reinhard, J. (1998) The persuasive effects of testimonial assertion evidence, in M. Allen and R. Preiss (eds) *Persuasion: Advances through Meta-analysis*. Cresskill, NJ: Hampton Press.

Reinhard, M-A., Messner, M. and Sporer, S. (2006) Explicit persuasive intent and its impact upon success at persuasion: The determining roles of attractiveness and likeability, *Journal of Consumer Psychology*, 16, 249–259.

Reinhard, M-A., Sporer, S., Scharmach, M. and Marksteiner, T. (2011) Listening, not watching: Situational familiarity and the ability to detect deception. *Journal of Personality and Social Psychology*, 101, 467–484.

Reinsvold, L. and Cochran, K. (2012) Power dynamics and questioning in elementary science classrooms, *Journal of Science Teacher Education*, 23, 745–768.

Remland, M. (2006) Uses and consequences of nonverbal communication in the context of organizational life, in V. Manusov and M. Patterson (eds) *The Sage Handbook of Nonverbal Communication*. Thousand Oaks, CA: Sage.

Remland, M. (2009) *Nonverbal Communication in Everyday Life*, 3rd edition. Boston, MA: Allyn and Bacon.

Reno, R. and Kenny, D. (1992) Effects of self-consciousness and social anxiety on self-disclosure among unacquainted individuals: An application of the social relations model, *Journal of Personality*, 60, 79–95.

Resnick, L. (1972) Teacher behaviour in an informal British infant school, *School Review*, 81, 63–83.

Reynolds, W. and Scott, B. (2000) Do nurses and other professional helpers normally display much empathy? *Journal of Advanced Nursing*, 31, 226–234.

Rhoades, B., Warren, H., Domitrovich, C. and Greenberg, M. (2011) Examining the link between preschool social-emotional competence and first grade academic achievement: The role of attention skills, *Early Childhood Research Quarterly*, 26, 182–191.

Richards, A. and Banas, J. (2015) Inoculating against reactance to persuasive health messages, *Health Communication*, 30, 451–460.

Richardson, D. and Hammock, G. (2007) Social context of human aggression: Are we paying too much attention to gender? *Aggression and Violent Behavior*, 12, 417–426.

Richins, M. (1983) An analysis of consumer interaction style in the marketplace, *Journal of Consumer Research*, 10, 73–82.

Richmond, V. and McCroskey, J. (2000) *Nonverbal Behavior in Interpersonal Relations*, 4th edition. Boston, MA: Allyn and Bacon.

Richter, L. and Kruglanski, A. (2004) Motivated closed mindedness and the emergence of culture, in M. Schaller and C. Crandall (eds) *The Psychological Foundations of Culture*. Mahwah, NJ: Lawrence Erlbaum.

Rider, E. and Keefer, C. (2006) Communication skills competencies: Definitions and a teaching toolbox, *Medical Education*, 40, 624–629.

Riesch, H. (2014) Why did the proton cross the road? Humour and science communication, *Public Understanding of Science*, 1–8. DOI: 10.1177/0963662514546299.

Riggio, R. (1992) Social interaction skills and nonverbal behaviour, in R. Feldman (ed.) *Applications of Nonverbal Behavioral Theory and Research*. Hillsdale, NJ: Lawrence Erlbaum.

Riggio, R. (2005) The Social Skills Inventory (SSI): Measuring nonverbal and social skills, in V. Manusov (ed.) *The Sourcebook of Nonverbal Measures: Going Beyond Words*. Mahwah, NJ: Lawrence Erlbaum.

Riggio, R. and Friedman, H. (1986) Impression formation: The role of expressive behavior, *Journal of Personality and Social Psychology*, 50, 421–427.

Rimal, R. (2002) Perceived risk and self-efficacy as motivators: Understanding individuals' long-tem use of health information, *Journal of Communication*, 51, 633–654.

Rindstedt, C. (2014) Conversational openings and multiparty disambiguations in doctors' encounters with young patients (and their parents), *Text and Talk*, 34, 421–442.

Rittle-Johnson, B. (2006) Promoting transfer: Effects of self-explanation and direct instruction, *Child Development*, 77, 1–15.

Roach, C. and Wyatt, N. (1999) Listening and the rhetorical process, in J. Stewart (ed.) *Bridges Not Walls*, 7th edition. Boston: McGraw-Hill.

Robbins, S. and Hunsaker, P. (2014) *Training in Interpersonal Skills: TIPS for Managing People at Work*, 6th edition. Harlow, Essex: Pearson Education.

Robbins, S. and Judge, T. (2013) *Essentials of Organizational Behavior*, 12th edition. Upper Saddle River, NJ: Pearson Education.

Robbins, S. and Judge, T. (2014) *Organizational Behavior*, 16th edition. Upper Saddle River, NJ: Pearson Prentice Hall.

Robertson, I. (2013) How power affects the brain, *The Psychologist*, 26, 186–189.

Robins, G. (2012) *Praise, Motivation and the Child*. Abingdon, Oxon: Routledge.

Robinson, J. (1998) Getting down to business: Talk, gaze, and body orientation during openings of doctor–patient consultations, *Human Communication Research*, 25, 97–123.

Robinson, J. (2006) Nonverbal communication and physician–patient interaction: Review and new directions, in V. Manusov and M. Patterson (eds) *The Sage Handbook of Nonverbal Communication*. Thousand Oaks, CA: Sage.

Robinson, J. and Heritage, J. (2006) Physicians' opening questions and patients' satisfaction, *Patient Education and Counseling*, 60, 279–285.

Robinson, J. and Stivers, T. (2001) Achieving activity transitions in physician–patients encounters: From history taking to physical examination, *Human Communication Research*, 27, 253–298.

Robinson, S., Sterling, C., Skinner, C. and Robinson, D. (1997) Effects of lecture rate on students' comprehension and ratings of topic importance, *Contemporary Educational Psychology*, 22, 260–267.

Roehling, M., Roehling, P. and Odland, L. (2008) Investigating the validity of stereotypes about overweight employees: The relationship between body weight and normal personality traits, *Group and Organization Management*, 33, 392–424.

Roese, N., Olson, J., Borenstein, M., Martin, A. and Shores, A. (1992) Same-sex touching behaviour: The moderating role of homophobic attitudes, *Journal of Nonverbal Behavior*, 16, 249–259.

Rogan, R. and Hammer, M.R. (1995) Assessing message affect in crisis negotiation: An exploratory study, *Human Communication Research*, 21, 553–574.

Rogers, C. (1951) *Client-centered Therapy*. Boston, MA: Houghton Mifflin.

Rogers, C. (1980) *A Way of Being*. Boston: Houghton Mifflin.

Rogers, C. (1991) *Client-centred Therapy*. London: Constable.

Rogers, E. (2003) *Diffusion of Innovations*, 5th edition. Free Press: New York.

Rogers, R. (2008) *Clinical Assessment of Malingering and Deception*, 3rd edition. New York: Guilford.

Rogers, W. (1978) The contribution of kinesic illustrators toward the comprehension of verbal behavior within utterances, *Human Communication Research*, 5, 54–62.

Roloff, M. (2014) Negotiation and communication: Explication and research questions, in C. Berger (ed.) *Interpersonal Communication*. Berlin: Walter de Gruyter.

Roloff, M. and Jordan, J. (1992) Achieving negotiation goals: The 'fruits and foibles' of planning ahead, in L. Putnam and M. Roloff (eds) *Communication and Negotiation*. Newbury Park: Sage.

Rose, J. (2011) Diverse perspectives on the groupthink theory – A literary review, *Emerging Leadership Journeys*, 4, 37–57.

Rose, Y. and Tryon, W. (1979) Judgements of assertive behavior as a function of speech loudness, latency, content, gestures, inflection and sex, *Behavior Modification*, 3, 112–123.

Rosenbaum, B. (2001) Seven emerging sales competencies, *Business Horizons*, 44, 33–36.

Rosenfarb, I. (1992) A behaviour analytic interpretation of the therapeutic relationship, *The Psychological Record*, 42, 341–354.

Rosenfeld, H. (1987) Conversational control functions of nonverbal behavior, in A. Siegman and S. Feldstein (eds) *Nonverbal Behavior and Communication*. Hillsdale, NJ: Lawrence Erlbaum.

Rosenfeld, H. and Hancks, M. (1980) The nonverbal context of verbal listener responses, in M. Kay (ed.) *The Relationship of Verbal and Nonverbal Communication*. The Hague: Mouton.

Rosenfeld, L. (2000) Overview of the ways privacy, secrecy, and disclosure are balanced in today's society, in S. Petronio (ed.) *Balancing the Secrets of Private Disclosures*. Mahwah, NJ: Lawrence Erlbaum.

Rosenfeld, L., Kartus, S. and Ray, C. (1976) Body accessibility revisited, *Journal of Communication*, 26, 27–30.

Rosengren, K. (2000) *Communication: An Introduction*. London: Sage.

Rosenshine, B. (1968) *Objectively Measured Behavioural Predictors of Effectiveness in Explaining*. Technical Report 4, Stanford: Stanford University Center for Research and Development in Teaching.

Rosenshine, B. (1971) *Teaching Behaviour and Student Achievement*. Windsor, Berks: National Foundation for Educational Research in England and Wales.

Rosenthal, R. (2006) Applying psychological research on interpersonal expectations and covert communication in classrooms, corporations, and courtrooms, in S. Donaldson, D. Berger and K. Pezdek (eds) *Applied Psychology: New Frontiers and Rewarding Careers*. Mahwah, NJ: Lawrence Erlbaum.

Rosenthal, R. and Jacobson, L. (1992) *Pygmalion in the Classroom*. New York: Irvington.

Roskos-Ewoldsen, D. and Monahan, J. (eds) (2007) *Communication and Social Cognition*. London: Routledge.

Rost, M. (2011) *Teaching and Researching: Listening*, 2nd edition. London: Routledge.

Roter, D. and Hall, J. (2006) *Doctors Talking with Patients/Patients Talking with Doctors: Improving Communication in Medical Visits*, 2nd edition. Westport, CT: Praeger.

Roth, H. (1889) On salutations, *Journal of the Royal Anthropological Institute*, 19, 164–181.

Rothwell, J. (2016) *In Mixed Company: Communicating in Small Groups*, 9th edition. Boston, MA: Cengage Learning.

Rotter, J. (1966) Generalized expectancies for internal versus external control of reinforcement, *Psychological Monographs, 80* (whole no. 609).

Rousseau, E. and Redfield, D. (1980) Teacher questioning, *Evaluation in Education*, 4, 51–52.

Routasalo, P. (1999) Physical touch in nursing studies: A literature review, *Journal of Advanced Nursing*, 30, 843–850.

Rowan, K. (2003) Informing and explaining skills: Theory and research on informative communication, in J. Greene and B. Burleson (eds) *The Handbook of Communication and Social Interaction Skills*. Mahwah, NJ: Erlbaum.

Rowe, M. (1969) Science, silence and sanctions, *Science and Children*, 6, 11–13.

Rowe, M. (1974a) Pausing phenomena: Influence on the quality of instruction, *Journal of Psycholinguistic Research*, 3, 203–233.

Rowe, M. (1974b) Wait-time and rewards as instructional variables, their influence on language, logic, and fate control. Part One – wait-time, *Journal of Research in Science Teaching*, 11, 81–94.

Rowitz, L. (2014) *Public Health Leadership: Putting Principles into Practice*. Burlington, MA: Jones and Bartlett Learning.

Ruback, R. and Juieng, D. (1997) Territorial defence in parking lots: Retaliation against waiting drivers, *Journal of Applied Social Psychology*, 27, 821–834.

Ruben, D. (1990) *Explaining Explanation*. London: Routledge.

Rubie-Davies, C. (2007) Classroom interactions: Exploring the practices of high- and low-expectation teachers, *British Journal of Educational Psychology*, 77, 289–306.

Rubie-Davies, C., Hattie J. and Hamilton, R. (2006) Expecting the best for students: Teacher expectations and academic outcomes, *British Journal of Educational Psychology*, 76, 429–444.

Rubin, D., Yang, H. and Porte, M. (2000) A comparison of self-reported self-disclosure among Chinese and North Americans, in S. Petronio (ed.) *Balancing the Secrets of Private Disclosures*. Mahwah, NJ: Lawrence Erlbaum.

Rubin, M. and Morrison, T. (2014) Individual differences in individualism and collectivism predict ratings of virtual cities' liveability and environmental quality, *The Journal of General Psychology*, 141, 348–372.

Ruddle, A. and Dilks, S. (2015) Opening up to disclosure, *The Psychologist*, 28, 458–461.

Rudman, L. and Glick, P. (2001) Prescriptive gender stereotypes and backlash toward agenic women, *Journal of Social Issues*, 57, 743–762.

Rudy, B., May, A., Matthews, R. and Davis, T. (2013) Youth's negative self-statements as related to social self-efficacy among differing relationships, *Journal of Psychopathology and Behavioral Assessment*, 35, 106–112.

Ruffner, M. and Burgoon, M. (1981) *Interpersonal Communication*. New York: Holt, Rinehart and Winston.

Ruiter, R., Kessels, L., Peters, G. and Kok, G. (2014) Sixty years of fear appeal research: Current state of the evidence, *International Journal of Psychology*, 49, 63–70.

Rumsey, M. (ed.) (2013) *The Oxford Handbook of Leadership*. Oxford: Oxford University Press.

Russell, J. (1971) *Motivation*. Dubuque, IA: W.C. Brown,

Russell, J. (1997) Reading emotions from and into faces: Resurrecting a dimensional-contextual perspective, in J. Russell and J. Fernandez-Dols (eds) *The Psychology of Facial Expression*. Cambridge: Cambridge University Press.

Rutherford, M. and Kuhlmeier, V. (eds) (2013) *Social Perception: Detection and Interpretation of Animacy, Agency, and Intention*. Cambridge, MA: MIT Press.

Rutledge, R., Skandali, N., Dayan, P. and Dolan, R. (2014) A computational and neural model of momentary subjective well-being, *Proceedings of the National Academy of Sciences*, 111, 12252–12257.

Rutter, D. and Quine, L. (2002) Social cognition models and changing health behaviours, in D. Rutter and L. Quine (eds) *Changing Health Behaviour*. Buckingham: Open University Press.

Ruusuvuori, J. (2001) Looking means listening: Coordinating displays of engagement in doctor–patient interaction, *Social Science and Medicine*, 52, 1093–1108.

Ryan, E., Anas, A. and Friedman, D. (2006) Evaluations of older adult assertiveness in problematic clinical encounters, *Journal of Language and Social Psychology*, 25, 129–145.

Ryan, E., Anas, A. and Vuckovich, M. (2007) The effects of age, hearing loss, and communication difficulty on first, impressions, *Communication Research Reports*, 24, 13–19.

Ryan, R., Curren, R. and Deci, E. (2013) What humans need: Flourishing in Aristotelian philosophy and self-determination theory, in A. Waterman (ed.) *The Best Within Us: Positive Psychology Perspectives on Eudaimonia*. Washington, DC: American Psychological Association.

Ryan, S., Oaten, M., Stevenson, R. and Case, T. (2012) Facial disfigurement is treated like an infectious disease, *Evolution and Human Behavior*, 33, 639–646.

Ryan, W., Legate, N. and Weinstein, N. (2015) Coming out as lesbian, gay, or bisexual: The lasting impact of initial disclosure experiences, *Self and Identity*, 14, 549–569.

Ryff, C. and Singer, B. (2000) Interpersonal flourishing: A positive health agenda for the new millennium, *Personality and Social Psychology Review*, 4, 30–34.

Sabia, J. and Rees, D. (2012) Body weight and wages: Evidence from add health, *Economics and Human Biology*, 10, 14–19.

Sailer, K. and McCulloh, I. (2012) Social networks and spatial configuration: How office layouts drive social interaction, *Social Networks*, 34, 47–58.

Salacuse, J. (1998) Ten ways that culture affects negotiating style. Some survey results, *Negotiation Journal*, 14, 221–239.

Salmon, P. and Young, B. (2011) Creativity in clinical communication: From communication skills to skilled communication, *Medical Education*, 45, 217–226.

Salter, A. (1949) *Conditioned Reflex Therapy*. New York: Capricorn Books.

Samovar, L., Porter, R. and McDaniel, E. (2012) *Intercultural Comunication: A Reader*, 13th edition. Boston, MA: Wadsworth Cengage.

Samp, J. and Solomon, D. (1998) Communicative responses to problematic events in close relationships I: The variety and facets of goals, *Communication Research*, 25, 66–95.

Samuelsson, C., Adolfsson, E. and Persson, H. (2013) The use and characteristics of elderspeak in Swedish geriatric institutions, *Clinical Linguistics and Phonetics*, 27, 616–631.

Sanchez, M. (2001) Effects of assertive communication between doctors and patients in public health outpatient surgeries in the city of Seville, *Social Behavior and Personality*, 29, 63–70.

Sanders, R. (2003) Applying the skills concept to discourse and conversation: The remediation of performance defects in talk-in-interaction, in J. Greene and B. Burleson (eds) *Handbook of Communication and Social Interaction Skills*. Mahwah, NJ: Lawrence Erlbaum.

Sanders, R. and Fitch, K. (2001) The actual practice of compliance seeking, *Communication Theory*, 11, 263–289.

Sandow, D. and Allen, A.M. (2005) The nature of social collaboration: How work really gets done, *Reflections*, 6, 1–14.

Sansone, C. and Harackiewicz, J. (eds) (2000) *Intrinsic and Extrinsic Motivation: The Search for Optimal Motivation and Performance*. San Diego: Academic Press.

Santen, S., Rotter, T. and Hemphill, R. (2008) Patients do not know the level of training of their doctors because doctors do not tell them, *Journal of General Internal Medicine*, 23, 607–610.

Sarafino, E. (2004) *Behavior Modification: Principles of Behavior Change*, 2nd edition. Long Grove, IL: Waveland Press.

Sarkova, M., Bacikova-Sleskova, M., Orosova, O. *et al.* (2013) Associations between assertiveness, psychological well-being, and self-esteem in adolescents, *Journal of Applied Social Psychology*, 43, 147–154.

Sas, L. (2002) *The Interaction between Children's Developmental Capabilities and the Courtroom Environment: The Impact on Testimonial Competency*. Research Report, Department of Justice,

Canada (http://www.judcom.nsw.gov.au/publications/benchbks/sexual_assault/articles/Sas-Interaction_between_children_and_courtroom.pdf) (accessed 2 December 2009).

Saucier, D., Webster, R., Hoffman, B. and Strain, M. (2014) Social vigilantism and reported use of strategies to resist persuasion, *Personality and Individual Differences*, 70, 120–125.

Saunders, C. and Caves, R. (1986) An empirical approach to the identification of communication skills with reference to speech therapy, *Journal of Further and Higher Education*, 10, 29–44.

Saunders, C. and Saunders, E. (1993) Expert teachers' perceptions of university teaching: The identification of teaching skills, in R. Ellis (ed.) *Quality Assurance for University Teaching*. Buckingham: Open University Press.

Saxton, T., DeBruine, L., Jones, B., Little, A. and Roberts, C. (2009) Face and voice attractiveness judgments change during adolescence, *Evolution and Human Behavior*, 30, 398–408.

Scanlon, L. (1994) *Narrative, Authority and Power: The Medieval Exemplum and the Chaucerian Tradition*. Cambridge: Cambridge University Press.

Schafer, M. and Crichlow, C. (2010) *Groupthink Versus High-Quality Decision Making in International Relations*. New York: Columbia University Press.

Schaller, M. (2008) Evolutionary bases of first impressions, in N. Ambady and J. Skowronski (eds) *First Impressions*. New York: Guilford.

Schatzman, L. and Strauss, A. (1956) Social class and modes of communications, *American Journal of Sociology*, LX, 329–338.

Scheflen, A. (1974) *How Behavior Means*. Garden City, NJ: Anchor.

Schegloff, E. (2007) *Sequence Organization in Interaction: Vol. 1: A Primer in Conversation Analysis*. Cambridge: Cambridge University Press.

Schegloff, E. (2000) Overlapping talk and the organization of turn-taking for conversation, *Language in Society*, 29, 1–63.

Schegloff, E. and Sacks, H. (1973) Opening-up closings, *Semiotica*, 8, 289–327.

Scherer, K. and Grandjean, D. (2007) Facial expressions allow inference of both emotions and their components, *Cognition and Emotion*, 22, 789–801.

Scherer, K., Clark-Polner, E. and Mortillaro, M. (2011) In the eye of the beholder? Universality and cultural specificity in the expression and perception of emotion, *International Journal of Psychology*, 46, 401–435.

Scherer, K., Johnstone, T. and Klasmeyer, G. (2003) Vocal expression of emotion, in R. Davidson, K. Scherer and H. Goldsmith (eds) *Handbook of Affective Sciences*. Oxford: Oxford University Press.

Schermuly, C. and Scholl, W. (2012) The Discussion Coding System (DCS) – a new instrument for analyzing communication processes, *Communication Methods and Measures*, 6, 12–40.

Schirmer, A. (2014) *Emotion*. London: Sage.

Schirmer, J., Mauksch, L., Lang, F. *et al.* (2005) Assessing communication competence: A review of current tools, *Family Medicine*, 37, 184–192.

Schlundt, D. and McFall, R. (1985) New directions in the assessment of social competence and social skills, in L. L'Abate and M. Milan (eds) *Handbook of Social Skills Training and Research*. New York: Wiley.

Schneider, M. and Bos, A. (2014) Measuring stereotypes of female politicians. *Political Psychology*, 35, 245–266.

Schneider, S. and Laurion, S. (1993) Do we know what we've learned from listening to the news? *Memory and Cognition*, 21, 198–209.

Schofield, T., Parke, R., Castaneda, E. and Coltrane S. (2008) Patterns of gaze between parents and children in European American and Mexican American families, *Journal of Nonverbal Behavior*, 32, 171–186.

Schroth, M. (1992) The effect of delay of feedback on a delayed concept formation transfer task, *Contemporary Educational Psychology*, 17, 78–82.

Schubert, J. (2000) Give sorrow words: Mourning at termination of psychoanalysis, *Scandinavian Psychoanalytic Review*, 23, 105–117.

Schüler, A., Arndt, J. and Scheiter, J. (2015) Processing multimedia material: Does integration of text and pictures result in a single or two interconnected mental representations? *Learning and Instruction*, 35, 62–72.

Schullery, N. (1997) Communication behaviors of employed females: A survey focusing on argumentativeness and women's supervisory roles in organizations, *Dissertation Abstracts International: Humanities and Social Sciences*, 58 (3-A), 0647.

Schulze, R. and Pishwa, H. (eds) (2015) *The Exercise of Power in Communication: Devices, Reception and Reaction*. Basingstoke: Palgrave Macmillan.

Schutz, A. (1998) Assertive, offensive, protective, and defensive styles of self-presentation: A taxonomy, *The Journal of Psychology*, 132, 611–628.

Schutz, W. (1955) What makes groups productive? *Human Relations*, 8, 429–465.

Schwab, S., Scalise, J., Ginter, E. and Whipple, G. (1998) Self-disclosure, loneliness and four interpersonal targets: Friend, group of friends, stranger, and group of strangers, *Psychological Reports*, 82, 1264–1266.

Schwartz, B. and Robbins, S. (1995) *Psychology of Learning and Behaviour*, 4th edition. New York: Norton.

Scheibe, S., Notthoff, N., Menkin, J. *et al.* (2014) Forewarning reduces fraud susceptibility in vulnerable consumers, *Basic and Applied Social Psychology*, 36, 272–279.

Schyns, B. and Schilling, J. (2013) How bad are the effects of bad leaders? A meta-analysis of destructive leadership and its outcomes, *The Leadership Quarterly*, 24, 138–158.

Science Daily (2007) Stereotype about female talkativeness unfounded, researchers report, July 6 (http://www.sciencedaily.com/releases/2007/07/070705152953.htm) (accessed 2 December 2009).

Scoboria, A. (2012) Facilitating don't know responses in interviews with children: A brief review, *Investigative Interviewing: Research and Practice*, 4, 6–13.

Scott, B. (1988) *Negotiating: Constructive and Competitive Negotiation*. London: Paradigm Press.

Sedikides, C. and Spencer, S. (2007) (eds) *The Self*. New York: Psychology Press.

Segerstrale, U and Molnar, P. (1997) Nonverbal communication: Crossing the boundary between culture and nature, in U. Segerstrale and P. Molnar (eds) *Nonverbal Communication: Where Nature Meets Culture*. Mahwah, NJ: Lawrence Erlbaum.

Segrin, C. (1992) Specifying the nature of social skill deficits associated with depression, *Human Communication Research*, 19, 89–123.

Segrin, C. (2000) Interpersonal relationships and mental health problems, in K. Dindia and S. Duck (eds) *Communication and Personal Relationships*. Chichester: Wiley.

Segrin, C. and Flora, J. (2011) *Family Communication*, 2nd edition. New York: Routledge.

Segrin, C. and Taylor, M. (2007) Positive interpersonal relationships mediate the association between social skills and psychological well-being, *Personality and Individual Differences*, 43, 637–646.

Segrin, C., Hanzal, A., Donnerstein, C., Taylor, M. and Domschke, T. (2007) Social skills, psychological well-being, and the mediating role of perceived stress, *Anxiety, Stress and Coping*, 20, 321–329.

Seih, Y., Buhrmester, M., Lin, Y., Huang, C. and Swann, W. (2013) Do people want to be flattered or understood? The cross-cultural universality of self-verification, *Journal of Experimental Social Psychology*, 49, 169–172.

Seiter, J. and Dunn, D. (2001) Beauty and believability in sexual harassment cases: Does physical attractiveness affect perceptions of veracity and the likelihood of being harrassed, *Communication Research Reports*, 17, 203–209.

Senate Report (2004) *Report on the U.S. Intelligence Community's Pre-War Intelligence Assessments on Iraq* (http://web.mit.edu/simsong/www/iraqreport2-textunder.pdf) (accessed 4 April 2014).

Sénémeaud, C., Mange, J., Fointiat, V. and Somat, A. (2014) Being hypocritical disturbs some people more than others: How individual differences in preference for consistency moderate the behavioral effects of the induced-hypocrisy paradigm, *Social Influence*, 9, 133–148.

Şener, A. (2011) Emotional support exchange and life satisfaction, *International Journal of Humanities and Social Science*, 1, 79–88.

Senju, A. and Johnson, M. (2009) The eye contact effect: Mechanisms and development, *Trends in Cognitive Sciences*, 13, 127–134.

Seppänen, J. (2006) *The Power of the Gaze: An Introduction to Visual Literacy*. New York: Peter Lang.

Serewicz, D. and Canary, M. (2008) Assessments of disclosure from the in-laws: Links among disclosure topics, family privacy orientations, and relational quality, *Journal of Social and Personal Relationships*, 25, 333–357.

Serewicz, M., Hosmer, R., Ballard, R. and Griffin, R. (2008) Disclosure from in-laws and the quality of in-law and marital relationships, *Communication Quarterly*, 56, 427–444.

Sevilla, C. (1999) *Disorder in the Court: Great Fractured Moments in Courtroom History*. New York: Norton.

Shaffer, D., Pegalis, L. and Cornell, D. (1992) Gender and self-disclosure revisited: Personal and contextual variations in self-disclosure to same-sex acquaintances, *The Journal of Social Psychology*, 132, 307–315.

Shah, J. and Kruglanski, A. (2000) Aspects of goal networks: Implications for self-regulation, in M. Boekaerts, P. Pintrich and M. Zeidner (eds) *Handbook of Self-regulation*, San Diego: Academic Press.

Shannon, C. and Weaver, W. (1949) *The Mathematical Theory of Communication*. Champaign, IL: University of Illinois Press.

Shapiro, D. (2000) Supplemental joint brainstorming: Navigating past the perils of traditional bargaining, *Negotiation Journal*, 16, 409–419.

Sharf, R. (2016) *Theories of Psychotherapy and Counseling: Concepts and Cases*, 6th edition. Boston, MA: Cengage Learning.

Sharkey, W. (1997) Why would anyone want to intentionally embarrass me? in R. Kowalski (ed.) *Aversive Interpersonal Behaviors*. New York: Plenum.

Sharpley, C., Jeffrey, A. and McMah, T. (2006) Counsellor facial expression and client-perceived rapport, *Counselling Psychology Quarterly*, 19, 343–356.

Sheard, A., Kakabadse, N. and Kakabadse, A. (2013) Destructive behaviours and leadership: The source of the shift from a functional to dysfunctional workplace? *International Journal of Social Science Studies*, 1, 73–89.

Shearman, S. and Yoo, J. (2007) 'Even a penny will help!' Legitimization of paltry donation and social proof in soliciting donation to a charitable organization, *Communication Research Reports*, 24, 271–282.

Sherif, M. (1936) *The Psychology of Social Norms*. New York: Harper and Row.

Sherman, L., Michikyan, M. and Greenfield, P. (2013) The effects of text, audio, video, and in-person communication on bonding between friends, *Cyberpsychology: Journal of Psychosocial Research on Cyberspace*, 7(2), article 1. DOI: 10.5817/CP2013-2-3.

Sherman, W. (1990) *Behavior Modification*. New York: Harper and Row.

Sheskin, M., Bloom, P. and Wynn, K. (2014) Anti-equality: Social comparison in young children, *Cognition*, 130, 152–156.

Shipstead, Z., Redick, T. and Engle, R. (2012) Is working memory training effective? *Psychological Bulletin*, 138, 628–654.

Shore, D. and Heerey, E. (2011) The value of genuine and polite smiles, *Emotion*, 11, 169–174.

Shotter, J. (2009) Listening in a way that recognizes/realizes the world of 'the other', *International Journal of Listening*, 23, 21–43.

Shrestha, P. and Menzel, N. (2014) Hispanic construction workers and assertiveness training, *Work: A Journal of Prevention, Assessment and Rehabilitation*, 49, 517–522.

Sidanius, J. and Pratto, F. (1999) *Social Dominance: An Intergroup Theory of Social Hierarchy and Oppression*. Cambridge: University of Cambridge Press.

Sigler, K., Burnett, A. and Child, J. (2008) A regional analysis of aseertiveness, *Journal of Intercultural Communication Research*, 37, 89–104.

Silberstang, J. and London, M. (2009) How groups learn: The role of communication patterns, cue recognition, context facility, and cultural intelligence, *Human Resource Development Review*, 8, 327–349.

Silver, R. (1970) *Effects of Subject Status and Interviewer Response Program on Subject Self-disclosure in Standardized Interviews*, paper presented at American Psychological Association Convention, Miami Beach, Florida, September 3–8 (http://eric.ed.gov/ERICDocs/data/ericdocs2sql/content_storage_01/0000019b/80/36/31/e6.pdf) (accessed 2 December 2009).

Simi, N. and Mahalik, J. (1997) Comparison of feminist versus psychoanalytic/ dynamic and other therapists on self-disclosure. *Psychology of Women Quarterly*, 21, 465–483.

Siminoff, A.L., Graham, G.A. and Gordon, N. (2006) Cancer communication patterns and the influence of patient characteristics: Disparities in information-giving and affective behaviors, *Patient Education and Counseling*, 62, 355–360.

Simons, T. and Tripp, T. (2007) The negotiation checklist, in R. Lewicki, B. Barry and D. Saunders (eds) *Negotiation: Readings, Exercise and Cases*, 5th edition. New York: McGraw-Hill.

Sims, R. and Sauser, W. (2013) Toward a better understanding of the relationships among received wisdom, groupthink, and organizational ethical culture, *Journal of Management Policy and Practice*, 14, 75–90.

Singh, D. and Young, R. (1996) Body weight, waist-to-hip ratio, breasts, and hips: Role of judgements of female attractiveness and desirability for relationships, *Ethology and Sociobiology*, 16, 483–507.

Singh, R., Onglatco, M., Sriram, N. and Tay, A. (1997) The warm–cold variable in impression formation: Evidence for the positive–negative asymmetry, *British Journal of Social Psychology*, 36, 457–478.

Sinha, V. (1972) Age differences in self-disclosure, *Developmental Psychology*, 7, 257–258.

Siraj-Blatchford, I. and Manni, L. (2008) 'Would you like to tidy up now?' An analysis of adult questioning in the English Foundation Stage, *Early Years*, 28, 5–22.

Skalski, P., Tamborini, R., Glazer, E. and Smith, S. (2009) Effects of humor on presence and recall of persuasive messages, *Communication Quarterly*, 57, 136–153.

Skarlicki, D., Folger, R. and Gee, J. (2004) When social accounts backfire: The exacerbating effects of a polite message or an apology on reactions to an unfair outcome, *Journal of Applied Social Psychology*, 34, 322–341.

Skelton, J. and Hobbs, F. (1999) Concordancing: Use of language-based research in medical communication, *The Lancet*, 353, 108–111.

Skinner, B. (1953) *Science and Human Behaviour*. London: Collier MacMillan.

Skinner, B. (1957) *Verbal Behavior*. New York: Appleton-Century-Crofts.

Skinner, B. (1971) How to teach animals, in R. Atkinson (ed.) *Contemporary Psychology*. San Francisco: Freeman.

Skinner, B. (1974) *About Behaviorism*. New York: Vintage Books.

Skinner, B. (1977) The force of coincidence, in B. Etzel, J. Le Blanc and D. Baer (eds) *New Developments in Behavioral Research: Theory, Method and Applications*. Hillsdale, NJ: Lawrence Erlbaum.

Skipper, Y. and Douglas, K. (2012) Is no praise good praise? Effects of positive feedback on children's and university students' responses to subsequent failures, *British Journal of Educational Psychology*, 82, 327–339.

Skogstad, A., Einarsen, S., Torsheim, T., Aasland, M. and Hetland, H. (2007) The destructiveness of laissez-faire leadership behaviour, *Journal of Occupational Health Psychology*, 12, 80–92.

Skowronski, J., Carlston, D. and Hartnett, J. (2008) Spontaneous impressions derived from observations of behaviour: What a long, strange trip it's been (and it's not over), in N. Ambady and J. Skowronski (eds) *First Impressions*. New York: Guilford.

Skubisz, C., Reimer, T. and Hoffrage, U. (2009) Communicating quantitative risk information, in C. Beck (ed.) *Communication Yearbook 33*. New York: Routledge.

Slater, M. and Rouner, D. (2002) Entertainment-education and elaboration likelihood: Understanding the processing of narrative persuasion, *Communication Theory*, 12, 173–191.

Smetana, J. (2008) 'It's 10 o'clock: Do you know where your children are?' Recent advances in understanding parental monitoring and adolescents' information management, *Child Development Perspectives*, 2, 19–25.

Smetana, J., Metzger, A., Gettman, D. and Campione-Barr, N. (2006) Disclosure and secrecy in adolescent–parent relationships, *Child Development*, 77, 201–217.

Smith, E. (1999) Traditions of touch in psychotherapy, in E. Smith, P. Clance and S. Imes (eds) *Touch in Psychotherapy: Theory, Research, and Practice*. New York: Guilford.

Smith, E. (2014) Evil acts and malicious gossip: A multiagent model of the effects of gossip in socially distributed person perception, *Personality and Social Psychology Review*, 18, 311–325.

Smith, E. and Mackie, D. (2007) *Social Psychology*, 3rd edition. Hove: Psychology Press.

Smith, F., Hardman, F. and Higgins, S. (2006) The impact of interactive whiteboards on teacher–pupil interaction in the National Literacy and Numeracy Strategies, *British Educational Research Journal*, 32, 443–457.

Smith, J., LaFrance, M., Knol, K. *et al.* (2015) Surprising smiles and unanticipated frowns: How emotion and status influence gender categorization, *Journal of Nonverbal Behavior*, 39, 115–130.

Smith, K., Shaw, G., Deacy, S. *et al.* (2011) *Achieving Best Evidence in Criminal Proceedings: Guidance on Interviewing Victims and Witnesses and Guidance on Using Special Measures*. London: Ministry of Justice (http://www.justice.gov.uk/downloads/victims-and-witnesses/vulnerable-witnesses/achieving-best-evidence-criminal-proceedings.pdf) (accessed 12 December 2014).

Smith, M., Hancock, J., Reynolds, L. and Birnholtz, J. (2014) Everyday deception or a few prolific liars? The prevalence of lies in text messaging, *Computers in Human Behavior*, 41, 220–227.

Smith, P. and McCulloch, K. (2012) Subliminal perception, in V. Ramachandran (ed.) *Encyclopedia of Human Behavior*, 2nd edition. London: Elsevier.

Smith, R. and Boster, F. (2009) Understanding the influence of others on perceptions of a message's advocacy: Testing a two-step model, *Communication Monographs*, 76, 333–350.

Smith, R. and Smoll, F. (2007) Social-cognitive approach to coaching behaviors, in S. Jowett and D. Lavallee (eds) *Social Psychology in Sport*. Champaign, IL: Human Kinetics.

Smith, S. and Wilson, S. (eds) (2010) *New Directions in Interpersonal Communication Research*. Thousand Oaks, CA: Sage.

Snaebjornsson, I. and Edvardsson, I. (2013) Gender, nationality and leadership style: A literature review, *International Journal of Business and Management*, 8, 89–103.

Snavely, W. and McNeil, J. (2008) Communicator style and social style: Testing a theoretical interface, *Journal of Leadership and Organizational Studies*, 14, 219–232.

Snyder, M. (1987) *Public Appearances, Private Realities*. New York: Freeman Press.

Snyder, M. and Omoto, A. (2001) Basic research and practical problems: Volunteerism and the psychology of individual and collective action, in W. Wosinska, R. Cialdini, D. Barrett and J. Reykowski (eds) *The Practice of Social Influence in Multiple Cultures*. Mahwah, NJ: Lawrence Erlbaum.

Snyder, M. and Stukas, A. (2007) Interpersonal processes in context: Understanding the influence of settings and situations on social interaction, in K. Fiedler (ed.) *Social Communication*. New York: Psychology Press.

Soetens, B., Braet, C., Dejonckheere, P. and Roets, A. (2006) 'When suppression backfires': The ironic effects of suppressing eating-related thoughts, *Journal of Health Psychology*, 11, 655–668.

Solan, L. and Tiersma, P. (2005) *Speaking of Crime: The Language of Criminal Justice*. Chicago, IL: University of Chicago Press.

Solano, C. and Dunham, M. (1985) Two's company: Self-disclosure and reciprocity in triads versus dyads, *Social Psychology Quarterly*, 48, 183–187.

Solomon, D. and Theiss, J. (2013) *Interpersonal Communication: Putting Theory into Practice*. New York: Rutledge.

Somech, A. (2005) Directive versus participative leadership: Two complementary approaches to managing school effectiveness, *Educational Administration Quarterly*, 41, 777–800.

Sommer, R. (1969) *Personal Space*. Englewood Cliffs, NJ: Prentice-Hall.

Song, H. and Schwarz, N. (2010) If it's easy to read, it's easy to do, pretty, good, and true, *The Psychologist*, 23, 108–111.

Song, L. (2011) Social capital and psychological distress, *Journal of Health and Social Behavior*, 52, 478–492.

Sopory, P. and Dillard, J. (2002) The persuasive effects of metaphor, *Human Communication Research*, 28, 382–419.

Sorenson, R., De Bord, G. and Ramirez, I. (2001) *Business and Management Communication: A Guide Book*, 4th edition. Upper Saddle River, NJ: Prentice-Hall.

Sorochinski, M., Hartwig, M., Osborne, J. *et al.* (2014) Interviewing to detect deception: When to disclose the evidence? *Journal of Police and Criminal Psychology*, 29, 87–94.

Sosik, J., Kahai, S. and Avolio, B. (2000) Leadership style, anonymity and creativity in group decision support systems: The mediating role of optimal flow, *Journal of Creative Behavior*, 33, 227–256.

Souter, K. (2011) *How You Can Talk to Anyone*. London: Hodder Education.

Spangenberg, E. and Greenwald, A. (2001) Self-prophecy as a behavior modification technique in the United States, in W. Wosinska, R. Cialdini, D. Barrett and J. Reykowski (eds) *The Practice of Social Influence in Multiple Cultures*. Mahwah, NJ: Lawrence Erlbaum.

Spangenberg, E., Sprott, D., Knuff, D. *et al.* (2012) Process evidence for the question–behaviour effect: Influencing socially normative behaviors, *Social Influence*, 7, 211–228.

Sparko, A. and Zebrowitz, L. (2011) Moderating effects of facial expression and movement on the babyface stereotype, *Journal of Nonverbal Behavior*, 35, 243–257.

Spector, P. (2012) Gender differences in aggression and counterproductive workplace behavior, in S. Fox and T. Lituchy (eds) *Gender and the Dysfunctional Workplace*. Cheltenham, Gloucestershire: Edward Elgar.

Spielmann, N. (2014) How funny was that? Uncovering humor mechanisms, *European Journal of Marketing*, 48, 1892–1910.

Spencer, J. and Lamb, M. (2012) *Children and Cross-Examination: Time to Change the Rules?* Portland, OR: Hart Publishing.

Spencer-Rodgers, J., Hamilton, D. and Sherman, S. (2007) The central role of entitativity in stereotypes of social categories and task groups, *Journal of Personality and Social Psychology*, 92, 369–388.

Spisak, B., Grabo, A., Arvey, R. and van Vugt, M. (2014) The age of exploration and exploitation: Younger-looking leaders endorsed for change and older-looking leaders endorsed for stability, *The Leadership Quarterly*, 25, 805–816.

Spitzberg, B. and Cupach, W. (2007) *The Dark Side of Interpersonal Communication*, 2nd edition. London: Routledge.

Spitzberg, B. and Cupach, W. (2011) Interpersonal skills, in M. Knapp and J. Daly (eds) *The Sage Handbook of Interpersonal Communication*, 4th edition. Thousand Oaks, CA: Sage.

Sprecher, S., Treger, S. and Wondra, J. (2013) Effects of self-disclosure role on liking, closeness, and other impressions in get-acquainted interactions, *Journal of Social and Personal Relationships*, 30, 497–514.

Stafford, T. and Dewar, M. (2014) Tracing the trajectory of skill learning with a very large sample of online game players, *Psychological Science*, 25, 511–518.

Stapleton, K. and Hargie, O. (2011) Double-bind accountability dilemmas: Impression management and accountability strategies used by senior banking executives, *Journal of Language and Social Psychology*, 30, 266–289.

Stavropoulou, C. (2011) Non-adherence to medication and doctor–patient relationship: Evidence from a European survey, *Patient Education and Counseling*, 83, 7–13.

Stefanko, P. and Ferjencik, J. (2000) Identification of dimensions of opener ability, *Studia Psychologica*, 42, 279–282.

Steil, L. (1991) Listening training: The key to success in today's organizations, in D. Borisoff and M. Purdy (eds) *Listening in Everyday Life*. Lanham, MD: University of America Press.

Stein, T., Frankel, R. and Krupat, E. (2005) Enhancing clinician communication skills in a large healthcare organization: A longitudinal case study, *Patient Education and Counseling*, 58, 4–12.

Stepanikova, I. (2014) Patient–physician communication, in *The Wiley Blackwell Encyclopedia of Health, Illness, Behavior, and Society*. Malden, MA: Wiley, pp. 1762–1767.

Sternberg, R. (1988) *The Triangle of Love*. New York: Basic Books.

Stets, J. and Burke, P. (2014) Social comparison in identity theory, in Z. Križan and F. Gibbons (eds) *Communal Functions of Social Comparison*. Cambridge: Cambridge University Press.

Steuten, U. (2000) Rituals among rockers and bikers, *Soziale Welt-zeitschrift fur Sozialwissenschaftliche Forschung und Praxis*, 51, 25.

Stevanoni, E. and Salmon, K. (2005) Giving memory a hand: Instructing children to gesture enhances their event recall, *Journal of Nonverbal Behavior*, 28, 245–266.

Stevens-Long, J. and McClintock, C. (2008) Co-presence and group processes in online management education, in C. Wankel and R. DeFillippi (eds) *University and Corporate Innovations in Lifelong Learning*. Charlotte, NC: Information Age Publishing.

Stewart, C. (2009) Message construction and editing, in W. Eadie (ed.) *21st Century Communication: A Reference Handbook*. Thousand Oaks, CA: Sage.

Stewart, C. and Cash, W. (2013) *Interviewing: Principles and Practice*, 14th edition. Boston, MA: McGraw-Hill.

Stewart, G., Dustin, S., Barrick, M. and Darnold, T. (2008) Exploring the handshake in employment interviews, *Journal of Applied Psychology*, 93, 1139–1146.

Stewart, J. and Logan, C. (1998) *Together: Communicating Interpersonally*, 5th edition. Boston, MA: McGraw-Hill.

Stewart, J., Zediker, K. and Witteborn, S. (2005) *Together: Communicating Interpersonally*, 6th edition. Los Angeles: Roxbury.

Stiglitz, J. and Bilmes, L. (2008) *The Three Trillion Dollar War: The True Cost of the Iraq Conflict*. New York: Norton.

Stivers, T. (2001) Negotiating who presents the problem: Next speaker selection in pediatric encounters, *Journal of Communication*, 51, 252–282.

Stivers, T. (2012) Physician–child interaction: When children answer physicians' questions in routine medical encounters, *Patient Education and Counseling*, 87, 3–9.

Stivers, T. and Majid, A. (2007) Questioning children: Interactional evidence of implicit bias in medical interviews, *Social Pschychology Quarterly*, 70, 424–441.

Stogdill, R. (1974) *Handbook of Leadership: A Survey of Theory and Research*. New York: Free Press.

Stone, J., Wiegand, A., Cooper, J. and Aronson, E. (1997) When exemplification fails: Hypocrisy and the motive for self-integrity, *Journal of Personality and Social Psychology*, 72, 54–65.

Strack, F. and Förster, J. (2009) *Social Cognition: The Basis of Human Interaction*. Hove: Psychology Press.

Straub, D. and Karahanna, E. (1998) Knowledge worker communications and recipient availability: Towards a task-closure explanation of media choice, *Organisational Science*, 9, 160–175.

Stricker, G. (1990) Self-disclosure and psychotherapy, in G. Stricker and M. Fisher (eds) *Self-disclosure in the Therapeutic Relationship*. New York: Plenum Press.

Stroebe, M., Schut, H. and Stroebe W. (2006) Who benefits from disclosure? Exploration of attachment style differences in the effects of expressing emotions, *Clinical Psychology Review*, 26, 66–85.

Stroebe, W. (2000) *Social Psychology and Health*, Buckingham: Open University Press.

Strömbergsson, S., Hjalmarsson, A., Edlund, J. and House, D. (2013) *Timing Responses to Questions in Dialogue*. Stockholm, Sweden: Department of Speech, Music and Hearing, KTH (http://www.speech.kth.se/prod/publications/files/3859.pdf) (accessed 26 November 2014).

Strömwall, L. and Granhag, P. (2007) Detecting deceit in pairs of children, *Journal of Applied Social Psychology*, 37, 1285–1304.

Strong, R. (2005) *Decisions and Dilemmas: Case Studies in Presidential Foreign Policy Making Since 1945*, 2nd edition. Armonk, NY: ME Sharpe.

Strong, S., Taylor, R., Branon, J. and Loper, R. (1971) Nonverbal behavior and perceived counselor characteristics, *Journal of Counseling Psychology*, 18, 554–561.

Strong, T. (2006) Reflections on reflecting as a dialogic accomplishment in counseling, *Qualitative Health Research*, 16, 998–1013.

Stronge, J., Ward, T. and Grant, L. (2011) What makes good teachers good? A cross-case analysis of the connection between teacher effectiveness and student achievement, *Journal of Teacher Education*, 62, 339–355.

Strongman, L. (2012) *Modern Nature: Essays in Environmental Communication*. Boca Raton, FL: Universal Publishers.

Stuhlmacher, A. and Linnabery, E. (2013) Gender and negotiation: A social role analysis, in M. Olekalns and W. Adair (eds) *Handbook of Research on Negotiation*, London: Edward Elgar.

Stulp, G., Buunk, A., Verhulst, S. and Pollet, T. (2013) Tall claims? Sense and nonsense about the importance of height of US presidents, *The Leadership Quarterly*, 24, 159–171.

Sturm, R. and Antonakis, J. (2015) Interpersonal power: A review, critique, and research agenda, *Journal of Management*, 41, 136–163.

Sue, D., Sue, D. and Ino, S. (1990) Assertiveness and social anxiety in Chinese-American women, *Journal of Psychology*, 124, 155–164.

Suganuma, M. (1997) Self-disclosure and self-esteem in old age, *Japanese Journal of Psychology*, 45, 12–21.

Suissa, J. (2013) Tiger mothers and praise junkies: Children, praise and the reactive attitudes, *Journal of Philosophy of Edication*, 47, 1–19.

Sullivan, G. and Goodfriend, W. (2013) The effects of controlling nonverbal intimacy, *Journal of Psychological Inquiry*, 18, 32–41.

Sullivan, H. (1953) *The Interpersonal Theory of Psychiatry*. New York: Norton.

Sullivan, H. (1954) *The Psychiatric Interview*. New York: Norton.

Sullivan, P. and Feltz, D. (2005) Applying social psychology to sports teams, in F. Schneider, J. Gruman and L. Coutts (eds) *Applied Social Psychology: Understanding and Addressing Social and Practical Problems*. Thousand Oaks, CA: Sage.

Suls, J. and Wheeler, L. (2012) Social comparison theory, in P. Van Lange, A. Kruglanski and E. Higgins (eds) *Handbook of Theories of Social Psychology*: Vol. 1. London: Sage.

Sun, Y., Shen, L. and Pan, Z. (2008) On the behavioral component of the third-person effect, *Communication Research*, 35, 257–278.

Suppes, A., Tzeng, C. and Galguera, L. (2015) Using and seeing co-speech gesture in a spatial task, *Journal of Nonverbal Behavior*, 39, 241–257.

Sutherland, K. and Wehby, J. (2001) The effect of self-evaluation of teaching behaviour in classrooms for students with emotional and behavioural disorders, *Journal of Special Education*, 35, 161–171.

Sutton, S. (1982) Fear arousing communication: A critical examination of theory and research, in J. Eiser (ed.) *Social Psychology and Behavioral Medicine*. New York: Wiley.

Swami, V. (2015) Cultural influences on body size ideals: Unpacking the impact of Westernization and modernization, *European Psychologist*, 20, 44–51.

Swami, V. and Furnham, A. (eds) (2007a) *The Body Beautiful: Evolutionary and Socio-cultural Perspectives*. Basingstoke: Palgrave Macmillan.

Swami, V. and Furnham, A. (2007b) *The Psychology of Physical Attraction*. London: Routledge.

Swami, V. and Tovée, M. (2006) Does hunger influence judgments of female physical attractiveness? *British Journal of Psychology*, 97, 353–363.

Swami, V., Furnham, A., Georgiades, C. and Pang, L. (2007b) Evaluating self and partner physical attractiveness, *Body Image*, 4, 97–101.

Swami, V., Neto, F., Tovee, M. and Furnham, A. (2007a) Preferences for female body weight and shape in three European countries, *European Psychologist*, 12, 220–228.

Swann, W. (2009) Self-verification theory, in H. Reis and S. Sprecher (eds) *Encyclopedia of Human Relationships*. Thousand Oaks, CA: Sage.

Swanson, S. and McIntyre, R. (1998) Assertiveness and aggressiveness as potential moderators of consumers' verbal behavior following a failure of service, *Psychological Reports*, 82, 1239–1247.

Sweeney, J. and Creaner, M. (2014) What's not being said? Recollections of nondisclosure in clinical supervision while in training, *British Journal of Guidance and Counselling*, 42, 211–224.

Swider, B., Barrick, M., Harris, T. and Stoverink, A. (2011) Managing and creating an image in the interview: The role of interviewee initial impressions, *Journal of Applied Psychology*, 96, 1275–1288.

Swift, J., Gooding, T. and Swift, P. (1988) Questions and wait time, in J. Dillon (ed.) *Questioning and Discussion: A Multidisciplinary Study*. Norwood, NJ: Ablex.

Takada, J. and Levine, T. (2007) The effects of the even-a-few-minutes-would-help strategy, perspective taking, and empathic concern on the successful recruiting of volunteers on campus, *Communication Research Reports*, 24, 177–184.

Tallman, K., Janisse, T., Frankel, R., Sung, S., Krupat, E. and Hsu, J. (2007) Communication practices of physicians with high patient-satisfaction ratings, *The Permanente Journal*, 11, 19–29.

Talwar, V. and Crossman, A. (2012) Children's lies and their detection: Implications for child witness testimony, *Developmental Review*, 32, 337–359.

Tamir, D. and Mitchell, J. (2012) Disclosing information about the self is intrinsically rewarding, *Proceedings of the National Academy of Sciences*, 109, 8038–8043.

Tang, D. and Schmeichel, B. (2015) Look me in the eye: Manipulated eye gaze affects dominance mindsets, *Journal of Nonverbal Behavior*, 31, 181–194.

Tannen, D. (1995) Asymmetries: Women and men talking at cross-purposes, in J. Stewart (ed.) *Bridges not Walls: A Book about Interpersonal Communication*. Boston, MA: McGraw-Hill.

Tannen, D., Kendall, S. and Gordon, C. (eds) (2007) *Family Talk: Discourse and Identity in Four American Families*. Oxford: Oxford University Press.

Taras, V., Steel, P. and Kirkman, B. (2012) Improving national cultural indices using a longitudinal meta-analysis of Hofstede's dimensions, *Journal of World Business*, 47, 329–341.

Tardy, C. (1988) Self-disclosure: Objectives and methods of measurement, in C. Tardy (ed.) *A Handbook for the Study of Human Communication*. Norwood, NJ: Ablex.

Tardy, C. (2000) Self-disclosure and health: Revisiting Sidney Jourard's Hypothesis, in S. Petronio (ed.) *Balancing the Secrets of Private Disclosures*. Mahwah, NJ: Lawrence Erlbaum.

Tardy, C. and Dindia, K. (2006) Self-disclosure: Strategic revelation of information in personal and professional relationships, in O. Hargie (ed.) *The Handbook of Communication Skills*, 3rd edition. London: Routledge.

Taylor, D. and Altman, I. (1987) Communication in interpersonal relationships: Social penetration processes, in M. Roloff and G. Miller (eds) *Interpersonal Processes: New Directions in Communications Research*. Newbury Park, CA: Sage.

Taylor, K., Mesmer-Magnus, J. and Burns, T. (2008) Teaching the art of negotiation: Improving students' negotiating confidence and perceptions of effectiveness, *The Journal of Education for Business*, 83, 135–140.

Taylor, O. (1997) Student interpretations of teacher verbal praise in selected seventh- and eighth-grade choral classes, *Journal of Research in Music Education*, 45, 536–546.

Taylor, P. (2002) A cylindrical model of communication behavior in crisis negotiations, *Human Communication Research*, 28, 7–48.

Taylor, S., Neter, E. and Wayment, H. (1995) Self-evaluation processes, *Personality and Social Psychology Bulletin*, 21, 1278–1287.

Teiford, J. (2007) *Social Perception: 21st Century Issues and Challenges*. New York: Nova Science Publishers.

Temple, L. and Loewen, K. (1993) Perception of power: First impressions of a woman wearing a jacket, *Perceptual and Motor Skills*, 76, 339–348.

Tenenbaum, H., Ford, S. and Alkhedairy, B. (2011) Telling stories: Gender differences in peers' emotion talk and communication style, *British Journal of Developmental Psychology*, 29, 707–721.

Ternes, M. and Yuille, J. (2008) Eyewitness memory and eyewitness identification performance in adults with intellectual disabilities, *Journal of Applied Research in Intellectual Disabilities*, 21, 519–531.

Tesser, A. (1988) Toward a self-evaluation maintenance model of social behavior, in L. Berkowitz (ed.) *Advances in Experimental Social Psychology, Vol. 21*. New York: Academic Press.

Tesser, A. (2001) Self-esteem, in A. Tesser and N. Schwarz (eds) *Blackwell Handbook of Social Psychology: Intraindividual Processes*. Oxford: Blackwell Publishers.

Tessonneau, A. (2005) Learning respect in Guadeloupe, in S. Muhleisen and B. Migge (eds) *Politeness and Face in Caribbean Creoles*. Amsterdam: John Benjamins.

Teyber, E. (2006) *Interpersonal Process in Therapy: An Integrative Model*, 5th edition. Belmont, CA: Thomson Brooks/Cole.

Thibaut, J. and Kelley, H. (1959) *The Social Psychology of Groups*. New York: Wiley.

Thomas, A. and Bull, P. (1981) The role of pre-speech posture change in dyadic interaction, *British Journal of Social Psychology*, 20, 105–111.

Thomas, K. (1976) Conflict and conflict management, in M. Dunnette (ed.) *Handbook of Industrial and Organizational Psychology*. Chicago, IL: Rand McNally.

Thomas, L. and Levine, T. (1994) Disentangling listening and verbal recall. Related but separate constructs? *Human Communication Research*, 21, 103–127.

Thomas, L. and Levine, T. (1996) Further thoughts on recall, memory, and the measurement of listening: A rejoinder to Bostrom, *Human Communication Research*, 23, 306–308.

Thompson, C. and Born, D. (1999) Increasing correct participation in an exercise class for adult day care clients, *Behavioral Interventions*, 14, 171–186.

Thompson, L. (1990) Negotiation behavior and outcomes: Empirical evidence and theoretical issues, *Psychological Bulletin*, 108, 515–532.

Thompson, L. (2014) *The Mind and Heart of the Negotiator*, 6th edition. Upper Saddle River, NJ: Pearson.

Thompson, T. (1998) The patient/health professional relationship, in L. Jackson and B. Duffy (eds) *Health Communication Research: A Guide To Developments and Directions*. Westport, CT: Greenwood Press.

Thompson-Leduc, P., Clayman, M., Turcotte, S. and Légaré, F. (2015) Shared decision-making behaviours in health professionals: A systematic review of studies based on the theory of planned behaviour, *Health Expectations*, 18, 754–774.

Thorne, A. (2000) Personal memory telling and personality development, *Personality and Social Psychology Review*, 4, 45–56.

Thyne, J. (1963) *The Psychology of Learning and Techniques of Teaching*. London: University of London Press.

Tice, D. and Wallace, H. (2005) The reflected self: Creating yourself as (you think) others see you, in M. Leary and J. Tangney (eds) *Handbook of Self and Identity*. New York: Guilford.

Tiersma, P. (2006) *Communicating with Juries: How to Draft More Understandable Jury Instructions*. National Center for State Courts, Williamsburg, VA (http://www.ncsconline.org/Juries/Communicating.pdf) (accessed 2 December 2009).

Timmers, R. and van der Wijst, P. (2007) Images as anti-smoking fear appeals: The effect of emotion on the persuasion process, *Information Design Journal*, 15, 21–36.

Tizard, B., Hughes, M., Carmichael, H. and Pinkerton, G. (1983) Children's questions and adult answers, *Journal of Child Psychology and Psychiatry*, 24, 269–281.

Tobin, K. (1987) The role of wait time in higher cognitive learning, *Review of Educational Research*, 57, 69–95.

Todorov, A., Olivola, C., Dotsch, R. and Mende-Siedlecki, P. (2015) Social attributions from faces: Determinants, consequences, accuracy, and functional significance, *Annual Review of Psychology*, 66, 519–545.

Tofade, T., Elsner, J. and Haines, S. (2013) Best practice strategies for effective use of questions as a teaching tool, *American Journal of Pharmaceutical Education*, 77 (http://www.ncbi.nlm.nih.gov/pmc/articles/PMC3776909/pdf/ajpe777155.pdf) (accessed 2 November 2014).

Togo, D. and Hood, J. (1992) Quantitative information presentation and gender: An interaction effect, *The Journal of General Psychology*, 119, 161–167.

Tomlinson, E. and Lewicki, R. (2015) The negotiation of contractual agreements, *Journal of Strategic Contracting and Negotiation*, 1, 85–98.

Tormala, Z. and Petty, R. (2007) Contextual contrast and perceived knowledge: Exploring the implications for persuasion, *Journal of Experimental Social Psychology*, 43, 17–30.

Tormala, Z., Clarkson, J. and Petty, R. (2006) Resisting persuasion by the skin of one's teeth: The hidden success of resisted persuasive messages, *Journal of Personality and Social Psychology*, 91, 423–435.

Torrecillas, F., Martin, I., De la Fuente, E. and Godoy, J. (2000) Attributional style, self-control, and assertiveness as predictors of drug abuse, *Psicothema*, 12, 331–334.

Tottie, G. (2014) On the use of *uh* and *um* in American English, *Functions of Language*, 21, 6–29.

Tourish, D. (1999) Communicating beyond individual bias, in A. Long (ed.) *Interaction for Practice in Community Nursing*. Basingstoke, Hampshire: MacMillan.

Tourish, D. (2013) *The Dark Side of Transformational Leadership*. London: Routledge.

Tourish, D. (2014) Leadership, more or less? A processual, communication perspective on the role of agency in leadership theory, *Leadership*, 10, 79–98.

Tourish, D. and Hargie, O. (2000) Communication and organisational success, in O. Hargie and D. Tourish (eds) *Handbook of Communication Audits for Organisations*. London: Routledge.

Tourish, D. and Hargie, O. (eds) (2004) *Key Issues in Organizational Communication*. London: Routledge.

Tourish, D. and Hargie, O. (2012) Metaphors of failure and the failures of metaphor: A critical study of root metaphors used by bankers in explaining the banking crisis. *Organization Studies*, 33, 1045–1069.

Tourish, D. and Pinnington, A. (2002) Transformational leadership, corporate cultism and the spirituality paradigm: An unholy trinity in the workplace, *Human Relations*, 55, 147–172.

Tourish, D. and Wohlforth, T. (2000) *On the Edge: Political Cults Right and Left*. Armonk, NY: ME Sharpe.

Tourish, D., Collinson, D. and Barker, J. (2009) Manufacturing conformity: Leadership through coercive persuasion in business organizations, *M@n@gement*, 12, 360–383.

Tourish, D., Pinnington, A. and Braithwaite-Anderson, S. (2007) *Evaluating Leadership Development in Scotland*. Aberdeen: Aberdeen Business School, The Robert Gordon University.

Townend, A. (2007) *Assertiveness and Diversity*. Basingstoke: Palgrave.

Tracy, K. and Coupland, N. (1990) Multiple goals in discourse: An overview of issues, *Journal of Language and Social Psychology*, 9, 1–13.

Tracy, R. and Robins, J. (2007) Self-conscious emotions: Where self and emotion meet, in C. Sedikides and S. Spencer (eds) *The Self*. New York: Psychology Press.

Trenholm, S. and Jensen, A. (2007) *Interpersonal Communication*, 6th edition. New York: Oxford University Press.

Trepte, S. and Reinecke, L. (2013) The reciprocal effects of social network site use and the disposition for self-disclosure: A longitudinal study, *Computers in Human Behaviour*, 29, 1102–1112.

Treviño, L. and Nelson, K. (2011) *Managing Business Ethics*, 5th edition. New York: Wiley.

Triesma, E. (1995) Dictionaries and death: Do capital jurors understand mitigation? *Utah Law Review*, 1, 20–69.

Trinidad, C. and Normore, A. (2005) Leadership and gender: A dangerous liaison? *Leadership and Organization Development Journal*, 26, 574–590.

Trolinder, D., Choi, H. and Proctor, T. (2004) Use of delayed praise as a directive and its effectiveness on on-task behaviour, *Journal of Applied School Psychology*, 20, 61–83.

Tsekeris, C. (2015) Contextualising the self in contemporary social science, *Contemporary Social Science: Journal of the Academy of Social Sciences*, 10, 1–14.

Tsintsadze-Maass, E. and Maass, R. (2014) Groupthink and terrorist radicalization, *Terrorism and Political Violence*, 26, 735–758.

Tskhay, K., Xu, H. and Rule, N. (2014) Perceptions of leadership success from nonverbal cues communicated by orchestra leaders, *The Leadership Quarterly*, 25, 901–911.

Tubbs, S. (1998) *A Systems Approach to Small Group Interaction*, 6th edition. Boston, MA: McGraw-Hill.

Tuckman, B. (1965) Developmental sequence in small groups, *Psychological Bulletin*, 63, 384–399.

Tuckman, B. and Jensen, M. (1977) Stages in small group development revisited, *Group and Organizational Studies*, 2, 419–427.

Turk, C. (1985) *Effective Speaking*. London: E. and F.N. Spon.

Turkat, I. and Alpher, V. (1984) Prediction versus reflection in therapist demonstrations of understanding: Three analogue experiments, *British Journal of Medical Psychology*, 57, 235–240.

Turner, J. (2014) The evolution of human emotions, in J. Stets and J. Turner (eds) *Handbook of the Sociology of Emotions: Volume II*. Dordrecht: Springer.

Turner, J. and Reinsch, L. (2007) The business communicator as presence allocator: Multicommunicating, equivocality, and status at work, *Journal of Business Communication*, 44, 36–58.

Turner, M., Tamborini, R., Limon, M. and Zuckerman-Hyman, C. (2007) The moderators and mediators of door-in-the-face requests: Is it a negotiation or a helping experience? *Communication Monographs*, 74, 333–356.

Turner, R. and Schabram, K. (2012) The bases of power revisited: An interpersonal perceptions perspective, *Journal of Organizational Psychology*, 12, 9–18.

Turney, C., Ellis, K., Hatton, N., Owens, L., Towler, J. and Wright, R. (1983) *Sydney Micro Skills Redeveloped: Series 1 and 2 Handbooks*. Sydney: Sydney University Press.

Tusing, K. and Dillard, J. (2000) The sounds of dominance: Vocal precursors of perceived dominance during interpersonal influence, *Human Communication Research*, 26, 148–171.

Tversky, A. and Kahneman, D. (1981) The framing of decisions and the rationality of choice, *Science*, 211, 453–458.

Twenge, J. (1998) Assertiveness, sociability, and anxiety, *Dissertation Abstracts International: The Sciences and Engineering*, 59 (2-B), 0905.

Twenge, J. (2014) *Generation Me: Why Today's Young Americans are More Confident, Assertive, Entitled – and More Miserable than Ever Before*. New York: Atria.

Uhlemann, M., Lea, G. and Stone, G. (1976) Effect of instructions and modeling on trainees low in interpersonal communication skills, *Journal of Counseling Psychology*, 23, 509–513.

UKCES (2012) *UK Commission's Employer Skills Survey 2011: UK Results* (http://dera.ioe.ac.uk/14574/1/ukces-employer-skills-survey-11.pdf) (accessed 2 April 2014).

Ury, W. (2007) *The Power of a Positive No: How to Say No and Still Get to Yes*. New York: Bantam.

Uzell, D. and Horne, N. (2006) The influence of biological sex, sexuality and gender role on interpersonal distance, *British Journal of Social Psychology*, 45, 579–597.

Vaillancourt, T. (2013) Do human females use indirect aggression as an intrasexual competition strategy? *Philosophical Transactions of the Royal Society of Biological Sciences*, 368. DOI: 10.1098/rstb.2013.0080.

Vandekerckhove, W. and Lewis, D. (2012) The content of whistleblowing procedures: A critical review of recent official guidelines, *Journal of Business Ethics*, 108, 253–264.

van de Ridder, J., Stokking, K., McGaghie, W. and Cate, O. (2008) What is feedback in clinical education? *Medical Education*, 42, 189–197.

van der Land, S. and Muntinga, D. (2014) To shave or not to shave? *HCI in Business: Lecture Notes in Computer Science*, 8527, 257–265.

Van Der Merwe, J. (1995) Physician–patient communication using ancestral spirits to achieve holistic healing, *American Journal of Obstetrics and Gynecology*, 1172, 1080–1087.

Van der Molen, H. and Gramsbergen-Hoogland, Y. (2005) *Communication in Organizations: Basic Skills and Conversation Models*. Hove: Psychology Press.

van Dick, R., Tissington, P. and Hertel, G. (2009) Do many hands make light work? How to overcome social loafing and gain motivation in work teams, *European Business Review*, 21, 233–245.

Vangelisti, A. and Caughlin, J. (1997) Revealing family secrets: The influence of topic, function, and relationships, *Journal of Social and Personal Relationships*, 14, 679–705.

Vangelista, A. and Hampel, A. (2010) Hurtful communication: Current research and future directions, in S. Smith and S. Wilson (eds) *New Directions in Interpersonal Communication Research*. Thousand Oaks, CA: Sage.

Van Kleef, G., De Dreu, C., Pietroni, D. and Manstead, A. (2006) Power and emotion in negotiation: Power moderates the interpersonal effects of anger and happiness on concession making, *European Journal of Social Psychology*, 36, 557–581.

Van Kleef, G., van Dijk, E., Steinel, W., Harinck, F. and Beest, I. (2008) Anger in social conflict: Cross-situational comparisons and suggestions for the future, *Group Decision and Negotiation*, 17, 13–30.

Van Slyke, E. (1999) *Listening to Conflict: Finding Constructive Solutions to Workplace Disputes*. New York: AMACOM.

Van't Riet, J. and Ruiter, R. (2013) Defensive reactions to health-promoting information: An overview and implications for future research, *Health Psychology Review*, 7, S104–S136.

Van Yperen, N. and Van de Vliert, E. (2001) Social psychology in organizations, in M. Hewstone and W. Stroebe (eds) *Introduction to Social Psychology*, 3nd edition. Oxford: Blackwell.

Venetis, M., Greene, K., Magsamen-Conrad, K. *et al.* (2012) 'You can't tell anyone but…': Exploring the use of privacy rules and revealing behaviors, *Communication Monographs*, 79, 344–365.

Verderber, K., Verderber, R. and Sellnow, D. (2014) *Communicate!* 14th edition. Boston, MA: Wadsworth, Cengage Learning.

Verner, C. and Dickinson, G. (1967) The lecture, an analysis and review of research, *Adult Education,* 17, 85–100.

Vernon, R., Sutherland, C., Young, A. and Hartley, T. (2014) Modeling first impressions from highly variable facial images, *Proceedings of the National Academy of Sciences*, 111, E3353–E3361.

Vijayalakshmi, V. and Bhattacharyya, S. (2012) Emotional contagion and its relevance to individual behavior and organizational processes: A position paper, *Journal of Business Psychology*, 23, 363–374.

Virtanen, I. and Isotalus, P. (2013) A clear mirror on which to reflect: Beneficial supportive communication in Finnish men's friendships, *Qualitative Communication Research*, 2, 133–158.

Vishwanath, A. (2006) The effects of number of opinion seekers and leaders on technology attitudes and choices, *Human Communication Research*, 32, 322–350.

Vittengl, J. and Holt, C. (2000) Getting acquainted: The relationship of self-disclosure and social attraction to positive affect, *Journal of Social and Personal Relationships,* 17, 53–66.

Vlăduțescu, S. (2014) Communication environment: Context/situation/framework, *Journal of Sustainable Development Studies*, 6, 193–204.

Vondracek, F. (1969) The study of self-disclosure in experimental interviews, *Journal of Psychology,* 72, 55–59.

Von Glinow, M., Shapiro, D. and Brett, J. (2004) Can we *talk*, and should we? Managing emotional conflict in multicultural teams, *Academy of Management* Review, 29, 578–592.

Vouloumanos, A. and Werker, J. (2007) Listening to language at birth: Evidence for a bias for speech in neonates, *Developmental Science*, 10, 159–164.

Vrij, A. (2001) Detecting the liars, *The Psychologist*, 14, 596–598.

Vrij, A. (2006) Nonverbal communication and deceit, in V. Manusov and M. Patterson (eds) *The Sage Handbook of Nonverbal Communication*. Thousand Oaks, CA: Sage.

Vrij, A. (2007) Deception: A social lubricant and a selfish act, in K. Fiedler (ed.) *Social Communication*. New York: Psychology Press.

Vrij, A. (2008) *Detecting Lies and Deceit: The Psychology of Lying and the Pitfalls and Opportunities*, 2nd edition. Chichester: Wiley.

Vrij, A. and Granhag, P. (2012) Eliciting cues to deception and truth: What matters are the questions asked, *Journal of Applied Research in Memory and Cognition*, 1, 110–117.

Vrij, A., Edward, K., Roberts, K. and Bull, R. (2000) Detecting deceit via analysis of verbal and nonverbal behavior, *Journal of Nonverbal Behavior*, 24, 239–263.

Wagner, L., Clopper, C. and Pate, J. (2014) Children's perception of dialect variation, *Journal of Child Language*, 41, 1062–1084.

Waldo, C. and Kemp, J. (1997) Should I come out to my students? An empirical investigation, *Journal of Homosexuality*, 34, 79–94.

Waldron, V., Cegala, D., Sharkey, F. and Teboul, B. (1990) Cognitive and tactical dimensions of conversational goal management, *Journal of Language and Social Psychology*, 9, 101–118.

Walker, J. (2001) *Control and the Psychology of Health*. Buckingham: Open University Press.

Walker, K. (1997) Do you ever listen? Discovering the theoretical underpinnings of empathic listening, *International Journal of Listening*, 11, 127–137.

Walker, M. and Antony-Black, J. (eds) (1999) *Hidden Selves: An Exploration of Multiple Personality*. London: Routledge.

Walker, N. and Hunt, J. (1998) Interviewing child victim-witnesses: How you ask is what you get, in C. Thompson, D. Herrmann, J. Read, D. Bruce, D. Payne and M. Toglia (eds) *Eyewitness Memory: Theoretical and Applied Perspectives*. Mahwah, NJ: Lawrence Erlbaum.

Wallach, J. (1986) *Looks That Work*. New York: Viking Penguin.

Wallihan, J. (1998) Negotiating to avoid agreement, *Negotiation Journal*, 14, 257–268.

Wang, J. (2006) Questions and the exercise of power, *Discourse Society*, 17, 529–548.

Wang, L., Northcraft, G. and Van Kleef, G. (2012) Beyond negotiated outcomes: The hidden costs of anger expression in dyadic negotiation, *Organizational Behavior and Human Decision Processes*, 119, 54–63.

Wänke, M. (2007) What is said and what is meant: Conversational implicatures in natural conversations, research settings, media, and advertising, in K. Fiedler (ed.) *Social Communication*. New York: Psychology Press.

Wanzer, M., Frymier, A. and Irwin, J. (2010) An explanation of the relationship between instructor humor and student learning: Instructional humor processing theory, *Communication Education*, 59, 1–18.

Ward, M., Doherty, D. and Moran, R. (2007) *It's Good to Talk: Distress Disclosure and Psychological Wellbeing*. Dublin, Ireland: Health Research Board.

Waring, E., Holden, R. and Wesley, S. (1998) Development of the marital self-disclosure questionnaire, *Journal of Clinical Psychology*, 54, 817–824.

Waring, H. (2012) Yes–no questions that convey a critical stance in the language classroom, *Language and Education*, 26, 451–469.

Warmelink, L., Vrij, A., Mann, S. and Granhag, P. (2012) Spatial and temporal details in intentions: A cue to detecting deception, *Applied Cognitive Psychology*, 27, 101–106.

Warner, L., Lumley, M., Casey, R., Pierantoni, W., Salazar, R., Zoratti, E., Enberg, R. and Simon, M. (2006) Health effects of written emotional disclosure in adolescents with asthma: A randomized, controlled trial, *Journal of Pediatric Psychology*, 31, 557–568.

Warren, L. and Hixenbaugh, P. (1998) Adherence and diabetes, in L. Myers and K. Midence (eds) *Adherence to Treatment in Medical Conditions*. Amsterdam: Harwood Academic Publishers.

Waterman, A. and Blades, M. (2011) Helping children correctly say 'I don't know' to unanswerable questions, *Journal of Experimental Psychology: Applied*, 17, 396–405.

Waterman, A., Blades, M. and Spencer, C. (2001) Is a jumper angrier than a tree? *The Psychologist*, 14, 474–477.

Waterman, A., Blades, M. and Spencer, C. (2004) Indicating when you do not know the answer: The effect of question format and interviewer knowledge on children's 'don't know' responses, *British Journal of Developmental Psychology*, 22, 335–348.

Watkins, M. (2006) *The New Leader's Guide to Effective Negotiation*. Boston: Harvard Business School Press.

Watson, K. and Barker, L. (1984) Listening behavior: Definition and measurement, in R. Bostrom and B. Westley (eds) *Communication Yearbook 8*. Beverly Hills, CA: Sage.

Watzlawick, P., Beavin, J. and Jackson, D. (1967) *Pragmatics of Human Communication*. New York: W.W. Norton.

Webb, P. (1994) Teaching and learning about health and illness, in P. Webb (ed.) *Health Promotion and Patient Education*. London: Chapman and Hall.

Weber, K., Martin, M. and Corrigan, M. (2006) Creating persuasive messages advocating organ donation, *Communication Quarterly*, 54, 67–87.

Weber, M. (1947) *The Theory of Social and Economic Organizations*. New York: Free Press.

Webster, P. (1984) *An Ethnographic Study of Handshaking*, unpublished doctoral dissertation, Boston, MA: Boston University..

Weger, H., Bell, G., Minei, E. and Robinson, M. (2014) The relative effectiveness of active listening in initial interactions, *International Journal of Listening*, 28, 13–31.

Weger, H., Castle, G. and Emmett, M. (2010) Active listening in peer interviews: The influence of message paraphrasing on perceptions of listening skill, *International Journal of Listening*, 24, 34–49.

Weingart, L., Prietula, M., Hyder, B. and Genovese, R. (1999) Knowledge and the sequential processes of negotiation: A Markov chain analysis of response-in-kind, *Journal of Experimental Social Psychology*, 35, 366–393.

Weinstein, N. and Sandman, P. (2002) Reducing the risks of exposure to radon gas: An application of the Precaution Adoption Process Model, in D. Rutter and L. Quine (eds) *Changing Health Behaviour*, Buckingham: Open University Press.

Weirzbicka, A. (2004) The English expressions good boy and good girl and cultural models of child rearing, *Culture and Psychology*, 10, 251–278.

Weisbuch, M., Slepian, M., Clarke, A., Ambady, N. and Veenstra-VanderWeele, J. (2010) Behavioral stability across time and situations: Nonverbal versus verbal consistency, *Journal of of Nonverbal Behavior*, 34, 43–56.

Weisbuch, M., Unkelbach, C. and Fiedler, K. (2008) Remnants of the recent past: Influences of priming on first impressions, in N. Ambady and J. Skowronski (eds) *First Impressions*. New York: Guilford.

Weiss, S. and Niemann, S. (2011) Measurement of touch behavior, in M. Hertenstein and S. Weiss (eds) *The Handbook of Touch: Neuroscience, Behavioral, and Applied Perspectives*. New York: Springer Publications.

Weitlauf, J., Smith, R. and Cervone, D. (2000) Generalization effects of coping-skills training: Influence of self-defense training on women's efficacy beliefs, *Journal of Applied Psychology*, 85, 625–633.

Wentzel, K. and Brophy, J. (2014) *Motivating Students to Learn*, 4th edition. New York: Routledge.

Wert, S. and Salovey, P. (2004) A social comparison account of gossip, *Review of General Psychology*, 8, 122–137.

West, C. (1983) Ask me no questions…an analysis of queries and replies in physician–patient dialogues, in S. Fisher and A. Todd (eds) *The Social Organization of Doctor–Patient Communication*. Washington, DC: Center for Applied Linguistics.

West, C. (2006) Coordinating closings in primary care visits: Producing continuity of care, in J. Heritage and D. Maynard (eds) *Communication in Medical Care Interaction between Primary Care Physicians and Patients*. Cambridge: Cambridge University Press.

West, M. (2012) *Effective Teamwork: Practical Lessons from Organizational Research*, 3rd edition. Malden, MA: Wiley.

Westmyer, R. and Rubin, R. (1998) Appropriateness and effectiveness of communication channels in competent interpersonal communication, *Journal of Communication*, 48, 27–48.

Westwood, S., Wood, J. and Kemshall, H. (2011) Good practice in eliciting disclosures from sex offenders, *Journal of Sexual Aggression: An International, Interdisciplinary Forum for Research, Theory and Practice*, 17, 215–227.

Wetherell, M. (1996) Life histories/social histories, in M. Wetherell (ed.) *Identities, Groups and Social Issues*. London: Sage.

Whaley, B. and Wagner, L. (2000) Rebuttal analogy in persuasive messages: Communicator likability and cognitive responses, *Journal of Language and Social Psychology*, 19, 66–84.

Wheelan, S. (2004) *Group Process. A Developmental Perspective*, 2nd edition. Boston: Allyn and Bacon.

Wheelan, S. (2005) *The Handbook of Group Research and Practice*. Thousand Oaks, CA: Sage.

Wheeless, L., Erickson, K. and Behrens, J. (1986) Cultural differences in disclosiveness as a function of locus of control, *Communication Monographs*, 53, 36–46.

Wheldall, K. and Glynn, T. (1989) *Effective Classroom Learning: A Behavioural Interactionist Approach to Teaching*. Oxford: Basil Blackwell.

Wheldall, K., Bevan, K. and Shortall, K. (1986) A touch of reinforcement: The effects of contingent teacher touch on the classroom behaviour of young children, *Educational Review*, 38, 207–216.

Whetzel, D. and McDaniel, M. (1999) The employment interview, in A. Memon and R. Bull (eds) *Handbook of the Psychology of Interviewing*. Chichester: Wiley.

Whitcomb, C. and Whitcomb, L. (2013) *Effective Interpersonal and Team Communication Skills for Engineers*. Hoboken, NJ: Wiley.

White, B. and Saunders, S. (1986) The influence on patients' pain intensity ratings of antecedent reinforcement of pain talk or well talk, *Journal of Behaviour Therapy and Experimental Psychiatry*, 17, 155–159.

White, C. and Burgoon, J. (2001) Adaptation and communicative design patterns of interaction in truthful and deceptive conversations, *Human Communication Research*, 27, 9–37.

White, J. and Gardner, J. (2012) *The Classroom X-Factor: The Power of Body Language and Non-verbal Communication in Teaching*. Abingdon, Oxon: Routledge.

White, J., Rosson, C., Christensen, J., Hart, R. and Levinson, W. (1997) Wrapping things up: A qualitative analysis of the closing moments of the medical visit, *Patient Education and Counseling*, 30, 155–165.

Whitney, G. (1990) Before you negotiate: Get your act together, in I. Asherman and S. Asherman (eds) *The Negotiating Sourcebook*, Amherst, MA: Human Resource Development Press.

Whitted, K. (2011) Understanding how social and emotional skill deficits contribute to school failure, *Preventing School Failure: Alternative Education for Children and Youth*, 55, 10–16.

Whitty, M. and Carr, A. (2006) *Cyberspace Romance: The Psychology of Online Relationships*. Basingstoke: Palgrave Macmillan.

Widener, C. (2005) Dos and don'ts at the podium, *Journal of Accountancy*, 200, 32.

Wiksell, W. (1946) The problem of listening, *Quarterly Journal of Speech*, 32, 505–508.

Wildermuth, S., Vogl-Bauer, S. and Rivera, J. (2007) Practically perfect in every way: Communication strategies of ideal relational partners, *Communication Studies*, 57, 239–257.

Wilderom, C., van den Berg, P. and Wiersma, U. (2012) A longitudinal study of the effects of charismatic leadership and organizational culture on objective and perceived corporate performance, *The Leadership Quarterly*, 23, 835–848.

Wildfeuer, J., Schnell, M. and Schulz, C. (2015) Talking about dying and death: On new discursive constructions of a formerly postulated taboo, *Discourse Society*, 26, 366–390.

Wilding, J., Cook, S. and Davis, J. (2000) Sound familiar, *The Psychologist*, 13, 558–562.

Wilke, H. and Wit, A. (2001) Group performance, in M. Hewstone and W. Stroebe (eds) *Introduction to Social Psychology*, 3rd edition. Oxford: Blackwell.

Wilkins, P. (2003) *Person-centred Therapy in Focus*. London: Sage.

Willard, J., Madon, S., Guyll, M., Scherr, K. and Buller, A. (2012) The accumulating effects of shared expectations, *European Journal of Social Psychology*, 42, 497–508.

Williams, A. and Nussbaum, J. (2001) *Intergenerational Communication Across the Life Span*. Mahwah, NJ: Lawrence Erlbaum.

Williams, E. and Akridge, R. (1996) The Responsible Assertion Scale: Development and evaluation of psychometric qualities, *Vocational Evaluation and Work Adjustment Bulletin*, 29, 19–23.

Williams, K. and Dolnik, L. (2001) Revealing the worst first: Stealing thunder as a social influence strategy, in J. Forgas and K. Williams (eds) *Social Influence: Direct and Indirect Processes*. Philadelphia: Psychology Press.

Williamson, T. (ed.) (2005) *Investigative Interviewing: Rights, Research, Regulation*. Uffculme, Devon: Willan.

Willis, F. and Dodds, R. (1998) Age, relationships and touch initiation, *The Journal of Social Psychology*, 138, 115–124.

Willis, J. and Todorov, A. (2006) First impressions: Making up your mind after a 100-ms exposure to a face, *Psychological Science*, 17, 592–598.

Wilmot, W. (1995) The transactional nature of person perception, in J. Stewart (ed.) *Bridges not Walls: A Book About Interpersonal Communication*. New York: McGraw-Hill.

Wilson, D. and Conyers, M. (2013) *Flourishing in the First Five Years: Connecting Implications from Mind, Brain, and Education Research to the Development of Young Children*. Lanham, MA: Rowman and Littlefield.

Wilson, G. (2004) *Groups in Context: Leadership and Participation in Small Groups*, 7th edition. Boston: McGraw-Hill.

Wilson, G. and Nias, D. (1999) Beauty can't be beat, in L. Guerrero and J. DeVito (eds) *The Nonverbal Communication Reader: Classic and Contemporary Readings*. Prospect Heights, IL: Waveland Press.

Wilson, J. (1990) *Politically Speaking: The Pragmatic Analysis of Political Language*. Oxford: Basil Blackwell.

Wilson, J. and Rule, N. (2015) Facial trustworthiness predicts extreme criminal-sentencing outcomes, *Psychological Science*, 26, 1325–1331.

Wilson, K. and Gallois, C. (1993) *Assertion and its Social Context*. Oxford: Pergamon Press.

Wilson, S. (2006) Communication theory and the concept of 'goal', in B. Whaley and W. Samter (eds) *Explaining Communication: Contemporary Theories and Exemplars*. Mahwah, NJ: Lawrence Erlbaum.

Wilson, S. (2010) Seeking and resisting compliance, in C. Berger, M. Roloff and D. Roskos-Ewoldsen (eds) *The Handbook of Communication Science*. Thousand Oaks, CA: Sage.

Wilson, S., Greene, J. and Dillard, J. (2000) Introduction to the special issue on message production: Progress, challenges and prospects, *Communication Theory*, 10, 135–138.

Wilson, S., Paulson, G. and Putnam, L. (2001) Negotiating, in W. Robinson and H. Giles (eds) *The Handbook of Language and Social Psychology*. Chichester: Wiley.

Wilson-Barnett, J. (1981) Communicating with patients in general wards, in W. Bridge and J. MacLeod Clark (eds) *Communication in Nursing Care*. London: Croom Helm.

Wiltermuth, S. and Heath, C. (2009) Synchrony and cooperation, *Psychological Science*, 20, 1–5.

Windschitl, M. (2001) Using simulations in the middle school: Does assertiveness of dyad partners influence conceptual change? *International Journal of Science Education*, 23, 17–32.

Wit, A. (2006) Interacting in groups, in O. Hargie (ed.) *The Handbook of Communication Skills*, 3rd edition. London: Routledge.

Witte, K. (1992) Putting the fear back into fear appeals: The extended parallel process model, *Communication Monographs*, 59, 329–349.

Wittebols, J. (2004) *The Soap Opera Paradigm: Television Programming and Corporate Priorities*. Lanham, MD: Rowman and Littlefield.

Wittnebel, L. and Boone, E. (2013) Reconciling differences in personal motivations and group expectations: Participation and completion of allied health and other cohort-based higher education programs, *Journal of Medical and Allied Health Sciences*, 2, 33–39.

Wojciszke, B. (2001) The consequences of being an influential minority in the context of social controversies in the emerging Polish democracy, in W. Wosinska, R. Cialdini, D. Barrett and J. Reykowski (eds) *The Practice of Social Influence in Multiple Cultures*. Mahwah, NJ: Lawrence Erlbaum.

Wolfe, C. (2007) Contingencies of worth, in R. Baumeister and K. Vohs (eds) *Encyclopedia of Social Psychology*. Thousand Oaks, CA: Sage.

Wolff, F., Marsnik, N., Tacey, W. and Nichols, R. (1983) *Perceptive Listening*. New York: Holt, Rinehart and Winston.

Wolff, K. (1950) *The Sociology of Georg Simmel*. New York: Free Press.

Wolpe, J. (1958) *Psychotherapy by Reciprocal Inhibition*. Stanford, CA: Stanford University Press.

Wolvin, A. (2009) Listening, understanding and misunderstanding, in W. Eadie (ed.) *21st Century Communication: A Reference Handbook*. Thousand Oaks, CA: Sage.

Wolvin, A. (ed.) (2010a) *Listening and Human Communication in the 21st Century*. Malden, MA: Blackwell.

Wolvin, A. (2010b) Listening engagement: Intersecting theoretical perspectives, in A.Wolvin (ed.) *Listening and Human Communication in the 21st Century*. Malden, MA: Blackwell.

Wolvin, A. and Coakley, C. (1996) *Listening*, 5th edition. Boston, MA: McGraw-Hill.

Wong, R. (2014) Same power but different goals: How does knowledge of opponents' power affect negotiators' aspiration in powerasymmetric negotiations? *Global Journal of Business Research*, 8, 77–89.

Wood, J. (2007) *Gendered Lives: Communication, Gender, and Culture*, 7th edition. Belmont, CA: Wadsworth.

Wood, J. (2009) Gender, in W. Eadie (ed.) *21st Century Communication: A Reference Handbook*. Thousand Oaks, CA: Sage.

Wood, J. (2013) *Interpersonal Communication: Everyday Encounters*, 7th edition. Belmont, CA: Wadsworth.

Wood, J. (2014) *Communication Mosaics: An Introduction to the Field of Communication*, 7th edition. Boston, MA: Wadsworth, Cengage Learning.

Wood, J., Perunovic, E. and Lee, J. (2009) Positive self-statements: Power for some, peril for others, *Psychological Science*, 20, 860–866.

Wood, R. and Williams, R. (2007) 'How much money do you spend on gambling?' The comparative validity of question wordings used to assess gambling expenditure, *International Journal of Social Research Methodology*, 10, 63–77.

Wood, T. (2001) Team negotiations require a team approach, *The American Salesman*, 46, 22–26.

Wood, T. (2013) Exploring the role of first impressions in rater-based assessments, *Advances in Health Sciences Education*, 19, 409–427.

Wood, W. and Quinn, J.M. (2003) Forewarned and forearmed? Two meta-analysis syntheses of forewarnings of influence appeals, *Psychological Bulletin*, 129, 119–138.

Woodbury, H. (1984) The strategic use of questions in court, *Semiotica*, 48, 197–228.

Woodward, G. and Denton, R. (2014) *Persuasion and Influence in American Life*, 7th edition. Long Grove, IL: Waveland.

Woodworth, R. and Marquis, D. (1949) *Psychology: A Study of Mental Life*. London: Methuen.

Woolfolk, A. (1998) *Educational Psychology*, 7th edition. Needham Heights, MA: Allyn and Bacon.

Woolfolk, A. (2005) *Educational Psychology*, 9th edition. Harlow, Essex: Pearson Prentice Hall.

Worchel, S. (1994) You can go home again. Returning group research to the group context with an eye on developmental contexts, *Small Group Research*, 25, 205–23.

Worland, P. (1998) Proctor feedback in a modified PSI course format: The effects of praise, encouragement and group information, *Dissertation Abstracts International: Section B: The Sciences and Engineering*, 59(6-B), 3107.

Worley, D., Titsworth, S., Worley, D. and Cornett-DeVito, M. (2007) Instructional communication competence: Lessons learned from award-winning teachers, *Communication Studies*, 58, 207–222.

Worthington, D. (2008) Exploring the relationship between listening style and need for cognition, *International Journal of Listening*, 22, 46–58.

Worthy, M., Gary, A. and Kahn, G. (1969) Self-disclosure as an exchange process, *Journal of Personality and Social Psychology*, 13, 59–63.

Wortley, R. (2012) Exploring the person–situation interaction in situational crime prevention, in N. Tilley and G. Farrell (eds) *The Reasoning Criminologist: Essays in Honour of Ronald V. Clarke*. London: Routledge.

Wragg, E. and Brown, G. (2001) *Explaining in the Secondary School*. London: RoutledgeFalmer.

Wright, C. and Nuthall, G. (1970) Relationships between teacher behaviors and pupil achievement in three experimental elementary science lessons, *American Educational Research Journal*, 7, 477–493.

Wright, D., Gaskell, G. and O'Muircheartaigh, C. (1997) How response alternatives affect different kinds of behavioural frequency questions, *British Journal of Social Psychology*, 36, 443–456.

Wright, P. (1980) Message-evoked thoughts: Persuasion research using thought verbalizations, *Journal of Consumer Research*, 7, 151–175.

Wright, R. and Powell, M. (2006) Investigative interviewers' perceptions of their difficulty in adhering to open-ended questions with child witnesses, *International Journal of Police Science and Management*, 8, 316–325.

Wu, L. Mattila, A. and Han, J. (2014) Territoriality revisited: Other customer's perspective, *International Journal of Hospitality Management*, 38, 48–56.

Wyer, R. and Gruenfeld, D. (1995) Information processing in interpersonal communication, in D. Hewes (ed.) *The Cognitive Basis of Interpersonal Communication*. Hillsdale, NJ: Lawrence Erlbaum.

Wyer, R., Xu, A. and Shen, H. (2012) The effects of past behaviour on future goal-directed activity, in M. Zanna and J. Olson (eds) *Advances in Experimental Social Psychology*. San Diego, CA: Elsevier.

Wynn, R. (1996) Medical students, doctors – is there a difference? *Text*, 16, 423–448.

Xu, Y., Kelly, A. and Smillie, C. (2013) Emotional expressions as communicative signals, in S. Hancil and D. Hirst (eds) *Prosody and Iconicity*. Amsterdam: John Benjamins.

Yager, G. and Beck, T. (1985) Beginning practicum: It only hurt until I laughed, *Counselor Education and Supervision*, 25, 149–156.

Yager, T. and Rotheram-Borus, M. (2000) Social expectations among African American, Hispanic, and European American adolescents, *Cross-Cultural Research*, 34, 283–305.

Yalom, I. (1995) *The Theory and Practice of Group Psychotherapy*, 4th edition. New York: Basic Books.

Yalom, I. and Leszcz, M. (2005) *The Theory and Practice of Group Psychotherapy*, 5th edition. New York: Basic Books.

Yan, W., Wu, Q., Liang, J. *et al.* (2013) How fast are the leaked facial expressions: The duration of micro-expressions, *Journal of Nonverbal Behavior*, 37, 217–230.

Yanai, H., Schushan-Eisan, I., Neuman, S. and Novis, B. (2008) Patient satisfaction with edoscopy measurement and assessment, *Digestive Deseases*, 26, 75–79.

Yang, Z., Tang, X., Duan, W. and Zhang, Y. (2015) Expressive writing promotes self-reported physical, social and psychological health among Chinese undergraduates, *International Journal of Psychology*, 50, 128–134.

Yao, B., Scott, G., McAleer, P., O'Donnell, P. and Sereno, S. (2014) Familiarity with interest breeds gossip: Contributions of emotion, expectation, and reputation. *PLoS ONE*, 9. doi:10.1371/journal.pone.0104916.

Yeatts, D. and Hyten, C. (1998) *High Performing Self-managed Work Teams*. Thousand Oaks, CA: Sage.

Yeschke, C. (1987) *Interviewing: An Introduction to Interrogation*. Springfield, IL: CC Thomas.

Yik, M. and Russell, J. (1999) Interpretation of faces: A cross-cultural study of a prediction from Fridlund's theory, *Cognition and Emotion*, 13, 93–104.

Ying, X., Li, H., Jiang, S., Peng, F. and Lin, Z. (2014) Group laziness: The effect of social loafing on group performance, *Social Behavior and Personality*, 42, 465–472.

Yoo, J. (2009) The power of sharing negative information in a dyadic context, *Communication Reports*, 22, 29–40.

Yoshioka, M. (2000) Substantive differences in the assertiveness of low-income African American, Hispanic, and Caucasian women, *The Journal of Psychology*, 134, 243–259.

Yukl, G. (2012) Effective leadership behavior: What we know and what questions need more attention, *Academy of Management Perspectives,* 26, 66–85.

Yukl, G. (2013) *Leadership in Organizations,* 8th edition. Upper Saddle River, NJ: Pearson Education.

Zahn, G. (1991) Face-to-face communication in an office setting: The effects of position, proximity and exposure, *Communication Research,* 18, 737–754.

Zajac, R., Gross, J. and Hayne, H. (2003) Asked and answered: Questioning children in the courtroom, *Psychiatry, Psychology and Law,* 10, 199–209.

Zamboni, B., Crawford, I. and Williams, P. (2000) Examining communication and assertiveness as predictors of condom use: Implications for HIV prevention, *AIDS Education and Prevention,* 12, 492–504.

Zaragoza, M., Belli, R. and Payment, K. (2006) Misinformation effects and the suggestibility of eyewitness memory, in M. Garry and H. Hayne (eds) *Do Justice and Let the Sky Fall.* Mahwah, NJ: Lawrence Erlbaum.

Zebrowitz, L. and Montepare, J. (2008) First impressions from facial appearance cues, in N. Ambady and J. Skowronski (eds) *First Impressions.* New York: Guilford.

Zelazniewicz, A. and Pawlowski, B. (2011) Female breast size attractiveness for men as a function of sociosexual orientation (restricted vs. unrestricted), *Archives of Sexual Behavior,* 40, 1129–1135.

Zemel, A. and Koschmann, T. (2011) Pursuing a question: Reinitiating IRE sequences as a method of instruction, *Journal of Pragmatics,* 43, 475–488.

Zhang, Q., Ting-Toomey, S. and Oetzel, J. (2014) Linking emotion to the conflict face-negotiation theory: A U.S.–China investigation of the mediating effects of anger, compassion, and guilt in interpersonal conflict, *Human Communication Research,* 40, 373–395.

Zhou, Y. and Humphris, G. (2014) Can reassurance hurt? *The Psychologist,* 27, 842–845.

Zimmer, J. and Anderson, S. (1968) Dimensions of positive regard and empathy, *Journal of Counseling Psychology,* 15, 417–426.

Zimmerman, B. (2000) Attaining self-regulation: A social cognitive perspective, in M. Boekaerts, P. Pintrich and M. Zeidner (eds) *Handbook of Self-regulation.* San Diego, CA: Academic Press.

Zirpoli, T. and Melloy, K. (2015) *Behavior Management: Applications for Teachers,* 7th edition. Boson, MA: Pearson.

Ziv-Beiman, S. (2013) Therapist self-disclosure as an integrative intervention, *Journal of Psychotherapy Integration,* 23, 59–74.

Zuker, E. (1983) *Mastering Assertiveness Skills.* New York: AMACOM.

Zuljan, M., Peklaj, C., Pečjak, S. *et al.* (2012) Didactic competencies of teachers from the learner's viewpoint, *Educational Studies,* 38, 51–62.

Author index

Subject index

Note: f denotes page numbers relating to figures.